THE ARDEN SHAKESPEARE

THIRD SERIES
General Editors: Richard Proudfoot, Ann Thompson,
David Scott Kastan and H.R. Woudhuysen

AS YOU LIKE IT

THE ARDEN SHAKESPEARE

ALL'S WELL THAT ENDS WELL	edited by G. K. Hunter*
ANTONY AND CLEOPATRA	edited by John Wilders
AS YOU LIKE IT	edited by Juliet Dusinberre
THE COMEDY OF ERRORS	edited by R. A. Foakes*
CORIOLANUS	edited by Philip Brockbank*
CYMBELINE	edited by J. M. Nosworthy*
HAMLET	edited by Ann Thompson and Neil Taylor
JULIUS CAESAR	edited by David Daniell
KING HENRY IV Part 1	edited by David Scott Kastan
KING HENRY IV Part 2	edited by A. R. Humphreys*
KING HENRY V	edited by T. W. Craik
KING HENRY VI Part 1	edited by Edward Burns
KING HENRY VI Part 2	edited by Ronald Knowles
KING HENRY VI Part 3	edited by John D. Cox and Eric Rasmussen
KING HENRY VIII	edited by Gordon McMullan
KING JOHN	edited by E. A. J. Honigmann*
KING LEAR	edited by R. A. Foakes
KING RICHARD II	edited by Charles Forker
KING RICHARD III	edited by Antony Hammond*
LOVE'S LABOUR'S LOST	edited by H. R. Woudhuysen
MACBETH	edited by Kenneth Muir*
MEASURE FOR MEASURE	edited by J. W. Lever*
THE MERCHANT OF VENICE	edited by John Russell Brown*
THE MERRY WIVES OF WINDSOR	edited by Giorgio Melchiori
A MIDSUMMER NIGHT'S DREAM	edited by Harold F. Brooks*
MUCH ADO ABOUT NOTHING	edited by Claire McEachern
OTHELLO	edited by E. A. J. Honigmann
PERICLES	edited by Suzanne Gossett
THE POEMS	edited by F. T. Prince*
ROMEO AND JULIET	edited by Brian Gibbons*
SHAKESPEARE'S SONNETS	edited by Katherine Duncan-Jones
THE TAMING OF THE SHREW	edited by Brian Morris*
THE TEMPEST	edited by Virginia Mason Vaughan and Alden T. Vaughan
TIMON OF ATHENS	edited by H. J. Oliver*
TITUS ANDRONICUS	edited by Jonathan Bate
TROILUS AND CRESSIDA	edited by David Bevington
TWELFTH NIGHT	edited by J. M. Lothian and T. W. Craik*
THE TWO GENTLEMEN OF VERONA	edited by William C. Carroll
THE TWO NOBLE KINSMEN	edited by Lois Potter
THE WINTER'S TALE	edited by J. H. P. Pafford*

* Second series

THE ARDEN SHAKESPEARE

AS YOU LIKE IT

Edited by
JULIET DUSINBERRE

The Arden website is at
http://www.ardenshakespeare.com

The general editors of the Arden Shakespeare have been
W. J. Craig and R. H. Case (first series 1899–1944)
Una Ellis-Fermor, Harold F. Brooks, Harold Jenkins and
Brian Morris (second series 1946–82)

Present general editors (third series)
Richard Proudfoot, Ann Thompson, David Scott Kastan and H.R. Woudhuysen

This edition of *As You Like It*, by Juliet Dusinberre
first published 2006 by the Arden Shakespeare

Typeset by DC Graphic Design Ltd

Arden Shakespeare is an imprint of Thomson Learning

Thomson Learning
High Holborn House
50–51 Bedford Row
London WC1R 4LR

Printed in China

British Library Cataloguing in Publication Data
A catalogue record for this book is available from the British Library
Library of Congress Cataloguing in Publication Data
A catalogue record has been requested

ISBN-13: 978-1904271-21-5 (hbk)
ISBN-10: 1-904271-21-9 (hbk)
NPN 9 8 7 6 5 4 3 2 1
ISBN-13: 978-1904271-22-2 (pbk)
ISBN-10: 1-904271-22-7 (pbk)
NPN 9 8 7 6 5 4 3 2 1

The Editor

Juliet Dusinberre is the author of the pioneering work in feminist criticism, *Shakespeare and the Nature of Women* (1975, 2nd edition 1996, 3rd edition 2003), of *Virginia Woolf's Renaissance: Woman Reader or Common Reader?* (1997), and of *Alice to the Lighthouse: Children's Books and Radical Experiments in Art* (1987, 2nd edition 1999). She is a Fellow of Girton College, Cambridge, and was its first M.C. Bradbrook Fellow in English.

For Bill

CONTENTS

Contents

LIST OF
ILLUSTRATIONS

GENERAL EDITORS' PREFACE

The Arden Shakespeare is now over one hundred years old. The earliest volume in the first series, Edward Dowden's *Hamlet*, was published in 1899. Since then the Arden Shakespeare has become internationally recognized and respected. It is now widely acknowledged as the pre-eminent Shakespeare series, valued by scholars, students, actors and 'the great variety of readers' alike for its readable and reliable texts, its full annotation and its richly informative introductions.

We have aimed in the third Arden edition to maintain the quality and general character of its predecessors, preserving the commitment to presenting the play as it has been shaped in history. While each individual volume will necessarily have its own emphasis in the light of the unique possibilities and problems posed by the play, the series as a whole, like the earlier Ardens, insists upon the highest standards of scholarship and upon attractive and accessible presentation.

Newly edited from the original quarto and folio editions, the texts are presented in fully modernized form, with a textual apparatus that records all substantial divergences from those early printings. The notes and introductions focus on the conditions and possibilities of meaning that editors, critics and performers (on stage and screen) have discovered in the play. While building upon the rich history of scholarly and theatrical activity that has long shaped our understanding of the texts of Shakespeare's plays, this third series of the Arden Shakespeare is made necessary and possible by a new generation's encounter with Shakespeare, engaging with the plays and their complex relation to the culture in which they were – and continue to be – produced.

THE TEXT

On each page of the play itself, readers will find a passage of text followed by commentary and, finally, textual notes. Act and scene divisions (seldom present in the early editions and often the product of eighteenth-century or later scholarship) have been retained for ease of reference, but have been given less prominence than in the previous series. Editorial indications of location of the action have been removed to the textual notes or commentary.

In the text itself, unfamiliar typographic conventions have been avoided in order to minimize obstacles to the reader. Elided forms in the early texts are spelt out in full in verse lines wherever they indicate a usual late twentieth-century pronunciation that requires no special indication and wherever they occur in prose (except when they indicate non-standard pronunciation). In verse speeches, marks of elision are retained where they are necessary guides to the scansion and pronunciation of the line. Final -ed in past tense and participial forms of verbs is always printed as -ed without accent, never as -'d, but wherever the required pronunciation diverges from modern usage a note in the commentary draws attention to the fact. Where the final -ed should be given syllabic value contrary to modern usage, e.g.

> Doth Silvia know that I am banished?
> (*TGV* 3.1.219)

the note will take the form

219 banished banishèd

Conventional lineation of divided verse lines shared by two or more speakers has been reconsidered and sometimes rearranged. Except for the familiar *Exit* and *Exeunt*, Latin forms in stage directions and speech prefixes have been translated into English and the original Latin forms recorded in the textual notes.

COMMENTARY AND TEXTUAL NOTES

Notes in the commentary, for which a major source will be the *Oxford English Dictionary*, offer glossarial and other explication of verbal difficulties; they may also include discussion of points of theatrical interpretation and, in relevant cases, substantial extracts from Shakespeare's source material. Editors will not usually offer glossarial notes for words adequately defined in the latest edition of *The Concise Oxford Dictionary* or *Merriam-Webster's Collegiate Dictionary*, but in cases of doubt they will include notes. Attention, however, will be drawn to places where more than one likely interpretation can be proposed and to significant verbal and syntactic complexity. Notes preceded by * discuss editorial emendations or variant readings from the early edition(s) on which the text is based.

Headnotes to acts or scenes discuss, where appropriate, questions of scene location, Shakespeare's handling of his source materials, and major difficulties of staging. The list of roles (so headed to emphasize the play's status as a text for performance) is also considered in commentary notes. These may include comment on plausible patterns of casting with the resources of an Elizabethan or Jacobean acting company, and also on any variation in the description of roles in their speech prefixes in the early editions.

The textual notes are designed to let readers know when the edited text diverges from the early edition(s) on which it is based. Wherever this happens the note will record the rejected reading of the early edition(s), in original spelling, and the source of the reading adopted in this edition. Other forms from the early edition(s) recorded in these notes will include some spellings of particular interest or significance and original forms of translated stage directions. Where two early editions are involved, for instance with *Othello*, the notes will also record all important differences between them. The textual notes take a form that has been in use since the nineteenth century. This comprises, first: line reference, reading adopted in the text and closing square bracket; then: abbreviated reference, in italic, to the earliest edition to adopt the accepted reading, italic semicolon and noteworthy alternative reading(s), each with abbreviated italic reference to its source.

Conventions used in these textual notes include the following. The solidus / is used, in notes quoting verse or discussing verse lining, to indicate line endings. Distinctive spellings of the basic text (Q or F) follow the square bracket without indication of source and are enclosed in italic brackets. Names enclosed in italic brackets indicate originators of conjectural emendations when these did not originate in an edition of the text, or when the named edition records a conjecture not accepted into its text. Stage directions (SDs) are referred to by the number of the line within or immediately after which they are placed. Line numbers with a decimal point relate to entry SDs and to SDs more than one line long, with the number after the point indicating the line within the SD: e.g. 78.4 refers to the fourth line of the SD following line 78. Lines of SDs at the start of a scene are numbered 0.1, 0.2, etc. Where only a line number and SD precede the square bracket, e.g. 128 SD], the note relates to the whole of a SD within or immediately following the line. Speech prefixes (SPs) follow similar conventions, 203 SP] referring to the speaker's name for line 203. Where a SP reference takes the form e.g. 38+ SP, it relates to all subsequent speeches assigned to that speaker in the scene in question.

Where, as with *King Henry V*, one of the early editions is a so-called 'bad quarto' (that is, a text either heavily adapted, or reconstructed from memory, or both), the divergences from the present edition are too great to be recorded in full in the notes. In these cases the editions will include a reduced photographic facsimile of the 'bad quarto' in an appendix.

INTRODUCTION

Both the introduction and the commentary are designed to present the plays as texts for performance, and make appropriate reference to stage, film and television versions, as well as introducing the reader to the range of critical approaches to the plays. They discuss the history of the reception of the texts within the theatre and scholarship and beyond, investigating the interdependence of the literary text and the surrounding 'cultural text' both at the time of the original production of Shakespeare's works and during their long and rich afterlife.

PREFACE

Early in the 1890s a schoolboy was given as a school prize a magnificent presentation copy of *As You Like It*, with an introduction by Edward Dowden and illustrations by Emile Bayard. It was bound in white vellum (embossed with gold and lined with green silk) and inscribed with his name, Charles Cecil. With what joy and hope he received it, and what it rewarded, no one now knows, for he was killed in July 1916 at the battle of the Somme, and rests for ever in the Ardennes.

In 1884 Frederick Bridge, organist and passionate lover of Shakespeare, christened his daughter Rosalind. He liked the name even if Jaques didn't. Our Rosalind, with her infectious cackle, certainly would never let anyone sing their song without a burden, and played her breeches part *allegro con brio*. Our family were old foresters.

I would like to thank the general editors, David Scott Kastan and Richard Proudfoot, for an immense amount of meticulous hard work on behalf of this edition; and Ann Thompson for asking me to undertake it, and for many years of support.

No edition of *As You Like It* can exist without aid from Richard Knowles's magnificent New Variorum edition (1977). I acknowledge with gratitude the work of many other modern editors, especially Agnes Latham (Arden, 1975), Alan Brissenden (Oxford, 1993), Michael Hattaway (New Cambridge, 2000) and Cynthia Marshall (Cambridge, 2004). The pioneering eighteenth-century editions, of which Edward Capell's is the most illuminating, have been a vital source of information.

David Bevington advised throughout, and generously read and commented on an early draft of the Introduction, as did my erstwhile colleague James Simpson, whose help has been indispensable; warm thanks also for detailed comments from John and Margaret Parry, Elizabeth Newlands and Veronica Cutler. Steven May read and generously encouraged my work on the date of the play, as did Gail Kern Paster, Barbara Mowat, William Sherman, James C. Bulman and Robert Miola. The input of Tom Lockwood, an invaluable research assistant (2001–2), has been vital to the whole project. If I have now got queer theory straight, it is entirely due to Anne Fernihough. The responsibility for any remaining errors is of course my own.

A research fellowship at the Folger Shakespeare Library in 1999 was a godsend; special thanks in addition to those already mentioned, to Georgianna Ziegler, Laetitia Yendle and Peter Blayney. I would like to thank Akiko Kusunoki and Hiroko Sato for a research fellowship (also in 1999) at the Centre for Women's Studies at the Tokyo Christian Woman's University.

Warmest acknowledgements for help over many years to the long-suffering, expert and amiable staff of Cambridge University Library, especially of the Rare Books, Manuscript and Anderson rooms; to Frances Gandy and the staff of Girton College library; and to Girton College for ongoing support and generosity with sabbatical leaves. Thanks are due also to Janet Birkett at the Theatre Museum, Covent Garden; the Shakespeare Centre Library, Stratford-upon-Avon; the staff of the Manuscripts room at the British Library; the Public Record Office at Kew, London; and Dom. Philip Jebb, the archivist at Downside School. Quotations from The Hulton Papers, BL Additional MS 74286, and from BL Additional MS 48126 are by permission of the British Library.

I owe a special debt of gratitude to Pierre-Jacques Lamblin, Director of the Bibliothèque municipale, Douai, for his careful reading of Appendix 4, for permission to print material from Bm de Douai, MS 787 Anglais, Douai (1694–5), and for his enthusiastic support of the whole project; also to Jacqueline Delporte and the staff of the Bibliothèque municipale who made my visit in 1999 so enjoyable. Michèle Willems of the University of Rouen kindly criticized Appendix 4.

Unpublished work was generously made available to me by Anne Barton, Tiffany Stern and David Kathman, who also commented helpfully on Appendix 2. Dennis Kay sent me before his death all his valuable lecture notes on *As You Like It*.

Many thanks to the numerous readers, editors and copy-editors who have worked on articles and essays on the play. Valuable advice on particular matters was given by Katherine Duncan-Jones, Wes Williams, Bernard Capp, Heather Dubrow, Ian and Sue Barlow, Luisella Simpson, Deana Rankin, Joanne Archibald, Jenny Mulrenan and many others.

Grateful thanks to the Arden Shakespeare for financial help; to Jessica Hodge, for unfailing support; to Margaret Bartley, its director; to Jane Armstrong, for keeping her head when all about her were in danger of losing theirs, and for tireless hard work; to Philippa Gallagher, her predecessor Giulia Vicenzi, Fiona Freel, Jocelyn Stockley and all the other members of the working team. Thanks also to Nicola Bennett. Hannah Hyam has been a marvellous co-mate in the Forest of Arden, exemplary in her good humour, efficiency and critical acumen; patient as Griselda but much more fun. Every aspect of this edition bears witness to the transforming touch of her superb copy-editing.

Edward and Beth and Martin Dusinberre offered specific comments on many aspects of the writing as well as hauling me out of some sloughs of despond. To my own William, whom I met in the Forest of Arden forty years ago, I owe both personally and professionally more than can ever be acknowledged.

Juliet Dusinberre
Girton College, Cambridge

INTRODUCTION

A BRIEF VIEW OF THE PLAY

As You Like It, with its cross-dressed heroine, gender games and explorations of sexual ambivalence, its Forest of Arden and melancholy Jaques, speaks directly to the twenty-first century. Although the play is rooted in Elizabethan culture – literary, social, political, aesthetic – Shakespeare has placed a prophetic finger on the pulse of the future. Amongst the myths of classical pastoral and of the biblical Garden of Eden are a group of displaced persons fleeing family disruption and political corruption. In raising profound questions about the nature of liberty, renewal and regeneration posed by the new environment of the Forest, Shakespeare has created a comedy of extraordinary flexibility and depth.

This edition sets *As You Like It* within its theatrical, cultural, social and historical contexts. The play's cross-dressed heroine, Rosalind, its language, its perfect exploiting of a theatrical medium, its connections with the Court and with theatrical controversy, and its philosophical and imaginative scope, all contribute to a phenomenal richness.

Probably written at the end of 1598, perhaps first performed early in 1599, and first printed in the First Folio in 1623, *As You Like It* marks the culmination of the golden decade of Shakespeare's plays in the 1590s. Even though moments in the earlier comedies anticipate the play, its novelty is still startling. It demonstrates a confluence of high and low culture, combining within one harmonious whole many different traditions. The folklore of Robin Hood and his merry men is married to the classical

1

ideal of the Golden Age, from both Virgil's *Eclogues* and Ovid's *Metamorphoses*. The refinement of pastoral, itself an intermingling of pagan and Christian traditions, is counterpointed with the *fabliau* ribaldry of Rabelais's *Gargantua and Pantagruel* (1532–4, well known in England in the 1590s[1]), and of Chaucer's Wife of Bath's Prologue and Tale (reprinted in 1598). At the end of the Tale, the knight allows his old wife the 'soverainte' and 'maistry' (fol. 37ᵛ) which women desire: 'For as you liketh, it suffiseth me' (fol. 38ᵛ); Shakespeare may have echoed the phrase in the title of a play which certainly allows one woman sovereignty.[2] Petrarchan love poetry is undercut by Touchstone's parody and Jaques's satire, and the play develops a rhythmic, fast-moving, imaginative prose beyond anything in Shakespeare's previous plays. The high romance world of Ariosto's *Orlando Furioso* (translated by Sir John Harington in 1591) coexists in *As You Like It* with dramatic traditions of performance and narrative inherited from the old mumming plays and from John Heywood's interludes for the court of Henry VIII. There are elements of fairy-tale (the three brothers, the eldest wicked, the youngest virtuous) deriving from the fourteenth-century *Tale of Gamelyn* and from a more immediate Elizabethan source: Thomas Lodge's prose novella, *Rosalynde* (1590).[3]

As You Like It is perfectly poised between the comedies of the 1590s and the romances of Shakespeare's post-tragic period: *Pericles* (1607–8), *Cymbeline* (1609–10), *The Winter's Tale* (1610–11), *The Tempest* (1611), *The Two Noble Kinsmen* (1612–13) and *Henry VIII* (1612–13). Valentine's joining of the outlaws in the forest in *The Two Gentlemen of Verona* (probably Shakespeare's

---

1 *Gargantua* was available in a new edition from Lyons in 1573. Many of Shakespeare's contemporaries – Sir John Harington, John Donne, Ben Jonson, Thomas Nashe, Gabriel Harvey – refer to Rabelais, and Huntington Brown suggests that Jonson might have introduced Shakespeare to his work (31–70; see also Ard², 71; Dusinberre, 'As *Who?*', 10–14).
2 Dusinberre, 'Rival poets', 76–7.
3 Reprinted in 1592, 1596 and 1598, 1604 and 1609; in the 1612 edition and subsequently in 1624, 1634 and 1642 the title *Rosalynde* was replaced by the subtitle *Euphues Golden Legacy* (see p. 80).

first comedy and perhaps his earliest play) offers a preview of Duke Senior and his exiled courtiers in the Forest of Arden. The relation of Julia and Silvia in the same play (though in some ways nearer to Viola and Olivia in *Twelfth Night* than to Rosalind and Celia) nevertheless marks out – in Julia's disguise as a page – the ground of Shakespeare's virtuoso capacity to convert the convention of boy actors playing women's parts from a restriction to a resource. In *A Midsummer Night's Dream* (1595–6), despite the different atmosphere of the wood outside Athens in which the lovers, fairies and eventually Theseus and Hippolyta all meet, the dramatist creates, as later in *As You Like It*, a 'green world' away from the court. *The Merchant of Venice* (1596–7) and *Much Ado About Nothing* (1598–9) feature in Portia and Beatrice powerful women who, like Rosalind, suggest parallels with Elizabeth I, before whose court – as well as at the public theatre – most of the comedies would have been performed. *Much Ado* develops in the sparring of Beatrice and Benedick a flexible witty prose, perfected in *As You Like It* in the interchanges between Rosalind and Celia, Rosalind (as Ganymede) and Orlando, and between Touchstone and everyone else.

In 1599 *Julius Caesar* heralded the great tragedies of the new century. *As You Like It*, with its interplay of familial and political disruption, foreshadows *King Lear*. The melancholy Jaques, at odds with his world, looks forward to *Hamlet* in 1600. The glow of comic festivity in *Twelfth Night* (performed at the Middle Temple at Christmas in 1602) is darkened by a certain distance from its own revelry. The earlier comedy is more at ease with its own merriment, although its gaiety is sharpened – especially in relation to the corruption of Duke Frederick's court – by a dash of the satirical and critical spirit which will animate *All's Well That Ends Well* (1602), *Measure for Measure* (1603) and *Timon of Athens* (1609), in which the forest of Timon's exile gives birth not to *joie de vivre* but to misanthropy. In Arden melancholy only spices and enhances the experience of mirth.

The special lyricism of *As You Like It* looks back to *Richard II* and forward to the pastoral fourth act of *The Winter's Tale* and to the Utopian setting of Prospero's isle. The wedding masque for Miranda and Ferdinand in *The Tempest* recalls Hymen and the wedding songs of the last scene of *As You Like It*. The pastoral masque in *Henry VIII*, where the king enters as a shepherd, is a reminder of the courtly dimension – taken for granted by educated Elizabethans – of the pastoral genre. The tournament in *Pericles*, with the unknown knight in rusty armour, conjures up the wrestling contest in which Orlando proves his fitness as chivalric hero. *As You Like It*, more allied to the last plays than any of the other comedies, nevertheless remains rooted in Shakespeare's comic world of the 1590s.

The outstanding comic creation of that theatrical decade, the rotund figure of Shakespeare's Falstaff, inhabits not comedy but history. Although some scholars have argued that Touchstone, the jester in *As You Like It*, was played by the actor Robert Armin, for whom the later roles of witty fool (Feste in *Twelfth Night*, the Fool in *King Lear*) seem in part to have been fashioned, others have expressed doubts.[1] This edition suggests that Touchstone may originally have been played by Shakespeare's clown, Will Kemp. The irreverent energy of Rabelais's *Gargantua and Pantagruel* courses through *As You Like It* – as it had also coursed through the veins of Shakespeare's fat knight – erupting not least in the uninhibited jokes of the 'ladies': 'I prithee', cries Rosalind, 'take the cork out of thy mouth that I may drink thy tidings.' 'So you may put a man in your belly,' retorts Celia, in an interchange (3.2.196–8) routinely cut in the nineteenth century.

Who played Rosalind in Shakespeare's theatre? The research of David Kathman into apprentices on the London stage has brought us nearer to answering that question.[2] In the team-world

---

1 See Ard², li–lv, for Agnes Latham's uncertainty about whether Kemp or Armin played the role of Touchstone. David Wiles (116–35) argues for Kemp's playing Falstaff; but David Scott Kastan points to the possibility of Thomas Pope's playing the role, with John Lowin assuming it later on (Kastan, '*1H4*', 78–9). According to *The Return from Parnassus, Part 2* (1601–2; line 1851), Kemp may have played Justice Shallow in *2 Henry IV* (see 3.2.54, 58n.), making his playing of Falstaff in *1 Henry IV* less likely.

2 Kathman, 'Apprentices', 'Sins', 'Boy actors'; see Appendix 2.

of early modern theatre companies, where women were acted by boys, there was no star to claim the role, as it has (since the Restoration) been claimed by every aspiring actress. Rosalind's dynamism leaps off the page. If she dominated Shakespeare's theatre, her real arena is in the mind of the audience, which she effortlessly subjugates and draws to her lodestone, just as the magnetic shepherd boy, Ganymede, draws Orlando to imagine the woman he loves.

The part of Rosalind dominates the play, but the domain of the Forest of Arden is equally compelling. The envy and constraint of Frederick's court sets the scene for the contrast of freedom and good fellowship in the Forest of Arden, an environment which exploits Elizabethan love of the hunt, dancing, singing and pastoral merriment. Literary pastoral, an artistic mode deriving from the classics, may be alien to a modern urban audience, but the Romantic and modern longing for an escape from city life flourishes in the same subsoil.

The magic circle of Elizabeth's court, like any elite group, drew its life-blood from exclusion; its mystique was nurtured and maintained by a ruthless and fluctuating discrimination between insiders and outsiders. Elizabeth's courtiers – the Earl of Essex, Sir John Harington, Sir Walter Ralegh, Sir Robert Cecil – all had their country estates to which they escaped to sulk, lick their wounds and evade trouble, or to which the queen peremptorily banished them as a mark of her disfavour. If in such circumstances life in the country seemed like exile, it looked more inviting when the queen went on her progresses and was royally and loyally entertained – at vast expense – by her nobles.

As You Like It has much in common with the pastoral entertainments mounted for the queen during the 1590s, in which (as earlier in Sir Philip Sidney's *The Lady of May* at Wanstead in 1578 or 1579[1]) the presence of the queen herself often became a central

---

1 Sidney's masque could have been performed in either year (Duncan-Jones, introduction to *The Lady of May*, 13). It included Robin Hood, as did other such entertainments (J. Wilson, 146n.).

element in the performance staged for her welcome. The entire court traversed the country in summertime for a taste of carefully orchestrated rustic living, when the monarch might meet the 'people' in a mode in which Elizabeth, richly endowed with the 'common touch', excelled. The role of Rosalind has some correspondence with that of the queen, who was the 'cynosure . . . of Elizabethan pastoralism'.[1] This correspondence may have originated in part in the 'January' and 'April' eclogues of Edmund Spenser's *Shepheardes Calender* (1579), where Colin Clout's love is named 'Rosalinde'. The poet explains through E.K.'s gloss for 'January' that '*Rosalinde*, is also a feigned name, which, being wel ordered wil bewray the very name of hys love and mistresse, whom by that name he coloureth' (p. 447). The well-ordering of the name 'Rosalinde' can produce the anagram 'Elisadorn'.[2] Inherent in Rosalind's mastery in the Forest of Arden is arguably Elizabeth (see Fig. 18) the royal 'shepherd' with her flock of English subjects. Rosalind in Arden is as much a 'Queene of shepheardes all' (*SC*, 'April', p. 455) as Elizabeth was in the Earl of Leicester's Kenilworth in 1575. The courtly mode of the pastoral allowed its practitioners a covert language of jokes and innuendoes which Shakespeare exploits in his pastoral play.

There is no record of a performance of *As You Like It* in the public theatre, despite popular unfounded conviction that it was first produced in the opening season of the Globe, 1599–1600. An extant document in the Public Record Office (see Fig. 9 and p. 43) lists the play among those owned in 1609 by the private theatre at Blackfriars. Most of Shakespeare's plays were staged both at court and in the public theatre, and *As You Like It* is probably no exception. But there is circumstantial evidence to suggest that there might have been a first performance before the Court early in 1599.

In 1972 William Ringler and Steven May suggested that an epilogue found by May in the commonplace book of Henry

---

1 Montrose, 'Elisa', 154; see also Patterson, 126–32.
2 Dusinberre, 'As *Who*', 16; Marcus, 'Heroines', 135–7, 145, 148; Goldberg, 152–3.

Stanford was probably by Shakespeare, a view accepted by G. Blakemore Evans when he printed it in the Riverside edition (1974, reprinted 1997), and more recently by Brian Vickers in *'Counterfeiting' Shakespeare*.[1] This edition suggests that the play which Ringler and May's epilogue followed may have been *As You Like It*. If so, it was performed on Shrove Tuesday, 20 February 1599, when the Court was at Richmond Palace.[2]

If this was the case, *As You Like It* would have received 'hall' staging, as *Twelfth Night* did in the Middle Temple in 1602. May has pointed out in private communication that there are no specific stage directions in the play which require the special resources of the public theatre. However, Shakespeare's adaptation of Lodge's *Rosalynde* demonstrates a sophisticated awareness of stage space, of audience interaction with the players, and of the players themselves as spectators of their own play. There is a high level of self-conscious performance, not just in the roles of Touchstone, the fool and entertainer, and Jaques, the cynical commentator on other people's follies (both Shakespearean inventions with no counterpart in Lodge). The courtship of Orlando and Rosalind is an extended play, and Rosalind and Celia are invited to watch the pageant of Silvius's rejection by the scornful Phoebe. The drama begins with a performance – in the wrestling of Charles and Orlando – and ends with two youthful Pages singing a beautiful Morley song, and a wedding masque to rival anything in the last plays. Its distinctive characters all speak their own distinctive language.

As You Like It provides a more varied palette of verse forms and prose rhythms than is present in any earlier play. Shakespeare recasts some of the best moments of *Love's Labour's Lost* in the new comedy. Orlando's poetry is recited by Rosalind and Celia and parodied by Touchstone in a sequence reminiscent of the reading of love sonnets composed in the earlier play by the four

1 Ringler & May. See Riv, Appendix B, 32: 1851–52; Riv², Appendix C, 32: 1978. Vickers, *'Counterfeiting'*, 427–9.
2 Dusinberre, 'Pancakes'; see pp. 37–41 below and Appendix 1.

lovesick courtiers, each eavesdropping on the previous speaker. Blank verse (mocked by Jaques as the affectation of a lover) is the medium not only for Duke Senior's beautiful meditation on the Forest of Arden (2.1.1–17), but also for Duke Frederick's harshest utterances. Orlando's Petrarchan verses are derided (though no doubt relished as well) by Rosalind for being too long, like a bad sermon, just as (in the guise of Ganymede) she scoffs at the claims of the great romantic lovers of classical mythology to die for love. The heroine makes short work of the tripping couplets in Phoebe's love-letter to Ganymede.

The play oscillates between verse and a lucid, expressive prose which is never far removed from the rhythms of poetry, necessitating difficult discriminations by editors on lines which in the First Folio text could be either. Shakespeare rewrites the love-longing of Petrarchan sonnet and Italian epic romance in vernacular prose, a medium particularly associated with women[1] and (in *As You Like It*) the fool, with whom Rosalind and Celia share outsider status. Viola, Juliet and Cleopatra express their love in poetry. But Rosalind – like Beatrice in *Much Ado* – fashions hers in prose, which in *As You Like It* comes of age as the medium of romantic love. The dramatist again proves prophetic, for the great love stories of the future will be charted not in epic romance but in the prose of a new literary form hospitable to women writers, the novel.

It is hard to recapture in the modern theatre the inflammatory potential of the play, especially in its use of the boy actor, which on the Elizabethan stage in 1599 offered audacious provocation to detractors who attacked the theatre for telling lies (like all poetry), for cross-dressing and for encouraging licentious assembly. Sidney's posthumously published *Apology for Poetry* (1595), at which Touchstone glances in 3.3, provided a resounding response to the tribe of Stephen Gosson (an unsuccessful playwright turned preacher). Lodge, author of *Rosalynde*, had been in the

---

1 Henderson & Siemon, 208; Lewalski, *Writing Women*; Hannay; Parker, 'Tongue'; Bruster; Dusinberre, *Women*, li–liii, lxix–lxx, 114, and *Woolf's Renaissance*, 164–8.

early 1580s one of the first to defend the theatre (see the untitled 'A reply') against Gosson's diatribes. Gosson proclaimed that music was an effeminizing and degenerate influence, a slur to which Thomas Morley, who wrote the contemporary setting of 'It was a lover and his lass' (5.3), responded as bitterly as Lodge did.

The use of the boy actor to impersonate women became the focal point of vituperation of the theatre, on the grounds that cross-dressing excited homoerotic feeling both in the actors on stage and in the audience.[1] (What the many women in the audience were expected to feel was not part of the argument.) Into this arena prances Rosalind, planning to court Orlando while cross-dressed as the shepherd boy Ganymede.

As You Like It touches some of the deepest chords of human experience. But it also draws elements of its unique vitality from particular circumstances, particular personalities and particular theatrical conditions in Shakespeare's own society.

FICTIONS OF GENDER

Rosalind and the boy actor

The part of Rosalind manifests an awareness of gender as performance which has become an indispensable part of contemporary understanding of Shakespeare. Feminist thought has highlighted the audacity and originality of Shakespeare's conception of Rosalind, analysing the ways in which the play participates in an Elizabethan questioning of attitudes to women. The narrative of Rosalind's stage history tells as much about women's roles outside the theatre as it does about their representation on stage. Rosalind is witty, voluble, educated and imaginative; spirited and energetic; a woman who faints at the sight of her lover's blood; an imperious shepherd; a powerful magician who arranges the marriages at the

---

1 Levine, 4, 19–25; Traub, 118–19. See M. Shapiro, Appendix C, for records of cross-dressing prosecutions. The compilers, Mark Benbow and Alastair D.K. Hawkyard, note: 'By the 1590s the court [Bridewell Court] was inundated with a flood of vagrants, and sexual misdemeanors were less threatening than the potential for instability arising from masterless men and women' (225).

end of the play; and a saucy boy who returns to speak the epilogue.

Shakespeare plays with gender by creating for the boy who acts Rosalind another fictional character whom he must perform: the shepherd boy in the Forest of Arden whom Rosalind chooses for her disguise as a man. The name she gives him, Ganymede, carries multiple associations in the play. In classical mythology Ganymede is the cup-bearer of Jove, whose passion for the youth he had seized and abducted to Olympus – when disguised as an eagle – incensed Juno. The name Ganymede is conventional to classical pastoral. However, it allows the playwright to explore the homoerotic as well as the heterosexual.[1] The corrupted form of Ganymede is 'catamite', a boy hired for his sexual services.[2] But where in other dramatic contexts a 'Ganymede' is tainted with the disreputable, in *As You Like It* this hinterland is playful. The name was also emblematic of 'intelligence, or rational thought' and formed part of the mythology of the Medici.[3]

Another significant aspect of Rosalind's choice of name in her disguise relates to the figure of Hymen, who presides over the wedding masque in 5.4. In book 9 of Ovid's *Metamorphoses*, Hymen officiates with Juno at the wedding of Iphis and Ianthe. Iphis, a girl, has been brought up as a boy, and can only marry Ianthe when Hymen allows her to change sex, as at the end of John Lyly's play *Galatea* (also probably developed from this moment in Ovid). Arthur Golding's 1567 translation of Ovid reads: '*The vowes that Iphys vowed a wench he hath performd a Lad*' (123ʳ).[4] The wedding at the end of *As You Like It* is a joyous heterosexual celebration in a way that neither Ovid's nor Lyly's is.

---

1   Szatek, 357–8; DiGangi, 23; Traub, 124–5; Orgel, *Impersonations*, 51.
2   Cf. Jonson, *Poetaster*: 'Fill us a bowl of nectar, Ganymede' (4.5.59). Jonson's Ganymede is addressed as 'catamite'. See Marlowe, *Dido*; cf. Marston, *Scourge*: 'Yon effeminate sanguine *Ganimede*, / Is but a Beuer [beaver, i.e. a bedcover] hunted for the bed' (Satire 7, p. 74).
3   Saslow, 17; see also Panofsky, 212.
4   E.K. Chambers gives details of a lost play, '*Iphis and Iantha*', attributed in the seventeenth century to 'WS' (Chambers, *ES*, 3.489; 4.397, 401; and especially *WS* 1.538).

The change of Ganymede into Rosalind inverts Ovid's narrative: the shepherd boy is transformed into the Duke's daughter, the difference being that the change is only play-acting; Ganymede was a girl all along.

Shakespeare's treatment of the fictions engendered by Rosalind's alter ego is by no means simple. Rosalind, playing the boy Ganymede, invents another woman: the imagined Rosalind of a brash youth, a girl whose waywardness will cure Orlando of his love. At the end the original Rosalind plays the boy who has played her, in an epilogue in which she speaks to men as a woman and to women as a boy.

Even before Rosalind chooses this audacious male persona for herself, the two girls play in 1.2 with the idea of putting on manhood. Touchstone urges them to swear by their (non-existent) beards. Stroking their chins, Rosalind and Celia obediently make a hypothetical oath. But the act is a daring reminder of a physical state. Flute in *A Midsummer Night's Dream* protests against acting a woman because he has 'a beard coming' (1.2.44–5). The absence of a beard announces that Rosalind and Celia are women. Yet it also draws attention to the bodies of the boys playing them. The coming of a beard would have meant the possibility of graduation to male adult parts. Flute would prefer to play the role of a 'wandering knight' (42) to a woman's part. The boy's hand strokes a smooth chin, where bristles would be at present unwelcome – here he is with a woman's part to perform – but ultimately welcome: manhood, with its releases, would be upon him. 'Why, God will send more if the man will be thankful,' cries Rosalind of the little-bearded Orlando (3.2.202–3).

When Rosalind at the end of 1.3 decides to put on a man's clothes, she announces that her heart will remain a woman's while her outside brags of manhood. Elizabeth said the exact opposite in her famous speech in 1588 to the troops at Tilbury before the Spanish Armada: 'I know I have the body but of a weak and feeble woman, but I have the heart and stomach of a king and of a king of England too' (Elizabeth I, *Works*, 326). Rosalind's

11

language for describing this duality of outer/inner – man/woman or woman/man – is not as straightforward as the queen's:

> in my heart,
> Lie there what hidden woman's fear there will,
> We'll have a swashing and a martial outside,
> As many other mannish cowards have
> That do outface it with their semblances.
>
> (1.3.115–19)

In the phrase 'mannish coward' Shakespeare devises a new linguistic form to describe a man with a woman's heart. The usual epithet would be 'effeminate'. 'Mannish' is only used in two other places in his plays, in *Cymbeline*[1] and in *Troilus and Cressida*, where 'A woman impudent and mannish grown' (3.3.219) means a woman who has stepped out of her place in the gender hierarchy, a 'masculine' woman. But a male coward – a 'mannish man', in Rosalind's formulation – apes manhood as much as does a woman dressed in a man's clothes.

When Rosalind enters the Forest of Arden, courage and manhood are at issue: 'I could find in my heart to disgrace my man's apparel and to cry like a woman, but I must comfort the weaker vessel, as doublet and hose ought to show itself courageous to petticoat' (2.4.4–7). In 3.4 Celia turns the tables on her. Rosalind declares that she will weep at Orlando's failure to keep his appointment, and her cousin retorts: 'Do, I prithee, but yet have the grace to consider that tears do not become a man' (2–3). The social and cultural constructions of gender are in *As You Like It* the equivalent of a wardrobe of garments to be put on and off at will. When Virginia Woolf entitled her mock-biography of her friend (and sometime lover) Vita Sackville-West *Orlando* (1928) – a figure who moves easily between male and female – she saluted the unstable fictions of gender.[2] The

---

1 See 4.2.235–6: 'though now our voices / Have got the mannish crack', where 'mannish' describes a man, but in a context replete with gender ironies, as the two princes sing over the dead Fidele (Imogen in disguise).

2 See Judith Butler: 'There is no gender identity behind the expressions of gender; that identity is performatively constituted by the very "expressions" that are said to be its results' (25; see also 128–41).

performance of gender in *As You Like It* creates, as the anti-theatricalists in the Elizabethan period feared that it would, a vision of liberty.

Later Rosalinds

The boy actor in the Elizabethan theatre liberated Shakespeare from many constraints which became obvious the moment women started to play his parts, of which a concern for propriety, particularly in language, is the most intrusive. It may also have been easier for a boy in Shakespeare's theatre to play the girl Rosalind than it has proved to be for a woman to play the boy Ganymede.

The audience of *As You Like It* falls in love with Rosalind. One must wonder whether her creator also did so. But with whom does one fall in love? A girl? A boy? In 1992 Benedict Nightingale described Samantha Bond's Rosalind (Thacker, RSC) as 'a kind of androgynous elf or sprite'; another reviewer declared: 'The English actress playing Rosalind is a gender all her own.'[1] For the Elizabethans this would have meant a monster, as later in *Hic Mulier, Haec Vir* – this (masculine) woman, this (feminine) man, from the two pamphlets of those titles published in 1620 – a creation of the sort dreaded by the anti-theatricalists. But androgyny carries its own pitfalls on stage. Camille Paglia points out that 'the androgynous Rosalind is prettified and demasculinized' (200). The great eighteenth-century actress Sarah Siddons seemed unable to become the 'boy' Ganymede. James Boaden, in his *Memoirs of Mrs. Siddons*, states that 'she ventured to appear upon the London stage [Sheridan, 1785] in a dress which more strongly reminded the spectator of the sex which she had laid down, than that which she had taken up' (2.166). Dressing as a boy emphasized womanhood to a delighted audience. The femininity of the actress was enhanced by her assumed masculine attire. Clement Scott wrote of the American actress Ada Rehan's performance of Rosalind in 1897 (Daly): 'The great feature of Miss Rehan's Rosalind is that she never for one moment forgets, or allows

1 Lindsay Duguid, cited in Smallwood, 128.

13

herself to forget, that she is a woman.'[1] Nobody wanted her to look like a boy, let alone be one.

Rosalind became for the Victorians the type of ideal woman, a view of her reinforced both by Helena Faucit's acting in the 1840s and by her later writing about the heroine in *On Some of Shakespeare's Female Characters* (1887).[2] But different strains can be heard in the chorus of acclaim as early as 1845, when the American actress Charlotte Cushman played Rosalind at the Princess's Theatre, London (Maddox); she was renowned for playing men, and had excelled as Romeo. One reviewer ran through celebrated performances of Rosalind in order to appraise Charlotte Cushman's:

> Mrs. Nesbit's Rosalind was a sweet piece of acting, full of honey; Madame Vestris's Rosalind is all grace and coquetry; Miss Helen Faucit's (by far the best of them) is full of wit, mirth, and beauty. But Miss Cushman *was* Rosalind. These were all water-colors; but Miss Cushman's Rosalind is in oils, with such brilliancy of light and shade, with such exquisitely delicious touches of nature and art, with such richness of variety and perfect congruity, that if we did not see Shakespeare's 'very Rosalind,' we never hope or wish to do so.
>
> (Stebbins, 54–5)

Rosalind, like Hamlet, seems to acquire an existence separate from the play itself.

Was this the case when Peter Lely painted in the mid-seventeenth century his *Young Man as a Shepherd* (see Fig. 1) – aristocratic, feminine, a picture which might suggest the influence of Rosalind as Ganymede? Since the early nineteenth century Penshurst, the seat of the Sidney family, has contained a portrait of Dorothy Jordan playing Rosalind, given by the actress to her daughter Sophia, who married into the family (see Fig. 2). The

1   *Stratford-upon-Avon Herald*, 20 August 1897.
2   Jackson, 16–17; Hamer, 107–12; Hankey, 58.

1   *Young Man as a Shepherd* (*c.* 1658–65) by Sir Peter Lely

picture suggests that Jordan, like Cushman, *was* Rosalind (although she was self-deprecating about her performance of the role). Nevertheless Jordan captured the boyishness to which the later Cushman had access through her acting of male parts. Almost the same claim, that Cushman *was* Rosalind, has been made for Fiona Shaw, intriguing in view of Shaw's playing – like Cushman – Shakespearean male roles: 'She appears not as a woman dressed as a man but as herself. It is not the costume which

2 *Mrs Jordan, as Rosalind, by Hamilton* (probably Gavin Hamilton, 1723–98): portrait of the eighteenth-century actress Dorothy Jordan as Rosalind

makes Shaw's Rosalind into a man; rather it is Shaw's personality which enlivens and supports both parts' (Goodman, 212, of Albery, 1989). The blurring of boundaries between the counterfeit and the real comes from the heart of *As You Like It*: 'Well then, take a good heart, and counterfeit to be a man' cries Oliver to a fainting Ganymede. 'So I do,' murmurs Rosalind, 'But i'faith, I should have been a woman by right' (4.3.172–5).

Shakespeare's Rosalind endlessly reinvents herself. In celebration in 1916 of the tercentenary of Shakespeare's death the *New York Times* carried a special supplement, which included on 5 March a double-page spread on 'The Heroines as Viewed from the Stage – and Seen as Modern Types, People of Today'. The actress Viola Allen wrote:

> Shakespeare's women . . . are about us here in New York all the while, and in London and Paris and all the cities of the civilized world . . . And there is Rosalind – how contemporary she is! She did not fold her hands and await the pleasure of circumstances. She was no Patient Grizel, virtuous only in compliance. She was that modern type, the woman of direct, brave, and intelligent action.

It would not be long before a different form of modernity entered the composition of the stage Rosalind.

Michael Redgrave reveals in his autobiography, *In My Mind's Eye*, that in playing Orlando at the Old Vic in 1936 when in his late twenties (see Fig. 3) he fell passionately in love and had an affair with his Rosalind, Edith Evans, who was then 48. Equally fascinating is the fact, only known in more recent years, of Redgrave's bisexuality. The complexities and gender ambivalences of the role of Rosalind are marvellously identified in this story. The role of Rosalind nurtures sexual multiplicity and Orlando could have called her, as Shakespeare calls the young man of the sonnets, the 'master mistress of my passion' (20.2). Redgrave writes:

> As Rosalind the girl, she [Evans] was less than persuasive. But when she changed into a boy her whole being seemed transformed. It was not that she looked in the least like a boy. The Watteau style which the designer had imposed upon the play was most unbecoming to her. But nothing mattered except her spell.
>
> (102–3)

3 Orlando (Michael Redgrave) and Rosalind (Edith Evans) in Esmé Church's production at the Old Vic, London, 1936

Did he fall in love with Rosalind, or did he fall in love with Ganymede, or was it some subtle admixture of the two, as perhaps it was also for Orlando?

Glen Byam Shaw's production of the play with Margaret Leighton as a boyish Rosalind, together with a set designed by the celebrated Motley team, was mounted in 1952, the year of the second Queen Elizabeth's accession. In a sense the young queen, forced out of her role as wife and mother, had to take on at a moment's notice the male disguise of authority which Rosalind, as Ganymede, jubilantly assumes. The war was over, a beautiful young woman was on the throne and much was said about a second Elizabethan age. But Leighton's Rosalind looked forward rather than back. Penny Gay, describing the production, observes that 'it's the foreignness, the un-Englishness of this new image of women that is such a threat to conservative critics: the transatlantic girl bicyclist or androgynous French *gamine* look, lacking feminine curves; intellectual, even' (51).[1] With the new modern Rosalind, especially in modern dress, other problems would arise.

The Rosalind of Vanessa Redgrave in 1961 (Elliott, RSC) was perhaps heir to her father's narrative of falling in love with the boy that Shakespeare has written into his heroine's part. Her boyish Rosalind was a triumph at the beginning of the swinging sixties. But Eileen Atkins, who played Rosalind for Buzz Goodbody's *As You Like It* (RSC, 1973), confessed that 'Modern dress is a nightmare for Rosalind . . . Impossible'.[2] The changeability of modern dress codes takes the life out of Rosalind's disguise. But a new kind of liberation is created by disregarding the traditional beauty of the pantomime-boy Rosalind, achieved by Juliet Stevenson (Noble, RSC, 1985) in a Chaplinesque costume which allowed her to elude conventional expectations of beautiful boys as well as of beautiful girls.

Clifford Williams's all-male production for the early National Theatre at the Old Vic in 1967, just one year before the legalization of homosexuality between consenting adults, apparently eschewed any engagement with the homoerotic issues which have subsequently become part of the critical literature of

---

1 Gay (48–81) analyses, with review excerpts, productions of the play in 1952–7, 1961–73, 1977–80 and 1985–90.

2 Hemming, 'Like a man'; but cf. Callaghan ('Buzz Goodbody', 169), on the audacity of 'Eileen Atkins' blue jeans unisex disguise . . . [which] thwarted those who desired a traditional interpretation'.

cross-dressed parts in Shakespeare. Nevertheless, its timing is bound with hindsight to seem indicative of the more open climate of the late 1960s. Declan Donnellan's Cheek by Jowl production in 1991 enters, a quarter of a century later, a more complex scene, with gay scholarship forming an important part of academic Shakespeare, and the more open attitude to homosexuality in society creating new possibilities for theatre performance. The production was packaged as witty and joyous rather than controversial, with a flamboyantly drag Audrey. In the Forest of Arden Adrian Lester's Rosalind trying to be macho was funny in a way that it never is with a woman playing the part. Lester recalls: 'People said I looked most like a woman when I was playing Rosalind trying to look like a man. When I stopped trying to look like a woman, I looked most like one' (see Fig. 4).[1] One might read Lester's success in part as a tribute to the way in which the text constructs femininity.

James Bulman suggests that the Cheek by Jowl production focused debates which animated the last quarter of the twentieth century, and that the response of many critics seemed to deny political issues at the heart of the production: 'It is time to bring Cheek by Jowl's *As You Like It* out of the closet' ('Gay Theater', 35). The scenes between Rosalind and Celia (Tom Hollander) raised many questions about the balance between the homosexual and the heterosexual in the relationship between the two girls. 'This elision of identities' (36) was even more pronounced in the courtship scenes between Orlando and Rosalind; eventually 'the scene was played unabashedly as two men pledging their love to one another' (37). Bulman concludes that Donnellan decided 'to use the gender elisions of *As You Like It* to foreground a contemporary political agenda' (38), and adds a telling explication: 'In 1991 . . . when AIDS was still regarded as God's revenge on homosexuals and homophobic violence was commonplace, it would have been impossible for a production as daring as this *not* to ground itself in gay political discourse' (41).

1 Cited in Hemming, 'Three Rosalinds'.

4   Rosalind (Adrian Lester) in Declan Donnellan's Cheek by Jowl all-male
    production at the Lyric Hammersmith, London, 1991

In 1599 *As You Like It* would also, beneath its pastoral tranquility, have had its own social and political agenda.[1] Even if for Shakespeare's contemporaries the terms in which the challenges were embodied were different, they can nevertheless be discerned in the play in attitudes to the theatre, to women, to gender, to the Court, and to the fate of the Earl of Essex, that luminary of Elizabethan cultural and political life. To imagine anything else is to fly in the face of the status of theatre in Shakespeare's period. Why were the anti-theatricalists frightened of theatre? Not just because it was more fun to go to a theatre than to go to a sermon. Why were playwrights put in prison? Because what happened on stage looked either seditious or transgressive. Satire was a key genre in the 1590s, as John Marston's *Scourge of Villainy* (1598), Lodge's *Fig for Momus* (1595), Joseph Hall's *Virgidemiarum* (1597, 1599), the *Satires* of John Donne (written in the 1590s), and many other writings demonstrate. Ben Jonson's *Every Man In His Humour* (1598), *Every Man Out of His Humour* (1599), his *Poetaster* (1602) and *Cynthia's Revels* (1601), Marston's *Histriomastix* (1599) and Thomas Dekker's *Satiromastix* (1602) all reflect this fashion (see Leishman, 42–7). Grace Tiffany has argued that the figure of Jaques is implicated in the fracas between Jonson and his fellow playwrights first mentioned in *The Return from Parnassus, Part 2*, and now called the 'War of the Theatres' (see Appendix 3). All the references to satire in *As You Like It* press against social and political boundaries[2] just as much as its gender games enter a potentially disruptive liminal territory. The updating in the modern theatre of the play's political and social contexts testifies to the natural capacity for rebirth inherent in any great work of art. The

---

1   See Kerrigan: 'There is no doubt that, as Richard Wilson (among others) has shown with *As You Like It*, mature Shakespearean comedy goes much further in internalizing and articulating political conflict than traditional criticism realised' (90).

2   In 1979 an all-male production of the play was staged by the Haiyuza Company in Tokyo in which the director, Toshikiyo Masumi, sanctioned the insertion of topical jokes by the actors. Though they were not especially successful, and Rosalind's were considered in bad taste (Shibata, 403), the spirit of the change speaks to a topical vitality which the play would have had in 1599.

survival of a drama four hundred years old must depend on its capacity to refashion itself in contemporary cultural language, otherwise it will surely grow something stale, as the pastoral passion of Silvius has for Touchstone.

Donnellan compared his enterprise in staging an all-male *As You Like It* to Japanese Kabuki theatre, in which the actors *become* women, but are also supremely the creation of make-believe.[1] In all-male Shakespeare the question of audience reception depends on the culture and history of the audience. Bulman cites Dominic Cavendish's remark that 'however good the performances, you never forget you are watching men'.[2] But students who had never seen the play before declared that after Act 1 they completely forgot that the part of Rosalind was being played by a man. For audience members familiar with the play, the ghosts of past Rosalinds are never completely exorcised from the stage. Adrian Lester's Rosalind is not free of Ashcroft's, or Edith Evans's, or Redgrave's, or of any other Rosalind whom audiences have identified with the part. But fresh eyes see, like Miranda, a brave new world.

As the millennium dawned *As You Like It* was performed in both Stratford-upon-Avon (Doran, RSC) with Alexandra Gilbreath as Rosalind, and at the Sheffield Crucible (Grandage) with Victoria Hamilton as the heroine. Hamilton put back into the part of Rosalind the range of feeling which Helena Faucit had claimed for it in the 1840s, when the tradition of tomboys and hoydens – of whom eighteenth-century actress Dorothy Jordan was the most admired – gave way to a more emotional and imaginative reading of the character. Hamilton also spoke Ganymede's lines as though she were improvising them, which gave a sudden freshness to the game of courtship. Reviewers' comments on Gilbreath's adventurous Rosalind were more reserved, but John Peter nailed an important element in her performance when he remarked that it was as if 'she had been brought to the edge of the

---

1 Hemming, 'Like a man'. See also Kawachi, 117–18; Kott, 11.
2 *Independent*, 5 January 1995, cited in Bulman, 'Gay Theater', 35.

magic forest called dangerous love and then not been encouraged to go any further' (cited in Smallwood, 133).

Dangerous love because Shakespeare's Rosalind is both boy and girl, and must realize Ganymede's brashness not simply as a female pretence of maleness. This is not what Rosalind does. She becomes a boy playing a woman's role: Ganymede playing Rosalind for Orlando to woo. But Ganymede's Rosalind is not our Rosalind; here is the mistress he invents for Orlando:

ROSALIND   . . . I will be more
> jealous of thee than a Barbary cock-pigeon over his hen, more clamorous than a parrot against rain, more new-fangled than an ape, more giddy in my desires than a monkey. I will weep for nothing, like Diana in the fountain, and I will do that when you are disposed to be merry. I will laugh like a hyena, and that when thou art inclined to sleep.

ORLANDO   But will my Rosalind do so?
ROSALIND   By my life, she will do as I do.

(4.1.139–48)

The wayward Rosalind is Ganymede's fictionalized capricious woman, just as Ganymede is our Rosalind's fictionalized brash boy with 'a swashing and a martial outside' (1.3.117), whom the heroine promised to impersonate at the beginning of the play. Orlando is dubious. He is deterred by Ganymede's Rosalind. But our Rosalind lends her own authority: how could Ganymede imagine anything but the real thing, because under the disguise she who speaks is Rosalind. It takes some skill for the actress to communicate to the audience that the 'real' Rosalind is not actually Ganymede's Rosalind, while claiming to her lover that of course they are the same thing, as physically – beneath the disguise – they are.

When Nina Sosanya played Rosalind in 2003 (Thompson) – the first black actress to take the part in the RSC – the Ganymede

5   Orlando (Martin Hutson), Rosalind (Nina Sosanya) and Celia (Naomi Frederick) in Gregory Thompson's production at the Swan Theatre, Stratford-upon-Avon, 2003

part of the role was virtuoso: smart, quick, physically lithe, and demonstrating a kind of ruthlessness which illuminates Orlando's gentleness (see Fig. 5). But the tenderness and relenting of the female Rosalind in love with Orlando were nowhere to be seen. When Orlando declared 'I would not have my right Rosalind of this mind, for I protest her frown might kill me', Rosalind's melting response, 'By this hand, it will not kill a fly' (4.1.100–2), sounded dry. Reviewers called Sosanya a tomboy, the Victorian equivalent of the 'mannish woman' of the Elizabethans. But Sosanya was not a tomboy. She was just too good at acting a boy to be able simultaneously to act a woman, which the actress playing Rosalind still must do even if she is a woman. In *As You Like It* both genders must be acted. That is the comedy's extraordinary challenge, which is played out in Rosalind's epilogue where the boy who has played Rosalind perhaps hardly wants to go back to being a lady. She wants to have the last word as a boy. Or does she?

A reconstruction (*Wie es euch gefällt*) by Michael Dissmeier of Veracini's opera *Rosalinda* (1744; see Appendix 5) was performed at the Staatskapelle, Weimar, in April 2002 during the Deutsche Shakespeare-Gesellschaft conference. The actors wore modern dress. The singer Franziska Gottwald, who played Rosalind disguised as the shepherd boy, Ganymede (Clelia in Veracini's opera), was so convincing that many of the audience believed she was a man until she began to sing. Not only had the actress mastered a masculine way of moving, she had also completely assimilated a set of masculine facial expressions and attitudes. Her entire body language belied femininity. Yet her femininity was convincing. The actress seemed to detach herself from the role she played. As Paglia observes: '[Rosalind] theatricalizes her inner life' (208).

As You Like It conjures into its orbit multiple sexualities; the homoerotic, whether in the courtship of Orlando and Rosalind or in Phoebe's passion for the scornful Ganymede (see Fig. 6), is in dialogue with heterosexuality. If the play finally celebrates and affirms heterosexuality, in the process it traverses the gamut of emotions and impulses. The complex performance of gender which the play requires may, as modern productions have shown, ultimately confound distinction between male and female, homoerotic and heterosexual, boy and girl, as Rosalind does in her epilogue.

Celia

It used to be thought that Celia, who shows spirit and initiative in the first act of the play, is overshadowed by Rosalind once they move into the Forest. Certainly Celia in Act 1 exhorts her melancholy cousin to merriment, stands up to her tyrannous father, and initiates the plan to flee to the Forest of Arden. Only with Rosalind's invention of the disguise of Ganymede does the audience glimpse the enabling verve accessed by Rosalind as she dons her male costume. Celia, on the other hand, arrives in the Forest exhausted. But her low spirits don't last long, and the plan to buy the shepherd's cottage is hers, not Rosalind's. Furthermore,

6   Rosalind (Peggy Ashcroft) and Phoebe (Miriam Adams) in Harcourt
     Williams's production at the Old Vic, London, 1932

although the courtship between Orlando and Rosalind moves
centre stage, Celia's role remains a vital one in reminding both the
heroine and the audience of the girl Rosalind beneath the disguise
of the boy Ganymede – a reminder even more important in
Shakespeare's theatre when the girl dressed as a boy was really a
boy: 'You have simply misused our sex in your love-prate! We
must have your doublet and hose plucked over your head and
show the world what the bird hath done to her own nest'
(4.1.189–92). It is easy to suggest that all the bawdy jokes belong
to Rosalind, but these lines of Celia's were still cut in 1952 when
Margaret Leighton played Rosalind. Don't they force an audience
to imagine genitals? And which sex of genitals are we – or certainly an Elizabethan audience – imagining?[1] Celia is a right royal
tease; when Rosalind moans 'Never talk to me, I will weep' at
Orlando's apparent defection (3.4.1), her cousin, quite recovered
from her 'feminine' fatigue on entry into the Forest, gives
Rosalind a dose of her own medicine: 'Do, I prithee, but yet have
the grace to consider that tears do not become a man' (2–3).

The relation between Celia and Rosalind is socially the most
equal of all the friendships between women in Shakespeare's
plays. Celia's concern for her cousin in the opening act, and her
tenderness to her over the swoon in 4.3, make it far more than a
sparring relationship. Oliver's narration of Orlando's bravery in
rescuing him from the lion, and the wound the hero sustained,
become a brilliant backdrop for what can only be created on stage
by the actors themselves – the falling-in-love of Oliver and Celia
and the shunting of the clamorously anxious Rosalind into a side-
alley (not unlike the one which Celia herself might have occupied
up till that moment if she had not resisted that supporting role).
It comes as a shock to register that Celia has no speech in Act 5.

This shortfall in Celia's part was remedied by the nineteenth-
century French novelist George Sand in her adaptation of *As You
Like It* (*Comme il vous plaira*), performed at the Comédie

1   Ronk, 261–2; for the general point about the body of the boy actor see Stallybrass,
    'Transvestism'.

Française in April 1856. Sand's experiments with cross-dressing and her advocacy of free love and of women's rights made *As You Like It* peculiarly her play. But the role of Celia, rather than of Rosalind, seems to have spoken to the novelist's own autobiography, as Adeline Tintner points out. Sand applauded Celia for logic and reason, and constructed a romance with Jaques, which Tintner sees as a prototype for Sand's love affairs with Alfred de Musset and Frédéric Chopin (341). This is a bizarre throw-back to Charles Johnson's *Love in a Forest* (1723; see Appendix 5), which concludes with the marriage of Jaques and Celia. But the celebration of Celia interestingly anticipates twentieth-century developments in the way the part is played.

With the advent of the modern woman's movement the role of Celia became charged with new life, evident in Janet Suzman's performance in 1968 (Jones, RSC), and subsequently in the partnership between Juliet Stevenson (Rosalind) and Fiona Shaw in 1985 (see Fig. 7), of which Stevenson remarked: 'I got snatches of a wonderful relationship between two women, Celia and Rosalind. There's no real parallel to their journey anywhere in Shakespeare. I had never seen this friendship fully explored.'[1]

When George Eliot wrote to her female friends, she often invoked the relation of Celia and Rosalind as a paradigm for closeness between women (Novy, *Engaging*, 45–6). This relationship can be exemplified in the letters of educated women in the Victorian period, expressed in an erotic language which underwrites Adrienne Rich's identification of a 'lesbian continuum'. Rich celebrates a 'primary intensity between and among women, including the sharing of a rich inner life, the bonding against male tyranny, the giving and receiving of practical and political support' (51). All Rich's criteria could apply to Celia and Rosalind in Act 1 of *As You Like It* as well as in the Forest of Arden.

A depth of feeling exists between the cousins which Shakespeare describes as the love between sisters (Stirm, 380–5).

---

1 Rutter, 97; see also S. Carlson.

7   Rosalind (Juliet Stevenson) and Celia (Fiona Shaw) on entry into the
      Forest of Arden, in Adrian Noble's RSC production at the Royal
      Shakespeare Theatre, Stratford-upon-Avon, 1985

Modern gender theorists argue that the fantasies of all individuals cross the boundaries of the heterosexual and homosexual,
occupying instead a 'queer' space. Queer theorists see in the love
of Celia and Rosalind an inherent eroticism (Jankowski, 147–9).
But where critics differ is on the question of how Orlando's presence affects the love between the two women. Theodora
Jankowski and others see disruption and disappointment as
Celia's affection has to give way to the heterosexual passion
between Rosalind and Orlando. But Jan Stirm celebrates Celia's
'ability to share sensuously [in Rosalind's pleasure] without sharing Rosalind's object of desire', pointing out that Celia remains
part of her cousin's passions through 'narrative control of
Rosalind's access to Orlando' (384). Celia is audience, commentator and agent in the mock marriage (4.1.119–27). In Act 5 not only
do the 'sisters' become even more closely bonded as prospective

sisters-in-law, but the brotherhood between Orlando and Oliver acquires a new generosity which aligns it with an ideal of sisterhood in the play.

Orlando

On stage there are at least two Rosalinds: the banished Duke's daughter, disguised after Act 1 as a shepherd boy, Ganymede, and the wayward mistress 'he' impersonates for Orlando. Equally there are two young men: Orlando, the youngest son of Sir Rowland de Boys, with whom the banished Rosalind is in love, and Ganymede, the fictional man of Rosalind's imagination. Shakespeare makes Orlando into a new man by contrasting him with the 'saucy lackey' (3.2.287) Rosalind invents.

The main difference between them consists in 'gentleness', a word used more in this play than in any other. Orlando is introduced in the first scene, even by his hostile elder brother, as 'gentle'. Shakespeare uses the word in its old sense of 'of noble birth', but also increasingly in *As You Like It* to describe a mode of behaviour which abjures the violent and aggressive – or, one might say, the cultural accoutrements of traditional 'masculinity'. There is no stage direction in the First Folio to indicate who makes the first physical attack in the struggle between Oliver and Orlando in 1.1, but most critics, editors and directors have believed Oliver to be the aggressor (see 1.1.49n.).

Gentleness is given priority over savagery in 2.7, when Orlando, seeking food for his old servant Adam, faint from hunger, bursts in, sword drawn, on the Forest supper of Duke Senior and his band of exiled courtiers. The Duke admonishes him:

> What would you have? Your gentleness shall force
> More than your force move us to gentleness.
>
> (2.7.103–4)

Orlando responds with compunction: 'Speak you so gently? Pardon me, I pray you. / I thought that all things had been savage here' (107–8). Gentleness persuades where force does not. Orlando is gentle even though he is denied the education of a gentleman, and this is a statement not just about birth but about the qualities of character which make him 'enchantingly beloved' (1.1.157). Duke Senior, having heard Orlando's apology for his rough behaviour, invites him to eat: 'And therefore sit you down in gentleness' (2.7.125). But Orlando has one more act to perform, the supremely gentle mission of fetching his failing servant, Adam, to the feast of plenty:

> Then but forbear your food a little while,
> Whiles like a doe I go to find my fawn,
> And give it food.
>
> (128–30)

Shakespeare could easily have made Orlando here into a lion fetching its cub, but he chooses instead a feminine image of the doe feeding her fawn (Erickson, 75), which makes its own comment on the male culture of hunting.

These characteristics were noticed by the nineteenth-century critic and scholar Mary Cowden-Clarke, one of the first professional female Shakespearean scholars (Thompson & Roberts, 84). Although Cowden-Clarke is eager to dissociate Orlando from 'effeminacy', she nevertheless describes his resignation to his fate in 1.2 as 'almost womanly', and declares that he treats the ailing Adam 'with almost feminine tenderness'. In rewriting the script of 'femininity' through Rosalind/Ganymede, Shakespeare has also rewritten the script of 'masculinity' as the Elizabethans knew it. Just as Rosalind explodes myths of feminine sexuality so the figure of Orlando revises the binaries of violent masculinity and gentle femininity.

Orlando's characteristic gentleness contrasts strongly with the male persona of Ganymede as imagined and played by Rosalind. Phoebe is indignant at Ganymede's falsehood to her: 'Youth, you have done me much ungentleness / To show the letter that I writ to you' (5.2.73–4). One way of reading the harshness of Rosalind's response – 'I care not if I have; it is my study / To seem despiteful and ungentle to you' (75–6) – would be to say that it marks traditional male conduct towards an importunate female. But of course Phoebe is also playing to a male script: the cruel courtly lady. Ganymede is cruel, but his cruelty is partly Rosalind's anger at Phoebe's ungentleness to Silvius, another man who is called 'gentle'. In this context the word is particularly interesting, as Silvius may be tender-hearted and kind, but there is no way in which he can also be well born.

Shakespeare recognized that it is not possible to have new women without new men. The 'macho' characteristics of Ganymede which Rosalind mapped out for her 'male' role in the first act of the play throw into relief the extent to which Orlando, despite his wrestling skills, is not such a man. Orlando sighs, having just fallen in love with Rosalind after the wrestling:

> O poor Orlando, thou art overthrown!
> Or Charles or something weaker masters thee.
>
> (1.2.248–9)

The language of the 'weaker' 'mastering' the stronger contradicts the standards of Charles the wrestler, whereby physical strength always masters weakness; Shakespeare's juxtaposition of *weaker* and *masters* creates a linguistic unit of gender instability.

In Rosalind's epilogue to *As You Like It* the boy actor who has been a catalyst for Shakespeare's redefining of gender in the play does not, however, address his audience as 'Gentles', as Puck does at the end of *A Midsummer Night's Dream*. Rosalind's final speech is not to ladies and gentlemen, but to women and men, that category of the modern world which demands gentle behaviour from both its players and its audiences, irrespective of birth. Orlando is 'gentle' because he is the son of a nobleman, Sir Rowland de Boys, but this pales into insignificance beside the newer meaning of the word, where gentleness is allowed to overcome force, just as the weaker wrestler (Rosalind) is allowed to overcome Orlando where Charles the professional wrestler could not.

Phoebe and Audrey

In one of the rudest moments in the play, Rosalind as Ganymede criticizes Phoebe's hands:

> I saw her hand – she has a leathern hand,
> A freestone-coloured hand – I verily did think
> That her old gloves were on, but 'twas her hands.
> She has a housewife's hand – but that's no matter.
> (4.3.24–7)

Phoebe's 'leathern hand' is that of a working girl, not an aristocrat, and the unpleasing implication here is that Rosalind castigates Phoebe from a position of class superiority. This may be part of Ganymede's unattractively brash male persona. But another possibility concerns the physique of the boy actors playing the parts of Rosalind and Phoebe. Both presumably have larger hands than girls would have. Either the boy playing Rosalind thinks his own hand superior, or Shakespeare wants to convince the audience of his aristocratic heroine's physical refinement through an unflattering comparison (Dusinberre, 'Women and boys', 15). The boy's body becomes part of the play in a way that it is not in Lodge's *Rosalynde* or Sidney's *Arcadia*. Theatre means bodies: those of the players and those of the audience.

As You Like It requires four main boy actors, and two extras to sing the song in 5.3. But the question of gender games, the fictionalizing of the body, is only ever discussed in relation to Rosalind. She is the one with the gender games. Celia must act Aliena but she is never remotely like a shepherdess, nor is she a boy. The boy playing Celia had to be a good enough actor to convince the audience that he could play no part except that of the princess.

Phoebe is histrionic to the extent that she acts out the part of the courtly lady spurning her lover, while she herself is only, according to Rosalind, 'in the ordinary / Of Nature's sale-work' (3.5.43–4). But there is never the slightest reference to the boy beneath the petticoats. Phoebe must remain unambiguously a woman who falls in love with Ganymede. All the ambiguity resides in whether she falls in love with a man or a woman or some mixture of both, as she seems to realize: 'There was a pretty redness in his lip' (121). Yet she convinces herself that 'He'll make a proper man' (116). This is the necessary preliminary to her wail in the last scene: 'If sight and shape be true, / Why then, my love adieu' (5.4.118–19). The gender games are played with her, but she herself is never that kind of player.

In the case of Audrey the absence of playfulness in the area of gender fictions is even more pronounced. There is no Audrey in Lodge's *Rosalynde*, and in Shakespeare's play Audrey, bawdry and body go together. In the final scene Audrey has nothing to say, but she has something to do: 'bear your body more seeming, Audrey', reproves her lover (5.4.68–9), when he is displaying his rhetorical skills to the Duke. It is usually thought that Touchstone criticizes Audrey for not acting in a proper manner in polite company. But this is not just a request for more seemly behaviour; it is a reminder to the boy actor that he is still supposed to be acting. The body to which he, as boy, applies his attention, is not his own but Audrey's, the girl whom he must play. However, in being himself, the boy is also being Audrey, a country girl liable to forget her manners. In fact the rebuke almost sounds like a reminder from a master to his apprentice in the course of a rehearsal (see 5.4.68–9n.). As in the case of Phoebe's 'leathern hand', Shakespeare exploits the fact that the boy's body is resistant to fiction, and makes a fiction out of that resistance. By contrast Rosalind's body exists only as a constant act of evasion. Is she man without and woman within, or is she woman without and man within? Is she neither, or is she both?

Elizabethan boy actors were trained to perform women, as the Induction to *The Taming of the Shrew* demonstrates (Ind. 1.104–32). The role of Rosalind taps many traditions of performance – the morality vice, the boy mummer, the Maid Marian of the Robin Hood ballads and plays, the '*eiron* hero of Aristophanic comedy . . . with his voyages to mock-utopias and frequent transvestist humour' (Soule, 131) and the sporting apprentice of Shrovetide festivals. The actor playing her celebrates a liminality characteristic of adolescence (the apprentice), of gender (playful movements between masculine and feminine), of sexuality (a counterpointing of the heterosexual and homosexual), and of class (Ganymede is a shepherd boy and Rosalind a duke's daughter). Rosalind creates erotic excitement through a fiction of male comradeship, with all the ambiguity and ambivalence which that bisexual model generates.

Passion, even in this supremely genial comedy, is itself subversive. It will climb the stairs to marriage incontinently or be incontinent before marriage. A girl's wishes always run before the priest (4.1.129–30). But in a theatre where women were played by boys Shakespeare has grasped a fundamental characteristic of passion, that it thrives on repression. Rosalind's doublet and hose force on both her and Orlando a repression of desire which operates as a gust of oxygen on dampened cinders. In our more liberated Western world this is one of the many challenges which the part of Rosalind still presents to the actress. No one knew more about repressed desire in 1599 than the queen, her maids of honour and her courtiers, before whom the play may first have been performed in the final fling of feasting and festivity that preceded the privations of Lent.

DATE

As You Like It was probably acted sometime between 1598 and 1600. Its absence from Frances Meres's list of plays in *Palladis Tamia* (1598) almost certainly precludes a date earlier than 1598.[1] The staying order of 1600 in the Stationers' Register (see pp. 120 ff.) means that it must have been ready to be printed in quarto, even though it never was. Lukas Erne has argued that the date of 1600 for the staying order, assuming a text available for printing at

---

1   *Love's Labour's Won* on Meres's list is probably not *As You Like It*, as argued by Mark Dominik; see Baldwin, *Evidence*.

a later date, would imply that the play was in performance eighteen months to two years earlier (Erne, 84), which would push the date back to late 1598 or early 1599.

This edition suggests a new and specific date for the play, of Shrove Tuesday, 20 February 1599. On 10 February the Court had moved to Richmond Palace to celebrate Shrove,[1] and the Chamberlain's Men performed a play on the night of Shrove Tuesday. The entry for the Chamberlain's Men in the Declared Accounts of the Treasurer of the Chamber notes payments made on 2 October 1599 for performances by the Chamberlain's Men at court during the preceding calendar year:

> To John Heminges and Thomas Pope servants vnto the Lorde Chamberleyne vppon the Councells warraunt dated at the Courte at Nonesuche sēdo die Ottobris 1599 for three Enterludes or playes played before her Ma[tie] vppon S[t] Stephens daye at night, Newyeares daye at nighte and Shrovetuesday at nighte laste paste xx[li] [£20] and to them more by waye of her Ma[tie] rewarde x[li] [£10]. In all amounting to xxx[li] [£30].[2]

The payment – including the queen's reward, a regularly granted extra for court performance – works out at ten pounds a play. Was the play performed by the Chamberlain's Men on Shrove Tuesday *As You Like It*?

It may have been, because the epilogue found by Ringler and May in Henry Stanford's commonplace book, and believed by them and other scholars probably to be by Shakespeare, fits *As You Like It* better than any other play. Stanford was tutor in the family of George Carey, Lord Hunsdon (Lord Chamberlain since 1597)[3] and the epilogue is addressed 'to y[e] Q. by y[e] players. 1598' (see Fig. 8, and Appendix 1 for the modernized version). May

---

1   PRO E351/543, fols 38ff.; Chamberlain, *Letters*, 45; Astington, 236.
2   PRO E351/543, fol. 55; reproduced in *Dramatic Records* 6, 31; See Dusinberre, 'Pancakes', 378; see also Astington, 236.
3   May reproduces the epilogue in *Stanford*, 162 (item 228), annotated on 373.

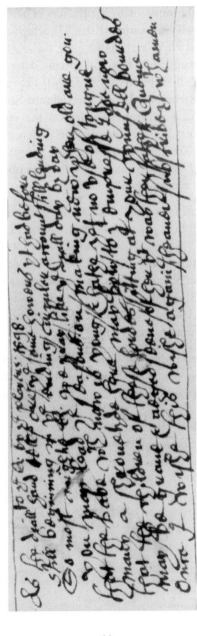

8 'to yᵉ Q. by yᵉ players. 1598', from the commonplace book of Henry Stanford, Cambridge MS Dd.5.75

demonstrated that 1598 is old-style dating (in which the new year begins on 25 March) so the epilogue was spoken in February 1599 (*Stanford*, xi–xv). The text is reproduced below. Line 6 states that this is 'Shrovetide', the period immediately preceding Lent (the commemoration of Christ's temptation in the wilderness) in the Christian calendar:

> As the diall hand tells ore / ye same howers yt had before
> still beginning in ye ending / circuler accompt still
> lending
> So most mightie Q. we pray / like ye Dyall day by day
> you may lead ye seasons on / making new when old are
> gon
> that the babe wch now is yong / & hathe yet no vse of
> tongue
> many a Shrouetyde here may bow / to y^t Empresse I
> doe now
> that the children of these lordes / sitting at your
> Counsell Bourdes
> may be graue & aeged seene / of her y^t was ther father
> Quene
> Once I wishe this wishe again / heauen subscribe yt
> wth amen.
> (Cambridge MS Dd.5.75, fol. 46)

The manuscript epilogue assures the queen of the loyalty of both players and courtly audience, and of the courtiers of the future (who are still at the present moment children). Both the Admiral's Men and the Chamberlain's Men performed at court at Shrove, 1599, the former on Shrove Sunday, 18 February, and the latter two days later on Shrove Tuesday. The court epilogue is more likely to have belonged to the Chamberlain's Men because of Stanford's connections with the Lord Chamberlain.

Henry Stanford was a poet, collector of miscellaneous writings and friend of Carey's daughter 'Bess', whom he helped to translate two sonnets by Petrarch (Duncan-Jones, 'Bess Carey'). He moved in literary, musical and theatrical circles through his connections with the Lord Chamberlain, and was probably acquainted with both Shakespeare and Jonson. He was also a Catholic; at his death in 1616 he was buried in St Anne's, Blackfriars, where many of those connected with the theatre (as also Catholics and Huguenots) lived, because it was not subject to city jurisdiction, having been monastic ground.[1]

If the epilogue in Stanford's book was spoken after what may have been a first court performance of *As You Like It*, a dreadful joke becomes funny. In 1.2 Touchstone enters, swearing by his honour that he is sent to fetch Celia:

ROSALIND   Where learned you that oath, fool?
TOUCHSTONE   Of a certain knight that swore by his
    honour they were good pancakes, and swore by his
    honour the mustard was naught. Now I'll stand to it:
    the pancakes were naught and the mustard was good,
    and yet was not the knight forsworn.

(1.2.61–6)

The joke is only funny on one day of the year: Shrove Tuesday, Pancake Day, when in the Great Hall at Richmond courtiers were probably feasting on pancakes while they watched a play. Pancakes for Shrove would have been filled with powdered (minced) beef and spiced with mustard, according to Elizabethan custom. Touchstone declares that the pancakes weren't much good but the mustard was fine.

Many preparations had been made, according to the Office of Works Accounts for Royal Palaces, for the reception of the queen and her courtiers at Richmond for Shrove 1599. Among them is an item in which workmen were paid 'for makeinge a larder to sett powdered meate in'.[2] The larder must have been a cold safe for

---

1   Stanford was originally employed as a tutor by the Pagets, a well-known recusant family, moving to the Carey household when Sir Thomas Paget's son William became George Carey's ward (Ringler & May; May, *Stanford*, ix).
2   PRO E351/3234. fol. 6ʳ.

meat. Why did they need a special larder for 'powdered meate'? They needed it because the entire court would be stuffing its face with pancakes on Shrove Tuesday. Had the meat kept fresh in the larder specially constructed for it? According to Shakespeare's clown it may have been a bit high. Did a courtier throw him a pancake for his jest?

Such a performance of *As You Like It* may not, of course, have been a first performance. But it probably was, because, as Tiffany Stern's research has shown, epilogues were provided for new plays to test the water for approval before confirming a 'run' (Stern, *Making*, 121). February 1599 was arguably an occasion when a new play for the queen would have been particularly appropriate. Shrove Tuesday 1599 would have marked the final celebratory performance for the fortieth year of the queen's reign before the theatres closed the next day (Ash Wednesday) for Lent. Without being in any specific sense an 'occasional' piece, *As You Like It* is geared to Elizabethan court taste. It boasts, in a pastoral drama full of music and witty word-play, a uniquely powerful heroine posing as a shepherd, Elizabeth's favourite image for her own rule.

Shakespeare knew that he would need many plays for his new Globe theatre opening in the late summer or early autumn. Leeds Barroll has demonstrated that the dramatist wrote plays when he could see that they were going to be performed (Barroll, 19–20). Might he not have tried out this ebullient comedy for court performance before playing it at the Globe in the autumn? The queen's approval would have been valuable, and it was given, for the players received her monetary 'reward' in addition to their standard payment.

To audiences and readers accustomed to the panache of Rosalind's epilogue in the First Folio the idea that another epilogue was spoken at the play's putative first performance sticks in the gorge. But Stern has demonstrated that epilogues were often only used once and then discarded. It is perfectly feasible that *As You Like It* might have been presented at court with an epilogue which was then virtually thrown away, or plundered by a member of the audience – in this case, Henry Stanford – and copied into a commonplace book, as a collector's item.[1] Moreover, the breezy egalitarian tone of Rosalind's epilogue, addressing 'men' and 'women' rather than 'gentlemen' and 'ladies', is less appropriate for court performance than it is for the public theatre. The only other play in the period in which a woman speaks an epilogue is Lyly's *Galatea*, and Galatea addresses the 'ladies and gentlemen' of the court deferentially, where Rosalind's insouciant offering of kisses indiscriminately to women and to men might have trodden on a royal toe.

Rosalind's epilogue seeks approval and ratification for the play. Is this play going to succeed? Is it worth continuing with it? Even that epilogue may not in fact have been performed more than once during Shakespeare's lifetime (Stern, 'Re-patching', 161). In a more restrained and decorous fashion the court epilogue by implication asks the same questions of the queen, requesting approval as was also customary. When the play was done and the reward given, the function of the epilogue had been served. A new performance would need new packaging in the form of a new (Rosalind's) epilogue.[2]

The supposition that *As You Like It* was first performed at the new public theatre, the Globe, when it opened in the autumn of 1599, grew from Fleay's suggestion in 1886 that Jaques's 'All the world's a stage' (2.7.140) echoes the motto round the new theatre's circumference: '*Totus mundus agit histrionem*' ('All the world plays the player'). However, the existence of the motto has been queried.[3] Jaques's 'All the world's a stage', if pronounced in

---

1 See Stern, 'Re-patching', 155: 'It was normal practice for audiences to plunder the performances they attended, removing particular types of text for future use elsewhere in non-play contexts'; see also 159: 'As with songs, stage orations flourished in books of poetry, sometimes even when "lost" from their play.'
2 See Stern, 'Small-beer', esp. pp. 182, 186, 194 and 197.
3 Fleay, 209, cited here from Stern, '*Totus*', 122. Cf. Dutton, 'Sign', 42–3. Stern points out that although Cam[1] (132) and Ard[2] (xxvii) adopt Fleay's suggestion ('*Totus*', 123), it is not endorsed by Knowles (373) or Cam[2] (63), and is ignored by Oxf[1].

February 1599, might have advertised the new Globe rather than reflected on its existence.[1] The next day (21 February, Ash Wednesday) the lease for the new theatre was signed by six of the Chamberlain's Men: Shakespeare, Richard Burbage, John Heminges, Augustine Phillips, Thomas Pope and William Kemp; as also by Cuthbert Burbage and Nicholas Brend (Schoenbaum, 210). A successful performance of *As You Like It* the previous night might have seemed like a good omen for the new venture.

The only specific documentary evidence for performances of *As You Like It* in Shakespeare's lifetime links the play not with the public theatre (the Globe) but with the private theatre at Blackfriars. A document dating from 1669 names it among plays from the old Blackfriars theatre assigned to Thomas Killigrew for the new Theatre Royal (see Fig. 9): 'A Catalogue of part of his Maties Servants Playes as they were formerly acted at the Blackfryers & now allowed of to his Maties Servants at ye New Theatre'.[2] One hundred and eight plays are listed, twenty-one by Shakespeare; *As You Like It* appears between *The Merchant of Venice* and *The Taming of the Shrew*. It is surprising that more has not been made of this document, in view of the many characteristics which might relate the play to the tastes of the Court and private theatres rather than to those of the public theatre audience.

Tradition claims that *As You Like It* may have been produced at court on 2 December 1603, when James I was at Wilton House – the Wiltshire home of Mary Sidney, the Countess of Pembroke. If so, it would have been the first Shakespeare play to be seen in the new reign of James I, and particularly appropriate because of James's passion for hunting and the play's connections with Sir Philip Sidney's *Old Arcadia* (Gibbons, esp. 158). William Cory in the nineteenth century alleged seeing a letter from the Countess of Pembroke to her son William Herbert, stating: 'We have the man

---

1 Cf. Dekker's *Old Fortunatus*, played at court at Christmas 1599, which may advertise the new Fortune theatre about to be built in 1600 (Dutton, 'Sign', 39).
2 PRO LC 5/12, fols 212–13. The King's Men in 1608–9 reacquired the Blackfriars theatre that the Burbages had leased in 1600 to the Children of the Chapel Royal (Hillebrand, 156; Schoenbaum, 264).

9   PRO LC 5/12, fols 212–13: plays granted to Thomas Killigrew for the
new Theatre Royal at Drury Lane in 1669. 'As you like it' is fourth from
the bottom in the middle column.

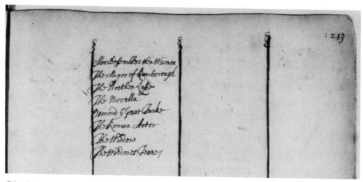

Shakespeare with us' (Knowles, 633). Sadly, the letter has not materialized. Leeds Barroll backs the tradition of a Wilton performance, however, using the list of plays performed at court in the 1604–5 season to suggest that plays which are not mentioned – *Twelfth Night* and *Hamlet*, *Henry IV*, *As You Like It*, and even *Troilus and Cressida* – may be absent because they had been played at court in 1603 (Barroll, 124). Lodge's *Rosalynde* was reprinted in 1604, which might suggest that the printer (James Roberts, who probably made the staying order for *As You Like It* (see pp. 121–2) and held the monopoly on printing play-bills) thought he would sell copies in the wake of a successful play.

If *As You Like It* was first performed before queen and court on 20 February 1599, new questions arise. Might Shakespeare have included in the play some awareness of the Shrovetide festival?[1] The new date would affect the casting of the part of Touchstone, often assigned by scholars to Robert Armin, who joined the company at the end of the year. In February 1599 the part of Touchstone would have been taken by Will Kemp. Later the role may have passed on to Robert Armin, as was the case with Dogberry in *Much Ado About Nothing*. Aspects of Touchstone's role in *As You Like It*, notably the satire directed at Sir Oliver Mar-text in 3.3 and its connections with the Marprelate

---

1 Anny Crunelle-Vanrigh's discussion of liminality in the play could be transposed into a Shrovetide context, because of the nature of the festival which takes place on the threshold of Lent; but she does not use Shrove in her argument. For liturgical correspondences in other Shakespeare plays see Hassel; Hopkins; Dean.

controversy (in which Kemp was a key player), make Kemp a likely candidate for the part.[1]

If *As You Like It* dates from February 1599, it may have been performed within months of *2 Henry IV*,[2] now thought to be the play named as 'Henry 5' in the staying order of 1600 (see p. 121 and n.), making more plausible some apparent connections between the two plays noted in the commentary. *Henry V*, composed at the latest by the summer of 1599, may have followed rather than preceded *As You Like It*. *Henry V* has many affinities with the comedies, not least in the motif of disguise which links its hero-king with tales of Robin Hood (Barton, 'King', 112), but also in Henry's comic wooing of the French Kate, which serves to cement Henry's Englishness (Gregerson). The French setting of the court in the opening act of *As You Like It*, and the alternative foreign location of the Forest, may serve a comparable purpose of highlighting the true Englishness of the Forest of Arden.

THE FOREST OF ARDEN

'Well, this is the Forest of Arden'

What must those first audiences, whether at court or in the new Globe, have thought of the Forest of Arden? Were they transported, as Rosalind and Celia and Touchstone are, to a natural place where the sorrows and envy and danger of Frederick's court are left behind? Did they find it, as later audiences have done, an escape from the city? Did they think of it as a fiction, a Utopian place (like Thomas More's ideal community in *Utopia*) that was 'nowhere' (see 2.7.2n.), or did they recognize it as a natural forest?

---

1 See Dusinberre, 'Touchstone'; Poole, 34 and n. 2 for Kemp and the Marprelates; see also Appendix 2. The belief that Kemp left the Chamberlain's Men before his Lenten dance in 1600 has been disputed by Nielson. Dutton argues that Kemp must have acted in *Julius Caesar*: 'What is the business of the Poet who tries to reconcile Brutus and Cassius, and is dismissed by the former with impatience at "jigging fools" (4.3.137), if it is not an opportunity for one of Kempe's trade-mark jigs?' (Dutton, *Licensing*, 34).

2 *2 Henry IV*, probably composed in 1598 (Riv², 52), may still in 1599–1600 have been in the repertory of the Chamberlain's Men (Knutson, *Shakespeare's*, 81); see 1.3.85n.

10 Map showing the 'old forrest of Arden' from Michael Drayton, *Poly-Olbion* (1612)

Scholars have debated whether Arden is Shakespeare's own Warwickshire Forest of Arden, or the Ardennes in Flanders (first suggested by Malone). Lodge's *Rosalynde* offers a third location, north of Bordeaux, which he also calls 'Ardennes'. Shakespeare is at pains to stress the Frenchness of the court in Act 1. Robin Hood is identified as 'of England' (1.1.111), Orlando as 'the stubbornest young fellow of France' (1.1.133–4). Le Beau is a French courtier – Celia greets him in French. The medieval *Chanson de Roland* (set in the court of Charlemagne) links the play to a continental chivalric tradition with which the Elizabethans were extremely familiar (see Fig. 11 and 2.7.198n.). The choice of the name 'Orlando' instead of 'Rosader' (as in Lodge's *Rosalynde*) derives from Ariosto's *Orlando Furioso* – a sixteenth-century Italian continuation of the *Chanson de Roland* (Orlando being the Italian form of Roland). The name of Orlando's father, Sir Rowland, is spelt 'Roland' three times in the First Folio. But Shakespeare's mother's maiden name was Arden, and the playwright must have expected audiences to identify an English setting for the Forest, which, however decimated it may have been in 1599, was still a well-known region (see Fig. 10).

Shakespeare's play embraces the literary and chivalric resonances of the Ardennes in France, together with a specific Elizabethan association of the area with the Earl of Leicester's campaign in Flanders in 1585–6 against the Spanish (on behalf of the Dutch Protestants). In this campaign Sir Philip Sidney was mortally wounded and Leicester's stepson, the Earl of Essex (barely twenty), made his military debut. These connections coexist with a rural English Forest of Arden in the dramatist's home county of Warwickshire, where William, possibly played by Shakespeare himself (see Appendix 2), courts Audrey. The French court in the first act is corrupt, and the English Arden of Duke Senior's court-in-exile a setting for renewed innocence and regeneration. If uncomfortable parallels could be drawn between Frederick's court and Elizabeth's, the French setting would be useful as a stalking-horse under the presentation of which the

11 *The Quintain*: drawing (*c.* 1581) by Antoine Caron of the sport of jousting with a quintain (see 1.2.240n.), reflecting celebrations for the marriage in 1581 of the Duc de Joyeuse and Marie de Lorraine

dramatist might, like the jester (5.4.104–5), shoot his wit with impunity.

The Forest of Arden, like Hamlet, like Falstaff, like Romeo and Juliet, has become a Shakespearean myth. Even the name of the Arden edition salutes it.[1] Many people across the world who have neither seen nor read *As You Like It* possess a pool of associations into which the words 'Forest of Arden' drop like a pebble, creating concentric ripples. Few writers have had this power, and an analysis of the elements which create the myth still fails to explain its magic. Rooted in Elizabethan culture – books, topology, economics, social customs, natural phenomena – the Forest of Arden in *As You Like It* has grown, like the biblical mustard-seed, into a vast tree which casts shadows over other cultures and other times. The setting of a play, it transcends the theatre. All the world is its stage.

The first evidence of this influence appears in *Poly-Olbion* (1612), the work of another Warwickshire poet, Michael Drayton. In the thirteenth song Drayton gives the Forest of Arden in the opening part of the poem her own voice – 'When thus of her owne selfe the Forrest spake' (213). Arden laments that she has been enclosed by landowners and encroached upon by building.[2] The Forest's ancient deer preserves have been desecrated. Drayton chooses three particular motifs to convey its character: an evocation of birds and birdsong; a vivid description of the hunting of a hart; and a detailed depiction of the forest hermit. Drayton's account is celebratory, nostalgic, and angry at the despoiling of an environment he considers his own. When Drayton claims that all continental literary Ardens derive from the ancient terrain of his birth,[3] he describes a region which even as early as 1612 may have

1   RP points out that 'the first three volumes of the first series, *Ham*, *KL*, *RJ*, 1899–1901, do not bear the series name, but *Tem*, 1901, does'.

2   *Poly-Olbion*, 213–14. Anne Barton points out that the Forest of Arden was apparently never Crown property, but only subject to Common Law, which tolerated encroachment on it ('Parks and Ardens', 353–4).

3   'Forest call'd *Arden*. The reliques of whose name in *Dene of Monmouth* Shire, & that *Arduenna* or *La Forest d'Ardenne*, by *Henault* and *Luxembourg*, shews likelihood of interpretation of the yet vsed *English* name of *Woodland*' (Drayton, *Poly-Olbion*, 223).

been the stuff of a new myth: Shakespeare's Forest of Arden. But in 1599 that myth was only in the making.

The Forest in *As You Like It* is breathtakingly beautiful, with great oak trees, running brooks, green pastures, banks of willows, flowers, birds, sheep and deer. But it is also a working environment, with shepherds, a goat-girl called Audrey, foresters and locals like Audrey's rustic suitor, William. Within that environment Shakespeare sketches the social tensions of his own time: the threat of enclosure of common land, which took away the means for an independent livelihood from men like Corin, who is working for another man, a 'churl'.[1] Marcia McDonald suggests connections with the English experience of dearth in 1599.[2] In 1817 William Hazlitt described the Forest as an 'ideal' realm, a description both true and misleading. The dramatist allows the ideal to blend into the actual, and the actual to attain to the ideal. Just as the binaries of the heterosexual and the homosexual, masculine and feminine are refracted and melt into each other within the figure of Rosalind, so in the Forest the polarity of real and ideal ceases to be illuminating.

In his essay 'Of Nature in Men' Francis Bacon declares that 'A Mans *Nature* is best perceiued in Priuatenesse, for there is no Affectation; in Passion, for that putteth a Man out of his Precepts; And in a new Case or Experiment, for there Custome leaueth him' (*Essays*, 161). Touchstone dislikes the Forest because it is private, the worst possible scenario for a jester, who must have an audience to entertain. Happily, he finds that the Forest, seemingly deserted, is in fact full of people, and most of them are watching him. Orlando and Rosalind are both put out of their precepts by passion, as are poor lovesick Silvius and deluded Phoebe. Once in the Forest, all the court characters, like the courtiers of Milan on Prospero's isle in *The Tempest*, are in a 'new Case or Experiment', which reveals their natures. But where

---

1 For a specific identification of this figure as 'old Carlot' see 3.5.109n., and see L. Parker for the absentee landowner John Quarles.
2 McDonald, 121–44. See also Barnaby; R. Wilson, esp. 5–6.

in *The Tempest* the island itself is a subjective terrain perceived differently by the corrupt and the virtuous, the Forest of Arden remains independent of those who arrive and those who depart. It has its own native inhabitants, both human and animal. In his treatment of the hunt Shakespeare delicately sets the traditions of aristocratic sport against a larger backdrop of the relation between men and beasts.

The hunt

Deer-hunting was an aristocratic sport and the right to hunt was conferred by the monarch. Elizabeth was a keen huntswoman who was still hunting in September 1600, when she was 67.[1] Hunting was considered the proper recreation for a gentleman and a training for war. Shakespeare's Forest of Arden had not formally been a royal hunting preserve since the reign of Henry II, although the area continued to be the scene of deer-hunting throughout the dramatist's lifetime. Elizabeth hunted at Kenilworth Castle in 1575; a legend claims that Shakespeare poached deer from Sir Thomas Lucy's deer park at Charlecote near Stratford-upon-Avon (Knowles, 639). Shakespeare's Forest of Arden offers a full-scale deer forest, which means an area not just devoted to trees, but complete with 'purlieus' (border grazing grounds consisting of coppices and little woods (Manwood, *Laws*, 126–68)) and pasture for sheep, goats, cows and horses – in other words, a varied rural terrain (Daley, 173).

The exiled lords in the Forest of Arden hunt for subsistence, a motive disallowed by a genuinely aristocratic hunter. Hunting was not, however, an activity solely confined to aristocrats. Foresters were employed to protect the environment for the deer, and to tend the woodland, as Drayton's forester (named, correctly, Silvius: 'of the woods'; see List of Roles, 15n.) makes clear in *The Muses' Elizium* (1630). These men are essential to the satisfactory practice of the hunt. In Shakespeare's play the term 'forester' applies

---

1 Berry, *Hunt*, 3, quoting a letter from Rowland Whyte to Sir Robert Sidney, 12 September 1600.

equally to the huntsmen and to their forest keepers. Huntsmen were under the control of the Forest Ranger, an office held by a nobleman and eagerly sought. This aspect of the Forest is far removed from a Romantic vision of solitary oaks (under which the melancholy Jaques reclines, lamenting the wounded stag; see Fig. 12). The deeply suggestive imaginative topos of forests which was to engage the Romantic poets, and, in music, Beethoven,[1] is antipathetic to the working and hunting environment of Shakespeare's play. Nevertheless, the dramatist evokes a possible imaginative realm for future times even as he locates the principal life of his own Forest of Arden in a different domain.

As You Like It also dramatizes dubiousness about hunting. During the sixteenth century the sport was under fire from humanists who attacked its cruelty and the aristocratic culture – including traditions of adulterous romantic love[2] – which accompanied it (Berry, *Hunt*, 160). There is no adulterous love in the Forest and the exiled Duke recognizes that he and his courtiers have invaded the natural environment and usurped the rights of its native inhabitants, the deer (its 'poor dappled fools', 2.1.22). But Jaques's concern for the deer does not prevent him from acting as a master of ceremonies when one is slaughtered – possibly by the Lord who reports Jaques's lament. The hunting song in 4.2 and the carrying of the slaughtered deer may have struck a jarring note in some Elizabethan ears, as it does in some modern ones. But it also points to a social unrest, focused on the control of the Forest, which lies in the hinterland of Shakespeare's play and is connected with its evocation of Robin Hood (R. Wilson; Fitter). As Edward Berry points out, 'Duke Senior and his men are technically poaching, since they live as outlaws, taking deer from land that is under the authority of Duke Frederick' (*Hunt*, 25), although Duke Frederick's rights are the dubious

---

1 See John Keats, 'When through the old oak forest I am gone' ('On sitting down to read King Lear once again', Keats, 211). For Beethoven see also Solomon, 42–5; and p. 67.
2 Hunting featured prominently in the medieval romances, which humanists blamed on 'idle Monkes, or wanton Chanons' (Ascham, 80; Dusinberre, *Women*, 144).

12 *Jaques and the Wounded Stag* (1830) by John Constable, from a mezzotint by David Lucas

ones of a usurper. A conservationist strain may even be detected in the wounded-deer sequence. Sir John Harington disliked deer-hunting on his estate and wrote epigrams about the more satisfying diet of nuts and fruit (see 2.1.62n.). When Orlando interrupts the Duke at supper, he is offered fruit.

The deer are displaced, but so are the people who live there. Rosalind buys the cottage Silvius wanted and becomes the object – at least temporarily – of Phoebe's affections. Touchstone pinches William's Audrey, probably literally as well as figuratively, and their union is seen as doomed by everyone except Audrey herself. Even the trees are scarred by the hunter, Orlando, in his pursuit of the heart (hart?); Jaques complains: 'I pray you, mar no more trees with writing love-songs in their barks' (3.2.252–3).

Hunting should nevertheless be seen in the play within the context of the projected plans of Duke Frederick to enter the Forest at the end of Act 5 with a mighty army. To hunt deer for food is not in the same order of killing as hunting men for revenge. The hunt is juxtaposed in *As You Like It* with the court, in which the malicious hunting of men is taken for granted – Oliver's hounding of Orlando, Duke Frederick's hounding of Oliver and banishment of Rosalind, not to mention his usurpation of his own brother's dukedom. In this realm envy and slander reign. Whispering, overhearing, spreading rumours, treating old servants like dogs, making sport out of an old man's grief at the near-fatal injuries inflicted on his three sons in a wrestling contest to amuse the idle court, are all part of a court culture which is transmuted in the Forest of Arden into the hunting of deer.

Robin Hood and his merry men

Shakespeare's Forest is in the Robin Hood tradition not only in its alternative court in the greenwood, but in its festivity and joyfulness. In the medieval *Little Geste of Robin Hood* Robin Hood's love of the forest environment – its birds and beasts, its freedom, its fresh air and its great trees – irradiates the text. The melancholy Jaques in *As You Like It* stands out because he is surrounded by merry men, as was Robin Hood; modern productions often make all the courtiers in Arden miserable, which distorts the play's mood and structure. Charles the wrestler introduces the exiled Duke with the evocative parallel: 'They say he is already in the Forest of Arden and a many merry men with him, and there they live like the old Robin Hood of England' (1.1.109–111). Not only are the exiled courtiers liberated from the envy, suspicion, treachery and violence of Duke Frederick's court, they are also liberated from hierarchy. The Duke's opening line greets his 'co-mates' (2.1.1), a word unique in Shakespeare. This aspect of the Forest is often disregarded, but is captured in the 'Drammatis Personae' (*sic*) of the Douai manuscript (dated 9 March 169$^{4/5}$, 1695 in new-style dating) where Duke Senior's lords are 'companions' but Duke Frederick's are 'attendants' (fol. 32^v; see Fig. 22 and Appendix 4). The communal spirit of Duke Senior's court in the Forest in the second act of the play is in sharp contrast to the court of Duke Frederick which the audience has witnessed in Act 1; this difference is true to the spirit of the Robin Hood ballads and plays.[1]

It is easy to underplay the significance of the Robin Hood legends in *As You Like It*. The social subversion of those stories – the attacks on civil and ecclesiastical authority, the flouting of convention by a cross-dressed Maid Marian (played by a man) – are in evidence in Shakespeare's comedy in its cross-dressed heroine, its questioning of primogeniture and its ribaldry against a representative of the clergy, Sir Oliver Mar-text.

In his parody of Orlando's love poetry Touchstone cries:

> They that reap must sheaf and bind,
> Then to cart with Rosalind.
>
> (3.2.104–5)

---

1 *As You Like It* may have been written for the enjoyment of the Essex circle as an answer to the crude Robin Hood plays of Anthony Munday and Henry Chettle – *The Downfall of Robert Earl of Huntingdon* and *The Death of Robert Earl of Huntingdon* (Bullough, 2.142). Other Robin Hood plays are George Peele, *Edward I* (1593), the anonymous *George a Green, Look about You* and *Wily Beguiled*, and Munday's Lord Mayor's Show, *Metropolis Coronata* (see 1.1.111n.).

An Elizabethan audience would immediately have recognized the custom of 'carting' obstreperous women. This formed part of the tradition of Maid Marian in the Robin Hood mummers' plays (Stallybrass, 'Liberty', 54–7). Natalie Zemon Davis includes Rosalind in her list of unruly women who were punished with carting and the allied custom of the skimmington ride, a ritual associated – like the parallel shaming of cuckolds – with Shrovetide sports and festivities.[1] In linking Rosalind to this tradition Shakespeare allows her gender games to move beyond the world of court pastoral into the arena of rumbustious and socially subversive folk festivals.

In *As You Like It* Orlando's revolt against his brother is given the backing of the play's moral authority (Montrose, 'Brother'). Interestingly that authority is chiefly vested in a servant, Adam. The quarrel between Orlando and Oliver over the denial of Orlando's inheritance and right to education becomes charged with ideas of illegitimacy: 'I am no villain,' rages Orlando. 'I am the youngest son of Sir Rowland de Boys; he was my father, and he is thrice a villain that says such a father begot villains' (1.1.53–5). Orlando refuses to accept Oliver's claim of a superiority attendant on being the eldest son:

> The courtesy of nations allows you my better in that you are the first-born, but the same tradition takes not away my blood, were there twenty brothers betwixt us. I have as much of my father in me as you, albeit I confess your coming before me is nearer to his reverence.
>
> (1.1.43–8)

In 2.3 Adam, the old retainer whom Oliver has unceremoniously cast off, claims that Oliver doesn't deserve the names of 'son' of Sir Rowland or 'brother' of Orlando (2.3.19–20) because of his base behaviour. This motif is bizarrely taken up by Duke Frederick, who has usurped his own brother's kingdom, when he

---

1 See 3.2.105n, 3.3.51-2n. See Zemon Davis, 'Women', 161; also her 'Misrule', 75, for an interpretation of the *charivari* (skimmington) as youth rebellion; Howard, 'Crossdressing', 426–7; Laroque, 100; Stallybrass, 'Liberty', 48–51.

caps Oliver's 'I never loved my brother in my life' with 'More villain thou!' (3.1.14–15). At the end of the play the potentially tragic theme of family disruption, which looks forward to *King Lear*, is turned aside by Oliver's repentance and the Duke's own conversion. But the challenge to primogeniture as a mode of thought and social practice is not expunged, any more than Rosalind's gender subversion is cancelled by her return to women's clothes. Oliver recovers his confiscated lands, but it is Orlando, the youngest brother, who inherits a dukedom. The renegotiation of social mores, of the precepts by which people live, is in the tradition of Robin Hood.

Finally, the traditional confrontation in the Forest between Robin Hood and representatives of the Church lies behind Touchstone's teasing of Sir Oliver Mar-text, the rural vicar whose name invokes the Puritan sectarians who attacked Bishops. The Forest of Arden had its own makers and marrers of text, and there is an inspired congruity in Touchstone's encounter with one of their representatives in a Warwickshire Arden. The meeting of the jester with a Mar-text in the Forest would have located Arden, at least for the Elizabethan civil and ecclesiastical authorities, firmly in Shakespeare's Warwickshire. The defiance of authority in the printing of unlicensed Marprelate tracts (Dutton, *Licensing*, 74) centred on Warwickshire, where Job Thro[c]kmorton was convicted at the Warwickshire Assizes in 1590 for taking part in illegal printing (L. Carlson, 17–18, 33).

When Amiens sings his song in 2.5, the line 'Under the greenwood tree' echoes the refrain from the old ballad of *A Little Geste of Robin Hood*. Those who heard it, both on stage and off, would have recognized that the three elements of Robin Hood's social revolt – Church, State and gender – were all present in Shakespeare's Forest of Arden.

Staging the Forest of Arden

The Forest of Arden in *As You Like It* is both the magic circle of the natural environment and the theatre into which the magician dramatist, shadowed by Rosalind, conjures his creatures. The play is full of audience address; the horned beasts mocked by Touchstone in 3.3 (see Fig. 13) are both the rams of Corin's flock and the fearful husbands who watch the play. Rosalind's epilogue is only the final recognition that the forest watches – as it watched Helena and Demetrius in *A Midsummer Night's Dream*: 'Nor doth this wood lack worlds of company' (2.1.222) – but also passes judgement: 'You have said,' remarks Touchstone dryly to the heroine, 'But whether wisely or no, let the forest judge' (3.2.118–19). The audience are arbiters of the jest, as of the play.

This is not the only place in *As You Like It* where Touchstone seems to imply a special capacity of 'judgement' in the audience, making one wonder whether Shakespeare intended the play, like *The Comedy of Errors* and *Twelfth Night*, for performance at the Inns of Court in front of the most intelligent young men in London, who were ostensibly embarked on a study of the law. When Touchstone prepares himself for marriage he announces: 'for here we have no temple but the wood, no assembly but horn-beasts' (3.3.45–6); the joke could be on an audience of members of either the Middle Temple (as for *Twelfth Night* in 1602), or the Inner Temple, or possibly of Lincoln's Inn.[1] There are a lot of legal usages and puns in the play which would have been particularly appreciated by the young bloods of the Inns of Court. But an even more appropriate setting may have been available to the Chamberlain's Men at Shrove, 1599.

If *As You Like It* was first staged at Richmond Palace, the idyllic rural retreat of Richmond would have meant that the audience participated in the experience not only of the players, taking time

---

1   Thomas Morley's *First Book of Airs* (containing 'It was a lover and his lass') is dedicated to Sir Ralph Bosville, of Lincoln's Inn; Lodge, Harington, Morley, Donne, and John Manwood, author of *A Treatise of the Laws of the Forest* (1598), were all Lincoln's Inn men, and Lodge's *Rosalynde* is dedicated to the 'Gentlemen of Lincoln's Inn'. Ralegh was a Middle Temple man. Leicester was a member of the Inner Temple, and on his death Essex, as his stepson, was invited to join the society (Hammer, 76).

Mr King, in the Character of Touchstone.

Right, many à Man has good horns.

Act III. Scene 2.

Publiſhd by J.Wenman 1ˢᵗ March 1777.

13   *Mr King, in the Character of Touchstone*: sketch by an unknown artist of the
     eighteenth-century comic actor Thomas King, showing a gesture to
     accompany the 'horns' speech at 3.3.44–58; facing the title page of a 1777
     edition of *As You Like It*

out from the London theatre to enjoy the country venue, but also of the characters in the play itself. When the Royal Shakespeare Company occupied its London winter home of the Barbican Theatre, its spring migration to Stratford-upon-Avon was itself a journey to the Forest of Arden, particularly piquant in 1992, when the first play to be performed was *As You Like It*. The players in that production were conscious that they were acting a play that would reflect their own escape from the city of London to Shakespeare's Warwickshire Arden. This is one key to any production of *As You Like It*. The play creates a special relation with its audience, who become not just watchers but participants.[1] What would that experience have been like if the play was staged in the Great Hall at Richmond in February 1599?

Richmond Palace, situated west of London, fronting the Thames, where the medieval Palace of Sheen had stood, was a rural palace, which functioned in some respects as a pastoral retreat – comparable to the Forest of Arden – for the Elizabethan court. It was a favourite location for royal hunting. The ancient friary, its gardens, and the 'Great Orchard' beyond the outer east wall can be seen in Anthony van den Wyngaerde's drawing of *c.* 1558 (see Fig. 14), which also shows deer grazing in the park to the west of the Palace. The rural location of the Palace is captured in a Flemish painting (*c.* 1620) depicting the towpath across the Thames and morris dancers (see Dusinberre, 'Pancakes', fig. 4). A herald's account dating from 1501, written for the marriage of Prince Arthur and Katharine of Aragon, describes the Palace as 'this erthely and secunde Paradise of our region of England'[2] – in other words, another Eden, a parallel invoked by Duke Senior in

---

1   However, Richard Proudfoot criticizes the actors in Bayley's production for the new Globe (1998) for not taking advantage of the 'many chances of rapport with their audience' (216).

2   The herald's account, entitled 'Here begynneth the note and trewth of the moost goodly behavior in the receyt of the Ladie Kateryne, daught͏ʳ unto Phardinand, the King of Espayn, yowen in mariage goinct to Prince Arthure, son and heir unto oʳ noble Soferynge of Englond King Henry the VII͏ᵗʰ, in the XVII yere of his reign', is reproduced in Grose, 2.249–331; for the herald's 'desc*rip*ci*o*n of the place of Rychemont', see 313–17.

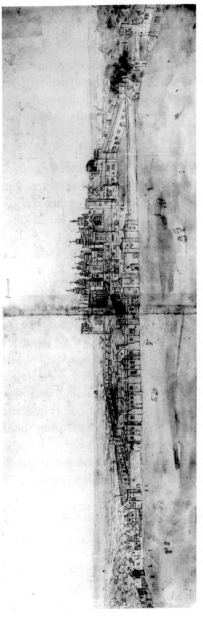

14 Drawing (*c.* 1558) by Anthony van den Wyngaerde of Richmond Palace from the north–east

the Forest of Arden at 2.1.5 (see n.): 'Here feel we not the penalty of Adam'.

Shakespeare's Forest is only in part naturalistic. Its flora and fauna include a palm-tree, an olive, a lioness, a gilded snake and perhaps a shoe-tree to match its palm-tree (see 3.2.125n., 171–2n.). Some of these are clearly 'literary' motifs: the olive (peace), the lioness (a royal beast) and the gilded snake (Eden/Egypt: sin and wisdom) can be found in Spenser's *Faerie Queene*. However, carved lions and grotesque beasts decorated the outer court at Richmond; the royal symbolism might have seemed as appropriate to the festive occasion at court as the physical environment was to the alternative court set up by Duke Senior in a different deer forest.

If the play was staged at Richmond various records suggest details of the scene. The Office of Works Accounts for 1598–9 record 'the making of tressells, tables, formes & dressers', which presumably refers to the furnishing of the Great Hall for a banquet.[1] The audience of banqueters would have lined the three sides of the performing area. According to the Parliamentary assessment of 1649 the hall was 'very well lighted', had 'a faire foote pace [dais] in the higher end thereof' and 'a skreene at the lower end thereof over which is a litle gallery' (Hart, 77). The queen would have sat on the 'dais' (raised platform) with select courtiers, as in the picture of Sir Henry Unton's wedding-feast (see Fig. 15). Steps leading to the platform would have allowed the players access to the main body of the hall for larger scenes. In the Unton picture the musicians sit at ground level below the platform, but at Richmond there was a gallery at the other end of the hall, opposite the queen.[2] In the centre of the Great Hall was a 'brick hearth for a charkoale fier' (Hart, 77), around which Duke

---

1 PRO E351/3234, fol. 6^r. See also *Dramatic Records* 10, xix–xxii; and Astington, 103: 'Early Elizabethan court staging . . . employed dispersed settings, with actors moving across the wider arena of the open floor of the room.'
2 PRO E351/3234, fol. 6^r, records as one of the works undertaken in 1598–9 the strengthening of the gallery with iron.

15 Detail from *The Wedding Feast of Sir Henry Unton* from the memorial
portrait of Henry Unton (*c.* 1596) by an unknown artist, showing the
players in a broken consort

Senior's co-mates could have gathered to defend themselves against the chiding of the winter wind.

The Great Hall at Richmond was distinctive in other ways, having been built in French-Burgundian style by Henry VII (Astington, 4, 35, 59). The 1501 herald describes a dynastic scene created by pictures (in fact sculptures, according to the later Parliamentary survey made in 1649, cited above) of the kings of the realm, positioned round the walls. There were also rich tapestries, 'rep⟨r⟩esentyng many noble batalls and seages, as of [Jerusalem], Troye, Albe and many other' (Grose, 2.315). The actor playing Rosalind could have glanced at the tapestries of Troy as the heroine made her joke against Troilus as 'one of the patterns of love' (4.1.91). Astington describes the Great Hall as 'an architectural and artistic endorsement of the historical pattern which had led to the fortunate outcome of the Tudor dynasty' (61). In *As You Like It*, the most dynastic of all Shakespeare's comedies, it would be possible to see old Sir Rowland as an almost legendary figure looking back to the Burgundian influences on the court of Henry VIII and, nearer home, to the figure of the Earl of Leicester (Dusinberre, '*AYL*', 415). In the version of *As You Like It* transcribed in the 1695 Douai manuscript Duke Senior is described in the list of characters as 'Old duke of Burgundy' (fol. 32ᵛ; see Fig. 22 and Appendix 4). Duke Senior loved old Sir Rowland, while Duke Frederick, the usurper, is his enemy. The play's retrospective mood would have been in tune with the setting of Richmond Palace, in which Henry VII's granddaughter Elizabeth had been born – and in 1603 would die – and which in many ways could hardly have provided a more perfect ambience for Shakespeare's pastoral comedy.

In subsequent eras much ingenuity has been expended on the creation of a perfect setting for *As You Like It*. Yet the history of its staging tells of disappointment as often as of delight. The ideal solution for a play set in the greenwood might seem to be outdoor performance, as the majority of the play's scenes take place out of doors. The eighteen-year-old John Gielgud played Orlando in an outdoor amateur production (Bell & McNeill) at St Leonards, Rye and Battle, East Sussex, in 1922.[1] In June 1933 the new Open Air Theatre in Regent's Park opened its first season with a production of *As You Like It* (Carroll) with Phyllis Nielson-Terry as Rosalind and George Grossmith as Touchstone. The audience watched from deckchairs, although the stage was covered. But *The Times* was dubious about open-air playing:

> The truth is that any Shakespearian play within four walls is a better thing than it can be in the most charming garden ever made. In the open air acting and production have to reckon with the distracting movement of the wind and the trees and the clouds in the sky, and perhaps it should also be assumed that the mind of the spectator, set to work out of doors, is apt to be expansive rather than precise.
>
> (20 June 1933)

A *Morning Post* reviewer recalled an outdoor staging in 1897 (in the grounds of the Shakespeare Memorial Theatre, Stratford-upon-Avon) of Augustin Daly's famous production with Ada Rehan as Rosalind: 'Rain began to fall just as the audience welcomed Miss Rehan, and Rosalind sighed: "I show more mirth than I am mistress of"' (21 June 1933).

An illusion of outdoor performance might seem to offer a good compromise. Werner Habicht describes an *As You Like It* staged in West Berlin in 1978 in a film studio, the first act taking place within a confined studio space but the rest of the play requiring the audience to

> share the hardships attending the nobler characters' escape to the woods. This meant a fifteen-minute, single-file walk on a dark, narrow, thorny, and labyrinthine path obstructed with (artificial) briars and puddles, through gusts of wind and patches of blinding light, and past such surprises as a wild bear and a sleeping hermaphrodite.
>
> (Habicht, 'Shakespeare', 299)

1   Robert Tanitch reproduces a fine photograph of this production in *Gielgud*, 18.

Eventually the audience arrived in an idyllic Arden, and relaxed in grandstand seats. 'But there was also the unromantic poverty of peasants' cottages, and there were little niches filled with botanical, zoological, and astronomical collections.' Other figures were imported to add local colour: not only Robin Hood and Robinson Crusoe, but also 'a roaring Wild Man running about the gallery behind the audience added menace'. In the end, Hymen's pageant wagon conveyed everyone back to 'the "real" world'. A 'total' experience was had by all (Habicht, 'Shakespeare', 299). But physical participation does not necessarily create imaginative participation.

Both the lush forest of Motley's design for Glen Byam Shaw in 1952 (Smallwood, 50–1) and David Thacker's realistic scene with a great tree (1992) looked back to an earlier naturalistic tradition with elaborate greenwood, at its most splendid in Macready's revival in 1842. Macready's production was accompanied with orchestral excerpts from Beethoven's Pastoral Symphony, in a novel linking of classic pastoral tropes (see Fig. 16). But more minimalist representations of the Forest, such as Adrian Noble's white ribbons and drapes (1985), are sometimes more evocative. In George Roman's 1977 production at Theatre Clwyd in Mold, North Wales, 'the austere setting, against a simple grid of steel mesh screens' created a 'metal cage' Arden (Thornber). However, austerity, like the Forest wind, can also freeze as well as liberate, as in Clifford Williams's 1967 Old Vic production, in which different shades of grey plastic stood in for old oaks and brawling brooks.

The problem for all directors is how to balance the intensely visual poetry of the play with the visual effects of set and design. Stage trees, wind and clouds passing can distract from the trees and clouds and sunshine of Shakespeare's verse and prose. *As You Like It*, like *Henry V*, requires the audience's imagination to work vigorously. The two plays were conceived at much the same time in the dramatist's mind, and they both require active input from the audience:

> And let us, ciphers to this great account,
> On your imaginary forces work.
>
> (*H5*, Prologue 17–18)

16 Playbill for Macready's 1842 revival at the Theatre Royal, Drury Lane, London, with Macready in the role of Jaques and incidental music from Beethoven's Pastoral Symphony

Entering imaginatively into the Forest of Arden is perhaps less easy for modern audiences than it would have been for Shakespeare's contemporaries, for whom rustic retreats were an everyday reality.

William Empson's review of a Cambridge University production at the Festival Theatre in 1928 identifies a not uncommon feeling that a production has failed to evoke either Shakespeare's Forest or its inhabitants:

> I can explain my feelings so little about this I must just say what they were; I was terribly depressed, and spent some time after I had got home hunting through the text to see if I could find all the Beauty which must surely have been cut. But no, the cutting was fairly tactful . . . Why is it that seeing Shakespeare or Beaumont at the Festival Theatre is like hearing your love-letters read out in a divorce court; you feel keenly only your own past lack of judgment, and it might all have been written by Sir James Barrie? Partly because the guts are taken out; . . . one ought to feel it was *brave* of them all to romp like that; Nature was not really kindly, and Nurse not in reserve.
>
> (Empson, *Reviews*, 86)

Bravery, audacity, the challenge of the unfamiliar: these are the hallmarks of Shakespeare's Forest. The audience needs to feel its danger as well as its escape from danger, its risk as well as its release. 'All the world's a stage' is not just a pretty Shakespearean tag. Shakespeare offered his play to the Elizabethan court with a sense of its significance beyond the world of entertainment, just as productions of *As You Like It* in the modern theatre have often tapped, even if unconsciously, the conditions of the times.

Nigel Playfair's production of 1919 marked a watershed in the history of performances of *As You Like It* at the Shakespeare Memorial Theatre in Stratford-upon-Avon. It flouted tradition in various ways, notably in dispensing with the stuffed deer that had habitually graced 4.2 (Playfair, 52–3). But something more significant than disregard for theatrical convention aroused the wrath of spectators. *As You Like It*, in which the enmity of political life is left behind by gentlemen (and ladies) flocking to the beneficent Forest where the rhythms of nature supplant the mechanics of court time, was surely chosen as a potentially restorative experience in that first post-World War I theatre season. What audiences wanted was a reassurance that in the world of art nothing had changed. Shakespeare would always be the same, stuffed deer and all.

In the same way the choice of *As You Like It* for the first post-war season in 1946 (Prentice) also carried its own special baggage, for Ruth Lodge, who played Rosalind, had played Cressida in *Troilus and Cressida* in a much-hailed production at the Westminster Theatre in 1939 (Smallwood, 11). The message offered to the audience, when the same actress plays Rosalind after the war is over, is unmistakable. In the Forest of Arden fire is for warmth not for the destruction of cities.

Another kind of political event could also be read into the performance history of *As You Like It*. This is a play about the dispossessed. Its staging in 1957 by Glen Byam Shaw, with Peggy Ashcroft as Rosalind (a part in which she had excelled in 1932 at the Old Vic under Harcourt Williams), must have allowed some audience members to meditate on the Hungarian uprising of the previous year, and the influx of Hungarian refugees into both Britain and America.

The sense of a play speaking to the contemporary world of refugees and exiles may colour perceptions of the 1936 film of *As You Like It* (the first speaking film of any Shakespeare play), directed in London by an Austrian Jewish refugee, Paul Czinner, whose wife, the Austrian Jewish actress Elizabeth Bergner, played Rosalind to the Orlando of the young Laurence Olivier. (The musical score was by the British composer William Walton.) The film was relentlessly fairy-tale. But its performance, by artists hounded from their native land by political persecution, provides a reminder of Shakespeare's theatre in 1599, when the precarious fortunes of the Earl of Essex had begun to overshadow courtly festivity. What looks to a modern, Western, democratic audience like a harmless frolic in the Forest has never been, for less liberated societies, just a play about a place where, like Celia, we willingly would waste our time.

In 1992 the RSC staged it at the Royal Shakespeare Theatre in Stratford simultaneously with Richard Brome's *The Jovial Crew* (1641) at the Swan.[1] Brome's play was first presented on the eve of the Civil War, and, in the words of Michael Billington's review, 'pits bourgeois security against vagrant freedom'. The vagrants 'romantically imagine a life of "liberty, mirth and ease". The reality . . . is different: sleeping rough is harsh, begging is difficult, and violent sexual assault always threatening'. Brome 'both celebrates and criticizes the myth of pastoral freedom' and in fact anticipates the plight of many cavalier supporters of Charles I, who would become displaced persons in the 1650s Interregnum (Billington, 'Beggars'). This is a version of the Forest of Arden subtly soured and localized by politics. Compared with *As You Like It*, *The Jovial Crew* seems bound in by its own political agenda. But the later play highlights the fact that politics is a presence in Shakespeare's comedy, and not just the fairy-tale politics of wicked rulers and treacherous brothers. *As You Like It* deals in a more poetic way with the displacement of individuals and the breaking of apparently insuperable barriers. If it grows in part from the conditions of its time, its breadth of vision allows it to tap not only the fantasies but also the social and political realities of other ages.

Social and political realities would not have been far from the minds of its first audiences in 1599, whether at court or in the public theatre. Beneath an impeccably sunny surface *As You Like It* touches on troubled territories, as a brief glimpse at one or two extra-theatrical players might demonstrate.

1 Paul Taylor, in the *Independent*, 24 April 1992, commented on the felicitous pairing of the two plays.

EARLY FORESTERS

The Earl of Essex

At Shrove 1599 special preparations had been made for the arrival of the noble guests at Richmond Palace. The two main court factions of Sir Robert Cecil – son of William Cecil, Lord Burleigh, whose death in 1598 was still fresh in the queen's mind – and of the Earl of Essex, appear to have been treated with equal honour. Workmen were paid for 'makeing twoe dores and cases for Sr Robte Cecills lodginge'. Essex's family were well provided for, with 'joystinge and boordinge a greate floore for the lady Walsingham [Essex's mother-in-law] and another for therle of Essex'.[1] Wives and children may also have been in attendance.

The special court epilogue from Henry Stanford's book speaks poignantly to the queen, as well as to the courtiers, of the continuity of loyalty at a time when Essex's future career still hung in the balance and his supporters still believed in his capacity for future triumph. Its reference to 'the babe wh^ch now is yong / & hathe yet no vse of tongue' has relevance in February 1599 to Essex's own family, in which there was at this time a babe-in-arms and another expected. The Lord Chamberlain was present, probably with his daughter Bess Carey, his ward William Paget and their tutor, Stanford. The Lord Chamberlain's mother-in-law, Lady Katharine Berkeley, who had consulted a magician in the Warwickshire Forest of Arden (see 5.2.59n.), may also have been present.[2]

Elizabethan court politics centred on the fortunes of the Earl of Essex. The hold which Essex exerted on the Elizabethan imagination began with his early prominence in Leicester's campaign on behalf of the Dutch Protestants against the Catholic Philip II

---

1 PRO E351/3234, fol. 6^r.
2 Lady Katharine's belief in the magician provides interesting testimony not only to the Forest as a site of magic, but to the contemporary existence of a geographical area popularly known as the 'Forest of Arden'. Berry argues that Lord Henry and Lady Katharine Berkeley may have been the originals for Petruchio and Kate in *The Shrew* (*Hunt*, 129–31).

of Spain in 1585–6; at the funeral of Sir Philip Sidney, fatally
wounded at the Battle of Zutphen in 1586, Essex bore the dead
hero's sword at Sidney's request (in his will). The pattern of
stormy personal and political relations between the queen and the
young earl emerged when he was a commander of the army in
Rouen in 1591, and was repeated throughout the decade. He made
a brilliant debut in a masque of his own writing at the Accession
tilts in 1595, but his successful expedition to Cadiz in 1596 was
tarnished by being unauthorized by his royal mistress.

The full impact of Essex's renown and charisma on
Elizabethan culture has yet to be charted, but it is evident that
Shakespeare, whose patron, the Earl of Southampton, was one of
Essex's closest confederates, alluded repeatedly to Essex's career
and personality in his plays. In *Richard II* Bolingbroke's skill with
the commons recalls Essex's known 'common touch'. In *Henry V*,
composed probably by June 1599,[1] and certainly before Essex
returned from Ireland, the Chorus transparently proclaims his
return in glory, comparing him to a Caesar, a passage absent from
the 1600 Quarto of the play. The reprinted first volume of
Richard Hakluyt's *Principal Navigations, Voyages, and Discoveries
of the English Nation* in 1598 carried a eulogy of his role in the
Cadiz expedition, which was excised from the volume in 1599
after the Irish disaster, on orders from the queen. It had obviously
been timed to tap the anticipated popularity of the earl on his
return. In *Julius Caesar* the fickleness of the crowd towards
Pompey at the opening of the play resonates on the favourite's fall
from grace in the summer of 1599. Later, in *Troilus and Cressida*,
probably first performed in 1601–2, the moody Achilles would be
modelled on the earl (Bevington, *TC*, 11–19). Hamlet, Coriolanus
and Antony all owe something to Essex's tragic history.

In February 1599 the atmosphere at court, according to contemporary witnesses, was strained, although no one could have
foreseen the precise chain of events that would lead to Essex's

---

1 T.W. Craik suggests the play was written between March 1599 and September of that
year (Craik, *H5*, 3).

unsuccessful rebellion and his subsequent execution in 1601. Nevertheless the danger from the earl's volatile temperament and consequent stormy relation with the queen was in evidence throughout the decade of the 1590s and contributed to the delay in February 1599 in his appointment as commander of the Irish expedition. However, the harmless sun and shade of the Forest of Arden might have looked more volatile by the autumn of 1599, when the evocation of an alternative court under an exiled 'Robin Hood', Duke Senior, could unintentionally have created uncomfortable parallels with the disgraced and discontented earl. This appears to have happened in the case of Thomas Dekker's *Old Fortunatus*, acted at court at Christmas 1599, and printed in 1600, in which, as Fredson Bowers points out, a leaf was torn out of a third of the contemporary copies. It contained a verse referring to the ambition nurtured in courts, which was possibly seen as a reference to Essex:

> In some Courts shall you see ambition
> Sit piercing Dedalus old waxen wings,
> But being clapt on, and they about to flie,
> Euen when their hopes are buried in the clouds,
> They melt against the Sunne of maiestie.[1]

The parallels with Amiens's song in 2.5 are noticeable and the same political inferences might have been made for Shakespeare's play.[2]

There is plenty of precedent for Elizabethan sensitivity to political innuendo after the event, when works acquired significances they may not have had when written – as Samuel Daniel argued for his play *Philotas* when called before the Privy Council in 1604 to answer for its unsuitably close resemblances to the fate of the Earl of Essex.[3] Essex's supporters would commission a

1 Fol. E2ʳ, reproduced in Bowers, 'Rebellion', 365; see also Dekker, *Works*, 2.109–10, 146.
2 *As You Like It* was not printed in quarto, so no leaf needed to be excised, but the cutting of this scene in the Douai manuscript may indicate that, for whatever reason, there was an early theatrical tradition of excision (see also p. 137 and Appendix 4).
3 See Pitcher, 119–21; Gazzard, 424–5. Pitcher (133, n. 9) supports Gazzard's view that Daniel did intend to draw parallels between Philotas and Essex.

special performance of *Richard II* by the Chamberlain's Men on the eve of his rebellion some two years later. Whether this was in fact Shakespeare's play has been debated, but recent scholarship inclines towards that identification. Elizabeth herself recognized parallels between the fate of the deposed king and challenges to her own pre-eminence: 'I am Richard II: know ye not that?' she observed to William Lambarde in 1601.[1]

Essex's role as a patron of drama, music and fencing – all of which are reflected in *As You Like It* – and his wayward and flamboyant courtship of the queen to whom he was both vassal and incipient rival, were part of a pattern in the 1590s which made him the lodestar of the Court.[2] That this was a precarious position to sustain needs no proof, and there were many who would caution him about his pride and intransigence in his handling of a monarch who, though fascinated by her young knight, was nevertheless determined to brook no master. He had in September 1598 put his hand to his sword when she boxed his ear, and by the following February her good favour had still not been recovered. At Richmond in February 1599 Essex awaited a final decision on his appointment to the position of commander of the Irish expedition to quell the rebels under the Earl of Tyrone, but Elizabeth expressed her disfavour through rancorous delay, only resolved in March when the appointment was finally confirmed. Even then Essex complained that being dispatched to Ireland was a form of exile from court. In this atmosphere of mistrust and discontent the Chamberlain's Men may have first performed *As You Like It*

---

1 Cited in Forker (*R2*), 5; see also Rasmussen; Dutton, *Mastering*, 118–20. Robert Armin, in *Fool upon Fool* (1600), tells a tale, which suggests the wide currency of the parallel between Elizabeth and Richard II, about William Hollis's fool, Jack Oates: 'Iacke Oates sitting at Cardes all alone, was dealing to himselfe at Wide ruffe, for that was the game hee ioyed in, and as he spide a knaue, ah knaue art there quoth hee? When he spide a king, king by your leaue quoth he: If he spied a Queene, Queene Richard art come quothe hee? and would kneele down and bidde God blesse her Maiesty, (meaning indeed our Queene, whom he heard Sir Wiliam Hollis his Maister so much to pray for' (1. sig. A4).

2 See Ruff & Wilson, 36: 'Essex became the living tragic archetype for a generation of inspired poets, dramatists and composers. That is the reason why he is ubiquitous in allusion in Elizabethan drama, verse and song.'

to queen and court, a play of incomparable geniality and good humour, in which the claims of courtly pleasure are pitted against the rival, and in the end ascendant, claims of rustic contentment. Amiens's songs counsel against ambition and treachery and celebrate the trust and comradeship of the greenwood.

Two of Essex's protégés – the official court miniaturist, Nicholas Hilliard, and the Italian fencing expert Vincentio Saviolo – grace the text of *As You Like It* (see 2.7.198n., 5.4.89n., 99–101n.). Hilliard's relation to the Earl of Essex goes back to a shared childhood as Protestant exiles in Geneva during the reign of the Catholic Mary Tudor (1553–8). In 1595 Essex helped the artist to pay for his house in Blackfriars.[1] Shakespeare drew on Saviolo's work on fencing for Touchstone's extravaganza in 5.4 on duelling.

Essex may also have acted as patron for a third and even more significant figure in Shakespeare's text, the musician and composer Thomas Morley, whose setting for the song 'It was a lover and his lass' is the only undisputed contemporary setting of any of Shakespeare's songs (Fellowes, *Madrigal*, vi). One of the dedicatory poems to Morley's immensely popular *A Plain and Easy Introduction to Practical Music* (1597) says that a great patron – a day-star – has found out '*a part where more lay vndiscouered*'. Elizabeth called Essex her 'evening star'. The earl may have become Morley's patron in 1595 after Morley took part in the spectacular masque which Essex mounted for the annual celebration of the queen's accession on 17 November.[2] Essex's generosity to Catholic musicians was well known and an admirable example of tolerance in a fanatical age. Morley (like the composer William Byrd) was a Catholic and (like his mentor) narrowly avoided charges of treason.[3] Shakespeare probably knew Morley personally because they were in 1598 neighbours in Bishopsgate.

---

1 Strong, 'Hilliard', 'Miniature'; Edmond, *Hilliard*, 28, 126.
2 *Sidney Papers*, 1.132, cited in Chambers, *ES*, 3.121.
3 Ruff & Wilson, 14–15; Hammer, 318n.; Scott-Warren, *Harington*, 88. For Morley's Catholicism see D. Brown, 54–5; Dart, 'Catholics', 92.

Fellowes pointed out that both their names figure 'in the Roll of Assessments for subsidies' for that year in the parish of St Helen's (*Madrigal*, vi).

Thomas Morley

Morley's connections with the Court and with theatrical performance make his links with *As You Like It* particularly intriguing. If *As You Like It* was played at Richmond Palace in February 1599 both Morley and Byrd would probably have been present to perform their musical duties in the choir for the Shrovetide and Lenten services. Morley could have produced his song 'It was a lover and his lass' – first printed in his *First Book of Airs* (1600) – in manuscript version for the players.[1]

The careers of Morley and Byrd were linked at several points. Despite their shared Catholicism, Morley succeeded Byrd as organist at the Anglican cathedral of St Paul's and after 1592 joined him as a Gentleman of the Chapel Royal – employed to sing in the queen's chapels for Anglican feast-days. This leniency to religious preference demonstrates some interesting royal priorities. The queen preferred impeccable music to impeccable Protestant dogma. Morley's promotion in 1592 to Gentleman of the Chapel Royal may have reflected the queen's delight at his consort music during the entertainment put on at Elvetham in 1591 for one of her progresses. In 1598 Byrd passed on his monopoly on the printing of music to Morley (*Records*, 1.lxiv and 65). Morley was also apparently acquainted with Henry Stanford, in whose commonplace book the court epilogue which may have been used for *As You Like It* was found. The book contains the text of two songs by Morley which are only known from the *First Book of Airs* (1600); Steven May suggests that Morley himself may have given them to Stanford or to the Lord Chamberlain, who possessed his own collection of songs by Morley and Dowland, to which the family tutor would have had access (May, *Stanford*, 313–14).

---

1 Its chorus, 'When birds do sing', may have found the composer catching the eye of his fellow singer and former master, William Byrd.

Another kind of music may make a connection between Morley and *As You Like It*. When Rosalind hears of Charles's brutal wrestling against the three brothers in 1.2 she cries: 'But is there any else longs to see this broken music in his sides?' (1.2.134–5); at that moment the actor playing Rosalind could have glanced at the musicians in the gallery of the Great Hall at Richmond. A 'broken consort' would almost certainly have been playing at intervals during the performance of the play while the Court feasted. Morley's *First Book of Consort Lessons*, published in 1599, was for the same group of instruments as performed at Elvetham, consisting of a treble and bass viol, bass recorder, lute, cittern and pandora, the whole known as a broken consort. The same consort of instruments can be seen playing for the masque for Sir Henry Unton's wedding (Poulton, 432; see Fig. 15). Shakespeare's own company were much involved in consort music. Thurston Dart has argued that this combination of instruments was used by the performers ('waits') at the Lord Mayor's banquets – Morley's book is dedicated to the Lord Mayor's Wayts; this group also played in both the private and public theatres:

> The two most famous Elizabethan comedians, Will Kemp and Ned [Richard] Tarleton, were both excellent musicians. Phillips the actor left his lute, cittern and pandora to one apprentice and his bass viol to another . . . The Lord Admiral's company in 1598 owned a lute and pandora, and the one feature which all six instruments of Morley's consort have in common is their portability.
>
> (Dart, *Consort*, 6)

When the Duke calls for music in *As You Like It* (2.7.174, 5.4.176), when music plays to accompany the rowdy hunting song in 4.2, or at the entrance of Hymen ('*Still Music*', 5.4.105.2), the most likely accompaniment would have been the broken consort for which Morley wrote his *Consort Lessons*.

Finally, the play is full of comments about how music should be performed, from Amiens's reluctance to sing in 2.5, to the Pages protesting against Touchstone's exacting standards in 5.3. If Will Kemp originally played the jester in this scene, his well-known musical expertise would have lent savour to Touchstone's salt. Morley's instructions in his *Practical Music* (1597) linger around the edges of Shakespeare's text. If the composer had been in that first audience he might have laughed at Touchstone's jibe that his song was badly sung and a waste of time.

REALMS OF GOLD

It would not be difficult to gain the impression from reading any commentary on *As You Like It* that this is a play which demonstrates that its author was dauntingly well read, and that the drama itself demands a well-read audience. Shakespeare's comedies are certainly full of well-read people. 'How well he's read, to reason against reading', observes the King dryly of Berowne in *Love's Labour's Lost* (1.1.94). Shakespeare had an extraordinary capacity for absorbing other writers' works, no doubt partly from actual reading, but also from their dissemination within the rich soil of Elizabethan oral culture (Mowat, 'Theater', 214). But though the play can be enjoyed in the study, it never creates the impression – unlike some of Ben Jonson's plays – that it was conceived there.

Scholars have become increasingly uneasy about the term 'sources' to identify works which Shakespeare 'adapted' for plots and characters and echoed in the metaphoric and linguistic medium of his plays. The more recent term 'intertextuality', which invests the power of recognition and interrelation in the reader, has proved useful in unravelling the literary threads in Shakespeare's textual web. But the word 'reader' removes the play from its natural habitat, the theatre. For this particular play the most felicitous metaphor for reading is journeying, as in John Keats's sonnet 'On First Looking into Chapman's Homer':

> Much have I travell'd in the realms of gold,
> And many goodly states and kingdoms seen.
>
> (Keats, 49)

The experience of reading a translation of Homer was for Keats one of exploring unknown lands. Lodge's *Rosalynde* was written when the author was on an Elizabethan 'privateering voyage in the Galleon Dudley in 1590' to the Canary Islands (Edwards, 46). The subtitle of *Rosalynde* was *Euphues Golden Legacy*. In his satirical poem *A Fig for Momus* (1595) Lodge used 'Golde' as an anagram for his own name, which Shakespeare may have known when he created from Lodge's novella his own golden world.

Shakespeare and Thomas Lodge

The ill-tempered outburst of the playwright Robert Greene about an 'upstart Crow, beautified with our feathers' (*Groatsworth*, ll. 939–43) could logistically have issued from the lips of Thomas Lodge. Several of Shakespeare's plays bear witness to the dramatist's enormous admiration for Lodge's *Rosalynde*. He drew on the novella, probably shortly after its first printing in 1590, in *The Two Gentleman of Verona* (1594) for the incident in which Julia and Silvia are attacked by outlaws (5.3).[1] He would use it again in *The Winter's Tale* (1610–11) for the description of Perdita as Flora (4.4.2–3, 10), which comes from Lodge's description of Ganimede/Rosalynde on her wedding-day.[2]

Lodge apparently never complained about Shakespeare's wholesale appropriation of his plot in *As You Like It*. The theatre

---

1   See Lodge, sig. K4ᵛ: 'Certaine Rascals that liued by prowling in the Forest, who for feare of the Prouost Marshall had Caues in the groaues and thickets, to shrowde themselues from his traines, hearing of the beautie of this faire shepheardesse Aliena, thought to steale her away, and to giue her to the King for a present, hoping, because the King was a great leacher, by such a gift to purchase all their pardons: and therefore came to take her and her Page away.'

2   Lodge, sig. P2ᵛ; see 5.4.105.2n.

had an established role as advertiser of literary works, and he may have been delighted with the enhanced publicity and sales of his book. Indeed *Rosalynde* might almost have been considered a book-text for Shakespeare's play, making the printing of a quarto unnecessary. Phoebe's quotation, 'Who ever loved, that loved not at first sight?' (3.5.83), inadvertently performs an advertising function for Christopher Marlowe's *Hero and Leander* (first published posthumously in 1598). But *As You Like It* quickly reveals that the dialogue between Shakespeare's play and Lodge encompassed more than the use of *Rosalynde* for the plot of the play, important though that was.

The two writers were probably acquainted. Lodge was involved in theatrical affairs from the early 1580s. He possibly had an even longer association with theatrical performance, as he had been brought up in the household of Henry Stanley, fourth Earl of Derby, as he states in his dedication of *A Fig for Momus* (1595) to Stanley's second son, William Stanley. William inherited the title of sixth earl after the death in 1593 of his elder brother, Ferdinando Strange, whose patronage of actors and entertainers was well known; Lodge retained close relations with the family, and may have derived from these early associations the interest in theatre which led to his defence of it early in the 1580s.[1] Lodge's *Rosalynde* was dedicated in 1590 to the Lord Chamberlain, Henry Hunsdon, under whose patronage Shakespeare and his fellows would later perform.

Shakespeare often allows into his dramas a figure who speaks with the voice of a writer whose work he has plundered.[2] In *As*

---

1 Lodge was probably born in 1558; he says he was a member of the Stanley household 'in my infancie', a phrase which could hardly be used in this period for a child over ten; thus his early contacts would probably have been with both Ferdinando and William. The connection is additionally intriguing in the light of Shakespeare's possible theatrical connections with the Derby family in the 1590s (Honigmann, *'Lost Years'*, 60).

2 The narrative voice of Plutarch, whose 'Life of Antonius' is the main source for *Antony and Cleopatra*, is discernible in the crusty tones of the Roman soldier Enobarbus; similarly in *Romeo and Juliet* the Friar's attitude to the lovers recalls Arthur Brooke, author of the poem *Romeus and Juliet* on which the play is largely based.

You Like It elements of Lodge's life history emerge in the figure of Jaques. Lodge, like Jaques, had passed a libertine youth. His conversion to Catholicism in the mid-1590s and his leaving England in 1597 to study medicine at Avignon offer an interesting gloss on Jaques the 'convertite' (5.4.182), who refuses to return home to the pleasures of the court. In fact Lodge never returned to the London literary scene nor to the theatre (although he died in 1625 treating plague cases in the city). But although these elements in Jaques might evoke Lodge, they may glance also at Ben Jonson (see Appendix 3); Jaques resists attempts to limit his identity to that of any one Elizabethan figure. Lodge was simultaneously a libertine defender of the stage, a wronged younger brother, a rejected lover, a pastoral poet, a satirist, a convert to Catholicism who turns away from the world, and the man who provided Shakespeare with his own Rosalind.

The role of wronged younger brother is relevant to Lodge's *Rosalynde*. The enmity between the brothers Saladyne and Rosader is as prominent in the narrative as the hostility between Oliver and Orlando (surfacing in slurs on legitimacy) with which *As You Like It* opens. Lodge's grandfather, William Lodge, was illegitimate, and the name 'lodge' was given to him as a convenient way of identifying the nameless place where he was born (A. Walker, 411). His son Thomas, the writer's father, having started life as an apprentice to the Grocers' Company, rose to be Lord Mayor of London (the first to wear a beard – a physical attribute which attracts recurrent jesting in the play) and was knighted. His triumph was not to be long lived; he lost his money, and his son Thomas entered Trinity College, Oxford, as a poor scholar. There was still, however, enough property around for heated disputes between the author of *Rosalynde* and his elder brother William, who denied Thomas money on the grounds of his dissolute life, and shut him out of his house.[1] It is not difficult to see the appeal that the story of Saladyne and Rosader would have had for Thomas Lodge (independent of its analogue in the story of the

---

1   A. Walker, 415, 420, 422–3; Sisson, *Lodge*, 4.

three brothers in the *Tale of Gamelyn*), nor to root the hostilities of the two brothers in Shakespeare's play in Lodge's biography as well as in his novella.

The way in which Shakespeare draws Lodge into the circle of the Forest, as he does many other writers – Marlowe, Harington, Ariosto, Chaucer, Rabelais – might suggest the model of good fellowship which Duke Senior promotes in his own followers, and which Keats contrasted with the rivalries between poets in his own time: 'Let us have the old poets and robin Hood', he wrote to John Hamilton Reynolds on 3 February 1818, enclosing his poem 'Lines on the Mermaid Tavern' (Keats, *Letters*, 102). Shakespeare's interaction with Lodge suggests not the rivalry and back-biting of the jealous Robert Greene, but the good-humoured jesting of two comrades, fellow-travellers or 'co-mates', making their way in the world.

In considering the way in which Lodge reworks Spenser's Rosalinde, great lady of the 'April' eclogue (see p. 6), Clare Kinney suggests that Lodge 'grants a voice to the silenced Rosalind of Spenser's work, in turn providing a prototype for the talkative Rosalind of *As You Like It*' (291). Lodge addressed *Rosalynde* to 'Gentleman *Readers*' (sig. A3ʳ). Shakespeare's Rosalind in the epilogue declares: 'I'll begin with the women' (11). When Shakespeare read *Rosalynde* he must have recognized that here was a narrative text, but also a dramatic one, crying out for theatre, for the body of the actor and the presence of an audience.

In *Rosalynde* Lodge gives his characters long meditations on their own mental states; he also provides great wedges of song and verse in which they express their emotion. In between there is a fairly snappy narrative. But Lodge's structural links are brittle compared with those of Shakespeare, who makes each type of writing depend intimately on those that surround it. Poetry becomes the vital competitor of prose: 'I'll rhyme you so eight years together, dinners and suppers and sleeping-hours excepted' (3.2.93–4). 'Nay then, God b'wi' you an you talk in blank verse,' growls Jaques to Orlando (4.1.28–9). 'Do you wish then that the gods had made me poetical?' asks a bewildered Audrey (3.3.20–1). 'Jove, Jove, this shepherd's passion / Is much upon my fashion!' cries Rosalind. 'And mine, but it grows something stale with me,' murmurs Touchstone, glancing over his shoulder at the audience (2.4.56–9). Even the songs are not allowed to stand on their own. The very act of singing becomes part of the process of self-dramatization: 'My voice is ragged: I know I cannot please you,' protests Amiens. 'I do not desire you to please me; I do desire you to sing,' retorts Jaques (2.5.13–15). The climax of these techniques is reached in the courting scenes, where there is no shadow of distinction between what is theatrical and what is real, between playing and being: 'But will my Rosalind do so?' asks a bemused Orlando. 'By my life, she will do as I do,' replies Ganymede (4.1.147–8). It would not have been difficult for Shakespeare to recognize that the most vital part of Lodge's narrative is its prose, and that his poetry sits leadenly on the page, copying the conventions of the time in a fashion something stale.

In *As You Like It* Shakespeare takes a number of well-established and often ancient poetic forms and juxtaposes them with a couple of girls and a clown talking a modern language:

> CELIA   Well said – that was laid on with a trowel.
> TOUCHSTONE   Nay, if I keep not my rank –
> ROSALIND   Thou loosest thy old smell.
>
> (1.2.102–4)

It is not surprising that the French courtier, Le Beau, is scandalized. Later on, a hero from the literary world of the *chansons de geste* enters, furnished like a hunter; he could be French, English, Italian, a Robin Hood or an Orlando. The dramatist gives both girls suitors who speak the old language, but he allows Rosalind to teach her suitor a new one (Garber, 'Education', 106; see 3.2.138–45n.). Shakespeare's play has at its heart a girl speaking to an Elizabethan audience in their own language: 'Men have died from time to time and worms have eaten them, but not for love' (4.1.97–9). Miraculously, after more than four hundred years, what she says is still our language. This is the signal difference between Shakespeare's play and Lodge's novella.

Shakespeare and Sidney

If Lodge provided Shakespeare with a plot, Sir Philip Sidney offered something more radical in a daring questioning of the roots of sexual identity, and a playful sporting with gender roles, which is in part stimulated by the presence of a female audience (Gibbons, 155–6). The *Old Arcadia* [1580] was written to be read aloud to the Countess of Pembroke and her ladies at Wilton, and their reactions inform the narrator's consciousness.[1] In one of the greatest mistimings of Providence or Fortune, Sidney missed *As You Like It* by thirteen years. If there is a shocking text in this period from the Puritan point of view, it isn't a play at all, but Sidney's *Arcadia*, in which the hero, Pyrocles, disguises himself as a woman. Both the *Old Arcadia* and the revised version (printed in 1593) contain the song in which Pyrocles declares that 'she' is 'Transformed in show, but more transformed in mind' (26).[2]

Sidney often seems uncertain about the nature of the change which takes place in his warlike hero once he dresses himself as the beautiful Amazon lady, Cleophila. It's not clear whether Pyrocles really does undergo some deep process of transformation; this must have been particularly interesting to Shakespeare as he created his own Rosalind. The dual nature of Pyrocles creates a highly comic interaction in the confrontation in *Old Arcadia* between Dametas, the brutish shepherd, and Pyrocles, disguised as Cleophila: '"Maid Marian," demands Dametas, "am I not a personage to be answered?"' (29). Receiving no response he gives

---

1 Both Wilton in Wiltshire (the home of the Countess of Pembroke, Sidney's sister) and Penshurst in Kent (the family home of Sidney's brother Robert) have connections with *As You Like It*, the former through the *Old Arcadia* and the latter through Jonson's '*To Penshurst*'; see 2.4.81n.; see also Fig. 2.

2 In the reworking of *Arcadia* for publication, the 'her' of the *Old Arcadia* becomes 'his' when the disguised Pyrocles is described, which has the effect of erasing Musidorus's erotic admiration for his friend with its suggestive Pygmalion image. The fluidity of gender presented in the *Old Arcadia* is thus subtly censored in the revised version printed after Sidney's death.

'her' a hefty blow. The title 'Maid Marian' is already double-edged, as in May games and morris dances Robin Hood's consort, Maid Marian, was always played by a man, so that, as Katherine Duncan-Jones notes, Sidney's text creates a dramatic irony.[1] Pyrocles' response to the attack is instantaneous:

> Cleophila no sooner felt the blow but that, the fire sparkling out of her eyes, and rising up with a right Pyrocles countenance in a Cleophila face, 'Vile creature,' said she, laying her hand upon her sword, 'force me not to defile this sword in thy base blood!'
>
> (29)

At this moment the outer may be the fair Amazon, but the inner is warlike Prince Pyrocles, hand to sword before you can say distaff, just as the Ganymede who swoons at blood is Rosalind within, however much she pretends to be counterfeiting. The question of transformation is a less simple one in the *Old Arcadia* than it is in Lodge's *Rosalynde*, a story in which Rosalynde simply becomes a brash boy called Ganimede.

One could say that Shakespeare's Rosalind speaks with Ganymede's voice but she is never truly transformed in mind: 'Dost thou think, though I am caparisoned like a man, I have a doublet and hose in my disposition?' (3.2.189–91), she demands of Celia during a display of 'feminine' impatience to know more of her lover. But something is either transformed or revealed in Rosalind's disposition when she changes into a man's clothes. Shakespeare owes to Sidney more than to Lodge the playfulness, but also the seriousness, which prevents one from deciding whether transformation or revelation predominates once Rosalind is cross-dressed.

Harington, Ariosto and Rabelais

Ben Jonson considered Sir John Harington's 1591 translation of Ariosto's *Orlando Furioso* (see Fig. 17) – the epic romance from

---

1 Sidney, *Old Arcadia*, 370, n. 29; see 1.2.261n.

17 The frontispiece to John Harington's 1591 translation of Ariosto's *Orlando Furioso*

which Shakespeare derived his hero's name – to be 'under all translations . . . the worst' ('Drummond', l. 26, p. 596), a view which may be slyly endorsed in *As You Like It* by various jokes at Orlando's poetry.[1] What makes it irresistible reading even now is Harington's prose notes and reflections at the end of each canto, where he has drawn into the circuit of the Italian chivalric romance epic his own modern world of family, friends, politics, morals, what you will. The result is a curious dialogue between the main text of Ariosto's poetry and the marginal text of Harington's translation. But it is a marginality which usurps its own subject because Harington's jottings are more fun to read than the main translated text.[2]

Harington, like Sidney in the *Old Arcadia*, aimed his translation of Ariosto in the first place at the queen's ladies, giving them the bawdy canto 28 for their amusement, an act of sauciness for which his royal godmother administered the equivocal punishment of banishing him to the country to translate the rest of the poem. His dual role as a writer is mirrored in *As You Like It*. On the one hand the play draws on Ariosto's high-culture Italian romance epic poem, on the other on Harington's low-culture work on the disposal of excrement, *The Metamorphosis of Ajax* (1596). The elaborate fountain Harington created for his own garden modelled on the fountain in Ariosto led him directly to the plumbing experiment of *Ajax*. Like Jonson and numerous other Elizabethans, Harington was an ardent admirer of Rabelais. His cousin Robert Markham wrote to Harington in 1598:

> Your book is almost forgiven, and I may say forgotten; but not for its lacke of wit or satyr . . . The Queen is minded to take you to her favour, but she sweareth that she

---

1 See 2.1.20n., 3.2.95n., 110n, 162–7 and nn. Harington's translation was apparently instrumental in giving Ariosto's poem the status of a classic (Javitch, 134–57).

2 Cf. the structure of *Much Ado*, in which the poetic romance of Hero and Claudio takes second place to the prose commentary of Beatrice and Benedick (Dusinberre, 'Much Ado', 240). Charles I wrote 'Betteris and Benedick' beside the title of the play in his copy of the Second Folio.

believes you will make epigrams and wirke *misacmos*[1]
again on her and all the Courte; she had been heard to say,
'that merry poet her godson, must not come to
Greenwich, till he hath grown sober and leaveth the
Ladies sportes and frolicks'.

(Harington, *Nugae Antiquae*, 2.287–8)

Harington's prose annotations to the cantos of Ariosto's work
familiarize and domesticate the poem; his prose in *Ajax* takes the
lowest of subjects and gives it a pretension to learning and wit in
true Rabelaisian fashion. For Rabelais's originality with the vernacular is to force into the world of high culture, education and
learning, subjects which had never been allowed within those
precincts.

Harington, like Touchstone, was always ready for a joke with
the ladies. It has been suggested that women provide the ideal
audience for Rabelais because of his subversion of intellectual and
rational authority through a celebration of the body (Bellard-
Thomson, 174). When Le Beau enters in 1.2, he is astonished to
find the ladies jesting with the clown about breaking wind
(1.2.104–5), a subject from which Harington, who had cam-
paigned to reduce the stench in Elizabethan mansions, was never
allowed to be free. When Rosalind overwhelms Celia with questions about Orlando in the Forest and demands 'Answer me in one
word,' her cousin complains: 'You must borrow me Gargantua's
mouth first. 'Tis a word too great for any mouth of this age's
size' (3.2.217–19). Rabelais's *Gargantua and Pantagruel* and
Harington's imitation of it in *The Metamorphosis of Ajax* root the
play in a carnivalesque tradition of humanist writing which allows
the body to undermine high culture.

The Forest of Arden has in its life-blood Rabelais's ideal
community, the Abbey of Thelema, a place designed to overthrow the concept of monasticism, and to create instead a kind

---

1 *Misacmos* is the pen-name used by Harington in *Ajax* – a slightly inexact Greek
coinage meaning 'hater of filth'; see *Ajax*, 80n.

of co-educational commune, whose motto is 'FAY CE QUE VOUDRAS': '*Do as thou wilt*' (see 1.1.62n.) – or, perhaps, as you like it. 'Thelema' is the Greek word for 'will', and is used in the New Testament by St Paul for the freedom attending on the new will of God (Dusinberre, 'As *Who?*', 11). The Abbey of Thelema eschews the monastic bells that keep the time, and allows true liberty and equality to men and women. Shakespeare's Forest also offers the freedom of doing as one likes: liberation from clocks and clerics, and from the constraints and conventions of the court.

In an essay on Rabelais, Primo Levi declares that

> in Pantagruel's vast inspiration and vast laughter is enclosed the dream of the [sixteenth] century, that of an industrious and productive humanity which . . . walks towards . . . the golden age described by the Latins, neither past nor distantly future but within reach.
>
> (Levi, 122)

For Rabelais, as Levi explains, the Golden Age, familiar from Virgil's fourth Eclogue and from Ovid's *Metamorphoses*, is attainable in the modern age provided temporal authority observes reason.

Golden worlds

In the Forest of Arden, Duke Senior and his alternative court 'fleet the time carelessly as they did in the golden world' (1.1.112–13). In Ovid's *Metamorphoses* the Golden Age was a time of everlasting spring with no laws, no punishment, no judges, no fear, no soldiers and peace everywhere (*Met.*, 1, pp. 2^{r-v}) – a classical equivalent of the Judaeo-Christian Paradise. In *As You Like It* none of these characteristics truly apply. But they have been transmuted into a golden age in the mind, in which the winter wind is nullified by the kindness and loyalty of friends, and contrasted with the envy of the court. The return of spring to the Forest heralds love. Work is not absent, but it is a source of true content to the country shepherd. Ovid's vision casts a golden glow over the Forest and its inhabitants – both native and exiled.

The Elizabethans promoted a mythology in which they saw themselves enjoying a new golden age presided over by the virgin queen Elizabeth (see Fig. 18), shadowed by Astraea in Virgil's fourth Eclogue, the Virgin of Justice, who would preside over the return of the golden world under Augustus Caesar.[1] Spenser's 'April' eclogue equates 'Elisa, Queene of shepheardes all' (*SC*, p. 455) with Flora, the classical goddess of Spring, in a deliberate imitation of Virgil's fourth Eclogue.[2] As principal actor in the Forest, Rosalind is more than just the heroine. She becomes by the end of the play – as the queen herself did for her subjects – the focal point for a new golden world of amity, justice, compassion and content. But the imaginative realm of the Golden Age had for the Elizabethans a compelling material counterpart.

The Elizabethan voyages of discovery, in which Lodge took part, are as integral to *As You Like It* as the myth of the Golden Age. Travel was for mythical and for real gold, the legendary realm of Sir Walter Ralegh's *El Dorado* and the limitless real wealth which it promises. In 'Colin Clout's Come Home Again' Spenser christened Ralegh – the most glamorous and controversial figure in the world of exploration – 'Shepheard of the Ocean', because of his poem to Elizabeth, 'The Ocean to Cynthia' (Koller, 44). The image of 'shepherd' was one Ralegh applied to himself not just in that poem; he wrote to Leicester of his own posting to Ireland in 1581: 'Were it not for that I knew hyme [Deputy *Grey*] to be on[e] of yours I would disdeyn it as miche as to keap sheepe' (*Letters*, 11). Rosalind's mockery of Jaques as traveller touches on aspects of a common Elizabethan experience – the affectations of the returned traveller in dress and speech, his discontent with his native land and arrogance about his superior knowledge of the

---

1 Yates, 4; Montrose, 'Elisa', 160.
2 Spenser died on 31 January 1599, just three weeks before the putative first performance of *As You Like It*. His influence on Shakespeare's pastoral play is so profound and pervasive that the play might almost be seen as a tribute to him.

18 *Elizabeth I* (1572), Nicholas Hilliard's earliest likeness of the queen, shown
    wearing her colours of black and white

world (see 4.1.30–4 and nn.) – but also on the traveller's actual
poverty. He has sold his lands to finance his travels, as Ralegh himself did (see 4.1.20n.). Jaques's metaphor for Touchstone's brain,
that it is 'as dry as the remainder biscuit / After a voyage'
(2.7.39–40), and his perception that the loving voyage of Audrey

and Touchstone is 'but for two months victualled' (5.4.189), recalls the common Elizabethan experience of sea-voyaging. Rosalind's love is as bottomless as the Bay of Portugal (4.1.197, 195–6), conjuring up Elizabethan expeditions connected with both Ralegh and Essex.

Many of the puns in the play seem to draw the colourful figure of Ralegh into its orbit. Ralegh, who originally spelt his name Rawly, was a country boy who made good. He was taunted as self-made by his rival and supplanter in the queen's affections, the Earl of Essex. The hostile court nickname, 'Fortune', is possibly glanced at in the jesting of Rosalind and Celia (see 1.2.40n.). Even Touchstone's virtuoso piece on the 'lie' may touch a raw area in Ralegh's history (5.4.68–101; see 68n.), when he lied to the queen about his secret marriage to her maid of honour, Bess Throckmorton. Be that as it may, the play's metaphors and dramatic structure are grounded in Elizabethan travel to exotic lands.

In *As You Like It* the question of real gold is almost as important as the imaginative realm of the golden world. The play opens with Orlando's complaint that a thousand gold crowns is a mean inheritance, an apparently justified grouse, as Adam later offers to finance him with savings amounting to half that sum (2.3.38). Rosalind and Celia are well equipped with gold to buy the shepherd's cottage (2.4.70, 99). But Jaques is the chief link with a moneyed world. Money is as central to his mental processes as philosophy is to the Duke's. What things cost ('his bravery is not on my cost', 2.7.80), what people owe ('Nay, I care not for their names: they owe me nothing,' 2.5.17–18), what they squander, beg ('renders me the beggarly thanks', 2.5.23–4), borrow and waste, are the small coin of his language and imagination. Elizabeth was a central part of the myth of the Golden Age for her courtiers and poets, but they were left in no doubt at all that she required real gold as well (Sherman, 87); their rewards were not just for a world of words.

Indeed, the Golden Age, as recounted by classical poets, was treated with apparent scepticism by some Renaissance thinkers.

Sir John Davies called it 'a fable' in *Nosce Teipsum* (1599, p. 75), although it was in the context that babes in the womb thought the world a fable, so perhaps he felt it to be in some sort true. Montaigne was unequivocally scathing. As he reflects in the essay 'Of the Cannibals' on the primitive societies newly accessible to Renaissance travellers, and observes their apparent lack of corruption, Montaigne remarks that they 'exceed all the pictures wherewith licentious Poesie hath proudly imbellished the golden age, and all her quaint inventions to faine a happy condition of man' (1.220). The derogative term 'licentious Poesie' is a reminder of another aspect of the golden world in *As You Like It*, poetry itself. Sidney used the metaphor to justify the poet against the attacks of Puritans such as Stephen Gosson, declaring in *An Apology for Poetry* that '[Nature's] world is brazen; the poet delivers a golden' (100). The question of what the poet delivers, and whether it is a fable – or, as Gosson and others would have argued, a lie – gives Touchstone the occasion for much wit at Audrey's expense in 3.3. The word 'truly' and its many ambiguities pepper Touchstone's speeches, together with its partner, 'if'. The question of the truth of the golden world and of its poetry runs throughout the play. *As You Like It* has its own place in the idealist tradition of poetry described by Sidney, in which the poet teaches through his creation of a better and more delightful world. 'Hereafter in a better world than this / I shall desire more love and knowledge of you,' remarks Le Beau (1.2.273–4), urging Orlando to flee the dangers of the Court, a moment which may be made ambiguous by the possible doubling of Le Beau's part with that of Jaques (see Appendix 2). If the two actors meet again in a better world, the Forest of Arden, Jaques's rebuff – 'let's meet as little as we can' (3.2.250) – would carry a special comic irony.

In that better world Shakespeare has provided his own method for trying the fables of licentious poesy, and particularly the central fable of a golden world which anticipates the biblical Garden of Eden. To do this he invents special touchstones: Jaques, Touchstone and Audrey; and a heroine for whom the world of poetry is always to some degree both suspect and subject to the world of prose. Yet in that new language of prose Rosalind forges her own realm of gold, accessible to women who had not read the classics and chivalric poetry.

PASTORAL

Genre: entertainments for Elizabeth

As You Like It is a pastoral drama which draws on Lily's court plays (*Galatea*, *Endymion*) as well as on the more popular romance of *Sir Clyomon and Sir Clamydes*, but its closest kinship is with the outdoor entertainments mounted for Elizabeth during her summer progresses.[1] Jean Wilson points out that 'the implication of the many pastoral presentations of Elizabeth is that the Golden World has returned with her' (23). When Orlando describes encountering a ragged man who turns out to be his brother Oliver, an audience would have recognized the familiar figure of a 'wild' man from these pageants (see 4.3.105n.).[2] Carefully placed fictitious hermits and magicians peopled the woodland environments of the country estates visited by the queen.[3] In Shakespeare's comedy Ganymede claims that an old courtly uncle taught him not only a fine accent but magic arts for transforming a boy into a girl; the uncle, in his later role as hermit, also manages to convert Duke Frederick (just in time) to the religious life. In the masque provided for Elizabeth at Kenilworth by the Earl of Leicester in 1575

---

1 The most famous royal entertainments took place at the Earl of Leicester's castle at Kenilworth in 1575, and at his country estate at Wanstead (Sidney's *Lady of May*, 1578/1579; see p. 5, n. 1); at the Earl of Hertford's seat at Elvetham in 1591; and at Cowdray (home of Lord Montague) in 1591.
2 Philippa Berry (90–2) traces the history of the 'wild' man from medieval folklore, his affinities with Robin Hood and misrule, and his presence in European medieval romance, pointing to the survival of the tradition in Ariosto, 'where the wild-man-like insanity inspired in the knight Orlando by unrequited love is a central element of the plot' (91). See also Leslie, 57; Hattaway, 80; Feuillerat, 200.
3 The role of hermit was often played by the Lord Treasurer, Lord Burleigh, who was centrally involved in these entertainments (P. Berry, 87–8, 95–107; J. Wilson, 148n.). Burleigh died on 4 August 1598.

95

the hermit had been, like Rosalind's fictitious uncle, 'in his youth an inland man' (J. Wilson, 42n.). Leicester may be shadowed in *As You Like It* in the figures of both Duke Senior and Sir Rowland de Boys.[1]

However, hermits were not just pageant or entertainment figures for the Elizabethans. They were still, in a society only newly Protestant, a part of religious culture. In the medieval epic romance *Girart de Roussillon* the pilgrimage to the Forest of Arden and the repentance and purging of the hero by the hermit is a central part of chivalric and crusading life, as also in the home-grown romance *Guy of Warwick*. This motif finds many echoes in Shakespeare's Forest, which surrounds all who enter it with images of pilgrimage and ends with the conversion of Duke Frederick and the resolve of Jaques to remain with him in the Forest. The journey, like a pilgrimage, is long, and causes not just weary legs but weary spirits. If the play were first performed on Shrove Tuesday, the day before the beginning of Lent on Ash Wednesday, the Forest could have acquired for the Elizabethans the associations of the veritable 'desert' in which Christ's temptations were played out during his forty-day fast.

If the hermit was in part a religious figure, he also symbolized the conflict for many Elizabethan courtiers between the challenges and dangers of court favour and the repose (and tedium) of the country, incisively anatomized by Touchstone at 3.2.13–20. The Earl of Essex, who had been brought up in Wales, used his country home at Wanstead to escape from the Court (Heffner, 16–25, 31–33). Pastoral retreat was for Elizabethan courtiers an inherently political gesture.

---

1 See 2.7.199n. and Dusinberre, '*AYL*', 415. Richard Barnfield's *The Affectionate Shepherd* contains an apostrophe to love which appears to use the name 'Rowland' for Leicester: 'By thee great Collin lost his libertie, / By thee sweet Astrophel forwent his joy; / By thee Amyntas wept incessantly, / By thee good Rowland liv'd in great annoy' (41). Here Collin is Spenser; Astrophel, Sidney; Amyntas, Tasso; and Rowland, Leicester. The word 'shadow' used in this sense is Spenserian, from the invocation to the queen in book 3 of *The Faerie Queene*; the poet 'Cannot your glorious pourtraict figure playne, / That I in colour showes may shadow itt, / And antique praises unto present persons fitt' (p. 155).

In *As You Like It* Rosalind's role in the Forest is that of both actor and audience, as was the queen's in entertainments that often contained topical and controversial material. Conducted on a tour of the grounds and gardens, Elizabeth would encounter, as if by accident, performers in a pageant in which she herself was expected to play a part. She might intervene (like Rosalind, the 'busy actor' (3.4.55) who interrupts the stormy wooing of Silvius and Phoebe in 3.5) in the action presented to her. In *The Lady of May* at Wanstead the queen, required to make a judgement at the end, chose not to fall in with the conclusion expected by both the author (Sidney) and her host (Leicester – Essex's stepfather) to the embarrassment of all (J. Wilson, 146n.). Elizabeth's double role as both performer and audience involved ambiguities which Michael Leslie explores in his analysis of the masque at Cowdray mounted by the Catholic Lord Montague in 1591: 'From being the audience she had been turned into an actor; from being the object of celebration she had been metamorphosed into the subject of theatre' (Leslie, 70). These ambiguities of role and tone are central to the mode of literary pastoral.

Corin and Touchstone

As You Like It explores issues raised by its own throwaway title. In pastoral poetry the poet is the shepherd. Shakespeare as poet can annex the image of shepherd to himself; but as playwright both for the Court and for the public theatre he is an entertainer, as is Touchstone. If the role of shepherd allows Shakespeare as poet to meditate on the true nature of contentment in the Forest of Arden, the role of entertainer makes him – like his own court jester – play to the audience, and hope that his play will please.

As You Like It goes to the heart of the dream of simple country life, which still remains potent in Western industrialized society of the twenty-first century. Our contemporary vision of rustic retreat is part of Shakespeare's play. But other aspects of Elizabethan pastoral do not translate so readily into contemporary terms. Pastoral was a courtly genre, cultivated by poets versed in

Theocritus, Virgil and Ovid, but it also represented a social reality. Courtiers in Shakespeare's audience owned country estates and knew the seasons of the year for the farming community. The meditations of Touchstone on the relative merits of court and country can be paralleled in Sir John Harington's own jottings about his love of Somerset (collected in *Nugae Antiquae*), but also in his equally pressing need to have a finger in the court pie. Our own comparative lack of access to a literary classical background is conceivably a less significant loss for appreciation of *As You Like It* than the absence of an internal rural calendar, which Shakespeare could take for granted in his audiences. Many city-dwellers were country migrants, a movement vastly on the increase in London at the turn of the sixteenth century. All of them would have experienced country life.

'And how like you this shepherd's life, Master Touchstone?' inquires the old shepherd Corin at the beginning of a dialogue crucial for the whole play. The court jester replies: 'Truly, shepherd, in respect of itself, it is a good life; but in respect that it is a shepherd's life, it is naught' (3.2.11–15). There are analogues to this confrontation between shepherd and courtier in Spenser's *Faerie Queene* (6.9.19–33) but Shakespeare replaces Spenser's courtier with a fool. Corin – as in the popular drama of *Sir Clyomon and Sir Clamydes* – is not a literary shepherd from Theocritus, but a man even more caught up in the economy of country living than Spenser's shepherds in *The Shepheardes Calender*.[1] Both works of Spenser lie in the hinterland of this interchange, but the confrontation of the clown (countryman) with another clown (the jester) – a pun which permeates the play – is startlingly original. The Elizabethans would have found the incongruity between the characters funny, whereas a modern audience sits gaping, trying to work out where to laugh.

---

1 See Bullough, 2.155–6, for the shepherd Corin in *Sir Clyomon and Sir Clamydes*, and its motif of a princess in disguise (Neronis), which Bullough relates to *As You Like It*.

The court jester, still in 1599 retained in some noble households (as in the Berkeley household, for example, and also in Elizabeth's own court), was already beginning to be an anachronism (Douce, *Illustrations*, 2.327), as Malvolio's hostility to Feste in *Twelfth Night* accurately records. His livelihood depended on making jokes out of anything to hand, including his benefactors, who allowed him – within reason – the liberty to do so, just as Rosalind and Celia allow Touchstone freedom to mock authority, but threaten the whip when mockery comes too near home (1.2.83–4). For maximum effect Touchstone needs a 'straight man', and in 3.2.11–82 Corin unwittingly plays that role, as do Jaques in the reported encounter in the Forest (2.7.12–42), Sir Oliver Mar-text in 3.3 and William in 5.1. Other men's follies are the fool's bread and butter and their only defence against him is to pretend indifference:

> He that a fool doth very wisely hit
> Doth very foolishly, although he smart,
> Not to seem senseless of the bob.
>
> (2.7.53–5)

The presence of the old shepherd is as much meat and drink to Touchstone as the advent of another country clown, William, a suitor to Audrey. But where the jester's wit sees William off the stage, the confrontation in the earlier scene ends with the old shepherd peacefully declining to compete: 'You have too courtly a wit for me, I'll rest' (3.2.67). The Elizabethans would have found in the shepherd, a man known for his silence, his self-sufficiency, the security of his function, a piquant contrast to the savvy jester, for whom words are a livelihood, and whose insecurities are manifold, for he must always please or his livelihood is gone, where the shepherd rests content if his sheep are so.[1]

---

1   Philip Hope-Wallace thought Patrick Wymark gave Touchstone, in the 'wholly unfunny' scene with Corin (3.2), 'an almost Falstaffian stature' (review of Elliot, RSC, Aldwych transfer 1962; cited in Smallwood, 146). The scene between Corin and Touchstone recalls the confrontation of Falstaff with Justice Shallow in *2 Henry IV* (see 3.2.54, 58n.).

In the dialogue between Corin and Touchstone in 3.2 the golden world of the Forest is subjected to a touchstone which tries its worth. 'Is it true?' is a question that can be asked equally of gold and of the fable of the golden world. The jester's answer is equivocal: yes and no. Whether the shepherd's life pleases you or not depends on where you are standing and what lens you are looking through, a position of philosophical Scepticism which entitles Touchstone to ask whether Corin has any philosophy. The jester receives an answer which can be fitted into a model of Natural philosophy (see 3.2.30 and n.), which is certainly unintended by the shepherd. But you wouldn't have to read a learned note to see that these two come from incompatible contexts. The axis on which the world of the shepherd turns is contentment, not pleasure, a distinction which lies at the heart of the play, wittily entitled 'as you like it'. The shepherd's content taps a pastoral tradition from David and Psalm 23 to Christ the Good Shepherd. Chat about damnation is the jester's defence against the shepherd's authority over his sheep, which comes not just with a shepherd's scrip and scrippage but with hefty biblical bag and baggage.

Borderlands: love and politics

Classical pastoral takes love between men for granted, and its prime function is to describe and celebrate that love. Karoline Szatek argues that 'the pastoral is a borderland that allows for the consideration of both alternative sexualities and alternative sexual lifestyles'.[1] It also provides a safe mode for criticizing those in power. George Puttenham questions whether it is the oldest form of poetry, because beneath a surface simplicity it conceals sophisticated allusions to sensitive material (*English Poetry*, 30–1).

In the prologue to *The Queen's Arcadia*, played before Anne of Denmark in Oxford in 1605, Samuel Daniel laments an increase in the political content of pastoral writing:

1 Szatek, 358–9. See also Crunelle-Vanrigh; Ronk, 268–9.

And all of vs are so transformed, that we
Discerne not an *Arcadian* by attyre,
Our ancient Pastorall habits are dispisd
And all is strange, hearts, clothes, and all disguisd.

(sig. B1ᵛ)

This tradition of pastoral writing as a disguise was analysed in 1935 by William Empson in *Some Versions of Pastoral* and has been scrutinized since by many scholars of the pastoral. Louis Montrose points to the Shrovetide revels at Gray's Inn in 1595 as an example of 'pastoral forms of political relationship'.[1] The modern theatre, unfamiliar with the political ramifications of literary pastoral from its earliest inceptions in classical writers, has lost the sense that an Elizabethan audience at a performance of *As You Like It* would have had, of 'greater matters' behind a rustic disguise.

Pastoral allows the poet, the alter ego of all shepherds, to have his say about court and church under the stalking-horse of innocent country pastimes, as Spenser does in his 'satirical' eclogues in *The Shepheardes Calender. As You Like It* belongs to this literary and social context. Its gender ambiguities are another aspect of its pastoral world. But a further parallel arises from the condition of exile. 'I am here with thee and thy goats, as the most capricious poet, honest Ovid, was among the Goths,' announces Touchstone to Audrey (3.3.5–7), approximating Ovid's exile among the Getes to his own in the Forest of Arden (see 3.3.7n.). Exile had a reality for the Elizabethans which can only be recaptured in the modern world by observing the plight of refugees. Those who travel to the Forest in Shakespeare's play are all asylum seekers, people for whom the Court has become dangerous, and for whom 'home' is a state approximating to vagabondage (McDonald, 121). All the courtiers in Arden are the equivalent of vagabonds, in that they have 'no fixed abode'; this links them with 'gipsies' or common

---

1   Montrose, 'Elisa', 157, refers to the Gray's Inn revel in BL MS Harley 541, excerpts of which are printed in Axton, 85–7.

travelling players, forcing their living on the 'common road' (2.3.33). This parallel would have been more apparent to an Elizabethan audience than it is to a modern one.

The state of exile is a well-established tradition of classical pastoral. The dispossessed shepherds in Virgil's first and ninth Eclogues reflect the poet's own displacement from his lands in Mantua and his plea to Augustus for their return. Virgil's first Eclogue announces the theme in Meliboeus's '*Nos patriam fugimus*' ('we flee from our homeland'); the Latin word *fugimus* encompasses both flight and the condition of banishment.[1] The pastoral poetry of the French Renaissance poet Clément Marot (named by Spenser in E.K.'s gloss to the 'January' eclogue) reinterpreted Virgil's *Eclogues* in the light of 'his personal history as a Lutheran exile' (Patterson, 107). Duke Senior is a political exile, as Prospero is in *The Tempest*, and as Bolingbroke is in *Richard II*. Gaunt counsels his son to imagine his exile in terms which transform bleakness to 'happy havens' (1.3.276; see 1.3.134–5n. below). Bolingbroke's retort, 'O, who can hold a fire in his hand / By thinking on the frosty Caucasus?' (294–5), looks forward to Orlando's protest against the *imagined* pleasures of courtship: 'I can live no longer by thinking' (5.2.49). Exile and banishment are a living part of both the Elizabethan political scene and Shakespeare's play.

Essex complained to the queen that his appointment to Ireland in March of 1599 was exile; in a letter written from Arbracken on 30 August 1599 he signed himself 'Y^r Maties / exiled seruant / Essex'.[2] *As You Like It*, perhaps first performed at one of the most significant turning-points of Essex's career, shortly before his

---

1 Virgil, *Eclogues*, 43, 72. See Heaney; Dusinberre, 'Rival poets', 73. In James Robert Carson's production of *As You Like It* at the Greenwich Theatre in 1992 'a big neon sign with a quote from a Virgilian eclogue "*Nos cedamus amori*" ("Let us yield to love") runs along the top of the acting area and it lights up with a blue glow when the song to Hymen is sung' (Paul Taylor, *Independent*, 6 May 1992).

2 Essex, 'Original Letters', letter 44, fol. 122. Robert Markham wrote to his cousin Sir John Harington of Essex's Irish appointment: 'he goeth not forthe to serve the Queenes realme, but to humor his owne revenge' (Harington, *Nugae Antiquae*, 2.288).

departure for Ireland,[1] has always been considered exempt from political influence because of its pastoral mode. But this is not how the Elizabethans viewed pastoral. In an age of censorship the pastoral mode provided a way of saying one's dangerous piece with relative safety.

At the heart of *As You Like It* lies an awareness that the true enemies of content are envy and ambition, both nurtured at court. Like John Heywood's interludes for Henry VIII,[2] Shakespeare's *As You Like It* may, under the mask of pastoral, have invited the moody Essex, the envious Ralegh, the calculating Cecil, and even the queen herself, to cool their passions and cherish their true friends. 'Who doth ambition shun / And loves to live i'th' sun', sings Amiens (2.5.33–4), a man whose name suggests concord and friendship (see List of Roles, 12n.). The sun of the queen's favour was a commonplace image among her courtiers, as in John Chamberlain's account of unsuccessful attempts to restore Essex to Elizabeth's favour in February 1600: 'For the bright sunshine that seemed so to dasell them was indeed but a glimmering light that was sodainly overshadowed again, and the skie as full of cloudes as before.'[3]

Sir Robert Cecil was later to vent his anxiety to Ralegh about whether, in the event of Essex's execution, his own son William would be in danger from the vengeance of Essex's son Robert. But Ralegh responded calmly: 'Humours of men succeed not [i.e. are not inherited], butt grow by occasions & accidents of tyme and poure [power]' (*Letters*, 186, February/March 1600). Or, as Rosalind tells Frederick: 'Treason is not inherited, my lord' (1.3.58). *As You Like It* celebrates loyalty stretching over more than one generation in the love that Duke Senior attests for Orlando's father, Sir Rowland de Boys. If treason is not inherited,

---

1 A performance of *As You Like It* at any point between 1598 and 1600, the recognized limits for its first performance, would have found Essex in equally sensitive political circumstances.

2 G. Walker, 100–7, esp. 106; Bevington, *Tudor Drama*, 65–73; Dusinberre, 'Rival poets', 75.

3 Chamberlain, *Letters*, 65, 22 February 1600; see 2.5.34n. and *AW* 5.3.32–6.

neither is hatred; Celia mocks Rosalind for claiming to love Orlando because her father did so. 'Doth it therefore ensue that you should love his son dearly? By this kind of chase I should hate him for my father hated his father dearly; yet I hate not Orlando' (1.3.29–32). The court epilogue in Henry Stanford's book offers to Elizabeth at the end of the play the future support of her courtiers' children.

There is no portrait of Essex in *As You Like It*, but the play captures the spirit which made Essex a lodestar for his own culture: insouciant, vital, exuberant, audacious. Various characters evoke his divided personality – the 'humorous' Duke Frederick (a word often used of Essex), the melancholy and satirical Jaques, and even the dual persona of Rosalind/Ganymede – but his image evokes Orlando, named from the world of epic romance which Essex cherished in his self-dramatization (Hammer, 199–212). Essex was, as any reading of his letters to Elizabeth demonstrates, a tremendous role-player, himself a Rosalind/Ganymede, now a woman to be wooed, now a brash young man.[1] In July 1599 Elizabeth wrote sternly to him about her dissatisfaction with his conduct in Ireland, adding: 'These things we would pass over but that we see your pen flatters you with phrases' (Elizabeth I, *Works*, 392). In 1599 the young earl, poised between triumph and disaster, could still be shadowed by a hero whose love for Rosalind ('sweet Rose'; see 1.2.22 and n.), associates him with Nicholas Hilliard's miniature, *Young Man among Roses*, now thought to be a portrait of Essex (see Fig. 19).[2] The play's mood of genial reconciliation seems to plead for a leniency which was never granted. Sir Thomas Egerton, the Lord Keeper, warned Essex in 1598: 'My verie good L. It is often seene, that a stander by seeth more then he that plaieth.'[3] The disguises of the pastoral mode allowed the actors to retain their innocence while the Court might glean

---

1 See Peter Beal's unconscious echo of Ganymede in describing Essex's letters in Sotheby's Catalogue for *The Hulton Papers* (Beal, 17, see Dusinberre, '*AYL*', 413).
2 Piper, 2.300–1; Strong, '*Young Man*', 56–7; Hammer, 68–9. For Hilliard's *Young Man* as the Earl of Southampton see Edmond, *Hilliard*, 87–91; see also 2.7.197n.
3 BL Add MS 48126, fol. 99.

19 *Young Man among Roses* (*c.* 1587) by Nicholas Hilliard, displaying the queen's emblem of the eglantine or sweet-brier (wild rose) and her colours of black and white

what it would from the green cornfield where the lover passed with his lass.

A wise man and a fool: Jaques and Touchstone

Jaques and Touchstone form a partnership in *As You Like It*. They are Shakespeare's inventions, and both in different ways use their wit as a scalpel to scrape the veneer off the surface of pastoral pleasure. Satire is intrinsic to the pastoral mode. It is one of the ways in which free speech is allowed. Shakespeare creates in Jaques a 1590s satirist, but pairs him with a fool whose wit punctures the pretensions of the wise man.[1] But their presence in the play also performs the important function of vastly extending Rosalind's role, by creating for her a speculative field for wit and observation lacking in Lodge's *Rosalynde*.[2]

The First Lord describes in the opening scene in the Forest of Arden (2.1) Jaques's delight at meeting a fool in the Forest; 3.3 is the only scene (before the final one) where that meeting takes place in front of the audience. Robert Smallwood suggests that 'the comparative weight that it gives to its Touchstone and its Jaques is a measure of a production's position on the scale of romantic optimism' (138). The two parts are weighed in a balance: on one side is merriment, on the other, melancholy. But equally on the one side is folly, and on the other, wisdom. Just as Jaques is described laughing for an hour at a lamenting Touchstone, thus reversing their roles, so the paradox of which character wears the fool's motley, and which the mantle of sage, lies, in the true fashion of Erasmus's *Praise of Folly*, at the centre of Shakespeare's comedy.

Shakespeare presents in 3.3 a classic encounter between the fool and the wise man. Jaques offers the counsel of the wise man – 'Get you to church, and have a good priest that can tell you what

---

1 See Samuel Beckett's prose novella *Company* (1980), which retains 'only the voices of Touchstone and Jaques, and that of the "deviser" (the Oberon, Rosalind, Prospero types) in his skeletal *mise-en-scène* for his own version of *As You Like It*' (Murphy, 147).
2 Berry, 'Rosalynde', 43.

marriage is' (3.3.77–9) – and Touchstone retorts with the wisdom of the fool:

> I am not in the mind but I were better to be married of him than of another, for he is not like to marry me well, and not being well married it will be a good excuse for me hereafter to leave my wife.
>
> (82–5)

But just as Erasmus's spokeswoman *Stultitia* (Folly) ironizes every *bêtise*, so that lies become truth and truth lies, so the clown is in the play the touchstone by which the wisdom of the wise is exposed as false currency. '"The fool doth think he is wise, but the wise man knows himself to be a fool",' intones Touchstone to a bemused William (5.1.31–2). The audience can see all too clearly that Jaques's longing for a motley coat and the licence of a fool comes from a firm belief in his own wisdom, punctured by the clown, who responds to his counsel by singing and dancing. When Jaques announces rudely to Orlando, 'I was seeking for a fool when I found you,' the hero retorts: 'He is drowned in the brook. Look but in and you shall see him' (3.2.277–80). Jaques likes Touchstone because he believes that his own wisdom is cast into relief by the fool's irrelevancies, just as his melancholy is highlighted (and relieved) by the fool's mirth. But Shakespeare allows his pose of false wisdom to be tried by the touchstone of true folly.

Jaques is a dissident in Shakespeare's play; a man susceptible neither to the pastoral world nor to the delights of love and marriage, an observer not a participator, the odd man out at a party. Such a man the Elizabethans described as 'melancholic', a fashionable malady in a *fin de siècle* world, which would be voluminously documented in Robert Burton's *Anatomy of Melancholy* in 1620. But it was also suffered seriously by a man at the heart of Elizabethan intellectual life – the ninth Earl of Northumberland, patron of Ralegh, limned by Hilliard (*c.* 1595) in melancholy pose, anticipating Isaac Oliver's miniature of Edward Herbert (*c.* 1613) by a stream; this representation may have been influenced by the beautiful word-painting of Jaques languishing by the brook in the Forest of Arden, into which the wounded deer weeps copious tears.[1]

However, the melancholic Jaques of the First Lord's reported speech in 2.1 is only half of Shakespeare's story. The excision – and exorcism from theatrical productions – of the acerbic, parodic gadfly satirist in 2.7 robs *As You Like It* of its critical edge (see pp. 22–3), as in William Charles Macready's 1842 revival: 'The effect of this is to pull Jaques's teeth. Shorn of his best invective, Macready's Jaques was probably just what his Victorian audience wanted him to be: noble, loving, wise, and fatherly tender' (Shattuck, 40). But it is not only Jaques's role which suffers from the cuts. In the Forest of Arden discomfort seasons sunshine and song. Jaques's request for a fool's licence to satirize everyone forms a vital part of the play's many-faceted surface. The belief that *As You Like It* is a fairy-tale of pure escape from the cares of the world, on a par with Mozart's comic operas (Helen Gardner's comparison, reiterated in programme notes and reviews), still prevails.[2] Leaving aside this questionable view of Mozart's operas, *As You Like It* has its own teeth removed when those of Jaques are drawn. Without Jaques's edge of cynicism, the Forest of Arden is too sweet. Its honey is improved by a dash of gall.

The cuts probably represented a later decline in the popularity of the satirical mode. If there was topical jesting on some of Ben Jonson's characteristics (see Appendix 3) it may have been perceived as 'old hat' by both players and audience once both the badinage between the theatres and the vogue for satire lost immediacy. But there is another aspect of Jaques's part which perhaps offended early sensibilities. In Charles Johnson's free adaptation, *Love in a Forest* (1723; see Appendix 5), Jaques is subjected to the ultimate taming and becomes a married man, the spouse of Celia, a motif which in George Sand's adaptation almost transforms the

1 Bath, 14–15; Ronk, 269. See 2.1.30n. and Oxf[1].
2 Gardner, '*AYL*', 59; see Billington, '*AYL*', on Gregory Thompson's 2003 production for the RSC: 'What it lacks is the pulsating passion that can turn Shakespeare's comedy into a transcendent, Mozartian experience.'

play to tragedy. When Debussy sketched an opera based on *As You Like It* – a project never realized – the introspective character of the melancholy Jaques fascinated him as much as the merriment of Rosalind, and he may have known Sand's passionate version of Jaques's history (Lockspeiser, 252). The transformation of the solitary contemplative into a lover highlights the importance in Shakespeare's play of Jaques as a *single* man, one who observes the coupling of others without ever wanting to be coupled himself.

If Jaques has any affections they are for men – Touchstone, the young Ganymede who repulses him unceremoniously, and even Orlando, to whom his incivility can be played as a kind of courtship. Smallwood (156) describes Derek Godfrey's portrayal (Hands, RSC 1980) of this sexual ambiguity – unusual in performances of Jaques. Reviewers offered conflicting interpretations of Jaques's apparent advance to Rosalind (during the dialogue at the opening of 4.1), spreading his cloak wide and offering to encompass her in it; some reviewers saw a homosexual advance to the boy Ganymede, others that Jaques had made a pass at the woman he perceived beneath the boy's clothes. The Platonic homoerotic dimension of the moment in a play which encompasses every gradation of love was noticed by Sally Aire in *Plays and Players* (Smallwood, 157). In Declan Donnellan's Cheek by Jowl production in 1991 this aspect of Jaques's character became central to the interpretation of the role by Joe Dixon, and is seen by Bulman as part of that production's political orientation ('Gay Theater', 38–9).

In the figure of Jaques Shakespeare draws an aggressively single man surrounded by couples coming to the ark to mate (5.4.35–6). The melancholy gentleman ends up planning to be confederate with the converted Duke Frederick in a pseudo-monastic Forest, reminiscent of the monastic nook to which the lover 'cured' by Rosalind's invented uncle allegedly retreated (3.2.400–3). The melancholy satirist's indifference to women and his marked preference for the company of men is one element in the multiple sexualities which the play evokes and celebrates. He won't stay for the wedding dance. He is for other measures.

In his exclusiveness Jaques is also a competitor. Smallwood observes that the play belongs to Rosalind 'but Jaques tries hard to pull it his way' (138). This is borne out by Macready's billing himself as a co-lead in the role of Jaques in his 1842 production (see Fig. 16), a custom followed throughout the nineteenth century. Henry Irving, who began by acting Oliver, made the role of Jaques his own. The capacity of the character to dominate the play is only restrained by the superior dominance of Rosalind, although the fool plays her a good second. For if anyone can confine Jaques within the limits of his own philosophical empire, it must be the fool, who is simultaneously the melancholy man's adversary and his ally.

Touchstone is a notoriously difficult role to play in the modern theatre. The history of the role illuminates the nature of the part, in which it is not what the actor says that matters, but who says it. The sucess of the part depends on the *persona* of the comic actor more than on anything Shakespeare gives him to say. In an otherwise favourable review of Peter Hall's production at the Theatre Royal, Bath, in 2003, Michael Billington observes: 'Michael Siberry can make little of the desperately unfunny Touchstone, reminding me of George Bernard Shaw's comment: "An Eskimo would demand his money back if a modern author offered him such fare"' (Billington, '*AYL*'). The Elizabethan clown Richard Tarlton (d. 1588) only had to be seen on stage for audiences to laugh. Shakespeare's comic actor of the 1590s, Will Kemp, was one significant heir to the Tarlton tradition. When Roy Kinnear, a television comedian, played Touchstone for the RSC in 1967 (Jones) Hilary Spurling wrote: 'If you want to make sense of the gobbledegook of Shakespearean clowns, all you need is a live clown' (Smallwood, 157).

Something of this relation to the audience was attempted by Richard McCabe in 1986 (Hytner) at the Royal Exchange, Manchester, when Touchstone was 'made to jolly along the audience by sitting down among them and putting his arms round old ladies'. The reviewer John Peter objected: 'This is fun, but it's not quite the play.'[1] But who is making the rules? At many points in the text Touchstone does address the audience. The actor Joe Melia, who played Touchstone in 1980 (Hands, RSC), remarked in conversation with Robert Smallwood 'how dismayed he had been by that first joke about the knight and the mustard and the pancakes: he had, he said, had far better material than that for an act on, I think it was, Yarmouth pier' (Smallwood, 154). In other words, the joke struck him as low-quality 'occasional' comedy. But 'occasional' comedy is meat and drink to Shakespeare's clown. The awful pancakes joke is funny on Pancake Day. The best Touchstones – Patrick Wymark in 1957 (Byam Shaw) comes immediately to mind – have always had a kind of music-hall rapport with the audience.

In June 1933 George Grossmith, a performer in revue at the Gaiety Theatre (*OCT*, 357), and son of the George Grossmith famed for turn-of-century performances in Gilbert and Sullivan for the D'Oyly Carte Opera Company, played Touchstone – to universal acclaim – in the new Open Air Theatre's opening production of *As You Like It* in Regent's Park (Carroll). One reviewer noted that 'his style is derived from musical comedy'; another stated that 'I have rarely seen a more nimble fool in the motley of this antic philosopher nor one who jangled to bells of folly and bandied quips and jests with better address. He skipped and pirouetted like a two-year-old.'[2]

What Grossmith recovered was a dancing Touchstone, which would have been the clown's mode if the part was initially played by Kemp, renowned for morris dancing. Kemp's *Nine Days' Wonder* (1600) describes his dancing from London to Norwich in Lent 1600. The tradition of clowning which he exemplifies 'does not have sharp, well-defined boundaries between actors and an audience but is rather a form of participatory scenario that combines dance, comic improvisation and athletic endurance with an atmosphere of festive spontaneity and informal hospitality'.[3] The

1 'Outside the rules', *Sunday Times*, 12 January 1986.
2 *Empire News*, Manchester, 25 June 1933, and *Star*, 20 June 1933.
3 Bristol, 142. See also Palmer.

part of Touchstone both requires and provides this interaction. It was no doubt easier to achieve where performances were given virtually in the round or on an apron stage; outdoor performance might also facilitate that easy interchange between player and audience which the part demands, and might explain Grossmith's spectacular success in Regent's Park. The absence in outdoor performance of a darkened auditorium allows a rapport between players and audience ideal for the role of the clown. The best Touchstones rise to the challenge of the part, which requires them to bridge the gulf between amateur and professional, between sophisticated wit and holiday foolery.

Touchstone's speeches often invoke the title of a well-known Elizabethan jig (see 3.3.70n., 77n., 91n., 5.4.64n.). Peter Holland has called the jig 'the most Bakhtinian and subversive form of the exuberant carnivalesque' and lamented that it has been 'suppressed from our discourse' in discussions of Elizabethan drama (59). In the case of Touchstone this may be partly because scholars have identified the role with Robert Armin, known as a singer (which Touchstone is not), not a dancer (which Touchstone is). But it has also been a consequence of a more general loss of dancing as a routine element of Shakespearean performance. Bruce Smith points out that the epilogue to *2 Henry IV* is spoken by 'a dancer with tired legs in the quarto text', understandably so, because 'Through the 1590s at least, the epilogue to most plays was performed if not spoken by dancers, in the form of a jig' ('E/loco', 131). Smith concludes:

> The sense of the play as a piece of choreography is no less palpable in epilogues spoken by Robin Goodfellow, Rosalind, and Prospero, who beg breath and movement from the audience to send on their way both the characters in the fiction and the actors who have personated them.
>
> (132)

If *As You Like It* was performed at court at Shrove, 1599, the actor most likely to speak the court epilogue after or during the dance which the Duke calls for is Touchstone, probably played, at least on that occasion, by Kemp, a writer of jigs and an expert dancer.

At the end of the play the fool returns to court, where he can make a living out of his folly. The satirist remains in the Forest, weeping tears into the brook where he sees a reflection: is it of a wise man or a fool?

'A SPEAKING PICTURE': READERS AND PAINTERS

Sir Philip Sidney called poetry a 'speaking picture'. Pictures are an important part of the poetry of *As You Like It*, and its after-life has borne fruit in art even more than in music. The pictorial aspects of the play make it especially enjoyable to read. Where *The Comedy of Errors*, or *The Two Gentlemen of Verona*, or even *Much Ado About Nothing* demand performance, the imaginative world of *As You Like It* is sometimes sold short in the theatre.

To attract readers was in 1623 the main concern of John Heminges and Henry Condell, the first editors of Shakespeare's *Comedies, Histories and Tragedies*. The First Folio, in which *As You Like It* was first printed, was an elegant volume produced as an act of homage to the playwright by his fellow shareholders. After dedicating the volume to the Earls of Pembroke and Montgomery, Heminges and Condell addressed a second dedication 'To the great Variety of Readers':

> From the most able, to him that can but spell:[1] There you are number'd. We had rather you were weighd. Especially, when the fate of all Bookes depends vpon your capacities: and not of your heads alone, but of your purses. Well! It is now publique, & you wil stand for your priuiledges wee know: to read, and censure. Do so, but buy it first.
>
> (sig A3^r)

1 See Masten, 'Pressing subjects', 77–8, for 'spell' meaning 'to peruse' or 'make out'.

They proceed to draw a contrast between audiences (at '*Black-Friers*', or the '*Cock-pit*') where 'these Playes haue had their triall alreadie' and readers, who must now judge them: 'But it is not our prouince, who onely gather his works, and giue them you, to praise him. It is yours that reade him . . . Reade him, therefore, againe, and againe' (sig. A3ʳ). Such loyalty could in 1623 only have been perceived in terms of the repeated reading of the Bible. Indeed the Puritan William Prynne complained bitterly in *Histrio-Mastix* (1633) – his attack on the stage – that Shakespeare's Folio was printed on as fine paper as the Bible (Kastan, *Book*, 5). For every adult who could remember plays performed before the dramatist's death in 1616, there must have been, in 1623 and thereafter, new readers for whom the first life of the play was on the written page. Anthony West claims that 'although there is no record to prove it, it is probably safe to conclude that the demand for the First Folio was such that it sold out in less than a decade, for the Second Folio appeared in 1632' (7). It was bought by 'noblemen and commoners of standing' (6).[1]

Intriguing evidence of the First Folio as a reading text exists in the copy annotated by a Scottish reader in the 1620s, probably William Johnstone. He mines the text for homiletic and sententious material, commenting on Jaques's admiration of Touchstone (2.7.12–57): 'Vanitie of the world / fooles detect wise mens errors safelie / We ripe and rot by houres' (in Yamada, 60; see also 1.3.118n., 3.2.11–82n.). The use of the Folio as a reading text would have been increasingly common as Puritan disapproval of the theatre became institutionalized, resulting in the closing of the theatres in 1642.[2] For the next eighteen years until the Restoration of Charles II in 1660 most people would have virtually no exposure to Shakespeare's plays on stage. The enthusiasm of the diarist Samuel Pepys for seeing plays as opposed to reading

1 For differences between readers see Hackel, 142. Cf. Marcus, *Puzzling*, 22; de Grazia. Hackel, 140–1, summarizes current debates on literacy figures.
2 Clare, 11. Clare stresses the survival of drama in various forms during the Interregnum (1–38).

them derives in part from his early experience of a society which outlawed theatre.

The traditional assumption has been that Shakespeare was not interested in plays as reading material, but only as texts for the theatre. Julie Peters calls this 'one of those enduring lies so convenient to the history of progress', arguing instead for a vital symbiotic relationship between the printing press and the theatre.[1] The making of presentation manuscript copies of plays meant that readers were courted as well as audiences.[2] Sir John Harington listed 109 plays in quarto which he owned in 1609; eighteen (three in duplicate) were by Shakespeare (Furnivall). Some of these may have been in manuscript. Lukas Erne argues that Shakespeare may have deliberately envisaged readers for his plays and that the 'plays work well on the page because they are in certain ways designed for readers' (225; see also 220–46).

As You Like It was not printed in quarto, although a quarto must have been available for print, for the play was 'staied' in the Stationers' Register, apparently in 1600 (see pp. 120–4). Aspects of the First Folio text suggest a wooing of the attention and delight of a reader as opposed to a playgoer. Whether these effects were authorial, or the consequence of the skills of Heminges and Condell, or of scribes – the scrivener Ralph Crane may be a vestigial presence in the text (see p. 126) – or of compositors, the fact remains that various devices enhance the pleasure of reading the play.

As You Like It is intensely visual (see Ronk). There are several long episodes of narrative reportage in the play: Jaques and the wounded stag (2.1.29–63); Oliver's account of his rescue by Orlando from the snake and the lioness (4.3.101–31); Rosalind's of Phoebe's lack of beauty (3.5.38–49); and Phoebe's of Ganymede's attractiveness (3.5.114–24). An audience doesn't need these last two passages because the originals are present to the eye. A reader must see with the eye of the mind.

1 Peters, 5. See also Erne, 7; Mowat, 'Theater', 216, 217.
2 Werstine, 85–6; Love, 65–70; Peters, 6.

The impulse which may have inspired both Nicholas Hilliard and Isaac Oliver to portraits of melancholy courtiers reminiscent of Shakespeare's Jaques reappears in the Romantic period in William Blake's drawing of 'Jaques and the wounded stag', first printed in John Bell's special edition of the Second Folio (see Oxf¹, fig. 4). Constable also retouched an etching of David Lucas's on the same theme (Merchant, 87–9 and plate 87a; see Fig. 12). Edward Dowden's edition of 1887 contains twelve illustrations by the French impressionist painter Emile Bayard, of which the most remarkable is of Hymen and the wedding masque, complete with baroque cherubs adorning the trees. Pictures of *As You Like It* may have inspired writers almost as much as the text. Hardy may have seen sketches in exhibition catalogues of 'rural festivities' (Altick, 9) drawing on *As You Like It* before choosing *Under the Greenwood Tree* as the title for his pastoral novella.

Erne has argued in relation to *Henry V*, *Hamlet* and *Romeo and Juliet* that Shakespeare invites a reader of his plays to imagine movements and gestures. *As You Like It* is rich in internal stage directions which help readers to visualize the action. F's placing of stage entries is often the consequence of theatrical conditions (see Ard², xii–xv), but there are two cases where the placing of an entry might attract the notice of a reader. The first, at 4.3.4.1, will be discussed in the context of the sample page (see pp. 129ff.). The second is at 5.2.12.1, where Rosalind enters as Ganymede after Oliver's lines to Orlando announcing his marriage to the shepherdess, Aliena (Celia in disguise): 'all the revenue that was old Sir Rowland's will I estate upon you, and here live and die a shepherd. *Enter* ROSALIND'. The arrival of Rosalind is not announced by Orlando until three lines later. Ganymede's entry on 'shepherd' slyly satirizes Oliver's pastoral dream because the shepherd boy whose lifestyle Oliver plans to imitate is a princess in disguise. This false shepherd exposes the artifice of the pastoral fiction. Changing the early entry obscures a subtlety which an Elizabethan audience might have noticed, but which is readily perceived by a reader.

The rhetorical balance and fine-tuning of the language of *As You Like It* might suggest reading aloud, a skill which the

Elizabethans practised enthusiastically. Sidney's *Old Arcadia* and Harington's translation of *Orlando Furioso* were both read aloud by their authors to admiring audiences. Harington at one point was employed as a virtually official reader to the queen (Nelson, 114–15). Playwrights apparently read their work in progress to actors, who then commented and made their own contributions to the text (Stern, *Rehearsal*, 101–12). Reading aloud may have been a resource for owners of the First and Second Folios during the Interregnum (1642–60), when the theatres were closed. But it is the reading of the play 'againe, and againe', as envisaged by the original editors, which reveals its finesse.

A number of language usages could only be appreciated by readers, as in Touchstone's pun on 'faining/feigning' in his dialogue with Audrey (see 3.3.18–19 and nn.); in the archaic dialect spelling of *'shoe'* for *'show'* (see 3.2.125 and n.); and in 'bawdrey' spelt 'baudrey', to rhyme for the eye as well as the ear with 'Audrey' (see 3.3.88–9 and n.). At 3.4.14 'cast', meaning 'thrown away', also invokes in the context of Diana the word 'chaste' (F2), which connects etymologically chastity and castigation (from the Latin *castigare*, to chasten, and *casta*, chaste). In the theatre these effects pass too quickly to be noticed, but in private reading they add an extra witty dimension to the language of the play.

Charles Lamb was not the only Romantic writer to feel that in some cases reading could be superior to watching: 'Stage was being pitted against page, the material performance against the imaginative freedom of reading' (Moody, 'Romantic', 41). The nineteenth-century actress Fanny Kemble never played Rosalind but was famous for her readings of the part. William Hazlitt, an ardent theatre-goer, suggested that in *As You Like It* 'the interest arises more out of the sentiments and characters than out of the actions or situations' (234). Hazlitt recognizes that the play enters the solitary individual consciousness possibly even more powerfully than it draws the audience into its orbit in the theatre. He draws attention to the culling of passages for books of extracts, and to the number of phrases which have become proverbial: 'If we were to give all the striking passages, we should give half the play' (237).

As You Like It has been appropriated by novelists. In the nine volumes of George Eliot's letters the novelist refers to the play eighteen times, and often appropriates a phrase: 'my favourite little epithet: "this working day world"'.[1] George Eliot used Rosalind for a number of purposes besides the model of female friendship already noted from her letters. But in her later fiction Eliot seems to have taken against Rosalind as a woman whose attractiveness guaranteed successful courtship. Dorothea's sister Celia in *Middlemarch* – a woman of spirit repressed by her elder sister – may have been named from *As You Like It*. In *Daniel Deronda* Gwendolen Harleth's flirting with the role of Rosalind (Novy, *Engaging*, 124) implies her creator's conviction that modelling oneself on a Shakespearean woman creates more problems than it solves.

Shakespeare's play is differently realized in Théophile Gautier's novel *Mademoiselle de Maupin* (1835), in which 'The dramatic and the psychological plots . . . turn on a production of *As You Like It*' (Garber, *Vested Interests*, 74). Gautier's treatment of cross-dressing looks forward to Virginia Woolf's *Orlando* (1929), for which, like Gautier, Woolf chose a male not a female protagonist. The masculinity of Woolf's hero/heroine exists in a liminal territory which he shares not only with Shakespeare's Orlando but with Rosalind in the Forest of Arden. When Gautier's hero plays Rosalind, both the narrator (d'Albert) and his mistress (Rosette) fall in love, just as Orlando, but also Phoebe, fall in love with Ganymede. The cross-dressed heroine (or hero, as in Gautier's novel) represents 'the space of desire' (Garber, *Vested Interests*, 75). At the end of *As You Like It* the epilogue allows the actor to enter as both boy and woman that enigmatic space colonized by Rosalind from the moment of her entry into the Forest of Arden.

In 2000 Susan Sontag recreated in the novel *In America* the Forest of Arden community set up by the Polish actress Helena Modrezejewska – known professionally in the USA as Helena Modjeska – when she and her fellow actors left Poland for California. Playing Rosalind at Booth's Theatre in New York in

---

1 *George Eliot Letters*, 1.44, cited in Novy, *Engaging*, 208, 7n.

20 Rosalind (Helena Modjeska). The Polish émigrée actress first played
Rosalind in New York at Booth's Theatre in 1882, and performed the role
many subsequent times until 1898

1882, Modjeska was able to bring to the part her own experience of exile, of foreignness, of liberated new woman and of old-world siren (see Fig. 20). At the beginning of the novel the members of a Polish theatre company (of which Modjeska is the star) discuss their plans to emigrate and a 'young actress', who plays Celia to Modjeska's Rosalind, exclaims:

> *Therefore devise with me how we may fly,*
> *Whither to go, and what to bear with us.*
> (Sontag, 22)

Modjeska, like many other actresses, made the part of Rosalind into 'an oblique form of autobiography' (Hankey, 58, on Helen Faucit).

When Charles I wrote 'Rosalind' next to its title in his copy of the 1632 Second Folio was he reminding himself of a performance he had seen, or of his private experience of reading the play?[1] Perhaps in 1623 some of the new readers of the First Folio who turned eagerly to the hitherto unprinted *As You Like It* might have felt, as Empson did in 1929, that an imagined Arden was even more beautiful than one represented in the theatre. After all, the love of Orlando for Rosalind depends on imagining a woman who is conceived in the mind. This is the condition of reading rather than of theatre-going.

TEXT

The staying order

As You Like It might have become available for reading as early as 1600 if the manuscript which appears to have been ready for print – and was therefore given a preliminary staying order in the Stationers' Register (on 4 August 1600) – had in fact subsequently been printed, but it was not.

---

1   West notes that 'Both Steevens and Malone believed it was the non-availability of a First Folio, rather than his preference for a more recent edition, that caused the King to acquire a Second Folio (now in the Royal Library at Windsor)' (1.12).

'Staying' was an alternative to 'entering' an item in the Stationers' Register prior to printing it. To 'stay' a work meant that no one else could print it, and most works which were stayed, as with the other three items named below, were subsequently confirmed as regular entries and printed thereafter. The staying order for *As You Like It* (Arber, 3.37) reads:

4. Augusti

As you like yt / a booke
HENRY *the* FFIFT / a booke
Euery man in his humour./ a booke   to be staied
The commedie of 'muche A doo about nothing'
    a booke /

Peter Blayney has demonstrated that the play named as *Henry V* in the order is in fact *2 Henry IV*,[1] a discovery which has a bearing on *As You Like It*, which at several points seems to recall moments in *2 Henry IV*. Roslyn Knutson infers that 'all four had recently been in production' and that 'Perhaps *2 Henry 4* had also been continued into 1599–1600' (Knutson, *Shakespeare's*, 80, 81), which would probably mean that it ran at some point more or less concurrently with *As You Like It*, making cross-references between the acting of the two plays a possibility.[2]

As the staying order, handwritten on a preliminary flyleaf (presumably in 1600), follows two entries for the Chamberlain's Men plays by James Roberts, Blayney argues that the order was also his, and that the Clerk of the Stationers' Company began a separate list with a play presented by Roberts on 27 May (Arber, 3.37), which he assumed would contain further entries later in the year (Blayney, 'Playbooks', 387). But although *Henry V* (i.e. *2 Henry IV*) and Ben Jonson's *Every Man In His Humour* were

---

1   Erne, 103n., citing Blayney, 'Exeunt pirates' (unpublished paper); see Clegg: 'as Blayney suggested, the 4 August notice may not have been for *Henry V* at all, since it was either already in print or being printed, given the proximity to the 14 August transfer of title. Instead, the 4 August reference was to *2 Henry IV*, whose title page closely resembled that of *Henry V*' (478).

2   See 1.3.85n. and 3.2.54, 58n.

confirmed as regular entries on 14 August 1600, and *Much Ado About Nothing* on 23 August, there is no entry for *As You Like It* until the general entry on 8 November 1622 by the publishers (Edward Blount and Isaac Jaggard) of the sixteen plays that had not been registered before. This was a necessary preliminary to the printing of the First Folio in 1623. Blayney assumes that the Clerk of the Stationers' Company was asked to search the records and confirmed that for fourteen of the plays there were no entries.[1] For those fourteen, a fee of seven shillings each was then paid. But no fee was paid for two plays, which were probably *Antony and Cleopatra*, registered by Blount himself in 1608 (but not printed, and apparently forgotten by him), and *As You Like It*. Blayney argues that the Clerk would have found the staying entry, which 'he would have interpreted as the provisional registration of *As You Like It* by James Roberts in 1600. After Roberts retired, William Jaggard acquired most of his publishing rights, and Isaac inherited William's rights' (Blayney, *Folio*, 21). *As You Like It* would thus have already been in his possession, and no fee would have been necessary.

Scholars have suggested various explanations for the staying order for *As You Like It*.[2] It used to be thought that plays were 'staied' to prevent their being either bought or 'pirated' by other companies wanting to act them. But Knutson's research discredits the piracy theory, demonstrating that companies offered new plays on comparable subjects rather than 'getting a printed quarto or pirating a playbook from another company's stock' ('Repertory', 469).[3] This could be borne out in the case of *As You Like It*, a play which may draw on popular taste for dramas about Robin Hood, evidenced by the Admiral's Men's staging of Anthony Munday and Henry Chettle's two Robin Hood dramas

---

1   Blayney, *Folio*, 18–21; Blayney includes a photograph of the 8 November 1622 entry containing 'As you like it', which heads the section on 'Comedyes' and is followed by 'All's well that ends well', 'Twelfe night' and 'The winters tale'.

2   A comprehensive survey of editions before 1977 is provided by Knowles, 353–64.

3   See also Blayney, 'Playbooks', 386–7; Dutton, *Licensing*, 91–3.

in 1598. The idea that the staying order represented a copyright claim by the Chamberlain's Men to prevent unauthorized publication is not credited by recent scholars (Clegg, 478). It is no longer believed, moreover, that the publication of a play would detract from its popularity with an audience and must therefore be delayed till that play was off the stage (Blayney, 'Playbooks', 386).

Blayney demonstrates that the end of May to October 1600 represents a 'peak period' for the number of plays entered in the Stationers' Register. He suggests that one of the key figures in the registrations was in fact James Roberts, and that the staying order for *As You Like It* was part of the general pattern ('Playbooks', 387), which perhaps makes it more surprising that the play was never printed. This impetus to print plays in quarto came from the players themselves, and may have been fuelled by the competition from the Children of Paul's, staging plays at the newly opened private Paul's theatre.[1] Lukas Erne believes that the Chamberlain's Men probably wanted *As You Like It* to be published, but were for some reason unsuccessful, possibly because with *The Merchant of Venice*, *Much Ado About Nothing*, *A Midsummer Night's Dream* and *The Merry Wives of Windsor* all in print in 1600 there was no further demand for another comedy (Erne, 103). This may have been the case, but if so, the decision to halt *As You Like It* still needs elucidation, as the play is so obviously a winner. The figures for the sale of plays certainly do not reinforce any view that this was a lucrative venture (Blayney, 'Playbooks', 389), and it seems therefore unlikely that the publication of plays had much to do with financial incentives such as the opening of the new Globe.

There may have been some censorship issue which impeded the printing of *As You Like It*. *Troilus and Cressida* was 'staied' until permission was received from the clerical authorities for its printing, and it is possible that *As You Like It* also required some kind of authorization which was not immediately forthcoming.

---

1 Suggested by Gary Taylor, in Blayney, 'Playbooks', 417, n. 6; see Erne, 102.

Alan Brissenden (Oxf[1]) considers a possible viewing of the staying order within the context of the prohibition against printing satires and epigrams instituted by the Archbishop of Canterbury and the Bishop of London on 1 June 1599. The Chamberlain's Men may not have been granted permission to print *As You Like It* because it contained satirical material centring on the figure of Jaques. Brissenden points to the sensitive political situation surrounding the Earl of Essex in 1599–1600 and remarks on the allusions to the queen's godson, Sir John Harington, and his tract *The Metamorphosis of Ajax*, suggesting four reasons why a 'corrector' under the terms of the Bishops' decree might have taken exception to printing *As You Like It*:

> First, the name Jaques itself, with its lavatorial/Harington associations; second, the fact that Harington was the Queen's godson; third, the satirical qualities of the role; fourth, the relationship of Harington with the Earl of Essex, who was out of favour with the Queen even before he went to Ireland. On his unexpected return in September Essex was taken into custody, and not released until the next August. It is to be noted that when the Quarto of Henry V, which had been stayed, was printed in 1600, it was without the choruses, which include lines referring favourably to Essex. These could be omitted from the text without structural damage; to remove Jaques without injuring the fabric of *As You Like It* would be virtually impossible, and so, it can be argued, it remained unpublished at that time.
>
> (Oxf[1], 3–4)

The acceleration of events after August 1600, which led to Essex's aborted rebellion at the end of January 1601 and his execution in the following month, might have made *As You Like It*, with its depiction of an alternative court in the Forest of Arden, seem politically sensitive.

The Folio text: provenance and editorial practices

As You Like It, first available to readers in the Folio text of 1623 (reprinted in 1632, 1664 and 1685), is the tenth of the fourteen plays listed in 'Comedies', the first section of the First Folio. It follows *The Merchant of Venice* and precedes *The Taming of the Shrew*. It occupies leaves Q2 to S3, and pages 185 to 207, although in all copies page 189 retains the wrong number 187. Charlton Hinman concluded that the print was set by three of the possible Folio compositors, whom he named 'B', 'C' and 'D'.[1] Although the alleged habits of the compositors are constantly being reassessed, involving some challenges to Hinman's work,[2] at the present time it is still useful to readers and editors to be aware of differences in sections of the text which appear to have arisen from compositorial activity.

As You Like It is a 'clean text', but its unproblematic and elegant presentation in the Folio has perhaps allowed various mistakes in the text to go unchallenged (*TxC*, 392). What follows represents some observations on the nature of the Folio text of *As You Like It*, and on some of the ways in which the material has been ordered in the present edition. This will be shown in detail in relation to the sample page 202.

My discussion of the text is in two parts. The first deals with editing as a textual activity. The second deals with the 'unofficial' editing that takes place in every performance of the play by directors in conjunction with actors, a process which makes all the agonizing decisions of textual editing partial and contingent on theatrical conditions. This was also the case in Shakespeare's theatre, as many scholars have demonstrated, notably Tiffany Stern in *Rehearsal from Shakespeare to Sheridan*.

---

1 Hinman, 1.182–200. Compositor B: 1.2.61–186, 2.4.68–3.4.13, 5.1.12–end (pp. 187, 192–8, 204–7, i.e. sigs Q4ʳ, Q6ᵛ–R3ᵛ, R6ᵛ–S2ʳ). Compositor C: 1.1.1–1.2.60, 3.4.14–5.1.11 (pp. 185–6, 199–203, i.e. sigs Q3ʳ⁻ᵛ, Q5ᵛa, R4ʳ–R6 ʳ). Compositor D: 1.2.187–2.4.67 (pp. 188–191, i.e. sigs Q4ᵛ–5ʳ, Q5ᵛb–Q6ʳ). Sig. Q5ʳ, misnumbered as page '187', falls in D's stint. D's share in the work is confined to a section of the first two acts, the rest of the play being set by B and C.
2 See for example McKenzie; Masten, 'Pressing subjects'.

125

I begin with a very brief summary of some of the main characteristics of the text and the theory about its provenance agreed
by most scholars.

As You Like It is divided in the Folio into acts and scenes. The
only change made by modern editors (to my knowledge) is the
separating of Orlando's speech at the beginning of 3.2 into a
separate scene, as in the New Cambridge edition (Cam^2). Plays
for the public theatre in Shakespeare's time were not divided
into acts and scenes, although they were for the Children's performances at the private theatre at Blackfriars, where music was
played between acts.[1] Music is played in *As You Like It* at the
ends of Acts 2 and 5, and in 4.2 (and there are songs in 2.5 and
5.3). *As You Like It* and nine out of the other eighteen plays
which appeared for the first time in the First Folio were divided
into acts and scenes, five of them (*The Tempest, The Two
Gentlemen of Verona, Measure for Measure, The Winter's Tale* and
probably *Cymbeline*) by the scrivener Ralph Crane.[2] T.H.
Howard-Hill has argued that Crane's role in the First Folio was
so pervasive that he might well be considered its earliest editor
in preference to Nicholas Rowe in his edition of 1709.[3] Traces of
his influence may be discerned in the text of *As You Like It*,[4]
although many characteristics of Crane texts are not present.
James Hirsh argues, however, that the divisions into acts and
scenes in the First Folio were created by two main agents, of
whom Crane was the principal, and includes *As You Like It* in
the list of plays probably divided by him (230ff.). Hirsh lists a
number of principles on which 'Divider A' (probably Crane)
operated, all of them convincing. However, the play's fine structure makes division into acts easy.

As You Like It moves fluidly between prose and verse, and it is
often not clear in the Folio which is intended. Editors continue to

1   Chan, 9–10; see also Taylor, 'Structure', 10–11; Dart, *Consort*, 6.
2   See *TxC*, 604. The four other new plays divided into acts and scenes are *TN, KJ, H8*
     and *Mac*. Of the remaining eight new plays, *CE, TS, AW, Cor* and *JC* have only act
     divisions; *3H6, Tim* and *AC* have no divisions at all.
3   Howard-Hill, 'Editor', 129; see also Honigmann, *Texts*, 75.
4   See 2.1.0.2n., 2.4.1n., 4.3.56n., 5.2.102n. and p. 383.

differ on how to align parts of the play, but the problem is largely a reader's not a theatre-goer's, and no absolute standard of correctness can be claimed.[1]

Many stage directions are (by modern standards) placed early. Agnes Latham suggests that the main reason is 'the time it took for an actor, entering upstage, to make his way down to the front' (Ard[2], xiii) and this would have been true in the hall staging suggested in this edition, as also in the Globe. The practice in the third Arden series of standardizing these entries sometimes obscures interesting elements in the original text.

Scholars are in general agreed that the text of *As You Like It* reflects a fair-copy transcript based on a book-keeper's theatrical copy rather than on Shakespeare's original manuscripts ('foul papers').[2] The text of *As You Like It* used in the printing of the First Folio was probably prepared before 1606. There are twenty-four references to God in the play,[3] suggesting that the copy used by the Folio editors probably predated the Act to Restrain Abuses of Players, 1606 (Act of Abuses), which resulted, in many plays, in the substitution of 'Heaven' for the deity. A high degree of consistency in the naming of the characters might suggest scribal copy rather than authorial papers, although it is interesting that the speech prefix for Touchstone (only given that name on his arrival in Arden) is always various forms of '*Clowne*'. Some errors in the text also might be attributed to scribal rather than compositorial error, as might certain anomalies relating to speech prefixes. At 2.3.16 (TLN 720) the prefix '*Orl.*' is omitted; fourteen lines later (2.3.29, TLN 733) the prefix '*Ad.*' is given where it should be '*Orl.*'. Various likely copying errors are noted in the commentary, as, for example, 'seauentie' (2.3.71, TLN 775) instead of 'seauenteene', which appears two lines later, and the repetition of 'obseruance' (5.2.92, 94, TLN 2503, 2505). There are also a

---

1 See *TxC*, 637–40, for a discussion of the principles involved, and 647–8 for Oxford's decisions on lineation with regard to *As You Like It*; for a discussion of the alignment of half-lines, see Bevington, *AC*, 266–70.

2 *TxC*, 392; Ard[2], xi; Taylor & Jowett, 241–2.

3 Knowles, 655; Taylor, 'Expurgation', 58, excludes ''Od's' at 3.5.44 and 4.3.17.

number of omissions of exit SDs, which could easily occur in a transcript from authorial papers, but would be less likely in a playhouse copy. At 1.1.89 (TLN 93) no exit is marked for Dennis, although he must leave the stage to call Charles the wrestler. At 1.2.275 (TLN 454) there is no exit for Le Beau, although Orlando bids him farewell. No exit is marked for Jaques at 4.1.29 (TLN 1947), although he announces his departure. Possibly in these two cases the character's adieus are allowed to stand in the place of a formal '*Exit*', but this practice might itself suggest a scribal transcription rather than a playhouse copy, where a book-keeper would certainly have exits marked for each character.

There may have been separate copy for the songs in 2.5, 2.7, 4.2 and 5.3 (Stern, 'Small-beer', 178–9), as well as for Orlando's verses – Celia enters at 3.2.119.1 '*with a writing*', and Orlando hangs his poem on a tree at the beginning of the scene – and for Phoebe's letter in 4.3. There are moments in the F text which might possibly be interpolations from actors, which then became part of the final text.[1]

Plays may have circulated in manuscript during Shakespeare's lifetime, as they did after 1625 (Dutton, *Licensing*, 100–9), in a manner akin to the circulation of manuscript poetry in the period.[2] When Giovanni Battista Guarini wrote his famous pastoral *Il pastor fido* many copies circulated in manuscript in Venice and, according to its first editor Giacopo Castelvetro, so many Londoners asked for a copy that he decided in 1590 to print it, alongside Torquato Tasso's *Aminta* (Henke, 47). This might suggest that the practice of circulating plays in manuscript was not uncommon in Shakespeare's London. The clean text of *As You Like It* might suggest a presentation copy to a nobleman or noble lady. The play would possibly have been a more valuable possession for presentation purposes if it were not simultaneously public property,[3] which might help to explain why it was not printed in 1600.

---

1 See 1.2.104n., 3.3.44n., 3.5.1n., 5.1.3–4n.; Stern, *Rehearsal*, 99–112.
2 If several manuscripts of a play were in circulation there might not have seemed an urgent need for actual publication (Blayney, 'Playbooks', 389).
3 Love, 67–8; Erne, 13–14; Loewenstein, 40.

The best way to understand the dilemmas of an editor, even in as clean a text as this, is to observe them in action. This edition reproduces page 202 of the Folio text of *As You Like It* (sig. R5ᵛ, set by Compositor C; see Fig. 21) to give some indication of the variety of typeface in F and the different kinds of decision an editor must make. The page begins with the concluding speeches of 4.1, when Celia berates Rosalind for her denigration of women in her courtship of Orlando (lines 190–206); then prints the hunting scene (4.2) with the celebratory song over the slaughtered deer; and concludes with 4.3.1–75, Silvius's delivery of the love-letter written by Phoebe to Ganymede (which he thinks mistakenly is a harsh upbraiding) up to the entrance of Oliver (who has only just arrived in the Forest) and the first two lines of his speech (74–5).

Page 202 is typical of the *As You Like It* text in its accuracy (there are no apparent mistakes), its lavish spacing and characteristic use of italics for proper names, stage directions, songs and poems. It demonstrates a variety of linguistic forms: prose between Celia and Rosalind, and between Jaques and the hunters; blank verse between Silvius the true lover and Rosalind as Ganymede, the shepherd boy; a song; prose for Rosalind's dismissal of Silvius; octosyllabic rhyming couplets for Phoebe's letter; and blank verse for the entrance of Oliver. The forms mirror the lightning dramatic changes on the page – from the daring gender joke (see p. 28) with which the page begins, the mumming plays' hunting ritual with the dissonant melancholy Jaques scorning the celebrations in which he nevertheless participates; a lovesick girl longing for a late lover, only to have to put a good face on the arrival of another girl's unwelcome swain; the reading of a letter whose text is different from what the bearer expected, and Rosalind's mean teasing of Silvius by pretending that Phoebe's declaration can be read as 'railing' (scorn). Rosalind retorts to her cousin's pity for the lovesick shepherd with a defiant accusation of Phoebe's perfidy. Another dramatic movement is signalled by the entry of a new arrival in Arden, Oliver (revealed on the next page

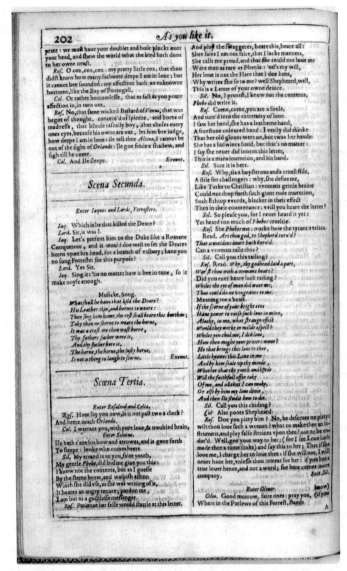

21 Page 202 from *Mr William Shakespeare's Comedies, Histories, & Tragedies* (1623), showing the hunting song in 4.2, Rosalind's reception of Phoebe's love-letter to Ganymede, and the return of Oliver

as penitent), whose impeccable blank verse may indicate from the outset his eligibility as a lover for Celia.

F's punctuation is heavy by modern standards, but nevertheless an exact transcript of this page would neither make it unreadable nor alter the sense. It demonstrates a number of the challenges that face the editor of this play, which include speech prefixes, stage directions, spelling, punctuation and the possible characteristics of the copy-text or texts.

Scholars believe that although there are some distinctive Shakespearean spellings, most of the spelling of F originates with either scribes or compositors. The scribe Ralph Crane used various distinctive spellings. Page 202 was, according to Hinman's analysis, set by Compositor C. Compositors are also known to have had characteristic spelling habits. Punctuation is equally thought to be in the main the work of compositors rather than the author. Here again there are exceptions. But the fact that the Folio text does not most of the time demonstrate the dramatist's hand in either spelling or punctuation ought not to preclude discussion of some of the fascinating aspects of spelling as it relates to the plays he has created.

At 4.3.39 Rosalind coins a verb out of Phoebe's name – 'She *Phebes* me', which follows Silvius's line 'Yet heard too much of *Phebes* crueltie'. The idea for this usage may originate in Silvius's opening line in 3.5 (set by Compositor C), which in F is missing a comma after 'do not': 'Sweet *Phebe* doe not scorne me, do not *Phebe*'. The half-line reiterates the injunction 'doe not scorne me'. When Rosalind remarks wryly 'She *Phebes* me: marke how the tyrant writes',[1] the heroine means 'She [Phoebe] scorns me', as she had scorned (or 'Phoebied') Silvius in the earlier scene. The claim becomes highly ironic when the adulatory letter containing Phoebe's love-suit to Ganymede is then read out loud. Phoebe's name is stressed at 2.4.40 when the lovesick Silvius exits, crying 'O Phoebe, Phoebe, Phoebe!', and is not likely to be forgotten by

---

1   4.3.39, middle of r.h. column, p. 202. In *Coriolanus* the name 'Aufidious' is used twice, at 2.1.125 and 127, before being metamorphosed to ''fidiussed' at 130 (RP).

an audience any more than by Rosalind herself. The later coinage of a verb from the name may have occurred to the playwright as the consequence of an actor's earlier omission of a pause after 'not' in 'do not Phoebe'.

The second question concerns a speech prefix. The SP '*Lord*' at 4.2.2 is usually edited to 'First Lord', so that the person who claims to have killed the deer becomes the same Lord who described Jaques's lament over the wounded stag in 2.1. This change is attractive because the ambiguities of Jaques's own position in this scene, after his reported moralizing on the velvet victim, can be reinforced by the ambiguities surrounding the speaker himself. There is also a problem of whether '*Forresters*' in the stage direction indicates a separate group of people, or whether it is a shorthand for '*Lords like Forresters*' as in the SD for 2.1. This edition assumes that foresters were attending on the exiled lords, and that when Jaques asks a forester for a song he is addressing not a lord but the foreman of the foresters, who would have organized the hunt. The song is therefore sung not by the Lord who killed the deer, but by the First Forester.

F's 'Musicke, Song' implies that music, probably in the form of a broken consort (see p. 78), accompanied the singing. The instruction 'Musicke' is to musicians, presumably offstage, while 'Song' is an instruction to the players. This distinction can also be seen at 2.7.174: 'Giue vs some Musicke, and good Cozen, sing.' Songs were often provided on separate sheets (see p. 128). The Douai manuscript provides no text for the song, stating only 'Musick and Song, after which Exeunt'.[1]

The words may belong to a song already in currency. James Boswell, in the Boswell–Malone edition of 1821, identified the earliest setting of this song in John Hilton's 1652 *Collection of Catches, Rounds, and Canons* (Hilton, 30). Richard Knowles (669) notes its presence in Folger MS V.a.409, fol. 17[r], but dates the copy at *c.* 1650, whereas Ross Duffin suggests *c.* 1625 (Duffin, *Songbook*, 434). A later hand has headed it '*A. Y.L.I.*'

---

1   fol. 45[v], similarly at 2.7.175, fol. 57[r]; see Appendix 4.

The catch in Folger MS V.a.409, like the one in Hilton's collection, does not contain F's problematic line '*Then sing him home, the rest shall beare this burthen*' (4.2.12–13), nor would its inclusion fit into the setting provided for the lines. Duffin argues that this line represents a spoken instruction from Jaques to the singer and surrounding lords (as in this edition), which has been unwittingly italicized and thus considered part of the song. This would explain its absence from the *c.* 1625 copy. Some editors have made the second half of the line, '*the rest . . . burthen*', into a stage direction, on the assumption that it has mistakenly crept into the main body of the song. In 2.5 this edition translates F's '*Altogether heere*' at TLN 926 (2.5.33) into a stage direction for all the lords to join in the song (see 2.5.38). Theobald suggested in 1733 that all the lords, except presumably the music-hating Jaques, should sing the song from '*Take thou . . . scorne*' (4.2.14) to the end. Duffin's research suggests that these lines would then be sung in a 'round':

> the text of the Folger manuscript matches that of the play more closely than does Hilton's version, and it includes some melodic variants – resulting, naturally, in harmonic variants because of the round – that relate more closely to earlier contrapuntal practice.
>
> (*Songbook*, 434)[1]

'The rest' of the lords carry the burden of the deer, the burden of horns, and possibly sing a 'bourdon' (accompanying bass line). Ariel's song in *The Tempest* carries a marginal note, which may be a non-italicized SD: 'Burthen dispersedly' (TLN 525; but see Vaughan & Vaughan, 1.2.382 SD).[2]

It seems likely that some version of the song, which may have been a popular hunting round, was in existence at the time of

---

1 The Folger version and Hilton's are compared in Duffin, 'Catching'.
2 The line of Ariel's song to which this SD is linked in *The Tempest* in F, '*Foote it featly heere, and there, and sweete Sprights beare the burthen*' (TLN 524–5), could also be a spoken prose line, mistakenly rendered as verse. Vaughan and Vaughan treat the line as part of the song (1.2.380–2). Jowett (111–12) suggests that the line may possibly reflect the intervention of the scrivener Ralph Crane, which would also create another connection between Crane and the text of *As You Like It*.

Shakespeare's play, if not earlier. John Chamberlain describes in 1617 (six years before the first printed text of *As You Like It*) 'a certaine song sunge by Sr John Finet, (wherin the rest bare the bourdon) of such scurrilous and base stuffe that yt put the K. out of his good humor, and all the rest that heard yt' (M. Butler, 161). Here it is evident that the line in brackets is descriptive, as probably in 4.2. This song apparently occurred in a masque of *Tom of Bedlam* but it is conceivable that the song from 4.2 was excerpted from the play for independent use, and reproduced in the Folger manuscript before finding its way into Hilton's catches. Its sentiments are arguably scurrilous enough to cause offence to the king.

There is also the question of the relation of the very short scene 4.2 to the rest of the playtext. F's spelling – unique to *As You Like It* – of the word 'Deare' (deer) at 4.2.1, 4 and 10 may support the view that a different copy-text was used for the whole scene (RP), not just for the song. However, it is not very likely that the scene is a later addition, partly because its omission would create a case of instant re-entry by Rosalind and Celia, which was not Shakespeare's usual practice (Bowers, 'Authority', 23). Moreover the song's frame of reference is in tune with Touchstone's disquisition on cuckoldry at 3.3.44–58. The spelling of 'Deare' at lines 1 and 4 of the text matches the spelling of the first line of the song. The copy for the song may have influenced the compositor who was setting up the scene in F. The consistency of the spelling may indicate that there was indeed a separate copy-text for the whole scene. However, the spelling could have derived also from Compositor C or from Shakespeare himself. Over seventy years later the Douai text (1695; see Appendix 4) preserves F's spelling. The Douai scribe has spelt 'deer' as 'dear' in both lines 1 and 4 (fol. 57ʳ), despite the fact that he omits the text of the song. 'Deare' creates a punning contingency between the hunted stag and the lover. The connection is reflected in the play's frequent use of the homonym (conventional to Petrarch sonneteers) of hart/heart (see 3.2.98, 239).

An earlier moment in *As You Like It* amplifies our sense of the literary resonances inherent in the spelling of 'Deare' on page 202. In 1.3, another scene set by Compositor C, 'dearly' is given its usual F spelling of 'deerelie' at 28 and 30 (TLN 488, 89), and 'deerely' a line later:

> *Ros.* The Duke my Father lou'd his Father deerelie.
> *Cel.* Doth it therefore ensue that you should loue his Sonne deerelie? By this kinde of chase, I should hate him, for my father hated his father deerely; yet I hate not *Orlando*.

Celia's 'deerelie' connects with the hunting word 'chase' and anticipates the move into the Forest of Arden in the next scene (2.1; see 1.3.30n.). The point is made in the Douai manuscript where the word is spelt 'chace' – the old term for a hunting forest (see Barton, 'Staging'). At 2.1.25, when the Duke talks of deer having 'their round haunches gored' (see n.), the image evokes the same equivalence of deer and human lover, and the slaughter of the deer encompasses metaphors of human sexuality. In Gregory Thompson's production for the RSC in 2003 the slaughtered deer in 4.2 was not a stuffed animal, as in nineteenth-century productions of the play, but the body of the sleeping Celia; the scene thus subtly anticipates the successful hunting of the heart by Oliver in the ensuing scene (4.3).

Another interesting case is the word 'boisterous', spelt 'boysterous' at 4.3.31 (TLN 2180), set by Compositor C – a spelling retained in the Douai manuscript (fol. 57ᵛ). At 2.3.32 (TLN 736) the word is set as 'boistrous' by Compositor D, also retained (as 'boisterous') in the Douai manuscript (fol. 41ʳ). Wherever the spelling at 4.3.31 originated, it acquires on this page some significance from the context, comparable to the significance of 'deare' in 4.2. The 'boysterous' style of the letter is indeed a male invention not only because Phoebe was played in Shakespeare's theatre by a boy, but because the hand of the male dramatist shapes the words of his female character. The letter's alleged ferocity may not suit a woman's gentle nature, but its literary language belongs in a male tradition of pastoral literary convention to which Phoebe as country shepherdess could have had no access. The sound of the syllable would be heard in the theatre, but the spelling 'boysterous' catches a reader's eye. If this is an accident, it is a happy one.

It is also worth noting some stage directions. Rosalind in both cases has a 'Read' direction for her reading of Phoebe's letter (4.3.40, 44). This contrasts with 3.2.82, where F supplies no SD for a 'writing' when Rosalind enters with Orlando's verses, although this is provided for Celia's entry at 119.1, together with an internal SD from Rosalind herself: 'Peace, here comes my sister reading.' The timing of Silvius's entry at the bottom left-hand corner of the page is intriguing. In F he enters after 'brain'. This may be a compositorial error, as the prose lines 'He hath . . . heere' (4.3.3–5) have been set in verse; the entry may therefore have been placed too early by two lines (and is placed later in this edition according to Arden house-style conventions). But F's early entry may also be correct. Celia has just spoken her line about Orlando's 'pure love and troubled brain' to explain Orlando's delay to an impatient Rosalind, when in comes the lovesick shepherd, who is subject to Cupid's bow and arrows while Orlando has taken his and gone not to hunt either the hart or his lady, but to (perhaps) sleep. It's a joke which is probably half-aimed at a reader, who can see the accuracy of the timing.

Page 202 thus represents in microcosm some of the fascinating puzzles and challenges which even the clean text of *As You Like It* presents to its editors.

Text and performance

One of the biggest changes in Shakespeare studies since the publication of the second Arden edition of *As You Like It* in 1975 has been the closing of the gap between text and performance, scholar and director/actors, the academy and the theatre. The role of director as editor of the text remains, however, the poor relation of this partnership. For all the agonizing which goes into the creating of a new edition, the decisions that have caused so much angst are often overturned within minutes by directors and actors when they start work on the real business in hand: the actual performing of the play.

In the case of *As You Like It* the discussion of the division into acts and scenes looks different if theatre directors are allowed into the debate. Early and later directors routinely altered the order of the scenes in the first three acts, sometimes moving 2.2 back into Act 1 (as in Thompson, RSC 2003), sometimes cutting 2.2 and 3.1, or replacing the earlier scene with the later one, in the interests of not disturbing the scenery for the Forest of Arden. This advantage nevertheless forfeits the play of contrast between Frederick's court and the alternative court in the Forest which 2.2 and 3.1 create. Two scenes dominated by music, 2.5 and 5.3, were also sometimes cut, and this may have started even in Shakespeare's time, where music in the public theatre was reduced in comparison with performances at court and in the private theatre at Blackfriars (see p. 126). William Percy gives instructions in his manuscript plays (written for the Children of Paul's but probably never performed) to cut the music between the acts for performance in the public theatre.

These cuts and alterations were dictated by theatrical convenience; others, as in the case of the part of Jaques, by preconceptions about the play as a whole, or about particular characters. In the nineteenth century many cuts in Rosalind's and Celia's speeches reflected a concern for propriety and the taste of audiences. But that a somewhat different play appears – almost always – on the stage from on the page deserves more recognition than it is perhaps in the interests of a scholarly editor to admit. In a comprehensive survey of the history of cutting the text of *As You Like It* for theatrical performance Knowles

observes that Michael Elliott's promptbook for the RSC production at the Aldwych Theatre, London (1962), represents 'on
the whole the nearest thing to an uncut version of the play'
(650). Elliott used the 1926 Cambridge edition, and only cut
Touchstone's remarks about the heathen philosopher (5.1.32–5).
However, an exception was, interestingly, Nigel Playfair's 1919
production, which Playfair claims was controversial for more
than the banishment of the stuffed deer:

> It was strange how it offended traditionalists for us to
> play 'As You Like It' without cutting a single word; and
> it only goes to show how easily tradition can choke its
> own fountain-head. But I was determined not to cut a
> single sentence.
>
> (51)

Possibly as early as the Restoration, and certainly by the time of
the play's revival in the theatre by Charles Fleetwood in 1741,
the only stable text of *As You Like It* was a reading text. A theatrical text even of so well-known a play is more fluid, temporary
and partial than the reading version studied by generations
of schoolchildren and students for public examinations might
suggest.

Was this always the case? What did the first audiences of *As
You Like It* see, or, more to the point, hear? They may have
heard, on at least one occasion, a different epilogue. Andrew
Gurr argues that 'no play texts survive from Shakespearian time
in a form that represents with much precision what was actually
staged'. Not only does he suggest routine cutting, but also that
'we need a much closer knowledge of staging practices and of
these dreadfully variable kinds of play book that we seek to
preserve in our fixated and too crystalline modern editions, over-
plugged as they are with facile assumptions about original
staging' (Gurr, 'Historicism', 72, 87). The earliest extant acting
edition was printed in Dublin in 1741, when it was acted at the
Theatre-Royal in Aungier-Street. This edition cuts some of

Jaques's part (his parody of Amiens's song in 2.5; the discussion of satire in 2.7; the dialogue with Rosalind in 4.1); the song 'It was a lover and his lass'; and the role of Hymen in 5.4. It also continues the practice begun by Charles Johnson in *Love in a Forest* (1723) of turning the First Lord's account of Jaques's lament over the wounded deer into direct speech, spoken by Jaques himself. The title-page carries a note: 'Collated with the oldest Copies and corrected, By Mr. Theobald.' But of what the 'oldest Copies' consisted is not known.[1] Did they also contain cuts?

Different types of conditions require different sorts of adjustment. The Douai manuscript predates the Dublin copy by almost fifty years. The three scenes which it cuts completely – 2.5, Amiens's first song and Jaques's parody of it; 5.1, Touchstone, Audrey and William; and 5.3, the two Pages singing 'It was a lover and his lass', with Touchstone – entail reductions in music and in the roles of Jaques and Touchstone, and the disappearance of William. The play was probably performed publicly in Douai, and may have been too long for the time available. The absence of 2.5 and 5.3 might suggest a lack of solo singers, although someone appears to have sung Amiens's song at the end of 2.7. Some of these cuts may reflect Restoration theatre practice, or may conceivably originate in differences between the public and private theatres in Shakespeare's time. The excised 5.1 resembles the 'grammar' scene in *The Merry Wives of Windsor*, which was cut for court performance; the singing Pages in 5.3 may have performed at court and at Blackfriars but not at the Globe. The existence of the Douai manuscript, and of many later prompt-books that cut and adapt passages in the play, is a salutary reminder that in the theatre the audience never has seen or heard exactly what is written in either the First Folio or any later edition, including this one.

---

1   See Stern, *Making*: 'these single plays [i.e. without quartos] often have internal indications that they once existed in variant, lost versions' (48–9).

EPILOGUE: 'ALL THE WORLD'S A STAGE'

'Princes, you know,' declared Elizabeth I, 'stand upon stages so that their actions are viewed and beheld of all men.'[1] The queen's sense of an audience asserts also her control of what happens on that stage, an omnipotence reflected in Shakespeare's Rosalind. As Camille Paglia observes: 'Behind her playfulness of language and personae is a pressure of magisterial will' (209).

The nineteenth-century actress Ellen Terry, who perhaps always regretted (like Fanny Kemble) that she had never played Rosalind, wrote in her *Four Lectures*:

> Don't believe the anti-feminists if they tell you, as I was once told, that Shakespeare had to endow his women with virile qualities because in his theatre they were always impersonated by men! This may account for the frequency with which they masquerade as boys, but I am convinced it had little influence on Shakespeare's studies of women. They owe far more to the liberal ideas about the sex which were fermenting in Shakespeare's age. The assumption that 'the woman's movement' is of very recent date – something peculiarly modern – is not warranted by history. There is evidence of its existence in the fifteenth century.
>
> (81)

There were no biological women on Shakespeare's stage. But Barbara Lewalski has suggested that the powerful female voices which Shakespeare gave actual women provided a model which spurred them to find a voice of their own:

> If we admit the power of literary and dramatic images to affect the imagination, we might expect the very presence of such a galaxy of vigorous and rebellious female characters to undermine any monolithic social construct

---

1 'Queen Elizabeth's first reply to the parliamentary petitions urging the execution of Mary, Queen of Scots, November 12, 1586' (Elizabeth I, *Works*, 189).

of woman's nature and role. There is some evidence that women took the oppositional support they needed or wanted from books and plays. Women of all social classes went to the theater and the Queen herself was passionate about it.

(Lewalski, 9–11)

In the nineteenth century the step from acting Rosalind to managing a theatre was taken by Eliza Vestris, who demonstrated her capacity for gender politics in her highly successful reign at the Olympic Theatre.[1] Nina Auerbach suggests that Ellen Kean and Marie Bancroft also 'inherited from their breeches roles the managerial power that the larger society reserved for men' (60).

But Shakespeare's Rosalind also envisages less lofty forms of power in her sporting with Orlando. When her lover announces that he must leave her, Ganymede's fictional Rosalind pouts: 'Ay, go your ways, go your ways. I knew what you would prove. My friends told me as much and I thought no less. That flattering tongue of yours won me' (4.1.170–3). With the formulation 'My friends', Shakespeare allows Rosalind to conjure up the gossip networks of women of the 'middling sort' described by Bernard Capp in his investigation of the ways in which such women asserted power in a man's world (Capp, *Gossips*, esp. 49–55). In the public theatre many of those 'gossips' would have been in Shakespeare's audience. The shepherd boy does not confine his Rosalind to an aristocratic world. The middling sort are also a vital part of his imagination and of his theatre.

As You Like It can encompass equally the court and the motley arena from which Shakespeare and the players also came and with which they were familiar – a world in which they could themselves be classed as vagabonds and gipsies, where apprentices could burst into a theatre on Shrove Tuesday and demand a play of their own choice (Laroque, 246). The role of Rosalind spans regality and rebelliousness, sovereignty and subversion. Edward Berry points out that

1 Moody, *Illegitimate*, 197–202, 207.

> As the director and 'busy actor' (III.iv.60) in her own 'play,' and the Epilogue in Shakespeare's, Rosalind becomes in a sense a figure for the playwright himself, a character whose consciousness extends in subtle ways beyond the boundaries of the drama.
>
> (Berry, 'Rosalynde', 44)

Samuel Beckett's subtle reinvention of *As You Like It* in *Company* embodies the same perception of an authorial power invested in Rosalind both '*within* the play' and '*beyond* [its] confines'. Rosalind's epilogue highlights the 'artificiality' of the work of art (Murphy, 148). The player in the end evades the play by recognizing that the forest is in fact a sea of faces, who can applaud or hiss, like or mislike. But that movement out of the drama into the theatre reminds the audience that they too are actors on a stage from which there is no easy exit.

Shakespeare creates in this play a partnership between the boy actor and his own role as dramatist, but also between Rosalind/Ganymede and the women in his audience. If for the duration of the play Elizabethan women had shared Rosalind's liberation into manhood, the apprentice actor in Shakespeare's company had also entered into the heroine's freedom and mastery of her world. Might he not have felt some wistfulness as he mused 'If I were a woman' before returning to being just an apprentice to a master player? Perhaps Flute in *A Midsummer Night's Dream* would rather play a knight than Thisbe, but the role of Rosalind is a different matter, bringing with it the power of the maker or deviser, as well as of the royal queen of shepherds. For if the adult players rehearsed their apprentices for the play, in *As You Like It* the apprentice has reversed those roles, teaching Orlando not only how to love, but how to act the lover.[1]

As You Like It speaks to worlds beyond its own time, as it will also speak to audiences and players of the future, with their own exits and entrances, their own Rosalinds and their own Forests of Arden.

---

1 Dusinberre, '*KJ*', 49–50; '*TS*', esp. 169–70, 182; 'Cleopatras', 55–7, 64. See S. Smith, 'Apprentices', esp. 153–5, and also McMillin, for the rehearsing of the boy apprentices by the sharers.

AS YOU LIKE IT

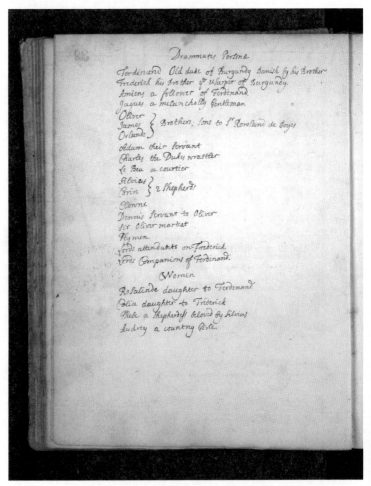

Drammatis Persona

Ferdinand Old duke of Burgundy Banish by his Brother
Friderich his Brother & usurper of Burgundy.
Amiens a follower of Ferdinand
Jaques a melancholly Gentleman
Oliver
James ⎱ Brothers, sons to Sr Rowland de Boyes
Orlando ⎰
Adam their servant
Charles the Duke wrastler
Le Beu a courtier
Silvius ⎱ 2 Shepherds
Corin ⎰
Clowne
Dennis servant to Oliver
Sir Oliver martext
Hymen.
Lords attendants on Frederick
Lords Companions of Ferdinand.

Women

Rosalinde daughter to Ferdinand
Celia daughter to Friderick
Phebe a Shepherdess beloved by Silvius
Audrey a country Girle.

22 'Drammatis Personae' from 'As You Like It', Bm de Douai, Ms 787
    Anglais, Douai (1694–5), the earliest extant 'List of Roles' for the play

144

LIST OF ROLES

ROSALIND	*daughter of Duke Senior*
CELIA	*daughter of Duke Frederick*
DUKE SENIOR (Ferdinand)	*living in exile*
DUKE FREDERICK	*his usurping brother*
ORLANDO	*youngest son of Sir Rowland de Boys* 5
OLIVER	*his eldest brother*
ADAM	*servant in the de Boys household*
DENNIS	*Oliver's servant*
CHARLES	*Duke Frederick's wrestler*
LE BEAU	*a courtier* 10
TOUCHSTONE	*a clown*
AMIENS	*a lord, follower of Duke Senior*
JAQUES	*a melancholy gentleman*
CORIN SILVIUS	*shepherds* 15
PHOEBE	*a shepherdess*
AUDREY	*a country girl*
SIR OLIVER MAR-TEXT	*a country vicar*
WILLIAM	*a country youth*
HYMEN	20
JAQUES DE BOYS	*second son of Sir Rowland de Boys*
LORDS	*attendant on Duke Frederick*
LORDS	*companions of Duke Senior*
FORESTERS	
Two PAGES	*attendant on Duke Senior* 25

Attendants

145

LIST OF ROLES This list is based, with minor changes of order, on the Douai MS of 169⁴ᐟ⁵ (1695 new-style dating), whose 'Drammatis Personae' (*sic*) provides the earliest list of roles, preceding Rowe's by some 15 years (see Fig. 22 and Appendix 4).

1 ROSALIND Shakespeare took the name of his heroine from Lodge's *Rosalynde*, his principal source, but he would also have found it in the 'April' eclogue of Spenser's *Shepheardes Calender* (1579), where the name seems to be intended to disguise a correspondence with the queen (see 1.2.22n. on *sweet Rose*), whom the eclogue celebrates. The name is always pronounced in modern English with a short final vowel, Rósalínd; in Orlando's verses it rhymes with *wind/lined/mind*. Cercignani (58–9) suggests that the rhymes indicate the normal Elizabethan pronunciation of the name with a long final vowel. It is set by Compositor D (who had just been setting *LLL*) as '*Rosaline*' (1.2.278; 1.3.0.1, 1, 87, 93; 2.4.0.1); see Knowles, 7.

2 CELIA Knowles (7) suggests that the name, which means 'heavenly', derives from Spenser's *Faerie Queene*, 1.10.4, where Dame Cælia, 'as thought / From heaven to come, or thither to arise', is the saintly mother of Fidelia (faith), Speranza (hope) and Charissa (charity). Shakespeare's choice of the name suggests a possible tribute to Elizabeth, true mother of the Protestant religion. Although F twice spells the name '*Cellia*' (on Q3ᵛ, set by Compositor C), Spenser's diphthong makes it plain that it is pronounced with a long *e*. In Lodge the corresponding character is called Alinda.

3 DUKE SENIOR (Ferdinand) unnamed in F, but see 4n. and 1.2.80n. for F's 'old *Fredericke*' at TLN 247, which Capell conjectured in his *Notes* (1.56) was probably a mistake for 'Ferdinand'. The Douai MS names Duke Senior 'Ferdinand' in the 'Drammatis Personae', but 'old Duke' in the SDs, and describes him as 'Old duke of Burgundy Banish by his

Brother', thus situating the play in the Ardennes, local to Douai. Rowe leaves a blank after 'Duke of'. In Lodge, Duke Senior is a king named Gerismond.

4 DUKE FREDERICK ('*Duke*' in F) F names the usurping Duke as Frederick only twice, '*Fredricke*' (1.2.223) and '*Frederick*' (5.4.152), or, according to some editors, three times. Theobald interpreted F's 'old *Fredericke*' as referring to Celia's, rather than Rosalind's, father (see 3n.). In the Douai MS he is called 'Duke' in the text and 'New Duke' in the SDs to 2.2 and 3.1, but in the 'Drammatis Personae' he appears as 'Frederick his Brother yᵉ Usurper of Burgundy'. In Lodge the equivalent character is a king, Torismond.

5 ORLANDO Orlando's name is the Italian form, used by Ariosto in *Orlando Furioso*, of the French 'Roland'. The hero of Lodge is named Rosader. The anglicized name of Orlando's father, Sir Rowland, spelt '*Roland*' in F at 1.2.212, 221 and 224, gives all three sons the chivalric pedigree of the knights of Charlemagne, chronicled in the *Chanson de Roland*. The patronym, 'de Boys' ('*de Boyes*' in F2–F4), is the anglicized form of 'de Bois' (of the woods). In Lodge the father of Saladyne and Rosader is named John of Bordeaux.

6 OLIVER The name Oliver comes from the *Chanson de Roland* and belongs to one of Roland's principal knights (not in any way a villain), who appears as the figure of Oliviero in Ariosto. But Shakespeare undermines the epic romance tradition by making Oliver initially a betrayer of his father's honour. The name invokes the olive tree, symbol of peace (see 3.5.76n.). The corresponding figure in Lodge is called Saladyne.

7 ADAM Named 'Adam the spencer' (steward) in the fourteenth-century *Tale of Gamelyn*, the old servant in Lodge acquires a surname, 'Adam Spencer'. Both function and patronym are dropped by Shakespeare, leaving

only the archetypal name Adam, with its Edenic echoes, to describe the old retainer of Sir Rowland's household.

8 DENNIS the anglicized name of the patron saint of France

9 CHARLES The name which Shakespeare chooses for the wrestler ('the Norman' in Lodge) almost seems like a joke at the expense of Charles the Great (Charlemagne), just as Dennis (see 8n.) rises no higher than a doorman.

10 LE BEAU F's 'the *Beu*' at 1.2.90 implies Celia's anglicized pronunciation (cf. Sir Rowland de Boys). The name may have been suggested by Hall's attack on the affected dress of the courtier in *Virgidemiarum* (1599) in the satire entitled '*Plus Beauque fort*' (4.4, p. 28).

11 TOUCHSTONE named '*Clowne*' in F. At 2.4.0.2 his entry is noted as '*Clowne, alias Touchstone*', which creates the possibility that his name, not used in the text until 3.2.12, is an Arden pseudonym corresponding to *Ganymede* and *Aliena*. A touchstone was 'a very smooth, fine-grained, black or dark-coloured variety of quartz or jasper (also called BASANITE), used for testing the quality of gold and silver alloys by the colour of the streak produced by rubbing them upon it' (*OED* 1). Cf. Sir John Harington's epigram, 'An Elegie of a poynted Diamond given by the Author to his wife at the birth of his eldest sonne' in 1589: 'The touch will try this Ring of purest gold. / My touch tryes thee, as pure though softer mold. / That metall pretious is, the stone is true, / As true, and then how much more pretious you' ('Epigrams 1600', fol. 2). See also Gosson, *Abuse*: 'The abuses of plaies cannot bee showen, because . . . for tryall [they] are neuer broughte to the touchstone' (21).

12 AMIENS The form of the name, which makes its owner *Lord of Amiens* (2.1.29), a city in the Ardennes, might appear to combine (in a false etymology) *ami* (Fr. = friend) and *amans* (Lat. = loving). Shakespeare may have had in mind the faithful knight Aimenon, who in the medieval epic *Girart de*

Roussillon accompanies the hero, Girart, in the Forest of Arden. 'Aymes' or 'Aymon' is Girart's brother, and the hero of a romance known to Shakespeare as *Quatre fils Aymon*, which was also adapted for the stage as *The Four Sons of Aymon* (Fraser, *AW*, 6). The Douai MS's description of Amiens as a 'follower' rather than an attendant lord underwrites the egalitarian fellowship of the Forest *co-mates . . . in exile* (2.1.1), but the Duke calls him *cousin* (2.7.174), which may imply that Amiens is his kinsman (but see also Appendix 2).

13 JAQUES Rowe made Jaques a 'lord' (like Amiens) attending on Duke Senior, but the earlier Douai MS, following the text more exactly, identifies him as 'a melancholly Gentleman' rather than a lord in the Duke's court. Cam[2] describes him as '*a melancholic traveller*'. In the play he is addressed as *Monsieur*, which may also be a tribute to his status as a gentleman (Touchstone greets him as *Master*) rather than as a lord (3.3.68). The name is anglicized in modern productions and *qu* pronounced as *kw*. The Elizabethans also probably pronounced it as two syllables: Jak-es. The name for a privy was a jakes, spelt 'iaques' in Q *KL* (sig. E1'), the usual Elizabethan spelling (*OED* jakes 1a, noted in Cam[2]; see 3.3.68n.). Jaques has no counterpart in Lodge.

14 CORIN Lodge's old shepherd, like Virgil's in his second Eclogue, is called Coridon. Shakespeare may have taken the name from the play *Sir Clyomon and Sir Clamydes*, printed in 1599 (see Bullough, 2.257–66; and p. 98).

15 SILVIUS The name means 'of the woods' (Lat. *silva* = wood); in Drayton, *Elizium* (1630), Silvius is a forester. But Silvius in *AYL*, though a forest-dweller, is a shepherd; as with most literary shepherds, he is more given to loving than to lambing.

16 PHOEBE Taken from Lodge, the name is the feminine form of Phoebus, used for the goddess of the moon, and current in compliments to the queen (see

Koller, 43). It signifies both chastity and inconstancy; cf. *RJ* 2.2.109: 'O swear not by the moon, th'inconstant moon'.

17 AUDREY Shakespeare's addition to Lodge of Audrey, the simple country girl who herds goats, establishes an authentic working environment in the Forest (see Clark, 62). The name adds to the number of connections between the play and Henry VIII; Sir John Harington's father, another John, was married first to an illegitimate daughter of Henry VIII (described in documents as 'base-born'). In some of the records she is called Ethelreda (or Esther) but in others, Audrey (Hughey, 17).

18 SIR OLIVER MAR-TEXT Sir Oliver is described at 3.3.39 as 'the vicar of the next village', which suggests an Anglican parish priest, but see 3.3.77–9n. *Mar-text* conjures up the Marprelate controversy consequent on a Puritan attack on Anglican bishops, which began in 1583 and was widely satirized in the theatre. *Sir* was translated from *Dominus*, a title used for a cleric without formal qualifications; see 3.2.309n. and Appendix 2.

19 WILLIAM Shakespeare's choice of his own name for his Forest-born rustic has led to the suggestion that he may have played the part himself; see Appendix 2.

20 HYMEN The name was used by the Elizabethans as a synonym for 'marriage', as in the entry under 'Marriage' in *England's Parnassus* (1600): '*Hymen* that now is god of nuptiall rights, / And crownes with honor loue and his delights' (no. 1099, p. 149, quoting stanza 91 of Chapman's 1598 completion of Marlowe's *Hero and Leander*).

21 JAQUES DE BOYS The second son of Sir Rowland de Boys, mentioned in Orlando's first speech (1.1.5), only appears in 5.4. In the Douai MS he is named 'James' both in the 'Drammatis Personae' and at 1.1.5, but at his entry at 5.4.148.1 he reverts to being the '2nd Brother' (F '*Second Brother*'). For pronunciation see 13n. He is named Fernandyne in Lodge.

22, 23 LORDS The Douai MS distinguishes the subordinate roles given to Duke Frederick's 'attendant' courtiers from the egalitarian one assigned to Duke Senior's 'companions' in the Forest of Arden.

24 FORESTERS Although the Lords are dressed as foresters, true foresters are also present to help with the hunt in 4.2.

25 PAGES The advent of Duke Senior's two Pages in 5.3 to sing 'It was a lover and his lass' means that the play required six boy actors (see Appendix 2).

AS YOU LIKE IT

1.1   *Enter* ORLANDO *and* ADAM.

ORLANDO   As I remember, Adam, it was upon this
fashion bequeathed me by will but poor a thousand
crowns, and, as thou sayst, charged my brother on his
blessing to breed me well; and there begins my sadness.
My brother Jaques he keeps at school and report speaks   5
goldenly of his profit. For my part, he keeps me
rustically at home or, to speak more properly, stays me
here at home unkept; for call you that keeping, for a
gentleman of my birth, that differs not from the
stalling of an ox? His horses are bred better, for besides   10

1.1.0.1 F has no indication of location at
the head of any of the scenes in the
play. Act 1 is set in France; 1.1 opens in
Oliver's orchard (39), sometimes
glossed as a 'garden', as in Lodge,
Shakespeare's main source. An orchard
(with apple trees) was the common
adjunct of a country house, appearing
in *JC* 2.1 (Brutus's orchard); *MA* 2.3
and 3.1.5; and *2H4* 5.3.1, where
Shallow invites Falstaff to eat an apple.
If trees or a tree were provided for the
scene (see 2.1n.), they would do double
duty for the Forest of Arden in Act 2.

2   **poor a** a mere (*OED* poor *a.* 4b); the
indefinite article intensifies the adjective (Abbott, 85; cf. *a many*, 110).
Although the motif of three brothers
suggests a folk-tale (*Gamelyn*; see
1.2.113 and n.), the small inheritance
(cf. Adam's offer, 2.3.38 and n.) contradicts the customary favour
bestowed on the youngest son (as on
Rosader in Lodge).

3   **charged** 'he' is implied (cf. 3.3.19n.)
4   **blessing** the benediction given by a
dying father to his eldest son
breed me bring me up; see 3.2.28n.
5   **Jaques** the second son of Sir Rowland
de Boys, in Lodge named
'Fernandyne', 'that liues a scholler in
Paris' (sig. P4ʳ); see List of Roles, 21n.,
5.4.148.1, 150.
school university; cf. *Ham* 1.2.113:
'back to school in Wittenberg' (as in
modern American usage).
6   **goldenly** glowingly (*OED* 1, the only
example till 1840). The epithet prepares the audience's ear for the *golden
world* at 113.
profit progress
7   **rustically** used disparagingly: as a
country yokel
properly precisely
stays detains
8   **unkept** not looked after, but also
'unkempt' compared with the well-
groomed horses (10)

1.1] *(Actus primus. Scoena Prima.)*   Location] *an Orchard / Rowe;* OLIVER*'s House / Pope; Orchard
of* Oliver's *House / Capell*   2 fashion] my father *Hanmer;* fashion he *(Ritson);* fashion: He */ Rann
(Blackstone);* fashion: 'a *Cam¹ (Furness)*   me by] me. By *Johnson*   poor a] a poore *F2*   5 Jaques]
James *Douai ms*   7 stays] stys *Warburton*

that they are fair with their feeding, they are taught
their manage and to that end riders dearly hired; but I,
his brother, gain nothing under him but growth, for the
which his animals on his dunghills are as much bound
to him as I. Besides this nothing that he so plentifully   15
gives me, the something that nature gave me his
countenance seems to take from me. He lets me feed
with his hinds, bars me the place of a brother and, as
much as in him lies, mines my gentility with my
education. This is it, Adam, that grieves me, and the   20
spirit of my father, which I think is within me, begins
to mutiny against this servitude. I will no longer endure
it, though yet I know no wise remedy how to avoid it.

Enter OLIVER.

11 **fair . . . feeding** handsome from a
good diet. Markham, *Horseman* (1607),
describes the fine diet necessary for the
training of horses (5.4, pp. 39–41; 6.4,
pp. 13–18), which contrasts strikingly
with the *husks* Orlando receives (35).
12 **manage** the final stage in the
breaking-in of a horse (Markham,
Horseman, 1.28, pp. 194ff.: 'Of
Managing, and the severall kindes
thereof'). Orlando contrasts his own
lack of training with the advanced
tutelage afforded to a horse. Sidney in
Old Arcadia [1580] criticizes the king
Basilius for putting his trust in the
boorish shepherd Dametas, as if 'an
ass will be taught to manage' (28), i.e.
acquire the skills of a trained horse.
dearly hired hired at considerable
expense
14 **bound** indebted
15–17 **Besides . . . from me** 'As well as
giving me abundance of nothing, he
deprives me, through his neglect, of
the good qualities [*something*] which

nature has bestowed on me.' The
antithesis of 'nothing' and 'something'
was a favourite Elizabethan paradox
(Colie, 219–72).
17 **countenance** (ill) looks and (lack of)
favour
18 **hinds** servants (*OED sb.*² 2); cf.
Jonson, *EMO* (1599), 1.3.65.1: '*Enter a
Hind.*'
bars debars; Orlando's predicament
mirrors an Elizabethan debate about
primogeniture (Montrose, 'Brother',
esp. 33–4; Sokol & Sokol, 313). Lodge
may have depicted in the hostility of
Saladyne (= Oliver) and Rosader (=
Orlando) his own enmity with his elder
brother, William (Sisson, *Lodge*, 4; see
also 2.3.23n. and pp. 82–3).
18–19 **as . . . lies** as far as he is able
mines undermines
gentility with good breeding along
with
20 **education** nurture (ironic); i.e. the
experience of eating with servants
instead of studying at the university

12 manage] *(*mannage*)*; manège *Oxf*   23.1] *after* 26 Collier²; *after* 24 Ard²

ADAM   Yonder comes my master, your brother.

ORLANDO   Go apart, Adam, and thou shalt hear how he   25
will shake me up.

OLIVER   Now, sir, what make you here?

ORLANDO   Nothing. I am not taught to make anything.

OLIVER   What mar you then, sir?

ORLANDO   Marry, sir, I am helping you to mar that which   30
God made, a poor unworthy brother of yours, with
idleness.

OLIVER   Marry, sir, be better employed and be naught
awhile.

ORLANDO   Shall I keep your hogs and eat husks with   35
them? What prodigal portion have I spent that I should
come to such penury?

25 **Go apart** one of many SDs contained within the text; see also *Stand aside* (3.2.120–1); *go off a little* (3.2.155); *Slink by* (3.2.245).

26 **shake me up** harass me – an anticipation of the scuffle which follows

27 **make you** are you doing; cf. 2.3.4, 4.3.61.

28 F's habitual division of 'any thing' makes the paradox of *nothing* and *something* more explicit; see 15–17n.
make taken by Orlando in the sense of 'fashioning something'; cf. 27.

29 **mar** spoil. The word-pair *make/mar* is an Elizabethan commonplace; see John Heywood, *Epigrams 300* (reprinted in 1598), no. 39: 'Of making and marring'.

30 **Marry** well, indeed; a corrupted form of 'by Mary'

31 **God made** Cf. 'Is he of God's making?' (3.2.199). Orlando's accusation that Oliver mars God's creation by denying his younger brother education ushers in a number of 'marred texts'. Orlando mars trees by carving Rosalind's name on them (3.2.9–10); Touchstone's parody mars Orlando's love poetry (3.2.98–109); Jaques mars Orlando's verses by *reading them ill-favouredly* (3.2.255), and parodies

Amiens's song (2.5.41n.); and Sir Oliver Mar-text mars the biblical text through his lack of learning (see 3.3.38–9n. and Owens, 23).

33–4 **be naught awhile** 'go to the devil' (Dent, N51.1); *naught* implies worthlessness (cf. 3.2.15) or even profligacy, but Oliver possibly also puns on the figure nought, representing 'a fool or a cipher' (3.2.282 and n.). Orlando ignores the jibe, taking *naught* to mean 'having nothing'.

35 **hogs . . . husks** an allusion to the parable of the Prodigal Son; see Luke, 15.16: 'And he wolde faine haue filled his bellie with yᵉ huskes, that the swine ate: but no man gaue *them* him' (Geneva Bible). The son wasted his father's substance with prodigal living, but repented and returned to ask his father to make him his hired servant, causing rejoicing and forgiveness; cf. *1H4* 4.2.34–5, *2H4* 2.1.144–5.

36 **prodigal** extravagant, wasteful. In Lodge, Sir John of Bordeaux admonishes his sons to save his legacies: 'Wherein if you be as prodigall to spend, as I haue beene carefull to get, your friendes wil greeue to see you more wastfull then I was bountifull' (sig. A4ᵛ).

OLIVER   Know you where you are, sir?

ORLANDO   O, sir, very well: here in your orchard.

OLIVER   Know you before whom, sir?   40

ORLANDO   Ay, better than him I am before knows me. I know you are my eldest brother, and in the gentle condition of blood you should so know me. The courtesy of nations allows you my better in that you are the first-born, but the same tradition takes not away my   45 blood, were there twenty brothers betwixt us. I have as much of my father in me as you, albeit I confess your coming before me is nearer to his reverence.

OLIVER   What, boy!

ORLANDO   Come, come, elder brother, you are too young   50 in this!

OLIVER   Wilt thou lay hands on me, villain?

---

39 **here . . . orchard** Orlando's precise answer undercuts Oliver's imperious rhetorical question.

42–3 **gentle . . . blood** estate of being well born; *gentle* also implies noble conduct and bearing. See also 156n., 2.3.2, 6 and pp. 31–2.

41 **knows** recognizes

44 **courtesy** conventions and customs; cf. Edmund's outburst against 'the plague of custom' and 'curiosity of nations' (*KL* 1.2.3–4).
   allows acknowledges

48 **his reverence** his honourable position and status. The reading should possibly be 'sir reverence', as 'sir' is easily misread as 'his' in secretary script; see 104n. See Greene, *Quip* (1592): 'For the eldest, he is a Ciuilian, a wondrous witted fellow, sir reuerence sir' (sig. E4ʳ). There may also be here an insulting scatological jest, as 'reverence' was a euphemism for excrement (Partridge, 'sirreverence', 188); see

Manningham, 45: 'One had fouled his finger with some reverence' (fol. 116: January 1601 [=1602]). Rabelaisian jokes, often stemming from Harington's *Ajax* (a tract on the author's invention of the water-closet), are part of the play's texture; see also 82n., and pp. 4, 86–9.

49 **boy** a denigrating reference to Orlando's youth; see also 161. Lodge has 'sir boy' (sig. B4ʳ); cf. *AC* 4.12.48. Editors have offered a variety of SDs here, casting Oliver as the likely aggressor (Sprague, 31–2). The elder brother may make only a menacing or rude gesture, such as the Elizabethan 'biting of the thumb'; cf. *RJ* 1.1.42–52.

50 **too young** too childish, a suitable retort to an insulting gesture

52 **thou** Calvo, 'Pronouns', points to the difficulty of categorizing the fluctuations between 'you' and 'thou' in late sixteenth-century dramatic texts,

---

48 reverence] revenue *Hanmer*   49 boy!] boy! *Strikes at him.* / *White²* (Staunton); boy! *menacing with his hand.* / *Johnson; assailing him* What, *Oxf*   50 Come] *seizing him by the throat* Come, *Oxf; putting a wrestler's grip on him* Come, *Ard²; at 51* this. *collaring him* / *Johnson*

ORLANDO   I am no villain. I am the youngest son of Sir
Rowland de Boys; he was my father, and he is thrice a
villain that says such a father begot villains. Wert thou   55
not my brother I would not take this hand from thy
throat till this other had pulled out thy tongue for
saying so. Thou hast railed on thyself.

ADAM   Sweet masters, be patient. For your father's
remembrance, be at accord.   60

OLIVER   Let me go, I say.

ORLANDO   I will not till I please. You shall hear me. My
father charged you in his will to give me good
education. You have trained me like a peasant,

identifying the use of 'thou' for insults
and contempt as well as for 'love, care
or affection' (13).

lay hands on assault, seize; an internal SD for Orlando at 50

52, 53 **villain** Oliver uses the word in its
modern (Machiavellian) sense: 'That
one may smile, and smile, and be a
villain' (*Ham* 1.5.108); cf. 2.2.2n. But
Orlando gives the term its old meaning
(villein = a peasant possessing a strip
of land which he pays for with the
duties of a vassal; see *KL* 3.7.77: 'My
villein?'). Cf. Essex's letter [1598] to
Sir Thomas Egerton, Lord Keeper: 'I
haue been contented to doe her
[Elizabeth I] the seruice of an Erle, but
can neuer serue her as a villaine or
slaue' (Essex, 'Two Letters', fol. 100;
see Dusinberre, '*AYL*', 418; McCoy,
96).

54–5 **thrice a villain** First, if Orlando is
a villein, i.e., a peasant, so is his brother Oliver; secondly he is a villain for
slandering his father; thirdly he is (in
Elizabethan thinking) a villain and a
villein because illegitimate.

58 **railed** poured scorn on, jibed at; a
word particularly associated with
the satirical performances of the
Children's companies at Blackfriars

and St Paul's. See 2.5.53, 3.2.270,
4.3.42, 43, 46.

59 **Sweet masters** Adam comes forward
(see 25n.).

59–60 **For . . . remembrance** for the
sake of your father's memory

60 **at accord** in agreement

62 **will not** a defiant refusal (*OED v.*[1] B
10a, 'purposes to, is determined to',
obs.); cf. 75. This use of *will* connects
the play with Rabelais's Abbey of
Thelema, over whose door was
inscribed 'FAY CE QUE VOUDRAS' ('*Do
as thou wilt*') (Rabelais, *Gargantua*,
1.87; Rabelais/Urquhart, 1.157). Cf.
4.1.104n., 5.2.70–1n. and p. 90.
Orlando puns on *will* meaning 'want
to' and *will* as testament (63).

please the first intimation of the
negotiation of 'pleasing', 'liking' and
'content', which lies behind the play's
throwaway title; see 1.3.134n. and pp.
97, 100.

You Orlando returns to the formal *you*
after the enraged *thou* of 55.

64 **peasant** uneducated feudal depen-
dant, as in *villain* (53); cf. *KL* 3.7.79:
'A peasant stand up thus?' Cf. Lodge:
'Though hee be a Gentleman by
nature yet forme him a new, and make
him a peasant by nourture' (sig. B3[r]).

53 villain] villein *Oxf*   54 Rowland] Roland *Cam²*   55 villains] villeins *Oxf*

obscuring and hiding from me all gentleman-like 65
qualities. The spirit of my father grows strong in me,
and I will no longer endure it! Therefore allow me such
exercises as may become a gentleman, or give me the
poor allottery my father left me by testament; with that
I will go buy my fortunes. 70

OLIVER   And what wilt thou do? Beg when that is spent?
Well, sir, get you in. I will not long be troubled with
you; you shall have some part of your will. I pray you
leave me.

ORLANDO   I will no further offend you than becomes me 75
for my good.

OLIVER   Get you with him, you old dog.

ADAM   Is 'old dog' my reward? Most true, I have lost my
teeth in your service. God be with my old master, he
would not have spoke such a word. 80

Exeunt Orlando [and] Adam.

OLIVER   Is it even so? Begin you to grow upon me? I will

Nashe caricatures Lodge in *Pierce Penniless* (1592), describing his wastrel existence and his defiant protest that 'nere a such Pesant as his Father or brother shall keepe him vnder' (1.170–1, ll. 32–4). Saladyne keeps his brother Rosader 'in such seruile subiection, as if he had been the sonne of any country vassal' (sig. B3ᵛ).

65 **obscuring . . . hiding from** The two verbs are virtually synonymous, the first Latin in root and the second Old English; for similar pairings see *Left and abandoned* (2.1.50), *sanctified and holy* (2.3.13), *Lose and neglect* (2.7.113) (Knowles).

68 **exercises** riding, fencing, tilting, as in *manage*, 12 (see n.)

69 **allottery** portion (*OED obs. rare*, only example), suggesting the haphazard nature of endowment by will

73 **will** both desires and inheritance (Var 1890); see 62n.

75–6 'I will not affront you more than is

appropriate for my own well-being.'

78–9 **old . . . service** 'Adam produces a quiet *asteismus* or "merry scoff," literalizing his master's metaphor and turning it against him . . . a case of the ingenious disguised as the ingenuous' (Elam, 169).

lost my teeth Cf. '*Sans* teeth, *sans* eyes, *sans* taste, *sans* everything' (2.7.167), and see *MA* 5.1.116–17: 'We had like to have had our two noses snapped off with two old men without teeth.'

79 **God . . . master** The normal form of 'goodbye' was 'God be with you', but Adam replaces 'you' with *my old master*, in a valediction not to Oliver, but to the old order, which the eldest son has betrayed in his rough treatment of a faithful servant.

80 **spoke** shortened past participle (Abbott, 343); cf. *ate* (1.3.71, 2.7.89), *broke* (2.4.37), *begot* (5.4.169).

81 **grow upon me** get out of hand

physic your rankness, and yet give no thousand crowns
neither. Holla, Dennis!

Enter DENNIS.

DENNIS   Calls your worship?

OLIVER   Was not Charles, the Duke's wrestler, here to   85
speak with me?

DENNIS   So please you, he is here at the door and
importunes access to you.

OLIVER   Call him in.   [*Exit Dennis.*]
'Twill be a good way – and tomorrow the wrestling is.   90

Enter CHARLES.

CHARLES   Good morrow to your worship.

OLIVER   Good Monsieur Charles. What's the new news at
the new court?

CHARLES   There's no news at the court, sir, but the old
news: that is, the old Duke is banished by his younger   95

---

82 **physic** administer medicine for
purging (the bowel); another possible
scatological reference, and a nudge at
Harington for *Ajax*; see pp. 88–9.
rankness the state of being over-
grown and stinking, used of weeds. Cf.
Ham 1.2.135–7: 'Fie on't, ah fie, 'tis an
unweeded garden / That grows to
seed; things rank and gross in nature /
Possess it merely.'

83 **neither** strengthens the preceding negative, but also provides the phrase with
a euphonious ending; cf. 1.2.27, 50.
Holla a shout to excite attention (*OED*
int. and *sb.* 2)

85 **wrestler** F's 'wrastle' and its variants
('wrastler', 'wrastling') survive as

dialect forms (Wright, *Dialect*, 6.551).

87 **at the door** of the walled orchard

88 **importunes** begs

90 **'Twill . . . way** addressed to the audience (cf. 153–62) in the half-comic
mode of the stage villain

92–3 **new . . . court** Cf. 1.2.91, 'With his
mouth full of news'. Word-play on *old*
and *new* raises audience awareness of
Frederick's usurpation. The new court
relies on gossip, rumour and overhearing (1.2.266–72 and 2.2), whereas the
old court in the Forest of Arden is nurtured by *old custom* (2.1.2; see 4.1.125,
127n.). *New court* implies a recent
change, despite the fact that the
usurpation is *old news*.

85, 160 wrestler] *(Wrastler)*   89 SD] *Johnson*   90 wrestling] *(wrastling)*   92 Good] Good morrow
Dyce² (Walker)

brother the new Duke, and three or four loving lords have put themselves into voluntary exile with him, whose lands and revenues enrich the new Duke; therefore he gives them good leave to wander.

OLIVER   Can you tell if Rosalind, the Duke's daughter, be   100
banished with her father?

CHARLES   O no; for the Duke's daughter, her cousin, so loves her, being ever from their cradles bred together, that she would have followed her exile or have died to stay behind her. She is at the court and no less beloved   105
of her uncle than his own daughter, and never two ladies loved as they do.

OLIVER   Where will the old Duke live?

CHARLES   They say he is already in the Forest of Arden and a many merry men with him, and there they live   110
like the old Robin Hood of England. They say many

---

96 **three or four** F's SD at 2.1.0.1–2 names '*two or three*' lords; see 2.5.0.1–2n., 2.7.0.1n.

99 **good leave** full permission

100, 102 **Duke's** Oliver still recognizes the old order, whereas Charles is henchman to the new.

104 *****she would have** F's 'hee' represents one of several pronominal errors (cf. 3.2.142n. on *her*, 5.4.112n.), probably made here by Compositor C in reading secretary script (commonly used in manuscript), where *h* and long *s* are easily confused (cf. 48 and n.); see Appendix 4.

109 **Forest of Arden** Act 1's French setting would suggest the Ardennes (Flanders in Shakespeare's time), but in Lodge the Forest is situated near Bordeaux. From Act 2 onwards Shakespeare develops the Englishness of the Forest; see 5.1.23n., p. 48 and Fig. 10.

110 **a many** See 2n.

111 **Robin Hood** Stories of the folk hero Robin Hood, leader of a band of forest outlaws, were part of popular culture in England from the Middle Ages, as was the *Chanson de Roland* on the continent (see List of Roles, 5n., for Orlando/Roland). For Shakespeare's interest in Robin Hood see *TGV* 4.1.36, *2H4* 5.3.103 and *TNK* Prologue 20–1. In Munday and Chettle's two Robin Hood plays, *Downfall* and *Death*, Robin Hood is identified with Robert Earl of Huntingdon, and the pastoral setting is used, as also in *AYL*, as a means of criticizing the court (Chaudhuri, 353–4); see pp. 100–6. Breton, *Pasquill's Pass* (1600), prays to be delivered 'From a delight in hunting after newes, / Or louing idle tales of Robin Hood' ('Pasquil's Precession', stanza 25, 1.8), which may refer to *AYL*.

of England emphasizes the French setting

---

100 Duke's] old Duke's *Hanmer*   102 Duke's] new Duke's *Hanmer*   104 she] *F3;* hee *F*   her] their *F3*   109 Arden] Ardenne *Oxf*

young gentlemen flock to him every day and fleet the
time carelessly as they did in the golden world.

OLIVER What, you wrestle tomorrow before the new
Duke?   115

CHARLES Marry, do I, sir, and I came to acquaint you
with a matter. I am given, sir, secretly to understand
that your younger brother Orlando hath a disposition
to come in disguised against me to try a fall. Tomorrow,
sir, I wrestle for my credit, and he that escapes me   120
without some broken limb shall acquit him well. Your
brother is but young and tender, and for your love I
would be loath to foil him, as I must for my own honour
if he come in. Therefore out of my love to you I came
hither to acquaint you withal, that either you might stay 125
him from his intendment or brook such disgrace well as

112 **flock** a significant word in legislation about vagabondage and unlawful assembly (see *Proclamations* (1600), 420, and Dusinberre, '*AYL*', 422); here it may evoke not only the subversiveness of the Robin Hood stories, but also the categorizing of stage players as vagrants (McDonald, 121); see 1.3.65n. and pp. 71, 101–2. Frederick's entry into the Forest with an army, reported by Jaques de Boys at 5.4.152–7, conveys the threat generated by the alternative court in Arden. However, the word also prepares the audience for Corin's sheep and the pastoral world.
fleet pass, rare transitive use of *fleet* (*OED v.*¹ 10d); cf. 2.4.94n.
113 **golden world** a time of eternal spring and innocence without labour or laws; see 2.1.5n., Ovid, *Met.*, 1, pp. 2ʳ⁻ᵛ, and cf. *Tem* 2.1.168–9: 'I would with such perfection govern, sir, / T'excel the Golden Age.' See pp. 90–5.
114 **What** well now; cf. 2.7.11.

119 **disguised** Orlando's birth would disqualify him from competition with an ordinary wrestler, but disguise allows him to accept the challenge; cf. *KL* 5.3.142–4, where Edmund 'By rule of knighthood' can refuse to fight the disguised and unknown Edgar. In modern productions Orlando is not usually disguised in 1.2.
try a fall technical description of the first bout of a wrestling contest; see 1.2.195n., 1.3.23–4n.
121 **acquit him** conduct himself
122 **young** Orlando's youth is emphasized throughout; see 1.2.146n. and Appendix 2.
tender vulnerable
for your love in consideration of your favour to me
123 **foil** overthrow, a wrestling term (*OED v.*¹ 4); cf. 1.2.179, 2.2.14.
125 **withal** a common adverbial form, here signifying 'with this matter'
126 **intendment** purpose, plan of action
brook endure

114+ wrestle] *(wrastle)* 115 Duke?] *F2;* Duke. *F* 116 came] come *F4*

he shall run into, in that it is a thing of his own search
and altogether against my will.

OLIVER   Charles, I thank thee for thy love to me, which
thou shalt find I will most kindly requite. I had myself   130
notice of my brother's purpose herein and have by
underhand means laboured to dissuade him from it,
but he is resolute. I'll tell thee, Charles, it is the
stubbornest young fellow of France, full of ambition,
an envious emulator of every man's good parts, a secret   135
and villainous contriver against me his natural brother.
Therefore use thy discretion; I had as lief thou didst
break his neck as his finger. And thou wert best look
to't; for if thou dost him any slight disgrace, or if he do
not mightily grace himself on thee, he will practise   140
against thee by poison, entrap thee by some treacherous
device, and never leave thee till he hath ta'en thy life by
some indirect means or other. For I assure thee (and
almost with tears I speak it) there is not one so young
and so villainous this day living. I speak but brotherly of   145
him, but should I anatomize him to thee as he is, I

127 **search** seeking
129 **thee** Oliver's second person can be
heard as an intimate tone which flatters Charles by making him into an ally
(Byrne, 54, cited in Knowles).
132 **underhand** Oliver seems unaware of
the critique he offers of his own conduct (132–60); cf. *natural* (136) and
brotherly (145).
134 **stubbornest** most immovably ruthless; cf. 2.1.19.
of France Cf. *of England*, 111 and n.
135 **emulator** disparager (*OED* 1a *obs.*);
Oliver accuses Orlando of his own vice
(cf. 159–60), in a first intimation of the
character of the *envious court* (2.1.4;
see 1.2.230, 253–5). For the envy
fuelled in 1599 by the rivalries in
Elizabeth's court between Essex and
Ralegh, see pp. 93, 103–4.

parts qualities
136 **natural** blood; used for a child born
out of wedlock – ironic in view of the
quarrel about legitimacy, 54–5 and n.
(cf. 1.2.48). Illegitimacy carries in this
period the slur of unreliability; see *KL*
1.2.11.
137 **had as lief** would as soon
140 **grace . . . thee** improve his credit by
discrediting you
practise plot, conspire, carrying (sin-
ister) Machiavellian associations for an
Elizabethan audience (Raab, 32–4,
51–76; see 2.3.26)
145 **brotherly** Oliver's unconscious irony
is a marker from comedy rather than
tragedy (see Scolnikov, 145); cf.
3.1.15n.
146 **anatomize** dissect, here used figuratively to mean 'analyse'; see 2.7.56n.

must blush and weep, and thou must look pale and wonder.

CHARLES   I am heartily glad I came hither to you. If he come tomorrow I'll give him his payment. If ever he go   150
alone again I'll never wrestle for prize more. And so God keep your worship.   *Exit.*

OLIVER   Farewell, good Charles. – Now will I stir this gamester. I hope I shall see an end of him; for my soul – yet I know not why – hates nothing more than he. Yet   155
he's gentle, never schooled and yet learned, full of noble device, of all sorts enchantingly beloved, and indeed so much in the heart of the world, and especially of my own people, who best know him, that I am altogether misprized. But it shall not be so long. This wrestler   160
shall clear all. Nothing remains but that I kindle the boy thither, which now I'll go about.   *Exit.*

150–1 **go alone** i.e. walk without crutches
154 **gamester** gambler (see 1.2.151n.) or 'frolicsome person' (Onions, 1, p. 91), but also possibly a 'playboy', as in *boy*, 49, 161. Oliver addresses the audience.
156 **gentle** refers here to Orlando's character rather than his birth; cf. 42–3n. 'The word "gentle" and its derivatives appear more than fifteen times' (Ruthrof, 10); see pp. 31–3.
    schooled . . . learned natural learning contrasted with book-learning; see *LLL* 1.1.86–7: 'Small have continual plodders ever won, / Save base authority from others' books.' The inherent 'natural' virtues of Orlando cannot be erased by poor nurture; cf. Lodge: 'nurture & art may do much, but that *Natura naturans* which by propagation is ingrafted in the hart, will be at last perforce predominant' (sig. B2ᵛ).

156–7 **noble device** chivalric behaviour associated throughout with Orlando; see 3.2.368n.
157 **enchantingly beloved** 'loved to a degree that could only be supposed to be the effect of spell or incantation' (Caldecott)
160 **misprized** undervalued, and therefore scorned (*OED* misprize *v.*¹). Oliver's envy and hostility provide potentially tragic material. *AYL*'s affinities with the last plays, especially *Per* and *WT* (Chaudhuri, 463; Ryan, 119; see pp. 3–4), are congruent with Guarini's conception of pastoral drama as a tragicomic form (see Kirsch, 7–15), manifested in his immensely popular pastoral play, *Il pastor fido* (1580–5; see p. 128).
161 **kindle** incite
    boy derogative, as at 49; cf. *gamester*, 154 and n.

152 SD] *after* Charles *153 Capell*   153 SP] *F2; not in F*

1.2   *Enter* ROSALIND *and* CELIA.

CELIA   I pray thee, Rosalind, sweet my coz, be merry.

ROSALIND   Dear Celia, I show more mirth than I am
mistress of.

CELIA   And would you yet were merrier.

ROSALIND   Unless you could teach me to forget a   5
banished father you must not learn me how to
remember any extraordinary pleasure.

CELIA   Herein I see thou lov'st me not with the full weight
that I love thee. If my uncle, thy banished father, had
banished thy uncle, the Duke my father, so thou hadst   10
been still with me I could have taught my love to take
thy father for mine. So wouldst thou, if the truth of thy

1.2 The location is probably still outdoors,
as the wrestling comes to the place
where Rosalind and Celia are (see
110–11, 137–9). From the start they are
'outside' the court psychologically as
well as physically, partly because they
are women, and partly because
of the ambiguous position of Rosalind,
with which Celia allies herself. The
dialogue between them is not found in
Lodge; their entry in mid-conversation
'quotes' the opening scene between
Orlando and Adam (Cam²).

1   **coz** a form of address used five times
in this scene, creating a contrast
between the amity of the female
cousins and the enmity between the
brothers in 1.1

4   *F prints this line as a continuation of
Rosalind's speech, and most editors,
following Rowe³, insert 'I': 'And would
you yet I were merrier'. But Jourdain
suggested that the SP '*Cel.*' has
dropped out of the text (cf. 2.3.16 t.n.).

This edition treats Rosalind's *Unless
. . . pleasure* as a response to Celia.

6   **learn me** teach me; cf. *Ham* 5.2.9,
'should learn us' (Q2), replaced in
F by 'teach us', suggesting that by
1623 'learn me' had begun to look old-
fashioned. Here the conjunction of
teach . . . forget . . . learn . . . remember
creates a rhetorical balance, which
inverts – for emotional emphasis – the
expected order of 'teach to remember',
'learn to forget'.

8   **thou lov'st** The change from *you* to
thou underlines Celia's devotion,
but also marks 'in-group membership'
in which she, as a Duke's daughter,
insists on equality with her dis-
inherited cousin (Calvo, 'Celia',
109). Celia would have followed
Rosalind into exile if Frederick had
not allowed Rosalind to remain for his
daughter's sake (1.1.104–5; see also
1.3.103n.).

10   **so** provided that

1.2] *(Scoena Secunda.)*   Location] *The Duke's Palace / Rowe; an Open Walk, before the Duke's Palace
/ Theobald*   4 SP] *this edn (Jourdain); not in F*   were] I were *Rowe³*

love to me were so righteously tempered as mine is to
thee.

ROSALIND   Well, I will forget the condition of my estate   15
to rejoice in yours.

CELIA   You know my father hath no child but I, nor none
is like to have, and truly when he dies thou shalt be his
heir, for what he hath taken away from thy father
perforce, I will render thee again in affection. By mine   20
honour I will! And when I break that oath let me turn
monster. Therefore, my sweet Rose, my dear Rose, be
merry.

ROSALIND   From henceforth I will, coz, and devise
sports. Let me see: what think you of falling in love?   25

CELIA   Marry, I prithee do, to make sport withal – but love
no man in good earnest, nor no further in sport neither

---

13 **righteously** rightly (*OED* 2 *ob*s., latest
example), with biblical resonance
tempered stretched, beaten out, as of
steel; harmonized as in music (the
'well-tempered clavier'); ordered,
through the moderation of excess (see
Aristotle, *Ethics*, 2. 54–8).

15 **condition . . . estate** state of my
worldly circumstances, both social and
economic; see 5.4.173 and cf. *TN*
1.3.106–7: 'she'll not match above her
degree, neither in estate, years, nor wit'.

17 **but I** except me (Abbott, 209: *I* for *me*)
nor none emphatic (Abbott, 406)

18 **like** likely

20 **perforce** by force, balanced with *in
affection*
render restore to

20–1 **By mine honour** A significant oath
which Touchstone reiterates both at 59
and in his jests, 62–78. Its use by Duke
Frederick at 1.3.85, when he banishes
Rosalind, contrasts with his daughter's
vow of loyalty to her cousin; see 76n.

22 **monster** the epitome of unnaturalness
and bestiality (cf. *KL* 4.2.51); a possible
reminder of the boy actor beneath
the woman's dress, as 'monster' was the

standard term of abuse used by detractors of the theatre for boys dressed as
women; cf. *TN* 2.2.34 and see
5.4.118n.

sweet Rose a contrast to *briers*
(1.3.12n.). The name means 'beautiful
rose' (Spanish = *rosa linda*), and may
connect Shakespeare's heroine with the
queen, who adopted the sweet-brier,
eglantine or wild rose as one of her
emblems (Strong, *Cult*, 71, 75–6). See
Fig. 19, *Young Man among Roses* (a
courtier garlanded with the queen's
eglantine; see p. 104). In Lady Russell's
entertainment at Bisham (1591) the
sewing consisted of 'Roses, Eglentine,
harts-ease, wrought with Queenes
stitch and all right' (J. Wilson, 45).

24–5 **devise sports** think of games. If
the play was initially performed at
Shrovetide the eagerness for sports
would mirror the festive season, when
schoolboys and apprentices were given
a special licence to devise sports
(as were boy actors; see Kathman,
'Apprentices'); see pp. 37–9, 141.

26 **make sport withal** amuse ourselves
with

> than with safety of a pure blush thou mayst in honour
> come off again.

ROSALIND   What shall be our sport then?   30

CELIA   Let us sit and mock the good housewife Fortune
from her wheel, that her gifts may henceforth be
bestowed equally.

ROSALIND   I would we could do so, for her benefits are
mightily misplaced – and the bountiful blind woman   35
doth most mistake in her gifts to women.

CELIA   'Tis true, for those that she makes fair she scarce
makes honest, and those that she makes honest she
makes very ill-favouredly.

ROSALIND   Nay, now thou goest from Fortune's office to   40
Nature's; Fortune reigns in gifts of the world not in the
lineaments of Nature.

28–9 **than . . . again** 'than you are able to
laugh off with an innocent blush
which shows that your honour was not
compromised'. The dramatist uses a
blush – which in the theatre must exist
in language rather than in physical
show – to signal the 'feminine' identity assumed by the boy actor (see
2.7.120n.; cf. *RJ* 2.5.70–1).

29 **come off** relinquish, give up

31 **housewife** pronounced 'hussif', a
woman in command of a household
(cf. 4.3.27), but also, colloquially, a
'hussy' – capricious and loose-
moralled 'wench'.

32 **wheel** spinning wheel, as in the classical image of the three Fates (*Parcae*)
spinning (as a housewife spins) human
destinies, but also the medieval emblem
of Fortune's wheel; cf. *KL* 2.2.171.

35 **blind woman** Fortune was depicted
as blind (like Cupid), or at least blind-
fold, to indicate her impartial distribution of favours and misfortunes; see
5.2.63n. on *fortune*, and *H5* 3.6.29–37.

38 **honest** chaste. Chastity and beauty
were traditionally at war (Dent, B163);
see 3.3.26–8.

39 **ill-favouredly** ugly; the adverbial
form used as an adjective (Kittredge)

40–1 **Fortune's . . . Nature's** a female
version of the nature/education debate
between Orlando and Oliver in 1.1; see
Lodge: '[Sir John of Bordeaux] whome
Fortune had graced with many fauors,
and Nature honoured with sundry
exquisite qualities, so beautified with
the excellence of both, as it was a question whether Fortune or Nature were
more prodigall in deciphering the riches of their bounties' (sig. A4ᵛ).

40 **Fortune's office** those things which
pertain to Fortune. The extended jesting between Celia and Rosalind may
have had a contemporary frame of reference in the rivalry between Ralegh
and Essex in the Elizabethan court (see
5.4.68n. and p. 93). Ralegh's nickname
was 'Fortune' (see 4.1.20n.), and Essex
used it to accuse him of being an
upstart. But Ralegh threw the term
back, claiming that Essex owed his
ascendancy to birth rather than merit
(Hammer, 67–8).

41 **gifts . . . world** material as opposed to
spiritual endowments

31 housewife] huswife *Capell;* hussif *Ard²*

162

Enter TOUCHSTONE.

CELIA   No? When Nature hath made a fair creature may
she not by Fortune fall into the fire? Though Nature
hath given us wit to flout at Fortune, hath not Fortune   45
sent in this fool to cut off the argument?

ROSALIND   Indeed there is Fortune too hard for Nature,
when Fortune makes Nature's natural the cutter-off of
Nature's wit.

CELIA   Peradventure this is not Fortune's work neither,   50
but Nature's, who, perceiving our natural wits too dull
to reason of such goddesses, hath sent this natural for
our whetstone; for always the dullness of the fool is the
whetstone of the wits. – How now, wit, whither wander
you?   55

42.1 Touchstone's early entry here allows him to hear Celia's next speech (cf. 4.1.25n. and p. 127).

44 **fall . . . fire** lose her virtue, hence incur the risk of hellfire; cf. *Mac* 2.3.19, 'everlasting bonfire'. Samuel Phelps's promptbook for his 1847 production has a prompter's note after *fire*: 'Touchstone laughs off S[tage]' (before entry at 46).

45 **wit** intelligence, sharpness (often with sexual connotations; see Oxf[1], Appendix A, and cf. 4.1.78, 159)
flout at mock; see 3.3.100, and cf. 5.1.13n., 17n. Flouting was the trade of the jester, but women (as outsiders) often share his skill (see p. 8).

46 **fool** foolish person, as opposed to *wit* (54), but also the professional fool, Touchstone
cut . . . argument interrupt our train of thought with his folly, which sharpens other people's wits; see 53n., 54n. Cf. Falstaff, *2H4* 1.2.9–10: 'I am not only witty in myself, but the cause that wit is in other men'.

48 **natural** illegitimate offspring; cf. 1.1.136n.

cutter-off curtailer of – as illegitimate children may intrude on the legitimate line of inheritance

51 **dull** stupid; but also blunt, after jokes about cutting, 48

53 **whetstone** stone for sharpening metal implements. See Jonson, *Cynthia's Revels* (1601): 'How happely hath Fortune furnisht him with a *Whetstone?*' (i.e. a jester, 1.5.710).
dullness . . . fool stupidity of the idiot (not the professional jester); cf. *dull fool* (3.2.112) and *TN* 1.5.81–3: 'I saw him put down the other day with an ordinary fool, that has no more brain than a stone.'

54 **whetstone . . . wits** See Part 2 of Robert Record's *Arithmetic*: *The Whetstone of Wit* (1557, reprinted 1596, cited by Wright), which Shakespeare would probably have used in school; see also Dent, W298.1.
How now familiar and jocular greeting
wit ironic

54–5 **whither wander you?** The phrase echoes the opening dialogue in Breton, *Will of Wit* (1597, reprinted 1599), 9ff.; cf. 4.1.156.

42.1] *after 46 Dyce* TOUCHSTONE] *Theobald[2]; Clowne F*   51 perceiving] *F2;* perceiueth *F*   52 hath] and hath *Malone*

TOUCHSTONE   Mistress, you must come away to your father.

CELIA   Were you made the messenger?

TOUCHSTONE   No, by mine honour, but I was bid to come for you.   60

ROSALIND   Where learned you that oath, fool?

TOUCHSTONE   Of a certain knight that swore by his honour they were good pancakes, and swore by his honour the mustard was naught. Now I'll stand to it: the pancakes were naught and the mustard was good,   65 and yet was not the knight forsworn.

CELIA   How prove you that in the great heap of your knowledge?

ROSALIND   Ay, marry, now unmuzzle your wisdom.

TOUCHSTONE   Stand you both forth now. Stroke your   70 chins and swear by your beards that I am a knave.

CELIA   By our beards – if we had them – thou art.

TOUCHSTONE   By my knavery – if I had it – then I were.

---

56 **Mistress** formal and peremptory; Touchstone parodies Frederick's style; see 1.3.38, and also 3.5.46, 58.

58 **messenger** Celia's question implies that the fool is an unsuitable emissary.

59 **by mine honour** Touchstone's oath initiates a volley of jests on *honour* and forswearing, 62–78; see 20–1n.

63 **pancakes** Pancakes were traditional fare for Shrove Tuesday, a time of pre-Lenten revel, when plays were given at court. Cf. *AW* 2.2.20–3: 'As fit . . . as a pancake for Shrove Tuesday'. (Dusinberre, 'Pancakes', 379–80 and pp. 40–1).

64 **mustard was naught** In Jonson, *EMO* (1599), the foolish Sogliardo's new coat of arms bears the motto '*Not without mustard*' (3.1.244, a possible reminder of Touchstone's phrase; see 76n.), often read as Jonson's mockery of Shakespeare's acquisition (in 1596) of a coat of arms from the Herald's Office on behalf of his father (see

Schoenbaum, 229 and Appendix 3).

66 **forsworn** perjured; see 74–5n.

69 **unmuzzle** release (as in removing a muzzle from a dog); Rosalind allows the fool his traditional freedom of speech.

72 **By . . . them** The two women are instructed to imagine themselves to be boys on the verge of manhood; see 3.2.201n. Cf. *MND* 1.2.44–5: 'let not me play a woman: I have a beard coming' (see Oxf¹). Cf. a jest by the famous clown Richard Tarlton: 'Sirra, what art thou? A woman, sayes Tarlton. Nay, that is a lye, say the watchman, women have no such beards' (*Tarlton's Jests*, 10). Touchstone's joke inaugurates a series of beard jests, which culminate at 5.4.69–101.

73 **if** Touchstone's first use of his favourite word (see 5.4.71–8, 95–101), and the hallmark of the play's sporting with the hypothetical (see Rackin, 'Crossdressing', 119).

But if you swear by that that is not, you are not
forsworn. No more was this knight swearing by his   75
honour, for he never had any; or if he had, he had sworn
it away before ever he saw those pancakes or that
mustard.

CELIA   Prithee, who is't that thou mean'st?

TOUCHSTONE [*to Rosalind*]   One that old Ferdinand, your   80
father, loves.

ROSALIND   My father's love is enough to honour him.
Enough! Speak no more of him. You'll be whipped for
taxation one of these days.

TOUCHSTONE   The more pity that fools may not speak   85

74–5 **swear . . . forsworn** Cf. 'A Sermon
Against Swearing and Perjury': 'what
perill and danger it is vainely to
sweare, or to be forsworne' (*Homilies*,
1.45; cited in Shaheen, 160).

76 **honour** Touchstone's satire on the
dishonourable knight can be read as a
covert attack on Frederick, who swears
by his honour after the dishonourable
banishment of the innocent Rosalind
(see 1.3.85n.); a possible reminder for
an Elizabethan audience of Falstaff's
famous disquisition on honour in *1H4*
5.1.129–40, which concludes 'Honour
is a mere scutcheon', i.e. a coat of
arms; see pp. 4, 366.

79 **Prithee, who** an ingenuous question
which may unwittingly suggest to both
Rosalind and the audience that the
fool's barb glances at the usurping
Duke Frederick

80 SD *Touchstone's *your father* means
Rosalind's father, Duke Senior (see
next note); the person Duke Senior
loves may be his own brother, recapitulating the theme of hostility between
brothers in 1.1, an interpretation
adopted by David Thacker in his 1992
RSC production.
*old Ferdinand (F 'old *Fredericke*')

F's 'old' might suggest Duke Senior,
but Frederick is the name of his
younger brother. This edition adopts
Capell's suggestion that F should
read 'Ferdinand' (*Notes*, 1.56; see List
of Roles, 3n., Fig. 22 and Appendix 4).

82 The assigning of Rosalind's retort
to Celia (Theobald) robs the story
of the dishonourable knight of its
specific barb, creating also the unlikely
situation that Rosalind doesn't
speak for 20 lines. Rosalind's rebuke
(consonant with her somewhat edgy
relationship with Touchstone) suggests that she has understood his
attack on her cousin's father, and leaps
to Celia's defence, withdrawing as she
does so the liberty she allowed the
fool at 69.

84 **taxation** fault-finding (*OED sb.*[3], citing this line); see 2.7.71n. There may
be a pun on the Latin word *tax* meaning 'the sound of a whip-stroke'
(Oxf[1]). Cf. *KL* 1.4.174–6: 'FOOL . . .
They'll have me whipped for speaking
true, thou'lt have me whipped for
lying, and sometimes I am whipped for
holding my peace.'

85–6 'More's the pity that fools are not
allowed to demonstrate wisdom by

80 SD] *Cam*[1]   Ferdinand] *Rann (Capell Notes); Fredericke F; Ferdericke F2*   82 SP] *Cel. / Theobald*
82–3 him. / Enough!] *Hanmer subst.;* him enough; *F*

wisely what wise men do foolishly.

CELIA By my troth, thou sayst true. For since the little
wit that fools have was silenced, the little foolery that
wise men have makes a great show.

Enter LE BEAU.

Here comes Monsieur Le Beau. 90

ROSALIND With his mouth full of news.

CELIA Which he will put on us as pigeons feed their
young.

ROSALIND Then shall we be news-crammed.

CELIA All the better; we shall be the more marketable. 95
Bonjour, Monsieur Le Beau, what's the news?

LE BEAU Fair princess, you have lost much good sport.

CELIA Sport? Of what colour?

LE BEAU What colour, madam? How shall I answer you?

telling the truth about the foolish
actions of wise men'; see 2.7.49–50.

87–9 Celia's defence of Touchstone is
implausible if she has just rebuked him
for free speech. Her championing of
his liberty offers a gloss on the clown's
devotion to her; see 1.3.129.

87–8 **little . . . silenced** These lines have
sometimes been used to date the play
after 1 June 1599, when the Bishops'
Order (from the Archbishop of
Canterbury and Bishop of London)
prohibited printing of satires and
called in existing ones to be burnt
(Arber, 3.677–8; McCabe, 188–9).
However, complaints about satire were
ubiquitous in the 1590s; see 2.7.71n.
Cf. Benedick's dismissal of both satire
('paper bullets of the brain', *MA*
2.3.231) and satirists: 'Dost thou think
I care for a satire or an epigram?'
(5.4.100–1).

89.1 The foolish courtier enters to speak
as the wise fool is silenced.

90 **Monsieur** Only Le Beau and Jaques
(2.5.9, 2.7.9) receive the French title;
see Appendix 2. Although Rosalind
and Celia mock Le Beau, he proves at
260–72 more substantial than his initial
manner suggests (Ard[2]). Nineteenth-
century stage tradition had him enter
with a falcon on his wrist (Shattuck,
16; Marshall).

92 **put** force (as in force-feeding)

94 **news-crammed** stuffed with news,
like plump pigeons; cf. *LLL* 5.2.315,
'This fellow pecks up wit as pigeons
peas', and *Ham* 3.2.95, 'promise-
crammed'.

95 **marketable** As pigeons fat with grain
are easy to sell, so women are easier to
market if accompanied by fat (fertile)
lands; cf. Rosalind to Phoebe: 'you are
not for all markets' (3.5.61).

97 **sport** entertainment; see 30.

98 **colour** sort, kind (*OED sb.*[1] 16a, first
example)

99 **How . . . you?** What do you mean?

86 wise men] *(Wisemen)*   89.1] *Sisson; after 90 F; after* marketable *95 Dyce*   90 Le] *F2; the F*
96 Bonjour] *(Boon-iour), Rowe*

ROSALIND   As wit and Fortune will.   100

TOUCHSTONE   Or as the Destinies decrees.

CELIA   Well said – that was laid on with a trowel.

TOUCHSTONE   Nay, if I keep not my rank –

ROSALIND   Thou loosest thy old smell.

LE BEAU   You amaze me, ladies. I would have told you of   105
good wrestling, which you have lost the sight of.

ROSALIND   Yet tell us the manner of the wrestling.

LE BEAU   I will tell you the beginning and, if it please your
ladyships, you may see the end, for the best is yet to do;
and here – where you are – they are coming to perform   110
it.

CELIA   Well, the beginning that is dead and buried?

---

101 **decrees** a common Elizabethan
usage: plural subject and singular verb
(Abbott, 333); see 1.3.54, 3.5.53–4n.

102 **laid . . . trowel** now proverbial

103 **rank** Touchstone puns on the practice of conferring knighthood (*rank*)
by the laying of a sword on a man's
shoulder; here it has been bestowed
with a trowel (i.e. by illegitimate
methods), a possible political reference
to the unauthorised knighting of
courtiers by the Earl of Essex, to the
queen's fury (Hammer, 223–4; McCoy,
87).

104 **loosest . . . smell** (you) let loose or
release a smell, i.e. fart (Oxf[1]);
Touchstone will break wind if
deprived of his rank; see 2.7.41n.
Rosalind's wit darts from *rank* meaning status to its associations with
noisome smells (see 2.7.46n.). For
flatulence and Shrove Tuesday see
Laroque, 47. The jest would have
acquired point after July 1599, when
Harington and others were knighted
by Essex in Ireland. The lines may
conceivably represent an interpolation
by the clown after that date (see p. 128),
when Harington – always dogged by
jokes about smells, following *Ajax* –

feared that his wrathful royal godmother would remove his newly
acquired title.

105 **ladies** The courtier is shocked by the
schoolboy humour of the *ladies*, a freedom facilitated by the fact that female
parts were acted by boys (Dusinberre,
Women, 269–70); see 130–2n.

109 **to do** to be done; cf. *Ham* 4.4.44: 'this
thing's to do'.

110–11 **where . . . it** The princesses, who
constitute the main action for the
theatre audience, become 'audience' to
the wrestling (see also 2.4.16.1n. and
5.4.149n.). Scolnikov notes the gender
division between the men within,
fighting 'with bare hands', and the
princesses without (148).

112 **dead and buried** a paradoxical playing with Le Beau's *beginning* and *end*
(108–9), in which the *beginning*
(instead of the customary 'end') is
dead and buried, because past. The
phrase would have been familiar to
Shakespeare from the Apostles' Creed:
'Was crucified, dead and buried'
(*BCP*, 'A Catechism', fol. 133[r]; see
4.1.200n.). Both Lodge and *Gamelyn*
begin, rather than end, with death and
burial.

---

101 decrees] decree *Douai ms, Pope*   104 loosest] losest *Rowe*   106+ wrestling] *(wrastling)*

LE BEAU   There comes an old man and his three sons –

CELIA   I could match this beginning with an old tale.

LE BEAU   Three proper young men of excellent growth   115
and presence –

ROSALIND   With bills on their necks: 'Be it known unto all
men by these presents.'

LE BEAU   The eldest of the three wrestled with Charles,
the Duke's wrestler, which Charles in a moment threw   120
him and broke three of his ribs, that there is little hope
of life in him. So he served the second and so the third.
Yonder they lie, the poor old man their father making
such pitiful dole over them that all the beholders take
his part with weeping.   125

ROSALIND   Alas!

TOUCHSTONE   But what is the sport, Monsieur, that the
ladies have lost?

LE BEAU   Why, this that I speak of.

TOUCHSTONE   Thus men may grow wiser every day. It is   130

---

113 **an . . . sons** from *Gamelyn*

114 **tale** a pun on 'tail' (end); cf. 2.7.28.

115 **proper** presentable, well-shaped, exemplary; cf. 3.5.56, and 116: 'He'll make a proper man' (see n.)

117 **bills** legal notices, but specifically wills (cf. Ard²); for legal language see p. 59. The three young men risk their lives and therefore carry intimations of their last testament with them. Lodge's Rosader bears 'his forrest bill on his necke' (sig. K4ʳ) – an implement for wood-cutting.

117–18 **Be . . . presents** Rosalind quotes the standard formula for the commencement of a legal will (*presents* means 'present writings'). Charlotte Cushman's 1859 promptbook contains the handwritten direction 'chaunting' (Moore, 1.2.95) to emphasize the formal status of the line. However, chanting cannot lend enchantment to the

heroine's word-games with *presents* and *presence* (116) – one of Rosalind's most dreadful puns (Stevenson, in Stevenson & Sosanya; see also Kökeritz, 95).

124 **dole** lamentation

124–5 **beholders . . . weeping** The onlookers, as in a theatre, share the protagonist's sorrow; cf. *TGV* 4.4.164–70. By contrast Lodge's old man 'neuer chaunged his countenance, but as a man of a couragious resolution, tooke vp the bodies of his sonnes without shewe of outward discontent' (sig. C2ʳ). Rosader acts to avenge the old father, whereas Orlando rebels against his own despised state.

130–2 **It . . . ladies** a demur deriving from both gender and class; the ladies are too sensitive ('feminine') and too well bred to be entertained by the suffering of others (see 105n.). Oxf¹ notes

---

119, 243 wrestled] *(wrastled)*   120, 161 wrestler] *(Wrastler)*

the first time that ever I heard breaking of ribs was
sport for ladies.

CELIA   Or I, I promise thee.

ROSALIND   But is there any else longs to see this broken
music in his sides? Is there yet another dotes upon rib-   135
breaking? Shall we see this wrestling, cousin?

LE BEAU   You must if you stay here, for here is the place
appointed for the wrestling and they are ready to
perform it.   *Flourish*

CELIA   Yonder sure they are coming. Let us now stay and   140
see it.

Enter DUKE [FREDERICK], *Lords*, ORLANDO,
CHARLES *and Attendants*.

DUKE FREDERICK   Come on. Since the youth will not be
entreated, his own peril on his forwardness.

ROSALIND   Is yonder the man?

LE BEAU   Even he, madam.   145

that 'the remarks of Touchstone and
Celia point up the barbarity of
Frederick's court, even though tournaments resulting in "breaking of ribs"
and worse injuries were watched by
ladies both in medieval times and at
the Accession Day tilts of Elizabeth's
reign'.

134 **any** anyone
    longs 'that' omitted for emphasis
(Abbott, 244)
134–5 **broken music** music for a broken
consort (see 2.7.174n.), a group particularly associated with Thomas Morley,
composer of 'It was a lover and his
lass' in 5.3 (see p. 78 and Fig. 15); used
here as a metaphor for 'broken ribs'. In
Armin, *Fool* (1600), the fool attacks a
bagpiper and a fiddler at a Christmas

feast and his victims languish in bed
declaring that 'Good Musicke or broken consorts they agree well together'
(1. sig. B2ʳ). Shakespeare often links
both 'broken music' and 'consort' (in
the musical sense) with violence
and/or the erotic: cf. *TC* 3.1.48–50;
H5 5.2.240–1; *RJ* 3.1.45–6.
135 **dotes** longs for, implying folly, but
there may also be a pun on the 'doh' of
the *sol fa* music scale; see 2.5.3–4n.
137 **here** The action comes to the audience (see 110).
139 SD The Duke's entry is signalled by
trumpets.
143 **his . . . forwardness** 'his own presumption and aggression create his
danger' (*OED* forwardness *sb.* 4, first
example in this sense)

134 see] set *Theobald (Warburton)*; feel *(Johnson)*   139 SD] *this edn (RP)*; *after 141 F*   141.1 FRED-
ERICK] *Malone*; *junior / Capell*   142–3] *Douai ms, Pope*; *F lines* intreated / forwardnesse. /

CELIA Alas, he is too young. Yet he looks successfully.

DUKE FREDERICK How now, daughter – and cousin. Are
you crept hither to see the wrestling?

ROSALIND Ay, my liege, so please you give us leave.

DUKE FREDERICK You will take little delight in it, I can   150
tell you; there is such odds in the man. In pity of the
challenger's youth I would fain dissuade him, but he
will not be entreated. Speak to him, ladies; see if you
can move him.

CELIA Call him hither, good Monsieur Le Beau.   155

DUKE FREDERICK Do so; I'll not be by.

LE BEAU Monsieur the challenger, the princess calls for
you.

ORLANDO I attend them with all respect and duty.

ROSALIND Young man, have you challenged Charles the   160
wrestler?

ORLANDO No, fair princess. He is the general challenger.
I come but in as others do, to try with him the strength
of my youth.

CELIA Young gentleman, your spirits are too bold for   165
your years. You have seen cruel proof of this man's
strength. If you saw yourself with your eyes or knew

---

146 **young** Orlando's youth (see
1.1.122n.) reinforces his innocence of
court corruption; cf. 160, 165, 172 and
2.3.2.

147 **cousin** a formal address, used generally for family relationships, but sometimes for friends (nobles)

148 **crept** 'Frederick's use of the word
indicates his (mistaken) perception of
the weakness of the women' (Oxf¹).

149 **liege** The title for a feudal overlord
reinforces the epic romance associations of the chivalric contest.

151 **odds in** advantage on the side of

(modern 'odds on', as in gambling);
see *gamester*, 1.1.154.
man i.e. Charles

152 **would fain** would gladly (*OED fain
v.*¹ 1 *obs.*)

157 **princess** This may be an uninflected
plural, referring to both women
(Abbott, 471) and carrying a singular
verb (Abbott, 333), or the word may
refer solely to Celia.

159 **them** Orlando may not know which
lady is the princess (see 258).

167 **If . . . eyes** It was a favourite
Renaissance paradox that the eyes look

147–8] *Pope; F lines* Cousin: / wrestling? /   147 daughter –] *Cam²;* daughter, *F;* daughter *Ard²*
151 you;] *Globe;* you *F*   man] men *Hanmer*   159 them] her *Douai ms, Rowe*   167 your] your own
Rowe²; our *Hanmer*

yourself with your judgement, the fear of your adventure would counsel you to a more equal enterprise. We pray you for your own sake to embrace 170 your own safety and give over this attempt.

ROSALIND Do, young sir. Your reputation shall not therefore be misprized. We will make it our suit to the Duke that the wrestling might not go forward.

ORLANDO I beseech you, punish me not with your hard 175 thoughts, wherein I confess me much guilty to deny so fair and excellent ladies anything. But let your fair eyes and gentle wishes go with me to my trial, wherein if I be foiled there is but one shamed that was never gracious, if killed, but one dead that is willing to be so. 180 I shall do my friends no wrong, for I have none to lament me; the world no injury, for in it I have nothing. Only in the world I fill up a place which may be better supplied when I have made it empty.

ROSALIND The little strength that I have, I would it were 185 with you.

CELIA And mine to eke out hers.

ROSALIND Fare you well. Pray heaven I be deceived in you.

CELIA Your heart's desires be with you. 190

outward and therefore do not see their owner; see Davies, *Nosce Teipsum* (1599): 'the eye, . . . Whose rayes reflect not, but spread outwardly, / Not seeing it selfe, when other things it sees' (5). See *TC* 3.3.96–112 and Dusinberre, '*TC*', 92–3.

173 **misprized** lowered in value; cf. 1.1.160n.

178 **trial** proof of valour, the standard language of chivalric endeavour (Laroque, 232–2); cf. *TNK* 2.5 and *Per* 2.2, where unknown knights distin-

guish themselves in public jousting (offstage in *TNK*) to win the lady, a motif familiar from entertainments mounted for Elizabeth on her progresses (J. Wilson, 28–35; see Fig. 11). In Lodge, Rosader's admiration for Rosalind precedes the wrestling, which is undertaken to win her favour, whereas Orlando's love for Rosalind follows his triumph (see 124–5n.).

179 **foiled** overthrown (in wrestling)

180 **gracious** full of the graces; see 1.1.156–60.

168 ¹your] our *Hanmer*   176 thoughts, wherein] thoughts. Therein *(Johnson)*

CHARLES   Come, where is this young gallant that is so
  desirous to lie with his mother earth?

ORLANDO   Ready, sir, but his will hath in it a more modest
  working.

DUKE FREDERICK   You shall try but one fall.   195

CHARLES   No, I warrant your grace you shall not entreat
  him to a second that have so mightily persuaded him
  from a first.

ORLANDO   You mean to mock me after; you should not
  have mocked me before. But come your ways.   200

ROSALIND   Now Hercules be thy speed, young man!

CELIA   I would I were invisible, to catch the strong fellow
  by the leg. [*Orlando and Charles*] *wrestle.*

ROSALIND   O excellent young man!

CELIA   If I had a thunderbolt in mine eye I can tell who   205

---

191 **gallant** flamboyant fellow (contemptuous); see 2.2.17.

192 **lie . . . earth** lugubrious sexual metaphor for death (making love to mother earth)

193 **will** determination, but also sexual drive, retorting to the innuendo of *lie with*

195 **try . . . fall** See 1.1.119n.; in wrestling one contestant must throw the other – a *fall* consisting in one party's 'back or one shoulder and the contrary heel touching the ground' (Lee & Onions, 2.456, cited in Cam²); see 1.3.23n.

196–8 **you . . . first** you will not want to persuade him to rise in time for a second bout after urging him so strongly to desist from the first

199–200 **You . . . before** If you intended to be fit to mock me after we have wrestled, you should not have provoked me beforehand.

200 **come your ways** come along

201 **Hercules** In Lodge the Norman wrestler (equivalent to Charles) 'looked lyke *Hercules* when hee ad-

uaunst himselfe agaynst *Achelous*' (sig. C1ᵛ); every time Achelous touched the ground he regained strength, but was overcome by Hercules' skill in keeping him airborne. See Moore, on John Buckstone's New York production (1871), when Charles was played by the 'Herculean' champion wrestler, James Mace: 'Grave doubts were suggested to the mind of the spectator as the gigantic Mace took a grip upon his opponent, whether he might not, as many another actor had done before him, take liberties with his author, and throw *Orlando* instead of being thrown . . . But the Shakespearian scholar finally triumphed over the champion and he allowed himself to be floored according to the text.'

be thy speed give you the pace and vigour for success

202 **invisible** Cf. Ariosto (11.4–8), where Angelica's magic ring allows her to become invisible.

205 **thunderbolt** Jupiter's weapon for aiding his protégés in battle

---

199 You] An you *Neil (Theobald)*   203 SD *Orlando and Charles*] *Malone subst.*   *wrestle*] *(Wrastle)*

should down. *Shout.* [*Charles is thrown.*]

DUKE FREDERICK

No more, no more.

ORLANDO   Yes, I beseech your grace:

I am not yet well breathed.

DUKE FREDERICK   How dost thou, Charles?

LE BEAU

He cannot speak, my lord.

DUKE FREDERICK   Bear him away.

[*Exeunt Touchstone and Attendants with Charles.*]

What is thy name, young man?   210

ORLANDO   Orlando, my liege, the youngest son of Sir
Rowland de Boys.

DUKE FREDERICK

I would thou hadst been son to some man else.

The world esteemed thy father honourable,

But I did find him still mine enemy.   215

Thou shouldst have better pleased me with this deed

Hadst thou descended from another house.

But fare thee well, thou art a gallant youth.

I would thou hadst told me of another father.

Exeunt Duke [Frederick, Le Beau and Lords].

208 **well breathed** warmed up

209 SD Touchstone's exit with Frederick at 219 would make him uncomfortably of the Duke's party, just as his remaining on stage during the love scene would be incongruous; see 219 SDn.

211–12 **son . . . Rowland** For connections with the medieval *Chanson de Roland* see List of Roles, 5n., 2.7.198n., and p. 65.

213 Duke Frederick's blank verse response to Orlando's prose marks his hostility; cf. 1.3.38n.

   some man else some other man.

Frederick's envy (see 230) contrasts with the cordiality of Torismond in Lodge: 'when they knew him to bee the yoongest sonne of Sir *Iohn of Bourdeaux*, the king rose from his seat and imbraced him' (sig. C2ᵛ).

215 **still** continually, always

217 **house** ancestry, lineage

219 SD F's '*Exit Duke.*' allows Frederick to sweep out solo, but his attendant '*Lords*' (141.1) are unlikely to remain on stage to intrude on the dialogue between Orlando and Rosalind, to which only Celia (as later in the Forest)

206 SD *Charles is thrown*] Rowe   207–8 Yes . . . breathed] *Oxf; prose F*   209–10 Bear . . . man] *prose Pope*   209 SD] *Capell subst.* (CHA. *is born off.*)   Touchstone and] *this edn*   212, 224   Rowland] (*Roland*), Rowe   219 SD] *Theobald subst. (Exit* Duke *with his train.*); Exit Duke. *F; Frederick / Malone; junior / Capell   Le Beau*] *Capell (*le BEU); Le Beau, Touchstone *Oxf*

CELIA

Were I my father, coz, would I do this?   220

ORLANDO

I am more proud to be Sir Rowland's son,

His youngest son, and would not change that calling

To be adopted heir to Frederick.

ROSALIND

My father loved Sir Rowland as his soul,

And all the world was of my father's mind.   225

Had I before known this young man his son

I should have given him tears unto entreaties

Ere he should thus have ventured.

CELIA   Gentle cousin,

Let us go thank him and encourage him.

My father's rough and envious disposition   230

Sticks me at heart. – Sir, you have well deserved.

If you do keep your promises in love

But justly as you have exceeded all promise,

---

is audience. Charles Macklin's part-book for 1741 marks Touchstone's exit here; see 209 SDn.

220–30 Rosalind and Celia remain together during these lines, while Orlando stands apart. At 231 they become one group; see 258n.

221 **proud** Orlando's patronym, 'de Boys', links Sir Rowland with Duke Senior, who has also been rejected by Frederick and is now *de bois* ('of the woods', i.e. the Forest of Arden).

222 **youngest son** Orlando's initial resentment of a niggardly inheritance (1.1.2–3) is obliterated by the challenge to his father's name; cf. 1.1.53–5. **calling** Orlando's destiny as a younger son, with overtones of religious vocation (see 3.3.100)

223 **adopted heir** recalls Celia's offer to Rosalind at 18–20

224 **My father** Rosalind's attention is arrested not by Celia's question at 220 but by Orlando's account of misfortunes similar to her own. Her invoking of her father's authority (cf. Elizabeth's references to Henry VIII in her speeches) marks her transition from a passive to an active role.

227 **given . . . entreaties** reinforced my pleading with tears

228 **Ere** before **Gentle** kind-hearted, rather than 'noble' (as in Cam[2]); cf. 267.

230 **rough** contrasts with *smooth*, 2.7.97

231 **Sticks** wounds

233 **But justly** as fairly **all promise** i.e. of valour. F2's 'all in promise' suggests the outstripping of rivals, of whom there are none in this scene, contrary to the conventional chivalric contest (see 178n.).

221 Rowland's] *(Rolands), Rowe*   231 deserved.] *Rowe[3] subst.;* deseru'd, *F*   232 love] *Hanmer;* loue; *F*   233 justly] justly, *Hanmer*   you have] you've here *Hanmer*   all] all in *F2*

Your mistress shall be happy.

ROSALIND   Gentleman,

[*giving him a chain from her neck*]

Wear this for me – one out of suits with fortune,   235

That could give more but that her hand lacks means.

Shall we go, coz?

CELIA   Ay. – Fare you well, fair gentleman.

ORLANDO

Can I not say, I thank you? My better parts

Are all thrown down, and that which here stands up

Is but a quintain, a mere lifeless block.   240

ROSALIND

He calls us back. My pride fell with my fortunes.

I'll ask him what he would. – Did you call, sir?

Sir, you have wrestled well and overthrown

---

234 **Your . . . happy** your beloved will be fortunate

234 **SD** See 3.2.176. The gift of a chain was the normal mark of royal approval for venturous exploits and represents one of many links between Rosalind and Elizabeth; see pp. 5–6, 11–12, 97, 140. In Lodge, Rosalynde sends a jewel to Rosader through a page (sig. C3ʳ).

235 **out of suits** out of favour
fortune more general than the personified deity of 31–55, and containing intimations of providence; see 2.1.19n, and cf. 5.2.63n.

236 **means** wealth. Rosalind could give him more – namely, her hand in marriage, the victor's traditional reward in the trial of chivalry – but lacks the power to do so.

237 **Fare . . . fair** a homonym. The verbal balance mirrors the ethical structure – the *fair* (beautiful but also virtuous people) *fare* well (prosper).

238 **parts** capacities

239 **thrown down** The first of many puns on 'overthrowing' and 'falling', which link wrestling and falling in love; see 241, 248, 1.3.20–6.

240 **quintain . . . block** A quintain was a wooden post used as a dummy opponent in chivalric jousting; cf. 3.4.38–40 and see Fig. 11. Orlando is bereft of words, like an inanimate block. In the *Revels Accounts* for 1578 for Shrovetide masques a payment is made for 'A Quinten. painted with A foole*s* head', (Feuillerat, 308). In Hall's *Virgidemiarum* the poet warns the courtier against duelling: 'Nor make thy *Quintaine* others armed head' (4.4, p. 32), where 'quintain' is used in the general sense of 'target'.

241 **He . . . back** usually played for laughter, as Orlando has not called them back. Jonson added an SD to the margin of the corrected Folio text (1616) of *Poetaster* (1602), '*She calls him back*' (4.10.79), and nine lines later '*He calls her back*' (4.10.88), which may reflect the stage success of this moment.
pride . . . fortunes a reminder of the Fortune debate (31–53), but also an anticipation of Rosalind's rising after a fall, i.e. pregnancy (see 1.3.23–4n.); a variation on 'Pride comes before a fall' (Dent, P581).

234 SD] *Theobald after coz 237*

More than your enemies.

CELIA   Will you go, coz?   244

ROSALIND

Have with you. – Fare you well. *Exeunt* [*Rosalind and Celia*].

ORLANDO

What passion hangs these weights upon my tongue?
I cannot speak to her, yet she urged conference.

Enter LE BEAU.

O poor Orlando, thou art overthrown!
Or Charles or something weaker masters thee.

LE BEAU

Good sir, I do in friendship counsel you   250
To leave this place, albeit you have deserved
High commendation, true applause and love.
Yet such is now the Duke's condition
That he misconsters all that you have done.
The Duke is humorous; what he is indeed   255
More suits you to conceive than I to speak of.

---

244 **Will . . . coz?** Celia interrupts the
mutual gaze of the lovers; cf. 4.3.181
(Whitworth, 393).
245 **Have with you** colloquial: 'All right,
I'm coming.'
246 **weights . . . tongue** See Forker, *R2*
3.4.71–2n., for 'the Elizabethan punishment of *la peine forte et dure* (the
piling of weights upon the chests of
accused felons, designed to force them
to plead guilty or not guilty; most died
under the torture)'.
247 **conference** conversation
249 **Or . . . or** either . . . or
   weaker masters thee an oxymoron
which identifies the paradox of love,
but also of gender. Rosalind, the 'weaker' sex (see 2.4.6n.), will play 'Master'
Ganymede, who, while allegedly help-

ing Orlando to 'master' (cure) his passion, will in fact 'overthrow' him.
251 **albeit** although
254 **misconsters** (miscònsters) miscon-
strues, misinterprets
255 **humorous** volatile, unpredictable
(i.e. moody, as in modern English); cf.
2.3.8. The four humours (*OED sb.* 2b)
arise from the four bodily fluids
(blood, water, phlegm and spleen),
which create temperament. The word
was made fashionable by Jonson's
'humour' plays: *EMI* (1598) and *EMO*
(1599); see Appendix 3. Cf. 3.2.19,
189n., 4.1.18, and Paster, 47–50.
256 is more fitting for you to imagine
than for me to speak of. Le Beau
hints at the risk of treachery from overhearing in Frederick's court; see 2.2.11.

245 SD] *Rowe; Exit. F*   247.1] *after 249 Dyce*

ORLANDO

I thank you, sir; and pray you, tell me this:
Which of the two was daughter of the Duke
That here was at the wrestling?

LE BEAU

Neither his daughter, if we judge by manners,   260
But yet indeed the taller is his daughter.
The other is daughter to the banished Duke,
And here detained by her usurping uncle
To keep his daughter company, whose loves
Are dearer than the natural bond of sisters.   265
But I can tell you that of late this Duke
Hath ta'en displeasure 'gainst his gentle niece,
Grounded upon no other argument
But that the people praise her for her virtues,
And pity her for her good father's sake;   270
And on my life his malice 'gainst the lady
Will suddenly break forth. Sir, fare you well.
Hereafter in a better world than this

---

258 **Which . . . daughter** Orlando apparently did not hear Rosalind's speech at 224; see 220–30n.

261 **taller** Shakespeare appears to follow Lodge: 'I (thou seest) am of a tall stature' (sig. D3ᵛ), but the word is frequently emended because it is inconsistent with Rosalind's claim to be *more than common tall* (1.3.112) and with Oliver's information about Celia, *the woman low* (4.3.86). Rosalind is *not very tall* (Phoebe's testimony at 3.5.119); Orlando's 'Just as high as my heart' (3.2.262) makes her, even allowing for a lover's extravagance, hardly a lamp-post. Variations in the height of different boy actors may have created inconsistencies in the text (see Appendix 2). Another meaning of tall

is 'bold', usually applied to men, as (satirically) to Sir Andrew Aguecheek (*TN* 1.3.20), but sometimes also to 'mannish' women (Cam², *OED* tall *a*. 2b 3). See Sidney, *Old Arcadia*, where the cowardly shepherd, Dametas, describes the warlike Pyrocles (disguised as the beautiful Cleophila) as 'the tallest woman in the parish' (30), creating a deliberate gender joke (see pp. 85–6).

264 **whose** referring to both women

268 **argument** reason or pretext

273–4 The Christian language of hope looks forward to the regenerated world of the Forest of Arden; cf. 3.2.34n., 4.1.112n. If the part of Le Beau were doubled with that of Jaques these lines might echo ironically during the

---

261 taller] lesser *Douai ms, Globe (Spedding)*; shorter *Rowe³*; smaller *Malone*; lower *Staunton*
270 good] old *Rowe³*

I shall desire more love and knowledge of you.   274

ORLANDO

I rest much bounden to you; fare you well.   [*Exit Le Beau.*]
Thus must I from the smoke into the smother,
From tyrant Duke unto a tyrant brother.
But heavenly Rosalind!   *Exit.*

1.3   *Enter* CELIA *and* ROSALIND.

CELIA   Why, cousin, why, Rosalind! Cupid have mercy!
Not a word?

ROSALIND   Not one to throw at a dog.

CELIA   No, thy words are too precious to be cast away
upon curs – throw some of them at me. Come, lame   5
me with reasons.

ROSALIND   Then there were two cousins laid up, when
the one should be lamed with reasons and the other
mad without any.

CELIA   But is all this for your father?   10

ROSALIND   No, some of it is for my child's father. O, how

distinctly unfriendly interchanges
between Jaques and Orlando in the
Forest of Arden; see Appendix 2 and
p. 94.

275 **bounden** indebted

276 **smoke . . . smother** equivalent to 'out
of the frying-pan into the fire' (Dent,
S570). The conventional concluding
couplet serves to highlight Orlando's
final (metrically irregular) sigh.

278 **heavenly** Petrarchan language; cf.
Orlando's poems in 3.2.

1.3 headed '*Scena Tertius*' in F. *Tertia*
would be the correct Latin form; the
compositor may have failed to change a
word ('*Tertius*') stored for reprinting.
There may, however, be a deliberate
Latin gender joke, matching a masculine adjective to a feminine noun, to

mirror the heroine's decision (at 113)
to metamorphose herself into a hero
(TL).

1 **Cupid** the god of love

3 **Not . . . dog** proverbial (Dent, W762)

5–6 **lame . . . reasons** disable me with
explanations (as stones would lame a
dog)

7–9 **Then there would be two cousins**
incapacitated, the one (Celia) by the
blows of reason, and the other
(Rosalind) by loss of it.

11 **child's father** the man whom I would
like to father my child. Often cut as
improper after the advent of women
actors, the phrase was not finally
accepted until Julia Arthur's production in 1898, the decade of the 'new
woman'.

275 SD] *Capell; after* 274 *Rowe* **1.3**] *(Scena Tertius.)* Location] *an Apartment in the* Palace
Theobald 1–2] *Rowe; F lines* mercie, / word? / 11 child's father] father's child *Rowe³*

full of briers is this working-day world!

CELIA   They are but burs, cousin, thrown upon thee in
holiday foolery. If we walk not in the trodden paths our
very petticoats will catch them.   15

ROSALIND   I could shake them off my coat; these burs
are in my heart.

CELIA   Hem them away.

ROSALIND   I would try, if I could cry 'hem' and have him.

CELIA   Come, come, wrestle with thy affections.   20

ROSALIND   O, they take the part of a better wrestler than
myself.

CELIA   O, a good wish upon you! You will try in time in

---

12 **briers** prickly trailing plants, i.e. the
common brier bush or hep tree, which
Londoners thought too ordinary to put
in their gardens (Gerard, *Herbal*,
1088); see 1.2.22n. on *sweet Rose*.
working-day as opposed to holiday;
cf. 14.

13 **burs** Celia urges Rosalind to treat her
troubles as little sticky seeds to be
played with, rather than swathes of
thorns to trip and scratch her, but
there may also be some innuendo; see
Maplet, *Forest*: 'The Burre of the
Greekes is called *Philanthros*, mannes
friend, for that it coueteth to catch
holde and to cleaue upon man his
Garment holding fast by such kinde of
roughnesse as it hath' (35). Cf. *TC*
3.2.107–8: 'They ['Our kindred', i.e.
Cressida] are burs, I can tell you;
they'll stick where they are thrown.'

14 **holiday foolery** festivity associated
with both holidays and some holy-days

15 **petticoats** (F 'petty-coates') a 'little'
(Fr. *petit*) coat or underskirt, a detail
which emphasizes the feminine role
played by the boy actor.

16–17 **burs . . . heart** Rosalind's pun on
bur as the name for the first spur on the
beam of a hart's antler (*Hunting*, 54–5)
anticipates Arden. She wishes the burs

were only on her coat, but in fact they
stick in her heart/hart; see 3.2.98n.

18 **Hem them away** cough them up

19 **try** attempt to. The word-play on *try*
and *cry* continues at 20 and 23; see nn.
hem a pun on *hem* and *him*. 'Hem' was
the trade call of a prostitute (Williams,
hem and *have*); see *2H4* 2.4.29, where
Doll Tearsheet's 'hem' indicates both
nausea and her profession.

20 **wrestle . . . affections** attempt to overthrow your passions; *wrestle* picks up on
try, 19. Cf. 1.2.195: 'You shall try but
one fall.' The pun on a fall in wrestling
and on falling in love symbolizes a rec-
onciling of aggression and romance not
present in Lodge (Ruthrof, 9).

23–4 **a good . . . fall** 'Here's good wishes
for your success. You will rise up within the allotted time of a "try" in scorn
of your fall.' Rosalind's stomach will
rise because she will 'fall pregnant'
(still in colloquial use) as a consequence of being thrown – in the act of
love – by a better wrestler than herself.
See also 1.2.241n. on *pride . . . fortunes*.

23 **try in time** A contestant in wrestling
can be 'knocked out of time' if he does
not rise and continue fighting within a
specified time limit; see 1.1.119,
1.2.195, 196–8 and nn.

---

20 wrestle] *(wrastle)*   21 wrestler] *(wrastler)*   23 try] cry *Sisson*

despite of a fall. But turning these jests out of service,
let us talk in good earnest. Is it possible on such a   25
sudden you should fall into so strong a liking with old
Sir Rowland's youngest son?

ROSALIND   The Duke my father loved his father dearly.

CELIA   Doth it therefore ensue that you should love his
son dearly? By this kind of chase I should hate him for   30
my father hated his father dearly; yet I hate not
Orlando.

ROSALIND   No, faith, hate him not, for my sake.

CELIA   Why should I not? Doth he not deserve well?

Enter DUKE [FREDERICK] *with Lords.*

ROSALIND   Let me love him for that, and do you love him   35
because I do. Look, here comes the Duke.

CELIA   With his eyes full of anger.

DUKE FREDERICK

Mistress, dispatch you with your safest haste
And get you from our court.

ROSALIND   Me, uncle?

---

24 **despite** scorn; see 2.5.41.
   turning . . . service dismissing these
   time-worn jokes as one would dismiss an
   old servant; cf. 1.1.78–9 and 2.3.41–2.
26 **sudden** 'impulse' implied (Abbott, 5)
   fall Celia has not yet turned the jest
   out of service.
   liking a predisposition towards loving
30 **dearly** heartily
   chase pursuit, hunting. 'Perhaps a
   pun following on "dear[ly]" and an
   intimation of the impending move to
   Arden' (Oxf¹); see p. 135.
   for because
31 **dearly** intensely, a *costly* hatred – a
   usage unique to Shakespeare (Onions,
   3, p. 54; cf. *CE* 2.2.129 and *Ham*
   4.3.41). But see Harington, 'To his

wife': 'For I can thus interpret if I will,
/ My dearest *Mall*, that is, my costliest
ill' ('Epigrams 1600', fol. 2).
33 **hate him not** i.e. love him
34 **Why . . . well?** Why should I not love
   him? Is he not deserving?
34.1 As the deserts of Orlando, the
   virtuous brother, are recognized, an
   undeserving brother, the usurping
   Duke, enters.
35 **for that** i.e. because he deserves well
38 **Mistress** a peremptory address; see
   1.2.56n.
   dispatch . . . haste 'leave as quickly as
   you can – for your safety'. 'The shift
   from prose to verse . . . underscores
   the sudden change from intimacy to
   formality' (Garber, 'Education', 105).

---

26 strong] strange *F3*   27 Rowland's] *(Roulands), Rowe*   34 I not?] I? *Theobald*   34.1] *after 37 Var
1785; after* do *36 Collier²*   FREDERICK] *Malone*   35–6] *Pope; F lines* you loue him / Duke. /

DUKE FREDERICK   You, cousin.
Within these ten days if that thou be'st found   40
So near our public court as twenty miles,
Thou diest for it.
ROSALIND   I do beseech your grace,
Let me the knowledge of my fault bear with me.
If with myself I hold intelligence,
Or have acquaintance with mine own desires,   45
If that I do not dream, or be not frantic –
As I do trust I am not – then, dear uncle,
Never so much as in a thought unborn
Did I offend your highness.
DUKE FREDERICK   Thus do all traitors.
If their purgation did consist in words,   50
They are as innocent as grace itself.
Let it suffice thee that I trust thee not.

---

39 **Me, uncle?** an incredulous and almost comic/pathetic response; cf. *LLL* 1.1.241, 243, Costard's repeated 'Me?'
cousin formal and hostile; cf. 1.2.147n., providing a metrical balance to *uncle*.

40, 46 **if that** if (Abbott, 287); cf. *When that*, 2.7.75.

41 **public** open, i.e. the lands and properties under court jurisdiction

42 **I . . . grace** Rosalind's courteous blank verse, completing Frederick's ungracious half-line, declares her equality with him; cf. Perdita's dignity in confronting Polixenes' rage (*WT* 4.4.444–8).

44 'If I know the workings of my own mind'. Rosalind affirms her truth by claiming self-knowledge, pointedly rejecting the associations of the word *intelligence* with spying. Macready's cutting of lines 46–9 (in the 1842 promptbook; see Shattuck) has a 'dumbing-down' effect on Rosalind's role.

45 or am familiar with my own passions

46 **frantic** mad

49 **offend** trespass or sin against; a weighty language congruous with *purgation* (50) and *grace* (51).

50 'If they could prove their innocence by talking'; cf. *WT* 3.2.21–7, where Hermione declares the futility of avouching her chastity.
purgation 'The word was used in theology (both of the purification of the soul in Purgatory and of the declaration of innocence on oath) and as a legal term, of the proving of innocence, particularly by ordeal' (Oliver); see 5.4.43–4n. On a different plane, 'purging' was the standard term for the evacuation of bodily waste; see 1.1.82n. Cf. *1H4* 5.4.164–5: 'I'll purge and leave sack and live cleanly, as a nobleman should do.'

51 **innocent as grace** as free from sin as the grace of God. The lines evoke the religious persecutions of the time; cf. 1.2.246n.

52 **suffice** be sufficient explanation

40 be'st] (beest)

181

ROSALIND

　Yet your mistrust cannot make me a traitor.

　Tell me whereon the likelihoods depends?

DUKE FREDERICK

　Thou art thy father's daughter, there's enough.　　　　55

ROSALIND

　So was I when your highness took his dukedom;

　So was I when your highness banished him.

　Treason is not inherited, my lord,

　Or if we did derive it from our friends,

　What's that to me? My father was no traitor.　　　　60

　Then good my liege, mistake me not so much

　To think my poverty is treacherous.

CELIA

　Dear sovereign, hear me speak.

DUKE FREDERICK

　Ay, Celia, we stayed her for your sake,

　Else had she with her father ranged along.　　　　65

---

54 **likelihoods** grounds for the hypothesis of treachery; cf. *AW* 1.3.120: 'Many likelihoods inform'd me of this before'. See also 1.2.101n.

55 **there's** that's

56, 57 **So was I** the rhetorical figure *isocolon* (repeated clause), used for emphasis and also, perhaps, pathos

58 **Treason . . . inherited** a particular fear at the turn of the century, both leading up to and following the Essex rebellion in 1601. Ralegh urged Sir Robert Cecil not to relent in his hostility towards the Earl of Essex through fear of reprisals by Essex's young son: 'Humours of men succeed not [i.e. are not inherited]' (Ralegh, *Letters*, 186: February/March 1600); see p. 103.

59 **friends** could also mean relatives (*OED* friend *sb.* and *a.* 3); a pointed allusion to Frederick's own perfidy to

his brother, which the Victorian actress Helena Faucit allowed to surface in the defiant 'My father was no traitor' (60; cited in Carlisle, 78). For 'false' and 'faithful' friends see Amiens's song, 2.7.182, 192 and nn.

61–2 **mistake . . . treacherous** 'do not misconstrue the situation by judging me to be a traitor because I am poor'. Cf. *misconsters*, 1.2.254.

63 **sovereign** a courteous and diplomatic appeal to the justice of a ruler rather than the favour of a father

64 **your** surly use of the formal *your* in response to *sovereign*

65 **ranged along** roamed about; a disrespectful phrase suggesting gipsies and vagabonds (cf. 1.1.112n., and see 2.3.32–3n.), which may also refer to the Crown office of Forest Ranger, in anticipation of the Forest of Arden in Act 2; see 4.3.75n.

---

54 likelihoods] likelihood *F2*　　depends] depend *Malone*

CELIA

I did not then entreat to have her stay;
It was your pleasure and your own remorse.
I was too young that time to value her,
But now I know her. If she be a traitor,
Why, so am I. We still have slept together,   70
Rose at an instant, learned, played, ate together,
And whereso'er we went, like Juno's swans,
Still we went coupled and inseparable.

DUKE FREDERICK

She is too subtle for thee, and her smoothness,
Her very silence and her patience   75
Speak to the people, and they pity her.
Thou art a fool. She robs thee of thy name,

67 **pleasure** choice; see Le Beau's testimony, 1.2.263–4.
remorse pity, but the word may also imply guilt; see 5.4.159n.
68 **that time** at that time. The childhood memories Celia shares with Rosalind (mentioned at 70–3; see Lodge, sig. D2ʳ) seem to contradict the apparent recentness of the usurpation (see 1.1.92–3n.), but underline the long-standing affection between the cousins (see 1.1.102–5). Cf. *MND* 3.2.198–214.
70, 73 **still** always
71 **ate** eaten (see 1.1.80n.)
72 **Juno's swans** The swan was sacred to Venus, but Thomas Kyd names 'Iunoes goodly Swannes' (*Soliman and Perseda*, 4.1.70–1, cited in Knowles). Ovid, *Met.*, 10, which contains the Ganymede story (p. 125 = 124)ᵛ; see 121, 122 and nn.), ends with Venus in her chariot borne by two harnessed swans (p. 134ᵛ). The reconciliation of Venus and Juno was part of Elizabeth's iconography; see also 5.4.139.
73 **coupled** yoked in the same harness, but also with the bonds of affection: hand in hand

74 **smoothness** plausibility (*OED* 3), associated with hypocrisy; see 5.4.45. Cf. *Tim* 3.6.91: 'Most smiling, smooth, detested parasites'; and Spenser, *FQ*, 1.1.35: '[Archimago] well could file his tongue as smooth as glas'. However, the word's primary meanings include 'civility' and 'courteousness', as contrasted with 'roughness'; see 1.2.230, 2.7.97.
75 **very silence** the very fact of her silence
patience long-suffering (trisyllabic); cf. 4.3.14n.
76 encourage public support for her out of compassion; Elizabeth won the people's favour in a similar fashion when forced by Mary Tudor to travel under arrest to Woodstock (Starkey, 148). In Lodge, Torismund is afraid that Rosalynde will marry a nobleman who will champion her rights to the throne (sig. D1ᵛ).
77 **Thou** registers exasperated affection
a fool stupid, but also 'too innocent' (Ard²); cf. St Paul's designation of Christians as fools for Christ: 'But God hathe chosen the foolish thi[n]gs of the worlde to confounde the wise'

71 ate] *(eate)*   74 subtle] *(subtile)*, *Rowe³*

183

And thou wilt show more bright and seem more
   virtuous
When she is gone. Then open not thy lips.
Firm and irrevocable is my doom   80
Which I have passed upon her. She is banished.

CELIA

Pronounce that sentence then on me, my liege;
I cannot live out of her company.

DUKE FREDERICK

You are a fool. You, niece, provide yourself.
If you outstay the time, upon mine honour   85
And in the greatness of my word, you die.

Exeunt Duke [Frederick] and Lords.

(1 Corinthians, 1.27, Geneva Bible).
Frederick's harshness to Celia was cut
by Macready (1842), Augustin Daly
(1889) and Julia Arthur (1898), perhaps in the interests of preserving a
'fairy-tale' *AYL*; see p. 108.

robs . . . name steals your reputation;
Frederick's envy of Rosalind (anticipated by Le Beau at 1.2.262–72) parallels Oliver's jealousy of Orlando at
1.1.159–60.

78 'And you will shine more, and appear
more full of admirable qualities.' Cf.
1H4, where Hal's reformation 'like
bright metal on a sullen ground . . . /
Shall show more goodly and attract
more eyes' (1.2.202–4). The unexpected alexandrine (12 syllables) gives the
line emphasis.
virtuous 'endowed with, or possessed
of, inherent or natural virtue or
power . . . Now *arch.*' (*OED* 6); see
3.2.8n.

80 **doom** judgement, sentence

82 **Pronounce . . . me** Lodge's
Torismund banishes Alinda as well as
Rosalynde (sig. D2ᵛ).

84 **You . . . fool** Marshall notes

Constance Benson's account (136–7)
of James Fagan's delivery of the line:
'You *are* a fool.' The formal *You*
expresses Frederick's anger; cf. 77n.
niece contrasts with *cousin* (39)
provide yourself make yourself ready

85 **outstay the time** stay beyond *ten days*
(40)
upon mine honour Frederick's oath
was mocked by Touchstone at 1.2.59.
Its placing here at a moment of dishonourable action recalls Prince John's
stress on his 'honour' when betraying
his oath to the rebels in *2H4* 4.2.55,
114; the same actor may have played
the parts of Prince John and of
Frederick (Dusinberre, 'Boys', 16;
Stern, *Rehearsal*, 15). Cf. Jenkins,
Ham 3.2.103n.: 'It is likely enough that
the roles of Caesar and Brutus in
Caes. (first performed in 1599) were
taken by the same actors as now played
Polonius and Hamlet'; see 2.7.32n,
3.2.54, 58n.

86 **greatness . . . word** power of my
command; cf. *R2* 1.3.213–15: 'How
long a time lies in one little word! /
. . . such is the breath of kings.'

80 doom] *(doombe), Rowe*   86 SD] *Malone subst.; Exit Duke, &c. F*

CELIA

O my poor Rosalind, whither wilt thou go?
Wilt thou change fathers? I will give thee mine.
I charge thee, be not thou more grieved than I am.

ROSALIND

I have more cause.

CELIA   Thou hast not, cousin.   90
Prithee, be cheerful. Knowst thou not the Duke
Hath banished me, his daughter?

ROSALIND   That he hath not.

CELIA

No, hath not? Rosalind lacks then the love
Which teacheth thee that thou and I am one.
Shall we be sundered? Shall we part, sweet girl?   95
No, let my father seek another heir!
Therefore devise with me how we may fly,
Whither to go and what to bear with us,
And do not seek to take your change upon you
To bear your griefs yourself and leave me out.   100
For by this heaven, now at our sorrows pale,
Say what thou canst, I'll go along with thee.

ROSALIND

Why, whither shall we go?

CELIA

To seek my uncle in the Forest of Arden.

---

91 **Prithee, be cheerful** Celia's injunction
recapitulates the opening motif of 1.2.
94 **am** The verb agrees with the nearest
pronoun.
99 'And do not try to take sole responsibility for your change of state'. F2's
'charge' matches *bear*, but *change* may
inspire Rosalind's plan for an Ovidian
metamorphosis into a man's shape.
Knowles notes a common confusion
between *r* and *n* in F's printing; see

also 3.2.138, 404 and tnn.
101 **heaven . . . pale** sky, now faded in
response to our sorrows; the onset of
twilight. Cf. 3.2.2–3. If the play was
first performed at court in February
1599, it was played 'at night' (see p. 37).
103 **whither . . . go** Cf. the Book of Ruth,
where Ruth vows to go with Naomi on
her journey: 'for whither thou goest, I
wil go' (1.16, Geneva Bible); see
3.5.102–4n. and 2.3.29.

94 thee] me *Theobald* thou] she *Rann (Capell Notes)* am] are *Douai ms, Hanmer (Theobald)*
99 change] charge *F2* 104 Arden] Ardenne *Oxf*

185

ROSALIND

Alas, what danger will it be to us,   105
Maids as we are, to travel forth so far!
Beauty provoketh thieves sooner than gold.

CELIA

I'll put myself in poor and mean attire,
And with a kind of umber smirch my face –
The like do you; so shall we pass along   110
And never stir assailants.

ROSALIND   Were it not better,
Because that I am more than common tall,
That I did suit me all points like a man?
A gallant curtal-axe upon my thigh,
A boar-spear in my hand, and in my heart,   115

---

107 The female fear of sexual assault
(*assailants*, 111), not just material rob-
bery, is borne out in *TGV* with
Proteus's threatened rape of Silvia
(5.4.59). The line is an example of
sententia, a pithy moral aphorism of a
formulaic character; see 2.7.17n.,
3.2.125n., 5.4.59–61n., 63n.

108 **mean** shabby

109 'and smear brown pigment on my
face' – i.e. umber from Umbria in Italy.
See 4.3.87: 'browner than her brother'.
Boy actors regularly applied white
make-up to appear feminine and
aristocratic (Callaghan, *Women*, 84–5);
see Jonson, *Poetaster*, 4.5.67–89. The
boy actor playing Celia would therefore
not in fact be applying brown pigment
on entry into the Forest, but removing
the white which disguised his natural
boyhood (see 3.2.378n.). The practice
of blacking the face for disguise was
traditional to forest poachers (E.P.
Thompson, 57–8; see Appendix 5);
Celia's line would thus have increased
the audacity of the girls' plan for forest
flight by connecting it with a familiar
form of social subversion. It is rare for

productions to show either woman
with a besmirched face.

110 **The . . . you** you do the same

111 **stir assailants** provoke attackers

112 **more . . . tall** See 1.2.261n.

113 **suit me** dress and equip myself
all points in every respect

114 **curtal-axe** cutlass, a short broad-blad-
ed sword. Lodge's Rosalynde plans to
carry a rapier, 'and if any knaue offer
wrong, your Page wil shew him the
poynt of his weapon' (sig. D3ᵛ), a bawdy
innuendo suppressed by Shakespeare.
thigh The arrival, with the Restoration
of Charles II in 1660, of women to play
Rosalind made the mention of a thigh
indecorous; Johnson, *Forest* (1723)
changed it to 'upon my side'.

115 **boar-spear** A broad spear with a
cross-bar, carried by Lodge's Rosader
in the boar-hunt (sig. Kᵛ). Shakespeare
had already used boar-hunting as a
symbol of sexuality in *VA*. Rosalind's
'masculinity' is advertised by her two
weapons, a *cutlass* and a *boar-spear*. As a
hunter of the boar, Ganymede should
wear russet, as opposed to the green
costume of the hunter of deer; see

---

109 smirch] smitch *F2*; smutch *F3*   114 curtal-axe] *(*curtelax*)*; curtelass *Capell*

Lie there what hidden woman's fear there will,
We'll have a swashing and a martial outside,
As many other mannish cowards have
That do outface it with their semblances.

CELIA

What shall I call thee when thou art a man?   120

ROSALIND

I'll have no worse a name than Jove's own page,
And therefore look you call me Ganymede.

3.2.238n. In fact Ganymede is a shepherd – as on Olympus (see 121n., 122n.) – not a hunter (Berry, *Hunt*, 166).

115–16 **heart . . . will** The problematic syntax may reflect Rosalind's excitement. Oxf places a full-stop after *will*, which solves the problem of the syntactical relation of *Lie* to the preceding line, but creates a new one of detaching lines 115–16 from 117–20, to which they clearly belong. The question of what is in the heart, compared with outward show, strikes a recurrent Shakespearean note; see *Ham* 1.2.85: 'But I have that within which passes show'; and *R3* 1.2.196: 'I would I knew thy heart.'

117 **swashing** swash-buckling; cf. *play the swaggerer*, 4.3.14. Cf. Lodge's Rosalynde: 'I wil play the man so properly, that (trust me) in what company so euer I come I wil not be discouered' (sig. D3ᵛ); and see 2.4.6–7, 4.3.172–3.

martial warlike, as Mars; cf. *Cym* 4.2.310: 'his Martial thigh'. In the teasing evocation of the homoerotic there may be a covert punning allusion to Martial, the classical epigrammist. Coleman points to Montaigne's use of Martial 'to open up homosexuality . . . [and] new dimensions around male and female roles in sexual matters' (139; see also 2.5.3–4n., 3.2.255n.).

outside external appearance; see 2.4.5., 4.3.163: *You a man?* Cf. *TN* 2.2.18: 'Fortune forbid my outside have not charm'd her!'

118 **mannish** ostentatiously manly – usually applied to masculine women

(see *TC* 3.3.219–21 and p. 12). Rosalind exposes the masquerade of 'masculinity' by using *mannish* to describe not a woman aping a man, but a man pretending to a 'manly' courage he does not possess. A 1620s Scottish reader annotated his copy of F: 'Mannish Cowards with a marshall owtside' (in Yamada, 59; see also 3.2.11–82n., 5.1.6n. and p. 114).

119 **outface it** brave it out
semblances appearances

121 **Jove's** Shakespeare – unlike Lodge – reminds his audience of Jove's passion for the boy Ganymede (Ovid, *Met.*, 10, p. 124ᵛ) (see 122n.), but also hints at 'the symbolic extension of the role to include omnipotence' (Berry, 'Rosalynde', 44); see also 2.4.56n., 3.2.8n., 3.5.83n.

page Lodge's Rosalynde volunteers herself as Aliena's page (sig. D3ᵛ), but Shakespeare creates the more equal relationship of brother and sister (Sen, 107–15); see 3.2.84n.

122 **Ganymede** Rosalind's choice of name was conventional to pastoral poetry (see Barnfield, *Shepherd* (1594), 8). Ganymede, a beautiful Trojan shepherd boy, seized by Jove (disguised as an eagle) and swept up to Olympus to be cup-bearer to the gods, was also associated with the zodiacal sign of Aquarius – January to mid-February (Owens, 26n.); he therefore came to represent Shrovetide festivity. The name is richly provocative of the fears of anti-theatricalists because of its homoerotic associations (see 121n. and Orgel, *Impersonations*, 51).

But what will you be called?

CELIA

Something that hath a reference to my state:
No longer Celia, but Aliena.   125

ROSALIND

But cousin, what if we assayed to steal
The clownish fool out of your father's court?
Would he not be a comfort to our travail?

CELIA

He'll go along o'er the wide world with me.
Leave me alone to woo him. Let's away,   130
And get our jewels and our wealth together,
Devise the fittest time and safest way
To hide us from pursuit that will be made
After my flight. Now go we in content   134
To liberty and not to banishment.   *Exeunt.*

---

124 **hath . . . state** refers to my (changed)
condition
125 **Aliena** The name (Lat. = stranger) is
from Lodge.
126 **assayed** tried; the word has associations with the testing of metal, appropriate as Celia thinks of summoning
Touchstone; see List of Roles, 11n.
127 **clownish fool** The word *clownish*
suggests a rusticity – despite the court
status of the fool – which in the Forest
Touchstone repeatedly repudiates,
distinguishing himself from the rustic
'clowns', Corin and William; see
2.4.63n., 5.1.11, 47–52n.
128 **comfort . . . travail** a pun on travel/
travail. Knowles notes that 'In this
play when the word refers to movement from place to place the spelling is
always *trauel(l)*' (see 4.1.17), but that
when it implies effort (sometimes with
the subsidiary meaning of labour in
childbirth) it is spelt 'trauaile', as here.

The conjunction of *comfort* and *travail*
echoes the *BCP* 'Holy Communion'
(1549), where the first of the 'comfortable woordes' addressed to the penitent reads: 'Come vnto me all that
trauell and bee heauy laden, and I shall
refreshe you' (fol. 118).
129 **o'er . . . world** an archetypal image
evocative of the epic questing journey,
both religious and secular
130 **Leave me alone** leave it to me
134–5 **Now . . . banishment** Celia
celebrates the power of the mind to
transform adversity; see 2.1.1–17. Cf.
R2 1.3.275–94, where Gaunt reasons
with Bolingbroke about his banishment: 'All places that the eye of
heaven visits / Are to a wise man ports
and happy havens'; see p. 102.
134 **content** a keynote word (see 3.2.24),
juxtaposed in the Forest of Arden with
pleasure and liking; see 2.3.68n.,
3.2.17n.

126 assayed] essayed *Oxf*   128 travail] travell *F3*   134 we in] *F2;* in we *F*

2.1   *Enter* DUKE SENIOR, AMIENS *and two or*
              three Lords [*dressed*] *as foresters.*

DUKE SENIOR
Now, my co-mates and brothers in exile,
Hath not old custom made this life more sweet
Than that of painted pomp? Are not these woods
More free from peril than the envious court?
Here feel we not the penalty of Adam,   5

2.1 In the absence of any stated location in
F the dress of the foresters may be sufficient indication of the change of scene
to the Forest of Arden. Some artificial
forestry would probably have been in
place at early performances, whether at
Richmond Palace, the Globe, or later at
the private Blackfriars theatre, and a
notice naming the Forest might also
have been used.
0.1–2 *two . . .* **Lords** See 1.1.96n. and cf.
2.5.0.1–2.
0.2 *dressed as foresters* F's punctuation,
with a comma after '*Amyens*', implies
that the Duke was probably not in the
green of a forester – a costume which
in the theatre, however, could equally
have indicated the Lincoln green of
Robin Hood's outlaws (see 2.7.0.2 and
nn.). Drayton's forester Silvius
declares: 'I am clad in youthfull
Greene, I other colours scorne, / My
silken Bauldrick beares my Beugle, or
my Horne, . . . / My Doghooke at my
Belt . . . / My Sheafe of Arrowes by,
my Woodknife at my Syde, / My
Crosse-bow in my Hand' (*Elizium*,
6.51–2). F's '*like*' is the form used by
the scrivener Ralph Crane (Jowett,
114); see 2.7.0.2 and p. 126. Foresters
were employed to keep the forest game
and tend the woodland (Drayton,
Elizium, 6.52), and they also assisted in
the formal hunt. See 4.2.9 SDn.
1 **co-mates** comrades. This word
(unique in Shakespeare) marks the

'Robin Hood' motif of equal fellowship
in the Forest (see pp. 56–8). The Douai
MS preserves an egalitarian mode for
the Duke's followers in its 'Drammatis
Personae' (see List of Roles, 22, 23, and
Fig. 22). See Valentine's description of
the outlaws in *TGV* 5.4.14 as 'mates',
implying the male bonding scorned by
Kate in *TS* 1.1.57–8: 'I pray you, sir, is
it your will / To make a stale of me
amongst these mates?'
exile stressed on the second syllable
(Cercignani, 38)
2 **old custom** ancient traditions of pastoral innocence, as in the Garden of
Eden and the classical myth of the
Golden Age, from Ovid, *Met.*, 1; see
also Tasso's pastoral drama *Aminta*
(Poggioli, 42–4). See 1.1.113n., and cf.
TGV 5.4.1–3.
3 **painted pomp** ceremonial display;
painted implies artifice, and is often
used derogatively of women wearing
cosmetics.
5 **not . . . Adam** The penalty of Adam,
according to Genesis, 3.19, was work,
whereas the Duke claims that it was
the change of seasons (6), which
marked both the Fall and the passing
of the perpetual spring of the classical
Golden Age (see 1.1.113n.). The point
is that rough weather in the Forest
cannot detract from its Edenic freedom from court corruption (see
Amiens's song, 2.7.175–94). 'Not' may
mean 'only'; see 3.3.82n.

2.1] *(Actus Secundus. Scoena Prima.)* Location] *a Forest* / *Rowe*; Arden FOREST *Theobald*   0.1 DUKE
SENIOR] Old Duke *Douai ms*   0.2 *dressed*] *Oxf   as*] *Oxf*; *like* F   5 not] but *Theobald*

The seasons' difference – as the icy fang
And churlish chiding of the winter's wind,
Which when it bites and blows upon my body
Even till I shrink with cold, I smile and say:
'This is no flattery. These are counsellors   10
That feelingly persuade me what I am.'
Sweet are the uses of adversity,
Which, like the toad, ugly and venomous,
Wears yet a precious jewel in his head;
And this our life, exempt from public haunt,   15
Finds tongues in trees, books in the running brooks,
Sermons in stones, and good in everything.

AMIENS

I would not change it. Happy is your grace

6 **fang** tooth; see 2.7.178.
7 **churlish chiding** rude scolding (of nature), contrasted with human chiding (2.7.64, 3.5.65).
  winter's wind The opening scenes in the Forest take place in a literal, not just a figurative, winter (see 2.6.15n., 5.4.171n.). The play moves gradually towards the spring of the final act.
8 **Which** at which; cf. Abbott, 272.
10 **counsellors** advisers; the importance of good counsellors and the danger of evil ones was a major topic in the education of rulers; cf. *R2* 2.1.241–2.
11 **feelingly** through physical sensation; cf. *KL* 4.6.145: 'I see it feelingly.'
   persuade . . . am convince me of my own insignificance; cf. *KL* 3.4.101: 'Is man no more than this?'
12 a homiletic adage (Dent, A42) with ancient roots in classical and Christian thought (e.g. *Imitation*, 1.12, pp. 22–3)
13 **venomous** The skin of the common toad is poisonous.
14 **precious jewel** The ruby between a toad's eyes gave rise to a superstition that a real jewel (toadstone) could be

found in a toad's head (Douce, *Illustrations*, 1.294–6).
15 **exempt . . . haunt** free from the intrusions of the crowd
16 **tongues** oratory; a metaphor for the voice of Nature, which becomes literal with the advent of Orlando's verses: '*Tongues I'll hang on every tree*' (3.2.124).
   books . . . brooks The stream becomes a source of contemplation comparable to reading a book, a claim exemplified in Jaques's meditations on the wounded stag, 44–63.
17 **Sermons in stones** the finding of homiletic edification in inanimate things. The Duke evaluates his pastoral retreat from the perspective of educated society, where books and sermons (a major source of enlightenment in Protestant worship; see 3.2.152–4) are readily available.
18 **I . . . it** This half-line is sometimes given to the Duke. Removing it from Amiens's speech can make him sound discontented and suggest disaffection amongst the exiled courtiers (cf. *Tem*

6 seasons'] *(seasons), Theobald;* Season's *Rowe*   10–11 'This . . . am.'] *Riv;* This . . . am. *F*
18 SP] *before* Happy *18 Dyce (Upton)*

190

That can translate the stubbornness of fortune
Into so quiet and so sweet a style.   20
DUKE SENIOR
Come, shall we go and kill us venison?
And yet it irks me the poor dappled fools,
Being native burghers of this desert city,
Should in their own confines with forked heads
Have their round haunches gored.

1 LORD   Indeed, my lord,   25

2.1), a mood contradicted, however, by
the testimony of Orlando's *all's contented followers* (5.2.14–15) as well as
by Amiens's character (see List of
Roles, 12n.).
Happy fortunate
19 **translate** transform; but there is also a
sense of translation into another language and idiom (cf. Parker, *Margins*,
149–50, and 20n.).
stubbornness of fortune The
Duke's stoical endurance of misfor-
tune recalls Rosalind (see 1.2.235).
20 **sweet a style** mellifluous note, continuing from *translate*; there may be a
joke on the flowing rhymes of
Harington's *OF* (1591); see pp. 86–8.
21 **venison** the meat of any wild animal,
including deer. See Dekker, *Lantern*
(1608): 'sometimes they [gipsies] eate
venison, and haue *Gray-hounds* that
kill it for them' (sig. E4ᵛ). Berry calls
the term 'evasive' of the issues of 'violent death and butchering' because it
had only recently become specific (to
deer's meat) rather than generic (any
meat) (*Hunt*, 172–3; cf. Watson, 81).
22 **poor dappled fools** an affectionate
humanizing of the deer into a fool
wearing a motley (*dappled*) coat; the
word 'fool' subtly feminizes the image,
as fools and women are often allies in
Shakespeare's plays (see Dusinberre,
Women, 114, and 1.2.45n. on *flout at*;
see also Berry, *Hunt*, 173).
23 **native burghers** indigenous citizens
of repute and civic power; a potential
class conflict with the invading

courtiers (Fitter, 202, 206; Berry,
Hunt, 172); see 27. *OED sb.* 1a quotes
Drayton: 'As those great burghers of
the forest wild, / The hart, the goat'
(*Man Moon*, 1619), which may imitate
this line.
desert city an oxymoron: a city
deserted by people but peopled by deer
(cf. 3.2.122–3n.); doubly ironic in view
of the number of people either in or on
their way to the Forest.
24 **confines** territory, limits
with by
forked heads (forkèd) bifurcated
arrows with barbed points (*OED*
forked *ppl. a.* 1g, 'of an arrow'), suggesting both antlers (1a, 'bifurcate,
branching') and the *forked heads* of the
hunters, implying cuckoldry; see Fig.
13 and 3.3.44–58, 4.2.10–19 (the hunting song).
25 **round haunches gored** The phrase
connects hunting and sexuality (Berry,
Hunt, 32–3; see 4.2.1, 4, 10n. and pp.
134–5), including, in a curious bisexual image, both male *burghers* and
potentially female (see 22n.) *dappled
fools*. Harington used the word 'hanch-
es' to describe his wife's thighs, but
omitted it from the scribal manuscript
of his epigrams out of (perhaps) propriety ('Epigrams 1600', fols 3–4; cf.
Epigrams 1618, 1.25).
25–64 The text used at the Aungier-
Street Theatre, Dublin, in 1741 (otherwise based on Theobald) gives the
two speeches of 1 Lord to Jaques, as
also occurs in Johnson's *Forest* (1723)

The melancholy Jaques grieves at that,
And in that kind swears you do more usurp
Than doth your brother that hath banished you.
Today my Lord of Amiens and myself
Did steal behind him as he lay along   30
Under an oak, whose antic root peeps out
Upon the brook that brawls along this wood;
To the which place a poor sequestered stag,
That from the hunter's aim had ta'en a hurt,
Did come to languish; and indeed, my lord,   35
The wretched animal heaved forth such groans

and many later productions; restored
to 1 Lord by Macready in 1842.
26 **melancholy** Jaques's 'humour': a
fashionable Elizabethan malady; see
also 30n. and cf. 2.5.9, 3.2.286,
4.1.3–18.
  that i.e. the wounding of the deer
27 **kind** mode of behaviour (i.e. the practice of hunting)
  usurp i.e. oust the deer from their
rightful territory (as also, of course,
the country dwellers; see 2.4.90n. and
cf. *Tem* 1.2.332-3).
29 **my ... Amiens** the only lord amongst
the Duke's followers to be given a title;
see List of Roles, 12n.
30 **lay along** stretched himself out, a
typically 'melancholic' pose (see pp.
53, 107, 116 and Fig. 12). See Nicholas
Hilliard's miniature of the ninth Earl
of Northumberland; and see also
Isaac Oliver's miniature of Lord
Herbert of Cherbury (reproduced in
Oxf[1], 29).
31 **oak** a symbol of constancy
(Ellacombe, 140–1, citing *Cor* 5.2.109)
  antic grotesque or comic as well as
ancient (F 'anticke'). The difference in
pronunciation is modern (Kökeritz,
334). The ancient (antique) – as at
4.3.103 – oak's grotesque root *peeps out*
on the brook like a comedian (antic)

entering a stage. See Jonson, *EMO*,
2.1.16, where Fastidius's boy is compared to a 'great antique clock' (Q1,
Q2, F; 'anticke' Q3). Ostovich suggests 'that "antic" is punningly intended, along with leering or simpering
stage business for the boy' (*EMO*,
p. 161n.). An Elizabethan theatrical
convention involved an actor (usually
a boy) concealing himself within a
hollow tree (Barton, 'Staging'). The
peeping root is easily metamorphosed
into a peeping boy (alias Ganymede?
see 3.2.245).
32 **brawls** flows rowdily and noisily (e.g.
over stones), babbles (*OED v.*[1] 3, first
example)
33 **sequestered** separated (from the
herd) (*OED ppl. a.* 1, first example),
but it may also mean 'removed from
office', which reinforces the human
associations of the passage (Berry,
Hunt, 175). Drayton's forester unherds
his chosen prey so that he can hunt
him effectively (*Elizium*, 6. 52).
35 **languish** sink and pine away, a
Petrarchan image carrying spiritual
overtones of the soul's longing for
God, as in the 'pilgrim' Psalm, 42.1:
'Like as ye hert desyreth ye water
brookes, so longeth my soule after the
(O God)' (Great Bible)

31 antic] *(anticke), Rowe (antick); antique Pope
Theobald*   34 hunter's] *(Hunters), Douai ms, Pope;* hunters'

That their discharge did stretch his leathern coat
Almost to bursting, and the big round tears
Coursed one another down his innocent nose
In piteous chase. And thus the hairy fool,   40
Much marked of the melancholy Jaques,
Stood on th'extremest verge of the swift brook,
Augmenting it with tears.

DUKE SENIOR   But what said Jaques?
Did he not moralize this spectacle?

1 LORD

O yes, into a thousand similes.   45
First, for his weeping into the needless stream:
'Poor deer,' quoth he, 'thou mak'st a testament
As worldlings do, giving thy sum of more
To that which had too much.' Then being there alone,

37 **leathern coat** (deer's) hide; the phrase links the deer with humans, but also continues the class distinction between nobles and citizens (see 23n.; cf. *velvet*, 50 and n.).

38–9 **tears . . . nose** Bath (17–18) traces the iconography of the weeping stag from the myth of Actaeon – the Greek hunter who was turned into a stag by the goddess Diana after he spied her bathing in a stream, and was torn apart by his own hounds (Ovid, *Met.*, 3) – referred to in many Elizabethan texts, e.g. Drayton, *Poly-Olbion*, 13.217, and Gascoigne's *Hunting*, 136–40. Jonson used the Actaeon myth for Essex's stormy relationship with Elizabeth (which arguably has its own place in Shakespeare's Forest) in *Cynthia's Revels* (1601): 'Here young *Acteon* fell, pursu'd, and torne / By *Cynthias* wrathe (more egar then his houndes)' (1.2.450–1); see Strong, 'Persian Lady', and pp. 72–6.

39 **Coursed** pursued

40 **piteous** arousing the compassion

Jaques feels for the wounded deer
chase pursuit (as hounds); cf. *Ham.* 3.2.273–4.
hairy fool a deer, not a woman (see 22n.)

41 **marked** (markèd) noted
Jaques The usually disyllabic name may either create a feminine ending or be pronounced as a monosyllable to fit the metre; see List of Roles, 13n.

42 **th'extremest verge** the very edge

44 **moralize** draw a moral from

46 **needless** having no need of (more water); cf. *Ham.* 4.7.185–6: 'Too much of water hast thou, poor Ophelia, / And therefore I forbid my tears.'

48 **worldlings** people whose values are shaped by their worldly wealth and consequence

48–9 **giving . . . much** donating their wealth to something which already has a superfluity

49 **there** omitted in F2 to regularize the pentameter, but F's alexandrine could suggest the lingering of the deer after the herd has galloped on

38 bursting] brosting *Douai ms*   46 into] in *Pope*   49 had] hath *Collier²*   much] *F2;* must *F*   there] *om. F2*

Left and abandoned of his velvet friend: 50
''Tis right,' quoth he, 'thus misery doth part
The flux of company.' Anon a careless herd,
Full of the pasture, jumps along by him
And never stays to greet him. 'Ay,' quoth Jaques,
'Sweep on, you fat and greasy citizens!   55
'Tis just the fashion. Wherefore do you look
Upon that poor and broken bankrupt there?'
Thus most invectively he pierceth through
The body of country, city, court,
Yea, and of this our life, swearing that we   60
Are mere usurpers, tyrants and what's worse,
To fright the animals and to kill them up
In their assigned and native dwelling-place.

50 **velvet** with a soft luxuriant coat; in Elizabethan London only aristocrats were allowed to wear velvet. 'Velvet' was also the name given to the soft furry growth on the new antlers of a young deer.
friend The singular form may glance (as also at 2.7.190) at the queen's relation to Essex; see 38–9n.
51 **part** set (us) apart from
52 **flux** superfluity, excess
careless unconcerned
53 **Full . . . pasture** having newly grazed
55 **fat** corpulent but also for deer 'ready to kill, fatted' (*OED a.* and *n.*² 1)
greasy sweaty, suggestive of the well-oiled flattery of 'fair weather' friends
57 **broken** ruined; cf. *R2* 2.1.257: 'The King's grown bankrupt like a broken man.'
58 **invectively** with satirical thrusts; an anticipation of Jaques's satire, 2.7.47–87.
59 **country** generic: the state of being countrified, rather than the specific topos of a country landscape

61 **mere** downright, absolute (*OED a.*² and *adv.* 4)
62 **kill them up** suggests both killing the deer and carving them up for eating. A dislike of hunting as blood-sport was part of humanist thinking and linked with anti-militarism; see Montaigne, 'Of Cruelty': 'I could never so much as endure, without remorce and griefe, to see a poore, silly, and innocent beast pursued and killed, which is harmeles and voide of defence, and of whom we receive no offence at all' (2.337 = 249); see Berry, *Hunt*, 188, and 2.7.129n.). Harington kept deer on his Somerset estate more as pets than as prey for hunters, and inveighed against meat-eating ('Against feasting', *Epigrams 1618*, 2.20, 41; and 'In defence of Lent', 'Epigrams 1600', fol. 27).
63 **dwelling-place** 'Dwell' carries biblical associations from Psalms, 23.5: 'I wyll dwell in the house of God' (Bishops' Bible); see Jonson's eulogy to the Sidney family in '*Penshurst*': 'their lords have built, but thy lord dwells' (Donaldson, *Jonson*, p. 285, l. 102).

50 friend] Friends *Rowe*   56 do] should *Oxf (RP)*   58 pierceth] pierces *Douai ms;* pierced *Hanmer*
59 of] of the *F2*   62 and to] and *Douai ms, Capell*

194

DUKE SENIOR

And did you leave him in this contemplation?

2 LORD

We did, my lord, weeping and commenting   65
Upon the sobbing deer.

DUKE SENIOR   Show me the place.
I love to cope him in these sullen fits,
For then he's full of matter.

1 LORD

I'll bring you to him straight.   *Exeunt.*

2.2   *Enter* DUKE [FREDERICK] *with* Lords.

DUKE FREDERICK

Can it be possible that no man saw them?
It cannot be! Some villains of my court
Are of consent and sufferance in this.

1 LORD

I cannot hear of any that did see her.
The ladies, her attendants of her chamber,   5
Saw her abed, and in the morning early

---

64 **contemplation** meditative strain, continuing the religious language of the speech
65 **commenting** in the role of a moral commentator; cf. *moralize*, 44.
67 **cope** meet with (cited in *OED v.*² 7)
68 **matter** substance, 'material for expression, something to say' (*OED sb.*¹ 9); see 2.5.31n. Jaques's fondness for *matter* may create a link here (see also 3.3.29n.) with Jonson, whose Prologue in *Cynthia's Revels* says his creator: '*his* Poesie; *which (he*

knowes) affoords, / Words aboue Action: matter, aboue wordes' (p. 9, ll. 236–7). See 5.4.183 and Appendix 3.
69 **straight** straightaway
2.2 This scene was often played as Act 1 scene 4 (followed by 2.3 as scene 5) to avoid a scene change; cf. 3.1 and see p. 137.
2 **villains** servants or dependants, but also rascals; cf. 1.1.52, 53n.
3 **have** agreed to and allowed this (i.e. Celia and Rosalind's escape)
4 **her** i.e. Celia

65 SP] *Ami. / Capell;* 1 *Lord. / Rann*   69 SP] 2. *Lor. F3*   **2.2**] *(Scena Secunda.)*   Location] *The Palace / Rowe*   0.1 DUKE] New Duke *Douai ms*   FREDERICK] *Pope; junior / Capell*   2 villains] villeins *Cam*²   5 ¹her] the *Douai ms*

They found the bed untreasured of their mistress.

2 LORD

My lord, the roynish clown, at whom so oft
Your grace was wont to laugh, is also missing.
Hisperia, the princess' gentlewoman,   10
Confesses that she secretly o'erheard
Your daughter and her cousin much commend
The parts and graces of the wrestler
That did but lately foil the sinewy Charles;
And she believes wherever they are gone   15
That youth is surely in their company.

DUKE FREDERICK

Send to his brother; fetch that gallant hither.
If he be absent bring his brother to me.
I'll make him find him. Do this suddenly!
And let not search and inquisition quail   20

---

7 **untreasured of** robbed of its treasure, a Shakespearean coinage (*OED* untreasure *v.*, citing this line), implying both the preciousness of the princess and her chastity; cf. *Cym* 2.2.42: 'The treasure of her honour'. Celia's flight causes consternation, where Rosalind's was expected.

8 **roynish** scurvy, coarse, boisterous (Fr. *rogneux*); cf. Nashe, *Strange News* (1592): 'clownish and roynish ieasts' (1.324, 9–10, cited in Ard²).

9 **wont** accustomed

10 **Hisperia** A character only named at this point. The eavesdropping, while convenient for the plot, is in keeping with the atmosphere of Frederick's court; cf. 2.3.26n. If there were a walk-on part played by a boy in 1.3, he could have been enlisted later to sing; see 5.3.5.1n. and Appendix 2.

13 **parts** qualities
wrestler trisyllabic

14 **foil** overthrow (in wrestling)
sinewy muscular

17 **his brother** i.e. Oliver
gallant (gállant) young swell, meaning Oliver; a hendecasyllabic line (11 syllables). Cam² inserts quotation marks, 'fetch . . . hither', in which case *gallant* applies to Orlando.

19 **make him** i.e. Oliver. Frederick's petulance is potentially comic; see 3.1.15n. Oxf¹ notes 'the confusing babble of pronouns'.
find him i.e. Orlando
suddenly without delay

20 **inquisition** close questioning; the usual word for the papal 'Holy Inquisition', which persecuted heretics, both Catholic and Protestant; see *Thomas, Lord Cromwell* (1602): 'Pride, the Inquisition, and this bellie euill, / Are in my iudgement, Spaines three headed diuell' (3.3.56–7) (RP).
quail hesitate, falter, suggestive of the suspect shrinking under *inquisition*

---

10 princess'] *(Princesse)*, *Capell*   13 wrestler] *(Wrastler)*   14 sinewy] *(synowie)*, *Douai ms*, *Rowe³*
17 brother] brother's *Capell*   fetch . . . hither] 'Fetch . . . hither.' *Cam²* *(Andrews)*

To bring again these foolish runaways.   *Exeunt.*

2.3   *Enter* ORLANDO *and* ADAM.

ORLANDO   Who's there?
ADAM
        What, my young master? O my gentle master,
        O my sweet master, O you memory
        Of old Sir Rowland! Why, what make you here?
        Why are you virtuous? Why do people love you?   5
        And wherefore are you gentle, strong, and valiant?
        Why would you be so fond to overcome
        The bonny prizer of the humorous Duke?
        Your praise is come too swiftly home before you.
        Know you not, master, to some kind of men   10
        Their graces serve them but as enemies?
        No more do yours. Your virtues, gentle master,

2.3 A return to the orchard of 1.1, just as 2.2 returns to Frederick's court. This scene's strong homiletic tone appealed to eighteenth- and nineteenth-century audiences (Oxf[1]) and creates a special aura around the figure of Adam (see also 2.6, 2.7.128–34, 168, 201–2).

2   **gentle** of disposition (see 6n. and cf. 1.1.42–3n.), contrasted with the *rough* character of both Oliver and Frederick.

3   **memory** living likeness; see 2.7.197–8 and nn.

4   **make you** are you doing

5   **Why** The questions which Adam poses in this speech and answers himself are examples of '*Antipophora*', the figure of '*Responce*': 'when we will seeme to aske a question to th'intent we will aunswere it our selues' (Puttenham, *English Poetry*, 170).

6   **wherefore** for what purpose

gentle, strong, . . . valiant Orlando is *gentle* (see 2n.) and *strong*, as well as *strong* and *valiant* – a David who has overcome a version of Goliath in Charles the wrestler. The line contributes to a rewriting of gender in the play; see pp. 31–3.

7   **fond** foolish

8   **bonny** robust, stout (*OED a.* 2a *obs.*)
      prizer prize-winner
      humorous moody, volatile; see 1.2.255n.

9   'Report of your valour has preceded you and endangers your homecoming.'

11   'their good qualities militate against them by arousing envy'
      them, a redundant object, reinforcing *men*, 10 (Abbott, 414)

12   **No more** so, thus

12–13 **Your . . . you** Your good qualities betray you in spite of themselves.

2.3] *(Scena Tertia.)*   Location] *Oliver's House / Rowe*   2 master?] *Ard[2]*; Master, *F*   4 Rowland] Roland *Cam[2]*   10 some] *F2;* seeme *F*

Are sanctified and holy traitors to you.
O what a world is this, when what is comely
Envenoms him that bears it!   15

ORLANDO
Why, what's the matter?

ADAM   O unhappy youth,
Come not within these doors! Within this roof
The enemy of all your graces lives.
Your brother – no, no brother, yet the son –
Yet not the son; I will not call him son   20
Of him I was about to call his father –
Hath heard your praises, and this night he means
To burn the lodging where you use to lie,
And you within it. If he fail of that
He will have other means to cut you off;   25

---

13 **sanctified and holy** a juxtaposition of words of Latin and Saxon origin; see 1.1.65n.
traitors Adam uses a language of religious martyrdom; cf. 2.2.20n. Cf. Rosalind, accused of treachery because of her 'graces' (Jamieson, 37); see 1.3.51n.

14 **what a world** Adam's expostulation recalls Le Beau's words at 1.2.273–4, sharpening the contrast with the beneficent Arden of 2.1.
comely handsome; generous

15 **Envenoms** poisons; reminiscent of the serpent's venom in the Garden of Eden

16 **matter** substance, i.e. the material grounds of Adam's outpourings. Cf. Gertrude to Polonius, *Ham* 2.2.95: 'More matter with less art.'
unhappy unfortunate

17 **roof** house; an example of the rhetorical figure *synecdoche* (the part for the whole); cf. 2.4.78. In Lodge, Rosader is locked out of his brother's house after

his triumph at the wrestling, although he breaks in and is befriended by the steward Adam Spencer, after which his elder brother Saladyne feigns renewed friendship (sigs C3^v–4^r).

18 **graces** virtues

19–21 Oliver is 'morally undeserving' and '*spiritually* illegitimate' (Montrose, 'Brother', 37).

23 **burn the lodging** from Lodge, but historically accurate; arson was a recognized mode of aristocratic feuding, imitated by the gentry and 'slow to change' (Capp, 'Arson', 204). Elam suggests a pun, indicative of Shakespeare's 'recasting the source material' (i.e. Lodge) (163), a suggestion made even more plausible by the fact that Lodge's grandfather was named, as an illegitimate son, after his 'lodging' (A. Walker, 411; see p. 82).
use are accustomed
lie dwell

24 **of** in

I overheard him and his practices.
This is no place; this house is but a butchery.
Abhor it, fear it, do not enter it!

ORLANDO

Why whither, Adam, wouldst thou have me go?

ADAM

No matter whither so you come not here.   30

ORLANDO

What, wouldst thou have me go and beg my food,
Or with a base and boisterous sword enforce
A thievish living on the common road?
This I must do, or know not what to do.
Yet this I will not do, do how I can.   35
I rather will subject me to the malice
Of a diverted blood and bloody brother.

ADAM

But do not so. I have five hundred crowns,

26 **overheard** Haber draws a distinction between the function of overhearing in a 'court' context, to reveal 'individual motives and plots' (as here), and in the Forest of Arden, 'to uncover emotions' (179n.); see 2.2.10n., 3.2.155n.
practices plots (with Machiavellian undertones; see 1.1.140n.); cf. *MM* 5.1.126: 'This needs must be a practice.'
27 **place** dwelling-place, home
butchery slaughter-house
29 **whither** Orlando's question parallels Rosalind's at 1.3.103 (see n.).
30 **so** provided that
31 **beg** Orlando recalls Oliver's scornful question: 'Beg when that is spent?' (1.1.71).
32–3 'or force a living for myself with the lawless violence of the baseborn, by robbing travellers on the common highway'. Orlando's repudiation of violence anticipates his remorse for aggression at 2.7.107–10; *thievish living*

and *common road* echo Elizabethan hostility to the players as vagabonds (see 1.3.65n., 2.5.54n. and Epilogue 9n.).
boisterous See 4.3.31n.
33 **common** ordinary, continuing the social implications of *base*; cf. *2H4* 2.2.161–2 (of Doll Tearsheet): 'as common as the way between Saint Albans and London'.
35 **do how I can** whatever I do
36 **I . . . me** I would prefer to submit myself
37 **diverted blood** kinship turned aside from its natural (brotherly) course; see 19–21n. Cf. Duke Frederick and his brother, Duke Senior (Montrose, 'Brother', 29).
bloody brother oxymoron, possibly recalling the murder of Cain by Abel
38 **do** Adam returns the word to its function as *deed* rather than as a mere counter in rhetorical word-play.
crowns gold coins: four crowns made a pound – the average price of a copy

28 ³it] in *Douai ms*   29 SP] *F2; Ad. F*   32 boisterous] *(boistrous)*   35 can.] *Rowe subst.;* can, *F*

The thrifty hire I saved under your father,
Which I did store to be my foster-nurse,   40
When service should in my old limbs lie lame
And unregarded age in corners thrown.
Take that, and He that doth the ravens feed,
Yea, providently caters for the sparrow,
Be comfort to my age. Here is the gold: 45
All this I give you. Let me be your servant.
Though I look old, yet I am strong and lusty,
For in my youth I never did apply
Hot and rebellious liquors in my blood,
Nor did not with unbashful forehead woo   50
The means of weakness and debility.

in 1623 of the First Folio (Blayney, *Folio*, 26; West, l. 18). A serving-man might have earned £2 a year; Adam's wages would have been higher if he was a steward as in Lodge (Cam²). See 1.1.2n. and p. 93.

39 **thrifty hire** economy (in saving wages) when hired (by your father)

41 'when the weakness of old age prevents me from serving you'

43 **Take that** i.e. the money
He The religious tenor of Adam's speech evokes pilgrimage; cf. *RJ* 1.4.112–13: 'But he that hath the steerage of my course / Direct my suit'.
ravens feed See Luke, 12.24: 'Consider the Rauens: for they nether sowe nor reape: whiche nether haue store house nor barne, & *yet* God fedeth them: howe muche more are ye better then the foules?' (Geneva Bible).

44 **Yea** a biblical word of affirmation which introduces the reference to Matthew
providently through divine ordering; see Matthew, 10.29: 'Are not two sparrowes solde for a farthing, and one of them shal not fall on the ground with-

out your Father?' (Geneva Bible). Cf. *Ham* 5.2.215–16, 'There is special providence in the fall of a sparrow', where Jenkins notes: 'The Elizabethans believed both in general providence . . . and . . . in a singular or *special providence* . . . The latter, along with its scriptural exemplification in the sparrow, was especially insisted on by Calvin (see *Institutes*, 1, esp. xvi.1, xvii.6).'

45 **comfort** with biblical associations; see 1.3.128n.

47 **lusty** robust, vigorous; cf. 52.

48 **apply** administer (*OED* 3) or employ (*OED* 6)

49 **rebellious** causing revolt; in Elizabethan physiology too much blood, heated by alcohol, would create an imbalance leading to intemperate behaviour (lust, choler); see Paster, 47, 62–5.

50 **Nor . . . not** double negative for emphasis (Abbott, 406); see 2.7.90, 3.5.26, 128.
unbashful forehead immodest brow, implying *horns* and thus unchastity

51 **means of** course of action leading to
weakness and debility a veiled reference to venereal disease

43 He] *(he) Capell*

Therefore my age is as a lusty winter,
Frosty but kindly. Let me go with you.
I'll do the service of a younger man
In all your business and necessities. 55
ORLANDO
O good old man, how well in thee appears
The constant service of the antique world,
Where servants sweat for duty not for meed.
Thou art not for the fashion of these times,
Where none will sweat but for promotion, 60
And, having that, do choke their service up
Even with the having. It is not so with thee.
But, poor old man, thou prun'st a rotten tree,
That cannot so much as a blossom yield
In lieu of all thy pains and husbandry. 65
But come thy ways, we'll go along together,
And ere we have thy youthful wages spent
We'll light upon some settled low content.

53 **Frosty but kindly** sharp but conducive to well-being; cf. 2.1.5–11, where the winter wind is biting but beneficent.
54 'I'll serve you as well as if I were a younger man'
57 **constant . . . world** the faithfulness of servants in the 'olden days' (cf. 2.1.2, *old custom*), congruent with the golden world of classical myth recreated in the Forest
58 ***Where servants** F's 'When seruice' may be an example of dittography from line 41, where the same phrase occurs. F's 'seruice' is frequently emended on the grounds that it also repeats the previous line.
  meed reward, possibly with a pun on 'mead' (an intoxicating drink made with honey) prompted by Adam's repudiation of strong liquor

59 **fashion . . . times** fashionable modern ways
60–2 **Where . . . having** 'in which no one will exert himself except for advancement, and then uses his new prosperity as a pretext for abandoning the duties which secured it'
63 **prun'st . . . tree** Orlando sees himself as fruitless; a reminder of the orchard setting.
64–5 Adam's care (*husbandry*) in pruning a dead tree will not even produce blossom, let alone fruit.
65 **lieu** consequence, literally place (Fr. *lieu*)
66 **come thy ways** come along
68 **light upon** find, happen on
  settled low content humble place for untroubled living – a pastoral image; see 1.3.134 and 3.2.17n.

57 service] favour *Collier²*; fashion *Keightley* 58 Where] *this edn;* When *F* servants] *this edn (Halliwell);* seruice *F;* labour *(Cam²)*

201

ADAM

Master, go on and I will follow thee
To the last gasp with truth and loyalty.   70
From seventeen years till now almost fourscore
Here lived I, but now live here no more.
At seventeen years many their fortunes seek,
But at fourscore it is too late a week.
Yet fortune cannot recompense me better   75
Than to die well and not my master's debtor.   *Exeunt.*

2.4   *Enter* ROSALIND *as Ganymede,* CELIA
              as Aliena and TOUCHSTONE.

ROSALIND   O Jupiter, how weary are my spirits!

69 **thee** affectionate; a servant's normal address to his master, usually observed by Adam, would be 'you'.

70 **last gasp** See 2.7.203n. for Adam's absence from the play after 2.7.

71 ***seventeen*** F's 'seauentie' is probably a misreading of 'seauenteē' (a common contraction of *n*; see 2.4.41n.), correctly printed at 73.

74 **too . . . week** too late, playing also on 'weak'

76 **not . . . debtor** Adam's plan would leave Orlando (the master) in his servant's debt, an inversion befitting the Forest of Arden.

2.4.0.2 TOUCHSTONE The clown's name is used for the first time in F on his entry into the Forest of Arden; see List of Roles, 11n.

1 **Jupiter** a suitable oath for Ganymede, *Jove's own page* (1.3.121); see 56.
weary . . . spirits F's 'merry' follows Lodge, where on arrival in Arden the two girls produce a picnic and 'fedde

as merely [merrily] as if they had been in Paris with all the kings delicates' (sig. D3'). Shakespeare's princesses, furnished with gold and jewels (70, 99, 1.3.131), but not used to providing their own meals, are hungry and dispirited (see Fig. 7). The Douai MS reads 'weary', the earliest record of this change (see Appendix 4). In lines from the Crane manuscript for Middleton's *A Game at Chess*, reproduced by Roberts ('Ralph Crane', 222), two consecutive words at 17 and 19 begin with *w* and *m* ('would make' and 'me with'), demonstrating the similarity between the letters in secretary script (and perhaps particularly in Crane's handwriting). Rosalind's enforced joviality (after *Jupiter*) in 4–8 may be ironic (Halliwell; Cam²) or part of her 'manly' role (Caldecott), but the lines, and Touchstone's response, suggest otherwise.

71 seventeen] *Rowe;* seauentie *F*   **2.4**] *(Scena Quarta.)*   Location] *The Forest / Rowe; the* FOREST *of* Arden / *Theobald*   0.1 *as*] *Ard²; for F; in Boys Cloathes for / Rowe*   0.2 *as*] *Ard²; for F; drest like a Shepherdess for / Rowe*   TOUCHSTONE] *Malone; Clowne,* alias *Touchstone F*   1 weary] *Douai ms, Theobald (Warburton);* merry *F*

TOUCHSTONE   I care not for my spirits if my legs were
   not weary.

ROSALIND   I could find in my heart to disgrace my man's
   apparel and to cry like a woman, but I must comfort the   5
   weaker vessel, as doublet and hose ought to show itself
   courageous to petticoat. Therefore courage, good
   Aliena.

CELIA   I pray you bear with me, I cannot go no further.

TOUCHSTONE   For my part, I had rather bear with you   10
   than bear you. Yet I should bear no cross if I did bear
   you, for I think you have no money in your purse.

2–3 **legs . . . weary** Touchstone's riposte
opposes body and spirit (cf. 10–11,
61n.), possibly a stock joke of Will
Kemp's – a celebrated dancer; cf. *2H4*
Epilogue: 'My tongue is weary; when
my legs are too, I will bid you good
night' (32–4; see Wiles, 128). See 15n.,
pp. 4, 45, 111–13 and Appendix 2.

4–5 **disgrace . . . woman** In Lodge the
equivalent lines are spoken to Saladyne
(= Oliver): 'Nay forward man (quoth
the Forrester), teares are the vnfittest
salue that any man can apply for to
cure sorrows, and therefore cease from
such feminine follies, as should drop
out of a womans eye to deceiue, not
out of a Gentlemans looke to discouer
his thoughts' (sig. K3ʳ). Shakespeare's
reassigning of the lines to the disguised Rosalind inaugurates the gender games of the Forest scenes,
enhanced in his theatre by boy actors
playing women's parts; see pp. 9–13.

6 **weaker vessel** St Peter's phrase for
women (1 Peter, 3.7) became proverbial (Dent, W655) and was frequently
satirized. See also *LLL* 1.1.259: '*For
Jaquenetta, so is the weaker vessel
called*'; Lyly, *Sappho and Phao* (1584),
1.4.31–2: 'I cannot but sometimes
smile to myself to hear men call us
weak vessels when they prove themselves broken-hearted [perjured]';
Greene, *Mamillia* (1583): 'They say, a
woma[n] is the weaker vessel, but sure

in my iudgement, it is in the strength
of her body, and not in the force of her
minde' (2.95, also 255; see Ard²). Cf.
Elizabeth's gender politics (see
Marcus, 'Heroines', 138, 146, and pp.
5–6, 11–12).

doublet and hose tight-fitting jacket,
worn (usually) with puffed breeches,
and stockings (hose), the standard
costume for an Elizabethan courtier (see
Fig. 19, and Fig. 6 for Rosalind's
disguise), used here to identify
manhood, just as *petticoat* (7) identifies
femininity; see 1.3.15n.

9 **cannot . . . no** double negative for
affirmation (Abbott, 406)

10–11 **bear . . . you** be patient with you
rather than carry you; another swift
change from spirit to body. See 99
SDn.

11–12 **Yet . . . purse** elaborate word-play
both on the Christian doctrine of bearing one's cross and on the 'crusado', a
coin stamped with a single cross (pic-
tured in Adams, *Tables*, 1594, sig. C3ʳ).
Its name recalls medieval crusades
against the Turks; see 4.3.33n. Cf. *Oth*
3.4.25–6: 'I had rather have lost my
purse / Full of crusadoes'. An apprentice (as Kathman has shown boy actors
formally to be; see Appendix 2), not
being a 'sharer' in theatre profits,
would have no money in his purse –
unlike the Duke's daughter whose part
he was playing.

ROSALIND   Well, this is the Forest of Arden.

TOUCHSTONE   Ay, now am I in Arden, the more fool I!
When I was at home I was in a better place, but   15
travellers must be content.

Enter CORIN *and* SILVIUS.

ROSALIND   Ay, be so, good Touchstone. Look you, who
comes here? A young man and an old in solemn talk.

CORIN
That is the way to make her scorn you still.

SILVIUS
O Corin, that thou knewst how I do love her!   20

CORIN
I partly guess, for I have loved ere now.

SILVIUS
No, Corin, being old, thou canst not guess,
Though in thy youth thou wast as true a lover
As ever sighed upon a midnight pillow.
But if thy love were ever like to mine –   25
As sure I think did never man love so –

---

13 a location SD, which may also prompt
the audience (in a non-illusionist theatre, Cam²), to imagine the Forest; cf.
H5 Prologue 23: 'Piece out our imper-
fections with your thoughts.'
14 **the . . . I** proverbial (Dent, F505.1)
15 **home** See Hall, *Virgidemiarum*: '[The
traveller] wishes for home a thousand
sithes a day' (4.6, p. 47).
16 **travellers** Touchstone's claim allies
him with Jaques (4.1.17ff.).
16.1 Corin and Silvius enter engrossed
in conversation, shunting the
characters already on stage into the
position of audience; see 1.2.110–11n.
The ensuing dialogue recalls that
between Cuddie and Thenot in the

'February' eclogue of Spenser's *SC*
(Cam²).
19 **scorn** Corin has obviously been advis-
ing Silvius against his doting behaviour
towards Phoebe. In Lodge, Montanus's
(= Silvius's) verses to his scornful mistress, Phoebe, carved on a pine tree, are
the first thing Rosalind and Celia
encounter in the Forest (sig. D4ʳ).
22 **No . . . old** Cf. Romeo's dismissal of the
Friar's advice: 'Thou canst not speak of
that thou dost not feel' (*RJ* 3.3.64). In
Lodge the dialogue between Montanus
and Coridon takes the form of 'A pleasant Eglog', i.e. rhymed verses, although
their length makes them more tedious
than pleasant (sigs E1ᵛ–4ʳ).

13, 14 Arden] Ardenne *Oxf*   14 am I] I am *Douai ms, Pope*   16.1] *after 18 Pope; after* Touchstone *17
Cam*   17–18] *Capell lines* here? / talk. /   26 did never] never did *Douai ms*

How many actions most ridiculous
Hast thou been drawn to by thy fantasy?

CORIN

Into a thousand that I have forgotten.

SILVIUS

O, thou didst then never love so heartily!　　　　　30
If thou rememb'rest not the slightest folly
That ever love did make thee run into,
Thou hast not loved.
Or if thou hast not sat as I do now,
Wearing thy hearer in thy mistress' praise,　　　　35
Thou hast not loved.
Or if thou hast not broke from company
Abruptly as my passion now makes me,
Thou hast not loved.　　　　　　　　　　　　　39
O Phoebe, Phoebe, Phoebe!　　　　　　　　*Exit.*

ROSALIND

Alas, poor shepherd, searching of thy wound
I have by hard adventure found mine own.

TOUCHSTONE　And I mine. I remember when I was in
love I broke my sword upon a stone and bid him take

---

28 **fantasy** imagination, shapes and
forms created by love (5.2.90), a
Platonic formulation familiar to the
Elizabethans from Ficino's immensely
popular *Commentary* (6.6, p. 115); cf.
MND 5.1.4–5: 'Lovers and madmen
have such seething brains, / Such
shaping fantasies'.
30 **never** may be elided to 'ne'er' to make
an iambic pentameter
33, 36, 39 **Thou ... loved** The short line
acts as a refrain, as in shepherds'
pastoral songs.
34 **sat** on the grass (see 3.4.45); an internal SD (Watkins, 175)

35 **Wearing** wearing out, exhausting
(*OED* wear *v.*[1] 10a)
37 **broke** broken (see 1.1.80n.)
40 SD In the Douai MS Corin exits with
Silvius, re-entering after *kinsman*, 64.
41 **searching of** probing
***thy wound** F's 'they would' probably
represents a misreading of contracted
n, i.e. a line over the *u* in 'woud' (see
2.3.71n.), 'thy' being adjusted to 'thy'
to agree with 'would'.
42 **adventure** enterprise, with a sense of
'coming to' (Lat. *advenire*)
44 **sword . . . stone** may be bawdy; cf.
cods, 49.

---

30 never] nere *Douai ms, Rowe* 31 rememb'rest] *(*remembrest*)* 35 Wearing] Wearying *F2*
mistress'] *(*Mistris*), Pope* 40 SD] *Exeunt F2* 41 thy wound] *Douai ms, Rowe;* they would *F;* their
wound *F2*

205

that for coming a-night to Jane Smile; and I remember   45
the kissing of her batlet, and the cow's dugs that her
pretty chopped hands had milked; and I remember the
wooing of a peascod instead of her, from whom I took
two cods, and, giving her them again, said with weeping
tears: 'Wear these for my sake.' We that are true lovers   50
run into strange capers. But as all is mortal in nature, so
is all nature in love mortal in folly.

ROSALIND   Thou speak'st wiser than thou art ware of.

TOUCHSTONE   Nay, I shall ne'er be ware of mine own wit
till I break my shins against it.   55

ROSALIND
Jove, Jove, this shepherd's passion

---

46 *batlet (F2) a Warwickshire dialect word for a butter paddle (Wise, 150, cited in Knowles). F's 'batler' is a paddle used for beating laundry. 'Dairying was a well-known courtship venue: a "creampot love" was a popular saying' (Mendelson & Crawford, 111).

47 chopped chapped; *a* and *o* are often interchangeable in dialect forms (Northall, *Word-Book*, xi).

48 peascod peapod, a customary love-gift to a woman. In Charlotte Cushman's promptbook a handwritten couplet faces this speech: 'If women they were small as they are little good / A Peascod would make them a gown and a hood' (Moore). *Peascod* transposed = codpiece (Williams); the line was often cut in the nineteenth century (Marshall).

49 cods peapods; a pun on *cods* = testicles

49–50 weeping tears Touchstone may parody a line of Rosader's: '*But weeping teares their want could not suffice*' (Lodge, sig. H3ᵛ, Theobald, xvii–xviii).

50 We . . . lovers Touchstone's courting of Jane Smile is in keeping with a possible performance of the role by

Kemp, who was ribbed for being 'amorous' (*Almond*, dedication).

51 capers escapades, high jinks, literally a leap; cf. *TN* 1.3.136–7: 'Let me see thee caper.'

51–2 But . . . folly 'Just as in the course of nature all will die, so are all natural creatures in love ready to die for their delusions'; an example of *chiasmus*, the rhetorical patterning of words in the shape of a cross (x): *mortal, nature / nature, mortal*

53 wiser . . . of more wisely than you are aware of; cf. *Almond*: 'thou hast spoke wiser then thou art aware of, for if a man should imagine of fruite by the rottenesse . . .' (sig. C3ʳ; Dusinberre, 'Topical', 243).

54 be ware of be wary of, as in 'beware', as opposed to 'aware', a clever riposte to Rosalind's patronizing taunt

55 break my shins proverbial (Dent, F543, noting *shins* as Shakespearean); wise men don't see the paltry obstacles with which fools obstruct their path.

56 Jove a saucy invocation from Ganymede (see 1.3.121n., 122n.), as the passion of shepherds in pastoral poetry is usually homoerotic; see 3.5.83n. and pp. 9, 10.

---

45 a-night] *(*a night*)*; a nights *F2*   46 batlet] *F2*; batler *F*   56–7] *prose Pope*

Is much upon my fashion!

TOUCHSTONE   And mine, but it grows something stale
with me.

CELIA

I pray you, one of you question yon man   60
If he for gold will give us any food.
I faint almost to death.

TOUCHSTONE   Holla, you clown!

ROSALIND   Peace, fool, he's not thy kinsman.

CORIN   Who calls?   65

TOUCHSTONE   Your betters, sir.

CORIN   Else are they very wretched.

ROSALIND [*to Touchstone*]

Peace, I say. – Good even to you, friend.

CORIN

And to you, gentle sir, and to you all.

---

57 **fashion** mode: both Rosalind's disguise and her feelings. Her rhyming
couplet fashionably imitates pastoral
poetry; cf. 3.2.248–9n.
58 **something stale** rather passé.
Touchstone's prose line ironically
'caps' Rosalind's stagy couplet.
60 *yon yonder (*OED* yond *a*[1])
61 **food** the body must be fed, a characteristic physical intervention in the
poetic discourse of love; cf. *RJ*
1.1.173: 'Where shall we dine?' See
also 2–3n. and 4.1.206n.
63 **clown** yokel; used disparagingly by
those who are not countrymen; see
5.1.11. Cf. Drayton, *Poly-Olbion*:
'From Villages repleate with ragg'd
and sweating Clownes' (13.217). In
Lodge, Coridon is called 'the Clown'
only once (sig. O3[r]), with belittling
effect.
64 **not thy kinsman** neither your relation nor a clown like you; see 1.3.127n.

The Douai MS here marks a re-entry
for Corin.
67 'If they were not (my betters) they
would   be   very   miserable.'
Touchstone's *betters* focuses on social
status, while Corin's reply implies
'superior in material wealth'; cf. the
shepherd's praise of 'money, means
and content' as the good things of life
(3.2.23–4).
68 **Peace, I say** virtually an aside to
Touchstone; cf. Hal to Falstaff: 'Peace,
chewet, peace' (*1H4*, 5.1.29).
Good even Rosalind greets Corin
courteously in blank verse, and the
shepherd answers in the same vein
(Ard[2]). In Lodge, Aliena politely
accosts the shepherds, asking lodging
for herself and her page (sig. E4[r]).
69 **gentle** kind, but also well-bred (after
Touchstone's rudeness)
sir Ganymede's disguise has worked
on the first witness of it.

60–2] *prose Ard*[2]   60 yon] *Douai ms, Capell;* yon'd *F*   64] kinsman.] kinsman. Enter Corin *Douai ms*
68 SD] *Cam*[2]   you] *F2;* your *F*

ROSALIND

    I prithee, shepherd, if that love or gold   70
    Can in this desert place buy entertainment,
    Bring us where we may rest ourselves and feed.
    Here's a young maid with travel much oppressed
    And faints for succour.

CORIN   Fair sir, I pity her

    And wish, for her sake more than for mine own,   75
    My fortunes were more able to relieve her.
    But I am shepherd to another man
    And do not shear the fleeces that I graze.
    My master is of churlish disposition
    And little recks to find the way to heaven   80
    By doing deeds of hospitality.
    Besides, his cote, his flocks and bounds of feed
    Are now on sale, and at our sheepcote now,
    By reason of his absence, there is nothing

71 **desert** deserted, unpopulated; see 2.1.23n.
   entertainment both welcome and sustenance
73 **maid . . . travel** young girl worn out with the effort of travelling; see 1.3.128n.
74 **succour** (lack of) help, specifically nourishment
75–6 Corin's refusal of Rosalind's request is 'unique in the whole bucolic tradition' (Poggioli, 38).
77 **shepherd . . . man** Corin is not his own master, but is employed by an absentee landlord (old Carlot; see 3.5.109n.), a situation which created major social tension (Thirsk, 93; Barton, 'Parks and Ardens', 356).
78 **fleeces** sheep (*synecdoche*; see 2.3.17 and n.)
   graze provide pasture for; see 82n.
79 **churlish** surly, unfriendly, from Middle English *ceorl*, a base-born

knave, but also miserly (*OED* 3 and churl *sb.* 6)
80 **recks** cares, as in 'reckless'; cf. *Ham* 1.3.51: 'recks not his own rede' (does not heed his own advice). F's 'wreaks' is a variant of 'recks'.
81 **hospitality** generosity, the duty of providing for travellers, associated with a more generous past. The passage anticipates Duke Senior's old-world hospitality to Orlando and Adam in 2.7 as the mark of true breeding. Cf. Jonson, '*Penshurst*' (*c.* 1611), where the Sidneys' 'liberal board' and 'hospitality' (Donaldson, *Jonson*, 284, ll. 59–60) is contrasted with modern meanness and ostentation.
82 **cote** cottage
   bounds of feed range of pasture (*OED* feed *sb.* 2b *obs.*)
83 **sheepcote** literally, sheep-pen, but here a shepherd's dwelling (Cam[2], and see 4.3.76)

73 travel] *(trauaile)*, *F3*   80 recks] *(wreakes)*, *Hanmer;* reaks *Riv*

That you will feed on. But what is, come see,   85
And in my voice most welcome shall you be.

ROSALIND

What is he that shall buy his flock and pasture?

CORIN

That young swain that you saw here but erewhile,
That little cares for buying anything.

ROSALIND

I pray thee, if it stand with honesty,   90
Buy thou the cottage, pasture and the flock,
And thou shalt have to pay for it of us.

CELIA

And we will mend thy wages. I like this place
And willingly could waste my time in it.

CORIN

Assuredly the thing is to be sold.   95
Go with me. If you like upon report
The soil, the profit and this kind of life,
I will your very faithful feeder be,
And buy it with your gold right suddenly.   *Exeunt.*

---

86 **voice** approbation, invitation (almost, vote; cf. *Cor* 2.3.1)
88 **swain** shepherd; poetic
but erewhile only just now
90 **if . . . honesty** if it is consistent with fair dealing. Despite this disclaimer, Rosalind's purchase of the cottage Silvius wanted to buy is a form of usurpation of the country by the court (see 2.1.27n.).
91 **pasture . . . flock** The Forest of Arden is a 'chase' (hunting ground) but also pasture for sheep (see Daley, 173).
92 **have** 'the money' is implied
of from
93 **mend** improve, increase

94 **waste** spend; but the idea of pastoral idleness also carries overtones of time wasted. See 2.7.113 and 5.3.45n.
96 **upon report** when you have heard more about it
98 **feeder** herdsman, shepherd (*OED sb.* 4a)
99 **right suddenly** immediately; *right* functions as an intensifier, as also at 2.7.202, 3.2.95, 266.
99 SD A prompter's note to Phelps's 1847 production at Sadler's Wells states: 'Celia on bank calls "Touchstone!" who re-enters and assists her off'; in that production the Clown had to bear the princess as well as bear with her (see 10, and Marshall).

93–4] *Capell; F lines* wages: / could / it. / ; *Rowe³ lines* wages; / waste / it. /

2.5   *Enter* AMIENS, JAQUES *and other*
                  [Lords *dressed as foresters*].

AMIENS (*Sings.*)
         Under the greenwood tree
         Who loves to lie with me
         And turn his merry note
         Unto the sweet bird's throat,
         Come hither, come hither, come hither!   5
ALL [*Sing.*]
         Here shall he see no enemy
         But winter and rough weather.
JAQUES   More, more, I prithee, more.
AMIENS   It will make you melancholy, Monsieur Jaques.
JAQUES   I thank it; more, I prithee, more. I can suck   10

2.5 This scene may not always have been performed even in Shakespeare's theatre, and was often later cut; see pp. 128, 137, 139 and Appendix 4.

0.1–2 *other* Lords addressed at 26; see 1.1.96, 2.1.0.1–2, and cf. 2.7.0.1n.

1 SP *13 confirms Amiens as the singer.

1 a Robin Hood refrain: 'We be yemen of this foreste / Vnder the grene wode tre' (*Robin Hood*, sig. E2ᵛ).

3–4 The singer answers the bird. 'Turning' was a technical musical term for the degrees of the singing scale in *sol fa* notation; Morley's *Practical Music* declares that pupils must learn to 'truly sing their turnings, which we commonly call the sixe notes, or *vt, re, mi, fa, sol, la*' (Dedication, iv; see p. 79). Cf. Hall, *Virgidemiarum* (1599): 'Whiles thredbare Martiall turnes his merry note / To beg of *Rufus* a cast winter cote' (6.1, p. 90; for Martial see also

1.3.117n., 3.2.255n.). Amiens's joyful free bird contrasts with Hall's impoverished flatterer repeating 'threadbare' verses to gain new clothes.

4 **throat** voice, warbling

5, 37 **Come hither** an invitation to the Lords to gather round; see also 48n.

6, 38, 49 SP, SD *The Lords sing the last two lines of each stanza of Amiens's song as a chorus (i.e. 6–7, 38–9 and 49–50).

6–7 Amiens's song reinforces Duke Senior's contrast (2.1.3–11) between the beneficence of inclement weather and the malevolence of court backbiting.

9 **melancholy** often associated with music; cf. *MV* 5.1.69: 'I am never merry when I hear sweet music.'
Monsieur See 1.2.90n., 3.2.286n.

10–12, 14–15, 29–32, 40–1 printed as verse in F, presumably to fill up space; prose better conveys Jaques's cynicism.

2.5] *(Scena Quinta.)* Location] *a desart Part of the Forest / Theobald* 0.1–56] *om. Douai ms* 0.1 JAQUES, AMIENS] *(Amyens, Iaques) other] Oxf; others F* 0.2 Lords . . . foresters] *Oxf* 1 SP] *Capell; not in F* SD] *Sisson;* Song. F 3 turn] *tune / Rowe³* 6, 38 SP] *Capell subst.; not in F* 6 SD] *Capell subst.* 6, 38] *Pope lines see / enemy /* 10–12] *Pope; F lines* prethee more, / song, / more. /

melancholy out of a song as a weasel sucks eggs. More,
I prithee, more!

AMIENS   My voice is ragged: I know I cannot please you.

JAQUES   I do not desire you to please me; I do desire you to
sing. Come, more, another *stanzo* – call you 'em *stanzos*?   15

AMIENS   What you will, Monsieur Jaques.

JAQUES   Nay, I care not for their names: they owe me
nothing. Will you sing?

AMIENS   More at your request than to please myself.

JAQUES   Well then, if ever I thank any man I'll thank you;   20
but that they call compliment is like th'encounter of
two dog-apes. And when a man thanks me heartily,
methinks I have given him a penny and he renders me
the beggarly thanks. Come, sing; – and you that will
not, hold your tongues.   25

---

11 **weasel** a predatory rodent, out of
keeping with the pastoral idyll

13–15 This interchange marks the opposition between Amiens, the man of
concord and loving (see 2.1.18n.) and
Jaques, the malcontent satirist, hater of
music (2.7.5, 4.2.8–9); cf. *JC* 1.2.203
(of Cassius): 'he hears no music'.

13 **ragged** 'harsh, discordant, rough'
(*OED a.*[1] 3b, first example); Amiens's
reluctance to sing marks courtly good
manners, satirized as affectation in
Jonson, *Poetaster*: ''Tis the common
disease of all your musicians that they
know no mean [moderation] to be
entreated, either to begin or end'
(2.2.188–9).

15 *stanzo* the fashionable Italian name for
a verse, first recorded by the *OED* in
Greene's *Menaphon* (1589), and first
used by Shakespeare in *LLL* 4.2.103
('stanza' as in Q, 'stanze' F).

16 **What you will** as you like (it) (proverbial, Dent, W280.5), the subtitle of

TN and the title of Marston's play
What You Will (performed 1600–1?),
both possible participants in the 'War
of the Theatres' with which *AYL* may
also have been connected; see
Appendix 3.

17–18 **names . . . nothing** a legal joke.
Payment of debts in the Inns of Court
was due on particular days, and the
names of those owing money were
noted in account books (Cressy, 10);
Nomina. Cic. (Cicero) is glossed in
Cooper, *Thesaurus* (1578), as 'The
names of debtes owen' (sig. Nnnn4ᵛ,
cited in Ard²). For Jaques's material-
ism see p. 93.

22 **dog-apes** baboons or male apes who
mimic each other; see 3.2.394n.

24 **the beggarly thanks** the effusive
thanks of a beggar for a small reward.
The redundant use of the definite article is common in Midlands dialect
(Northall, *Word-Book*, 239); cf. *the
arm's end*, 2.6.10, and see 3.5.109n.

14–15] *Pope; F lines* me, / sing: / stanzo's? /

AMIENS   Well, I'll end the song. Sirs, cover the while. The
    Duke will drink under this tree; he hath been all this
    day to look you.

JAQUES   And I have been all this day to avoid him; he is
    too disputable for my company. I think of as many   30
    matters as he, but I give heaven thanks and make no
    boast of them. Come, warble, come.

AMIENS (*Sings.*)

>   Who doth ambition shun
>   And loves to live i'th' sun,
>   Seeking the food he eats   35
>   And pleased with what he gets,
>   Come hither, come hither, come hither!

---

26 **Sirs** several lords are implied; see
0.1–2n.
cover the while in the meantime
spread the cloth (for the Duke's
meal). In *Hunting* a woodcut (91,
reproduced in Berry, *Hunt*, 5) shows
the hunters sitting on the ground with
the queen (replaced by James I in the
1616 edition) on a raised mound covered with material. A simple cloth on
stage would solve the problem, perceived by some editors, that in the next
scene when Adam is starving the meal
remains visible to the audience.

28 **look** look for

30 **disputable**   argumentative.   See
Duncan-Jones, *Ungentle*, 122–5, for
connections between Jaques and
Jonson; see also Appendix 3.

31 **matters** questions of material significance; Jaques's use of the word links
him with Bacon's Natural philosophy,
which insisted on the primacy of
material forms: 'Here, therefore, is
the first distemper of learning, when

men study words and not matter'
(*Advancement*, 24); see 2.1.68n.,
3.2.30n. and 3.3.29n.

31–2 **give . . . boast** Cf. *MA* 3.3.19–20:
'give God thanks, and make no boast of
it' (Knowles).

32 **warble** sing, with some sense of
affected trilling; cf. *LLL* 3.1.1–2:
'Warble, child, make passionate my
sense of hearing.'

33 **ambition** the curse of courts, contrasted with pastoral content; see
2.7.43n. and 3.2.70–4n.

34 **i'th' sun** in the open air, away
from the confines of the indoor and
envious court; the sun was also frequently used as a metaphor for
royal favour. Cf. *AW* 5.3.33–4: 'KING
For thou may'st see a sunshine and a
hail / In me at once.' See Harington's
report of Sir Christopher Hatton's
warning: 'If you have any suite to
daie, I praye you put it aside. *The sunne
dothe not shine*' (*Nugae Antiquae*,
2.220–1).

---

27 drink] Dine *Rowe*   29–32] *Pope; F lines* him: / companie: / giue / them. / come. /   33 SP]
Capell; All / Hudson; not in F   SD] *Sisson; Song. Altogether heere. F; They sing 'altogether here'
Cam¹*   34 live] *lye F4*

212

ALL [*Sing.*]

> Here shall he see no enemy
> But winter and rough weather.

JAQUES   I'll give you a verse to this note that I made   40
yesterday in despite of my invention.

AMIENS   And I'll sing it.

JAQUES   Thus it goes. [*Gives Amiens a paper.*]

AMIENS [*Sings.*]

> If it do come to pass
> That any man turn ass,   45
> Leaving his wealth and ease
> A stubborn will to please,
> Ducdame, ducdame, ducdame!

ALL [*Sing.*]

> Here shall he see gross fools as he
> An if he will come to me.   50

AMIENS   What's that 'ducdame'?

JAQUES   'Tis a Greek invocation to call fools into a circle.

---

40   **note** tune
41   **despite** scorn
      invention creation; Miola notes that
      the word derives from Cicero, *De
      Inventione*: '*Inventio* . . . [is] . . . the
      first of five steps in the construction of
      an oration or literary work' (Jonson,
      EMI, 242). Jaques claims that his par-
      ody trivializes his poetic inspiration by
      a 'marring' of text (see 1.1.31n.).
43   SP *F's repetition of '*Amy.*' is prob-
      ably a mistake.
44   SP, SD *Many editors and directors
      have Jaques speak his parody, but 42
      authorizes Amiens to sing; see 2.7.4,
      where Jaques is described as 'merry,
      hearing of a song'.
45   **ass** fool; probably also a pun on 'arse'
48   **Ducdame** trisyllabic; a nonsense
      word to summon the Lords, as *Come*

hither, 5, 37. In 1891 Strachey
suggested connections with gipsy cant
– another possible link with Jonson,
who was fascinated by gipsies (see
Gypsies, 1621). In Dekker, *Satiromastix*
(1602), another play involved in the
'War of the Theatres' (see 16n.),
Horace (= Jonson) is described as
'the poore saffron-cheeke Sun-burnte
Gipsie' (1.2.367).
51   SP If Amiens sings the song F's SP is
      redundant, unless the Lords have sung
      the chorus, which this edition assumes.
52   **Greek invocation** nonsense incanta-
      tion; cf. 'Pedlars' Greek', i.e. 'rogues'
      cant' (Ard²) and *TN* 4.1.17, 'foolish
      Greek' (i.e. jester).
      fools . . . circle a conjuring image,
      making fools of the circle of listening
      lords; cf. Orlando's tricking of Jaques

---

38 SD] *Capell subst.; All together here* Ard² *opp.* 37   38–9 *no . . . weather] Pope; &c.* F   40–1] *Pope;
F lines* note, / Inuention. /   43 SP] *F2; Amy.* F   SD] *Sisson subst.*   44 SP] *Sisson; not in* F   SD]
Sisson   44–5] *F3; one line* F   48+ Ducdame] *Duc ad me* / *Hanmer*   49 SP] *this edn;
not in* F   SD] *this edn*   49] *Pope lines* see / he, /

I'll go sleep if I can; if I cannot, I'll rail against all the
first-born of Egypt.

AMIENS   And I'll go seek the Duke; his banquet is   55
prepared.   *Exeunt.*

2.6   *Enter* ORLANDO *and* ADAM.

ADAM

Dear master,
I can go no further. O, I die for food!
Here lie I down and measure out my grave.
Farewell, kind master.

ORLANDO

Why, how now, Adam? No greater heart in thee?   5
Live a little, comfort a little, cheer thyself a little. If this

---

at 3.2.279–80. The satirical barb also
grazes the theatre audience, gathered
round to watch the play (see 5.4.34n.).
The emblem of the circle was a
Jonsonian favourite (Donaldson,
Magic, 28–31; see also Bevington,
'Review', 317).
53 **rail** inveigh; see 1.1.58n.
54 **first-born of Egypt** a reference to the
plague on the first-born of Egypt in
Exodus, 11.5, but also possibly to gipsies. Cf. Dekker, *Lantern*: 'Gipsies . . .
call themselues Egyptians, others in
mockery call them Moone-men . . .
because . . . the Moone is neuer in one
shape two nights together, but wanders
vp and downe Heaven, like an Anticke'
(sig. E3ᵛ); cf. *1H4* 1.2.25. Jaques satirizes both the exiled courtiers and
Shakespeare's own players – also seen,
like gipsies, as antics and vagabonds –
in a typically Jonsonian 'own goal'
trajectory; see 1.1.112n., 2.3.32–3, and
pp. 71, 102.
55 **banquet** Withals's *Dictionary* (1599)
defines *banquet* as any meal (sig. H2ʳ),

but cf. *OED sb.*[1] 3, 'a course of sweet-
meats, fruit, and wine'. Only drink
(27) and fruit (2.7.99) are mentioned,
but something more substantial would
be required to relieve the starving
Adam, even if it were only bread.
2.6 In F the scene is set in blank verse.
Pope's decision to turn it into prose is
usually adopted by editors on the
assumption that Compositor B turned
prose into verse to fill up space
on page 192 of F so that 2.7 could
begin page 193 (Var 1890). This edition assumes that the exhausted Adam
speaks in free verse (as in F) and that
Orlando's first line is a verse response,
quickly turning to informal prose (as
Pope) for the encouragement of his
servant.
2 Cf. Celia's weariness on entering
Arden (2.4.9, 62, and see Fig. 7).
5 **heart** courage; cf. 4.3.164, 172.
6 Rosalind enters Arden acquiring manhood, while Orlando enters in a nurturing and maternal role (Erickson, 74;
see 2.7.129n. and see pp. 31–2).

55–6] *Pope; F lines* Duke, / prepar'd. /   **2.6]** *(Scena Sexta.)*   Location] *Another part of the forest /
Malone*   1–4] *this edn; F lines* further: / downe, / master. / ; *prose Pope*   5] *prose Pope*

uncouth forest yield anything savage I will either be
food for it or bring it for food to thee. Thy conceit is
nearer death than thy powers. For my sake, be
comfortable; hold death awhile at the arm's end. I will   10
here be with thee presently, and if I bring thee not
something to eat I will give thee leave to die. But if thou
diest before I come, thou art a mocker of my labour.
Well said, thou look'st cheerly, and I'll be with thee
quickly. Yet thou liest in the bleak air. Come, I will bear   15
thee to some shelter and thou shalt not die for lack of a
dinner if there live anything in this desert. Cheerly,
good Adam.   *Exeunt.*

2.7   *Enter* DUKE SENIOR, [AMIENS] *and* Lords
          [*dressed*] *as outlaws.*

DUKE SENIOR
I think he be transformed into a beast,

---

7 **uncouth** wild and uncivilized;
unknown (*OED* A 1 *obs.*)
savage wild (Fr. *sauvage*), implying
animals hunted for food
8 **food for it** prepares the way for the
lioness, 4.3.146
8–9 **Thy . . . powers** 'Your imagination
[*conceit*] convinces you that you are
closer to death than you really are'
(*powers* = physical capacity).
10 **comfortable** willing to be comforted;
cf. 1.3.128n.
awhile for a time
at . . . end at arm's length; see 2.5.24n.
11 **presently** immediately
14 **Well said** well done, not necessarily
implying speech; cf. *AC* 4.5.28.
cheerly (F cheerely) cheerful
15 **liest . . . air** A wintry Arden is not
merely metaphor; see 2.1.7n.

bear See 2.7.167.1n. for Orlando's
carrying of Adam.
17 **desert** unpopulated place
Cheerly cheerfully (cf. 14)
2.7.0.1 **Lords** F's '*Lord*' may refer to the
speaking part, but the phrase '*and others*' (see 2.1.0.1–2, '*two or three* Lords')
may have been omitted. Amiens –
unnamed here – is invited to sing by
the Duke (174).
0.2 'Outlaws' and 'foresters' would have
been indistinguishable in the theatre,
which may account for inconsistency
in the text; for '*like*' see 2.1.0.2n.
outlaws beyond the aegis of the law
(because in the Forest); a word always
used to describe Robin Hood's men.
Cf. *TGV* 4.1, 5.3, where, however,
Valentine's followers are felons.
1 **he** i.e. Jaques – a characteristic

6–18] *Pope; F lines* thy selfe a little. / sauage, / thee: / powers. / a while / presently, / eate, / diest /
labor. / cheerely, / liest / thee / die / dinner, / Desert. / *Adam.* / **2.7**] *(Scena Septima.)* Location]
Another part of the FOREST *Johnson*   0.1 DUKE SENIOR] Old Duke *Douai ms*   AMIENS] *Capell*   Lords]
Rowe; Lord F   0.2 *dressed*] *Oxf*   as] *Oxf; like F*   outlaws] *(Out-lawes); foresters Oxf*

For I can nowhere find him like a man.

1 LORD

My lord, he is but even now gone hence;

Here was he merry, hearing of a song.

DUKE SENIOR

If he, compact of jars, grow musical,   5

We shall have shortly discord in the spheres.

Go seek him, tell him I would speak with him.

Enter JAQUES.

1 LORD

He saves my labour by his own approach.

DUKE SENIOR

Why, how now, Monsieur! What a life is this

That your poor friends must woo your company!   10

What, you look merrily.

Shakespearean opening, where a character is not directly named, which creates for the audience an impression of intercepting a conversation already under way; see 3.1, 5.2.

transformed . . . beast an educated joke, recalling the myths of Actaeon (Ovid, *Met.*; see 2.1.38-9n.), and of Circe (in Homer's *Odyssey*). The Renaissance credo that men were distinguished from beasts by the possession of reason (Ficino, *Mind*, 206) is placed under scrutiny in the Forest of Arden; cf. 101, 4.3.49n.

2 **nowhere** The two words *no where* in all Folios suggest *utopia*, 'no place' (Greek = *ou topos*) or 'good place' (*eu topos*), as in Thomas More's *Utopia*; see Berry, *Hunt*, 168.
   like shaped like
3 **but even** only just
4 **merry . . . song** Jaques's habitual melancholy has been transformed into

mirth by his mockery of Amiens's song, another opening (as in 1.2, 1.3, 2.4, 2.5, 3.4, 4.1) which juxtaposes merriment and melancholy.

5 **compact of jars** composed of discords and dissonances; see 2.5.13–15n. The image had currency at court, for John Chamberlain wrote to Dudley Carleton on 15 February 1599 of the discontents fomenting around the queen's delay in commissioning Essex to Ireland: 'The jarres continue as they did, if not worse, by daily renewing, and our musicke runs so much upon discords that I feare what harmonie they will make of it in the end' (*Chamberlain*, 44; see pp. 72–6).

6 **discord . . . spheres** In the Ptolemaic universe the spheres circled the heavens making a music which was believed to be necessary for harmony on earth.

9 **What a life** what sort of existence

7.1] *after 8 Dyce*

JAQUES

A fool, a fool! I met a fool i'th' forest,
A motley fool – a miserable world!
As I do live by food, I met a fool,
Who laid him down and basked him in the sun,   15
And railed on Lady Fortune in good terms,
In good set terms – and yet a motley fool!
'Good morrow, fool,' quoth I. 'No, sir,' quoth he,
'Call me not fool till heaven hath sent me fortune.'
And then he drew a dial from his poke,   20
And looking on it with lack-lustre eye
Says very wisely, 'It is ten o'clock.

12–34 Jaques's eulogy enhances the fool's role in the play and recalls the apostrophizing in Rabelais's *Tiers Livre* (Rabelais/Urquhart, 3.444–52, 475–80) of Triboulet, fool to Louis XII and Francis I (Welsford, 147–8).

13 motley 'His dress should be a party-coloured garment' (Douce, *Illustrations*, 1.309); cf. Armin, *Fool*: 'Motley his wearing, yellow or else greene' (1. sig. A3ᵛ), suggesting a variegated weave rather than separate segments of different-coloured cloth (see also Knowles); see 34, 3.3.72n., 5.4.41. a miserable world Cf. 3.2.270–1, where Jaques invites Orlando to 'rail against our mistress the world and all our misery'. Jaques remembers just in time, amidst laughing at the fool, his own role as melancholy satirist.

16 Lady Fortune Touchstone's raillery gives Fortune a higher social status than she is allowed by Celia, to whom she is merely a *housewife*; see 1.2.31n. and cf. 3.2.270n.

17 good set terms formulaic maxims used in rhetoric (Ard²; see Thorne, 9–10). See Bacon's section on *Formulae* in *Advancement*: 'decent and apt passages or conveyances of speech, which may serve indifferently [i.e. equally appropriately] for differing subjects' (150), indexed by Kitchin as 'set passages' (239); see 1.3.107, 5.4.59–61, 63n.

18–19 No . . . fortune Touchstone (as Jaques reports) declares that before he can be called a fool fortune must favour him. The Latin proverb *Fortuna favet fatuis* (Fortune favours fools) was a favourite with Jonson (see *EMI*, 147).

20 dial an elaborate pocket timepiece and navigational instrument, as depicted in the frontispiece to Harington's *OF* (see Fig. 17 and Appendix 1). Touchstone may possibly draw out the much rarer pocket sundial.
poke bag

21 lack-lustre dull, disaffected (*OED*, *a*. and *n*., first example)

22–5 It . . . eleven Time hangs heavily in the Forest for the court jester (a heavy tale/tail); cf. *tedious*, 3.2.18.

13 fool . . . world!] *Theobald subst.;* Foole (a miserable world:) *F*   15 basked] baked *Douai ms*

Thus we may see', quoth he, 'how the world wags.
'Tis but an hour ago since it was nine,
And after one hour more 'twill be eleven.   25
And so from hour to hour we ripe and ripe,
And then from hour to hour we rot and rot,
And thereby hangs a tale.' When I did hear
The motley fool thus moral on the time,
My lungs began to crow like chanticleer,   30
That fools should be so deep-contemplative,
And I did laugh *sans* intermission
An hour by his dial. O noble fool,
A worthy fool! Motley's the only wear!

DUKE SENIOR
What fool is this?   35

JAQUES
O worthy fool! – One that hath been a courtier,

---

23 **wags** goes on, as a dog wags its tail;
possibly a jest at Harington, whose dog
Bungay is depicted in his frontispiece
next to his pocket dial (see Fig. 17)

26–7 **we ripe . . . we rot** the cycle of
nature (Dent, R133). Cf. Spenser, *SC*,
E.K.'s emblem to 'November': 'For
although by course of nature we be
borne to dye, and being ripened with
age, as with a timely harvest, we must
be gathered in time, or els of our selves
we fall like rotted ripe fruite fro the
tree' (p. 483); cf. *KL* 5.2.11: 'Ripeness
is all.'

28 **hangs a tale** a tail (an end); cf.
1.2.114.

29 **moral** either a verb: moralize; or an
adjective: the moral character of the
fool (Furness)

30 **chanticleer** the traditional name for a
cock (from the story of Reynard the
Fox) used by Chaucer for his braggart
cock, 'Chaunteclere', in 'The Nun's
Priest's Tale': 'In all the land, of crowing nas his pere [peer]' (fol. 85ᵛ). Cf.

91n. and see *Tem* 1.2.386: 'The strain
of strutting chanticleer'.

31 **deep-contemplative** profoundly
meditative, the condition of the wise
man Jaques feels himself to be; see pp.
106–8.

32 *sans* **intermission** without a break;
sans (Fr. = without) bespeaks affectation, although the anglicized word had
been in use since Chaucer (Douce,
Illustrations, 1.301); see 167. Cf. *LLL*
5.2.416: '*Sans "sans"*, I pray you.' The
title page of the Quarto *LLL* states
that the play was performed at court in
1598. An audience's memory of
Berowne, another French lord – possibly played by Burbage as Jaques may
also have been (see Appendix 2) – may
lie behind Jaques's linguistic affectation; see 1.3.85n.

35–87 cut in the Douai MS; see Appendix
4 and p. 108.

36 **O worthy fool** Jaques ignores the
Duke's question in order to continue
his eulogy. Furness (Var 1890) noted

---

23 we may] you may *Douai ms;* may we *Pope*   31 deep-contemplative] *(*deepe contemplatiue*)*
34 A] O *Cam (Anon)*   35–87] *om. Douai ms*   36 O] A *Cam (Anon)*

And says if ladies be but young and fair
They have the gift to know it. And in his brain,
Which is as dry as the remainder biscuit
After a voyage, he hath strange places crammed   40
With observation, the which he vents
In mangled forms. O that I were a fool!
I am ambitious for a motley coat.

DUKE SENIOR
   Thou shalt have one.

JAQUES   It is my only suit,

an anonymous suggestion that 33 should read 'O worthy fool' and this line 'A worthy fool' (Knowles), but F is characteristic of Jaques.

38–42 **And . . . forms** a description of the fool's mental processes which justifies the use of the term *motley-minded* (see 5.4.41n.); Touchstone's wayward combination of wisdom and folly, symbolized by his parti-coloured garment, contrasts with the later claim of Feste in *TN* 1.5.53–4: 'I wear not motley in my brain'.

39 **dry** applicable to the fool's witty commonplaces as well as to stale biscuits; cf. Jonson, *EMO*: 'a drie bisket jest' (Induction, 164).
   remainder biscuit provisions left at the end of a voyage – a reminder of the experiences of Elizabethan travellers; cf. 2.4.16n. and see 5.4.189–90n. In Hall's *Virgidemiarum* (1599) the foreign traveller is mocked, in a satire which transparently pillories Ralegh, for 'his parch'd Bisket' (4.6, p. 48; see 4.1.20n.).

40 **strange places** The *loci communes* (common places; see Ard² and Thorne, 11–12) of rhetoric transmute in the fool's brain to odd and unfamiliar *topoi*, like the exotic territories discovered by travellers.

40–1 **crammed . . . observation** cf.

news-crammed, 1.2.94. The traveller's brain is stuffed with reflections on his voyages, just as his stomach is crammed with stale food.

41 **vents** lets out or evacuates, suggesting breaking wind (Lat. *ventus*): the physical consequence of *crammed*; but also the 'hot air' both of the over-voluble traveller eager to recount his adventures and of the foolish jester. Sir William Cornwallis describes jesting as 'onely tollerable in them whose natures must of force haue that vent, which vse it as some bodies do breaking of winde' ('Of Jests and Jesters', Essay 13, sigs H2ᵛ–3ʳ). See *rank*, 46 and n. and 1.2.104n., and cf. *TN* 4.1.9: 'I prithee vent thy folly somewhere else.'

42 **mangled forms** disordered shapes; possibly a printing metaphor, describing mis-collated 'formes' (pages), or broken type. The *good set terms* of Touchstone's speech at 17 have become jumbled (see 38–42n.).

42–3 **O . . . coat** Jaques's eulogy of the fool emblazons his belief in his own wisdom.

43 **ambitious** Jaques, a supreme ironist, aspires not to wealth, power or position, but to the liberty of the fool.

44 **suit** plea, i.e. legal suit, and a suit of clothes; cf. 4.1.80–1n.

37–8 if . . . it] 'If . . . it.' *Oxf*

Provided that you weed your better judgements   45
Of all opinion that grows rank in them
That I am wise. I must have liberty
Withal, as large a charter as the wind
To blow on whom I please, for so fools have,
And they that are most galled with my folly,   50
They most must laugh. And why, sir, must they so?
The why is plain as way to parish church.
He that a fool doth very wisely hit
Doth very foolishly, although he smart,
Not to seem senseless of the bob. If not,   55
The wise man's folly is anatomized

45–7 **Provided . . . wise** as long as you
disabuse yourselves of the prejudice
that I am a wise man.

46 **rank** gross (homonym with *grows*),
often including foul smells; see
1.2.104. See *vents*, 41 and n.

47 **liberty** freedom, but also crossing the
border into *licence*, 68. Cf. *MM* 1.3.29:
'Liberty plucks justice by the nose'.

48 **Withal** in addition
charter licence, contract; a legal term,
with a pun on *liberty* (licence)
wind Cf. *H5* 1.1.48: 'The air, a char-
tered libertine, is still'; see *liberty* (47)
and *libertine* (65). See also John, 3.8:
'The winde bloweth where it listeth'
(Geneva Bible, cited in Ard²), i.e. where
it pleases or *as it likes*. Jaques comes
close to calling himself a windbag. Cf.
Amiens's song 'Blow, blow, thou winter
wind' (175), and Duke Senior's eulogy
of the biting wind (2.1.6–11) as less venomous than flattery (flatulence? see 41).

49 **so fools have** a reference to the special
licence of the 'allowed fool' (*TN*
1.5.91); see 1.2.83–9, and cf. *KL*
1.4.191: 'this your all-licensed fool'.

50 **galled** (gallèd) provoked, an image from
riding; cf. *R2* 5.5.94: 'Spurred, galled
and tired by jauncing Bolingbroke'.

51 **And . . . so?** Jaques creates a dialogue
with himself; see 83.

52 'The reason is as easy to find as a well-
trodden footpath leading to a church'
(in days when church-going was com-
pulsory).
as way For the omission of the article
see Abbott, 83.
parish church suggests an English
church; see 3.2.152nn., 309n., 3.3.39n.,
77–9n.

53–5 **He . . . bob** 'He who is wounded by
the fool's well-aimed blow behaves very
stupidly if he does not pretend – even
while he is smarting under the wound –
that the shaft has missed its mark.'

55 *****Not to** Theobald's addition of *Not* to
a metrically short line makes the meaning clear while regularizing the scansion and creating the rhetorical figure
epanalepsis (beginning and ending a
line with the same word, as at 91). The
wise man's defence against the fool's
jibe lies in his apparent indifference to
it (but cf. Cam²).
bob knock, light glancing blow;
'"rap", jibe, taunt' (Onions, 19).

56 **anatomized** exposed as in an anatomy lesson; cf. *KL* 3.6.73–4: 'Then let
them anatomize Regan'.

52 why] way *Rowe²*   55 Not to seem] *Theobald;* Seeme *F;* Seem aught but *Oxf;* If he seem *Cam²*
56 wise man's] *(*Wise-mans*);* wiseman's *Ard²*

Even by the squandering glances of the fool.
Invest me in my motley. Give me leave
To speak my mind, and I will through and through
Cleanse the foul body of th'infected world,   60
If they will patiently receive my medicine.

DUKE SENIOR

Fie on thee! I can tell what thou wouldst do.

JAQUES

What, for a counter, would I do but good?

DUKE SENIOR

Most mischievous foul sin in chiding sin.
For thou thyself hast been a libertine,   65
As sensual as the brutish sting itself,
And all th'embossed sores and headed evils

---

57 **squandering** extravagant, literally 'wandering about' (*OED ppl. a.* 2, first example)
glances looks; but also the glancing arrow of the fool's taunt, which shies off his victim without wounding him.
58 **Invest** clothe in official robes
58–9 **Give . . . mind** Free speech was the luxury of fools in a repressive society, and was associated with unruly women; cf. Kate's claim in *TS* 4.3.75: 'Your betters have endur'd me say my mind' (Dusinberre, '*TS*', 179–80).
60 **Cleanse . . . foul . . . infected** medical language typical of 1590s satire, linking Jaques as satirist with Marston, Hall, Donne, Lodge and Jonson; see pp. 22, 124.
62 **Fie on thee** for shame
63 **counter** a base metal coin of no value (cf. *WT* 4.3.36: 'I cannot do 't without counters'); possibly also punning on the hunting term: 'When a hound hunteth backwards the same way that the chase is come, the[n] we say he hunteth *Counter*' (*Hunting*, 114). Cf. *Ham* 4.5.110: 'O, this is counter, you false Danish dogs.' Jaques's moral

satire turns back on himself, because he also has been a libertine.
64 **foul sin** i.e. hypocrisy, because of Jaques's own debauched history. For connections between this attack on Jaques and the 'purge' alleged by 'Kempe' to have been administered to Jonson by Shakespeare in *2 Parnassus*, see Appendix 3.
65 **libertine** debauched person. The word also describes the adherents (including Donne and Montaigne) of Libertine or Natural philosophy associated with Epictetus, Cicero and Seneca (Ornstein, 133); see 2.1.68n., 3.2.30n. Renaissance Libertines 'appropriated Nature as their goddess and the Golden Age as their ideal' (Bredvold, 493).
66 **brutish sting** sting of an animal, with implications of lust
67 **embossed sores** (embossèd) scabs, indicative of venereal disease
headed evils boils which have come to a head and are about to break out (*OED* headed *a.* and *pa. ppl.* 4, only example); cf. Thersites, *TC* 2.1.2–6.

---

57 squandering] *(squandring)*

That thou with licence of free foot hast caught
Wouldst thou disgorge into the general world.

JAQUES

Why, who cries out on pride   70
That can therein tax any private party?
Doth it not flow as hugely as the sea
Till that the weary very means do ebb?
What woman in the city do I name,
When that I say the city-woman bears   75
The cost of princes on unworthy shoulders?
Who can come in and say that I mean her,
When such a one as she, such is her neighbour?

---

68 **with . . . foot** ranging about freely; an
activity banned in time of plague to
prevent the spread of infection. See
60n.
licence liberty, but also lack of discipline; see 47n., 58–9n.
70 **cries . . . pride** a fulmination against
pride – a pastime of both Church and
State in this period. Marston's
Histriomastix (1599) – a play implicated in the 'War of the Theatres' (see
Appendix 3) – contains a character
called 'Pride'.
71 **tax** accuse; cf. *taxation*, 1.2.84 and n.
Jaques offers the standard satirist's
disclaimer. Cf. Lodge, *Fig*: 'where I
reprehend vice, I purposely wrong no
man' (sig. A3ʳ); Jonson, *EMO*: 'The
happier spirits in this fair-filled
Globe . . . And are too wise to think
themselves are taxed / In any general
figure' (quarto, new ending, Appendix
A, p. 377, ll. 36–9). But despite the
disclaimers, McCabe (192) suggests
that it was the ease of identifying
individuals in satire which prompted
the Bishops' censorship in June
1599 (see 1.2.87–8n.). Essex dreaded
satirists and feared the players

'shortly . . . will play me in what forms
they list upon the stage' (Birch, 2.445);
cf. 4.1.20n. for Hall's jibe at Ralegh in
Virgidemiarum.
party individual
72–82 Pride flows like *the sea*, and is
maintained by waves of spending – the
extravagance of city-women – involving *cost* (76, 80) and *mettle* (metal); see
82n.
73 **the . . . ebb** 'the very resources which
create pride decrease from weariness,
as waves diminish with the ebbing tide'
means highlights the second meaning
of *tax*, i.e. to exact money; a *tax* on
pride eventually exhausts pride itself.
74 **woman . . . city** particular woman; cf.
private party, 71.
75 **When that** if
city-woman generic
76 **cost of princes** the price of extravagant dressing above her station (a topical Elizabethan lament with ancient
precedents; cf. 2.1.50n.); possibly also
an allusion (disguised as an attack on
city women) to antagonism between
city money and court extravagance.
78 when her neighbour's extravagance
matches her own

73 weary very means] very very means *Pope;* wearer's very means *Singer;* very means, weary, *(RP)*
75 city-woman] *(City woman)*

Or what is he of basest function,
That says his bravery is not on my cost –   80
Thinking that I mean him – but therein suits
His folly to the mettle of my speech?
There then – how then, what then? Let me see wherein
My tongue hath wronged him. If it do him right,
Then he hath wronged himself. If he be free,   85
Why then my taxing like a wild goose flies
Unclaimed of any man. But who comes here?

Enter ORLANDO [*with sword drawn*].

ORLANDO

Forbear and eat no more!

JAQUES   Why, I have ate none yet.

ORLANDO

Nor shalt not till necessity be served.   90

JAQUES   Of what kind should this cock come of?

---

79 **function** office, occupation
80 **bravery** finery
   on my cost paid for by me
81–2 **suits . . . speech** makes his foolishness fit my description of it (a pun on
   suits as 'fits' and a 'suit of clothes')
82 **mettle** quality, spirit, with a pun on
   'metal' (gold), which is paid and spent
   in the maintaining of pride. Cf. *KL*
   1.1.69–70: 'Sir I am made of that self
   mettle [the selfe same mettall, Q] as
   my sister, / And prize me at her
   worth', where 'prize' implies price as
   well as value.
83 **There . . . how then** Well, what about
   it? Cf. 51n.
84 **do him right** makes a just accusation
85 **wronged himself** slandered himself
   (by denying the truth)
   free blameless

86–7 My accusation flies off like a wild
   goose whom no one has hit, so it can't
   be claimed as a prize by any hunter; cf.
   the proverbial 'wild goose chase'
   (Dent, W390).
89 **ate** eaten
90 **Nor shalt not** The second person singular implies command, anger and
   possibly scorn (see 1.1.52n.).
91 The rhetorical figure *epanalepsis*
   (see 55n.) emphasizes Jaques's disre-
   spect.
   cock implying that Orlando crows
   (brags); see 30n. Theatres were used for
   cock-fighting and bear-baiting on non-
   playing nights (Scott-Warren, 'Bear-
   gardens', 64); see 3.2.187–8n. For cocks
   and Shrove Tuesday sports see
   Laroque, 61. Jaques hints that Orlando
   has strayed into the wrong show.

---

82 mettle] metal *Theobald*   83 There] Where *Hudson² (Malone)*   then –] *Cam¹ subst.;* then, *F;* then;
Theobald then,] then? *Theobald* then?] *Theobald;* then, *F*   87.1 *with sword drawn*] *Theobald*
89 ate] *(*eate*)*

DUKE SENIOR

Art thou thus boldened, man, by thy distress?
Or else a rude despiser of good manners,
That in civility thou seem'st so empty?

ORLANDO

You touched my vein at first. The thorny point   95
Of bare distress hath ta'en from me the show
Of smooth civility; yet am I inland bred
And know some nurture. But forbear, I say!
He dies that touches any of this fruit
Till I and my affairs are answered.   100

JAQUES   An you will not be answered with reason, I must
die.

DUKE SENIOR

What would you have? Your gentleness shall force
More than your force move us to gentleness.

ORLANDO

I almost die for food – and let me have it.   105

DUKE SENIOR

Sit down and feed and welcome to our table.

ORLANDO

Speak you so gently? Pardon me, I pray you.
I thought that all things had been savage here

92 **boldened** emboldened
94 **empty** Orlando is as empty of courtesy as his stomach is of food.
95 **touched my vein** hit upon my condition, as of a surgeon opening a vein
   thorny point Cf. *briers*, 1.3.12.
96–7 **show . . . civility** appearance of
   civilized and courteous manners; cf.
   1.3.74n.
97 **inland bred** brought up in the court;
   see 3.2.333 and p. 96.
98 **nurture** good breeding; cf. 1.1.19–20.
100 **answered** answerèd; perhaps similarly accented by Jaques at 101 in mockery of Orlando's blank verse (Cam²)

101 **An** if
   reason Malone saw *reason* (Fr. *raison*)
   as a pun on 'raisin' (Fr. = grape) as
   Monsieur Jaques helps himself to the
   fruit; see 2.5.55n.
103 **What . . . have?** What do you want?
   gentleness . . . force The reversed
   order in 104 creates the rhetorical
   figure *chiasmus* (see 2.4.51–2n.).
107 **gently** kindly, but also as a nobleman
108 **had** would have
   savage wild and uncivilized; see 2.6.7.
   Cf. *H5* 5.2.59–60: 'But grow like sav-
   ages, as soldiers will / That nothing do
   but meditate on blood'.

97 inland] *(in-land)*   103–4] *Pope; F lines* haue? / your force / gentleness. /

And therefore put I on the countenance
Of stern commandment. But whate'er you are, 110
That in this desert inaccessible,
Under the shade of melancholy boughs,
Lose and neglect the creeping hours of time –
If ever you have looked on better days,
If ever been where bells have knolled to church, 115
If ever sat at any good man's feast,
If ever from your eyelids wiped a tear,
And know what 'tis to pity and be pitied –
Let gentleness my strong enforcement be,
In the which hope, I blush and hide my sword. 120
DUKE SENIOR
True is it that we have seen better days,

109 **put I on** I assumed
countenance both look and manner
110 **commandment** giving of orders
112 **melancholy** an early instance of the 'pathetic fallacy'; the shade of the boughs induces melancholy in the human witness of it; see pp. 53, 107, 116 and Fig. 12.
114, 115, 116, 117 **If ever** The rhetorical figure *anaphora* – words repeated at the beginning of a phrase or clause – creates the effect of a liturgy; see 122–6.
115 **bells . . . church** not in Lodge; see 122n. The bells of St Mary Overies church close to the Globe could have been heard by an audience during a performance (Kay).
knolled combines the tolling of the bell to summon the faithful to church, and the knell for the dead; see *Tem* 1.2.403: 'Sea nymphs hourly ring his knell.'
116 **good man's feast** F's 'good mans' suggests that hospitality is provided by a man of virtue and compassion (cf. Cam²: 'goodman's', i.e. 'host's'). Cf.

Matthew, 22.2–14, the parable of the lord who, when his followers disdained to attend his feast, dispatched his servants into the highways and byways to seek out the dispossessed (as both Orlando and the banished Duke are here).
118 **pity** both chivalric and Christian, as in Theseus's compassion for the Theban widows in Chaucer's 'Knight's Tale': 'This gentle duke downe fro[m] his horse [courser] stert / With hert pitous' (fol. 1ʳ); dramatized by Shakespeare in *TNK* 1.1.
120 **I blush** Blushing is usually associated with women (see 1.2.28–9n.), but here Orlando blushes for shame (not rage as in Lodge; e.g. sig. B3ᵛ). Harington protested that blushing as a sign of chastity and modesty ought to be as welcome in men as in women: 'how happie may this realme be, if it may have a King that will blushe' (*Succession*, 87); cf. 3.4.16n.
121–4 liturgical patterning echoing 114–18

113 Lose] *F4;* Loose *F*   116 good man's] *(*good mans*)*; goodman's *Cam²*

And have with holy bell been knolled to church,
And sat at good men's feasts, and wiped our eyes
Of drops that sacred pity hath engendered;
And therefore sit you down in gentleness   125
And take upon command what help we have
That to your wanting may be ministered.

ORLANDO

Then but forbear your food a little while,
Whiles like a doe I go to find my fawn,
And give it food. There is an old poor man   130
Who after me hath many a weary step
Limped in pure love. Till he be first sufficed,
Oppressed with two weak evils, age and hunger,
I will not touch a bit.

DUKE SENIOR   Go find him out,
And we will nothing waste till you return.   135

ORLANDO

I thank ye, and be blest for your good comfort.   [*Exit.*]

---

122 **holy bell** See 115; church bells were
rung for services, weddings and funer-
als, as well as for midsummer, new year,
and Christian holy-days. They were
supposed to have a protective effect
against devils and spirits (Cressy,
69–70). Both references to bells were
cut in the Douai MS, possibly on the
grounds that the subject was too holy
for a profane play; see Appendix 4.
126 **upon command** at your own urgent
request, sanctioned by our authority
127 **wanting** need
ministered served, but also with a
pun on the ministry of a church; cf.
TN 1.5.84, where Malvolio's taunt to
Feste, 'minister occasion', prompts the
terms of the fool's revenge as Sir
Topas: 'the minister is here' (4.2.94).
129 **doe . . . fawn** Orlando casts himself
as a female deer finding food for her

youngling (Erickson, 75; see 2.6.5n.), a
contrast with the masculine setting in
which men hunt *stags* (see 2.1.62n.)
and fear *horns* (3.3.44–58 and
4.2.14–19).
132 **Limped** Cf. Adam's evocation of age
and youth, winter and springtime,
2.3.47–53; cf. *RJ* 1.2.26–8: 'Such comfort as do lusty young men feel / When
well-apparell'd April on the heel / Of
limping winter treads'.
sufficed satisfied
133 **weak evils** evils which cause weakness (Oxf[1])
136 **ye** either an especially polite form to
the Duke (Abbott, 236), or thanks
addressed to the whole company, as
Orlando's original challenge had been;
a common biblical form in keeping
with the language of the preceding
dialogue

123 good men's] *(good mens)*; goodmen's *Cam*[2]   135 you] your *Douai ms, Theobald*[3]   136 SD] *Douai ms, Rowe*

DUKE SENIOR

Thou seest we are not all alone unhappy.
This wide and universal theatre
Presents more woeful pageants than the scene
Wherein we play in.

JAQUES   All the world's a stage,   140
And all the men and women merely players.
They have their exits and their entrances,
And one man in his time plays many parts,
His acts being seven ages. At first the infant,

137 **Thou seest we** The singular *Thou*,
dictated by the solemnity of the senti-
ment and enhancing the musicality
of the line, should be addressed not
just to Jaques, who answers it, but
to the assembled company of exiled
courtiers.
   alone unhappy the only unfortunate
ones
139 **pageants** plays (see 3.4.48), from the
pageant-wagon on which the Guilds
performed the medieval mystery plays;
by Shakespeare's time, any kind of
dramatic performance. Cf. *TGV*
4.4.157: 'When all our pageants of
delight were played'.
   scene continues the theatrical
metaphor; see *acts*, 144 and n..
140–67 **All . . . everything** This great
speech, based on both classical and
medieval sources, acts as a focal point
in both the play's self-consciousness
about dramatic performance and its
implicit defence of the theatre against
detractors. Lodge had penned the
earliest defence (*c.* 1580) against the
attacks of Stephen Gosson (1579), and
in *Margarite* (1596) he compares life to
a play and discusses the stages of
man's life (Knowles). Jaques's speech
may have given the familiar image new
currency. Withals's *Dictionary* (1599)
describes 'A theatre, Theatrum . . .
This lyfe is a certaine enterlude or

playe, the world is a stage ful of change
euery way, Euery man is a player, and
therein a dealer' (sig. I5ʳ, also cited in
Douce, *Illustrations*, 1.299). Harington
may allude to *AYL* in a letter to Cecil in
1605: 'that the world is a stage and we
that live in it are all stage players . . .
I playd my chyldes part happily, the
scholler and students part to
neglygently, the sowldyer and cowrtyer
faythfully, the husband lovingly, the
countryman not basely nor corruptly'
(*Letters*, 31, cited in Gurr, *Playgoing*,
98). Jaques's highlighting of life as a
'role' prepares the ground for the
masquerade of courtship between
Orlando and Rosalind in 3.2.
141 **players** actors; see p. 42 for conjec-
tures about Jaques's speech and the
date of the play.
142 **exits** F's italicized '*Exits*' mark the
technical status of the word as stage
direction, as opposed to the descriptive
'entrances' (not italicized).
144 **acts** divisions as in a play, 'not necessarily numbered five' (Hirsh, 223); the
word follows on from *scene*, 139.
Appropriately for this speech, Act 2 is
divided (whether by author, scribe or
playhouse book-keeper) into seven
scenes.
   seven ages The notion of the ages of
man has an ancient pedigree from
Pythagoras, who named four, and

140 play in] play *Douai ms, Rowe*

Mewling and puking in the nurse's arms;   145
Then the whining schoolboy, with his satchel
And shining morning face, creeping like snail
Unwillingly to school; and then the lover,
Sighing like furnace, with a woeful ballad
Made to his mistress' eyebrow; then a soldier,   150
Full of strange oaths and bearded like the pard,
Jealous in honour, sudden and quick in quarrel,
Seeking the bubble reputation
Even in the cannon's mouth; and then the justice,
In fair round belly with good capon lined,   155
With eyes severe and beard of formal cut,
Full of wise saws and modern instances;

Aristotle, three (Cuffe, *Ages*, 115–16); Hippocrates was allegedly the first to name seven (Knowles); see Pont, *Reckoning* (1599), for the relation between the age of the world and the ages of man: 'Others count the ages of the World by seavens' (38); 'commonly, every seaventh yeare, some notable change or accident falleth out in mans life' (41). Pont specifically includes the Golden Age as the first, 'because in it the worlde was governed in innocencie . . . as the Poets recorde' (39); cf. 4.1.87n.

145 **Mewling and puking** wailing (almost 'mewing', as a kitten) and vomiting (*OED* mewl *v.*, puke *v.*, both first examples). Strout (283) notes the predominance of male roles in Jaques's list.

147, 149 **like snail . . . like furnace** See 52n. on *as way*. The image may derive from the poet Maurice Scève (Ormerod, 325).

150 **mistress' eyebrow** a typically Petrarchan extravagance. Kastan and Vickers (165) suggest Shakespeare's familiarity with 'the tradition of the *blason anatomique*', and more specifi-

cally with a collection of poems entitled *Les Blasons anatomiques du corps fémenin*, presented to the Duchess of Ferrara by Clément Marot in 1536; Scève contributed a piece on the 'Eyebrow', selected as the best by the Duchess. See also 3.2.1–10n.

151 **strange** outlandish
    pard leopard

152 **sudden** impetuous, unpredictable

153–4 **bubble . . . mouth** The cannon mouth inflates the bubble of reputation with the same breath with which it fires the bullets which destroy both life and fame.

155 **capon lined** A capon is a castrated cock, halfway in size between chicken and turkey. The justice's stomach is lined with the fat chicken on which he has dined, just as the fair robe which covers his round paunch is lined with fur.

156 **formal cut** trimmed appropriately for the dignity of his office in contrast to the unkempt beard of the active soldier, 151

157 **wise saws** sage sayings, precepts; cf. *TN* 3.4.377: 'We'll whisper o'er a couplet or two of most sage saws.'

145 the] his *Douai ms, Ard¹*   150 mistress'] *(*Mistresse*), Theobald*   a] the *Dyce² (Robson)*   155 good] fat *Douai ms*

And so he plays his part. The sixth age shifts
Into the lean and slippered pantaloon,
With spectacles on nose and pouch on side,   160
His youthful hose well saved, a world too wide
For his shrunk shank, and his big manly voice,
Turning again toward childish treble, pipes
And whistles in his sound. Last scene of all,
That ends this strange eventful history,   165
Is second childishness and mere oblivion,
Sans teeth, *sans* eyes, *sans* taste, *sans* everything.

Enter ORLANDO *bearing* ADAM.

DUKE SENIOR
Welcome. Set down your venerable burden

modern recent, new (Theobald), not, *pace OED* A 4, 'ordinary, commonplace' (citing this line)
instances arguments or examples, used to defend a legal case; cf. 3.2.49, 54, 58.
159 pantaloon baggy trousers worn by an old man over his emaciated calves (*shrunk shank*, 162), hence the name for the stock comic figure in the Italian *commedia dell'arte*; cf. *TS* 3.1.36: 'beguile the old pantaloon'.
160 pouch purse
161 The stockings which the young man thriftily saved for his old age are now too big for him.
a world much
163 childish treble the high-pitched voice of a child. Jonson's '*Epitaph on S [alamon] P [avy]*', the child actor, says he 'did act . . . / Old men so duly / As, sooth, the Parcae thought him one' (Donaldson, *Jonson*, p. 270, ll. 13–17).
treble, pipes F's 'trebble pipes' allows *pipes* to function both as a noun – a high voice operating as a musical pipe – and as a verb (see 164n.): making a

shrill noise as from a wind-pipe. Cf. *TN* 1.4.32: 'thy small pipe'.
164 whistles Wilson, in his *Rhetoric* ('Pronunciation', fols 111ᵛ–112ᵛ), berates children for indistinct articulation, and condemns 'evill voices': 'One pipes out his wordes so smalle, through defaulte of his winde pipe, that ye would thinke he whisteled' (fol. 112ᵛ); see 5.3.12n.
166–7 a bleak description of old age belied by Orlando's tenderness as he enters bearing Adam
166 mere total; see 2.1.61n.
167 *Sans* without; see 32n.
167.1 See 2.6.15–16. One of Shakespeare's brothers, probably Gilbert, allegedly said in old age that he had seen the playwright carried on stage by another actor; it was therefore deduced that Shakespeare played Adam (Var 1778, 1.204, citing William Oldys; see also Capell, *Notes*, 1.60). The Douai MS (1695) has the earliest SD for Orlando's carrying of Adam; see Appendix 4.
168–70 The whole of this scene is in blank verse with the exception of two

163 treble, pipes] *Douai ms, Theobald;* trebble pipes, *F*   167.1 bearing] *Douai ms, Oxf; with F*   168–9] *Douai ms, Rowe³; prose F*

And let him feed.

ORLANDO

I thank you most for him.

ADAM   So had you need;   170

I scarce can speak to thank you for myself.

DUKE SENIOR

Welcome, fall to. I will not trouble you

As yet to question you about your fortunes.

Give us some music, and good cousin, sing.

AMIENS *(Sings.)*

Blow, blow, thou winter wind,   175

Thou art not so unkind

    As man's ingratitude.

Thy tooth is not so keen

---

lines from Jaques which are of studied rudeness (91 and 101–2). At the climax of his courtly civility the Duke would probably speak in blank verse. Orlando's line could complete 169 (Cam²) or start a new line, which would be completed by Adam's half-line (170), rhyming *need* with the Duke's *feed* (169), as here.

168 **venerable** worthy of reverence: cf. Jaques's belittling description of the pantaloon, 158–166. Johnson quotes Ovid's *venerabile onus* (*Met.*, 13.624–5), describing Aeneas's bearing of his father Anchises from the flames of Troy.

172 **fall to** begin eating, 'tuck in'

174 **music** possibly played by a broken consort, which consisted of six instruments: treble and bass viol, bass recorder, lute, cittern and pandora, a 'very unusual combination' for which Morley's *Consort Lessons* (1599) were composed (Dart, *Consort*, 3–7); see 1.2.134–5n., p. 78 and Fig. 15.

cousin a courteous greeting between

nobles implying kinship (see List of Roles, 12n.) and recalling the allegiance between the female cousins, Celia and Rosalind. The Duke's welcome to Orlando contrasts with Frederick's rejection of him (1.2.213–19).

175–94 Amiens's song recapitulates the Duke's opening speech in 2.1, bringing Act 2, with its modulations between mirth and melancholy, to a harmonious finale.

175 **wind** probably pronounced here with a long *i*, as in *unkind* (176), despite the survival in the period of a pronunciation with a short *i* (Cercignani, 58–9)

176 **unkind** cruel, but also unnatural; cf. *KL* 3.4.70.

178 **tooth** a word apparently associated with the wounds inflicted by satire; an artistic recall of 2.1.6–8. Hall's first three books of satires are entitled 'toothless' and the second three 'biting'.

keen sharp; see 3.5.32.

170–1 So . . . myself] *Cam² lines* speak / myself. / SD] *Johnson;* Song *F;* Musick and song *Douai ms*

175–94] *om. Douai ms*   175 SP] *Johnson; not in F*
176–7] *Pope; one line F*   178–9] *Pope; one line F*

Because thou art not seen,
   Although thy breath be rude.   180
Hey-ho, sing hey-ho, unto the green holly.
Most friendship is feigning, most loving mere folly.
   Then hey-ho, the holly!
   This life is most jolly.

Freeze, freeze, thou bitter sky,   185
That dost not bite so nigh
   As benefits forgot.
Though thou the waters warp,
Thy sting is not so sharp
   As friend remembered not.   190
Hey-ho, sing hey-ho, unto the green holly.

---

179 not seen The wind does not hide ingratitude behind a smiling face; the only sign of its presence is its abrasive breath. Cf. 2.5.6–7.

180 rude rough, but also unmannerly; cf. *KL* 4.2.30–2: 'O Goneril, / You are not worth the dust which the rude wind / Blows in your face.'

181, 183, 191, 193 *Hey-ho This spelling, implying jollity, has been adopted in place of 'Heigh ho', also used in F for sighing (Oxf¹); see 4.3.167n., and 5.3.17. The expression may come from nautical usage (*OED* Hey-ho *int.*, quoting this line).

181, 191 green holly evocative both of Christmas, with sacred connotations related to the word 'holy', and of many pagan festivities and superstitions (as well as of Robin Hood's greenwood)

182 feigning pretending. For false friends, see 1.3.59n.; for lovers and poets, see 3.3.18–19n. In Lodge, Sir John of Bordeaux warns his sons: 'let time be the touchstone of friendship, & then friends faithful lay them vp for iewels' (sig B1ʳ); see 192n. Cicero's *De*

Amicitia (on faithful friendship) was translated into English in 1550 by John Harington the elder (father of the queen's godson), while he was imprisoned in the Tower for loyal service to the Princess Elizabeth. Fidelity over two generations is the condition of Orlando, son of old Sir Rowland (as it was also of a number of Elizabethans, including Harington, Sir Robert Cecil and Essex); see p. 103 and Appendix 1.

186 nigh near

188 warp ruffle – describing the dark ripple caused by a gust of wind, possibly also with a pun on the 'warping' or changing of favour, as in *WT* 1.2.365: 'My favour here begins to warp'; cf. also 3.3.81 below, the warping of timber. The line may allude to the fall of Ralegh from the queen's favour, as her nickname for him was 'water' (the Elizabethan pronunciation of 'Walter').

189 sting of the biting wind, but also the pain of the forgotten friend

190 friend remembered not the act of forgetting a friend, as well as the friend who is forgotten; see 2.1.50n.

181, 183, 191 Hey-ho] *(Heigh ho), Cam¹*   182 feigning] *Rowe; fayning F; faining F3*   183 Then] *Rowe; The F*   185–6] *Pope; one line F*   188–9] *Pope; one line F*   191–4 hey-ho . . . jolly] *Cam¹; &c. F*

Most friendship is feigning, most loving mere folly.
Then hey-ho, the holly!
This life is most jolly.

DUKE SENIOR
If that you be the good Sir Rowland's son,   195
As you have whispered faithfully you were,
And as mine eye doth his effigies witness,
Most truly limned and living in your face,
Be truly welcome hither. I am the Duke

192 **feigning** The repetition is stronger
after the innuendoes of the previous
lines. The atmosphere in the
Elizabethan court in 1599 might have
made this song a particularly poignant
one, at least for a court audience.
Robert Markham wrote to Harington
in 1598: 'The heart of man lieth close
hid oft time; men do not carrye it in
their hand, nor should they do so that
wish to thrive in these times and in
these places' (Harington, *Nugae
Antiquae*, 2.290–1).

195 *be F's 'were' has been emended to
'are' by editors (see t.n.); but the subjunctive form, *be*, is not only correct
after *If that* (Abbott, 298), but also creates a pattern with the imperative *Be* at
the beginning of 199.

197 **effigies witness** testifies to likeness,
as in the Latin inscription on an Isaac
Oliver miniature (1596): *Viva & vera
effigies Arundelli Talbot* ('the living and
true likeness of Arundel Talbot') (see
Edmond, *Hilliard*, plate 30). A dedicatory poem first printed in F2 is entitled
'Vpon the Effigies of my worthy
Friend, the Author Master William
Shakespeare, and his Workes', where
the word seems to refer to the Folio
engraving of Shakespeare. An audience
would hear the commoner 'effigy's',
suggesting a death-mask, which
prompts *living* (198).

198 **limned** painted; limning was a spe-

cial technique of colour painting in
miniature, derived from Flemish and
Burgundian manuscript illumination,
and particularly associated in the 1590s
with the court miniaturist Nicholas
Hilliard (see Fumerton, 66–7; see
3.2.91, 92n., 4.3.85n. and p. 76). Cf.
Marston, *Antonio and Mellida*: 'I fear it
is not possible to limn so many persons
in so small a tablet as the compass of
our plays afford' (9). Orlando is the
portrait in little of his father, Sir
Rowland. The scene ends on a note of
retrospective admiration for the chivalry of old Sir Rowland (invoking the
Chanson de Roland) at the same time as
it conjures up, by association with the
Burgundian limners, the court of
Henry VIII (Dusinberre, 'Pancakes',
397; see also List of Roles, 5n.).

199 **welcome** Duffin suggests that
Shakespeare makes a 'witty connection' between the Duke's welcome to
Sir Rowland's son and the titles of two
famous jigs which shared the same
tune, 'Lord Willoughby's Welcome
Home' and the 'Rowland' jig
(*Songbook*, 350), the latter probably
dating from Leicester's campaign in
the Low Countries; see pp. 72–3 and
Appendix 2.

199–200 **Duke . . . father** In Lodge,
Gerismond, like Torismond, is a king
not a duke, but in 1599 a displaced
king might have seemed impolitic.

195 be] *this edn;* were *F;* are *Hudson²* *(Dyce²)*   Rowland's] Roland's *Cam²*   196 were] are *Hudson²*
(Dyce²)   199 I am] I'm *Pope*

That loved your father. The residue of your fortune   200
Go to my cave and tell me. – Good old man,
Thou art right welcome as thy master is.
[*to Lords*] Support him by the arm.
                    [*to Orlando*] Give me your hand
And let me all your fortunes understand.   *Exeunt.*

3.1   *Enter* DUKE [FREDERICK],
                    Lords and OLIVER.

DUKE FREDERICK
Not see him since? Sir, sir, that cannot be.
But were I not the better part made mercy

200 **residue** rest, remainder
201 **cave** mentioned again at 5.4.194; that the action is never set within the cave might suggest that the play was not initially written to employ a 'discovery space' (SM).
202 **Thou** to a servant
    right heartily; see 2.4.99n.
203 **him** Adam, who disappears here from the play, perhaps because he was required for another role (see Appendix 2); but some modern productions indicate his death in the Forest. Steven Pimlott (RSC, 1996) introduced a grave with flowers, evocative of Poussin's painting *Les Bergers d'Arcadie* (1638–40), in which rustics in a forest come across a tomb inscribed *Et in Arcadia sum* ('I [death] also am present in Arcadia'); see Cam², fig. 5.
    your to an equal
204 **your fortunes** the vicissitudes of your life, but the word reminds a reader, if not an audience, of the debates

between Rosalind and Celia about Fortune at 1.2.31–54. The Douai MS's 'thy fortunes' suggests, as does Cam², that the Duke here addresses Adam, but it is more likely that the final words of the scene are spoken to its hero, Orlando. The act which began when his fortunes were at their nadir after Frederick's hostility ends with them in the ascendant.

3.1 This scene was often cut in productions with elaborate forest scenery; cf. 2.2 and see p. 137.
1   The scene begins in mid-conversation (cf. 2.7, 5.2), recapitulating Frederick's rage in 2.2. The confrontation between the two villainous brothers – Frederick and Oliver – contrasts with the comradeship of Duke Senior and Orlando at the end of 2.7 (Oxf¹). In Lodge's narrative Saladyne here repents (at length, sig. G2ᵛ).
    him Orlando
    Sir, sir Frederick blusters.
2–4 **But . . . present** 'If I were not in the

202 master] *F2;* masters *F*   203 1SD] *Oxf; To Orlando* Support *Cam²; not in F*   2SD *Oxf; To Adam* Give *Cam²; not in F*   your] thy *Douai ms*   3.1] *(Actus Tertius. Scena Prima.)*   Location] *the Palace / Rowe*   0.1 DUKE] new Duke *Douai ms*   FREDERICK] *Malone; junior / Capell*   1 Not . . . since] 'Not . . . since' *Cam²*   see] seen *Collier²*

233

I should not seek an absent argument
Of my revenge, thou present. But look to it!
Find out thy brother wheresoe'er he is;   5
Seek him with candle. Bring him dead or living
Within this twelvemonth, or turn thou no more
To seek a living in our territory.
Thy lands, and all things that thou dost call thine
Worth seizure, do we seize into our hands,   10
Till thou canst quit thee by thy brother's mouth
Of what we think against thee.

OLIVER

O that your highness knew my heart in this:
I never loved my brother in my life.

DUKE FREDERICK

More villain thou! Well, push him out of doors,   15
And let my officers of such a nature
Make an extent upon his house and lands.
Do this expediently, and turn him going.   *Exeunt.*

main a merciful man I would wreak my
revenge on you, instead of looking for
someone who is not here.'
3   **argument** pretext
4   **look to it** peremptory: get moving
6   **Seek . . . candle** Search thoroughly,
     even in dark corners; *candle* recalls the
     'bell, book and candle' of a lykewake –
     a traditional night-long vigil over a
     corpse – and prompts 'Bring him dead
     or living'.
7   **turn** return
10   **Worth seizure** of sufficient value to be
     worth taking; Oliver's lands are restored
     at 5.4.166. In Lodge, Torismond's
     displeasure with Saladyne is fuelled
     by a wish to possess his lands (sig.
     G2ʳ).
11   'until you can exonerate yourself by

producing your brother as witness'
14   a nefarious and irreligious statement
15   **More villain thou!** a comic volte-face
     considering Frederick's own 'brother-
     ly' behaviour; cf. 2.2.19n. Cf. Oliver,
     1.1.145n.
16   **officers . . . nature** people employed
     in this kind of work
17   **Make an extent** make a valuation (for
     the purposes of confiscation). Malone
     pointed out that the term translates
     the legal *extendi facias*, which empow-
     ers a sheriff to appraise lands for the
     payment of debt.
18   **expediently** speedily (*OED adv.* 2
     obs., no other examples); but also
     implies 'with politic care'
     turn him going turn him back in his
     tracks

3.2   *Enter* ORLANDO [*with a writing*].

ORLANDO

Hang there, my verse, in witness of my love.
And thou, thrice-crowned queen of night, survey
With thy chaste eye, from thy pale sphere above,
Thy huntress' name that my full life doth sway.

3.2 This pivotal central scene, which opens with the hanging of Orlando's verses on a tree (as in Lodge and Ariosto), is structured on a series of dialogues. The old shepherd and the court jester weigh the relative merits of court and country; Rosalind and Celia discuss Orlando; Orlando and Jaques talk about Rosalind. Finally Rosalind (as Ganymede) and Orlando debate the waywardness of a fictional 'Rosalind'.

1–10 sometimes printed as a separate scene (Pope, Cam²). Orlando's speech is in the form of a *dizain*: a ten-line poem popular in France, particularly associated with the poet Maurice Scève, who was admired by Sidney (de Mourgues, 12–23; see also 2.7.150n.). Shakespeare, like Puttenham, may have known the verse form through Scève's *Délie* (1544), a sequence of 449 *dizains* which associate the heroine with Diana (Ormerod, 326–7). Orlando's poem may remain on the tree throughout the scene (see 82.1n.).

1 Hang there The verses may have been attached either to a stage tree, or, in the public theatre, to a pillar (Stern, *Making*, 23–4); or to a 'music tree', probably a post with branches where music could be displayed and instruments hung – a version of the modern music stand. See Percy, *Fairy Pastoral* (MS, *c.* 1600): 'Highest, aloft, and on the Top of the Musick Tree the Title THE FAERY PASTORALL, *Beneath him pind on Post of the Tree The Scene* ELUIDA FOREST' (p. 94).

2 thrice-crowned queen (crownèd) Orlando refers to the threefold nature of the moon goddess: Diana (Artemis), huntress and protector of chastity; Proserpina (Hecate, Lucina) queen of the underworld and patron of child-birth; and Cynthia or Phoebe, the moon (see List of Roles, 16n.). In Lyly's *Endymion* (1588) the hero falls in love with the moon, a transparent compliment to the queen. Diana, Cynthia and (Bel)Phoebe were all names by which Elizabeth was celebrated (E.C. Wilson, 96–25). In Lodge, Rosader's passion evokes the queen's iconography: 'when I looke on *Floraes* beauteous tapestrie, checkered with the pride of all her treasure, I call to minde the faire face of *Rosalynd*, whose heauenly hue exceeds the Rose and the Lilly in their highest excellence' (H3ʳ); see 5.4.105.2n. For Rosalind and Elizabeth see 1.2.234 SDn. and pp. 5–6, 91).

4 thy huntress' name Rosalind, imagined as one of Diana's nymphs. Cf. Lodge: 'Is shee some Nymph that wayts vpon *Dianaes* traine' (sig. G3ᵛ). Drayton, *Poly-Olbion*, connects the goddess Diana with Arden: 'DEANAE. ARDVINNAE' (13.233). Cf. Jonson's salutation to the queen in the song to Diana in *Cynthia's Revels*, 5.1.3275: 'Qveene *and* Huntresse, *chaste and fayre*'; see 3.4.14n.; for the apostrophe (*huntress'*) see Abbott, 471.
full whole
sway govern – used especially in

3.2] *(Scena Secunda.)* Location] *The Forest / Rowe*   0.1 *with a writing*] *Capell subst.*   1 love.] love: *fixing it to a Tree. / Capell*   4 huntress'] *(Huntresse), Capell*

235

O Rosalind, these trees shall be my books,   5
And in their barks my thoughts I'll character,
That every eye which in this forest looks
Shall see thy virtue witnessed everywhere.
Run, run, Orlando, carve on every tree   9
The fair, the chaste and unexpressive she!   *Exit.*

Enter CORIN *and* TOUCHSTONE.

CORIN   And how like you this shepherd's life, Master
   Touchstone?
TOUCHSTONE   Truly, shepherd, in respect of itself, it is a
   good life; but in respect that it is a shepherd's life, it is
   naught. In respect that it is solitary, I like it very well;   15

---

astrological contexts; cf. *TN* 2.5.109:
'M.O.A.I. doth sway my life.'
6 **barks** Ariosto's Orlando carves
Angelica's name on trees; but see also
Spenser, *FQ*, 3, for Belphoebe's similar
carving of Timias's name (Koller, 48).
character inscribe
7 an ironic reference to the theatre audience; see also 119n., 2.7.140–67n. Cf.
MND 2.1.222: 'Nor doth this wood
lack worlds of company'.
8 **virtue** 'The power or operative influence inherent in a supernatural or
divine being. Now *arch.* or *obs.*' (*OED*
sb. 1a). See 1.3.78n. on *virtuous*, and cf.
Mac 4.3.156, 'strange virtue'. This
meaning of the word is consonant with
Rosalind's claim to special power at
5.2.69 (Goldberg, 153); it accords with
her 'princely potency' (Paglia, 202) and
encompasses her association with *Jove*
at 1.3.121 (Berry, 'Rosalynde', 44).
10 **unexpressive** inexpressible (Abbott,
442)
11–82 A 1620s Scottish reader annotated
this scene in his copy of F: 'Conference
of courtlie foole and a good wittie /
ship sheepheard Contentments &

discontent / Innocence of a sheepheards
life' (in Yamada, 63; see 1.3.118n.,
5.1.6n. on *Mar-text* and p. 114). Cf. the
dialogue in Spenser, *FQ*, 6.9.19–33,
between the old shepherd Meliboe and
Sir Calidore (modelled on Sidney or
Essex? see Heffner, 7–38, and p. 98).
11 **Master** Corin uses a respectful title to
a gentleman (modern 'Mr'), and the
'you' form, where Touchstone calls
him *shepherd* and uses *thou*, 13, 19
(Kittredge); cf. 83.
14, 15, 16 **in respect** considering
15 **naught** worthless
  solitary as in the contemplative life
16 **private** lacking company (Lat. *priva-
tus* = deprived), i.e. without access to
'public' life and therefore unappealing,
especially to a court jester; a word
loaded with political implications for
the Elizabethans. Essex's Accession
Day pageant in 1595 embodied the
choices of public and private activity,
and he was constantly advised on this
uneasy balance by Elizabeth's senior
courtiers (Gazzard, 446; see pp. 5, 96).
Daniel's *The Praise of Private Life*
(1603), a translation of Petrarch's *De*

10.1 TOUCHSTONE] *Malone; Clowne F*   11 Master] *(M*ʳ*), Var 1773;* M. *F3*

but in respect that it is private, it is a very vile life. Now
in respect it is in the fields, it pleaseth me well; but in
respect it is not in the court, it is tedious. As it is a spare
life, look you, it fits my humour well; but as there is no
more plenty in it, it goes much against my stomach.   20
Hast any philosophy in thee, shepherd?

CORIN   No more but that I know the more one sickens the
worse at ease he is; and that he that wants money,
means and content is without three good friends; that
the property of rain is to wet and fire to burn; that good   25
pasture makes fat sheep; and that a great cause of the
night is lack of the sun; that he that hath learned no wit
by nature nor art may complain of poor breeding or
comes of a very dull kindred.

TOUCHSTONE   Such a one is a natural philosopher. Wast   30
ever in court, shepherd?

Vita Solitaria, presents the dichotomy
in dialogue form, raising the question
of whether the translator imitated this
scene (Dusinberre, 'As *Who?*' 14).
vile low, a condition to be despised
17 **pleaseth me well** The dialogue cen-
tres on the difference between pleasure
(what you like, 11, 15), and content
(what satisfies you, 24, 70–4) and
probes the play's deceptively casual
title: as you *like* it (see also 1.3.134,
2.3.68, 3.3.3, 5.2.15n., 112n., 5.4.128n.,
Epilogue 13, 16, 18, and p. 100).
18 **spare** frugal
19 **humour** constitution, mood; see
1.2.255n.
20 **stomach** inclination; appetite
21 **thee** See 11n.; Touchstone patronizes
Corin throughout the dialogue.
22 **No more but** only
24 **means** capacity
25 **property** innate character
27 **wit** understanding
28 **art** skill
*poor breeding Corin, a sheep-
breeder, knows that poor grafting

produces a poor breed, whereas for the
courtier *breeding* means 'education'
(1.1.4, 10, 3.3.76); for a comparable
physical frame of reference see
4.1.164. F's 'good' is probably a scribal
error, copied from 'good friends' (24)
and 'good pasture' (25–6), especially as
'good breeding' is a stock phrase.
29 **dull kindred** stupid (extended) family
30 **natural philosopher** a pun on the
'natural' wisdom of the uneducated (i.e.
a *clown*, 2.4.63), and the insight of a
philosopher of the Natural or Libertine
school, which elevated Reason and
Nature above divine revelation in accordance with Stoic and Epicurean thought
(Williamson, 277–81); see 2.7.65n. The
term Natural philosophy also encompassed the pioneering study of the
physical universe (including matter; see
2.5.31n.) by Montaigne, Donne, Bacon,
Harriot and Harington; the latter
was considered a Natural philosopher
for his expertise in plumbing both
fountains and lavatories; see p. 88.
Touchstone's teasing of the old

28 poor] *this edn*; good *F*; bad *Hanmer*   30–1] *Pope*; *F lines* Philosopher: / Shepheard? /

CORIN   No, truly.

TOUCHSTONE   Then thou art damned.

CORIN   Nay, I hope.

TOUCHSTONE   Truly, thou art damned, like an ill-roasted   35
egg, all on one side.

CORIN   For not being at court? Your reason?

TOUCHSTONE   Why, if thou never wast at court thou
never sawst good manners; if thou never sawst good
manners then thy manners must be wicked, and   40
wickedness is sin and sin is damnation. Thou art in a
parlous state, shepherd.

CORIN   Not a whit, Touchstone. Those that are good
manners at the court are as ridiculous in the country as
the behaviour of the country is most mockable at the   45
court. You told me you salute not at the court but you
kiss your hands. That courtesy would be uncleanly if
courtiers were shepherds.

TOUCHSTONE   Instance, briefly. Come, instance.

CORIN   Why, we are still handling our ewes, and their fells,   50
you know, are greasy.

shepherd for advanced sceptical views
comically inverts the pastoral image of
the shepherd as an archetype for Christ;
see p. 100.

34 **hope** hope of salvation; see
1.2.273–4n. and 4.1.112n. See
Augustine, *City*: 'If anyone accepts the
present life in such a spirit that he uses
it with the end in view of that other life
. . . for which he hopes . . . such a man
may . . . be called happy even now,
though rather by future hope than in
present reality' (19.20, p. 881).

35 **Truly** The first of Touchstone's
games with *truly*, used here to verify a
palpable lie; see 3.3.17n.

36 **all . . . side** lop-sided, and therefore
ill-cooked

38–41 **Why . . . damnation** Touchstone

delivers a classic syllogism in which
each proposition follows logically, but
reaches a false conclusion, in this case
because he uses *manners* in its earlier
and wider sense of 'morals'; cf. *TN*
1.5.44–7: 'Anything that's mended is
but patched: virtue that transgresses is
but patched with sin, and sin that
amends is but patched with virtue. If
that this simple syllogism will serve,
so.'

42 **parlous** perilous (archaic)

43 **Not a whit** not at all

46 **salute not** do not kiss on the cheek

49, 54, 58 **instance** argument, example
(see 2.7.157n.)

50 **still** always, continually
   fells fleeces (*OED* fell *sb.*[1] 3, first
   example)

37 reason?] *Oxf;* reason. *F*

TOUCHSTONE   Why, do not your courtier's hands sweat?
And is not the grease of a mutton as wholesome as the
sweat of a man? Shallow, shallow. A better instance, I
say. Come.   55

CORIN   Besides, our hands are hard.

TOUCHSTONE   Your lips will feel them the sooner –
shallow again. A more sounder instance, come.

CORIN   And they are often tarred over with the surgery
of our sheep, and would you have us kiss tar? The   60
courtier's hands are perfumed with civet.

TOUCHSTONE   Most shallow man! Thou worm's meat in
respect of a good piece of flesh indeed! Learn of the
wise and perpend. Civet is of a baser birth than tar, the

---

52 **your** generic (Hope, 82–3); cf. *your
writers* (5.1.43), and see 5.4.60–1.
*courtier's F's 'courtiers' could be
singular or plural, but the singular cor-
responds to *a man* (54), and Corin's
courtier's hands (61).

53 **mutton** a sheep, not just its meat,
chosen for its alliteration with *man*

54, 58 **Shallow** superficial, unconvincing;
a lawyer's term for unsound proof,
hence the name Justice Shallow in *2H4*.
In *2 Parnassus* (1601–2) the character
'Kempe' claims that he played the part
of 'a foolish justice of peace' (l. 1851;
noted in Shaaber, 656, citing Malone).
If Kemp played Touchstone the jester's
reiteration of the word 'shallow' might
have reminded the audience of Kemp's
earlier performance as Justice Shallow
(cf. 1.3.85n. on *upon mine honour* and
see p. 99n.; for Kemp see Appendix 2).

56 **hard** horny from work; cf. *MND*
5.1.72: 'Hard-handed men'.

57 **lips will feel** hard hands will be felt
more by the person kissing them; possibly a bawdy double entendre on
female 'labia' (vulva), following *hard*,
56 (cf. 5.1.35n.)

58 **more sounder** double comparative
(Abbott, 11); cf. 3.3.54.

59 **tarred . . . surgery** Tar was used in
the dressing of cuts (*surgery*) made
accidentally while shearing fleece. In
Drayton, *Elizium*, the shepherd carries
'My Tarboxe, and my Scrip' (6.56); see
159n.

61, 64 **civet** an expensive perfume made
from the anal gland of a cat; see 65.

62, 69 **shallow man** man of weak judgement

62 **worm's meat** miserable specimen.
The distinction between a man and a
worm recalls Psalm 22 (containing
Christ's words from the Cross), v. 6:
'But as for me, I am a worme & no
ma[n]' (Great Bible).

63 **good . . . flesh** decent figure of a man;
cf. *MA* 4.2.80–1: 'as pretty a piece of
flesh'.
indeed in truth. There may be a play
on 'in deed', developing from the possibly bawdy innuendoes on *hard* and *lips*.

64 **perpend** literally, hang in there; pay
attention.
baser birth a clever reversion to the
argument about breeding; see 28n.

---

52 courtier's] *(Courtiers)*, *Capell;* courtiers' *Theobald⁴*   61 courtier's] *(Courtiers)*, *Pope;* courtiers'
Ard¹   62 shallow man] shallow, Man *Rowe*   worm's meat] *(wormes meate)*, *Capell;* Worms-meat
Rowe; worms' meat *Gilman*

very uncleanly flux of a cat. Mend the instance,   65
shepherd.

CORIN   You have too courtly a wit for me, I'll rest.

TOUCHSTONE   Wilt thou rest damned? God help thee,
shallow man! God make incision in thee, thou art raw!

CORIN   Sir, I am a true labourer. I earn that I eat, get that   70
I wear; owe no man hate, envy no man's happiness; glad
of other men's good, content with my harm; and the
greatest of my pride is to see my ewes graze and my
lambs suck.

TOUCHSTONE   That is another simple sin in you: to bring   75
the ewes and the rams together and to offer to get your
living by the copulation of cattle; to be bawd to a bell-
wether and to betray a she-lamb of a twelvemonth to a
crooked-pated old cuckoldly ram, out of all reasonable

---

65 **flux** secretion
Mend improve, correct

67 Corin's retreat paradoxically marks the
triumph of the self-respecting and
self-sufficient shepherd over the witty
but parasitic court jester.

69 **incision** make a cut (as in *surgery*, 59)
to let blood, or to test the *worm's meat*
(62) to see if it is properly cooked
raw inexperienced (uncooked); follows
meat (62) and *ill-roasted* (35). 'Raw'
also described country people not used
to the city (cf. modern 'green'); see
Whetstone, *Mirror*: 'A light yongman,
which com[m]eth (rawly) out of ye
coun[t]rey' (sig. H1ᵛ). The 'raw' element in Ralegh's West Country origins
may have made him sensitive about his
name, 'Rauley', which he changed to
Ralegh after he had been knighted
(*Letters*, lviii).

70–4 Cf. Spenser's Meliboe, *FQ*, 6.9.20,
21: 'The fields my food, my flocke my
rayment breed; / No better doe I
weare, no better doe I feed. /
Therefore I doe not any one envy, /
Nor am envyde of any one therefore'
(p. 404). Cf. Daniel, *Praise*: '[The
country dweller] envieth noe man, nor

hateth any bodie, but contente with his
fortune, holdeth himself secure' (331).
'Content' had a religious, but also,
probably, a political significance; see
2.5.33n. See H. Smith, 'Contentation'
(reprinted 1599): 'if you see a man
contented with that he hath, it is a
great signe that godlines is entred into
him' (sigs B4ʳ⁻ᵛ). Corin's rhythms
anticipate Lear's speech to poor Tom
on the heath: 'Thou ow'st the worm no
silk, the beast no hide, the sheep no
wool, the cat no perfume' (*KL*
3.4.101–3).

74 **lambs suck** Lambing in Elizabethan
England began on April Fool's Day (1
April; Thirsk, 187), a date appropriate
to this dialogue.

75 **simple** foolish

77 **cattle** animals: cf. 397.
bawd go-between, procurer

77–8 **bell-wether** The old belled ram,
leader of the flock; see Drayton,
Elizium, 6.56.

79 **crooked-pated** with a curled brow
cuckoldly The new ram cuckolds the
superannuated bell-wether.

79–80 **out . . . match** beyond any
possible compatibility

match. If thou be'st not damned for this, the devil   80
himself will have no shepherds. I cannot see else how
thou shouldst scape.

Enter ROSALIND [*as Ganymede, with a writing*].

CORIN   Here comes young Master Ganymede, my new
mistress's brother.

ROSALIND [*Reads.*]

> *From the east to western Inde*   85
>   *No jewel is like Rosalind.*
> *Her worth being mounted on the wind*
>   *Through all the world bears Rosalind.*
> *All the pictures fairest lined*

81 **will have no** will not accept any –
witty, as Christ himself was the 'Good
Shepherd' (see 62, 69n.)

82 **scape** escape (damnation)

82.1 Rosalind may take from the tree the
verses which celebrate her name (4; see
85–92), hung there by Orlando (1); but
more probably she enters with a paper
plucked from a profusion of tongues
on trees.

83 **Master** Corin gives Ganymede, a
shepherd boy, the same title as
Touchstone, the court jester; see 11n.

84 **brother** the first reference to the relationship between Ganymede and Aliena

85 *east . . . Inde* Hakluyt's new edition
(1598–1600) of *Navigations* includes in
volume 3 accounts of expeditions to
both the East Indies (India and the
Malayan islands) and the West Indies
(the Spanish Americas). Both Indies
were renowned for wealth; John
Chamberlain wrote to Dudley Carleton
on 10 October 1600: 'The carraques
are come home very rich from the East
Indies' (*Chamberlain*, 88).

86, 88, 90, 92 *Rosalind* For pronunciation, see List of Roles, 1n.

87 *mounted . . . wind* In Chapman's
translation of Homer's *Odyssey* (in
circulation in manuscript in the
1590s) Jove sends two eagles 'mounted
on the winds' (bk 2, p. 22) to the
court of Telemachus. The Olympian
echo underlines the majesty accorded
to Rosalind in Orlando's verse (see
2n.), also probably suggested by
Lodge's Rosader, who has 'let mine
eye soare with yᵉ Eagle against so
bright a Sun, that I am quite blind'
(sig. G4ʳ).

89 *lined* the drawing of lines in black; a
pun on 'limned' (see 2.7.198n.); *Rosa
lined* – the outline of Rosalind. See
Harington, *OF*: '*I thinke our countryman
(I meane Mʳ Hilliard) is inferiour to
none that liues at this day . . . my selfe
haue seen him, in white and blacke in foure
lynes only, set downe the feature of the
Queenes Maiesties countenaunce; that it
was eue[n] thereby to be knowne*' (bk 33,
p. 278).

79 cuckoldly] cuckoldy *Theobald³*   80 be'st] *(*bee'st*)*   82.1] *this edn; after 84 F   as Ganymede*] *Oxf
with a writing*] *Rowe subst.; she takes Orlando's paper from the tree: reading* / *Verity*   83 Master] *(*Mʳ*),
Malone;* M. *F2;* Monsieur *Cam²*   85 SD] *Rowe subst.   Inde*] *Jude F4*   89 lined] *(*Linde*); limn'd /
Johnson*

Are but black to Rosalind.   90
Let no fair be kept in mind
But the fair of Rosalind.

TOUCHSTONE   I'll rhyme you so eight years together,
dinners and suppers and sleeping-hours excepted. It is
the right butter-women's rank to market.   95

ROSALIND   Out, fool!

TOUCHSTONE   For a taste –
If a hart do lack a hind,
Let him seek out Rosalind.
If the cat will after kind,   100
So be sure will Rosalind.

---

90 *black* the lines of the drawing, but also
meaning ugly; cf. 3.5.47, and 4.3.35,
where the word describes the blackness
of ink as well as of the letter's cruel
content (see n.). Cf. *Son* 127 to the
dark lady: 'In the old age black was not
counted fair' (1). The Elizabethan
ideal of beauty required a fair complexion and grey eyes.

91 **fair* beauty, as well as a fair complexion; F's *'face'* is too 'local' for the scope
of Orlando's praise; *r* was easily misread as *c* in secretary script. Hilliard
advised: 'when you begin your picture,
choose your carnations [flesh colour]
too fair, for in working you may make
it as brown as you will, but being chosen too brown you shall never work it
fair enough' (*Limning*, 97, 96). No picture can be coloured beautifully
enough to compete with the beauty of
Rosalind; see 4.3.85n.

93 **eight years together** for the space of
eight years

95 **right** true
   butter-women's . . . market line of
   dairy-wives   chanting   traditional
   rhymes while riding to market to sell
   butter (see Mendelson & Crawford,
   210, 212, also woodcut, 307–8). The

jogging of the mount resembles
Touchstone's jog-trot verse (98–109;
Holdsworth, 197). Taylor suggests
that the popular satirical conception of
a butterwoman was of a 'whore' or
scold, in which case she joins the ranks
of 'unruly women' and anticipates
Touchstone's 'Then to cart with
Rosalind' at 105 ('Butterwomen', 188,
192). However, Arden was known for
its   dairying   (Thirsk,   91),   and
Touchstone's jibe may be, from a
Warwickshire dramatist, a local rather
than a literary joke.
rank line, as at 4.3.78 (*OED sb.*[1] 1a).
But a 'line' may also be determined by
'rank' in the sense of social status.

96 **Out** get away; also, possibly, 'you have
put me out', i.e., out of her part in
reciting the verses. Cf. 4.1.69.

97 **taste** sample or savour (of my skill);
'poet-tasters' (dilettante poets) were
satirized by Jonson in *Poetaster*
(1602).

98 **hart . . . hind** Touchstone mocks the
Petrarchan homonym of *hart/heart*
(see 239n. and 1.3.16–17n.); the male
deer (dear) needs a female (hind).

100 **after kind** pursues (like Rosalind) its
own species

91 *fair*] *Globe (Walker); face* F   92 *fair of*] *most fair* F3; *Face of* / *Rowe*[3]   95 butter-women's]
butter-woman's *Douai ms, Johnson*

242

Winter garments must be lined,
　　So must slender Rosalind.
They that reap must sheaf and bind,
　　Then to cart with Rosalind.   105
Sweetest nut hath sourest rind,
　　Such a nut is Rosalind.
He that sweetest rose will find
　　Must find love's prick – and Rosalind.
This is the very false gallop of verses. Why do you   110
infect yourself with them?

ROSALIND   Peace, you dull fool, I found them on a tree.

TOUCHSTONE   Truly, the tree yields bad fruit.

ROSALIND   I'll graft it with you, and then I shall graft it
with a medlar. Then it will be the earliest fruit i'th'   115

---

102 ***Winter** F's '*Wintred*' is an error
from Compositor B, caused by so
many words ending in *-d*.
lined given a lining (cf. 2.7.155),
prompting a bawdy change of meaning
in 103 from '*lined*' (89), meaning
'drawn'. The female sheath provides a
lining for a male sword.

104 **sheaf and bind** make the corn into
sheaves and gather them together in
stooks (bunches of standing sheaves)

105 **to cart** The dried sheaves are put in
a cart for threshing. Rosalind will be
punished for sexual misdemeanours by
carting, allied in popular folk customs
with the skimmington ride, a procession intended to humiliate 'a miser,
henpecked husband or a wife-beater
. . . a shrew or unchaste woman'
(Chambers, *MS*, 1.154, cited in
Donaldson, *World*, 40); see also R.
Wilson, 13, and pp. 56–7.

106 proverbial (Dent, N360); also a possible reference to Rosalind's disguise as
Ganymede: a sweet inside and a sour
rind

109 **love's prick** the thorn of the rose

(bawdy); cf. *RJ* 2.4.111–12: 'the bawdy
hand of the dial is now upon the prick
of noon'.

110 **false gallop** rollocking rhythm, suitable for a horse but not for refined
verses; see Nashe, *Strange News*
(1592): 'I would trot a false gallop
through the rest of his ragged Verses'
(1.275, ll. 7–8).

111 **infect yourself with** as with the
plague; see *marks*, 355, 358 and n.

112 **dull** stupid

113 **bad fruit** biblical: 'a corrupt tre
bri[n]geth forthe euil frute', and
'Therefore by their frutes ye shal
knowe them' (Matthew, 7.17, 20,
Geneva Bible)

114 **graft** insert new stock into

115–17 The medlar is a species of pear.
See Harington, *Salernum* (1608):
'Good *Medlers* are not ripe, till seeming rotten' (102, cited in Oxf¹); see also
2.7.26–7 and n. In Lodge, Saladyne
denies that he will prove 'soone ripe
and soone rotten' (sig. N2ʳ), like some
inconstant lovers. The word was spelt
the same as *meddler* and punned with

---

102 Winter] *F3; Wintred F*   114 graft] *(graffe), Malone*   115 medlar] *(Medler), Cam;* meddler
Sisson

country, for you'll be rotten ere you be half ripe, and
that's the right virtue of the medlar.

TOUCHSTONE   You have said. – But whether wisely or no,
let the forest judge.

Enter CELIA [*as Aliena*] *with a writing.*

ROSALIND   Peace, here comes my sister reading. Stand   120
aside.

CELIA [*Reads.*]
  Why should this a desert be,
  For it is unpeopled? No!
  Tongues I'll hang on every tree
  That shall civil sayings show: 125

---

it. See Heywood, *Epigrams 400*, no. 89:
'Of medlars': 'To feede of any fruite at
any feast, / Of all kyndes of medlers,
meddle with the least. / Meddle not
with great medlars. For no question, /
Medling with great medlars, maketh ill
digestion.'

117 **right virtue** proper quality (Onions,
'virtue' 3, p. 242). See Douce,
Illustrations: 'It is well known that the
medlar is only edible when *apparently*
rotten. This is what Shakespeare
means by *right virtue*. If a fruit be fit to
be eaten when rotten and *before it is
ripe*, it may in one sense be termed *the
earliest*' (1.302).

119 **forest judge** Touchstone appeals to
the audience to decide whether his or
Rosalind's joke is the funnier; see 7n.

120–1 **reading. Stand aside** an internal
SD

122–3 *Why . . . unpeopled* See 7n. Donne
wrote to his brother-in-law in 1614:
'We are condemned to this desart of
London for all this summer, for yt ys
company not houses which distinguishes between city and desarts'
(*Loseley*, 345). Habicht notes 'the

medieval identification of wood and
wilderness, of forest and desert, which
can be traced from Old Saxon poets to
Sidney's *Arcadia* [and] is paradoxically
unfolded in Shakespeare's *AYL*'
('Tree', 82).

123 *For* because

124 *Tongues* his poems, which speak of
his love; cf. *tongues in trees*, 2.1.16.

125 *civil* of import for the civilized, i.e.
cultivated (see *civility*, 2.7.97), as
opposed to wild (see *savage*, 2.6.7)
sayings sententiae: wise maxims clothed
in figurative language; see 133–4n. and
5.4.63n.
show F's '*shoe*', a dialect spelling of
show, unique in Shakespeare's lexicon
and spelt in its modern form at 137,
creates an eye-rhyme with '*Noe*' (123,
TLN 1324; see p. 117). The word in its
original spelling puns on 'show' (man-
ifest) and 'shoe' (contain), as a shoe
contains a *tongue* (leather flap, *OED sb.*
14f). It also draws the attention of a
reader to a chain of images connected
with shoes (127–9), and perhaps gives
rise to another joke: this is a 'shoe-tree'
which bears *tongues* just as a 'palm-

---

117 medlar] (Medler), *Cam* 119.1 *as Aliena*] *Oxf* 122 SD] *Dyce* a] *Douai ms, Rowe; not in F* be,]
be? *Rowe* 125 show] (shoe), *F4*

Some, how brief the life of man
   Runs his erring pilgrimage,
That the stretching of a span
   Buckles in his sum of age;
Some, of violated vows   130
   'Twixt the souls of friend and friend.
But upon the fairest boughs,
   Or at every sentence' end,
Will I 'Rosalinda' write,
   Teaching all that read to know   135
The quintessence of every sprite
Heaven would in little show.

tree' bears handwriting (see 171–2n.). The use of a wooden shoe-tree to keep shoes in shape is recorded considerably later in the *OED* but such a device must have been known, and indeed used, by the Elizabethans.

126 *brief . . . man vita brevis, ars longa*, 'life is short, art long', a comment on pastoral itself; see Keats's 'Ode to a Grecian Urn' (Keats, *Poems*, 365–6).

127 *erring* wandering (Lat. *errare*), but also subject to error (sin)
   pilgrimage spiritual journey; cf. 2.3.43n.

128 *span* the width of an outstretched hand, here used both for measuring (*OED sb.*[1] 2), and for the duration of life (*OED sb.*[1] 4a); see Psalms, 39.5: 'thou hast made my dayes as it were a spanne long' (Great Bible). In the context the word suggests the stretching of shoe-leather to fit the foot.

129 *Buckles* fastens (the pilgrim's shoe) with a buckle
   sum of age compass of years

130 *Some,* The comma, not inserted in most editions, is necessary for the parallel construction with 126; *sayings* is implied.

133–4 *sentence' . . . Rosalinda* Rosalind's

name will complete both every civil saying (Lat. *sententia*), as in a legal sentence or case, and also every clause (sentence) or phrase, as it does at 86, 88, 90 and 92 (a feature deftly parodied by Touchstone at 99, 101, 103, 105, 107 and 109). Finally, '*Rosalinda*', with its feminine ending, will provide the feminine ending to Orlando's case (grammatical, but also legal; see Epilogue, 7n.) or chase (pursuit; see 1.3.30n.).

136 *quintessence* elixir, or distillation. Davies, *Nosce Teipsum*, describes the function of the soul: 'From their grosse *matter* she abstracts the *formes* / And drawes a kind of *Quintessence* from things' (p. 24).
   sprite spirit. In Hall's *Virgidemiarum* (1597) the poet conjures Mercury to 'bring *Quintessence* of *Elixir* pale, / Out of sublimed spirits minerall' (2.4, p. 38).

137 (which) heaven would demonstrate in the microcosm (i.e. the little world of Rosalind). Cf. Chapman's dedication of his translation of seven of the books of Homer's *Iliad* to the Earl of Essex (1598): 'so much quintessence to be drawn from so little a project' (Homer/Chapman, 9).

133 *sentence*] *(sentence), Douai ms, Johnson*[2]

> *Therefore heaven Nature charged*
> *That one body should be filled*
> *With all graces wide-enlarged.*   140
> *Nature presently distilled*
> *Helen's cheek but not her heart,*
> *Cleopatra's majesty,*
> *Atalanta's better part,*
> *Sad Lucretia's modesty.*   145
> *Thus Rosalind of many parts*

138–45 Orlando distills the essence of Rosalind from stories of legendary women; see 140–5nn. Ronk points to the 'written' and 'read' portrait of Rosalind, which creates 'a text-book of language and stories and myths and rhetorical flourishes' (267). See Garber, 'Education': 'One of Rosalind's tasks . . . will be to make him speak to her in the natural language of men and women' (106).

138 *charged* commanded (F2 '*chang'd*'; see 1.3.99n.)

140 *all graces* both the virtues and beauty of all the excellent women in the ancient world, and the Graces who attended the Muses at Olympus; cf. Lodge: 'all in general applauded the admirable riches that Nature bestowed on the face of *Rosalynde*: for vppon her cheekes there seemed a battaile betweene the Graces, who should bestow most fauours to make her excellent' (sigs C1ʳ⁻ᵛ). Behind Orlando's eulogy lies Botticelli's *La Primavera*, picturing the Graces attending on Flora, goddess of spring, together with Spenser's 'April' eclogue in *SC*, which celebrates 'Elisa, Queene of Shepheardes all' (p. 455) as Flora (Montrose, 'Elisa', 160–1).

wide-enlarged assembled from a wide variety of sources

142 *Helen's cheek* Helen of Troy's beauty; cf. *Son* 53.7–8: 'On Helen's cheek all art of beauty set / And you in

Grecian tires are painted new'. This sonnet, with its apostrophizing of the young man in many different likenesses – 'Describe Adonis, and the counterfeit / Is poorly imitated after you' (5–6) – parallels Orlando's practice here. The counterfeit or feigned images of legendary women made by poets imitate Rosalind, a being devised not by art, but by 'Nature' (138) and 'Heaven' (137), a bold statement from the poet Shakespeare, the creator of both Rosalind and her poet-lover. Cf. *AC* 2.2.210–11 and 5.2.96–9.

*her F's '*his*' may be a common misreading of a manuscript '*hir*' (see also 5.4.112 and n.).

heart affections, i.e. faithlessness

144 *Atalanta's better part* her beauty, enhanced by her running; see Ovid, *Met.*, 10, p. 132 (cited in Malone), where Hippomenes 'More woondred at her beawtye than at swiftnesse of her pace' (cf. 269). However, the poet seems short of invention here, and the words fit the metre, so perhaps Atalanta's foot ekes out a lame line; see 165–7n.

145 *Sad* sober (see 207–8n.); also steadfast, constant (*OED* 2 *obs.*)

Lucretia Ravished by the Roman prince Tarquin, Lucretia, exemplary and beautiful wife of Collatine, chose to kill herself rather than live dishonoured (see *Luc*), an action which led to the fall of the Tarquins.

138 *charged*] chang'd F2   140 *wide-enlarged*] (wide enlarg'd)   142 *her*] Douai ms, Rowe; his F

> *By heavenly synod was devised,*
> *Of many faces, eyes and hearts*
> *To have the touches dearest prized.*
> *Heaven would that she these gifts should have,*   150
> *And I to live and die her slave.*

ROSALIND O most gentle pulpiter, what tedious homily of love have you wearied your parishioners withal, and never cried: 'Have patience, good people!'

CELIA How now! Back, friends. – Shepherd, go off a little;   155 go with him, sirrah.

TOUCHSTONE Come, shepherd, let us make an honourable retreat, though not with bag and baggage

---

147 *synod* council, often with ecclesiastical overtones, but here it is an assembly of mythical figures

149 *touches* features or traits (Onions, 4, p. 229); but also the detailed brush strokes especially associated with the art of limning. See 2.7.198n., 5.4.27; cf. *Son* 17.8: 'Such heavenly touches ne'er touched earthly faces'.

150 *would* willed, decreed

152 **gentle pulpiter* Spedding's suggested emendation of F's 'Iupiter' carries on the ecclesiastical context of *synod*, and anticipates *homily* (recalling *civil sayings*), *parishioners* (153) and *people* (154). The epithet *gentle* is more appropriate for Celia than for Jupiter. 'Iupiter', not printed in italics as is customary for proper names, may be a compositor's response, on analogy with Rosalind's oath, *O Jupiter* (2.4.1), to the unusual *pulpiter*. The emendation is handwritten in the margin of the promptbook used by Helena Modjeska in December 1882, possibly its first use in the theatre. Abbott, 443, cites 'pulpiter' (not noted as an emendation) as an example of the appending of *-er* to a noun to signify an agent.

homily sermon. The Elizabethan *Book of Homilies* was read in church every Sunday, and no doubt congregations, summoned compulsorily, were heartily sick of it.

153 **withal** with (ending a clause)

155 **Back, friends** move back, friends. Theobald's emendation to *back-friends* (false friends, *OED* backfriend 1 *obs.*) has been widely accepted, but creates an atmosphere of spying which is alien to the Forest (see 2.3.26n.). Charlotte Cushman's 1847 promptbook has a note: 'Touchstone close behind Celia reading over her shoulder. She starts with surprize and drops the paper' (Moore); in Daly's 1889 production, he was 'ordered off after peering over Celia's shoulder and reading in dumb-show; as he exited, he continued to mime the act of reading' (promptbook). In Declan Donnellan's 1991 production for Cheek by Jowl the joke was 'Corin's crush on Celia; here he brought her a flower' (Marshall).

---

152 pulpiter] *Cam (Spedding);* Iupiter *F; Juniper / Warburton*   tedious] a tedious *Douai ms, Capell*   154 'Have . . . people'] *Capell;* haue . . . people *F*   155 Back, friends] *Knight²;* backe friends *F;* back-friends *Theobald*

yet with scrip and scrippage.   *Exit [with Corin].*

CELIA   Didst thou hear these verses?   160

ROSALIND   O yes, I heard them all, and more too, for
some of them had in them more feet than the verses
would bear.

CELIA   That's no matter – the feet might bear the verses.

ROSALIND   Ay, but the feet were lame and could not bear   165
themselves without the verse, and therefore stood
lamely in the verse.

CELIA   But didst thou hear, without wondering, how thy
name should be hanged and carved upon these trees?

ROSALIND   I was seven of the nine days out of the wonder   170
before you came; for look here what I found on a palm-

---

159 **scrip and scrippage** Touchstone
coins the phrase to match *bag and baggage* (158). A *scrip* (shepherd's pouch)
was also carried by pilgrims; see
Ralegh, 'The passionate man's pilgrimage': 'My staff of Faith to walk
upon, / My scrip of joy, immortal diet'
(*Writings*, 53.2–3). Corin has the shepherd's staff of a pilgrim, and
Touchstone his *scrip* or Fool's *poke*
(2.7.20) for collecting tips (which,
however, he never does, unlike Feste in
TN). For pilgrimage motifs in the play
see pp. 95–6.
162–3 **more . . . bear** i.e. too many (metrical) feet to scan correctly
162 **feet** metrical units. 'The conversation [between Celia and Rosalind] may
be thought of as a prose equivalent to
the Theocritan/Virgilian singing
match often imitated by Elizabethan
pastoralists [i.e. Spenser, Sidney]'
(Kinney, 309).
164 **the feet . . . verses** a return to
human feet, capable of carrying verses
165–7 **feet . . . in the verse** Human feet
had to use the verse as a prop, thus
through their lameness (as metrical
units) spoiling the scansion. Bevington

compares Lyly, *Endymion*, 4.2.30–1:
'the metrical irregularity of Tophas's
verse'.
170 **seven . . . wonder** see Heywood: 'A
woonder lasteth but nine dayes'
(*Epigrams 300*, no. 139). Seven of those
days have passed but Rosalind is still in
a state of wonder (Capell, *Notes*, 61).
171–2 **palm-tree** Many explanations
(see Knowles) have been offered for a
palm-tree in Arden, including the suggestion that it is an old name for the
willow (*Salix caprea*, Ellacombe, 205;
see *osiers*, 4.3.78). But this is a tree
whose fruit (Orlando's verses) has
been created in the palm of a hand,
because it bears *handwriting*; see
Maplet, *Forest*, 56: 'The *Palme tree*, is
bespred with boughes plentifullye, and
the same in a maner resembling the
small lynes in our hande.' Cf. 125n. on
show. Maplet also compares the palm-
tree to a phoenix, one of Elizabeth's
cherished emblems: 'The Greekes in
their language call it [the palm-tree]
Phoenix, fetched & borrowed as I
think, from *Phoenix* the Birde of
Arabie.' The palm-tree, like the
phoenix, is hermaphrodite – '*Plinie*

---

159 SD *Exit*] Exeunt *Douai ms   with Corin*] *Rowe subst.*   170 the wonder] wonder *F2*

tree. I was never so berhymed since Pythagoras' time
that I was an Irish rat, which I can hardly remember.

CELIA   Trow you who hath done this?

ROSALIND   Is it a man?   175

CELIA   And a chain that you once wore about his neck –
change you colour?

ROSALIND   I prithee, who?

CELIA   O Lord, Lord, it is a hard matter for friends to
meet; but mountains may be removed with earthquakes   180
and so encounter.

ROSALIND   Nay, but who is it?

CELIA   Is it possible?

sayth, that there is hereof both Male
and Female' – and thus an appropriate
bearer of verses addressed to
Rosalind/Ganymede, about to become
the 'master mistress' of Orlando's passion (see 4.3.17n.).

172–3 **berhymed** . . . **rat** In Jonson's
Apologetical Dialogue, appended to the
1602 quarto of *Poetaster*, 'the Author'
protests that he could easily destroy
his detractors: 'Rhyme 'em to death, as
they doe Irish rats / In drumming
tunes' (150–1, p. 269). Cf. Sidney,
Apology: 'Nor to be rhymed to death,
as is said to be done in Ireland' (142).
Rosalind's speech through the play 'is
permeated with startling animal
references' which enhance rather than
tarnish her image (Roberts, *Wild*, 94).

172 **Pythagoras** a reference to
metempsychosis – Pythagoras's doctrine of the transmigration of souls (cf.
TN 4.2.57–9). But there may also be a
joke on numbers, i.e. metre; cf. Jonson,
EMI, 3.4.174–6: 'Signor Pythagoras,
he that's all manner of shapes, and
Songs and Sonnets, his fellow there.'

173 **Irish** Cam[1] (p. 158) suggests a veiled
reference to the Irish crisis of 1599 (cf.
5.2.106n. and see pp. 75, 102–3).
hardly remember Nobody else can

remember it, either: one of Rosalind's
most obscure jokes.

174 **Trow you** do you know, can you
guess

176 **chain** . . . **neck** See 1.2.234 SDn.

180–1 **mountains** . . . **encounter** The
image contradicts the proverbial difficulty of friends meeting by declaring
that immovable mountains may be
brought together by earthquakes.
Halliwell (Tollet) cites Pliny's *Natural
History*: 'a great strange wonder of the
earth; for two hils encountred together,
charging as it were, and with violence
assaulting one another, yea and
retyring again with a most mighty
noise' (2.83.39). Cf. Matthew, 17.20: 'if
ye haue faith . . . ye shal say vnto this
mountaine, Remoue hence to yonder
place, & it shal remoue' (Geneva
Bible); and 1 Corinthians, 13.2: 'yea, if
I had all faith, so that I colde remoue
mountaines and had not loue, I were
nothing' (Geneva Bible). The faith of a
lover functions in the same way as religious faith (see 5.4.1–4 and nn.).

183 **Either** 'Is it possible you don't
know?', or 'Is it possible that Orlando
can be in the Forest?' The latter would
fit Celia's exclamations of wonder,
186–8.

172 Pythagoras'] *(Pythagoras), Douai ms subst., Keightley*

ROSALIND Nay, I prithee now, with most petitionary
vehemence, tell me who it is.   185

CELIA O wonderful, wonderful, and most wonderful
wonderful, and yet again wonderful, and after that out
of all hooping!

ROSALIND Good my complexion! Dost thou think,
though I am caparisoned like a man, I have a doublet   190
and hose in my disposition? One inch of delay more is
a South Sea of discovery. I prithee tell me who is it

184–5 **petitionary vehemence** the
importunacy of one who presents a
petition
186–7 **most wonderful wonderful**
The first *wonderful* functions as an
adverb: most wonderfully wonderful;
the comic exaggeration and whooping
sound prompt 'out of all hooping'
(187–8). The word *wonderful* is
stronger than in modern English,
involving something almost miraculous; see 5.4.137, *wonder*. See *TN*
5.1.221: 'Most wonderful!'; *Tem*
1.2.427: 'O, you wonder!'; *WT*
5.2.15–16: 'a notable passion of wonder'; cf. 170. In the Douai MS Celia
speaks 'wonderful' twice, and then the
lines are cut to 199: 'Is he of God's
making?', a practice commonly followed in the nineteenth century to
erase the risqué jesting of the 'ladies';
see 1.2.105n.
187–8 **out ... hooping** out of all limit. In
cock-fighting a hoop was used to confine the birds within a small space to
force them to fight; cf. 2.7.91n. and *AC*
2.3.37n. Barrels containing liquor were
also bound with metal hoops, which
perhaps prompts Rosalind's drinking
images, 194–7. But *hooping* (whooping) also refers to the crowing sound
made by a cock; it could mean both
cheering (as here) and jeering; see *Cor*
4.5.80–1: 'And suffer'd me by th' voice
of slaves to be / Whoop'd out of

Rome'. The word is always spelt without a *w* in F.
189 **Good my complexion!** an oath: 'by
the truth of my looks and character',
i.e. as a woman. 'Complexion' meant
both the colour of the face and temperament (see 3.5.117n.), both determined by the distribution of fluids in
the body (see 1.2.255n.); for example, a
ruddy complexion indicated a sanguine temperament in which blood
predominated.
190 **caparisoned like** wearing the trap-
pings of
191 **disposition** Rosalind's assertion that
her clothes do not change her nature
contrasts with Perdita's: 'sure this robe
of mine / Does change my disposition'
(*WT* 4.4.134–5), though in Perdita's
case the regal robes of queen of the
sheep–shearing reveal her hidden
royalty.
191–2 **One . . . discovery** Rosalind
urges Celia to find the shortest and
quickest way to reveal the identity of
the writer of the love-poetry; *discovery*
is the normal word for 'exploration'.
Elizabethan travellers longed to find a
direct passage to the South Sea and
China (see Hakluyt, *Navigations*,
3.742). Rosalind's parallel, obscure in
detail, captures the emotions, which
fired the South Sea projects (cf.
5.2.63n.), of being on the brink of a
revelation of new land.

186–7 wonderful wonderful] wonderful-wonderful *Oxf* 188 hooping] hoping *F4;* whooping *Var*
1773 192–3 it quickly] *this edn;* it quickly, *F;* it, quickly, *Rowe*

quickly and speak apace. I would thou couldst stammer,
that thou mightst pour this concealed man out of thy
mouth as wine comes out of a narrow-mouthed bottle   195
– either too much at once or none at all. I prithee take
the cork out of thy mouth that I may drink thy tidings.

CELIA   So you may put a man in your belly.

ROSALIND   Is he of God's making? What manner of man?
Is his head worth a hat? Or his chin worth a beard?   200

CELIA   Nay, he hath but a little beard.

ROSALIND   Why, God will send more if the man will be
thankful. Let me stay the growth of his beard, if thou
delay me not the knowledge of his chin.

CELIA   It is young Orlando, that tripped up the wrestler's   205
heels and your heart both in an instant.

ROSALIND   Nay, but the devil take mocking! Speak sad
brow and true maid.

CELIA   I'faith, coz, 'tis he.

ROSALIND   Orlando?   210

CELIA   Orlando.

---

193 **apace** as quickly as you can; cf. 3.3.1.

195 **wine . . . bottle** Rosalind's image is in decorum for Ganymede's role as cup-bearer to the gods; see 1.3.122n. In Withals's *Dictionary* the entry for 'Sweet Wine' reads: '*Misceri decet hoc a Ganymede merum*. You mingle delicate Wine and principall honie together, which delicate wine ought to be tempered and made of none but Ganymedes' (sig. D7ᵛ).

197 **tidings** news

198 **man . . . belly** The shape of the bottle and the wine coming out of it lead inevitably to Celia's bawdy joke.

199 **Is . . . making?** Is he a genuine man? – a question perhaps prompted by Ganymede's awareness of his own aping of manhood; see 3.5.116n.

200 **worth** worthy of

201 **beard** the badge of manhood (see Fisher, 177ff.); see also 1.2.72n. When Lodge's Rosader 'felt haire on his face, and perceiuing his beard to bud, for choler hee began to blush, and swore to himselfe he would be no more subiect to such slauerie' (sig. B3ᵛ). But the wearing of a beard may also have had some connections with social class (see 362–3n. and 5.4.70n.).

203 **stay** wait for

204 **chin** In *H5* 3.4.33 'chin' is confused by Katherine with 'sin', a jest possibly also intended here.

207–8 **sad . . . maid** seriously and truthfully – a youthful oath, as 'cross your heart and swear to die'

---

205 wrestler's] *(*Wrastlers*)*

ROSALIND   Alas the day, what shall I do with my doublet
and hose? What did he when thou sawst him? What
said he? How looked he? Wherein went he? What
makes he here? Did he ask for me? Where remains he?   215
How parted he with thee? And when shalt thou see him
again? Answer me in one word.

CELIA   You must borrow me Gargantua's mouth first. 'Tis
a word too great for any mouth of this age's size. To say
ay and no to these particulars is more than to answer in   220
a catechism.

ROSALIND   But doth he know that I am in this forest and
in man's apparel? Looks he as freshly as he did the day
he wrestled?

CELIA   It is as easy to count atomies as to resolve the   225
propositions of a lover; but take a taste of my finding
him and relish it with good observance. I found him
under a tree, like a dropped acorn –

---

215 **makes he** is he doing
218 **Gargantua's mouth** i.e. large
enough to answer all Rosalind's questions in one word (mouthful).
Gargantua was a giant in Rabelais's
Gargantua who consumed legendary
quantities of food and drink; see p. 89.
221 **catechism** The 'Catechism' for children was printed in the *BCP* and
required rehearsed answers of 'yes' or
'no' to questions relating to the articles
of Christian belief. Rosalind's catechism demands fuller answers than
Celia has learnt.
223 **freshly** vigorously
225 **atomies** tiny particles. The word,
which occurs twice in *AYL* (see 3.5.13)
and in no other Shakespeare play, may
suggest the territory of the research
conducted by Ralegh's navigator,
Thomas Harriot, into the atom and
into optics, with particular relation to

the refraction of light and the nature
of vision (Rosen, 5; Jacquot, 107–8;
Shirley, *Harriot*, 383–6).
226 **propositions** hair-splitting distinc-
tions; a legal term
226–7 **taste . . . relish** Celia continues to
embroider the eating and drinking
metaphors associated with both
Ganymede and Gargantua; see 195,
218, and cf. 97.
227 **observance** attention (Onions, 3, p.
150)
228–9 **acorn . . . Jove's tree** Golding
translates Ovid's *glans Iouis* as
'Iupiters Acorne', but the Elizabethans
did not call the oak 'Jove's tree'
(Gerard, *Herbal*, 1158). In Gerard's
Herbal (1252) 'Iupiters Acorne' is a
walnut – a 'royal' tree, and one of
Elizabeth's emblems (Strong, 'Persian
Lady', 315–16). See Spenser, *SC*,
'December': 'The stately Walnut-tree',

218 Gargantua's] Garagantua's *Douai ms, Pope*   224 wrestled] *(*Wrastled*)*   225 atomies] Atomes
F3; attomes *Douai ms*

ROSALIND   It may well be called Jove's tree when it drops
forth such fruit.   230

CELIA   Give me audience, good madam.

ROSALIND   Proceed.

CELIA   There lay he stretched along like a wounded
knight –

ROSALIND   Though it be pity to see such a sight, it well   235
becomes the ground.

CELIA   Cry holla to thy tongue, I prithee: it curvets
unseasonably. He was furnished like a hunter –

ROSALIND

O ominous, he comes to kill my heart!

---

484). This would make better sense of
230, where the heroine seems to relish
an edible nut. However, in Cooper's
Thesaurus, 'Glans Iouis' is glossed as 'A
cheasten' (chestnut) (sig. I.ii.5'), a nut
which is also edible, and fits the colour
of Orlando's hair (3.4.10).

229–30 *drops forth such F2's addition
of 'such' is justified by the use of the
same phrase at 4.3.34.

231 audience hearing, attention; cf.
5.4.149.

236 becomes enhances the beauty of

237 holla 'A term of manege, by which
the rider restrained and *stopp'd* his
horse' (Malone, cited in Knowles)
curvets Celia compares Rosalind's
interruptions to the stopping and
starting of a horse which is being
trained to jump, although in fact it is
she herself who is forced to stop and
start when she wants to bound aloft in
her story. See Markham, *Horseman*:
'the motion is a kinde of dancing
which the horse is made to vse his
fore-legges a good height from the
ground, and his hinder legs not halfe
so much, prauncing vp and downe all
in one place' (2.22, p. 239).

238 unseasonably inappropriately
furnished equipped and dressed
(probably in green; see 2.1.0.2n.); see
Epilogue 9. The correct dress for a
hunter of deer included 'good bootes
and high, with an horne about his
necke. *Phoebus* saith, that they ought to
be cladde in greene when they hunt
the Hart or Bucke, & in russet when
they hunt the Bore, but that is of no
great importance, for I remit the colors
to the fantasies of me[n]' (*Hunting*,
101); see 1.3.115n.

239 kill my heart (F '*Hart*') See 98n.
Modernization of spelling obscures
Rosalind's pun (when read, though not
when heard). As Ganymede, she
adopts, in a standard Petrarchan trope,
the male stance of the wounded deer,
recalling Jaques's lament at 2.1.33–64;
cf. Orsino's 'That instant was I turn'd
into a hart' (*TN* 1.1.21). But cf. also *JC*
3.1.207–8: 'O world, thou wast the
forest to this hart, / And this indeed,
O world, the heart of thee' (cf.
4.2.3–4n.), where the metaphor may
arise from associations with *AYL*,
written in the same year (1599); see
5.2.30–1n. and p. 73.

---

230 forth such] *F2;* forth *F;* such *Douai ms, Capell*   237 holla] halla *Rowe*   thy] *Rowe;* the *F*
239 heart] *(*Hart*), Rowe*

CELIA   I would sing my song without a burden – thou   240
    bring'st me out of tune.

ROSALIND   Do you not know I am a woman? When I
    think, I must speak. Sweet, say on.

Enter ORLANDO *and* JAQUES.

CELIA   You bring me out. Soft, comes he not here?

ROSALIND   'Tis he! Slink by and note him.   245

JAQUES   I thank you for your company but, good faith, I
    had as lief have been myself alone.

ORLANDO
    And so had I, but yet for fashion' sake
    I thank you too for your society.

JAQUES   God b'wi' you, let's meet as little as we can.   250

ORLANDO   I do desire we may be better strangers.

---

240 **burden** (F 'burthen') either a chorus or refrain, or a *bourdon*, i.e. a bass line sung on a single note; see also 4.2.13.

241 **out of tune** Rosalind's interruptions distort the melody by sounding a false bass, but also spoil the rhythm by interrupting the flow of the words; *tune* can mean both musical pitch and musical time; see 5.3.43n.

242–3 **woman . . . speak** A mocking use by Ganymede of a stock satirical jibe about women's garrulity (see also 4.1.162), used by Rosalind to justify feminine importunacy, but also comically reminding Shakespeare's audience of the boy who plays her.

244 **bring me out** make me forget my lines; see 96n., 4.1.69. Shakespeare may incorporate into his text a moment from rehearsal (see 3.5.1n.); see *Ham* 2.1.51–2: 'By the mass, I was about to say something. Where did I

leave?' (Stern, *Rehearsal*, 100n., citing also Pennington, 60). Cf. *Cor* 5.3.40–2: 'Like a dull actor now / I have forgot my part and I am out, / Even to a full disgrace.'

245 **Slink by** creep past, an internal SD; see 1.1.25n.

247 **as lief** as soon
    myself alone by myself (Abbott, 20)

248–9 Editors since Pope have printed these lines as prose, but Orlando's fashionable propensity to blank verse is later mocked by Jaques (4.1.28–9).

248 **for fashion' sake** because it is the custom, or modish; cf. 2.4.57n.

250 *****God b'wi' you** F's 'God buy you' is probably a misreading of 'God bwy', a short form of 'God be with you'.
    let's . . . can a free-speaking fool's inversion of polite manners. Cf. 1.2.83–9, 2.7.58–9; see also 1.2.273–4n.

245 Slink] slip *Douai ms*   him.] him. Cel. *and* Ros. *retire / Theobald*   246–7] *Pope; F lines* faith / alone. /   248–9] *prose Pope*   248 fashion'] *(fashion), Craig;* fashions *Douai ms;* fashion's *Var 1785*
250 God b'wi' you] *(God buy you), Dyce;* adieu *Douai ms;* God be with you *Var 1773;* Good bye, you *Collier;* Goodbye *Oxf¹*

JAQUES I pray you, mar no more trees with writing love-
songs in their barks.

ORLANDO I pray you, mar no more of my verses with
reading them ill-favouredly.   255

JAQUES Rosalind is your love's name?

ORLANDO Yes, just.

JAQUES I do not like her name.

ORLANDO There was no thought of pleasing you when
she was christened.   260

JAQUES What stature is she of?

ORLANDO Just as high as my heart.

JAQUES You are full of pretty answers. Have you not been
acquainted with goldsmiths' wives, and conned them
out of rings?   265

ORLANDO Not so; but I answer you right painted cloth,

---

255 **reading them ill-favouredly** See
Harington, '*To* Sextus, *an ill reader*':
'For shame poynt [= punctuate] better,
and pronounce it cleerer, / Or be no
Reader, *Sextus*, be a Hearer' (*Epigrams
1618*, 3.6); cf. 3.5.1n. Both dramatist
and epigrammist allude to a famous
Martial epigram (1.39, cited in Douce,
Illustrations, 1.302; see also Scott-
Warren, *Harington*, 21); see 1.3.117n.
on *martial* and 2.5.3–4n..

257 **just** correct

262 For Rosalind's height see 1.2.261n.

264 **goldsmiths' wives** a courtier's scorn
of citizen taste (cf. *1H4* 3.1.242–52).
Sometimes seen as an allusion to
Robert Armin, who was a member of
the Goldsmiths' Guild; but many
actors belonged to the Guilds while
pursuing careers as players rather than
practising the skills associated with
the Guild (Kathman, 'Apprentices'),
which may make a specific reference
here unlikely.

conned learned by heart (Old English
cunnan, to know); cf. *TN* 1.5.168–9: 'I
have taken great pains to con it'.

265 **rings** The 'posy' (i.e. poesy) of a ring
was 'one verse, or two at the most, but
the shorter the better, we call them
Posies, and do paint them now a dayes
vpon the backe sides of our fruite
trenchers of wood, or vse them as
deuises in rings and armes and about
such courtly purposes' (Puttenham,
English Poetry, 47). Jaques suggests
that Orlando has learnt his elegant
answers from such a source. Cf. *Ham*
3.2.147: 'Is this a prologue, or the posy
of a ring?' Donne's Rabelaisian joke-
catalogue, *The Courtier's Library*,
ridicules the poet Sir John Davies,
member of the Middle Temple: '*The
Justice of England.* Vacation exercises
of John Davies on the Art of forming
Anagrams approximately true, and
Posies to engrave on Rings' (47–8; see
Manningham, 8).

266 **right** See 2.4.99n.

painted cloth Hangings painted with
ballads, stories or biblical texts were
used to decorate both inns and the private dwellings of ordinary citizens
(Watt, 194–8).

252 more] moe *Sisson*   254 more] *F2;* moe *F*

from whence you have studied your questions.

JAQUES   You have a nimble wit; I think 'twas made of
Atalanta's heels. Will you sit down with me, and we two
will rail against our mistress the world and all our   270
misery?

ORLANDO   I will chide no breather in the world but
myself, against whom I know most faults.

JAQUES   The worst fault you have is to be in love.

ORLANDO   'Tis a fault I will not change for your best   275
virtue. I am weary of you.

JAQUES   By my troth, I was seeking for a fool when I
found you.

ORLANDO   He is drowned in the brook. Look but in and
you shall see him.   280

JAQUES   There I shall see mine own figure.

ORLANDO   Which I take to be either a fool or a cipher.

JAQUES   I'll tarry no longer with you. Farewell, good

---

269 **Atalanta's heels** See 144n. Jaques
reluctantly admires Orlando's speedy
retorts, but hints that his 'sprinting'
wit will soon tire; cf. *MA* 1.1.136–7.

270 **rail . . . world** The malcontent
inveighs against the world as a disap-
pointed lover might rail against a faithless love; cf. Lady Fortune, 2.7.16.

272 **breather** living person; cf. *Son*
81.11–12: 'And tongues to be your
being shall rehearse, / When all the
breathers of this world are dead'.

276 **weary of you** a dismissal usually
reserved for the professional fool; see
AW 4.5.55, 'I begin to be aweary of
thee', and *TN* 4.1.1–22.

277–8 **fool . . . you** Either Jaques
counters Orlando's slur, or the insult
is involuntary, as Jaques was in fact
looking for Touchstone when he found
Orlando. In Ariosto, Orlando belongs
to the tradition of *en enamorado simple*
(Don Quixote's label): 'the fool in

love' (Dusinberre, 'As *Who?*', 12n.).

279–81 Orlando invokes the myth of
Narcissus who fell in love with his own
reflection. Cf. the Stationers' Register
entry, '*NARCISSUS* the fountaine of
Self Loue' (Arber, 3.71), for Jonson,
Cynthia's Revels. For reflections in the
mirror of self, see 3.5.55n.

281 **figure** image, but also a mathematical
figure, which gives Orlando the cue
for *cipher* (see 282n.); cf. *1H4* 1.3.208:
'He apprehends a world of figures
here'.

282 **cipher** nought, i.e. a figure 0 (like a
reflected face), but also naught (worthless), like a fool; see 1.1.33–4n. Cf.
KL 1.4.126: 'This is nothing, fool.'
Orlando implies that Jaques's pose of
wisdom is mere folly; cf. 5.1.31–2. The
word *cipher* could be a cue for Orlando
to yawn, in which the mouth becomes
an O.

283 **tarry** stay

Signior Love.   [*Exit Jaques.*]

ORLANDO   I am glad of your departure. Adieu, good   285
Monsieur Melancholy.

ROSALIND   I will speak to him like a saucy lackey and
under that habit play the knave with him. – Do you
hear, forester?

ORLANDO   Very well; what would you?   290

ROSALIND   I pray you, what is't o'clock?

ORLANDO   You should ask me what time o'day. There's
no clock in the forest.

ROSALIND   Then there is no true lover in the forest, else
sighing every minute and groaning every hour would   295
detect the lazy foot of time as well as a clock.

---

284 **Signior Love** a jibe at Italy, home of
Petrarchan passion; see 277–8n.

286 **Monsieur Melancholy** Orlando's
emphasis on Jaques's Frenchness highlights his alienation from an English
Forest hospitable to lovers; see
5.4.193n. and p. 109; see also pp. 46, 48.

287–8 **I . . . him** spoken to Celia before
Rosalind moves forward to accost
Orlando

287 **saucy lackey** impudent serving-boy

288 **habit** disguise

play the knave act the part of a rogu-
ish youth

289 **forester** The word here is synonymous with *hunter*; see 238n. In Lodge,
Ganymede addresses Rosader as a
lovesick forester: 'Reading the sonnet
ouer, & hearing him name *Rosalynde*,
Aliena lookt on *Ganimede* and laught,
and *Ganimede* looking backe on the
Forrester, and seeing it was *Rosader*,
blusht: yet thinking to shrowd all
vnder her pages apparell, she boldly
returned to *Rosader*' (sig. G3ᵛ).
Ganymede addresses Orlando as one
of the employed 'men' rather than as a
nobleman; cf. Touchstone's accosting
of Corin, 2.4.63.

291 **what is't o'clock?** What time is it?
Cf. Falstaff's first question in *1H4*:
'Now, Hal, what time of day is it, lad?'
(1.2.1).

293 **no clock** In Rabelais's Abbey of
Thelema 'It was decreed that in this
new structure there should be neither
Clock nor Dial . . . for (said *Gargantua*)
The greatest losse of time that I know,
is to count the hours' (Rabelais/
Urquhart, 1.52, 146; see Dusinberre,
'As *Who?*', 14, and Appendix 1).

295 **minute . . . hour** Cf. Lodge: 'for
Loue measures euerie minute, and
thinkes houres to bee dayes, and dayes
to bee moneths, till they feede theyr
eyes with the sight of theyr desired
obiect' (sig. K4ᵛ); cf. *WT* 1.2.289–90:
'wishing clocks more swift? / Hours,
minutes? noon, midnight?'

296 **lazy foot** because it moves so slowly
(for the lover); Rosalind may still be
playing with lame verses and
Atalanta's feet; but she also rewrites a
literary trope of Petrarchan love poetry, which Shakespeare himself uses in
Son 19.6 ('swift-footed time'), and is
challenged by Orlando, well versed in
the idiom, at 297.

---

284 SD] *Rowe; after 286 Douai ms, Capell*   286 Melancholy.] melancholy! Cel. *and* Ros. *come forward.*
/ *Theobald*   287–8 I . . . him] *marked as aside to* Cel. *Capell*

ORLANDO   And why not the swift foot of time? Had not
that been as proper?

ROSALIND   By no means, sir. Time travels in divers paces
with divers persons. I'll tell you who Time ambles   300
withal, who Time trots withal, who Time gallops
withal and who he stands still withal.

ORLANDO   I prithee, who doth he trot withal?

ROSALIND   Marry, he trots hard with a young maid
between the contract of her marriage and the day it is   305
solemnized. If the interim be but a se'nnight, Time's
pace is so hard that it seems the length of seven year.

ORLANDO   Who ambles Time withal?

ROSALIND   With a priest that lacks Latin, and a rich man
that hath not the gout; for the one sleeps easily because   310
he cannot study, and the other lives merrily because he
feels no pain; the one lacking the burden of lean and
wasteful learning, the other knowing no burden of
heavy tedious penury. These Time ambles withal.

ORLANDO   Who doth he gallop withal?   315

ROSALIND   With a thief to the gallows; for though he go
as softly as foot can fall, he thinks himself too soon
there.

ORLANDO   Who stays it still withal?

298 **proper** fitting or decorous

299, 300 **divers** various

302 **withal** with, in place of 'with whom'

306 **se'nnight** week, seven-night (cf. fortnight = fourteen nights)

307 **hard** laboured

309 **priest . . . Latin** a hedge-priest or uneducated priest, a term anticipating the arrival of Sir Oliver Mar-text on stage in the next scene. *Latin* does not necessarily imply a Catholic priest, as all educated clergymen would have known Latin.

310 **gout** a malady which causes lameness and was believed to be connected with drinking too much wine

313 **wasteful** suggests both being wasted away (lean) with study, and that study itself is a waste of good living time; cf. *LLL* 1.1.74–6.

314 **penury** poverty; Rosalind plays on the sounds of 'pain' and 'penury', both of which are avoided by the rich man.

317 **softly** slowly (Onions, 2, p. 202), suggesting both the thief's reluctance and the stealth of his craft

319 stays it] stays he *Douai ms;* stands he *Collier²*

ROSALIND   With lawyers in the vacation; for they sleep   320
between term and term and then they perceive not how
time moves.

ORLANDO   Where dwell you, pretty youth?

ROSALIND   With this shepherdess, my sister, here in the
skirts of the forest, like fringe upon a petticoat.   325

ORLANDO   Are you native of this place?

ROSALIND   As the coney that you see dwell where she is
kindled.

ORLANDO   Your accent is something finer than you could
purchase in so removed a dwelling.   330

ROSALIND   I have been told so of many. But indeed, an
old religious uncle of mine taught me to speak, who
was in his youth an inland man – one that knew
courtship too well, for there he fell in love. I have heard
him read many lectures against it, and I thank God I am   335

---

320 **vacation** the period between legal
terms (see 321n.)

321 **term** The legal year was divided into
terms, noted in Adams, *Tables*, sig.
Bvʳ: Hillary (23 January to 12 or 13
February), Easter (17 days after Easter
till the Monday after Ascension day),
Trinity (the twelfth day after Whitsun
for a further 19 days), and Michaelmas
(9 or 10 October till 28 or 29
November).

323 **pretty** personable, attractive; applicable to young men as well as to young
women. The phrase *pretty youth* or *fair
youth* (370, 4.3.6), or *Fair sir* (2.4.74),
accompanies most addresses to
Ganymede, reminding the audience of
Rosalind's 'feminine' beauty (3.2.10);
see 3.5.114, 4.1.1n.

325 **skirts** the usual word for the edges or
borders of a forest (see 4.3.75n.). See
Hunting, 90: 'For somewhiles Harts do
lye . . . in the borders or skirts of the
Forrest, in some little groues or cop-
pises'; see also 5.4.157. The simile

which follows ('like fringe upon a petticoat') metamorphoses the skirts of
the forest into the skirts of a woman, a
'feminine' marker particularly necessary when Ganymede was played by a
boy actor.

like fringe See 2.7.52n. on *as way*.

327 **coney** mountain rabbit

328 **kindled** conceived and born (used
for animals with proliferating young);
often cut in nineteenth-century editions as improper

329 **finer** more refined

330 **removed** remote

332 **old religious uncle** The hermit was
a part of the traditional epic lore of the
Forest of Arden; see pp. 50, 95–6.
Rosalind's uncle is also a magician (see
5.2.59n., 5.4.33).

333 **inland** nurtured at court

334 **courtship** courtly manners, including the art of wooing a lady

335 **read many lectures** make many
sermons, but also offer many admon-
ishments or reproofs

326 native] a native *Var 1773*   335 lectures] *(Lectors)*, *F3;* Lecturs *F2*

not a woman, to be touched with so many giddy
offences as he hath generally taxed their whole sex
withal.

ORLANDO   Can you remember any of the principal evils
that he laid to the charge of women?   340

ROSALIND   There were none principal – they were all like
one another as ha'pence are, every one fault seeming
monstrous till his fellow-fault came to match it.

ORLANDO   I prithee, recount some of them.

ROSALIND   No. I will not cast away my physic but on   345
those that are sick. There is a man haunts the forest that
abuses our young plants with carving 'Rosalind' on
their barks; hangs odes upon hawthorns and elegies on
brambles; all, forsooth, deifying the name of Rosalind.
If I could meet that fancy-monger I would give him   350
some good counsel, for he seems to have the quotidian
of love upon him.

---

336 **not a woman** Ganymede at his
    sauciest; see 242 and n.
    giddy frivolous, irresponsible; cf.
    5.2.5. Cf. *MA* 5.4.106–7: 'for man is a
    giddy thing, and this is my conclu-
    sion'. The word can also imply 'lecher-
    ous'; see 4.1.142.
337 **taxed** accused; see 2.7.71.
    whole sex The medieval literary genre
    of satire on women was associated
    with a celibate clergy; Chaucer's Wife
    of Bath (fol. 36ʳ) tears the page out of
    the satire on women which her fifth
    husband, a 'clerk' (i.e., cleric), insists
    on reading to her. Dispraise of women
    (as well as praise) formed a part of
    humanist literary culture in the six-
    teenth century (Dusinberre, *Women*,
    esp. 175–9).
340 **laid . . . of** included in the prosecut-
    ing documents in a court case against
345–6 **I . . . sick** See Matthew, 9.12: 'The
    whole nede not a physicion, but thei

that are sicke' (Geneva Bible).
345 **cast away** waste
    physic medicine
347 **our** proprietorial, as if from a native
    of the forest
348 **odes** poems of praise, usually to a
    high subject
    elegies love poems, not laments for
    the dead (*OED* elegy 2), from Ovid's
    Amores, translated by Marlowe (first
    printed 1598) – 'Toyes and light
    Elegies my darts I tooke' (Marlowe,
    Elegies, 2.1.21). Their verse form was
    that of the Latin elegiac couplet (a
    hexameter followed by a pentameter);
    see also 3.3.6n. on *honest Ovid*.
349 **deifying* F's 'defying' is probably a
    compositor's error; the two words are
    connected again at 4.3.32 (see n.).
350 **fancy-monger** coiner of fantasies;
    also one who incites love; see 4.3.100,
    3.5.30.
351 **quotidian** daily

342 ha'pence] *(*halfe pence*)*, *this edn*   343 monstrous] most monstrous *Hudson²* *(Walker)*
349 deifying] *F2;* defying *F*

ORLANDO   I am he that is so love-shaked. I pray you tell
me your remedy.

ROSALIND   There is none of my uncle's marks upon you.   355
He taught me how to know a man in love, in which cage
of rushes I am sure you are not prisoner.

ORLANDO   What were his marks?

ROSALIND   A lean cheek, which you have not; a blue eye
and sunken, which you have not; an unquestionable   360
spirit, which you have not; a beard neglected, which
you have not – but I pardon you for that, for simply
your having in beard is a younger brother's revenue.
Then your hose should be ungartered, your bonnet
unbanded, your sleeve unbuttoned, your shoe untied,   365
and everything about you demonstrating a careless
desolation. But you are no such man. You are rather

353 **love-shaked** shivering with the fever
of love
355, 358 **marks** distinguishing characteristics (cf. *TGV* 2.1.16–29, *LLL*
3.1.12–22). Red marks or 'tokens' were
one sign of the plague (Pepys, 6.93n.)
and an Elizabethan audience might
have recognized a sequence of words
suggesting the 'infection' of passion,
i.e. *physic* (345), *sick* (346), *love-shaked*
(353); see 111 and cf. *TN* 1.5.289:
'Even so quickly may one catch the
plague?'
356–7 **cage of rushes** a prison from
whose soft bars escape is easy
359 **a blue eye** In folk songs the lover is
usually blue-eyed; but Rosalind may
comment on 'a blueness about the
eyes' (Steevens) caused by insomnia.
360–1 **unquestionable spirit** moody,
disconsolate, unwilling to be ques-
tioned (*OED* unquestionable 3a, only
example)
362–3 **simply . . . revenue** Rosalind
nearly blows her disguise by revealing
her awareness that Orlando is the

younger brother, in beard as in income
(see 201n. and 5.4.70n.). Class was an
element in the regulations governing
the wearing of beards at Lincoln's Inn
in the sixteenth century: 'Item, that
none under the degre of a knight ["Or
Bencher", n.], being in comons, ware
any berde above iii weaks growinge'
(*Black Books*, I. 321).
364 **hose . . . ungartered** stockings
falling carelessly down your legs; cf.
Ham 2.1.78–9: 'his stockings foul'd, /
Ungarter'd and down-gyved to his
ankle'.
364–5 **bonnet unbanded** hat without a
hatband, indicating slovenliness
366–7 **careless desolation** indifference
to appearance caused by abandonment
to passion; Lodge's Rosader, unlike
Orlando, 'registred his melancholy
passions: they saw the sodaine change
of his looks, his folded armes, his passionate sighes' (sig. G3ᵛ). Montanus's
appearance at the wedding, when he
thinks he has lost Phoebe, epitomizes
that of the forsaken lover (sig. O4ᵛ).

357 are] *F2;* art *F*   363 in] no *F2*

point-device in your accoutrements, as loving yourself
than seeming the lover of any other.

ORLANDO   Fair youth, I would I could make thee believe   370
I love.

ROSALIND   Me believe it? You may as soon make her that
you love believe it, which I warrant she is apter to do
than to confess she does. That is one of the points in
the which women still give the lie to their consciences.   375
But in good sooth, are you he that hangs the verses on
the trees, wherein Rosalind is so admired?

ORLANDO   I swear to thee, youth, by the white hand of
Rosalind, I am that he, that unfortunate he.

ROSALIND   But are you so much in love as your rhymes   380
speak?

ORLANDO   Neither rhyme nor reason can express how
much.

ROSALIND   Love is merely a madness, and I tell you
deserves as well a dark house and a whip as madmen do;   385
and the reason why they are not so punished and cured

---

368 **point-device** fastidiously attentive to
detail (*OED* B *adj.*, citing this line); cf.
1.1.156–7n. Cf. *LLL* 5.1.18–19: 'point-
device companions'. A 'device' was the
impresa or decorated shield with which
the knight entered to joust (Strong,
Cult, 135; see Fig. 11), familiar to the
Elizabethans from the tournaments
staged annually on Elizabeth's
Accession Day, 17 November. The
epithet underlines the chivalric context
which surrounds Orlando.
    accoutrements trappings (of a
knight)
373 **warrant** guarantee
374 **confess she does** either 'recognize
your love for her' or 'acknowledge her
love for you', or perhaps both
375 **give . . . to** contradict
    consciences their inmost convictions;
cf. *Ham* 3.1.83: 'Thus conscience does

make cowards of us all'.
376 **in good sooth** in good faith, truly; a
'citizen' oath more suitable for a shepherd boy than for a Duke's daughter;
see *1H4* 3.1.242–52.
378 **white hand** characteristic of a
nobly born woman: has Ganymede
besmirched his hands for disguise (see
1.3.109n.)? Cf. Phoebe's *housewife's
hand* (4.3.27 and n.).
382 **rhyme nor reason** a common tag; see
CE 2.2.48: 'When in the why and the
wherefore is neither rhyme nor reason'.
384 **Love . . . madness** Cf. *MND*
5.1.7–8: 'The lunatic, the lover, and
the poet / Are of imagination all compact'.
385 **dark house** Cf. the protest of the
'mad' Malvolio, infatuated with Olivia,
TN 4.2.29–30: 'They have laid me
here in hideous darkness.'

---

368 point-device] *(*point deuice*)*

is that the lunacy is so ordinary that the whippers are in
love too. Yet I profess curing it by counsel.

ORLANDO   Did you ever cure any so?

ROSALIND   Yes, one, and in this manner. He was to   390
imagine me his love, his mistress, and I set him every
day to woo me. At which time would I – being but a
moonish youth – grieve, be effeminate, changeable,
longing and liking, proud, fantastical, apish, shallow,
inconstant, full of tears, full of smiles; for every passion   395
something and for no passion truly anything, as boys
and women are for the most part cattle of this colour;
would now like him, now loath him; then entertain
him, then forswear him; now weep for him, then spit at
him; that I drave my suitor from his mad humour of   400
love to a living humour of madness, which was to
forswear the full stream of the world and to live in a
nook merely monastic. And thus I cured him, and this
way will I take upon me to wash your liver as clean as a

---

393 **moonish** moody, governed by the
moon; see 5.2.106nn.
effeminate a Ganymede joke
394 **liking** loving
fantastical full of extravagant fancies
(see 3.3.99n.).
apish inclined to imitate. Cf. *MM*
2.2.121–3: 'like an angry ape / Plays
such fantastic tricks before high heav-
en / As makes the angels weep'.
397 **cattle . . . colour** creatures of this
kind. In Lodge, Ganimede makes the
parallel speech on arrival in Arden:
'what mad cattel you women be' (sig.
D4ᵛ).
400 **drave** drove (archaic, north-country
form)
401 **living** vital
madness In Ariosto, Orlando goes
mad for love of Angelica.
402–3 **forswear . . . monastic** renounce

the full life of the secular world for the
cell of a monk. Anti-monasticism constituted a vital element in Reformation
thought, popularized from Erasmus's
Folly and many other sources
(Dusinberre, *Women*, 30–1, 40–6; see
3.3.53n. on *Is . . . blessed?*, 5.4.179).
This line would have had extra point
when the play was performed after
1609 at the private theatre at
Blackfriars, a converted monastery;
see pp. 6, 43.
402 **world** the antithesis to the single life
of the monastery, particularly in relation to marriage – a choice of 'the
world' rather than the sanctified calling of single life; see 5.3.4–5n.
403 **nook** corner
404 **liver** believed to be the seat of the
passions; see *Tem* 4.1.56: 'the ardour of
my liver'.

404 clean] cleare *F2*

sound sheep's heart, that there shall not be one spot of   405
love in't.

ORLANDO   I would not be cured, youth.

ROSALIND   I would cure you, if you would but call me
Rosalind and come every day to my cote and woo me.

ORLANDO   Now by the faith of my love, I will. Tell me   410
where it is.

ROSALIND   Go with me to it and I'll show it you; and by
the way you shall tell me where in the forest you live.
Will you go?

ORLANDO   With all my heart, good youth.   415

ROSALIND   Nay, you must call me Rosalind. Come, sister,
will you go?   *Exeunt.*

3.3   *Enter* TOUCHSTONE, AUDREY *and*
                    JAQUES [*behind*].

TOUCHSTONE   Come apace, good Audrey – I will fetch
up your goats, Audrey. And how, Audrey? Am I the

---

405 **sound sheep's heart** Ganymede
keeps decorum in his role as shepherd.
407 **would not** do not want to
409 **cote** cottage
416 **Rosalind** The name of Rosalind
both begins and ends the scene, which
opens with the lover proclaiming his
love and closes with his undertaking a
cure he is certain won't work.
sister a triumphant exit line after the
success of Ganymede's disguise
3.3 This scene was cut in many eight-
eenth- and nineteenth-century productions, although reinstated by
Macready in 1842. The role of Sir
Oliver Mar-text was still subsequently
often cut, perhaps because its comedy,
deriving originally from jokes about
the Elizabethan Marprelate controversy, in which the office of bishop was

attacked by some extreme religious
sectarians (see List of Roles, 18n., p. 58
and Appendix 2), seemed too rooted in
Elizabethan topicality.
0.1–2 Jaques is not seen by Touchstone
until line 67 when he comes forward,
offering to give Audrey away at the
wedding ceremony.
1   **Come apace** come along, hurry up.
For traditional stage business see
Macready's note: 'No apple, – or
turnip munching – mind, Audrey!'
(Shattuck, facing 62).
1–2 **fetch up** round up
2   **And how** colloquial: 'what do you
think?'; F3's 'now' is attractive, as the
scene opens with Audrey rounding up
her goats watched by an impatient
Touchstone, who offers to do it for her
and finally secures her attention.

3.3] *(Scoena Tertia.)*   Location] *Another part of the forest / Dyce*   0.1 TOUCHSTONE] *Malone; Clowne
F*   0.2 *behind*] *Dyce; watching them / Johnson; at a Distance, observing them / Capell*   2 how] now *F3*

man yet? Doth my simple feature content you?

AUDREY   Your features, Lord warrant us! What features?

TOUCHSTONE   I am here with thee and thy goats, as the   5
most capricious poet, honest Ovid, was among the
Goths.

JAQUES [*aside*]   O knowledge ill-inhabited, worse than
Jove in a thatched house.

3   **feature** form, proportions, shape
(*OED sb.* 1a, usually singular). The
question would have been particularly
funny from Shakespeare's clown,
Robert Armin, a man of diminutive
stature and grotesque appearance; see
pp. 4, 112.
content Touchstone enters into the
language of Arden, enquiring not
whether he pleases Audrey, but
whether his appearance gives her satis-
faction; see 3.2.17n.

4   **Lord warrant us!** Good heavens! –
literally, God protect us (*OED* warrant
v. 1 *obs.*)

6   **capricious** lascivious. Touchstone
plays on the Latin for goat
(*caper/capri*, Upton, 246), a byword
for lust; cf. *KL* 1.2.127, 'goatish
disposition', and *Oth* 3.3.406: 'Were
they as prime as goats, as hot as
monkeys'.
honest Ovid The word *honest* means
both chaste (women) and truthful or
honourable (men); cf. 5.3.7, 4. Ovid is
*dis*honest on both counts. He was
exiled for the unchaste *Ars Amatoria*.
His *Amores* (see 3.2.348n.) were called
in for burning by the Bishops' Order
(Marlowe, 7; Bate, 159) and are named
by Lodge's Aliena during both
Rosader's and Saladyne's wooing (sigs
G3^v–4^r, H4^r, M4^v). Cf. Sidney's entry
in *England's Parnassus*: 'Yet neuer
shall my song omit / Her thighes, for
Ouids song more fit' (286. 2012).
Montaigne accuses Ovid of dishonesty

for his fiction of the Golden Age (see
p. 94).

7   **Goths** pronounced 'goats' in
Elizabethan English: 'The Goths, are
the *Getae*: Ovid. *Trist.*5.7' (Upton,
246), i.e. the tribe of the Getes, who
lived near the Black Sea, where Ovid
was exiled.

8 SD   No asides are marked in F; Jaques's
interjections function almost as a chorus heard by the audience but not by
Touchstone and Audrey.

8   **ill-inhabited** poorly housed, because
in a fool's head, but also a pun on the
fool's 'habit' (clothes); see 2.7.13n.
Douce notes: '[The Fool should]
wear asses' ears to his hood, which
is probably the head dress intended by
Shakspeare [*sic*], there being no allusion whatever to a cock's head or
comb' (*Illustrations*, 1.310).

9   **Jove . . . house** When Baucis and
Philemon entertained Jupiter in their
thatched cottage they did not recognize
him (Ovid, *Met.*, 8, pp. 106^r–107^v); cf.
MA 2.1.88–9. The story was often
invoked by Elizabeth's hosts on her
royal progresses, as in Lady Russell's
entertainment at Bisham, 1592: '*Jupiter*
came into the house of poore *Baucis*,
and she vouchsafeth to visite the bare
Farmers of her subjects' (J. Wilson,
45); cf. John Florio's dedication to *A
World of Words*: 'that I and my poore
studies, like *Philemon* and *Baucis*, may
in so lowe a cottage entertaine so high,
if not deities, yet dignities' (sig. a3^r).

4 features . . . features] feature . . . feature *Rann*   8, 29, 42 SDs] *Johnson*

TOUCHSTONE   When   a   man's   verses   cannot   be   10
understood, nor a man's good wit seconded with the
forward child, understanding, it strikes a man more
dead than a great reckoning in a little room. Truly, I
would the gods had made thee poetical.

AUDREY   I do not know what poetical is. Is it honest in   15
deed and word? Is it a true thing?

TOUCHSTONE   No, truly; for the truest poetry is the most
faining, and lovers are given to poetry, and what they
swear in poetry may be said, as lovers, they do feign.

10–11 **cannot be understood** Ovid complained that the Goths didn't understand his poetry (Bate, 159).

11 **seconded with** reinforced by

12 **forward** precocious

13 **great . . . room** often taken to refer to Marlowe's death in 1591 in a Deptford inn during a scuffle, allegedly over his failure to pay a bill. However, the *great reckoning* may be a scatological joke – Hanmer emended to 'reeking' – with *little room* a euphemism for a privy ('jakes', see 68n.). Harington invented his water-closet to 'find meanes to amend the ill savours in Ritchmond and Greenwich' (*Apology* [for *Ajax*], 209), which were the natural consequence of much feasting (great reckonings in little rooms); see Dusinberre, 'As *Who?*', 13–16.

Truly The word *truly* acts as a refrain (at 17, 22, 26, 32) in a passage of sustained word-play on poetry and lies; cf. 3.2.35n.

14 **poetical** capable of understanding poetry

15–16 **honest . . . true** The debate about poetry and lies underpins the whole play, and was central to attacks on the theatre. See Sidney's rebuttal: 'Now for the poet, he nothing affirms, and therefore never lieth' (*Apology*, 123); cf. Harington's 'Apology of Poetry'.

17 **No, truly** a paradoxical answer; Touchstone's negative is immediately undermined by his affirmative *truly*; cf. 3.2.35n. and 3.4.19n. 'The way Touchstone's argument deconstructs the assertion of his "truly" is symptomatic of the scepticism which the whole play extends to questions of truth in language' (Bath, 31).

18–19 **faining . . . feign** True poetry demonstrates the greatest desire or love, but it also represents the greatest fantasy, which extreme Protestants condemned as lies; see 4.1.96n. Touchstone puns *faining* – desiring or longing (*OED* fain *v.*¹ 3 *obs.*) – with *feign*, meaning to pretend, or to create fictions (*OED* 2c); see 21n., 24n. and 42n. Empson, *Versions*, compares *MND*: '"Thou hast by moonlight at her window sung / With faining voice verses of feigning love" (1.1.30–1, *TLN* 60–61) . . . He feigns true love because he would fain possess her' (113); see p. 117. Cf. Spenser, 'An Hymn in Honour of Love': 'And to his fayning fansie represent / Sights never seene, and thousand shadowes vaine' (*Hymnes*, 595), where 'fayning', i.e. 'desiring', also means 'fabricating'.

19 **may** 'it' is implied; cf. 1.1.3n.

lovers . . . feign 'Lovers write poems, and what they vow in their poems may

13 reckoning] reeking *Hanmer*   18 faining] feigning *Rowe*   19 may] it may *Collier*² *(Mason)*

AUDREY   Do you wish then that the gods had made me   20
poetical?

TOUCHSTONE   I do truly, for thou swear'st to me thou art
honest. Now if thou wert a poet I might have some
hope thou didst feign.

AUDREY   Would you not have me honest?   25

TOUCHSTONE   No, truly, unless thou wert hard-
favoured; for honesty coupled to beauty is to have
honey a sauce to sugar.

JAQUES [*aside*]   A material fool.

AUDREY   Well, I am not fair, and therefore I pray the gods   30
make me honest.

TOUCHSTONE   Truly; and to cast away honesty upon a
foul slut were to put good meat into an unclean dish.

AUDREY   I am not a slut, though I thank the gods I am
foul.   35

TOUCHSTONE   Well, praised be the gods for thy foulness:
sluttishness may come hereafter. But be it as it may be,
I will marry thee. And to that end I have been with Sir
Oliver Mar-text, the vicar of the next village, who hath

be considered fiction in terms of their
loving.' See 3.5.19 and Rosalind's challenge to Orlando at 3.2.380–1. Sidney
protested: 'But *truly* many of such
writings as come under the banner of
unresistible love, if I were a mistress,
would never persuade me they were in
love; so coldly they apply fiery speeches, as men that had rather read lovers'
writings . . . than that *in truth* they feel
those passions' (*Apology*, 137–8, my
emphasis).

21   **poetical** i.e. dishonest (according to
your definition of poetry) – not as stupid a question as Touchstone has led
one to expect of Audrey

24   **didst feign** were lying – about your
chastity (honesty); see 6n.

26–7   **hard-favoured** ugly

28   **honey . . . sugar** i.e. too much of a
good thing

29   **material** full of matter, i.e. obser-

vations of substance; see Jonson,
Poetaster, in which the dramatist uses
the epithet 'material' for his own alter
ego, the poet Horace (5.1.128). See
2.1.68n.

32–3   **to cast . . . dish** Chastity is wasted
on an ugly slattern, as good meat is
spoilt by being in a dirty dish.

33   **foul** ugly, with possibly an implication
of dirty and disreputable

34–5   'I don't sleep around, but I am
grateful to God for my homely looks.'

35   **foul** plain, having 'homely' looks
(Halliwell)

37   **sluttishness . . . hereafter** with luck
loose living will follow – a throwaway
line for the audience

38–9   **Sir Oliver Mar**-text *Mar-text*
recapitulates the theme of 'making and
marring' (see 1.1.29n., 31n.).

39   **vicar . . . village** implies an Anglican
parish priest, but see 77–9n.

promised to meet me in this place of the forest and to   40
couple us.

JAQUES [*aside*]   I would fain see this meeting.

AUDREY   Well, the gods give us joy!

TOUCHSTONE   Amen. – A man may, if he were of a
fearful heart, stagger in this attempt, for here we have   45
no temple but the wood, no assembly but horn-beasts.
But what though? Courage! As horns are odious, they
are necessary. It is said, many a man knows no end of
his goods; right. Many a man has good horns and
knows no end of them. Well, that is the dowry of his   50
wife – 'tis none of his own getting. Horns? Even so.

---

41 **couple** join in wedlock; see *BCP*, 'Of
Matrimony': 'For be ye well assured,
that so many as be coupled together
otherwayes then Gods worde doth
allowe: are not ioyned of God, neyther
is theyr matrymonye lawfull' (fol.
136').

42 **would fain** would be glad to; see
1.2.152n.

44 **Amen. – A man** The liturgical *Amen*
prompts Touchstone's *A man*. The
natural entry for Sir Oliver would
be after *Amen* (see Appendix 4).
Touchstone's *horns* monologue could
represent an ad lib, a practice for
which the comic actor Will Kemp was
famous (Stern, *Rehearsal*, 102). The
clown Richard Tarlton (d. 1588)
performed a 'horns' comic set-piece
involving repartee with the audience
(see 51–2n.), on one occasion 'holding
up two fingers to a man in the
audience' (*Tarlton's Jests*, 14–15, cited
in Mann, 59–60; see Fig. 13).
However, Shakespeare may create
deliberately an illusion of extempore
speech in accordance with the
rhetorical practice of 'copiousness'
(see Cave, *Cornucopian*, 125–34, and

57–8n.; see Thorne, 9–10, for the
influence of Erasmus's *De Copia* on
AYL).

45 **heart** but also 'hart', which then
prompts *horn-beasts* (46, Kökeritz,
112)

46 **temple . . . wood** Classical deities are
invoked by *temple*, but this is also an
audience-conscious remark, suggesting possible performance at the Inns of
Court ('Temples'); see p. 59.
horn-beasts deer, but Touchstone
also aims his bolt at the possible 'cuckolds' in the audience; cf. *Oth* 4.1.62–4.

48–9 **knows . . . goods** does not know the
extent of his property

50 **knows . . . them** doesn't know how
many times he has been cuckolded

51 **getting** endeavouring, but also beget-
ting

51–2 **Horns? . . . alone?** The jester sets
up an internal question-and-answer
pattern; see 44n. Fear of horns is
endemic in satire against women,
but one analogue to this speech occurs
in Rabelais's *Tiers Livre* (Rabelais/
Urquhart, 3.38, p. 411). Like the
'carting' of unruly women, the humi-
liation of cuckolds was part of the

44–58 A man . . . want] *om. Douai ms*   44 may] might *Collier²*   51–2 Horns? Even so. Poor men
alone?] *Theobald subst.;* hornes, euen so poore men alone: *F*

Poor men alone? No, no, the noblest deer hath them as
huge as the rascal. Is the single man therefore blessed?
No. As a walled town is more worthier than a village, so
is the forehead of a married man more honourable than   55
the bare brow of a bachelor. And by how much defence
is better than no skill, by so much is a horn more
precious than to want.

Enter SIR OLIVER MAR-TEXT.

Here comes Sir Oliver. Sir Oliver Mar-text, you are
well met. Will you dispatch us here under this tree or   60
shall we go with you to your chapel?

ritual of Shrove Tuesday sports
(Laroque, 100, 285; see 3.2.105n.).
52 **noblest deer** another barbed quip for
a court audience; see 4.2.16n.
53 **rascal** 'the young, lean, or inferior
deer of a herd, distinguished from the
full-grown antlered bucks or stags'
(*OED n.* and *a.* 4 *obs.*). Cf. *1H6*
4.2.48–9: 'If we be English deer, be
then in blood: / Not rascal-like to fall
down with a pinch'. Berry argues that
rascal was especially associated with
Falstaff both in *1H4* and in *MW*
(*Hunt*, 134–8).
Is . . . blessed? 'Is a bachelor in a
more laudable and happy state?'
Touchstone's question dominated the
Reformation debate by Luther,
Erasmus and others about the relative
merits of marriage and celibacy (see
3.2.402n.; also 5.4.179). Cf. *MND*
1.1.74–8, where Theseus threatens
Helena with the state of 'single
blessedness' if she refuses Demetrius.
54–6 **As . . . bachelor** 'As a properly
defended town is more honourable and
prosperous than an undefended country village, so the [horned] brow of a
married man [albeit caused by a faith-

less wife] is still more worthy of
respect than the unadorned forehead
of a bachelor.' This is somewhat on the
lines of 'nothing [nought] venture,
nothing [nought] gain' (Dent, N319).
Touchstone rewrites the defence of
marriage as a defence of cuckolds.
54 **walled** a feature of medieval towns
more worthier See 3.2.58n.
56–7 **defence . . . no skill** The married
man's horns can be used to defend
himself, whereas the bachelor's lack
of them suggests also his lack of the
skills required of a married man; cf.
4.1.55–6n.
57–8 **a . . . want** a horn on your head
is better than no horn at all. The
plenteousness of horns leads the clown
to the horn of plenty – the rhetorical
figure of *cornucopia*, deriving from
Quintilian (see Cave, *Cornucopian*,
173–82); see 44n. Cf. Palmer (38) for
Kemp's use of the same cornucopious
method in *Nine Days' Wonder*.
60, 69 **well met** welcome
60 **dispatch us** fix us up quickly
61 **chapel** a place of meeting for
worship (not a consecrated church);
see 77–9n.

58.1] *after* Oliver. *59 Douai ms, Dyce*

SIR OLIVER MAR-TEXT   Is there none here to give the
woman?

TOUCHSTONE   I will not take her on gift of any man.

SIR OLIVER MAR-TEXT   Truly she must be given or the   65
marriage is not lawful.

JAQUES [*Advances.*]   Proceed, proceed. I'll give her.

TOUCHSTONE   Good even, good Master What-ye-call't,
how do you, sir? You are very well met. God'ild you for
your last company. I am very glad to see you. Even a toy   70
in hand here, sir – nay, pray be covered.

JAQUES   Will you be married, motley?

TOUCHSTONE   As the ox hath his bow, sir, the horse his
curb and the falcon her bells, so man hath his desires;

62–3 give the woman The first question
put by the priest at the beginning of
the marriage service in *BCP*: 'who
geveth this woman to be maried to this
man?' (fol. 137ʳ). The usual giver is the
bride's father; see 5.4.7.

64 a deliberate bawdy misinterpretation,
implying that he will not accept
Audrey if she has already 'given' herself to another; cf. 5.1.8.

68 What-ye-call't a circumlocution for a
'jakes' (privy), i.e. Jaques (see List of
Roles, 13n.), creating links with
Harington's *Ajax* (Grimble, 130;
Dusinberre, 'As *Who?*', 11–12;
Bednarz, 109); see 13n. on *great . . .
room.*

69 God'ild you God reward you; a corruption of 'God yield you (reward)'
(*OED* yield *v.* B7, and see *OED* god 8);
see 5.4.54 and Cercignani, 362.

70 last company the meeting described
by Jaques at 2.7.12–43.
a toy a slight thing; also used 'for any
slight or unworthy composition [and]
. . . in a somewhat more specific way for
frivolous dramatic devices' (Baskervill,

88 and n.). In Cambridge MS Dd.2.11,
which contains the Shakespearean
'Heartsease' (*RJ*) and 'Robin' (*Ham*),
'A Toy' appears on fol. 37ʳ, 'The
Squirrills Toy' on 77ʳ, and 'Kempes
Jigge' on 99ᵛ. Touchstone's use of *toy*
may cue in singing and dancing. Cf.
Marston, *Scourge* (1598): 'A hall, a hall,
/ Roome for the Spheres, the Orbes
celestiall / Will daunce *Kemps Jigge*'
(Satire 10.2, p. 106; see 77n., 5.4.64n.,
pp. 111–13 and Appendix 2).

71 in hand in the process of being made
my own
be covered put your hat on – patronizing; cf. 5.1.17, 18.

72 motley i.e. (professional) fool; see
2.7.13n.. Cf. *Son* 110.1–2: 'Alas, 'tis
true, I have gone here and there, /
And made myself a motley to the
view'.

73 bow the curved wooden yoke used to
harness an ox for ploughing

74 curb 'Strap passing under the lower
jaw of a horse and fastened to the bit'
(Cam²)
bells the bells attached to the falcon's

62+ SP] *(Ol.)*, *Rowe*   67 SD] *Malone; discovering himself / Johnson*   68 Master] *(Mʳ)*, *Douai ms,
Rowe³;* M. *F2;* Monsieur *Oxf*   69 God'ild] *(goddild)*, *Douai ms, Theobald;* God 'ield *Var 1778*
71 sir –] sir. *Jaques removes his hat Oxf;* Sir: *F*   73 bow] bough *Capell*   74 her] his *F3*

and as pigeons bill, so wedlock would be nibbling.   75

JAQUES   And will you, being a man of your breeding, be
married under a bush like a beggar? Get you to church,
and have a good priest that can tell you what marriage
is. This fellow will but join you together as they join
wainscot; then one of you will prove a shrunk panel   80
and, like green timber, warp, warp.

TOUCHSTONE   I am not in the mind but I were better to
be married of him than of another, for he is not like to
marry me well, and not being well married it will be a
good excuse for me hereafter to leave my wife.   85

JAQUES

Go thou with me
And let me counsel thee.

leg, which enable the falconer to recapture her
so . . . desires Man is constrained by
marriage from unbridled sexual
appetite; cf. 1 Corinthians, 7.9: 'It is
better to marrie the[n] to burne'
(Geneva Bible).
75 **bill** intertwine their beaks in a mating
routine (billing and cooing)
76 **breeding** nurture, education
77 **under . . . beggar** i.e. without church
ceremony. 'Beggers Bush', the title of
a jig (see Fig. 9), may have been a cue
for Touchstone to dance, as Kemp may
have done in Day's *Parliament of Bees*
(performed *c.* 1600): 'With Jack droms
Intertai[n]ment, he shall dance / the
Jigg calld beggers bushe' (Day, *Bees*,
1.ii, p. 37; see Baskervill, 149). Day's
Travels of Three English Brothers (1602)
contains a scene with Kemp (2.55–9).
77–9 **church . . . is** Jaques implies that
Sir Oliver does not preside over a consecrated church, which 'vicar of the
next village' (39, see n.) might contradict. His objection is probably not only

to Sir Oliver's lack of learning, but to a
cobbled-up informal contract without
proper church ceremony (see 4.1.125,
127n.).
79–80 **join wainscot** line up wooden
panels (in joinery); compared with the
ill-joining of couples in matrimony
and the marring of texts implied by Sir
Oliver's name (Parker, *Margins*, 88).
Cf. 5.4.133.
80 **shrunk panel** ill-fitting through the
use of unseasoned (*green*, 81) wood;
Parker notes 'the failed phallicism of
its "shrinking" rather than (more
snugly) "fitting"' (*Margins*, 88).
81 **warp** Cf. 2.7.188n.
82 **not . . . but** only of the opinion that
(cf. Fr. *ne . . . que*); see 2.1.5n.
were would be
84 **well . . . well** i.e. legally
86–7 set in one prose line by Pope and
most later editors on the grounds that
the division in the line may be compositorial; but F's short lines allow a sententious 'false' exit, which is then parodied by Touchstone; see 3.5.137–40n.

82–5] *marked as aside Capell*   86–7] *one line Pope*

TOUCHSTONE

Come, sweet Audrey,
We must be married, or we must live in bawdry.
Farewell, good Master Oliver. Not   90
  [*singing and dancing*]
                    O sweet Oliver,
                    O brave Oliver,
              Leave me not behind thee.
But

                    Wind away,   95
                    Be gone, I say,
              I will not to wedding with thee.
              [*Exit Touchstone with Audrey and Jaques.*]

SIR OLIVER MAR–TEXT   'Tis no matter.

88–9 **Audrey . . . bawdry** Touchstone's rhyming couplet completes Jaques's two lines, making a four-line gag. He may have started singing here, even before moving on to the 'sweet Oliver' refrain from a popular jig. See 91n. Macready, although restoring the scene, cut 'Or we must live in bawdry' (i.e. sin). For the eye-rhyme of F's 'baudrey' see p. 117.

90 **Not** Most editors make Touchstone speak *Not* before breaking into song.

91 SD Capell denies the presence of a song (first suggested by Warburton), but claims that the words should be accompanied by the Clown's 'dancing about Sir Oliver with a harlequin gesture and action' (*Notes*, 63).

91 **O sweet Oliver** a 'ballat' entered in the Stationers' Register in 1584; the word 'ballad', like *carol* (5.3.28), implied singing and dancing, and was virtually

synonymous with 'jig' (Baskervill, 10, 13–14). The association of the 'O sweet Oliver' jig with Kemp dated from his attendance on the Earl of Leicester, Sidney and Essex in the Low Countries during the Dutch campaign, 1585–6 (Bald; Baskervill, 181–3; see Appendix 2). 'Sweet Oliver' appears in Jonson's *EMI*, 3.3.110, and in his '*Execration*' (1632): 'All the mad Rolands, and sweet Olivers' (366, l. 70).

94 **But** spoken, not sung

95 **Wind** possibly 'wend' (go), but the word may also mean 'turn', implying the turning outwards of the dancer at the top of a set in country dancing, who is then followed in a line by the dancers behind him or her, a movement technically known as 'casting off'. Touchstone, followed by Audrey and Jaques, casts off the country cleric, and may also exit dancing with Audrey; see 5.1.62n.

---

88 SP] *Malone; Ol. F; Clo. F2*   88–9] *prose Pope*   90 Master] *(M^r), Var 1778;* M. *F2;* Sir *Douai ms, Var 1773*   Not] *as part of verse line 91 Capell*   91–3] *Capell; prose F*   91 SD *singing] Cam^l (Warburton)   and dancing] Cam^l (Capell Notes)*   94 But] *as part of verse line 95 Capell*   95–7] *Capell; prose F*   95 Wind] wend *Collier^2 (Johnson)*   97 SD] *Capell subst.*   98 'Tis] *aside* 'Tis *Oxf*

Ne'er a fantastical knave of them all   99
Shall flout me out of my calling.   *Exit.*

3.4   *Enter* ROSALIND [*as Ganymede*]
                 and CELIA [*as Aliena*].

ROSALIND   Never talk to me, I will weep.

CELIA   Do, I prithee, but yet have the grace to consider
     that tears do not become a man.

ROSALIND   But have I not cause to weep?

CELIA   As good cause as one would desire; therefore weep.   5

ROSALIND   His very hair is of the dissembling colour.

CELIA   Something browner then Judas's. Marry, his kisses
     are Judas's own children.

ROSALIND   I'faith, his hair is of a good colour.

CELIA   An excellent colour – your chestnut was ever the   10
     only colour.

99–100 The Douai MS arranges Sir
Oliver's lines as verse. The rhyme on
all/call(ing) completes the volley of
rhyming begun by Jaques at 86–7,
which launched Touchstone into the
'sweet Oliver' jig; see 88–9n. Sir
Oliver's lines could be read either as
the hedge-priest's having the last word
against the fool, or as the fool's triumph in transforming the hedge-
priest into a versifier (and therefore a
liar?).

99 **fantastical** fanciful, grotesque; see
Cornwallis: 'Fantasticknesse, is the
Habiliment of youth . . . Customes
Enemie, It is greene thoughtes in
greene yeers' ('Of Fantasticknesse',
Essays, 1.24, sig. L7ʳ). Harington,
Apology [for *Ajax*], defends himself
against charges of having written 'a

mad fantasticall booke' (219).

100 **flout** mock. See 1.2.45n., 5.1.13n.,
17n.
   calling vocation: particularly of religious sects

3.4.3 **tears . . . man** Celia's revenge on
Rosalind's brag of manhood; see
2.4.4–7.

6 **dissembling** deceitful

7 **Judas's** The betrayer of Christ was
often represented as having red hair
and a red beard (Caldecott); see
Marston, *Insatiate Countess* (1613): 'I
ever thought by his red beard he would
prove a Judas' (2.2.36; see Halliwell).
   kisses Judas's kiss in the Garden of
   Gethsemane betrayed Christ to the
   High Priest.

10 **chestnut** auburn, as Judas's hair; see
3.2.228–9n.

99–100] *Douai ms, this edn; prose F*   100 SD] *Capell; Exeunt F*   **3.4**] *(Scoena Quarta.)*   Location] *a
Cottage in the* Forest *Theobald*   0.1 *as Ganymede*] *Oxf*   0.2 *as Aliena*] *Oxf*   5–8] *Pope; F lines* desire,
/ weepe. / haire / colour. / then Iudasses: / children. /   10–13] *Pope; F lines* colour: / colour: /
sanctitie, / bread. /

ROSALIND   And his kissing is as full of sanctity as the
touch of holy bread.

CELIA   He hath bought a pair of cast lips of Diana – a nun
of winter's sisterhood kisses not more religiously; the   15
very ice of chastity is in them.

ROSALIND   But why did he swear he would come this
morning and comes not?

CELIA   Nay certainly there is no truth in him.

ROSALIND   Do you think so?   20

CELIA   Yes. I think he is not a pick-purse nor a horse-
stealer – but for his verity in love I do think him as
concave as a covered goblet or a worm-eaten nut.

ROSALIND   Not true in love?

CELIA   Yes, when he is in, but I think he is not in.   25

ROSALIND   You have heard him swear downright he was.

CELIA   'Was' is not 'is'. Besides, the oath of a lover is no

---

12–16 the only lines in *AYL* cut by the
Jesuit William Sankey in his official
papal censorship (1641–2) of the
copy of F2 owned by the Valladolid
monastery in Spain (Frye, 276, 280);
also excised from the Douai MS (see
Appendix 4). Orlando is often associated with religious language; see
2.3.12–13.

13 **holy bread** bread sanctifed for use in
Holy Communion (*BCP*); in Catholic
ritual the host is placed directly in the
mouth, like a kiss, arguably a shocking
image for anti-theatricalists, in that it
connects the Eucharist and dramatic
representation (see D. Hawkes, 263).

14 **cast** a pun on the twin meanings 'discarded' and 'chaste' (F2 'chast', Lat.
casta; see p. 117); perhaps also a plaster
cast used in modelling
Diana See 3.2.2n., 4n.

15 **winter's sisterhood** a community of
nuns. Wintry coldness is a metaphor
for their vow of chastity (cf. *MND*
1.1.72–3: 'To live a barren sister all

your life, / Chanting faint hymns to
the cold fruitless moon'). Celia mis-
chievously imagines Orlando as a nun.

16 **chastity** identified mainly with
women (see 3.3.6n. on *honest Ovid*); cf.
Harington: 'I doubte . . . how this wanton age of ours will brook to have a
man praised for chastitie' (*Succession*,
86–7).

19 **Nay certainly . . . no** ironic and teasing mixture of negative and affirmative; cf. 3.3.13n. on *Truly*. Cf. *AC*
1.1.1.

21 **pick-purse** pick-pocket; the theatre
was considered by its opponents to be
a den of thieves.

23 **concave** curved, hollow – the curved
surface which reflects a distorted
image. Covered goblets were used as
drinking vessels for hunting parties, as
in the woodcut from *Hunting* (91); they
were also used for the Eucharist
(see 13).
worm-eaten nut possibly a walnut or
a chestnut; see 3.2.228–9n.

---

14 cast] chast *F2*   24 love] Ioue *F4*   27 'Was' . . . 'is'] *Hanmer;* Was . . . is *F*   of a] *F2;* of *F*

stronger than the word of a tapster: they are both the
confirmer of false reckonings. He attends here in the
forest on the Duke your father.   30

ROSALIND   I met the Duke yesterday and had much
question with him. He asked me of what parentage I
was. I told him of as good as he, so he laughed and let
me go. But what talk we of fathers when there is such a
man as Orlando?   35

CELIA   O, that's a brave man! He writes brave verses,
speaks brave words, swears brave oaths and breaks them
bravely quite traverse athwart the heart of his lover, as
a puny tilter, that spurs his horse but on one side,
breaks his staff like a noble goose. But all's brave that   40
youth mounts and folly guides.

Enter CORIN.

Who comes here?

CORIN
Mistress and master, you have oft enquired

---

28 **tapster** barman
29 **reckonings** accounts
34 **fathers** breezy, unlike Lodge's
Rosalynde, who first meets her father
at her wedding and is moved by his
reduced state (sig. P2ᵛ)
36, 37 **brave** ostentatiously fine
38 **traverse athwart** across, broadside on;
to break one's lance in this way instead
of lengthways in a jousting tournament
was a disgrace (see Fig. 11).
39 **puny** (Fr. *puis ne*) 'raw, inexperienced'
(*OED a.* and *n.* A 3 – not 'small and
insignificant' as in *OED* puisne *a.* 3,
quoting this line; but see also A 1a,
'junior, inferior in rank'). In 1598
Essex declared that if he had not been
given command at the siege of Rouen

in 1591 he would have 'seene my
Punies leapt ouer my head' (*Apology*,
sig. B1ʳ). Cf. Harington: 'I am but a
punie of Lincolnes Inne' (*Ajax*, 164).
tilter jouster
but . . . side in a lop-sided manner, i.e.
ineffectually
43–52 Cf. Lodge's Coridon: 'Oh Mistres
(quoth Coridon) you haue a long time
desired to see *Phoebe* the faire shepheardesse whom *Montanus* loues: so
now if it please you and *Ganimede* to
walke with mee to yonder thicket,
there shall you see *Montanus* and her
sitting by a Fountaine, he courting her
with his Countrey ditties, and she as
coy as if she held loue in disdaine'
(sig. L4ᵛ).

---

29 confirmer] confirmers *Douai ms, Pope*   39 puny] (puisny), *Capell*   41.1] *Folger; after 42 F*

After the shepherd that complained of love,
Who you saw sitting by me on the turf,   45
Praising the proud disdainful shepherdess
That was his mistress.

CELIA   Well, and what of him?

CORIN

If you will see a pageant truly played
Between the pale complexion of true love
And the red glow of scorn and proud disdain,   50
Go hence a little and I shall conduct you,
If you will mark it.

ROSALIND   O come, let us remove –
The sight of lovers feedeth those in love.
Bring us to this sight, and you shall say   54
I'll prove a busy actor in their play.   *Exeunt.*

3.5   *Enter* SILVIUS *and* PHOEBE.

SILVIUS

Sweet Phoebe, do not scorn me, do not, Phoebe.
Say that you love me not, but say not so
In bitterness. The common executioner,
Whose heart th'accustomed sight of death makes hard,

---

44 **complained** lamented, as in the literary form of the (female) love 'complaint' (Kerrigan, vii), deriving from
Ovid's *Heroical Epistles*
45 **sitting . . . turf** See 2.4.34 and n.
50 **red glow** an expression of anger or
choler – a rush of blood to the face
52 **mark** pay attention to
   remove move away, used intransitive-
ly
54 **sight** spectacle, but also the site
(i.e. place) where the scene will be
enacted

55 Cf. Puck, *MND* 3.1.74–5: 'What, a
play toward? I'll be an auditor; / An
actor too perhaps, if I see cause.'
3.5.1 **do not, Phoebe** F's omission of a
comma before '*Phebe*' makes it possible
to hear a verb in 'do not Phebe',
which may anticipate Rosalind's
coinage at 4.3.39, *She Phoebes me*, and
could reflect an actor's 'pointing' of
the line in rehearsal; see Stern: 'performance . . . emerges as a major forum
for revision' (*Rehearsal*, 112); see pp.
131–2.

---

54 you shall] you both shall *Douai ms*   3.5] *(Scena Quinta.)*   Location] *another part of the* Forest
Theobald   1 not, Phoebe] *F3;* not *Phebe F*

Falls not the axe upon the humbled neck   5
But first begs pardon. Will you sterner be
Than he that dies and lives by bloody drops?

Enter ROSALIND *[as Ganymede],* CELIA *[as Aliena]*
and CORIN. *[They stand aside.]*

PHOEBE
I would not be thy executioner;
I fly thee for I would not injure thee.
Thou tell'st me there is murder in mine eye.   10
'Tis pretty, sure, and very probable
That eyes, that are the frail'st and softest things,
Who shut their coward gates on atomies,
Should be called tyrants, butchers, murderers.
Now I do frown on thee with all my heart,   15
And if mine eyes can wound, now let them kill thee.
Now counterfeit to swoon – why now fall down!
Or if thou canst not – O, for shame, for shame –
Lie not, to say mine eyes are murderers.
Now show the wound mine eye hath made in thee.   20
Scratch thee but with a pin, and there remains

---

5 **Falls not** does not let fall
6 **pardon** forgiveness
7 The executioner lives by the blood of the beheaded prisoner. The rhetorical figure *hysteron proteron* inverts the expected word order (Knowles).
11 **pretty** adjective, as at 114. Oxf[1] retains F's punctuation, 'pretty sure', thus making *pretty* an intensifier.
13 **coward gates** eyelids; the tiniest speck causes the eyelids to blink in (timorous) self-protection.
atomies the tiniest particles; see

3.2.225n.
16 **kill** See 4.1.102n.
17 **counterfeit** pretend; the standard word for acting (see 4.3.166, 167)
swoon Phoebe's scornful sketch of the lover's feigned swoon contrasts with Rosalind's real swoon; see 4.3.155 SD, 157n.
19 **Lie not** Phoebe, literal rather than literary (cf. 3.3.15), designates as a lie Silvius's poetic image of eyes which wound (10–14; see Dusinberre, *Women*, 158–9); cf. 5.2.24.

7 dies and lives] deals, and lives *Theobald (Warburton)*; lives and thrives *Hanmer*; lives and dies *Keightley (Tollet)* 7.1 as Ganymede] *Oxf* as Aliena] *Oxf* 7.2 They stand aside] *Capell subst.* 11 pretty,] *Theobald*; pretty *F* 14, 19 murderers] *(murtherers), F2* 17 swoon] *(swound), Rowe[3]*

Some scar of it; lean thou upon a rush,
The cicatrice and capable impressure
Thy palm some moment keeps. But now mine eyes,
Which I have darted at thee, hurt thee not,   25
Nor I am sure there is no force in eyes
That can do hurt.

SILVIUS
                    O dear Phoebe,
If ever – as that ever may be near –
You meet in some fresh cheek the power of fancy,   30
Then shall you know the wounds invisible
That love's keen arrows make.

PHOEBE   But till that time
Come not thou near me. And when that time comes,
Afflict me with thy mocks, pity me not,
As till that time I shall not pity thee.   35

ROSALIND [*Advances.*]
And why, I pray you? Who might be your mother,

---

22 *lean thou Editors have offered various emendations to restore the regular
iambic pentameter line (see t.n.). The
insertion of *thou* matches Phoebe's
imperious *Come not thou*, 33.
23 cicatrice scar, deep impression
capable impressure indented marks
retained by a sensitive or receptive surface
24 some moment for some time
(Abbott, 21; *OED* some *a.*[1] B 4c)
25 darted retains its original force, of a
dart's being thrown in order to wound;
cf. *arrows*, 32. See *KL* 2.2.354–5: 'You
nimble lightnings, dart your blinding
flames / Into her scornful eyes!'
26 Nor . . . no See 2.3.50n.
30 meet subjunctive: were to meet, after
If
power of fancy ability to arouse love;
see 3.2.350n.
32 keen sharp; see 2.7.178.

34 Afflict hurt, wound; Silvius, silent in
Act 5, honours his promise to keep
faith with Phoebe when her love turns
out to be a woman, rather than taking
this cue to triumph over her disappointment; see 5.4.148n.
34–5 Phoebe rejects pity, while Rosalind
(as opposed to the shepherd boy
Ganymede, whose voice she ventrilo-
quizes for Phoebe's benefit, see
4.3.65–9n.), celebrates it. See
4.1.102nn.
36 Rosalind's interruption makes her, as
promised, *a busy actor* (3.4.55) in the
play between Silvius and Phoebe.
Who . . . mother? Phoebe's cruelty is
a slander to women; see 4.3.33n. and
4.1.189–92. Cf. Troilus's protest
against Cressida's faithlessness, *TC*
5.2.135–6: 'Let it not be believed, for
womanhood! / Think, we had moth-
ers' (Dusinberre, *Women*, 149).

---

22 lean thou] *this edn;* Leane *F;* Leane but *F2;* or lean *(RP)*   23 capable] palpable *Collier*[2]   36 SD]
Capell subst. after you 36

That you insult, exult, and all at once
Over the wretched? What though you have no beauty –
As by my faith I see no more in you
Than without candle may go dark to bed –   40
Must you be therefore proud and pitiless?
Why, what means this? Why do you look on me?
I see no more in you than in the ordinary
Of Nature's sale-work. 'Od's my little life,
I think she means to tangle my eyes too!   45
No, faith, proud mistress, hope not after it.
'Tis not your inky brows, your black silk hair,
Your bugle eyeballs, nor your cheek of cream,
That can entame my spirits to your worship.
You foolish shepherd, wherefore do you follow her   50
Like foggy south, puffing with wind and rain?

38 **What** Even
no beauty In Lodge, Phoebe is
described as '(the fairest shepherdesse
in all *Arden*, and he the frolickst swaine
in the whole forrest) she in a petticote
of scarlet, couered with a green mantle,
& to shrowd her from the Sunne, a
chaplet of roses: from vnder which
appeared a face full of Natures excellence' (sig. L4ʳ). Capell castigated
Theobald for omitting 'no', because
the point of Rosalind's remarks is that
Phoebe is nothing much to look at
(*Notes*, 64).

40 It is not worth producing a candle to
display Phoebe's (negligible) beauty as
she goes to bed, nor would her good
looks illumine the darkness; cf. *RJ*
5.3.85–6: 'her beauty makes / This
vault a feasting presence, full of light'.

42 Rosalind's questions provide the internal SD for Phoebe's ogling of
Ganymede; see 71.

43 **ordinary** noun: unexceptionable ware

44 **Nature's sale-work** the cheap goods

Nature displays for sale, i.e. the least
valued
'Od's a corruption of 'God save'
(*OED* god 8b) – one of Ganymede's
laddish oaths

45 **tangle** ensnare; the word suggests
being caught in a net, which leads on
to *black silk hair*.

46, 58 **mistress** Cf. 1.2.56n.

47 **inky . . . black** i.e. not beautiful; cf.
131 and see 3.2.90n.

48 **bugle** black and glassy, also possibly
protuberant: a bugle is 'a tube-shaped
glass bead, usually black' (*OED sb.*³ 1;
see also 2 *attrib.*, 'Made of . . . or
resembling, bugles').
cheek of cream as in 'peaches and
cream' complexion (cf. '*Helen's cheek*',
3.2.142). Phoebe does not sound as
unprepossessing as Rosalind makes
out.

50 **wherefore** why

51 **foggy south** the south wind, warm
and moist and therefore inducing fog,
reminiscent of the experience of

38 no] *om. Theobald (L.H.);* some *Hanmer;* mo *Malone;* more *Var 1793*   45 tangle] angle *Johnson*
my] mine *F2*

You are a thousand times a properer man
Than she a woman. 'Tis such fools as you
That makes the world full of ill-favoured children.
'Tis not her glass but you that flatters her,   55
And out of you she sees herself more proper
Than any of her lineaments can show her.
But, mistress, know yourself; down on your knees,
And thank heaven fasting for a good man's love.
For I must tell you friendly in your ear: 60
Sell when you can, you are not for all markets.
Cry the man mercy, love him, take his offer;
Foul is most foul, being foul to be a scoffer.
So take her to thee, shepherd. Fare you well.

Elizabethan sailors (see Ralegh, *Letters*, 181). Silvius is wet, windy, blinded with the mists of passion and becalmed in his pursuit of Phoebe. Cf. *Cym*, where Cloten curses Posthumous's voyage: 'The south-fog rot him' (2.3.132).

puffing Silvius's sighs; cf. 3.2.295.

52 **properer** finer, better appointed – Rosalind's (i.e. a woman's) assessment. Cf. 116 and see 3.2.199n.

53–4 **fools . . . makes** singular verb after a plural subject (see 1.2.101n.), probably influenced by the singular pronoun, *you*

54 **ill-favoured** ugly

55 **glass** The trope of the mirror (deriving from both Plato and Seneca), which might either create self-knowledge, or reflect self-love (see 3.2.279–81n. and *Son* 3)

56 **out of you** from your image of her

57 **lineaments** features and figure

58 **know yourself** Rosalind's command would have been familiar to educated Elizabethans from many different sources. See 55n.; Davies, *Nosce Teipsum*; and 1.2.167n.

59 **heaven** possibly a euphemistic substitute for 'God' (F's usual form in *AYL*), predating the profanity law of 1606 (Act of Abuses; cf. 4.1.177–8n. and see p. 127); *good* may have been intended to echo 'God'.

fasting in penitential spirit, as in Lent

61 **markets** See Celia's jest (1.2.95) on *marketable* women. Cf. Lodge's Phoebe (to Montanus): 'Wel sir, if your market can be made no where els, home againe, for your Mart is at the fayrest' (sig. M2ᵛ). Aliena protests against Montanus's urging of Ganimede to love Phoebe, 'seeing if *Ganimede* marry *Phoebe* thy market is cleane mard [spoilt]' (sig. O1ᵛ).

62 **Cry . . . mercy** offer the man your apologies; see 5.4.147–8.

63 **scoffer** a maker of scornful jests and mocks; cf. *rail*, 4.3.42, 43, 46. In Withals's *Dictionary* 'A scoffer' appears under *Minstrells and dauncers* as a type of player, all comprehended under the term *Histrio* or *mimus*: an actor (sig. L3ᵛ). 'Scoffer' was used for public political and religious abuse; in *Gamelyn* the hostile clergy scoff at the bound and helpless Gamelyn (e.g. ll. 480ff., p. 169).

64 **take . . . thee** take her as wife

54 makes] make *Pope*   55 flatters] flatter *Rowe*   59 love.] love; *Phebe kneels to Rosalind Cam¹*

PHOEBE

    Sweet youth, I pray you chide a year together!   65

    I had rather hear you chide than this man woo.

ROSALIND   He's fallen in love with your foulness, [*to*

    Silvius] and she'll fall in love with my anger. If it be so,

    as fast as she answers thee with frowning looks, I'll

    sauce her with bitter words.   70

    – Why look you so upon me?

PHOEBE

    For no ill will I bear you.

ROSALIND

    I pray you do not fall in love with me,

    For I am falser than vows made in wine.

    Besides, I like you not.

               [*to Silvius*] If you will know my house,   75

    'Tis at the tuft of olives here hard by.

    Will you go, sister? Shepherd, ply her hard.

    Come, sister. Shepherdess, look on him better,

    And be not proud. Though all the world could see,

    None could be so abused in sight as he.   80

    Come, to our flock.   *Exeunt* [*Rosalind, Celia and Corin*].

---

65 **a year together** for a whole year

70 **sauce . . . words** taunt

71 **look . . . me** an internal SD for Phoebe to make eyes at the shepherd boy; see 42n. and Fig. 6. Rosalind returns to blank verse after the colloquial throw-away lines of 68–70.

74 **vows . . . wine** the unreliable promises of the inebriated; an analogy appropriate to Ganymede as Jove's cup-bearer

75 SD Ganymede's direction is necessary for Silvius's delivery of Phoebe's letter to him at 4.3.7.

76 **tuft of olives** group of olive-trees (see 4.3.76), the olive as symbol of peace here possibly overriding the naturalism of the Forest. Cf. Spenser's 'April' eclogue, where Chloris 'Of Oliue braunches beares a Coronall: / Oliues bene for peace' with which to crown 'Elisa, Queene of shepheardes all' (*SC*, p. 455). The two princesses live outside the hunting area of the Forest, in an environment devoted to rustic peace. The word *olives* may also prepare the audience for the return of Oliver, bearing peace, not war.

79–81 Rosalind marks her exit with a rhyming couplet and a half-line; see 141n.

80 **abused** deceived

---

66 hear] (*here*), *Rowe*   67–70] *Pope; F lines* shee'll / fast / sauce /   67 your] her *Douai ms, Hanmer*   67–8 SD] *Singer²*   68 she'll] you'll *Keightley*   71] *Oxf; one verse line* Her . . . me? *F; prose Pope*   75 SD] *Oliver (Moberley); not in F*   81 SD] *Theobald; Exit. F*

PHOEBE

    Dead shepherd, now I find thy saw of might:
    'Who ever loved, that loved not at first sight?'

SILVIUS

    Sweet Phoebe –

PHOEBE   Ha? – What sayst thou, Silvius?

SILVIUS

    Sweet Phoebe, pity me.   85

PHOEBE

    Why, I am sorry for thee, gentle Silvius.

SILVIUS

    Wherever sorrow is, relief would be.
    If you do sorrow at my grief in love,
    By giving love your sorrow and my grief
    Were both extermined.   90

PHOEBE

    Thou hast my love, is not that neighbourly?

---

82 **Dead shepherd** Marlowe – first identified in Capell, *Notes*, 1.64. By 1632, with F2's 'Deed', the reference already seems lost.

saw sage saying; see 2.7.157.

83 **'Who. . . sight?'** Phoebe's rhyming couplet burlesques the elegant couplets of Marlowe's *Hero and Leander*, first published posthumously in 1598; see 4.1.91–7 and nn. See Jonson, *EMI*, 3.4.65: "Sheart, this is in *Hero and Leander*' (see p. 81). In Marlowe's poem Leander's passion for Hero is compared to Jove's for his cup-bearer, Ganimede: '*Ioue*, slylie stealing from his sisters bed, / To dallie with *Idalian Ganimed*' (Marlowe, *Hero and Leander*, ll. 147–8). The passage ends: 'Where both deliberat, the love is slight, / Who ever lov'd, that

lov'd not at first sight?' (ll. 175–6). Phoebe's quotation releases homoerotic innuendoes into a scene (originally played by boy actors) in which a woman falls in love with another woman (see Fig. 6). Shakespeare slyly mocks Marlowe by giving his lines to a girl who is neither Hero nor heroine.

84 **Ha?** 'Not an arresting ha! but the vague and questioning interjection with which someone emerges from a daydream' (Ard[2])

90 **extermined** exterminated, extinguished

91 **neighbourly** a mischievous play on Christ's reformulation of the Ten Commandments: 'Thou shalt loue thy neighbour as thy self' (Matthew, 19.19, Geneva Bible)

82 Dead] Deed *F2;* Troth *Douai ms;* Dear *Theobald 1741*   83 'Who . . . sight?'] *Hanmer;* Who . . . sight? *F*

SILVIUS

　　I would have you.

PHOEBE   Why, that were covetousness!

　　Silvius, the time was that I hated thee –

　　And yet it is not that I bear thee love –

　　But since that thou canst talk of love so well,   95

　　Thy company, which erst was irksome to me,

　　I will endure, and I'll employ thee too.

　　But do not look for further recompense

　　Than thine own gladness that thou art employed.

SILVIUS

　　So holy and so perfect is my love,   100

　　And I in such a poverty of grace,

　　That I shall think it a most plenteous crop

　　To glean the broken ears after the man

　　That the main harvest reaps. Loose now and then

　　A scattered smile, and that I'll live upon.   105

---

92 **have** possess
　　were would be
　　covetousness The tenth command-
　　ment, 'Thou shalt not covet', is given a
　　specifically sexual gloss in Dering's
　　Catechism (1590): 'Heere the Lorde in
　　plaine wordes doth forbid al inward
　　desire, whatsoeuer is vnlawful to be
　　done, although we neuer consent vnto
　　it, as the rebellion of the fleshe, all
　　corruption of the olde man, all blot
　　of originall sinne' (sig. B1ʳ). Cf.
　　H. Smith: '[Covetousness is that]
　　which I may call the Londoners
　　sinne' ('Contentation', sig. Aiiʳ). In
　　KJ 4.2.29 – the only other occurrence
　　in Shakespeare – 'covetousness' has
　　its modern sense of envious emula-
　　tion.
93 **I hated thee** Cf. Marlowe's *Dido*
　　(1594): 'Yet boast not of it, for I love

thee not, / And yet I hate thee not'
(Dido to Aeneas, 3.1.170–1).
96 **erst** previously
100 **perfect** complete, as well as without
　　flaw
101 **grace** The theological concept of
　　grace (a divine conferring of the Holy
　　Spirit) continues the biblical allusions.
　　Cf. Sylvanus in Montemayor's *Diana*
　　(tr. 1598), returning to Diana the
　　verses by his rival: 'which wordes, like
　　holy relikes, I kept in my minde' (7).
102–4 **That I . . . reaps** See the Book of
　　Ruth (2.2), where Ruth, 'gleaning the
　　ears of corn after the man who owns it,
　　hopes to find grace in his sight'
　　(Fraser, '*Genesis*', 125); see 1.3.103n.
104 **Loose** release
105 **scattered** dropped carelessly, as in
　　the scattering of *broken ears* for the
　　gleaner

101 I] *om. F2*　　104 Loose] lose *F4*

PHOEBE

   Knowst thou the youth that spoke to me erewhile?

SILVIUS

   Not very well, but I have met him oft,

   And he hath bought the cottage and the bounds

   That the old Carlot once was master of.

PHOEBE

   Think not I love him though I ask for him.   110

   'Tis but a peevish boy – yet he talks well.

   But what care I for words? Yet words do well

   When he that speaks them pleases those that hear.

   It is a pretty youth – not very pretty –

   But sure he's proud, and yet his pride becomes him.   115

   He'll make a proper man. The best thing in him

   Is his complexion; and faster than his tongue

   Did make offence, his eye did heal it up.

   He is not very tall, yet for his years he's tall;

   His leg is but so-so, and yet 'tis well.   120

   There was a pretty redness in his lip,

---

106 *erewhile** just now; for F's 'yerewhile' (Old English *æhwilum*) see Cercignani, 362.

109 **the old Carlot** F's '*Carlot*' appears to be a proper name (Knowles; but see *OED* carlot, *obs. rare*, a churl), which may refer to the notorious land-encloser and absentee landlord John Quarles, 'a citizen and draper of London' (L. Parker, 57; see 2.4.77n.). Quarles bought the manor of Cotesbach on the Warwickshire/Northamptonshire border from the Earl of Essex in 1596; his enclosure policies and exploitation of his tenants caused full-scale rioting over the next dozen years (L. Parker, 56–73; Thirsk, 234). Silvius probably uses a French pronunciation (Carlo) which would approximate to 'Carl'. For this use of the definite article see 2.5.24n.

116 **proper** real, fine, i.e. the genuine article (which Ganymede certainly is not); dramatic irony at Phoebe's expense

117 **complexion** demeanour, as well as colour of the face; ironic, as the admired complexion belongs to a woman; cf. 3.2.189n. and *TN* 1.4.30–4.

117–18 **faster . . . up** no sooner had his sharp words inflicted a wound than his (winning) eye healed it

119 For Rosalind's height see 1.2.261n.

120 **so-so** See Touchstone's gloss on William's usage, 5.1.27–8.

121 **redness . . . lip** Cf. *TN* 1.4.31–2: 'Diana's lip / Is not more smooth and rubious'.

109 Carlot] *(Carlot);* carlot *Var 1778*

A little riper and more lusty red
Than that mixed in his cheek. 'Twas just the difference
Betwixt the constant red and mingled damask.
There be some women, Silvius, had they marked him   125
In parcels as I did, would have gone near
To fall in love with him; but for my part
I love him not – nor hate him not. And yet
I have more cause to hate him than to love him,
For what had he to do to chide at me?   130
He said mine eyes were black and my hair black,
And now I am remembered, scorned at me.
I marvel why I answered not again.
But that's all one – omittance is no quittance.
I'll write to him a very taunting letter   135
And thou shalt bear it. Wilt thou, Silvius?

SILVIUS

Phoebe, with all my heart.

PHOEBE

I'll write it straight.
The matter's in my head and in my heart;

---

122 **lusty** vigorous (cf. 2.3.47), but also
hinting at sexual energy (see 4.2.18);
ironic in view of Ganymede's sexual
identity
124 **constant** uniform
damask a rich material embroidered
with different shades, here, of red and
white; see *Son* 130.5: 'I have seen roses
damasked, red and white'. Cf. *TN*
2.4.113: 'her damask cheek'.
125 **marked** scrutinized
126 **In parcels** in sections, item by item;
cf. *TN* 1.5.239–43.
gone near been on the point of (*OED*
near *adv.*² 15a)
128 **nor . . . not** See 2.3.50n.
130 **For . . . do** for what reason had
he

132 **I am remembered** I remember;
reflexive form (cf. Fr. *je me suis
rappelée*)
134 **omittance . . . quittance** Phoebe's
silence, when she omitted to answer
Ganymede's insults in kind, was not an
agreement to forgive his rudeness.
Quittance ('acquittance') is used for the
cancelling of a debt after it has been
satisfactorily paid (see Barlement's
Colloquia, 1586, reprinted 1598:
'A Quittance', sig. R6'); cf. Dent,
F584.
137–40 The scene ends with four (virtually) rhyming lines (Cercignani, 114),
two short (*heart/straight*) and two long
(*heart/short*), followed by a half-line;
cf. 3.3.86–7n.

129 I have] *F2;* Haue *F*   135 taunting] *(tanting)*, *F4*

I will be bitter with him and passing short.   140
Go with me, Silvius.   *Exeunt.*

4.1   *Enter* ROSALIND *[as Ganymede],* CELIA
                 [as Aliena] and JAQUES.

JAQUES   I prithee, pretty youth, let me be better
    acquainted with thee.
ROSALIND   They say you are a melancholy fellow.
JAQUES   I am so; I do love it better than laughing.
ROSALIND   Those that are in extremity of either are   5
    abominable fellows and betray themselves to every
    modern censure worse than drunkards.
JAQUES   Why, 'tis good to be sad and say nothing.
ROSALIND   Why then, 'tis good to be a post.
JAQUES   I have neither the scholar's melancholy, which is   10
    emulation; nor the musician's, which is fantastical; nor
    the courtier's, which is proud; nor the soldier's, which
    is ambitious; nor the lawyer's, which is politic; nor the
    lady's, which is nice; nor the lover's, which is all these;
    but it is a melancholy of mine own, compounded of   15

---

140 **passing** extremely
141 Ending a scene with an extra half-
    line, though common in the last plays,
    is uncommon as early as 1599 (RP).
4.1.1 **pretty youth** See 3.2.323n. Both
    men (Jaques and Orlando) and women
    (Phoebe)   are   captivated   by
    Ganymede's looks.
5 **extremity** excess
6 **abominable** appalling; F's 'abhom-
    inable' is the common form of the
    word at this time, based on the false
    etymology of *ab homine* (not of man).
6–7 **betray . . . censure** expose them-
    selves to every common judgement; cf.
    183.

11 **fantastical** indulging in fantasies
    (often related to love); see 3.3.99n.
13 **politic** expedient; usually a pejorative,
    associated with Machiavelli. Cf. 5.4.45.
14 **nice** fastidious, particular
15–18 **compounded . . . sadness** made
    up of many ingredients, distilled
    from many elements, and indeed the
    mingled reckoning of my travels, in
    which my frequent meditation enfolds
    me with a most volatile heaviness
15 **compounded** constituted, made up
    or combined (*OED* compound *v.* 1);
    used by Hobbes, *Philosophy*, 3, in
    connection with 'computation'; see
    17n.

4.1] *(Actus Quartus. Scena Prima.)* Location] *the Forest / Rowe* 0.1 *as Ganymede*] *Oxf*
0.2 *as Aliena*] *Oxf*   1 me be] *F2;* me *F*   2 thee] you *Douai ms, Ard¹*   6 abominable] *(abhominable), F3*

many simples, extracted from many objects, and indeed
the sundry computation of my travels, in which my
often rumination wraps me in a most humorous sadness.

ROSALIND   A traveller! By my faith, you have great reason
to be sad. I fear you have sold your own lands to see   20
other men's. Then to have seen much and to have
nothing is to have rich eyes and poor hands.

JAQUES   Yes, I have gained my experience.

16 **simples** medicinal herbs (see *RJ*
5.1.40, where the Apothecary is
'Culling of simples'); or 'ingredients'
(Onions, 199).
  extracted drawn out, or distilled (as
from particular plants)
17 **sundry** 'Consisting of different elements, of mixed composition' (*OED a.*
4b, *obs. rare*)
  *computation reckoning, in a
general rather than numerical sense
(*OED* 2 *obs.*, last example Hobbes,
Philosophy, 1656). Hobbes's analysis of
'*Computation*' (used as a synonym
for 'RATIOCINATION') in Part I of his
treatise entitled '*Computation OR
Logique*', illuminates the way in which
the word might be seen to mirror
Jaques's concerns: 'Now to compute, is
either to collect the sum of many
things that are added together, or to
know what remains when one thing is
taken of another' (2). Hobbes explains
that a man 'by looking fully and
distinctly upon [an Idea] . . . conceaves
all that he has seen as one thing'. As a
consequence, 'the Idea he has now, is
compounded of his former Ideas' (3, my
emphasis; see 15n.). Jaques's melancholy is, in his *computation* (reckoning), *compounded* (made up) of *sundry*
(mixed) elements. The decision to
replace F's 'contemplation' with this
older sense of the word 'computation'
(from the reading in the Douai MS:
see Appendix 4) has been taken in the
face of opposition.
  travels Jaques becomes the type of the
Elizabethan traveller to exotic lands
(Thorne, 14).
  in which *computation* is implied
17–18 ***my often rumination** my frequent reflection (literally, chewing the
cud); see 4.3.100. Cf. *Son* 64.11: 'Ruin
hath taught me thus to ruminate'. F's
'by' may be a simple typographical
error since *b* and *m* lie in contiguous
compartments of the compositor's
case' (Knowles).
18 **humorous** volatile; see 1.2.255n.
  sadness heaviness or melancholy
20 **sold . . . lands** This was Ralegh's
situation when he undertook his
expedition to Guiana in 1595
(Hakluyt, *Navigations*, 3.627ff.). See
Hall's *Virgidemiarum*: 'Ventrous
Fortunio his farme hath sold, / And
gads to *Guiane* land to fish for
gold' (4.3, p. 24), 'his land morgag'd'
(4.6, p. 48); see 1.2.40n., 2.7.71n. and
pp. 91–3.
23 **Yes** used emphatically to contradict
what has been said (as Fr. *si*); see
5.3.45.

16 objects,] objects; *Boswell–Malone*   17 computation] *Douai ms, this edn;* contemplation *F;*
contemplations *F3*   ¹my] *om. F3*   travels,] travels; *Boswell–Malone*   in] on *Johnson; and Malone;
om. Boswell–Malone*   which] which, *Collier (Malone)*   ²my] *F2;* by *F*   18 rumination] *Rowe;*
rumination, *F*   me in] me, in *Boswell–Malone*

Enter ORLANDO.

ROSALIND   And your experience makes you sad. I had
rather have a fool to make me merry than experience to   25
make me sad – and to travel for it too.

ORLANDO
Good day and happiness, dear Rosalind.

JAQUES   Nay then, God b'wi' you an you talk in blank
verse.   [*Exit.*]

ROSALIND   Farewell, Monsieur Traveller. Look you lisp   30
and wear strange suits; disable all the benefits of your
own country; be out of love with your nativity and
almost chide God for making you that countenance you
are, or I will scarce think you have swam in a gondola.

25 **fool . . . merry** F's early entry for
Orlando means that Rosalind's *fool* can
be aimed at her lover; see 1.2.42.1n.
and p. 127.

26 **travel** The two meanings of F's
'trauaile', journeying and making an
effort, are equally balanced.

28 **an** if

28–9 **blank verse** the metre of a lover,
therefore scorned by Jaques; see
3.2.248–9n., 4.3.178–9n. Jaques highlights the artificial medium in which
he exists; cf. *TN* 3.4.376–7.

29 SD F2's '*Exit*' gives Jaques the exit line;
cf. 3.2.284. The delaying of his exit
until after *gondola* (34) allows Jaques to
hear Rosalind's jibe, but distracts attention from her greeting of Orlando.

30 **Monsieur Traveller** Rosalind mocks
Jaques's French airs.
Look you take care you
lisp affect a foreign accent

31 **strange suits** outlandish outfits. In
1596 Essex admonished his cousin, the
Earl of Rutland, against 'affectation,
which is a generall fault amongst
English Trauellers; which is both dis-
pleasing & ridiculous'; a later letter

warns: 'Wee Travellers shall be made
sport of in Comedies' (Essex, *Travel*,
48–9, 81).

31–2 **disable . . . country** denigrate and
disregard the advantages of your
native land; see Thorpe's dedication of
Marlowe's *Lucan* (1600) to Edward
Blount: '[to] censure scornefully
inough, and somewhat like a trauailer'
(Marlowe, *Lucan*, 93). Rosalind's
defence of Englishness positions her in
the contemporary debate about the
'mother tongue' associated with translation (see Florio, dedication to
Montaigne's *Essays*, and 5.1.49n. on
common) and with early dictionaries
(see Cawdrey, *Table* (1604); 5.1.47–52
and nn.; and p. 8).

32 **be. . . nativity** despise your origins

33–4 **making . . . are** giving you the
appearance that you have, i.e. of being
English

34 **swam** floated; an irregular participle
(Abbott, 344)
gondola '*a kinde of small boates like our
wherries vsed in Venice*' (Florio, *World*,
153). There may be a jibe at the playwright Marston, who made much of

26 travel] *(*trauaile*)*, *F3;* travall *Douai ms*   28 God b'wi' you] *(*God buy you*)*, *Rowe;* adieu *Douai ms;*
Goodbye *Oxf*¹   29 SD] *F2; after* gondola *34 Hudson*   34 gondola] *(*Gundello*)*, *Pope;* Gondallo *Rowe*

Why, how now, Orlando, where have you been all this　35
while? You a lover? An you serve me such another trick,
never come in my sight more!

ORLANDO　My fair Rosalind, I come within an hour of my
promise.

ROSALIND　Break an hour's promise in love? He that will　40
divide a minute into a thousand parts, and break but a
part of the thousand part of a minute in the affairs of
love, it may be said of him that Cupid hath clapped him
o'th' shoulder, but I'll warrant him heart-whole.

ORLANDO　Pardon me, dear Rosalind.　45

ROSALIND　Nay, an you be so tardy, come no more in my
sight. I had as lief be wooed of a snail.

ORLANDO　Of a snail?

ROSALIND　Ay, of a snail, for though he comes slowly he
carries his house on his head – a better jointure, I think,　50
than you make a woman. Besides, he brings his destiny
with him.

ORLANDO　What's that?

ROSALIND　Why, horns – which such as you are fain to be

being half-Italian, but had never been
to Italy; in *Antonio and Mellida* (performed in 1599?) characters break into
Italian (4.1.191–208).

35 **how now** See 1.2.54n. In Lodge,
Aliena rebukes Rosader: 'Why how
now gentle forrester, what winde hath
kept you from hence?' (sig. K4ᵛ).

43–4 **clapped . . . shoulder** Dorsch
glosses 'shoulder-clapper' (*CE* 4.2.37)
as an ironic reference to 'an arresting
officer or bailiff, who is like a friend
who claps you on the back or shoulder'.

44 **warrant him** offer surety for his
being
heart-whole unsmitten

47 **lief** soon

50 **jointure** The endowment of a house
as part of the material settlement of

marriage, which will be held jointly,
and left to the wife on her husband's
death. Orlando, as a dispossessed
younger brother, is a less eligible suitor
than a snail, who brings his house
(shell) on his head.

51 **make** might make

54 **horns** a cuckoldry joke; a snail hides
his horns in his shell; cf. *KL*
1.5.27–30: 'I can tell why a snail has a
house . . . / Why, to put's head in, not
to give it away to his daughters and
leave his horns without a case'. Cf.
3.3.44–58 and nn. Ganymede invites
Orlando to participate in a 'men only'
dialogue about women's unchastity, an
invitation which he rejects (57–8).
fain glad, with ironic overtones; cf.
3.3.18–19n.

42 thousand] thousandth *Rowe*　44 heart-whole] (heart hole)　51 make] can make *Hanmer*

beholding to your wives for; but he comes armed in his   55
fortune and prevents the slander of his wife.

ORLANDO   Virtue is no horn-maker and my Rosalind is
virtuous.

ROSALIND   And I am your Rosalind.

CELIA   It pleases him to call you so, but he hath a Rosalind   60
of a better leer than you.

ROSALIND   Come, woo me, woo me – for now I am in a
holiday humour and like enough to consent. What
would you say to me now, an I were your very, very
Rosalind?   65

ORLANDO   I would kiss before I spoke.

ROSALIND   Nay, you were better speak first, and when
you were gravelled for lack of matter you might take
occasion to kiss. Very good orators when they are out,
they will spit, and for lovers lacking (God warrant us)   70

---

55 **beholding** under obligation, behold-
en; see Abbott, 372.
55–6 **armed . . . fortune** already
equipped with his destiny of horns,
but also fortified by his horns
56 **prevents** pre-empts (literally, 'comes
before', Lat. *prevenire*), and therefore
prevents in the modern sense
57 **Virtue** chastity
58 **virtuous** chaste (*OED a.* 2b, 'Of
women'). 'In a forest with horns
behind every tree and a Touchstone
behind every verse, Orlando remains
true to his own image of Rosalind'
(Berry, 'Rosalynde', 50).
59 **your Rosalind** After an almost too
convincing performance (as Ganymede)
of the laddish fiction of 'Rosalind', the
heroine claims the virtue of the 'true'
Rosalind.
61 **leer** complexion or feature (*OED, sb.*[1]
2). Celia fears that her cousin's play-
acting will break down.
63 **holiday humour** festive mood; see

1.3.14. Zemon Davis sees the phrase as
a warning to Orlando about the limits
of his control over Rosalind ('Women',
161). Cf. Lodge and Greene, *Looking-
Glass* (1594), 591–4: 'She [i.e. my wife]
will call me rascall, rogue, runnagate,
varlet, vagabond, slave, knave: why,
alas, sir, and these be but holiday
termes, but if you heard her working-
day words, in faith, sir, they be rattlers
like thunder, sir' (p. 125).
like enough very likely
64 **very very** real, true
68 **gravelled** grounded, a metaphor from
either the falling off a horse onto
gravel (Hudson), suitable to Orlando
as hunter, or the grounding of a boat in
sand (*OED gravel v.* 3 *obs.*), appropriate to the voyaging images in this scene
68, 71 **matter** content or substance; see
2.1.68n.
69 **occasion** opportunity
are out forget their lines (see 75); see
3.2.96, 244n.

55 beholding] beholden *Pope*   63 holiday] *(holy-day), Capell*

matter, the cleanliest shift is to kiss.

ORLANDO How if the kiss be denied?

ROSALIND Then she puts you to entreaty and there begins new matter.

ORLANDO Who could be out, being before his beloved 75 mistress?

ROSALIND Marry, that should you, if I were your mistress, or I should think my honesty ranker than my wit.

ORLANDO What, of my suit?

ROSALIND Not out of your apparel and yet out of your 80 suit. Am not I your Rosalind?

ORLANDO I take some joy to say you are because I would be talking of her.

ROSALIND Well, in her person, I say I will not have you.

ORLANDO Then, in mine own person, I die. 85

ROSALIND No, faith, die by attorney. The poor world is

---

70 **spit** i.e. while they think what to say next. Charlotte Cushman substituted 'Hem! Hem!' (Moore, 49). See Jonson, *Cynthia's Revels* (1601), 3.1.1272–9, for comparable advice from Amorphus to Asotus, the sottish courtier, on how to conceal from his lady that he has forgotten his courtship lines.

71 **shift** course of action, device; cf. *TS* Induction 1.125: 'An onion will do well for such a shift'.

75 **out** prompts Ganymede's innuendo on nakedness (80)

77 **that should you** you would be

78 **honesty . . . wit** 'chastity greater than my (sexual) skill'; see *rank*, 2.7.46, and *wit*, 1.2.45 and nn. In Ganymede's Jonsonian revision of values, *honesty* (truth and chastity) is less admired than a sharp wit (particularly in sexual matters); a line cut for coarseness in nineteenth-century productions; cf. 155–64n.

79 **suit** wooing; both a legal plea and also a suit of clothes

80–1 **Not . . . suit** not undressed, but unable to proceed with your courting, or perhaps, remember your part. Rosalind here hastily denies Ganymede's risqué invocation of a naked Orlando.

84–5 Ganymede, acting the role of Rosalind, rejects Orlando, who, playing himself, will die.

84 **in her person** playing the part of the true Rosalind; ironic, as it also means 'playing myself'

86 **by attorney** by proxy; *OED sb.*[1] 2: 'One duly appointed . . . (by *letter* or *power of attorney*) to act for another . . . either *generally* . . . or in some *specific* act, which the principal, by reason of absence, is unable to perform in person. Hence the contrast between "in person" and "by attorney".' Cf. 128n. In Jonson, *Cynthia's Revels*, Amorphus prays to Mercury to defend them all '*From making loue by Attourney*' (*Palinodia*, 3004), a process Jonson may have imitated from *AYL*.

---

70 warrant] *Cam¹ subst. (Anon)*; warne *F*; warns *Johnson²*   80–1] *Pope; F lines* suite: / *Rosalind?* /

almost six thousand years old, and in all this time there
was not any man died in his own person (videlicet, in a
love-cause). Troilus had his brains dashed out with a
Grecian club, yet he did what he could to die before,   90
and he is one of the patterns of love. Leander, he would
have lived many a fair year though Hero had turned
nun, if it had not been for a hot midsummer night; for,
good youth, he went but forth to wash him in the
Hellespont and, being taken with the cramp, was   95
drowned, and the foolish chroniclers of that age found
it was Hero of Sestos. But these are all lies. Men have

87 **six thousand years** The table in the
Bishops' Bible (1568) claims that the
world was '5503. yeres and sixe mon-
ethes' old' (sig. *vi'). Ralegh demonstrated that according to the Gregorian
calendar (adopted amidst protest in
1599) the world is 5548 years old,
although the Julian calendar makes
it older (*History*, 777ff.). Pont notes
'that common opinion, holden of
manie . . . that the World should
stande 6000. years, and thereafter
should be dissolved' (*Reckoning*,
35–6).

88–9 **died . . . love-cause** expired in person (as opposed to 'by proxy'), namely
(*videlicet*), from a broken heart

89 **love-cause** case (legal), cause (the reason for love) and course (the progress
of the love affair); see *MND* 1.1.134:
'The course of true love never did run
smooth'. See 96n. on *chroniclers*; cf.
5.4.50.
Troilus son of the Trojan king, Priam,
and a by-word for fidelity because of
his love for Cressida

90 **Grecian club** a blunt (wooden)
weapon (see 5.2.39n.), wielded by a
Greek adversary

91 **patterns of love** models of true love;
cf. *MA* 5.2.30–5. Phoebe rejects Montanus

in Lodge thus: 'Wert thou (Montanus) as
faire as Paris, as hardy as Hector, as constant as Troylus, as louing as Leander,
Phoebe could not loue, because she cannot
loue at all' (sig. M2').
Leander a Greek youth drowned while
pursuing his love for Hero, a vestal
virgin of Venus, a love-affair celebrated
in Marlowe's *Hero and Leander* (see
3.5.83n.), the story loosely based on the
Greek poet Musaeus and on Ovid,
Heroides, 18 and 19

92 **though** even if

94 **went but forth** went out only
wash him wash; reflexive (Abbott,
296)

95 **Hellespont** the stretch of sea between
mainland Greece and the island of
Sestos

96 **chroniclers** compilers of records;
Hanmer's emendation of F's
'Chronoclers' to 'coroners' is consistent with Rosalind's legal language.
However, the false tale told by chroniclers (i.e. the 'historians' – Ovid,
Musaeus and Marlowe) of the fictional Leander's drowning rekindles
the 'poetry and lies' debate; see
3.3.15–16n, 18–19nn.
found gave the verdict (that)

97 **it** i.e. the cause of death

96 chroniclers] *(Chronoclers), F2;* coroners *Hanmer*   97 Sestos] *F2;* Cestos *F*

died from time to time and worms have eaten them, but not for love.

ORLANDO I would not have my right Rosalind of this mind, for I protest her frown might kill me. 100

ROSALIND By this hand, it will not kill a fly. But come, now I will be your Rosalind in a more coming-on disposition, and ask me what you will, I will grant it.

ORLANDO Then love me, Rosalind. 105

ROSALIND Yes, faith, will I, Fridays and Saturdays and all.

ORLANDO And wilt thou have me?

ROSALIND Ay, and twenty such.

ORLANDO What sayst thou? 110

ROSALIND Are you not good?

ORLANDO I hope so.

98–9 **died . . . love** See 173n. Enobarbus is the only Shakespearean character to die of a broken heart (*AC* 4.10.36). The actress Juliet Stevenson recounts that Adrian Noble, in his 1985 RSC production, wanted her to play Rosalind's lines mournfully, instead of debunking the 'whole myth of romanticism' (Rutter, 111); however, in a BBC broadcast in 2003 she acknowledged reverting to a more wistful interpretation (Stevenson & Sosanya).

100 **right** real, true

101 **mind** opinion
frown might kill Orlando vouches for the true lover's susceptibility to the traditional cruelty of the courtly lady; see 3.2.401n.

102 **By . . . fly** Rosalind's rewriting of the script of the cruel mistress provides another reminder of Rabelais's model of the Abbey of Thelema, which proposes a new fellowship between men and women (Dusinberre, 'As *Who*?', 19).
By this hand a solemn oath anticipating the mock-marriage; see 115n.
kill a contrast with Phoebe's cruelty to

Silvius (3.5.16), for which Ganymede castigates her (3.5.36–41); see pp. 25, 32–3.

103–4 **coming-on disposition** encouraging mood: modern 'come-on', occasioned by a *holiday humour*, 63.

104 **what you will** whatever you like – a possible echo of Rabelais's '*Fay ce que voudras*' (Do as thou wilt), suggesting Elizabethan sexual connotations of 'will' (see 5.2.39n. and *Son* 135). Rosalind's invitation receives a chaste response; see 3.4.16n.

106 **Fridays and Saturdays** fast days (*Fridays*) and feast days (*Saturdays*), as in holy-day/holiday

107 **all** every day

108 Orlando's question echoes the priest's opening question: 'Wilt thou . . . ?', from the marriage ceremony ('Of Matrimony') in *BCP* (fols 136ᵛ–7ʳ), prompting Rosalind to initiate the mock-ceremony (114).

109 **such** men like you

112 **hope** a chivalric statement of Christian humility; see 1.2.273–4n., 3.2.34n.

ROSALIND   Why then, can one desire too much of a good
thing? Come, sister, you shall be the priest and marry
us. Give me your hand, Orlando. What do you say,   115
sister?

ORLANDO   Pray thee, marry us.

CELIA   I cannot say the words.

ROSALIND   You must begin: 'Will you, Orlando –'

CELIA   Go to. – Will you, Orlando, have to wife this   120
Rosalind?

ORLANDO   I will.

ROSALIND   Ay, but when?

ORLANDO   Why now, as fast as she can marry us.

ROSALIND   Then you must say: 'I take thee, Rosalind, for   125
wife.'

ORLANDO   I take thee, Rosalind, for wife.

ROSALIND   I might ask you for your commission. But I do
take thee, Orlando, for my husband. There's a girl goes

113–14 **can . . . thing** In becoming
proverbial Rosalind's question has lost
its irony.

114–15 **marry us** In Lodge the marriage
is Aliena's idea: 'And thereupon (quoth
Aliena) Ile play the priest, from this
daye forth *Ganimede* shall call thee husband, and thou shalt cal *Ganimede* wife,
and so weele haue a marriage. Content
quoth *Rosader*, and laught. Content
quoth *Ganimede*, and chaunged as red
as a rose: and so with a smile and a
blush, they made vp this iesting match,
that after proued to a marriage in
earnest: *Rosader*, full little thinking hee
had wooed and woonne his Rosalynde'
(sig. I4ᵛ); see 119–127nn.

115 **Give . . . hand** both literally and figuratively, i.e. in marriage (see 102n.).
Masten suggests that the moment
'stages the "rehearsal" of the marriage' at 5.4.112 ('Ganymede', 156).

119–21 The questions are from *BCP*, 'Of
Matrimony'.

120 **to wife** as your wife; see *BCP*, 'to thy
wedded wyfe' (fol. 136ᵛ).

125, 127 **I take thee** The vows exchanged
between Orlando and Rosalind here
constitute *sponsalia per verba de prae-
senti* – spousals, i.e. betrothal, through
words (spoken) in the present – made
binding by the presence of a witness,
Celia. This informal mode of contract
was increasingly frowned on for lacking church ceremony (see Ard²,
Appendix B; and see 3.3.77–9n.). See
T. Hawkes, 43, for the respect accorded in Arden to 'lore', as here (cf. *old
custom*, 2.1.2), over 'law'. However, the
false identity of Ganymede would nullify the contract, as it does for Jonson's
Morose in *Epicoene* (1609).

128 **commission** 'warrant or instrument
conferring . . . authority' (*OED sb.*¹ 3a);
see 86n.

129–30 **goes . . . priest** Traditionally the
priest speaks the vows, which are
repeated by the bride.

---

119 'Will you, Orlando –'] *Capell;* will you *Orlando. F*   123 Ay] *om. F3*   125–6 'I . . . wife.'] *Capell;*
I . . . wife. *F*   128 I . . . commission] *Pope; verse F*

before the priest, and certainly a woman's thought runs   130
before her actions.

ORLANDO   So do all thoughts – they are winged.

ROSALIND   Now tell me how long you would have her
after you have possessed her?

ORLANDO   For ever and a day.   135

ROSALIND   Say 'a day' without the 'ever'. No, no,
Orlando, men are April when they woo, December
when they wed. Maids are May when they are maids,
but the sky changes when they are wives. I will be more
jealous of thee than a Barbary cock-pigeon over his   140
hen, more clamorous than a parrot against rain, more
new-fangled than an ape, more giddy in my desires than
a monkey. I will weep for nothing, like Diana in the
fountain, and I will do that when you are disposed to be
merry. I will laugh like a hyena, and that when thou art   145

---

137 **April** the prime of life and love (see
Son 3.10 and 5.3.19); see Aliena to
Saladyne (Lodge, sig. N1ᵛ).
138 **May** a month of brilliant but unreliable weather; see *Son* 18.3: 'Rough
winds do shake the darling buds of
May'.
   maids unmarried girls (virgins)
140 **jealous** possessive, demanding of
exclusive rights
   Barbary cock-pigeon a special variety of black or dun-coloured pigeon,
introduced from Barbary in North
Africa (Knowles; *OED* barb *sb.*³ 2);
Ganymede's racist joke is happily too
obscure to be understood in the modern theatre, but looks forward to Iago's
rhetoric, e.g. *Oth* 1.1.110.
141 **parrot** See Breton, '*Praise*': 'In the
parler she is a parrat; she learnes but
what is taught her, and an almond will
please her' (169).
142 **new-fangled** obsessed with novelty;
cf. Elizabeth I's declaration that she

would not 'tolerate newfangleness' in
religion (*Works*, 183).
   giddy volatile generally, but also in
sexual matters; see 3.2.336n.
143 **monkey** renowned for lechery
143–5 **weep . . . merry** For Ganymede's
fiction of 'Rosalind' here, see p. 24; cf.
AC 1.3.4–7: 'If you find him sad, / Say
I am dancing; if in mirth, report /
That I am sudden sick.'
143–4 **Diana   . . .   fountain** In
Montemayor's *Diana* the forsaken
shepherd remembers that his faithless
love, Diana, wept false tears into the
fountain while vowing eternal love.
145 ***hyena** F's 'Hyen' may be a mistake
(Cam²), or an obsolete form of the
word (Knowles). A hyena's bark, like a
jackal's, sounds like a laugh; a hyena
could also 'counterfeit a man's voice'
and was thought to be androgynous
(Harley, 335–6, see also Douce,
Illustrations, 1.307). See Ovid, *Met.*,
15: 'Much rather may we woonder at

---

133 you would] would you *Theobald²*   136 'a day' . . . 'ever'] *Bevington;* a day . . . euer F   145 hyena]
*(*Hyen*)*   thou art] you are *Rowe³*

inclined to sleep.

ORLANDO   But will my Rosalind do so?

ROSALIND   By my life, she will do as I do.

ORLANDO   O, but she is wise.

ROSALIND   Or else she could not have the wit to do this –   150
the wiser, the waywarder. Make the doors upon a
woman's wit and it will out at the casement. Shut that
and 'twill out at the keyhole. Stop that, 'twill fly with
the smoke out at the chimney.

ORLANDO   A man that had a wife with such a wit, he   155
might say, 'Wit, whither wilt?'

ROSALIND   Nay, you might keep that check for it till you
met your wife's wit going to your neighbour's bed.

ORLANDO   And what wit could wit have to excuse that?

---

the *Hyēn*, if we please, / Too see how
interchangeably it one whyle doth
remayne / A female, and another
whyle becometh male againe' (p. 192ᵛ).
Ganymede's evocation of Rosalind
makes her noisy, laughing and androgynous; see also 3.2.171–2n. and
4.3.17n., 18n.

thou a sudden, unwary change to the
intimate form, which Rosalind subsequently masks with her satire

146 **sleep** The propensity of wayward
wives to interrupt sleep – as in the title
of Brathwait's compilation, *Art Asleep?*
(1640) – whether by laughing, as here, or
by garrulity, is a stock motif of medieval
satire against women (Dusinberre,
Women, 175–98).

148 **By my life** a heartfelt oath (cf.
5.2.68) as opposed to a *pretty* one
(177), an affirmation of the true
Rosalind behind the fiction of
Ganymede

150 **wit** See 78n., 1.2.45n. Ganymede is
quick to translate Orlando's *wise* into a
sexual register.

151 **Make . . . upon** 'To shut, close, bar

(a door). Now *arch.* and *dial.*' (*OED*
make *v.*¹ 37); cf. *CE* 3.1.93: 'the doors
are made against you'.

152, 153, 154 **at** by way of

152 **casement** window

155–64 In eighteenth- and nineteenth-
century productions the 'cuckoo'
song from *LLL* (5.2.882–917) usually
replaced these suggestive lines. However, the eighteenth-century actress
Dorothy Jordan (see Fig. 2) 'sang it
"with her two fingers held up over the
head of Orlando" to form a cuckold's
horns' (cf. Fig. 13); the song was
omitted by Helena Faucit in 1839
(Carlisle, 70, citing Robson, 142).

156 **Wit, whither wilt?** Cf. Breton's *Will
of Wit* (1599) in which Will and Wit
search for each other: '*Wit*. Whither
away? *Will*. Where I may' (p. 10); see
1.2.54–5n.; dubiously cited in *OED*
wit *sb.* 2e as the earliest example of a
'phr[ase] addressed to a person who is
letting his tongue run away with him'.

157 **check** restraint, rebuke

159 And what ingenuity could sexual
desire find to excuse that (fault)?

146 sleep] weep *Warburton (Theobald)*   151 doors] Doors fast *Rowe³*   158 met] meet *Johnson²*

ROSALIND   Marry, to say she came to seek you there. You   160
shall never take her without her answer unless you take
her without her tongue. O, that woman that cannot
make her fault her husband's occasion, let her never
nurse her child herself, for she will breed it like a fool!

ORLANDO   For these two hours, Rosalind, I will leave   165
thee.

ROSALIND   Alas, dear love, I cannot lack thee two hours.

ORLANDO   I must attend the Duke at dinner. By two
o'clock I will be with thee again.

ROSALIND   Ay, go your ways, go your ways. I knew what   170
you would prove. My friends told me as much and I
thought no less. That flattering tongue of yours won

---

160 **there** i.e. in your neighbour's bed
162 **without her tongue** Cf. *LLL*
1.1.119–23: '*That no woman shall come
within a mile of my court . . . On pain of
losing her tongue*' (Dusinberre, *Women*,
159–60).
163 **make . . . occasion** either 'make her
husband the cause of [her own misde-
meanour]', or 'convert her own fault
into an accusation or charge on her
husband' (Capell, *Notes*, 1.65). Cf.
Chaucer, 'Merchant's': 'That though
they been in any gilt ytake / With face
bolde, they shullen hemselue excuse /
And bear hem down that would hem
accuse' (fol. 30ᵛ; see A. Thompson, 63).
164 **nurse** breast-feed
breed rear (see 3.2.28n.) – an appropriate image for Ganymede, a shepherd boy
like a fool i.e. the child will imbibe
folly with its mother's milk; cf. *dull
kindred*, 3.2.29. Cf. *RJ* 1.3.67–8, Nurse
to Juliet: 'Were I not thine only nurse /
I would say thou hadst suck'd wisdom
from thy teat.'
165 **two hours** Cf. *Within an hour*, 4.3.99.

will must; see 168.
167 **lack** do without
170 **Ay, go your ways** well, have it your
own way; see Tasso and Tasso, *Of
Marriage* (1599): 'If thou ridest about
thy businesse abroade into the
Countreys, shee then sayth; it is an
excuse and deuise, onely to shunne and
flie from her companie: and if thou
stay not still spending thy time idlely
by her, as no wise man will or ought,
except hee be out of his wittes: why
then thou hast quite forgotten and
abandoned her for euer' (sig. D4ʳ).
Ganymede's assumed waywardness
enters the same territory as the Tassos'
satire, described in the Bishops' Order
of 1599 (see 1.2.87–8n.) as 'the booke
against woemen', so called either for its
sexual focus (Boose, 196) or for its
scurrility against women (McCabe,
190).
171 **prove** turn out to be
My friends Ganymede conjures up
cliques of 'gossips', often satirized on
the Elizabethan and Jacobean stage
(see p. 141).

---

163 occasion] accusation *Hanmer*

me. 'Tis but one cast away, and so, come death! Two
o'clock is your hour?

ORLANDO   Ay, sweet Rosalind.   175

ROSALIND   By my troth, and in good earnest, and so God
mend me, and by all pretty oaths that are not
dangerous, if you break one jot of your promise or
come one minute behind your hour, I will think you the
most pathetical break-promise and the most hollow   180
lover and the most unworthy of her you call Rosalind
that may be chosen out of the gross band of the
unfaithful. Therefore beware my censure and keep
your promise.

ORLANDO   With no less religion than if thou wert indeed   185
my Rosalind. So adieu.

ROSALIND   Well, Time is the old justice that examines all
such offenders, and let Time try. Adieu.   *Exit [Orlando]*.

CELIA   You have simply misused our sex in your love-
prate! We must have your doublet and hose plucked   190
over your head and show the world what the bird hath
done to her own nest.

---

173 **'Tis . . . away** it's only one person
lost: mock resignation
come death The fictional Rosalind is
as quick to die as Cleopatra (*AC*
1.2.151: 'she hath such a celerity in
dying'). Rosalind mocks her own anti-
romantic stance at 98–9.

177–8 **oaths . . . dangerous** A curious
statement to follow the oath *God mend
me* (176–7), which would in 1606
have been prohibited by the Act of
Abuses (see 3.5.59n.). Chambers
points out: 'Profanity was "dangerous"
long before a Jacobean parliament
made it so' (*ES*, 1.241); Ganymede's
alleged awareness of danger does not
inhibit his invocation of the deity.

178 **jot** iota; the smallest Greek letter

180 **pathetical** pathetic – affectionate

rather than scornful; cf. *LLL* 4.1.147:
'most pathetical nit'.

182 **gross band** coarse crowd or mob

183 **censure** judgement (here implying
condemnation)

185 **religion** the binding quality of a
religious vow

187–8 **Time . . . try** Cf. 'Time tries all'
(Dent, T336).

190 **plucked** pulled off, as in plucking
the feathers from a bird

191–2 **bird . . . nest** Shakespeare reworks
a scatological proverb (Dent, B377; cf.
Lodge, sig. D4ᵛ) into a jest about
gender, made more ambivalent in his
own theatre by the presence of the boy
actor; see p. 28 and cf. 3.5.36n
for Rosalind's protest that Phoebe's
cruelty to Silvius betrays women.

188 SD *Orlando*] *Rowe*

ROSALIND   O coz, coz, coz, my pretty little coz, that thou
   didst know how many fathom deep I am in love! But it
   cannot be sounded – my affection hath an unknown   195
   bottom, like the Bay of Portugal.

CELIA   Or rather bottomless, that as fast as you pour
   affection in, it runs out.

ROSALIND   No, that same wicked bastard of Venus that
   was begot of thought, conceived of spleen and born of   200
   madness, that blind rascally boy that abuses everyone's
   eyes because his own are out, let him be judge how deep
   I am in love. I tell thee, Aliena, I cannot be out of the

193 **coz** The resumption of the joyous and affectionate nickname of 1.2 marks Rosalind's return to her own role, but also frames her new-found love for Orlando with the old love between the two women (see pp. 29–31).

194 **fathom deep** A fathom was a nautical measurement of depth; see *Tem* 1.2.397: 'Full fathom five thy father lies'.

195 **sounded** measured (especially of the measurement of the depth of water at sea); cf. *2H4* 4.2.50–1: 'You are too shallow, Hastings, much too shallow, / To sound the bottom of the after-times.'

195–6 **unknown bottom** of a depth impossible to gauge; cf. 'Sir Walter Ralegh to Queen Elizabeth': 'Our passions are most like to floods and streams, / The shallow murmur, but the deep are dumb. / So, when affections yield discourse, it seems / The bottom is but shallow whence they come' (Ralegh, *Writings*, 33.1–4).

196 **Bay of Portugal** 'The sea off the coast of Portugal between Oporto and the headland of Cintra. The water is very deep, attaining 1400 fathoms within 40m of the coast' (Sugden, 420; see Ralegh, *Letters*, 74; cf. Marlowe,

Tamburlaine 1 (1590), 3.3.258–9). The scene ends, as it began, with the experiences of Elizabethan travellers.

197–8 **as fast . . . out** an image of a sieve. The sieve was one of Elizabeth's emblems, appearing in many of her portraits as a symbol of purity associated with the Roman Vestal, Tuccia, who had to carry a sieve without spilling a drop of water (Strong, *Cult*, 153; Yates, 114–17; see 1.2.234 SDn.). By 1599 both Ralegh and Essex had experienced the running-out of the queen's affection.

200 **begot . . . conceived . . . born** a probably unconscious linguistic echo of the Apostles' Creed: 'conceived of the holy ghost, borne of the virgin Mary' (*BCP*, 'A Catechism', fol. 133ʳ; cf. 1.2.112n.), rendered innocuous by the introduction of Cupid (*wicked bastard*, 199).

spleen the seat of melancholy, one of the four humours (*OED sb.* 2b), allied therefore with *madness*

203 ***I tell** F's 'ile' (TLN 2121) is probably a case of dittography, the scribe having copied 'Ile' from line 2122 (204), where it lies almost directly below the first example. Rosalind's asseveration requires the present tense.

198 in, it] *F2;* in, in *F*   203 ²I] *Hudson² (Cam);* ile *F*

sight of Orlando. I'll go find a shadow and sigh till he
come.   205
CELIA   And I'll sleep.   *Exeunt.*

4.2   *Enter* JAQUES, Lords *and* Foresters.

JAQUES   Which is he that killed the deer?
1 LORD   Sir, it was I.
JAQUES   Let's present him to the Duke like a Roman
conqueror, and it would do well to set the deer's horns
upon his head for a branch of victory. Have you no   5

---

204 **shadow** shady place – under a tree –
where Celia plans to sleep; but the
same word is used for an actor, thus
recalling for the audience the role-
playing of the whole scene. Cf. *MND*
5.1.417: 'If we shadows have offended'.
206 **sleep** the demands of the body, which
underpin the air and fire of ardent love,
rooting it in the natural physical world
(Dusinberre, *Women*, 167–70); cf.
4.3.4n. and 2.4.61n. In *TGV* Speed
complains: 'though the chameleon
Love can feed on the air, I am one that
am nourished by my victuals, and
would fain have meat' (2.1.159–61).
4.2 The celebratory bringing home of the
slaughtered deer and accompanying
song were traditional to the hunt. The
ritual derived also from the old mumming plays, in which mummers
dressed in animal skins, as well as from
the carnival shaming of cuckolds, and
skimmington rides (Hutton, 47–8;
Laroque, 234); see 3.2.105n., p. 57 and
Appendix 5.
1, 4, 10 **deer** F's 'Deare' (set by
Compositor C), a spelling unique in
Shakespeare to this scene, prompts a
reader to associate deer and lovers; see
2.1.25n. and pp. 134–5.

2 **SP** The witness of Jaques's lament in 2.1
may kill the deer; see pp. 53, 132.
3–4 **Roman conqueror** i.e., with a gar-
land round his head; see Elyot,
Governor: 'a garlande or some other
lyke token, to be gyuen in signe of
victorie [after hunting]' (fol. 72ᵛ). The
association of Caesar with the hunt
was traditional; see 3.2.239n. In
Munday and Chettle, *Death*, the
slaughtered stag wears Caesar's collar
(Berry, *Hunt*, 182), as does the deer (an
image for Anne Boleyn) in Wyatt's
sonnet xi, 'Whoso list to hunt': '*Noli*
me tangere for Caesar's I am' (77).
Rosalind invokes the Roman again
when describing the onset of passion
between Celia and Oliver (see 5.2.30–1
and n.).   References to Caesar often
resonate on the fortunes of the Earl of
Essex (cf. *H5* 5.0.28–34 and see J.
Shapiro, 145).
5 **branch** as with the laurel or bay
wreath celebrating victory; but the
branching of antlers is symbolic of
cuckoldry. Cf. *WT* 1.1.23–4: 'such an
affection which cannot choose but
branch now', where 'branch' ominous-
ly prefigures accusations of infidelity.
Harington wrote to Hugh Portman in

4.2] *(Scena Secunda.)*   Location] *The same / Capell; Another part of the forest / Malone*   0.1 Lords
and Foresters] *(and Lords, Forresters), Douai ms, Rowe; and Lords, in the habit of foresters / Malone;
and* Lords, *in the habit of Foresters, with a dead deer / White; AMIENS and other lords appear, dressed as
foresters Cam¹; and* LORDS, FORESTERS *bearing the antlers and skin of a deer Cam²*   1, 4, 10 deer]
(Deare), F3   2 SP] *Malone; Lord. F; 1. F. / Capell*

song, forester, for this purpose?

1 FORESTER   Yes, sir.

JAQUES   Sing it. 'Tis no matter how it be in tune so it
make noise enough.   *Music*

1 FORESTER [*Sings.*]

What shall he have that killed the deer?   10
His leather skin and horns to wear.

JAQUES   Then sing him home; the rest shall bear this
burden.

ALL [*Sing.*]

Take thou no scorn to wear the horn –
It was a crest ere thou wast born.   15

1598 to congratulate him on starting a family, adding: 'may they bring you more peace than the branches which adorn your neighbour Hattons brows' (*Nugae Antiquae*, 2.68–9).

9 **noise** For Jaques's scorn of music see 2.5.14–15, 2.7.5–6nn.

9 SD F's 'Musicke' in roman type before 'Song' (TLN 2136) may represent a cue for playing by a broken consort, a group sufficiently able to make enough din to cover banquet (or other) noises (Dart, 5–6; see 1.2.134–5n., 2.7.174n., p. 78 and Fig. 15). The song, together with Jaques's rudeness about the singer (8–9), might suggest Amiens's presence, but a genuine hunting-song is more likely to be sung by the forester responsible for the conduct of the hunt, with a chorus of lords; see p. 132.

11 **leather skin** a hunter's pragmatic language, contrasting with the romantic overtones of *velvet*, 2.1.50

12 SP *suggested by Duffin; see 12–13n.

12–13 **Then . . . burden** Duffin argues that the omission of F's line in a copy of the catch (Folger MS V.a.409, *c.* 1625) implies that it is not part of the song, suggesting that Jaques invites the attendant lords to provide a chorus to the forester's song for the triumphal procession with the slaughtered game at the end of the hunt (*Songbook*, 434). The half-line *The . . . burden* has sometimes been included in the song, and sometimes treated as an SD; see t.n. and pp. 132–4.

12 **bear** carry (horns); endure (cuckoldry); sing (the bass line or chorus)

13 **burden** bass line or chorus; see 3.2.240n.

15 **crest** on the deer's forehead; but also a coat of arms, as in the crest granted to the Earl of Essex's father in 1572, of a 'stag *trippant*' (Dusinberre, '*AYL*', 413).

---

7 SP] *Neilson; Lord. F; F. Douai ms; For. / Rowe; 2. F. / Capell; 2. Lord. / Malone; 1 LORD Staunton; Amiens Cam¹*   9 SD] *(Musicke, Song.); Musick and Song, after which Exeunt Douai ms*   10–20] *om. Douai ms*   10 SP] *Neilson; LORDS Oliver; not in F*   SD] *Sisson; Song. F*   12–13] *as prose this edn (Duffin); as a line of song F; om. Knight; as SD Collier; Then . . . home / as a line of the song, the . . . burthen / om. Capell; Halliwell lines bear / burthen. / ; Then . . . home as a line of song, the . . . bur-then in margin Theobald; Then . . . home as a line of dialogue, the . . . burthen as SD Harbage (Brenneke)*   12 SP] *this edn (Duffin); not in F*   14 SP, SD] *Theobald subst.; at 18 Capell subst.*   the horn] *the horn, the horn, the horn, Theobald*

301

          Thy father's father wore it
          And thy father bore it.
          The horn, the horn, the lusty horn
          Is not a thing to laugh to scorn!   *Exeunt.*

4.3   *Enter* ROSALIND [*as Ganymede*]
                    and CELIA [*as Aliena*].

ROSALIND   How say you now, is it not past two o'clock?
    And here much Orlando.
CELIA   I warrant you, with pure love and troubled brain he
    hath ta'en his bow and arrows and is gone forth to sleep.

                    Enter SILVIUS [*with a letter*].

    Look who comes here.   5
SILVIUS

    My errand is to you, fair youth.
    My gentle Phoebe did bid me give you this.
    I know not the contents, but as I guess

---

16 **Thy father's father** Capell sees the
reference to earlier generations as a
device to prevent *ad hominem* applica-
tion of the song's satire (*Notes*, 1.66);
see 5n., and cf. 3.3.46n., 52n.

18 **lusty** vigorous (see 2.3.47), also invoking desire (see 3.5.122n.).

4.3.1 How . . . now what can you say now
2 **much** ironic, i.e. no (*OED a.* 2f). In
Lodge, Aliena and Ganimede muse on
Rosader's delay: 'Some while they
thought he had taken some word
vnkindly, and had taken the pet: then
they imagined some new Loue had
withdrawne his fancie' (sig. K4ʳ).

3 **warrant** assure

4 **sleep** teasing: true lovers should be

insomniac; see 3.2.359n.

4.1 F's early SD (after *brain*, 3; see Fig. 21
and p. 136) may be an error by
Compositor C, as lines 3–5, *he . . . here*,
are set in verse. But the early entry
would increase the comedy by reward-
ing the wish of both the heroine and
the audience to see Orlando, with the
unwelcome alternative of drippy
Silvius of *troubled brain*.

8, 21 **contents** contènts (Cercignani, 38);
a suggestion of the *dis*contents which
the letter will create. Lodge's
Montanus surmises that Phoebe has
written a love-letter to Ganimede
because her health has collapsed from
lovesickness (sigs N3ʳ–Oʳ).

4.3] *(Scoena Tertia.)*   Location] *The same / Capell; The Forest Var 1793*   0.1 *as Ganymede*] *Oxf*   0.2
as Aliena] *Oxf*   1–5] *Pope; F lines* clock? / *Orlando.* / brain, / forth / heere. /   2 here much
Orlando] here's no Orland *Douai ms*   4.1] *Sisson; after* brain *3* F; *after 5* Pope   *with a letter*] *Cam²*
7 this.] this: *gives a Letter. / Capell*

By the stern brow and waspish action
Which she did use as she was writing of it,   10
It bears an angry tenor. Pardon me,
I am but as a guiltless messenger.

ROSALIND

Patience herself would startle at this letter
And play the swaggerer. Bear this, bear all!
She says I am not fair, that I lack manners;   15
She calls me proud, and that she could not love me,
Were man as rare as phoenix. 'Od's my will,
Her love is not the hare that I do hunt.
Why writes she so to me? Well, shepherd, well,
This is a letter of your own device.   20

SILVIUS

No, I protest, I know not the contents.
Phoebe did write it.

ROSALIND   Come, come, you are a fool,
And turned into the extremity of love.
I saw her hand – she has a leathern hand,

9 **action** gestures
11 **tenor** drift, import (*OED sb.*[1] A I 1a)
12 **but as** only (Abbott, 130)
13 **startle** be startled or shocked (*OED v.* 3a); give a start
14 **play the swaggerer** act the braggart; Rosalind, extolled for *patience* at 1.3.75, here pretends to imagine the figure of Patience provoked into swash-buckling (see 1.3.117).
16 **and that** and (asserts) that
17 **phoenix** a unique bird, conjuring up a unique (and self-propagating) man such as the disguised Ganymede; the phoenix consumes itself in fire and is born again from its own ashes; see 3.2.171–2n. In Lodge, Rosader describes Rosalynde as 'the Phenix of all that sexe' (sig. G4[r]).
'Od's my will abbreviation of 'God's (will) is my will'; see 3.5.44n.

18 **hare** Hares were alleged to be hermaphrodite; see 4.1.145n. Beagling – the hunting on foot of the hare – was assigned to specially chosen boys (beagles) at the Elizabethan court, so Ganymede's image is in decorum, but also conjures up the boy actor who plays the role; cf. *TN* 2.3.176, of Maria: 'She's a beagle, true-bred'.
19 **well** very good, well done (satirical)
20 **device** devising, invention
21 **protest** deny the allegation
23 **the extremity** th'extremity; cf. 2.1.42.
24 **her hand** not her handwriting
leathern hand brown and thick-skinned, as of a working woman (see *housewife*, 27), but also possibly a cunning exploitation of the boy actor's body – the apprentice's hands rather than the lady's; see p. 34.

11 tenor] *(tenure)*, *Douai ms, Theobald (*tenour*)*   13 letter] letter, *After reading the letter / Hanmer*
22 it.] it, with her own fair hand *Rann (Mason)*

A freestone-coloured hand – I verily did think   25
That her old gloves were on, but 'twas her hands.
She has a housewife's hand – but that's no matter.
I say she never did invent this letter;
This is a man's invention and his hand.

SILVIUS   Sure, it is hers.   30

ROSALIND

Why, 'tis a boisterous and a cruel style,
A style for challengers. Why, she defies me,
Like Turk to Christian. Women's gentle brain
Could not drop forth such giant-rude invention,
Such Ethiop words, blacker in their effect   35
Than in their countenance. Will you hear the letter?

25 **freestone-coloured** tawny-coloured, like Cotswold stone; cf. 'the white hand of Rosalind' (3.2.378–9).

27 **housewife's** (hand) of a woman who works in the house (see 1.2.31n.).

29 **man's invention** The letter sent by Phoebe demonstrates a masculine harshness, but also betokens masculinity because penned by the boy who acts her and composed by the male dramatist.

31 **boisterous** rough, unruly. F's spelling of 'boysterous' (set by Compositor C) carries on the joke on boyishness at 29; cf. 'boistrous', 2.3.32 (set by Compositor D). No claim is being made for 'significant' spelling – i.e. intended by either author, compositor or scribe – in the original (see Howard-Hill's caveats in *Crane*, esp. 4–8), but rather for the registering of a possible effect of F's spelling on a reader; cf. the jokes about spelling in *LLL* 5.1.17–25, and see pp. 135–6.

32 **style for challengers** manner of writing suitable for duellists, anticipating Touchstone's sallies at 5.4.46ff.; cf. *TN* 3.2.41–2: 'a martial hand'.
    defies upbraids me; in fact Phoebe's

letter deifies Ganymede: **god** (40), *god-head* (44); see 3.2.349n.

33 **Turk to Christian** Turks were renowned for cruelty. The victory of Christians over the Turks at the Battle of Lepanto in 1571 became an official day of celebration (Cressy, 91). Elizabethan audiences might recall the confrontation of Turk and Christian in the mumming plays.
    Women's Rowe's emendation to 'Woman's' alters the tone by making a group identification into a generic one (see 3.5.36n.).
    gentle not *cruel* (see 31)

34 **giant-rude** grossly ill-mannered

35 **Ethiop** Ethiopian; used as a by-word for both blackness and barbarity
    blacker . . . effect more disagreeable in their import; see 3.2.90n.

36 **countenance** appearance, i.e. the black ink which gives Phoebe's cruelty material form; a covert reminder of Ganymede's judgement on Phoebe's looks (3.5.131)
    letter In Shakespeare's theatre letters were usually held by the book-keeper in separate copy from the main text of the play (Stern, 'Small-beer', 178–9;

25 freestone-coloured] *(freestone coloured)*   27 housewife's] *(huswiues); hussif's Ard²*   31 boister-
ous] *(boysterous)*   33 Women's] Woman's *Rowe*   34 giant-rude] *(giant rude)*

SILVIUS

   So please you, for I never heard it yet,

   Yet heard too much of Phoebe's cruelty.

ROSALIND

   She Phoebes me. Mark how the tyrant writes.

   (*Reads.*)

        Art thou god to shepherd turned,   40

        That a maiden's heart hath burned?

   Can a woman rail thus?

SILVIUS   Call you this railing?

ROSALIND (*Reads.*)

        Why, thy godhead laid apart,

        Warr'st thou with a woman's heart?   45

   Did you ever hear such railing?

        Whiles the eye of man did woo me,

        That could do no vengeance to me.

   – Meaning me a beast –

        If the scorn of your bright eyne   50

        Have power to raise such love in mine,

        Alack, in me what strange effect

        Would they work in mild aspect?

        Whiles you chid me, I did love,

        How then might your prayers move?   55

see p. 128) and could therefore be lost or misplaced. Rosalind has, in a sense, been given the *wrong* letter – a love-letter instead of the promised rebuke.

37 **So please you** yes, please

39 **She Phoebes me** She scorns me. This coinage echoes Silvius's *Phoebe's* in the previous line, and may also look back to 3.5.1, printed in F as 'do not *Phebe*' (see n.). 'The stress is on *me*: "She Phebes *me* (as well as you)"' (Knowles).

42 **rail** scoff. See 3.5.63n.

47, 54 *Whiles* while

48 *vengeance* harm, mischief (Johnson)

49 **beast** in opposition to '*eye of man*', 47; cf. 2.7.1n. Rosalind deliberately misunderstands Phoebe's compliment that Ganymede is a god not a man.

50 *eyne* eyes: poetic, archaic plural

52 *effect* consequences

53 *mild aspect* (aspèct) the favourable or clement disposition of the stars, bestowing good fortune; cf. *Son* 26.10: 'Points on me graciously with fair aspect'.

40, 44 SDs] *(Read.)*   53 *mild*] sweet *Douai ms*

> He that brings these lines to thee
> Little knows this love in me;
> And by him seal up thy mind,
> Whether that thy youth and kind
> Will the faithful offer take   60
> Of me, and all that I can make,
> Or else by him my love deny,
> And then I'll study how to die.

SILVIUS
   Call you this chiding?

CELIA   Alas, poor shepherd.

ROSALIND   Do you pity him? No, he deserves no pity. –   65
   Wilt thou love such a woman? What, to make thee an
   instrument and play false strains upon thee? Not to be
   endured! Well, go your way to her, for I see love hath
   made thee a tame snake, and say this to her: that if she
   love me, I charge her to love thee. If she will not, I will   70
   never have her unless thou entreat for her. If you be a
   true lover, hence and not a word, for here comes more
   company.   *Exit Silvius.*

56 *these lines* As F's '*this loue*' is copied in
the next line, this edition assumes a case
of dittography, and follows the reading
in the Douai MS (see Appendix 4).
   these F's '*this*' may be an error resulting from the frequent manuscript
spelling of 'these' as 'theis' (RP).
Howard-Hill notes that the scrivener
Ralph Crane 'invariably uses the
spellings *theis* or *y^eis*' for 'these' (Crane,
5); see 5.2.102n. and p. 126.
   lines RP points out that 'line' is mis-
printed as 'loue' in Q1 of *E3* (1596),
2.1.142: 'That loue [line] hath two
falts, grosse and palpable' (Tucker
Brooke, 75n.).
57 *Little knows* because the letter is
sealed
58 *seal . . . mind* make up your mind and

send your reply sealed in a letter
59 *kind* nature, sort
61 *make* do
65–9 **Do . . . snake** Ganymede's scorn
transforms Lodge, where both
Ganimede and Aliena admire
Montanus's selfless devotion, which
causes him – after the reading of
Phoebe's letter – to plead with his rival
to love her. The girls then plot how to
make Phoebe requite Montanus's passion (sig. O').
67 **instrument** agent; musical instrument
   strains melodies, sounds; cf. *JC*
4.3.255: 'And touch thy instrument a
strain or two?'
69 **tame snake** contemptuous: a poor
specimen. The epithet prepares the ear
for the 'green and gilded snake' at 107.

56 these lines] *Douai ms, this edn; this loue F*   57 this] *that / Rowe²*   67 strains] *strings F2*

Enter OLIVER.

OLIVER

Good morrow, fair ones. Pray you, if you know,
Where in the purlieus of this forest stands   75
A sheepcote fenced about with olive-trees?

CELIA

West of this place, down in the neighbour bottom;
The rank of osiers by the murmuring stream,
Left on your right hand, brings you to the place.
But at this hour the house doth keep itself –   80
There's none within.

OLIVER

If that an eye may profit by a tongue,
Then should I know you by description,
Such garments and such years: 'The boy is fair,

---

74 Stern (*Making*, 107) suggests that the audience does not recognize Oliver, and therefore learns his transformed identity at the same moment as Rosalind and Celia (132), who have never seen him before, a situation which creates various options for directors: 'is he ragged and hairy, as he describes himself in line 101 [105]? Or has he donned the "fresh array" mentioned in line 138 [142]?' (Marshall). A reader obviously sees the SP, and therefore, as with the twins in *CE*, recognizes Orlando's brother.

75 **purlieus** a legal term for an area on the outskirts of a forest (*OED* purlieu 1, quoting this line, the only example in Shakespeare; see p. 52), whose inhabitants were exempt from its jurisdictions (Manwood, *Laws* (1598), ch. 20, pp. 170ʳ–87ʳ) – a suitable lodging for the disguised truant princesses (see 3.2.324–5 and 3.2.325n.). The Forest 'Ranger' was responsible for the protection of wild beasts of the Forest who had strayed into the purlieus, and must be returned to their haunts in the Forest proper (*Laws*, 186ᵛ–7ʳ; see 1.3.65n.). In Heywood, *Weather* (1533), 'the Ranger' announces: 'I come for my selfe and suche other mo, / Rangers and kepers of certayne places / As forestes, parkes, purlews and chasys / Where we be chargyd wyth all maner game' (ll. 411–14, p. 194).

76 **sheepcote** shepherd's cottage (see 2.4.83n.)
   olive-trees symbol of peace; see 3.5.76n.

77 **bottom** a hollow, or low-lying place

78–9 'If you leave the line of willows (by the stream) on your right hand, the path will bring you to the house.'

78 **rank** row, line
   osiers willows

80 **doth keep** looks after

82 if an eye can see as a consequence of having been told what to look for

84 **such years** i.e. the right ages

---

77 bottom;] *Rann (Capell Notes);* bottom *F*   84–7 'The . . . brother.'] *Theobald;* the . . . brother: *F*

Of female favour, and bestows himself   85
Like a ripe sister; the woman low,
And browner than her brother.' [*to Rosalind*] Are not
    you
The owner of the house I did enquire for?

CELIA

It is no boast, being asked, to say we are.

OLIVER

Orlando doth commend him to you both,   90
And to that youth he calls his Rosalind
He sends this bloody napkin. – Are you he?

ROSALIND

I am. What must we understand by this?

OLIVER

Some of my shame, if you will know of me
What man I am, and how and why and where   95
This handkerchief was stained.

CELIA   I pray you tell it.

85 **female favour** Ganymede resembles a woman in features, likeness and beauty; cf. 5.4.27. The miniaturist Nicholas Hilliard explains 'favour' as the combination of 'Complexion Proportion Countenance', adding that 'Favour and likeness are both one in some sense, as if one would say of a picture after the life that it hath the very favour . . . or the very likeness of the party' (*Limning*, 79, 78); see 2.7.198n. and p. 76.
   bestows bears

86 **ripe** in the prime of beauty
   sister The gender ambiguity surrounding Rosalind is increased by Oliver's arrival, in preparation for the denouement in 5.4.
   low short; see 1.2.261n. and 4.1.193.

87 **browner** more tanned; see 1.3.109n.

88 **owner** F's singular may be a mistake for *owners*, but Thirsk's tables (442–5) suggest that it would be more likely for the man (Ganymede) to own the cottage, and hence for Oliver to address them.

89 Celia may regain some of the assertiveness of Act 1 in claiming joint ownership of the cottage. In Lodge, Aliena falls in love with Saladyne when he rescues her from the forest outlaws (sig. L1r). Celia's answering of a question addressed to her cousin may be another cue for her falling in love at first sight; see 178–9n.

90 **doth . . . him** sends his greetings; Lodge's Saladyne brings the message to the women, but not the news of Rosader's wounds (incurred while he defended them against outlaws).

92 **napkin** handkerchief.
   Are you he? to Ganymede

86 ripe sister] right forester *Hudson²* (*Lettsom*)   the] but the *F2*   87 SD] *this edn*   88 owner] owners *Douai ms, Halliwell (Capell Notes)*   95 why] when *Douai ms*   96 handkerchief] (handkercher), *Hanmer*

OLIVER

When last the young Orlando parted from you,
He left a promise to return again
Within an hour, and pacing through the forest,
Chewing the food of sweet and bitter fancy,   100
Lo, what befell. He threw his eye aside,
And mark what object did present itself.
Under an oak, whose boughs were mossed with age
And high top bald with dry antiquity,
A wretched ragged man, o'ergrown with hair,   105
Lay sleeping on his back; about his neck
A green and gilded snake had wreathed itself,
Who with her head, nimble in threats, approached
The opening of his mouth. But suddenly
Seeing Orlando, it unlinked itself   110
And with indented glides did slip away
Into a bush; under which bush's shade

99 **Within an hour** Cf. *two hours*,
   4.1.165.
100 **Chewing . . . of** ruminating on; see
   4.1.17–18n.
   fancy love-longings; see 3.2.350n.
101 **threw . . . aside** glanced sideways; a
   baroque use of language, creating 'a
   sort of surreality' (de Mourgues, 74)
102 **mark** note, listen carefully to
103 ***an oak** F's 'old' (before *oak*) creates
   a hypermetrical line and is probably
   redundant in view of *mossed with age*
   (covered with moss through the passage of time) and *dry antiquity*. See
   2.1.31n.
104 **high top** highest branches
   bald leafless
   dry antiquity lacking through age the
   sap to produce leaves at the top of the
   tree
105 a 'wild' man, familiar from many folk
   sources and from pastoral entertain-

ments for Elizabeth, as at Kenilworth
in 1575 where the queen 'listened to an
out-of-door dialogue between a Savage
Man – the medieval folk-personage
known as the "wodwose" – and the
classical Echo' (Chambers, *ES*, 1.123;
see 5.4.157n. and p. 95).
107 **gilded** golden; the sheen on the
   snake's scales
   snake symbol of wisdom (Egyptian),
   or of evil (Judaic)
   wreathed coiled
108 **nimble in threats** suggesting the
   darting movement of the snake's
   forked tongue, wrongly identified as
   the source of its venom
110 **unlinked** uncoiled; the linked scales
   of the snake's skin expand as it slides
   away
111 **indented** sinuous, interlocking
   glides gliding movements (*OED sb.*,
   first example 1596)

99 an hour] two hours *Hanmer*   100 food] cud *Staunton (Scott)*   103 oak] *Douai ms, Pope;* old
Oake *F*   107 gilded] *(guilded)*   112 which] whose *F2*   bush's] *(bushes);* branches *Douai ms*

A lioness, with udders all drawn dry,
Lay couching, head on ground, with catlike watch
When that the sleeping man should stir. For 'tis   115
The royal disposition of that beast
To prey on nothing that doth seem as dead.
This seen, Orlando did approach the man
And found it was his brother, his elder brother.

CELIA

O, I have heard him speak of that same brother,   120
And he did render him the most unnatural
That lived amongst men.

OLIVER   And well he might so do,
For well I know he was unnatural.

ROSALIND

But to Orlando: did he leave him there,
Food to the sucked and hungry lioness?   125

OLIVER

Twice did he turn his back and purposed so;
But kindness, nobler ever than revenge,

---

113 **lioness** a royal beast, but also biblical, as in Psalms, 91.13: 'Thou shalt set
  thy foote vppon the Lion and Adder:
  the young Lion and the Dragon thou
  shalt treade vnder thy feete' (Bishops'
  Bible). The lion and the snake give
  Orlando the status of romance hero
  and Christian knight. Shakespeare creates 'a complex and unsentimental
  awareness of the animal and human
  worlds as implicated in both nurturing
  and killing' (Berry, *Hunt*, 186).
  with . . . dry having suckled its young,
  and therefore needing food
114 **couching** anglicizes the heraldic
  'lion couchant', i.e. reposing on all
  fours, crouching
117 Cf. Lodge: 'Lyons hate to pray on
  dead carkasses' (sig. K^r), from Pliny,

8.16, p. 201: 'The Lion alone of all
wilde beasts, is gentle to those that
humble themselues vnto him, and will
not touch any such vpon their submission, but spareth what creature soeuer
lieth prostrate before him.'
118 **This** i.e. the lioness's readiness to
  spring when the man awakened
121 **render** give an account of
  unnatural transgressing against kinship bonds
125 **sucked** having fed its young
126 **Twice** Rosader in Lodge only turns
  his back once on the lion (sig. K1^v).
127 **kindness** loyalty to kind, as well as
  the act of kindness; see *unnatural*
  (121), and *kindly* (139). Cf. Bacon, 'Of
  Revenge': 'Certainly, in taking
  Reuenge, A Man is but euen with his

---

114 couching] crouching *Dyce^3*   119 elder] eldest *Theobald^2*

And nature, stronger than his just occasion,
Made him give battle to the lioness,
Who quickly fell before him, in which hurtling   130
From miserable slumber I awaked.

CELIA

Are you his brother?

ROSALIND   Was't you he rescued?

CELIA

Was't you that did so oft contrive to kill him?

OLIVER

'Twas I, but 'tis not I. I do not shame
To tell you what I was, since my conversion   135
So sweetly tastes, being the thing I am.

ROSALIND

But for the bloody napkin?

OLIVER   By and by.

Enemy; But in passing it ouer, he is Superiour: For it is a Princes part to Pardon' (*Essays*, 4, p. 19). Berry cites the homily 'Of Faith' (*Homilies*, sigs Liii^r–Giv^r), which stresses that charity rather than revenge is the true mark of faith, in this case Orlando's faith to his love ('Rosalynde', 51).

128 **nature** the natural bond between brothers
    his Orlando's
    just occasion good opportunity, but also an opportunity for justifiable revenge

129 **give battle to** attack

130 **hurtling** the reeling and fall of the wounded lioness

131 **I awaked** The shift to the first person pronoun transforms the narrative into Oliver's own story: his redemptive awakening from spiritual wretchedness (Cam^2).

133 **contrive** plot

134 **'Twas . . . not I** a statement of repentance and transformation, both Ovidian and Christian; see Galatians,

2.20: 'Thus I liue *yet*, not I now, but Christ liueth in me' (Geneva Bible).

135 **conversion** The religious language is consonant with the pilgrimage and penance traditions of the Forest of Arden; see pp. 95–6). Oliver has put off the 'old' man (i.e. Adam) and has become 'new' (see 2 Corinthians, 5.17, and Forker, *R2* 5.3.145 and n.), as Duke Frederick later does (Fraser, 'Genesis', 126–7). In Lodge, Saladyne's conversion comes at the equivalent of 3.1: 'I go thus pilgrime like to seeke out my brother, that I may reconcile my self to him in all submission, and afterward wend to the holy Land' (sig. K3^r).

136 **being . . . am** The phrase, with its implications of self-knowledge, often suggests elements of regeneration (Garber, 'Education', 109). See Parolles, *AW* 4.3.327–8: 'Simply the thing I am / Shall make me live'; and cf. Iago's menacing 'I am not what I am' (*Oth* 1.1.64).

137 **But for** what about

When from the first to last betwixt us two
Tears our recountments had most kindly bathed –
As how I came into that desert place –   140
I'brief, he led me to the gentle Duke
Who gave me fresh array and entertainment,
Committing me unto my brother's love,
Who led me instantly unto his cave;
There stripped himself and here, upon his arm,   145
The lioness had torn some flesh away,
Which all this while had bled. And now he fainted,
And cried in fainting upon Rosalind.
Brief, I recovered him, bound up his wound,
And after some small space, being strong at heart,   150
He sent me hither, stranger as I am,
To tell this story, that you might excuse
His broken promise; and to give this napkin,
Dyed in his blood, unto the shepherd youth
That he in sport doth call his Rosalind.   155
          [*Rosalind faints.*]

CELIA
    Why, how now, Ganymede – sweet Ganymede!

---

139 **recountments** a Shakespearean
    coinage: recounting of our adventures,
    possibly also 'encountering'
    kindly with kindness, but also *of kind*;
    see 127n.
140 **As** as to
141 **I'brief** (F 'I briefe') in brief; antici-
    pates *Brief*, 149
    gentle noble, compassionate
142 **array** raiment, garments – the word
    used in the parable of the Prodigal Son
    for the clothes with which the Father
    decked his penitent offspring (see
    1.1.35n.)
    entertainment hospitality
143 **Committing** assigning, entrusting

147 **fainted** Orlando's 'manly' role as
    hunter is not compromised by his
    fainting.
150 **strong at heart** hearty: both coura-
    geous and physically robust
153–4 In Lodge, Rosader recognizes his
    brother Saladyne when his own nose
    bleeds (sig. K1'), a folk superstition.
154 **Dyed** The use of this word to
    describe the red of the blood on the
    handkerchief may, by suggesting its
    homonym, 'died', play a part in
    Rosalind's faint.
    ***his** F's erroneous 'this' is probably
    induced from *this story* and *this napkin*
    in the previous two lines.

141 I'] *Oliver;* I *F;* In *F2*   154 his] *F2;* this *F*   155 SD] *Pope*

OLIVER

Many will swoon when they do look on blood.

CELIA

There is more in it. Cousin – Ganymede!

OLIVER   Look, he recovers.

ROSALIND   I would I were at home.   160

CELIA   We'll lead you thither.

– I pray you, will you take him by the arm?

OLIVER

Be of good cheer, youth. You a man?

You lack a man's heart.

ROSALIND   I do so, I confess it.

Ah, sirrah, a body would think this was well   165
counterfeited. I pray you tell your brother how well I
counterfeited. Heigh-ho –

OLIVER   This was not counterfeit: there is too great

---

157   Oliver's folk wisdom is at least as true
of men as of women. The moment
harks back to Phoebe's scornful command to Silvius to swoon (3.5.17).
Rosalind's swoon is genuine, but gives
rise to much badinage about counterfeiting. Hodgdon sees Rosalind's faint
as '"outing" her female character –
and her "hidden" desire' (184). Julia
Arthur noted in her promptbook in
1899 (the decade of the 'new woman'):
'Rosalind is not the kind of woman to
faint *dead away* at the sight of a little
blood. So she does not fall to stage'
(see also Marshall). In Lodge, Aliena,
not Ganymede, *almost* swoons
after Saladyne has rescued her and
Ganimede from 'rascals' who wound
Rosader (sig. L1ʳ).

158   **Cousin – Ganymede!** Celia's agita-
tion leads her to forget to act the part
of Ganymede's sister (Johnson).

159–61   All three characters drop into
prose in the stress of the moment.

160   a famous comic line; cf. Falstaff at the
battle of Shrewsbury: 'I would 'twere
bedtime, Hal, and all well' (*1H4*
5.1.125).

162   The resumption of blank verse signifies a return to composure and to the
maintaining, at least by Celia, of
Rosalind's disguise.

165   **sirrah** Rosalind either addresses
Oliver in man-to-man familiarity to
pretend that the swoon was a performance, or she pretends to congratulate
herself on her own performance.
a body an onlooker, any one

166   **counterfeited** acted

167   **Heigh-ho** Rosalind relapses into
swoon; see 2.7.181, 183, 191, 193n.

168–9   **there . . . complexion** your
colour bears witness too incontrovert-
ibly; see 3.5.117n.

---

158 Cousin – Ganymede] *Johnson;* Cosen *Ganimed* F; Cousin! Ganymede! *Cam²*   159–61] *Var 1793*
lines home. / thither: – /; *Boswell–Malone lines* recovers. / thither: – /   159 recovers.] recovers.
Raising her / *Collier²*   162] *prose Ard²*   163–4] *prose Pope*   165 sirrah] sir *Douai ms, Pope*

testimony in your complexion that it was a passion of
earnest.   170

ROSALIND   Counterfeit, I assure you.

OLIVER   Well then, take a good heart, and counterfeit to
be a man.

ROSALIND   So I do. But i'faith, I should have been a
woman by right.   175

CELIA   Come, you look paler and paler. Pray you, draw
homewards. Good sir, go with us.

OLIVER

That will I, for I must bear answer back
How you excuse my brother, Rosalind.

ROSALIND   I shall devise something; but I pray you   180
commend my counterfeiting to him. Will you go?   *Exeunt.*

5.1   *Enter* TOUCHSTONE *and* AUDREY.

TOUCHSTONE   We shall find a time, Audrey; patience,
gentle Audrey.

169–70 **of earnest** genuine
172–3 **take . . . man** buck up and
pretend to be a man; cf. 1.3.115–19,
2.4.5–7.
175 **by right** if allowed my true rights;
the voice of Rosalind behind
Ganymede's acting
176–7 Celia's last lines in the play; see pp.
28–9.
   draw homewards let's go home
together; 'draw', often used in the
sense of yoked beasts pulling a vehicle
(Onions, 'draw' 1, p. 64), revives the
pastoral setting. Cf. Spenser, 'January':
'the pensife boy . . . / Arose, and
homeward droue his sonned [sunned]
sheepe' (*SC*, p. 447).
178–9 Oliver's return to blank verse may
be an indication of his new status as a
lover; see Stern: 'A sudden change
from prose to verse in a player's part

can reveal . . . the moment when a
character is supposed to fall in love'
(*Rehearsal*, 11).
181 **commend my counterfeiting** The
swoon and jokes about acting are
Shakespeare's invention. In Lodge,
Rosader himself reports his adventures to Ganimede (sig. K4ᵛ).
   Will you go? a recapitulation of
Celia's urging departure on the
lovesick Rosalind at 1.2.244 (see n.)
5.1 The scene is cut in the Douai MS, and
may also have been cut – as was *MW* 4.1,
with another (un)grammatical William
(see Melchiori, 32) – for court or private
theatre performance (see p. 139).
William may possibly have been played
by Shakespeare (see Appendix 2).
1–2 **patience,   gentle   Audrey**
Ganymede has just invented his own
roasting in an allegedly hostile letter

178–9] *prose White*   **5.1**] *(Actus Quintus. Scena Prima.)*   Location] *the Forest / Rowe*   0.1–63] *om.
Douai ms*   0.1 TOUCHSTONE] *Malone; Clowne F*

314

AUDREY   Faith, the priest was good enough, for all the old
gentleman's saying.

TOUCHSTONE   A most wicked Sir Oliver, Audrey, a most   5
vile Mar-text! But Audrey, there is a youth here in the
forest lays claim to you.

AUDREY   Ay, I know who 'tis. He hath no interest in me in
the world.

Enter WILLIAM.

Here comes the man you mean.   10

TOUCHSTONE   It is meat and drink to me to see a clown.
By my troth, we that have good wits have much to
answer for. We shall be flouting; we cannot hold.

WILLIAM   Good ev'n, Audrey.

AUDREY   God ye good ev'n, William.   15

WILLIAM   And good ev'n to you, sir.

TOUCHSTONE   Good ev'n, gentle friend. Cover thy head,

---

from Phoebe, but Touchstone is obviously getting a real one from an impatient and ungentle (in all senses of the
word) Audrey.

3–4 **old gentleman** i.e. Jaques. If the
part was written for Burbage (who may
in 1599 have seemed too old for the
young Orlando; see Appendix 2) this
may be an apprentice's jest at the master actor; however, Audrey is young
enough for everyone to look old to her.
For *gentleman*, see List of Roles, 13n.

4   **saying** remarks; but possibly a shortened form of 'gainsaying', i.e. repudiation or contradiction. See *WT* 1.2.19:
'I'll no gainsaying'.

6   **vile** 'having a bad influence or evil
effect' (Onions, 2, p. 242); a butt for
vilification (scoffing, ridicule)
Mar-text annotated by a 1620s reader
(see 1.3.118n.) in his copy of F:
'Marriage by a martext' (at 3.3.59ff., in

Yamada, 64). The word may have been
used as a common noun in 1599, dying
out later (RP), or it may have become
current for a time – perhaps until the
closing of the theatres in 1642 – from
this reference in *AYL*.

8   **interest** legal right to

11   **clown** Touchstone dissociates himself
from *rustic* clowns; see 1.3.127n.,
2.4.63n.

13   **flouting** mocking; see Puttenham:
'when we deride by plaine and flat
contradiction' (*English Poetry*, 159).
See 17n. and cf. 1.2.45.
hold restrain ourselves

15   **God . . . ev'n** a dialect greeting (*OED*
good even *obs.*)

17   **gentle** ironic: of noble birth and
breeding. The terms, applied to the
rustic William, are an example of
'*Antiphrasis*, or the Broad floute'
(Puttenham, *English Poetry*, 159).

9.1] *Sisson; after 10 F; after 13 Dyce*   16 And] *Taking off his hat* And *Cam²*

cover thy head. Nay, prithee be covered. How old are
you, friend?

WILLIAM   Five-and-twenty, sir.   20

TOUCHSTONE   A ripe age. Is thy name William?

WILLIAM   William, sir.

TOUCHSTONE   A fair name. Wast born i'th' forest here?

WILLIAM   Ay, sir, I thank God.

TOUCHSTONE   'Thank God' – a good answer. Art rich?   25

WILLIAM   Faith, sir, so-so.

TOUCHSTONE   'So-so' is good, very good, very excellent
good – and yet it is not, it is but so-so. Art thou wise?

WILLIAM   Ay, sir, I have a pretty wit.

TOUCHSTONE   Why, thou sayst well. I do now remember   30
a saying: 'The fool doth think he is wise, but the wise
man knows himself to be a fool.' The heathen

17, 18 **Cover thy head** Put your hat on;
see 3.3.71.

20 **Five-and-twenty** Shakespeare in
1599 turned thirty-five. '5.1.17–59 can
be read as a dialogue between
Shakespeare's older and younger
selves' (Duncan-Jones, *Ungentle*, 25;
see also Bednarz, 117–21).

21, 22 An uncorrected version of this
page in the Barton copy of F in the
Boston Public Library prints the SP
'*Orl.*' instead of *Clo.* [TOUCHSTONE] at
21, and '*Clo.*' instead of *Will.*
[WILLIAM] at 22. The correction may
indicate, according to Hinman, that
'Forme R1:6ᵛ was manifestly proof-
corrected' (1.261–2). See Knowles,
322; Blayney, *Folio*, 15.

21 **A ripe age** in the prime of life

23 **fair name** If the part were played by
Shakespeare there may be a pun on
'good name' meaning reputation.

born i'th' forest at this point defin-
itely Warwickshire Arden; see p. 48
and Fig. 10.

29 **pretty** ready; the self-satisfaction of
William (cf. Dogberry, *MA* 3.5.32–9)
sets him up for the fool's put-
down.

31–2 '**The . . . fool**' The aphorism
occurs in Heywood's 'Of weening
and wotting': 'Wise me[n] in olde
tyme would weene them selues
fooles: / Fooles now in new tyme
wil ween them selues wise' (*Epigrams
500*, no. 1). Heywood includes himself
in his jest: 'Made by *Iohn Heywood*, to
these fooles euerychone, / And made
of *Iohn Heywood*, when hee weeneth
him selfe none'. See p. 103.

32–3 **heathen philosopher** unidentified;
part of Touchstone's random learning,
which presents Socrates' wisdom in
mangled forms; see 2.7.42n.

---

21 SP] *Fc (Clo.); Orl. Fu*   22 SP] *Fc (Will.); Clo. Fu*   25] *Pope; F lines* answer: / rich? /   26 Faith]
(ˆFaith)   28 Art thou wise] *verse F*   31–2 'The . . . fool.'] *Malone;* The . . . Foole. *F*   wise man]
(wiseman)   32 The] *By this William's mouth is wide open with amazement* The *Cam¹ (Capell Notes)*

philosopher, when he had a desire to eat a grape, would
open his lips when he put it into his mouth, meaning
thereby that grapes were made to eat and lips to open.   35
You do love this maid?

WILLIAM   I do, sir.

TOUCHSTONE   Give me your hand. Art thou learned?

WILLIAM   No, sir.

TOUCHSTONE   Then learn this of me: to have is to have.   40
For it is a figure in rhetoric that drink, being poured out
of a cup into a glass, by filling the one doth empty the
other. For all your writers do consent that *ipse* is 'he'.
Now you are not *ipse*, for I am he.

WILLIAM   Which he, sir?   45

TOUCHSTONE   He, sir, that must marry this woman.
Therefore, you clown, abandon (which is, in the

---

35 **lips to open** to receive the grape; as in
Lodge, Phoebe's scoff to Montanus:
'Phoebe is no lettice for your lips, and
her grapes hangs so high, that gaze at
them you may, but touch them you
cannot' (sig. M2ᵛ). There may also be a
bawdy reference here to the female
labia (see 3.2.57n.). Elizabethans might
have heard an echo of *BCP*,
'Euensong': 'O Lord, open thou our
lippes'; cf. 4.1.200n.

41 **figure in rhetoric** 'amplification'
(Quintilian, *Institutio Oratoria*, 8.4.10,
cited in Knowles)

43 **your** generic; see 3.2.52n.
consent agree together (*OED v.* 2 *obs.*)

43–4 **that . . . he** Touchstone claims that
the Latin pronoun *ipse* means 'he', and
that William cannot be *ipse*, i.e. the 'he'
who will marry Audrey, because he
himself (*ipse*) is that 'he'. In Lily's
Grammar the section on pronominal
construction declares: '*IPSE, ex pro-
nominibus solùm trium personarum sig-
nificationem repraesentat: vt:* Ipse vidi.
Ipse videris. Ipse dixit' (281) ('*Ipse* is the
only one of the pronouns which may

stand for the signifying of three persons: as, I myself see. You yourself will
see. He himself said.'). Touchstone is
not the only 'he', because *ipse* can
apply to all three grammatical (and
actual) persons.

45 **Which he, sir?** a good question. The
grammatical joke may also contain a
gender jest – of which Lily himself
makes several in the *Grammar* –
because all three characters may be
'he' in theatrical reality, as Audrey was
played by a boy.

47–52 Touchstone's elaborate counterpointing of Latin words for the educated, with native ones for the uneducated, demonstrates his status as court
jester as opposed to country clown; cf.
Armado, *LLL* 4.2.5–7, 14–16.

47, 50 **abandon** was obviously thought to
be a superior word; cf. Spenser, *SC*,
'October', where Piers urges Cuddie to
give up pastoral poetry in favour of
epic: 'Abandon, then, the base and
viler clowne; / Lyft up thy selfe out of
the lowly dust, / And sing of bloody
Mars, of wars, of giusts' (p. 477).

vulgar, 'leave') the society (which in the boorish is
'company') of this female (which in the common is
'woman'); which together is: 'abandon the society of   50
this female', or, clown, thou perishest! Or to thy better
understanding, diest. Or (to wit) I kill thee, make thee
away, translate thy life into death, thy liberty into
bondage. I will deal in poison with thee, or in bastinado
or in steel. I will bandy with thee in faction; I will   55
o'errun thee with policy. I will kill thee a hundred and
fifty ways! Therefore tremble and depart.

AUDREY   Do, good William.

WILLIAM   God rest you merry, sir.   *Exit.*

Enter CORIN.

CORIN   Our master and mistress seeks you. Come away,   60
away.

Cawdrey's early dictionary, *Table* (1604), advertised on the title page as for '*the benefit & helpe of Ladies, Gentlewomen, or any other unskilfull persons*' (sig. A1ʳ), begins with 'Abandon, cast away, or yeelde vp, to leaue, or forsake' (sig. B1ʳ). Touchstone's condescension to the uneducated embraces both William and Audrey, and also women and apprentices in the audience.

48 **vulgar** common, the vernacular speech of the ordinary person; see Lyly, *Endymion*, 1.3.75 (and n.): 'the untamed, or as the vulgar sort term it, the wild mallard?'
boorish rough, uneducated

49 **female** For the same joke about genteel and common language, see *LLL* 1.1.252–3.
common everyday (see 48n.), and, like the vernacular, accessible to everyone (a bawdy innuendo when applied,

as here, to women as well as language); see Florio's dedication 'To the curteous Reader' of his translation of Montaigne: 'Learning cannot be too common, and the commoner the better' (Montaigne, sig. A5ʳ).

52 **to wit** to clarify

53 **translate** transform; see 2.1.19n.

54 **deal in** make use of
bastinado beating with a stick

55 **steel** a sword or rapier
bandy exchange blows and words; cf. *KL* 1.4.82, 'bandy looks': '*bandy* meant striking the ball to and fro in games such as tennis' (Foakes).
in faction in a spirit of dissension

56 **o'errun . . . policy** overwhelm you with plots

60 **seeks** The singular verb may here be occasioned by the proximity of *mistress*; it is also possibly a mistake caused by the misreading of a secretary script *k* (see Abbott, 339).

60 seeks] seek *Rowe*

TOUCHSTONE   Trip, Audrey, trip, Audrey! I attend, I
attend.   *Exeunt.*

5.2   *Enter* ORLANDO *and* OLIVER.

ORLANDO   Is't possible that on so little acquaintance you
should like her? That but seeing, you should love her?
And loving, woo? And wooing, she should grant? And
will you persever to enjoy her?

OLIVER   Neither call the giddiness of it in question, the   5
poverty of her, the small acquaintance, my sudden
wooing nor her sudden consenting. But say with me, I
love Aliena. Say with her that she loves me. Consent
with both that we may enjoy each other. It shall be to
your good, for my father's house and all the revenue   10
that was old Sir Rowland's will I estate upon you, and
here live and die a shepherd.

Enter ROSALIND [*as Ganymede*].

ORLANDO   You have my consent. Let your wedding be

---

62 **Trip** run; also dance – possibly a cue
for Touchstone and Audrey to exit
dancing. Cf. 3.3.91n.; and see *TN*
2.3.42: 'Trip no further, pretty sweet-
ing'. See also Milton, 'L'Allegro':
'Come, and trip it as you go / On the
light fantastic toe' (33–4, p. 38).
62, 63 **attend** am coming (*OED v.* 7b)
5.2.2 **her** Aliena
4 **persever** persèver
4, 9 **enjoy** possess
5 **giddiness** irresponsibility, instability
(see 3.2.336), both for the suddenness
of the passion and for Celia's rustic
status as shepherdess
6 **poverty** Celia has not disclosed her
birth, which makes it unlikely also that

she has let Oliver into the secret of
Rosalind's disguise; see 18n.
7–8 **I love Aliena** In Lodge, Saladyne's
declaration to Aliena is in direct
speech: 'By the honor of a Gentleman
I loue *Aliena*, and wooe *Aliena*, not to
crop the blossomes and reiect the tree,
but to consamate my faithfull desires,
in the honorable ende of marriage'
(sig. N2ʳ).
11 **estate** settle, entail
12.1 The entry on the cue of *shepherd* of
Ganymede – a Duke's daughter disguised as a shepherd boy – ironizes
Oliver's aristocratic pastoral dream
(see p. 116). 'The genre of pastoral is
designed to deceive' (Ronk, 269).

62–3] *Pope; F lines* attend. / attend. /   **5.2**] *(Scoena Secunda.)*   Location] *The same / Capell*   7 nor
her] *Douai ms, Rowe;* nor F   11 Rowland's] Roland's *Cam²*   12.1] *after* followers *15 Collier; after 16*
Hudson   as Ganymede] *Oxf*   13–16] *Pope; F lines* consent. / I / followers: / looke you, / *Rosalinde. /*

319

tomorrow. Thither will I invite the Duke and all's
contented followers. Go you and prepare Aliena; for 15
look you, here comes my Rosalind.

ROSALIND   God save you, brother.

OLIVER   And you, fair sister.   [*Exit.*]

ROSALIND   O my dear Orlando, how it grieves me to see
thee wear thy heart in a scarf!   20

ORLANDO   It is my arm.

ROSALIND   I thought thy heart had been wounded with
the claws of a lion.

ORLANDO   Wounded it is, but with the eyes of a lady.

ROSALIND   Did your brother tell you how I counterfeited 25
to swoon when he showed me your handkerchief?

ORLANDO   Ay, and greater wonders than that.

ROSALIND   O, I know where you are. Nay, 'tis true. There
was never anything so sudden but the fight of two rams,
and Caesar's thrasonical brag of 'I came, saw and   30
overcame.' For your brother and my sister no sooner
met but they looked; no sooner looked but they loved;

---

14 **all's** all his
15 **contented** happy, satisfied (see
1.3.134n., 2.1.18n.). The word adds to
the harmonious *consenting* of 7–8 and
prepares the way for the play's
masque-like conclusion.
17 **brother** brother-in-law
18 **sister** sister-in-law. Oliver, following
Orlando's cue of *Rosalind* (16), greets
Ganymede as a lady.
20 **thee** the intimate form, as Ganymede
plays Rosalind greeting her lover
heart a verbal quibble on *heart* and
'hurt', as in Sidney's *Old Arcadia*: 'My
heart was wounded, with his wounded
heart, / For as from me on him his
hurt did light . . . / Both equal hurt
. . . / My true love hath my heart.' Cf.

'to wear one's heart on one's sleeve'
(*OED* 54f, first example *Oth* 1.1.62–4).
scarf sling
24 Orlando, literal at 21, now recognizes
the Petrarchan conceit of wounding
with eyes; cf. Phoebe, 3.5.15–16.
28 **where you are** what you mean
29 **fight** F4's 'sight' is an easy misreading
of *f* for long *s*, but the point is the suddenness with which rams *fight*.
rams Rosalind sustains the decorum
of her role as a shepherd boy.
30 **thrasonical** as Thraso in Terence's
Roman comedies, an example of the
stock figure of the braggart soldier
(*miles gloriosus*)
30–1 **I . . . overcame** Caesar's boast
('*veni, vidi, vici*'), used by Puttenham

---

18 SP] *Orl. F3* SD] *Capell; Exit* OLIVER *Halliwell (Pinkerton) after 16* 26 swoon] *(sound), Rowe³;*
swound F4 handkerchief] *(handkercher), F4* 29 fight] *sight F4* 31 overcame] *F2;* ouercome *F*

no sooner loved but they sighed; no sooner sighed but they asked one another the reason; no sooner knew the reason but they sought the remedy; and in these 35 degrees have they made a pair of stairs to marriage, which they will climb incontinent or else be incontinent before marriage. They are in the very wrath of love and they will together. Clubs cannot part them. 40

ORLANDO   They shall be married tomorrow, and I will bid the Duke to the nuptial. But O, how bitter a thing it is to look into happiness through another man's eyes! By so much the more shall I tomorrow be at the height of

to illustrate the figure '*Asyndeton*, or the Loose lang[u]age', which he declares to be 'in a maner defectiue because it wants good band or coupling' (*English Poetry*, 145). The rhetorical figure mirrors the dramatic situation: passion will create looseness unless the 'good band or coupling' of Oliver and Celia is quickly supplied (through marriage). Caesar's boast – a favourite with Shakespeare; see *2H4* 4.3.41–2 and *LLL* 4.1.70 – was used by Hakluyt in 1598 to describe Essex's triumph in Cadiz, pages of which were 'ordered suppressed' (*STC* 18041) after the failure of the Irish expedition (see p. 73); for Caesar see also 3.2.239n.

36 **degrees** steps – the rhetorical figure *gradation*: 'Gradacion is when a sentence is disseuered by degrees, so that the worde, which endeth the sentence goyng before, doeth begin the next' (Wilson, *Rhetoric*, fol. 104ʳ = 100ʳ); as here, 32–5: 'looked . . . looked; loved . . . loved; sighed . . . sighed; reason . . . reason'. The progress of passion imitates the pattern of language (Oxf¹).

pair of stairs flight of stairs; 'As though one should go vp apaire of staiers, and not leaue til he come at the

toppe' (Wilson, *Rhetoric*, fol. 104ʳ = 100ʳ). The pair of lovers (Celia and Oliver) construct a *pair of stairs* to marriage.

37 **incontinent** precipitately; cf. Puttenham, *English Poetry*, 'Loose lang[u]age' (145).

38 **incontinent . . . marriage** make love before the marriage ceremony, thus showing lack of proper restraint

39 **wrath** heat and vehemence
will are determined to join (see 70–1n.); also suggests the noun *will*, the motor drive of the libido (see 4.1.104n.). Cf. *TC* 2.2.61–2: 'I take today a wife, and my election / Is led on in the conduct of my will'.
Clubs A club is a heavy wooden cudgel, associated in folklore with giants (cf. 4.1.90); see also *OED* 3 *obs.*, 'A staff or baton used as an official and restrictive "pass"' (to prevent entry), which may be the sense here. Nothing will impede the course of Celia and Oliver towards union.

43 **through . . . eyes** reminiscent of Celia's caveat to the apparently foolhardy young wrestler at 1.2.167 (see n.)

43–6 **By . . . happy** 'My sorrow will be increased in proportion to my brother's happiness tomorrow.'

321

heart-heaviness, by how much I shall think my brother   45
happy in having what he wishes for.

ROSALIND   Why then, tomorrow I cannot serve your turn
for Rosalind?

ORLANDO   I can live no longer by thinking.

ROSALIND   I will weary you then no longer with idle   50
talking. Know of me, then – for now I speak to some
purpose – that I know you are a gentleman of good
conceit. I speak not this that you should bear a good
opinion of my knowledge, insomuch I say I know you
are. Neither do I labour for a greater esteem than may   55
in some little measure draw a belief from you, to do
yourself good and not to grace me. Believe then, if you
please, that I can do strange things. I have since I was
three year old conversed with a magician, most
profound in his art and yet not damnable. If you do love   60

---

45 **heart-heaviness** melancholy, sadness; a beautiful compound which, together with *height*, allows the actor to sigh as he speaks.

47 **serve your turn** help you, also potentially bawdy; cf. *LLL* 1.1.282–3: 'This maid will not serve your turn, sir. / This maid will serve my turn, sir'.

49 **thinking** imagining. See Lodge: 'Let the forrester [Rosader] a while shape himselfe to his shadow, and tarrie fortunes leysure, till she may make a Metamorphosis fit for his purpose' (sig. I.4).

53 **conceit** imagination and mental powers

54 **insomuch** insofar as

55–7 **Neither . . . me** 'I don't exert myself in order to gain renown, but to enable you to believe in my ability to do you good.'

57 **Believe** Rosalind invokes Orlando's faith; see 5.4.1, 3. Cf. *WT* 5.3.94–5: 'It is requir'd / You do awake your faith.'

57–8 **if you please** a reminder of the play's title and central themes

58 **strange** magical, outside nature; cf. 5.4.125n.

59 **conversed** communicated, associated **magician** See 3.2.332n. In Lodge, Ganimede assures Rosader: 'I haue a friend that is deeply experienst in Negromancy and Magicke, what art can do shall be acted for thine aduantage' (sig. O3). Lady Katharine Berkeley had in 1581 consulted a forest magician: 'by ill advice, [she] wrote a secret lre [letter] to one old Bourne, then dwelling in the forrest of Arden in Warrwickshire, who (though falsly) was with many reputed a conjurer, witch, or foreteller of events, and of the periods of Princes lives' (Smyth, 2.379); see p. 72n.

60 **damnable** devilish (see 66n.); cf. Prospero, a 'white' or neoplatonic mage. For Rosalind's special powers see 3.2.8n.

---

45 heart-heaviness] *(*heart heauinesse*)*   59 year] years *F4*

Rosalind so near the heart as your gesture cries it out,
when your brother marries Aliena shall you marry her.
I know into what straits of fortune she is driven and it
is not impossible to me, if it appear not inconvenient to
you, to set her before your eyes tomorrow, human as   65
she is, and without any danger.

ORLANDO   Speak'st thou in sober meanings?

ROSALIND   By my life I do, which I tender dearly, though
I say I am a magician. Therefore put you in your best
array, bid your friends; for if you will be married   70
tomorrow you shall, and to Rosalind if you will.

Enter SILVIUS *and* PHOEBE.

Look, here comes a lover of mine and a lover of hers.

---

61 **near the heart** intensely
   gesture demeanour and actions; cf.
   3.2.355–69.
   cries it out proclaims
63 **straits** narrow stretch of water, a
   metaphor for hardship reminiscent of
   Elizabethan voyaging
   fortune Rosalind's 'fortune' – as
   opposed to Providence – keeps her
   terms of reference safely within classical rather than Christian bounds,
   advisable for her justification of white
   magic.
   driven sustains the *straits* image;
   Rosalind's ship is driven by the wind
   into a dangerous channel.
64 **inconvenient** inappropriate
65–6 **human . . . is** in her natural condition, not as a spirit conjured up by
   (dangerous) arts (Johnson)
66 **danger** spiritual rather than physical
   peril. It was believed that the devil
   could become an incubus and take
   human form in order to deceive his
   victims; see 5.4.34n.

67 **in sober meanings** seriously; a
   request for literal truth
68 **By my life** one of Ganymede's most
   serious oaths, coming from the heart of
   Rosalind; see 4.1.148n.
   tender dearly hold dear, consider
   precious
68–9 **though . . . magician** 'though I
   might seem to be exempt from risk
   because of my claim to supernatural
   powers'. The anonymous play *The
   Wisdom of Doctor Dodypoll*, staged by
   the Children of Paul's in 1599–1600,
   features 'a pastoral episode with an
   enchanter that evokes Ganymede's
   story of a forest magician in *As You
   Like It*' (Knutson, 'Repertory', 477).
70 **array** attire; cf. 4.3.142n.
70–1 **for . . . will** 'because if you want to
   be married tomorrow you shall be, and
   to Rosalind if you want to marry her'.
   A clear distinction is made between
   future intention (*shall*) and the dictates
   of the will (both passion and determination).

PHOEBE

> Youth, you have done me much ungentleness
> To show the letter that I writ to you.

ROSALIND 75

> I care not if I have; it is my study
> To seem despiteful and ungentle to you.
> You are there followed by a faithful shepherd.
> Look upon him; love him; he worships you.

PHOEBE

> Good shepherd, tell this youth what 'tis to love.

SILVIUS 80

> It is to be all made of sighs and tears,
> And so am I for Phoebe.

PHOEBE

> And I for Ganymede.

ORLANDO

> And I for Rosalind.

ROSALIND

> And I for no woman.

SILVIUS 85

> It is to be all made of faith and service,
> And so am I for Phoebe.

PHOEBE

> And I for Ganymede.

---

73 **ungentleness** unkindness, an injury resulting from ignoble behaviour; cf. *LLL* 5.2.623: 'This is not generous, not gentle, not humble.'

74 **writ** obsolete form of the past tense (not a participle); cf. *Son* 116.14: 'I never writ'.

75 **care not** Ganymede's cruelty to Phoebe contrasts with Orlando's kindness to 'Rosalind'.
study meditated desire

76 **despiteful** scornful, spiteful

77 **faithful shepherd** a possible reference to Guarini's *Il pastor fido* (GKH; see also 5.4.14); see p. 128.

80–101 a passage of liturgical patterning,

making extensive use of the rhetorical figures of *parison* (repeated adjacent words, e.g. *And I for*, 82–4, 87), *anaphora* (a word repeated at the beginning of a phrase, e.g. *All*, 91–4) and *isocolon* (repeated clauses of the same length, e.g. *And so am I for*, 95–8, and *why blame . . . you*, 99–101); see Vickers, 'Rhetoric', 87.

80 **sighs and tears** the badges of true Petrarchan and chivalric love; see 90–4n.

85 **faith** a key word in Act 5; see 5.4.1n., 3n.
service a word from the religion of love; see *observance* (92), *obedience* (94).

ORLANDO

And I for Rosalind.

ROSALIND

And I for no woman.

SILVIUS

It is to be all made of fantasy,   90
All made of passion, and all made of wishes,
All adoration, duty and observance,
All humbleness, all patience and impatience,
All purity, all trial, all obedience,
And so am I for Phoebe.   95

PHOEBE

And so am I for Ganymede.

ORLANDO

And so am I for Rosalind.

ROSALIND

And so am I for no woman.

PHOEBE [*to Rosalind*]

If this be so, why blame you me to love you?

SILVIUS [*to Phoebe*]

If this be so, why blame you me to love you?   100

ORLANDO

If this be so, why blame you me to love you?

90–4 In the literary and social revisions of the Forest the true shepherd (alias poet? see p. 97) Silvius, unlike 'false Ganymede' (Wordsworth, *The Prelude* (*1805*), 8.187), speaks of love – in the traditions of Petrarch and Dante – as a sacred worship of the beloved.

90 **fantasy** longings, imaginings; see 2.4.28n.

92 **observance** service and homage; cf. *MND* 1.1.167: 'To do observance to a morn of May'. Editors have sometimes emended the word to 'obedience', to prevent F's repetition at 94

(see n.); 'obeisance' is also a possible emendation. Cf. *TS* Induction 107: 'And call him "madam", do him obeisance'. But *observance* fits the reverent devotion implied in *adoration* and *duty*.

94 **purity . . . trial** The testing required for chivalric but also Christian love. Cf. Milton, *Areopagitica*: 'That which purifies us is trial, and trial is by what is contrary' (2.515).
*obedience the condition of *trial*; F's repeated 'obseruance' is probably an example of dittography.

92 observance] obedience *Collier²*   94 obedience] *Douai ms, Cowden Clarke (Malone);* obseruance *F;* obeisance *Singer (Ritson)*   99, 100 SDs] *Pope*

ROSALIND　　Who do you speak to, 'Why blame you me to love you?'

ORLANDO

To her that is not here nor doth not hear.

ROSALIND　　Pray you no more of this, 'tis like the howling　　105
of Irish wolves against the moon. [*to Silvius*] I will help
you if I can. [*to Phoebe*] I would love you if I could.
– Tomorrow meet me all together. [*to Phoebe*] I will
marry you, if ever I marry woman, and I'll be married
tomorrow. [*to Orlando*] I will satisfy you, if ever I　　110
satisfied man, and you shall be married tomorrow. [*to
Silvius*] I will content you, if what pleases you contents
you, and you shall be married tomorrow. [*to Orlando*]

102 *Who F's 'Why' may be copied from the middle of the line, or caused by a misreading of a copytext 'who' as 'whie', a spelling associated with the scribe Ralph Crane (Roberts, 'Ralph Crane', 221; see 4.3.56n. on '*these*', and p. 126).

102–3 Why . . . you? Rosalind masks her own speech to Orlando under the guise of quoting him, thus preserving the symmetry of the quartet.

106 Irish wolves In Lodge, Ganimede tells Montanus (Silvius) that 'in courting Phoebe, thou barkest with the Wolues of Syria against the Moone' (sig. N4ᵛ). Shakespeare's substitution of *Irish* for 'Syrian' may point to a topical allusion to the Irish expedition of 1599 (Cam¹, p. 158; cf. 3.2.173). Spenser observed (in *View*) that the Irish thought some men would be transformed annually into wolves, and paid special honour to the moon in the hopes of avoiding this fate (Schleiner, 5–6, 8). The lovers' howling to the moon recalls Lyly's *Endymion* and Elizabeth as moon goddess; see

3.2.2n., 4n.

against the moon by moonlight, literally, 'facing, in full view of' the moon (*OED prep.* 1a)

109 **if . . . woman** In Lodge, Phoebe promises to renounce Ganimede if reason dictates, and he vows in return that 'I wil neuer marry my selfe to woman but vnto thy selfe' (sig. O2ᵛ).

110 **satisy** you make you content. In *WT* 1.1.232–4 Leontes takes the word in its sexual sense, also hinted at here.

110–11 **if . . . satisfied** a poignant evocation of the hypothetical (cf. 5.4.101), in which the poet challenges the audience to trust the truth of his fictional Rosalind, even though the Epilogue will return her not just to the role of Ganymede but to the boy who acts them both. Cf. Ovid, and also Lyly's *Galatea*, where there is a magical sexchange (see pp. 10–11).

111 **satisfied** were to satisfy

112 **content . . . pleases . . . contents** 'as you like it', i.e. what pleases you may not in fact content you; see 1.3.134n., 3.2.17n.

102–3] *verse* Pope　102 Who] *Rowe*; Why F　¹to] *Rowe*; too F　106 SD] *Douai ms, Capell subst.*; *To Orlando Johnson subst.*　107 SD] *Douai ms, Johnson subst.*　108 all together] *(altogether)*　108, 110, 111–12 SDs] *Pope subst.*　111 satisfied] satisfy *Dyce² (Douce)*　113, 114 SDs] *Douai ms, Johnson subst.*

As you love Rosalind, meet. [*to Silvius*] As you love
Phoebe, meet. – And as I love no woman, I'll meet. So   115
fare you well. I have left you commands.

SILVIUS

    I'll not fail, if I live.

PHOEBE   Nor I.

ORLANDO   Nor I.   *Exeunt.*

5.3   *Enter* TOUCHSTONE *and* AUDREY.

TOUCHSTONE Tomorrow is the joyful day, Audrey,
    tomorrow will we be married.

AUDREY I do desire it with all my heart; and I hope it is
    no dishonest desire, to desire to be a woman of the
    world?   5

Enter two Pages.

Here come two of the banished Duke's pages.

1 PAGE Well met, honest gentleman.

TOUCHSTONE By my troth, well met. Come, sit, sit, and
    a song.

5.3 Morley's 'It was a lover and his lass' in
the *First Book of Airs* (1600) is the only
extant contemporary setting of a
Shakespeare song. In Lodge, '*A blyth
and bonny country Lasse, / heigh ho the
bonny Lasse*' (sigs P3ᵛ–4ʳ) is sung at
Rosalynde's wedding by the shepherd
Coridon. Morley's song 'is both courtly and rustic – a lute-song by a court
musician and a song sung in the Forest
as songs were sung to Elizabeth in the
entertainments offered on her progresses' (Chaudhuri, 179); see pp.
76–7, 137.

4 **dishonest** unchaste

4–5 **woman . . . world** a married woman

(Dent, W637); cf. *AW* 1.3.17–19: 'if I
may have your ladyship's good will to
go to the world, Isbel the woman and I
will do as we may', i.e. marry, a
formulation related to the Reformation
debate on monasticism and the
marriage of priests. See Erasmus's
colloquy 'The Virgin Averse to
Matrimony': 'He that would avoid
every Thing that offends him must
needs go out of the World' (*Colloquies*,
150; Dusinberre, *Women*, 42). Cf.
3.2.402n.

5.1 *two* **Pages** a surprising introduction
of two youthful attendants on Duke
Senior; see Appendix 2.

5.3] *(Scoena Tertia.)* Location] *The same / Capell* 0.1–47] *om. Douai ms* 0.1 TOUCHSTONE]
Malone; Clowne F 5 world?] world. *F4* 5.1] *Sisson; after 6 F*

2 PAGE   We are for you, sit i'th' middle.   10

1 PAGE   Shall we clap into't roundly without hawking or
          spitting or saying we are hoarse, which are the only
          prologues to a bad voice?

2 PAGE   I'faith, i'faith, and both in a tune like two gipsies
          on a horse.   15

PAGES (*Sing.*)

          It was a lover and his lass,
             With a hey and a ho and a hey nonino,

10 **sit i'th' middle** The song begins with the threesome seated, but may move to dancing (with Touchstone in the middle); see 17, 23, 29, 35n.

11 **clap into't roundly** get started right away without preamble; possibly a pun on singing a round (see 14n.)
hawking clearing the throat raucously, usually followed by spitting (*OED* hawk *v.*³ 1)

12 **hoarse** possibly a pun on *horse*, 15 (see also Watson, 90); see Wilson, *Rhetoric*: 'An other is hource in his throte, that a manne would thinke, he came latelie from scouryng of harnesse' (fol. 112ʳ). This sentence in Wilson follows the one which Shakespeare quotes at 2.7.164; see n.

12–13 **the only prologues** the only way of preparing the ground for, and excusing, a poor voice; sometimes emended to 'only the prologues', to mean 'merely the excuse for'

14 **in a tune** may mean 'in tune', especially in view of Touchstone's criticism of the Pages' performance. Fellowes suggested that the correct reading was 'in attune', meaning in unison ('Lover', 204–6), but the expression was not in use till 1850 (*OED* attune *sb. rare*). The boys may

have sung a line each – 'in turn' (a possible emendation) – and joined in the chorus. If Touchstone and the Pages also got up and danced the 'hay' (see 17, 23, 29, 35n.), it is more likely that they sang alternately than in unison.
gipsies skilled riders, often associated with the singing of jigs (Baskervill, 149)

16 SD F has only 'Song' with no instruction for 'Musicke' (cf. 4.2.9 SDn.), which suggests that the song was not accompanied by a broken consort (see 2.7.174n.). If Kemp played Touchstone, he might have played the lute in this scene; see Appendix 2.

17, 23, 29, 35 **hey nonino** a common singing refrain; cf. *MA* 2.3.68. Morley's text prints 'haye' instead of 'hey', a spelling which may suggest the country dance called the 'hay', which required three people in figure-of-eight formation (Naylor, 54); cf. *LLL* 5.1.145: 'and let them dance the hay'. The description of the song as a *carol* (see 28n.) implies singing and dancing (cf. 3.3.91n.), traditional for May Day and appropriate for the play's movement into spring.

12 the only] only the *Collier*² *(Capell Notes)*   14 a tune] tune *F3;* attune *(Fellowes)*   16 SP] *Oliver; not in F*   SD] *Sisson;* Song. *F*   17, 23, 29, 35 ¹hey] haye *Morley*   and a ho and] with a hoe and *Morley;* with a ho with *Adv. ms*   hey nonino] haye nonie no *Morley, Adv. ms*

That o'er the green cornfield did pass,
    In spring-time, the only pretty ring-time,
When birds do sing, hey ding a ding a ding,   20
    Sweet lovers love the spring.

Between the acres of the rye,
    With a hey and a ho and a hey nonino,
These pretty country folks would lie,
    In spring-time, the only pretty ring-time,   25
When birds do sing, hey ding a ding a ding,
    Sweet lovers love the spring.

This carol they began that hour,
    With a hey and a ho and a hey nonino,
How that a life was but a flower,   30
    In spring-time, the only pretty ring-time,
When birds do sing, hey ding a ding a ding,
    Sweet lovers love the spring.

---

18 **green cornfield** a field of unripe wheat, which would be green from February to early May. Barton notes 'Arden's gradual abandonment of traditional pastoral economy, based on sheep and cattle, in favour of "green cornfield[s]" and "acres of the rye"' ('Parks and Ardens', 356; see also Thirsk, 94).

19 **spring-time** the season of love (4.1.137), and of the Golden Age; see 1.1.113n. and p. 90.
   ***ring-time** The exchange of rings for betrothals (especially associated with May Day) also suggests the peal of bells (F '*rang*') conveyed in the

descending scales of Morley's refrain 'hey ding a ding a ding', which 'permeates the whole texture' (Greer, 34). The song summons the betrothed couples to their weddings – and by implication to church (Gargàno, 16 – the text used for Visconti's 1948 production). Oxf¹ also suggests dancing in a ring; cf. 17, 23, 29, 35n., 28n.

20 **birds** a possible joke from Morley at his former tutor, William Byrd, a fellow Gentleman at the Chapel Royal, who may have been present if the play was performed at Richmond at Shrove 1599; see p. 77.

28 **carol** a song with dancing; see 3.3.91n.

---

18 cornfield] *(corn feild);* corne fields *Morley*   19 In] *Morley, Adv. ms, Knight; In the* F   19, 25, 31, 37 spring-time] *(spring time)*   19 pretty ring] *Morley (*pretiring*), Adv. ms, Rann (Var 1778); pretty rang* F*; pretty spring / Johnson; pretty rank Var 1773*   20 a ding a ding] *Morley (*ading ading*), Adv. ms, this edn; a ding, ding* F   24 folks would] *fooles would Morley;* fools did *Adv. ms*   25, 31 In] In the F3   25–7, 31–3, 37–9 the . . . spring] *Cam¹; &c.* F   30 a life] *our life / Hanmer*

And therefore take the present time,
    With a hey and a ho and a hey nonino,   35
For love is crowned with the prime,
    In spring-time, the only pretty ring-time,
When birds do sing, hey ding a ding a ding,
    Sweet lovers love the spring.

TOUCHSTONE   Truly, young gentlemen, though there   40
was no great matter in the ditty, yet the note was very
untunable.

1 PAGE   You are deceived, sir, we kept time, we lost not our
time.

TOUCHSTONE   By my troth, yes. I count it but time lost   45
to hear such a foolish song. God b'wi' you, and God
mend your voices. Come, Audrey.   *Exeunt.*

---

34 **take . . . time** seize the moment – the *carpe diem* theme of pastoral poetry; cf. *TN* 2.3.48–9: 'Present mirth hath present laughter / What's to come is still unsure'. The song's final stanza, *And therefore take*, is mistakenly placed second in F; Fellowes suggests that the Pages only sang stanzas 1 and 4 ('Lover', 206).

36 **crowned** (crownèd) given its full glory
  prime spring (It. *la primavera*; Fr. *printemps*); also the prime of life

41 **matter** content, substance
  ditty used by Morley specifically for a light song – madrigal or canzonet (*Practical Music*, 204). Lodge's *Rosalynde*, 'taking up her Lute that lay by her . . . warbled out this dittie' (sig. D1ʳ), which is indeed a *foolish* one.

42 **untunable** out of tune. Touchstone's complaint appears to be about intonation, but the Page takes *untunable* to mean 'out of time' (see 43; see also 3.2.241n.). Puttenham identifies rhymes which 'make the meeters tun-

able and melodious', as in 'clauses, finishing in words of like tune' (i.e. rhyme), but warns that 'a rime of good simphonie should not conclude his concords with one & the same terminant sillable, as *less, less, less*' (*English Poetry*, 144–5).

43 **kept time** observed the correct rhythm. In Morley's *Practical Music* 'tune' is used for both time and melody. Withals's *Dictionary* translates 'to tune' as 'persono . . . temporo' ('to sound . . . to keep time') (sig. L2ᵛ).

45 **time lost** a waste of time; see 2.4.94n., 2.7.113. Cf. Morley's dedication of the *First Book of Airs* to Sir Ralph Bosville (of Lincoln's Inn): 'Which as they were made this vacation time [recess between legal terms], you may use likewise at your vacant howers', i.e. to fill 'empty' time.

46 ***God b'wi' you** See 3.2.250n.; the modernizing of this adieu to 'Goodbye' (Oxf¹) erases the rhetorical balance of Touchstone's parting shot.

34–9] *Morley, Adv. ms, Johnson (Thirlby); after 21 F*   34] Then prettie louers take the time *Morley, Adv. ms*   37 In] In the *Rowe*   42 untunable] untimeable *Theobald*   46 God b'wi' you] *(*God buy you*), Rowe;* Goodbye *Oxf¹*   47 SD] *Exeunt severally Oxf*

5.4   *Enter* DUKE SENIOR, AMIENS, JAQUES,
                 ORLANDO, OLIVER [*and*] CELIA [*as Aliena*].

DUKE SENIOR

    Dost thou believe, Orlando, that the boy
    Can do all this that he hath promised?

ORLANDO

    I sometimes do believe and sometimes do not,
    As those that fear to hope, and know to fear.

Enter ROSALIND [*as Ganymede*], SILVIUS *and* PHOEBE.

ROSALIND

    Patience once more whiles our compact is urged.   5
    [*to Duke Senior*] You say if I bring in your Rosalind
    You will bestow her on Orlando here?

DUKE SENIOR

    That would I, had I kingdoms to give with her.

5.4.1 **believe** The issue of faith underpins the action of the final scene; see
5.2.57n.
   the boy Ganymede
3 Orlando wavers between faith and
doubt, invoking the language of religion as well as of love; see *Imitation*,
for the man who is 'tossed betweene
hope, and feare' (1.25, p. 64). Cf. 186n.
4 ***fear . . . fear** are afraid to hope, and
know what it is to fear. Cf. *Son*
119.3–4: 'Applying fears to hopes and
hopes to fears, / Still losing when I saw
myself to win'. F's 'feare they hope'
seems unidiomatic, hence the history
of emendation recorded in the t.n.; 'to'
may have been misread by Compositor

C as 'they', written as a common
scribal contraction. The words *hope*
and *fear* continue the religious termi-
nology of Orlando's previous speech;
cf. Lodge's sonnet sequence, *Phillis*: 'I
hope and feare, *I* pray and hould my
peace' (sonnet 35, sig. G4ᵛ).
5 **whiles** while
   compact (compàct) agreement
   urged brought forward for ratification
(*OED* urge v. 1)
7 **bestow** give in marriage: usually a
father's duty (see 3.3.62–3n.)
8, 10 **would** subjunctive following *That*
(Abbott, 368)
8 **had I** if I had; subjunctive following
would

5.4] (*Scena Quarta.*)   Location] *another Part of the* Forest *Theobald*   0.1 DUKE SENIOR] Old Duke
Douai ms   0.2 *as Aliena*] *Oxf*   4 that] who *(Mason)*   fear to hope] *Collier²;* feare they hope *F;* think
they hope *Hanmer;* fear their hap *Warburton;* fear, they hope *Theobald⁴;* fear their hope *Capell*
(Heath); fearing hope *(Mason)*   know to] *this edn;* know they *F;* hope they *Douai ms;* know their
Warburton; hoping *(Mason);* hope their *Keightley (Lettsom)*   4.1 *as Ganymede*] *Oxf*   5 urged] heard
Collier²   6 SD] *Rowe*

ROSALIND [*to Orlando*]

And you say you will have her when I bring her?

ORLANDO

That would I, were I of all kingdoms king.   10

ROSALIND [*to Phoebe*]

You say you'll marry me if I be willing?

PHOEBE

That will I, should I die the hour after.

ROSALIND

But if you do refuse to marry me

You'll give yourself to this most faithful shepherd?

PHOEBE   So is the bargain.   15

ROSALIND [*to Silvius*]

You say that you'll have Phoebe if she will?

SILVIUS

Though to have her and death were both one thing.

ROSALIND

I have promised to make all this matter even.

Keep you your word, O Duke, to give your daughter,

You yours, Orlando, to receive his daughter.   20

Keep you your word, Phoebe, that you'll marry me,

Or else, refusing me, to wed this shepherd.

Keep your word, Silvius, that you'll marry her

If she refuse me; and from hence I go   24

To make these doubts all even.   *Exeunt Rosalind and Celia.*

9   **have** take as wife
10 **were I** even if I were. Orlando assumes that Rosalind is still the impoverished banished princess.
12 **will** am determined to; contrasts with *would*, 8, 10; Phoebe has no doubt that Ganymede will prove a fit husband.
    should even if I had to
    hour dissyllabic for the metre
17 **both one** one and the same; Silvius echoes Phoebe's vow to Ganymede (12).

18 **make . . . even** balance the accounts (*OED* even *a*. 10b); see 107, 146n.
    matter business
19, 21, 23 **Keep . . . word** *isocolon* (see 5.2.80–101n.)
21 **you your** Rosalind's echo of the previous lines is in keeping with liturgical patterning of the speech.
24 **refuse** subjunctive after *if*
25 **make . . . even** resolve all these uncertainties

9, 11, 16 SDs] *Rowe³*   21 you] *om. Rowe³*   25 SD *Exeunt*] *Theobald; Exit F*

DUKE SENIOR

  I do remember in this shepherd boy
  Some lively touches of my daughter's favour.

ORLANDO

  My lord, the first time that I ever saw him
  Methought he was a brother to your daughter.
  But my good lord, this boy is forest-born   30
  And hath been tutored in the rudiments
  Of many desperate studies by his uncle,
  Whom he reports to be a great magician,
  Obscured in the circle of this forest.

Enter TOUCHSTONE *and* AUDREY.

JAQUES   There is sure another flood toward, and these   35
couples are coming to the ark. Here comes a pair of
very strange beasts, which in all tongues are called
fools.

TOUCHSTONE   Salutation and greeting to you all.

JAQUES   Good my lord, bid him welcome. This is the   40

---

27 **lively touches** life-like brush-strokes;
see 3.2.149n.
  favour looks; see 4.3.85n.
29 **Methought** it seemed to me (impersonal construction, Abbott, 297)
31 **tutored . . . rudiments** Cf. Marlowe, *Faustus*, B-Text (1616), 1.2.155, for the instructions in magic offered to Faustus.
32 **desperate studies** studies carrying the risk of contamination by the devil; undertaken by those who despair of their faith, thought to be the unforgivable sin against the Holy Spirit. Cf. Marlowe, *Faustus*, B-Text, 1.1.69–72, and 1.3.87, 'desperate thoughts'.
33 **magician** See 5.2.59–60 and nn.
34 **Obscured** (obscurèd) concealed by darkness
  circle . . . forest The phrase encompasses the environment of the forest, the circle of the audience (see 3.2.7n. and Epilogue 11) and the circle in which a magician conjures spirits (see 2.5.52n.) in an image capable of provoking traducers who considered theatre a form of black art.
35 **toward** in the offing
36 **ark** Noah's ark, where one pair of each species of beast was allowed on board to survive the flood
37 **tongues** languages
39 Touchstone's formal greeting, set here as prose (prose or verse in F), may be an irregular blank verse line, marking both Touchstone's status as lover (Stern, *Rehearsal*, 11; see 4.3.178–9n.) and his claim to court breeding among the *country copulatives* (see 55–6n., 70n.).

34.1] *Douai ms, Rowe³; after* 33 F   TOUCHSTONE] *Malone; Clowne* F

333

motley-minded gentleman that I have so often met in
the forest. He hath been a courtier, he swears.

TOUCHSTONE   If any man doubt that, let him put me to
my purgation. I have trod a measure; I have flattered a
lady; I have been politic with my friend, smooth with   45
mine enemy; I have undone three tailors; I have had
four quarrels and like to have fought one.

JAQUES   And how was that ta'en up?

TOUCHSTONE   Faith, we met and found the quarrel was
upon the seventh cause.   50

JAQUES   How, seventh cause? – Good my lord, like this
fellow.

DUKE SENIOR   I like him very well.

TOUCHSTONE   God'ild you, sir, I desire you of the like. I
press in here, sir, amongst the rest of the country   55
copulatives, to swear and to forswear according as

---

41 **motley-minded** parti-coloured, i.e.
full of variegated impulses and information; see 2.7.13n., 38–42n.

43–4 **put . . . purgation** Touchstone
picks up *swears* and uses it in its
legal sense of proving one's innocence
by oath; but in this play the word *purgation* carries scatalogical overtones
from Rabelais and Harington (see
1.3.50n.).

44 **measure** a stately dance based on the
precise length of a step

45 **politic** diplomatic, with undertones of
cunning; see 4.1.13n.
smooth suave; see 1.3.74n.

46 **undone** bankrupted, through extravagant ordering of finery not paid for (cf.
2.7.80n.)

47 **like** was likely

48 **ta'en up** settled; see 97n.

50 **cause** pretext (legal); see 4.1.89n.

54 **God'ild you** God reward you; see
3.3.69n.

desire . . . like I desire to be liked by
you. See Watson: 'he [Touchstone]
desires a like [similar] liking; he would
like him [the Duke] to do something
like like him [Touchstone]' (89).
Touchstone treats the Duke as his
equal.
of For word order see Abbott, 174;
cf. *MND* 3.1.180–1: 'Good Master
Peaseblossom, I shall desire you of
more acquaintance'.

55–6 **country copulatives** rustic lovers
or mates, as in the 'mating' of the natural world (cf. 3.2.77). Touchstone, a
court jester in the company of a duke,
includes in this category not only
Silvius and Phoebe but also Ganymede
and Aliena, claiming – in a special joke
for the audience – social superiority
over the Duke's disguised daughter
and niece.

56 **forswear** break one's oath; see
1.2.74–5n.

49 Faith] (*Faith*)   54 God'ild] God thancke *Douai ms;* God 'ield *Var 1778*   you of] of you *Hanmer*

334

marriage binds and blood breaks; – a poor virgin, sir, an ill-favoured thing, sir, but mine own; a poor humour of mine, sir, to take that that no man else will. Rich honesty dwells like a miser, sir, in a poor house, as your   60
pearl in your foul oyster.

DUKE SENIOR   By my faith, he is very swift and sententious.

TOUCHSTONE   According to the fool's bolt, sir, and such dulcet diseases.
                                                                        65

JAQUES   But for the seventh cause – how did you find the quarrel on the seventh cause?

TOUCHSTONE   Upon a lie seven times removed – bear

---

57 **blood** passion; cf. *LLL* 4.3.213: 'Young blood doth not obey an old decree'.

59 **will** wants; the jester erases the competing clown, William (5.1).

59–61 **Rich . . . oyster** an example of *sententia* (a sage sound-bite – see 1.3.107n. and 2.7.17n.), which reinforces the debate on beauty and honesty at 3.3.25–37. Audrey is plain and chaste, but Touchstone may get tired of her (see 189–90, 3.3.82–5).

63 **sententious** skilled in uttering *sententiae*; see Puttenham, '*Of Figures sententious, otherwise called Rhetoricall*': 'To be furnished with all the figures that be *Rhetoricall*, and such as do most beautifie language with eloquence & sententiousnes' (*English Poetry*, 163). 'Eloquence' was the manner of oratory, 'sententiousness' its moral content; cf. 3.2.125n. on '*sayings*'.

64 **According . . . bolt** The fool's aphoristic wisdom is ephemeral and often ill aimed; see Heywood: 'A fooles bolte is soone shot, and fleeth oftimes fer, / But the fooles bolte and the marke, come few times ner' (*Epigrams 300*, no. 185; see also Dent, F514). The last verse of Tarlton's 'Jigge of a horse loade of Fooles' declares: 'A fooles bolt is soone shott: is't so?' (*Tarlton's Jests*,

xxvi), implying that Tarlton's own wit is soon spent. Touchstone's use of the catch-phrase, which is also a jig-title (Baskervill, 104), may cue in impromptu capering; cf. 3.3.70n., 77n.

65 **dulcet diseases** literally, sweet diseases, i.e. venereal disease, picked up by the shooting of the bolt in an infected area; Jonson uses the phrase '*Insipere dulce*' (the verb coined from 'incipere') to mean 'A sweet thing to be a fool' (see *EMI*, 3.4.53 and n.).

68 **lie** There may be some glancing at Ralegh here; see also 1.2.40n., p. 93. Manningham's *Diary* records the pun 'Raw Ly' by Henry Noel: '(Raw Ly) / The foe to the stommacke, and the word of disgrace, / Shewes the gent. name with the bold face' (162, fol. 83: December 1602); see 3.2.69n. on *raw*. Ralegh's poem 'The Lie' is a biting satire on contemporary life; in his *History* (1614) Ralegh attacks the practice of 'giuing the lie' and duelling as a corrupt French fashion (546), but distinguishes between 'a courteous and courtlike kind of lying' (547) and 'serious' lying (*History*, 5.3.17.2, 544–51).

removed avoided, or obviated (with an '*if*' ; see 95–101)

68–9 **bear . . . seeming** The usual Shakespearean meaning of *seeming*

your body more seeming, Audrey – as thus, sir. I did
dislike the cut of a certain courtier's beard. He sent me   70
word if I said his beard was not cut well, he was in the
mind it was. This is called the 'retort courteous'. If I
sent him word again it was not well cut, he would send
me word he cut it to please himself. This is called the
'quip modest'. If again it was not well cut, he disabled   75
my judgement. This is called the 'reply churlish'. If
again it was not well cut, he would answer I spake not
true. This is called the 'reproof valiant'. If again it was
not well cut, he would say I lie. This is called the
'countercheck quarrelsome' – and so to the 'lie   80
circumstantial' and the 'lie direct'.

JAQUES   And how oft did you say his beard was not well
cut?

TOUCHSTONE   I durst go no further than the lie

(ppl.) implies a species of show (e.g.
AC 2.2.219) or hypocrisy (e.g. *MA*
4.1.55). Onions, '"seeming" ppl. adj.',
offers this line as the only example
of the word's meaning 'becomingly'
(3, p. 192). Touchstone reminds
Audrey to keep in her part (i.e. keep
up appearances both socially and the-
atrically); see p. 35 and Stern,
Rehearsal, 98. Cf. Stoppard,
Rosencrantz, where the Player rebukes
the boy acting the Player Queen for
forgetting his role: 'Stop picking your
nose, Alfred'.
70 **certain courtier's beard** Jokes about
beards are a staple of Elizabethan
drama (see Lyly, *Midas*, 3.2.41–8,
pp. 263–4). But Touchstone's extravaganza on beards and duelling may
have more to do with social class than
with facial hair, despite the large
number of different cuts of beard worn
in Shakespeare's London (Fisher, 159).

The fool poses as a courtier who can
criticize the fashion of an equal's beard
and challenge him to a duel – a
procedure only permissible to the well
born. Jonson's 'duel' in 1598 with his
fellow actor Gabriel Spenser, whom he
killed, was 'a contradiction in terms'
because neither combatant 'was entitled
to bear arms' (Riggs, 50; see also 'Ben
Jonson', and Appendix 3). Lodge's
father, whose social ascent was from
apprentice to Lord Mayor of London,
was the first in that office to wear a
beard, arousing public disapproval, perhaps for social presumption (Sisson,
Lodge, 19; A. Walker, 415, 420, 422–3).
75 **quip** sarcastic or sharp retort; cf. *TGV*
4.2.12 and see Greene's *Quip for an
Upstart Courtier* (1592).
75–6 **disabled my judgement** accused
me of having no discrimination
80 **counfercheck** contradiction
84, 85 **durst** dared

80 to the] *F2;* to *F*

circumstantial, nor he durst not give me the lie direct;   85
and so we measured swords and parted.

JAQUES   Can you nominate in order now the degrees of
the lie?

TOUCHSTONE   O sir, we quarrel in print, by the book, as
you have books for good manners. I will name you the   90
degrees: the first, the retort courteous; the second, the
quip modest; the third, the reply churlish; the fourth,
the reproof valiant; the fifth, the counter-check
quarrelsome; the sixth, the lie with circumstance; the
seventh, the lie direct. All these you may avoid but the   95
lie direct and you may avoid that too with an 'if'. I knew
when seven justices could not take up a quarrel, but
when the parties were met themselves, one of them
thought but of an 'if': as, 'if you said so, then I said so';
and they shook hands and swore brothers. Your 'if' is   100
the only peacemaker; much virtue in 'if'.

JAQUES   Is not this a rare fellow, my lord? He's as good at
anything, and yet a fool.

---

85 **give . . . direct** call me a liar

86 **measured swords** compared the
length of our weapons (*OED* measure
v. 2j, first example); see Appendix 3.

87 **nominate** list, propose
degrees steps (see 5.2.36) or different
levels. Jaques's questions and
Touchstone's response parody the
rules of rhetoric.

89 **in print** according to printed words or
maxims
by the book according to the rules; cf.
RJ 1.5.110: 'You kiss by th' book.'
Touchstone quarrels according to
printed rules for fencing fashionable in
the 1590s (see Jonson, *EMI*, p. 11 and
2.1.5–7n.). The lines suggest a specific
reference to *Vincentio Saviolo His
Practice* (1595); see p. 76.

95 **avoid** escape, nullify

97 **take up** resolve (*OED* take *v.* 93u *obs.*,
quoting this line)

99–101 '**if**' See Saviolo, *Of Honor* (sigs
R4ᵛ–T4ᵛ): 'Conditionall lyes be such as
are giuen conditionally: as if a man
should saie or write these woordes. If
thou hast saide that I haue offered my
Lord abuse, thou lyest: or if thou saiest
so heerafter, thou shalt lye.' Saviolo
recommends not allowing the challenged person to escape with 'Ifs and
Ands' (sig. S3ʳ).

100 **swore brothers** vowed amity

101 **virtue** *OED* *sb.* 9a: 'efficacy or
power' (especially relating to precious
stones – as in 'touchstone'); also
9c: 'Efficacy of a moral nature'. Cf.
Son 81.13: 'such virtue hath my pen'.

99 'if you . . . so'] *Capell;* if you . . . so: *F*

DUKE SENIOR   He uses his folly like a stalking-horse and
under the presentation of that he shoots his wit.   105

Enter HYMEN [*with*] ROSALIND *and* CELIA
[*both undisguised*]. *Still music.*

HYMEN

Then is there mirth in heaven
When earthly things made even
    Atone together.
Good Duke, receive thy daughter.
Hymen from heaven brought her,   110

---

104 **stalking-horse** See Drayton, *Elizium*: 'Then vnderneath my Horse, I staulke my game to strike' (6.52), i.e. deceiving one's prey under the *presentation* (105), or false show, of a riderless horse.

105 **shoots his wit** hits his target by means of a sharp intelligence disguised as foolishness

105.1 HYMEN Shakespeare turns to the classical deity for the onstage weddings, in a sequence which is more pageant than epiphany (Bate, 161). Hymen may wear yellow, as in Ovid, *Met.*, 10, 'From thence in saffron colourd robe flew *Hymen* through y⁰ ayre' (p. 123ᵛ), and Jonson, *Hymenaei* (1606), ll. 42–3. See Appendix 2.

105.2 *both undisguised* In Lodge, Ganimede appears at the wedding day 'neat in a sute of gray' (sig. O3ᵛ). Gerismond, 'noting well the phisnomy of Ganimede, began by his fauours to cal to mind the face of his Rosalynd' (sig. P2ʳ); cf. Duke Senior, 26. Ganimede then leaves and returns as Rosalind in a 'gowne of green' (sig. P2ᵛ) – the traditional dress of a Maid Marian in the Robin Hood plays (see 1.1.111n. and pp. 56–7, 85–6). In her new attire 'Rosalynde seemed *Diana*

triumphing in the Forrest: vpon her head she wore a chaplet of Roses, which gaue her such a grace, yt she looked like *Flora* pearkt in the pride of all hir floures' (sig. P2ᵛ); see 3.2.2n. and cf. Perdita: 'Flora / Peering in April's front' and 'Most goddess-like prank'd up' (*WT* 4.4.2–3, 10).

Still music quiet and slow; probably interlude music from a broken consort (Dart, *Consort*, 3–7; see 176, 2.7.174n.). The music forms the background here to a recitation rather than a song (not marked until 139 SD).

106 **mirth** the triumph of joyful merriment over melancholy (see 2.7.4n.), almost a credo for comedy, as mirth acquires the spiritual status of a heaven-sent gift; cf. *Mucedorus* (1598), Induction, ll. 37–40 (RP).

107 **made even** balanced, evened out; see 18n., 146n.

108 **Atone** make one (at-one); see Chapman, *Masque*: 'Sweete *Hymen*; *Hymen*, Mightiest of Gods, / Attoning of all-taming blood the odds; / Two into One, contracting' (sig. E4ʳ). 'Attoning' is an act both of union and of temperance, which 'evens' the odds in the blood (cf. *Tem.* 4.1.52–3).

105.1 *with*] *Cam¹*   ROSALIND] Rosalind *in Woman's Cloths* / *Rowe*   105.2 *both undisguised*] *Capell subst.*   106 SP] *Hymen sings Cam¹*

338

Yea, brought her hither,

That thou mightst join her hand with his,

Whose heart within his bosom is.

ROSALIND [*to Duke Senior*]

To you I give myself, for I am yours.

[*to Orlando*] To you I give myself, for I am yours.   115

DUKE SENIOR

If there be truth in sight, you are my daughter.

ORLANDO

If there be truth in sight, you are my Rosalind.

PHOEBE

If sight and shape be true,

Why then, my love adieu.

ROSALIND

I'll have no father, if you be not he.   120

I'll have no husband, if you be not he.

Nor ne'er wed woman, if you be not she.

HYMEN

Peace, ho. I bar confusion.

---

112 *her hand* See 3.2.142n. on *her*.
Masten argues that F's 'his' is a deliberate recognition of the 'joining' of
Orlando with a boy actor, which would
suggest that Rosalind is not wearing
wedding clothes ('Ganymede', 156; see
4.1.115n.).

113 **Whose** i.e. Rosalind's heart, not
Orlando's. In Petrarchan love poetry
the exchange of hearts deliberately
confuses ownership; see 5.2.20n.

116, 117 **If . . . sight** The figure of *isocolon*, a reiterated clause, gives the
moment of recognition solemnity.

118 **shape** The word invokes Ovidian
metamorphosis; cf. *TGV* 5.4.107–8.

120–2 The moment of triumphant apoth-
eosis is rooted in the fantasies of the
counterfeit theatrical world, where
Ganymede can indeed metamorphose
into Rosalind, but after the conclusion
of the scene will return as boy not girl
(see Rackin, 'Crossdressing', 118–19).

123 **bar** forbid
confusion 'Rosalind's disguise, the
very essence of the dangerous
mimetism of festival-time, has been a
source of carnival misrule which is
now banished in the ceremonial conclusion' (Laroque, 234).

112 her] *F3; his F* with] *and Douai ms* 113 his] *her Malone* 114 SD] *Douai ms (*to ye D.*)*, *Rowe*
115 SD] *Douai ms*, *Rowe* To] *Or.* To *F3* 117 sight] *shape Rann (Johnson)* 118–19] *Douai ms,*
Pope; one line F

'Tis I must make conclusion
   Of these most strange events.   125
Here's eight that must take hands
To join in Hymen's bands,
   If truth holds true contents.
[*to Celia and Oliver*]
You and you no cross shall part.
[*to Rosalind and Orlando*]
You and you are heart in heart.   130
[*to Phoebe*]
You to his love must accord
Or have a woman to your lord.
[*to Audrey and Touchstone*]
You and you are sure together
As the winter to foul weather.
Whiles a wedlock hymn we sing,   135
Feed yourselves with questioning,
That reason wonder may diminish
How thus we met, and these things finish.

---

124 **make conclusion** Cf. Lyly, *Galatea*, Epilogue, 1: ''tis only I that conclude all' (p. 108).

125 **strange** magical, to be wondered at; see 5.2.58. Cf. *MND* 5.1.1–2: 'HIP-POLYTA 'Tis strange, my Theseus, that these lovers speak of. / THESEUS More strange than true.'

128 A line which represents the ethical climax of the play's debating of plea-sure and content, and of poetry and lies. For 'if' as affirmation see *Son* 116.13–14: 'If this be error and upon me proved, / I never writ, nor no man ever loved.'

129 SD usually directed to Rosalind and Orlando, but it would be more appro-priate for Celia and Oliver, as the highest in rank in the assembly, to be addressed first; Jaques de Boys has not yet brought news of Duke Frederick's conversion and resignation of his dukedom.

129 **cross** vexation or ill-fortune, carrying Christian overtones, but with a possible pun; cross-dressing is capable of pro-viding a 'cross' in matrimony, as later in Jonson's *Epicoene* (1609), where the 'silent' woman is revealed as a boy.

130 echoes Hymen's 'heart within his bosom is', 113

131 **accord** agree

132 **to** for

133 **sure together** firmly joined

135 **we sing** an internal SD; cf. 2.7.174.

136 **Feed** satisfy

137 **wonder** a sense of the miraculous; see 3.2.186–7n.

129 SD] *this edn*; *To* Orlando *and* Rosalind *Johnson*   130 SD] *this edn*; *To* Oliver *and* Celia *Johnson*
131 SD] *Johnson*   133 SD] *Johnson subst.*

SONG

Wedding is great Juno's crown,
   O blessed bond of board and bed.   140
'Tis Hymen peoples every town,
   High wedlock then be honoured.
Honour, high honour and renown
To Hymen, god of every town.

DUKE SENIOR

O my dear niece, welcome thou art to me   145
Even daughter; welcome in no less degree.

PHOEBE

I will not eat my word, now thou art mine,
Thy faith my fancy to thee doth combine.

Enter [JAQUES DE BOYS, *the*] *second brother.*

139 **Juno** goddess of marriage; see 1.3.72n.
140 **blessed** blessèd
141 **peoples** who populates. Cf. *MA* 2.3.232–3: 'the world must be peopled'.
   every town The introduction of *town* opens a vista beyond the stage and looks forward to Rosalind's epilogue.
142 **High** solemn
   honoured honourèd
146 **Even** 'as' is implied. The cousins, whose mutual love has created equality between them, are now equal in the Duke's love. In Lodge, Gerismond embraces Alinda for her loyalty to his daughter (sig. P3ʳ). Knowles suggests '*even-daughter*, "one who is as much as a daughter to me"'; see *OED* even- 2 *obs.*
147 **eat my word** go back on my promise

(Dent, W825); Phoebe's contrition and keeping of faith derives, in a more homely fashion, from Lodge (sig. P3ʳ), but also follows Ganymede's injunction at 3.5.62.
148 'Your fidelity combines with my fantasy to make me love you'; see 3.5.34n. The frequent omission of Phoebe's retraction in modern productions eliminates the wonderfully original touch of Phoebe's humanizing. No reaction to Phoebe's volte-face is allowed to Silvius; Montanus in Lodge is 'as frolicke as *Paris* when he hanseled his loue with *Helena*' (sig. P3ʳ).
   combine almost a chemical usage implying the coming together of distinct elements, *faith* and *fancy*, to make a new compound, *love*; see *compounded*, 4.1.15.

139 SD] *Choric song Cam¹*   146 Even daughter; welcome] *Oxf;* Euen daughter welcome *F;* Even daughter, welcome *F4;* Even daughter-welcome *Theobald;* Even-daughter welcome, *Oxf¹ (Knowles)*
148.1 JAQUES DE BOYS] *Rowe*

JAQUES DE BOYS

> Let me have audience for a word or two.
> I am the second son of old Sir Rowland   150
> That bring these tidings to this fair assembly.
> Duke Frederick, hearing how that every day
> Men of great worth resorted to this forest,
> Addressed a mighty power, which were on foot
> In his own conduct, purposely to take   155
> His brother here and put him to the sword;
> And to the skirts of this wild wood he came,
> Where meeting with an old religious man,
> After some question with him, was converted
> Both from his enterprise and from the world,   160

149 **audience** hearing, attention. A new actor takes the stage, turning the performers into spectators; cf. 1.2.110–11n.

150 **second son** See 1.1.5n. and List of Roles, 21n.

151 **tidings** news
fair assembly gracious gathering; possibly also including the audience (see 3.3.46n.)

152–3 a brief reminder of the potentially threatening scenario of an alternative court; see 1.1.112n.

153 **resorted** made their way

154 **Addressed** assembled
a mighty power a great army; in Lodge the wedding party is broken up and the bridegrooms and Gerismond leave to do battle with Torismund, who is killed (sigs P4^{r-v}). Shakespeare – in the true tradition of pastoral – converts the violent and vengeful (Oliver and Frederick) into the peaceable.
on foot foot soldiers

155 **In . . . conduct** under his own leadership
purposely with the specific intention
take seize, arrest

156 **put . . . sword** kill him

157 **skirts** edges; see 3.2.325n.
wild wood The term, with its fairy-tale and *chanson de geste* echoes, recalls pastoral entertainments put on for Elizabeth on her progresses (see p. 95); see also the 'wild man' suggested by the figure of Oliver at 4.3.105 (see n.).

158 **old religious man** a traditional hermit; see 3.2.332n. Drayton's hermit in *Poly-Olbion* was one 'Who in the strength of youth, a man at Armes hath been; / Or one who of this world the vilenesse hauing seene, / Retyres him from it quite' (13.217).

159 **question** questioning, discussion
was converted See 1.3.67 for Frederick's (surprising) remorse. See Montrose: 'With striking formal and thematic economy, Shakespeare realizes his change of plot as change *within* character' ('Brother', 43). See 4.3.135n. for Oliver's conversion.

160 **enterprise** undertaking
world earthly and material concerns; see *BCP*, 'Order for Baptism': 'renounce the world, the flesh and the devil'.

149+ SP] *Rowe*; 2. *Bro. F*   150 Rowland] Roland *Cam²*

His crown bequeathing to his banished brother,
And all their lands restored to them again
That were with him exiled. This to be true
I do engage my life.
DUKE SENIOR   Welcome, young man.
Thou offer'st fairly to thy brothers' wedding: 165
To one his lands withheld, and to the other
A land itself at large, a potent dukedom.
First, in this forest let us do those ends
That here were well begun and well begot;
And after, every of this happy number   170
That have endured shrewd days and nights with us
Shall share the good of our returned fortune,
According to the measure of their states.
Meantime, forget this new-fall'n dignity
And fall into our rustic revelry.   175

---

161 **crown** a relic from Lodge, where Torismond (Frederick) and Gerismond (Duke Senior) are both kings. Dukes could wear coronets but not crowns.
162 ***them** F's 'him' may be a misreading of 'hem' (old form of 'them').
163 **exiled** stressed on the second syllable
164 **engage** stake; the normal term for accepting a challenge
165 **offer'st fairly** bring fine gifts
  to on the occasion of
166 **To . . . withheld** to Oliver, the restoration of his confiscated lands; from Lodge (sig. P4ᵛ)
167 **at large** in its entirety
  potent powerful; Duke Senior will assign his dukedom to Orlando when he marries Rosalind. In Lodge, Gerismond creates Rosader his 'heire apparant to the kingdome' (sig. P4ᵛ).
168 **do those ends** complete those purposes and conclude those activities

169 **well begun** undertaken in a good spirit
  begot begotten; conceived or set in motion
170 **after** afterwards
  every every one
171 **shrewd** cold, biting, referring both to weather – cf. *Ham* 1.4.1: 'The air bites shrewdly, it is very cold' – and to fortunes; see 2.1.7n. on *winter's wind*.
172 **returnèd**; the line is a hendecasyllable ending with a spondee (two syllables stressed equally): *fortune*.
  fortune good fortune
173 **measure . . . states** degrees of their wealth and consequence ('estate'; see 1.2.15n.)
174 **new-fall'n dignity** favour or status recently acquired or bestowed
175 **fall into** throw ourselves into (see also 177); cf. 2.7.172.
  rustic revelry country jollity, festivities

---

162 them] *Douai ms, Rowe;* him *F*   165 brothers'] *(brothers), Johnson²;* brother's *F4*   166 To one]
To th'one *Douai ms*   174 new-fall'n] *(new-falne)*

Play, music! And you brides and bridegrooms all,
With measure heaped in joy to th' measures fall.

JAQUES

Sir, by your patience.
[*to Jaques de Boys*]   If I heard you rightly,
The Duke hath put on a religious life
And thrown into neglect the pompous court.   180

JAQUES DE BOYS

He hath.

JAQUES

To him will I; out of these convertites
There is much matter to be heard and learned.
[*to Duke Senior*] You to your former honour I
    bequeath:
Your patience and your virtue well deserves it.   185
[*to Orlando*] You to a love that your true faith doth
    merit;

176 **Play, music!** an internal SD; see
  105.2n. on '*Still music*'. The Duke's
  command is 'stayed' (Cam¹), i.e.
  arrested or contravened, by Jaques at
  178.
177 **measure heaped** a vessel (such as a
  cup) filled to overflowing; cf. *AC*
  1.1.1–2: 'Nay, but this dotage of our
  general's / O'erflows the measure.'
  measures dances; see 44n., 191.
  fall join in with the dance figure and
  the melodies of the music; resonant of
  the 'fall' of the wrestler at 1.2.195,
  248, and of the heroine's falling
  in love with a better wrestler than
  herself.
178 **by your patience** with your permission; Jaques asks leave to speak before
  the musicians play for the dance.
179 **religious life** the life of a monk or
  hermit; see 4.3.135n., and cf.
  3.2.402–3n.
180 **pompous** ceremonious

182 **convertites** the recently converted;
  cf. 159n. Jaques's interest in conversion may recall Jonson (see 2.5.30n.,
  48n., 52n. on *fools . . . circle*), who converted to Catholicism while in prison,
  1598–9 (see Appendix 3), or Lodge,
  who also converted to Catholicism in
  the 1590s.
183 **matter** information of substance;
  see 2.1.68n.
184–9 **You . . . victualled** Jaques, unlike
  Hymen, appears to address only the
  men, although at 186, 187 and 188,
  You could conceivably be addressed to
  each couple.
184 **honour** respect, but not his title; see
  167n. on *potent*.
185 **virtue** both moral and physical
  strength (It. *virtù*); cf. 3.2.8n.
186 **faith. . . merit** devotion and trust
  earns. Both words carry religious connotations of salvation; cf. 3n., and
  3.5.101n.

178 patience.] patience . . . *he stays the music Cam*¹   SD] *Cam*¹   184, 186, 187, 188, 189 SDs] *Rowe*
185 deserves] deserve *Pope*

344

[*to Oliver*] You to your land and love and great allies;
[*to Silvius*] You to a long and well-deserved bed;
[*to Touchstone*] And you to wrangling, for thy loving
    voyage
Is but for two months victualled. – So to your
    pleasures,   190
I am for other than for dancing measures.

DUKE SENIOR
    Stay, Jaques, stay.

JAQUES
    To see no pastime, I. What you would have
    I'll stay to know at your abandoned cave.   *Exit.*

DUKE SENIOR
    Proceed, proceed! We'll begin these rites   195
    As we do trust they'll end, in true delights.
                        [*Music and dance.*] *Exeunt* [*all but Rosalind*].

---

188 **well-deserved** deservèd
189–90 **voyage . . . victualled** the
    food supply will only hold out for
    two months – a final traveller's joke
    from Jaques; cf. *remainder biscuit*,
    2.7.39.
191 **measures** concerns, activities; see
    Appendix 3.
192 **Stay** remain (to enjoy the celebration
    with us); cf. *LLL* 2.1.192: 'I cannot
    stay thanksgiving' ('remain to thank
    you', Woudhuysen).
193 **I** The position of *I* at the end of the
    clause (cf. Fr. *moi*) is characteristic of
    Monsieur Jaques's isolated sense of
    self; see 3.2.286n. See Cave, *Pré-*
    Histoires, 119, for Montaigne's use of
    this marker of subjectivity, and
    2.7.65n. for other connections between

Jaques and Montaigne.
194 **stay** wait
    cave See 2.7.201n.
195–6 **begin . . . end** a return to the *old tale*
    of 1.2.114; see Appendix 1.
195 **We'll** disyllabic
    rites ceremonies, both the festivities
    and the wedding rituals
196 **trust . . . true** Trust, truth and
    delight – reminiscent of the purpose of
    poetry: 'to teach and delight' (Sidney,
    Apology, p. 101) – brings full circle the
    play's concern with poetry and lies,
    pleasure and content.
196 SD Elizabethan plays ended with
    jigs, which were the special province of
    the comedian Richard Tarlton, and
    subsequently of Will Kemp; cf.
    3.3.77n., 5.3.14n.

---

195 We'll] We will *F2*   rites] *Rowe*; rights *F*   196 trust . . . end,] *Pope*; trust, . . . end *F*; trust . . .
end *Douai ms, Rowe*   SD *Music and dance*] *Cam¹*; *A Dance* / *Capell*   Exeunt] *Craig*; *Exit F*; om. *F2*
all . . . Rosalind] *Ridley subst.*

[EPILOGUE]

ROSALIND   It is not the fashion to see the lady the
Epilogue, but it is no more unhandsome than to see the
lord the Prologue. If it be true that good wine needs
no bush, 'tis true that a good play needs no epilogue.
Yet to good wine they do use good bushes, and good   5
plays prove the better by the help of good epilogues.
What a case am I in then, that am neither a good
epilogue, nor cannot insinuate with you in the behalf
of a good play. I am not furnished like a beggar,
therefore to beg will not become me. My way is to   10

Epilogue 1–2 fashion . . . Epilogue See
3n. The only other epilogue spoken
(perhaps) by a girl concludes Lyly's
Galatea, although the speaker,
Galatea, could at that point be either a
boy or as a girl – obvious to an audience, but not to a reader (see Rackin,
'Crossdressing', 125).

2 **unhandsome** unbecoming

3 **lord the Prologue** The speaker of the
prologue starts the play, and good
manners require ladies to take first
place; see 1–2n.

3–4 **good . . . bush** proverbial; 'A branch
or bush of ivy (perhaps as the
plant sacred to Bacchus) hung up
as a vintner's sign' (*OED* bush
sb.[1] 5a; Knowles). Harington recalls,
in '*Of his translation of* Ariosta', a
friend's (perhaps Shakespeare's?)
reproof of his eagerness for applause:
'And with this prouerbe prou'd it
labour lost: / Good Ale doth need no
signe, good Wine no bush' (*Epigrams
1618*, 1.73; see Dusinberre, 'As *Who*?',
14–15).

4 **needs no epilogue** Cf. *MND*
5.1.350–1: 'No epilogue, I pray you;
for your play needs no excuse.'

7 **case** situation; a legal dilemma or
actionable state (cf. 3.2.133–4n.); also
perhaps the female 'case' or outside in
which the boy actor finds himself

8 **insinuate with you** wind my way into
your good opinion

9 **furnished** dressed; see 3.2.238n. 'The
"ambivalent figure" of Rosalind . . .
refuses to choose between actor and
character or between male and female'
(Rackin, 'Androgyny', 124). The
Victorian actress Helena Faucit disliked speaking the epilogue: 'In it one
addresses the audience neither as
Ganymede nor as Rosalind, but as
one's own very self. Anything of this
kind was very repugnant to me, my
desire being always to lose myself in
the character I was representing'
(*Characters*, 285). In the 1936 film
Paul Czinner created a 'floating-
world' mirage of alternating shots of
Rosalind in her wedding-dress and
Ganymede in doublet and hose.
like a beggar i.e. to plead for alms; a
final provocation to anti-theatricalists
who attacked players as vagrants; see
2.3.32–3n.

10 **become** be appropriate to

EPILOGUE] *Theobald*[2]

conjure you, and I'll begin with the women. I charge
you, O women, for the love you bear to men, to like as
much of this play as please you. And I charge you, O
men, for the love you bear to women (as I perceive by
your simpering none of you hates them), that between   15
you and the women the play may please. If I were a
woman I would kiss as many of you as had beards that
pleased me, complexions that liked me and breaths

---

11 **conjure** See 5.2.69. Donaldson compares the ending of Jonson's *EMI* (in
which Shakespeare acted): 'Well, then,
I conjure you all here to put off all dis-
contentment' (5.3.450). Rosalind's use
of the word *conjure* 'moves . . . between
its legal and magical sense'
(Donaldson, 'Myths', 17–18, citing
OED conjure *v.* 3; see Appendix 3).
charge exhort

11–16 **I . . . may please** possibly imitated and turned into bawdy innuendo in
Webster's Induction to Marston's
Malcontent (1604): 'Gentlemen, I
could wish for the women's sake you
had all soft cushions: and gentlewomen, I would wish that for the
men's sakes you had all more easy
standings' (14); see Dusinberre, 'As
Who?', 21n.

12 **O women** Rosalind's exhortation
mocks Gosson's fear of women in the
audience as provokers of licentious
behaviour (Sedinger, 72).
like Cf. Lodge, Dedication to the
Gentleman Readers: 'If you like it, so:
and yet I will bee yours in duetie, if
you be mine in favour'. See Jonson,
Epilogue to *Cynthia's Revels*: 'By *God
'tis good, and if you lik't, you may*'
(3054); and cf. 4.1.86n. For similar
phrases in Tasso's *Aminta* and
Guarini's *Il pastor fido* see Knowles, 9.

13 **please** both 'like' and 'content'

16–17 **If . . . woman** Often cut since the
advent of women actors in Restoration

theatre, these lines remain central to
interpretations of the play (see
Hodgdon, 194; Erickson, 79; Belsey,
181) despite the fact that the epilogue
may possibly only have been delivered
at a first performance (probably in the
public theatre; see pp. 41–2 and Stern,
Making, 120–1). Cheek by Jowl offered
a new dimension in 1991 as Adrian
Lester 'toyed with the audience . . .
teasing them with the possibility of
homoerotic contact' (Bulman, 'Gay
Theater', 41). Goldberg identifies
Rosalind's power with that of the
queen: 'We do not know where these
words end, what final reality they point
to, of which of the referents that pleasant
"if" makes most real. Most real, most
royal' (153).

17 **beards** flattery of the male audience –
in the tradition of epilogues – by reference to a marker of both gender and
class (see 5.4.70n.)

18 **complexions** both looks and expression (see 3.5.117)
liked pleased

18–19 **breaths . . . not** breath which
didn't make me turn away in disgust.
The new ending by Jonson for the
quarto of *EMO*, 'So many as have
sweet minds in their breasts'
(Appendix A, l. 37, p. 377), may
suggest that Jonson was influenced in
his rewriting of his original
unsuccessful epilogue (spoken at the
Globe in 1599) by hearing Rosalind's

---

13 please] pleases *F3;* shall please *Douai ms*   ¹you] them *Hanmer*   15 simpering] *(simpring)*   hates]
hate *Pope*   them),] them) to like as much as pleases them, *Hanmer*

that I defied not. And I am sure as many as have good
beards, or good faces, or sweet breaths will for my   20
kind offer, when I make curtsy, bid me farewell.   *Exit.*

FINIS

winning address to the audience;
see Appendix 3 (pp. 368–9), and
Dusinberre, 'Pancakes', 404–5.

21 **curtsy** a courtesy, in which the
Elizabethan player (in roles of either
sex) bent his knee. Rosalind is still in
her wedding dress, but 'what lingers,
like the smile of the Cheshire Cat'
(Garber, *Vested Interests*, 75) is her
evocation of the shepherd boy
Ganymede, whose performance as girl,
as boy, the forest now must judge.

21 SD] *Exeunt. F2*

APPENDIX 1

A COURT EPILOGUE, SHROVETIDE 1599

William Ringler and Steven May conjectured that the verse lines which seem to present an epilogue to a play and are transcribed on fol. 46 of Henry Stanford's commonplace book (Cambridge MS Dd.5.75; see Fig. 8) were probably by Shakespeare (see pp. 6–7, 37–9). The dramatist uses the same trochaic verse form in 'more than twenty songs and poems in his plays, from the earliest to the latest', including Puck's epilogue to *A Midsummer Night's Dream* and Prospero's epilogue to *The Tempest*.[1] Consistent with Shakespeare's practice is the uninflected genitive in the penultimate line ('ther father Quene'), as in *Antony and Cleopatra*: 'Oh *Anthony*, you haue my Father house' (TLN 1483, 2.7.129). All the words in the epilogue except 'circuler' (line 2) are to be found in Shakespeare's lexicon.

A competitor for the authorship of this piece might be Ben Jonson. The word 'circuler' occurs twice in his poems. But the way in which Jonson uses it, to describe perfection and infinitude,[2] differs from its use in the epilogue. The epilogue's 'circuler accompt' (l. 2) creates a metaphorical frame of reference comparable to Shakespeare's '*Cyphers to this great Accompt*' (*Henry V*, Prologue, TLN 17). It is true that the 'circle' was a favourite Jonsonian figure (see 2.5.52n.) and that Jonson's '*Epigram 128*', to William Roe, plays, as the epilogue does, with beginnings and endings:

---

1   Ringler & May, 139; May & Ringler; see also Dusinberre, 'Pancakes', 377.
2   In '*The Mind*', in Donaldson, *Jonson*, 419–21 (ll. 31–2), and '*The Vision of Ben Jonson, On the Muses of his Friend, M. Drayton*', 457–9 (l. 19); see also Donaldson, *Magic*, 28–31, and Bevington, 'Review', 317.

There may all thy ends,
As the beginnings here, prove purely sweet,
And perfect in a circle always meet.[1]

But '*Epigram 128*' postdates the verses in Henry Stanford's commonplace book by more than ten years. Roe's travels followed Jonson's testimony in court on his behalf in 1610 (Herford & Simpson, 1.223–30, esp. 228).

In February 1599 it is unlikely that a Jonson play would have been performed at court, because at the end of January 1599 Jonson was in prison for debt (following his disgrace for killing a fellow player in September 1598). He was released by the payment of a fine by one of his fellow players, and renewed his connections with the Bricklayers' Guild (Riggs, 49–54), returning to the theatre when *Every Man Out of His Humour* was produced at the Globe in the late autumn of 1599.

Both Jonson and Thomas Dekker used the trochaic form. Dekker's plays *Old Fortunatus* and *The Shoemaker's Holiday* were performed at court (at Richmond) on 27 December 1599 and 1 January 1600, but these dates are too late for the epilogue in Stanford's book.

The hypothesis of Shakespearean authorship of the epilogue raises the more tantalizing question of the play it might have followed. Tiffany Stern's research emphasizes that epilogues were used for new plays, to test approval of them (see p. 42). February 1599 is a possible date for *Much Ado About Nothing*. It is a few months earlier than modern scholars presume for *As You Like It* (see pp. 36, 43). But the epilogue splices more convincingly onto the end of *As You Like It* than onto the end of *Much Ado* and its contents connect piquantly with the pastoral play. With the addition of the court epilogue, the (modernized) text would appear as follows:

---

1   Donaldson, *Jonson*, 273–4 (ll. 6–8); see Dusinberre, 'Pancakes', 386–7.

JAQUES

    Sir, by your patience.

    [*to Jaques de Boys*]   If I heard you rightly,

    The Duke hath put on a religious life

    And thrown into neglect the pompous court.   180

JAQUES DE BOYS

    He hath.

JAQUES

    To him will I; out of these convertites

    There is much matter to be heard and learned.

    [*to Duke Senior*] You to your former honour I

        bequeath:

    Your patience and your virtue well deserves it.   185

    [*to Orlando*] You to a love that your true faith doth

        merit;

    [*to Oliver*] You to your land and love and great allies;

    [*to Silvius*] You to a long and well-deserved bed;

    [*to Touchstone*] And you to wrangling, for thy loving

        voyage

    Is but for two months victualled. – So to your

        pleasures,   190

    I am for other than for dancing measures.

DUKE SENIOR

    Stay, Jaques, stay.

JAQUES

    To see no pastime, I. What you would have

    I'll stay to know at your abandoned cave.   *Exit.*

DUKE SENIOR

    Proceed, proceed! We'll begin these rites   195

    As we do trust they'll end, in true delights.   *Exeunt.*

[EPILOGUE]

As the dial hand tells o'er

The same hours it had before,

Still beginning in the ending,

Circular account still lending,

So most mighty Queen we pray,   5
Like the dial day by day,
You may lead the seasons on
Making new when old are gone;
That the babe which now is young
And hath yet no use of tongue   10
Many a Shrovetide here may bow
To that Empress I doe now,
That the children of these lords
Sitting at your council boards
May be grave and aged seen   15
Of her that was their fathers' Queen.
Once I wish this wish again
Heaven subscribe it with amen.

Exit.

The epilogue follows seamlessly the Duke's couplet about beginning and ending. The play ends, but the wedding rites begin. 'Beginning in the ending' (l. 3) traces the circular movement of the play from court to country and back to court again, while recalling the 'old tale' of 1.2.114 and its end, which is 'dead and buried' (112). The *OED* (circular 7) records 'cyclic' as a very rare and now obsolete later meaning for circular, of which some traces are present in the epilogue's use of the word.

In the epilogue the 'dial hand' tells over the hours. There may be no clock in the Forest (see 3.2.293n.), but there is a dial, which Touchstone pulls from his bag to tell the time. Dials were coveted possessions for the Elizabethans. Sir John Harington had his portrait depicted on the frontispiece of his translation of Ariosto's *Orlando Furioso* with his pocket dial (see Fig. 17). The Earl of Essex had a special pocket dial made in 1593, which he probably used on the voyage to Cadiz in 1596 (Bruce, 353), and which bore a motto that would not have been out of place in Duke Frederick's court: '*Invidia virtutis comes*' ('Envy the companion of virtue').[1] The word 'dial' features in *The Comedy of Errors* ('By this I think the dial points at five', 5.1.118); in *Romeo and Juliet* ('for the bawdy hand of the dial is now upon the prick of noon', 2.4.111–12); and in *1 Henry IV*, in Hotspur's speech before Shrewsbury ('If life did ride upon a dial's point, / Still ending at the arrival of an hour', 5.2.83–4). But if Stern's arguments about epilogues as dispensable adjuncts to first performances is accepted, then all these plays are too early for Stanford's epilogue.

In February 1599 a distinctive feature of the 'outer court' at Richmond Palace, where the play which the epilogue followed was performed, was the 'great dyall', elaborately ornamented, which had been repaired and painted by the court painter, Leonard Fryer (appointed in the previous year), in preparation for the arrival of the queen and her courtiers for Shrove (Colvin, 4.222–34, esp. 230). This remarkable structure preceded the renowned later dials at Hampton Court (Colvin, 4.146). The shaft of the dial was twelve foot long and six foot deep, the 'whole dyall' being twelve foot wide and fourteen foot deep.[2] The dial would have been something of a marvel for the court audience in 1599. The epilogue's image of a dial's hand could be seen as a graceful acknowledgement of this magnificent structure at Richmond.

The epilogue addresses itself to the queen, with promises of loyalty from an audience of lords and their families (see p. 72). The epilogue's pious commitment of a new generation, 'the children of these lords' (l. 13), to the queen's service is fitting for

1 See Hammer, 20n.
2 PRO E351/3234, fol. 6ʳ. The full entry for Leonard Fryer's work on the dial reads: 'liii s iiij d [53s. 4d.] for paintinge & workinge of a great dyall in the utter courte beinge prymed & stopped 7 tymes ouer & the houres and letters guylded with fyne golde with her Majesties letters & the date of our lorde god, and a greate compertmente, and there in wrytten greate Romaine letters in fyne golde with an ordennance of Jasper and stone woorke in oyle colours in length xii foote and depth vi foote, the whole dyall conteyninge xii foote wyde and xiiij foote deepe.' These lines, which are from the Accounts of the Office of Works for 1 October 1598 to 30 September 1599, are only partially quoted in Colvin's printed version, and not in Dramatic Records 10, 17; see Dusinberre, 'Pancakes', 384–5.

Shakespeare's most dynastic comedy (see p. 65, 2.7.198n.), but also potentially poignant. The Countess of Essex in February 1599 had a babe-in-arms who 'hath yet no use of tongue' (l. 10); the rebellion of 1601 was already a shadow on the Shrove festivities, and, like the children of many of Essex's supporters, his own son would fight in the next generation against his king[1] (see 1.3.58n. and p. 103). If *As You Like It* was presented, as were the interludes of John Heywood to Henry VIII, as a festive celebration with its own undertones of political admonition, then Stanford's epilogue makes a discreet point about loyalty, as arguably does *As You Like It* (see 2.7.182n.), thus bringing Shakespeare's most harmonious comedy to a fitting conclusion.

It is not likely that the court epilogue would have been spoken by Rosalind. It might have been delivered by Touchstone, still on stage, or Jaques might have returned to speak it. If the former, in February 1599 the speaker would almost certainly have been Kemp (see Appendix 2). It cannot be proved that this epilogue belonged to a first court performance of *As You Like It*. But it may have done.

---

1   Robert (then third Earl of Essex), who would have been just eight years old in 1599 (Hammer, 54n), was killed in 1643 leading the Parliamentary army against Charles 1.

APPENDIX 2

CASTING AND DOUBLING

There are eighteen adult speaking parts in *As You Like It*, and six boys' parts, two of which are for pages who sing in one scene only (5.3) – a scene which may have been cut in performances in the public theatre (see p. 137). With the standard practice of doubling in the Elizabethan theatre this number could have been reduced to ten adult actors (not including attendants required in 1.2, 1.3, 2.1, 2.5, 2.7 and 4.2) and six boys (see Table 1).[1]

T.J. King suggests that hired men never doubled in main parts, but that principal actors did sometimes double minor parts, although probably not if they were playing a long lead part (King, 11); boy actors probably doubled small female parts, but not if they were playing major roles (6). Phoebe and Audrey could have played female attendants or ladies of Frederick's court in the first act. Neither of them could have doubled the roles of the singing Pages in 5.3. Doubling may have been arranged on purely mechanical principles in Shakespeare's theatre, or it may have taken into account various correspondences between the parts an actor played. Some possible doublings on the grounds of dramatic significance are suggested below.

Oliver

As the marrer of the text of his younger brother's education (see 1.1.29n.), Oliver may have been doubled with the ignorant hedge-priest, Sir Oliver Mar-text.

---

1   King; Ringler; Bradley.

Table 1   Distribution of actors for doubling

Adult actor	1.1	1.2	1.3	2.1	2.2	2.3	2.4	2.5	2.6	2.7
1	Orlando	Orlando				Orlando			Orlando	Orlando
2	*Adam					*Adam			*Adam	*Adam
3	*Oliver									
4	*Dennis									
5	*Charles	*Charles								
6		Touch					Touch			
7		*Le Beau								
8		*Duke F	*Duke F		*Duke F					
9				Duke S						Duke S
10				Amiens				Amiens		Amiens
11				*1 Lord	*1 Lord			*Lords		*1 Lord
12				*2 Lord	*2 Lord					
13							*Corin			
14							Silvius			
15								*Jaques		*Jaques
16										
17										
18										
19										
Boy actor										
1		Rosalind	Rosalind				Rosalind			
2		Celia	Celia				Celia			

* indicates possible doubling

Adult	3.1	3.2	3.3	3.4	3.5	4.1	4.2	4.3	5.1	5.2	5.3	5.4
1		Orlando				Orlando				Orlando		Orlando
2												
3	*Oliver							*Oliver		*Oliver		*Oliver
4												
5												
6		Touch	Touch						Touch		Touch	Touch
7												
8	*Duke F											Duke S
9												Amiens
10												
11							[*1 Lord]					
12							[*Forester]					
13		*Corin		*Corin	*Corin				*Corin			
14					Silvius			Silvius		Silvius		Silvius
15		*Jaques	*Jaques			*Jaques	*Jaques					*Jaques
16			*Mar-text									
17									*William			
18												*Hymen
19												*J de Boys
Boy												
1		Rosalind		Rosalind	Rosalind	Rosalind		Rosalind		Rosalind		Rosalind
2		Celia		Celia	Celia	Celia		Celia				Celia
3			Audrey						Audrey		Audrey	Audrey
4					Phoebe					Phoebe		Phoebe
5											1 Page	
6											2 Page	

* indicates possible doubling

357

Le Beau

Le Beau's Frenchness might suggest a doubling with Jaques, the only other character given the title of 'Monsieur' (see also 1.2.273–4n. and p. 94).

Duke Frederick

Sometimes doubled in modern productions with Duke Senior, this part could be linked with Jaques de Boys, who announces the Duke's conversion at 5.4.158–60.

William

The role may have been doubled with Adam. Scholars have seen jokes on the playwright's Warwickshire origins.[1]

Hymen

The part is often doubled in the modern theatre with Corin; other possibilities would be Adam and Charles the wrestler.

Table 1 demonstrates that some significant roles carry very few appearances and lines. Duke Senior is only on stage in three scenes (2.1, 2.7 and 5.4), yet his moral authority, and the number of times he is mentioned by other characters, make him more central to the play than the mere length of his part suggests. Phoebe also only appears in three scenes (3.5, 5.2 and 5.4), but the discussion of Silvius's love for her in 2.4, and the reading out loud of her long love-letter to Ganymede in 4.3, give her a larger role than the number of her lines would suggest. Duke Frederick only appears in four scenes (1.2, 1.3, and the two very short scenes, 2.2 and 3.1, the latter sometimes cut), yet the testimony of Jaques de Boys in 5.4 of the usurping Duke's arrival in the Forest, his conversion to the religious life and decision to stay, completes the part as though the actor were present on stage. However, Adam, prominent in the first two acts, is not mentioned after his disappearance at the end of Act 2.

1 Jones; H. Cooper; Duncan-Jones, *Ungentle*, 25–6; Bednarz, 117–21.

Who played these parts in Shakespeare's theatre? Shakespeare and other members of the Chamberlain's Men – Richard Burbage, Augustine Phillips, John Heminges and Thomas Pope – signed the lease for the new Globe theatre on 21 February 1599 (old-style dating 1598), together with Will Kemp. If *As You Like It* had been played at Richmond Palace the previous night – Shrove Tuesday, 20 February (see pp. 37–41 and Appendix 1) – the men listed as signatories of the Globe lease would have played in *As You Like It*. But we might also be able to add some names from the cast list appended to the 1616 Folio version of Ben Jonson's *Every Man In His Humour* – seen on 20 September 1598 by Toby Matthew[1] – which names the signatories of the Globe lease (excluding Kemp) but also Henry Condell, William Sly, Christopher Beeston and John Duke. Most of these men (though not necessarily, in 1598, Beeston and Duke) would have been sharers in the company;[2] hired men and boys are not named.

Other names are also newly available, including those of some boy actors, thanks to David Kathman's research into 'the handwritten "plot" of *The Second Part of the Seven Deadly Sins* (Dulwich College MS XIX)', which he believes refers to a play in the repertoire of the Chamberlain's Men as late as 1597–8, not, as previously believed, before 1591. Kathman shows that most of the names listed for *Deadly Sins 2* – Pope, Phillips, Burbage, Heminges, Shakespeare, Sly, Kemp and Richard Cowley – belong to players in Shakespeare's company.[3] The only one in this first list ('Sharers') who may not be in the company by the beginning of 1599 is Bryan, who may have left it early in 1597. Condell, Beeston and Duke, who appear in the Chamberlain's Men list for *Every Man In*, also appear on

---

1   Toby Matthew to Dudley Carleton: 'a new play called Every Man's Humour', *Calendar of State Papers Domestic*, Eliz. 268:61, cited in Jonson, *EMI*, 1.
2   David Kathman points out (private communication) that Beeston may not have been a sharer as early as 1598, when he was only eighteen, and that Duke may never have been a sharer.
3   Kathman disputes both Chambers' assigning of *Deadly Sins 2* to the Admiral's Men, and W.W. Greg's suggestion that it was 'an amalgamation of Strange's and the Admiral's' ('*Sins*', 13, referring to Chambers, *ES*, 3.497 and Greg, 19).

Kathman's second list of 'Hired men/older apprentices' for *Deadly Sins 2*; Beeston and Duke may not still have been in Shakespeare's company after *Every Man In*. John Sincler (Sinclo), also named in *Deadly Sins 2*, was well known as Shakespeare's 'thin' actor;[1] other names are John Holland, Robert Pallant, Thomas Goodale and (Thomas ?) Vincent.

Kathman's third list identifies boy actors. Alexander Cooke was bound apprentice to Heminges in 1597, and stayed until he was made free of the Grocer's Company on the expiry of his indentures in 1606 (Heminges is named as his master in his will, 1614). Nicholas Tooley may have been Burbage's apprentice.[2] Robert Gough does not appear on the apprentice lists of the Guilds, but he married Phillips's sister in 1603 and was the legatee of Pope, so was probably connected with the Chamberlain's Men for some time. Thomas Belte was also bound as apprentice to Heminges in 1595;[3] his indentures would have expired in 1604, when he may still have been with the Chamberlain's Men. 'Ned' may just possibly, as (the often unreliable) Frederick Gard Fleay suggested, have been Shakespeare's brother, Edmund (sixteen years his junior), who would have been eighteen or nineteen early in 1599, as he was christened on 3 May 1580 (Kathman, 'Apprentices', 30). The identity of 'Will' (perhaps Ostler? perhaps Ecclestone?) is uncertain. *As You Like It*, if played in February 1599, is a year later than Kathman's latest possible date of the 'winter of 1587–8' for *Deadly Sins 2* (31) and only five months after *Every Man In*.

Table 2 and accompanying notes tentatively propose an original cast list for Shakespeare's comedy.

1   Gaw, 'John Sinclo'. Sincler was thin rather than small, as Kathman claims ('*Sins*', 23; see Dusinberre, '*TS*', 170–4).
2   He was probably born in Antwerp in 1582–3, and subsequently lived in Warwickshire. See Kathman, '*Sins*', 29; see also Edmond, 'Burbages'.
3   Kathman, '*Sins*', 28; see also 'Apprentices'.

Table 2   Hypothetical cast list for *As You Like It*[1]

Actor	No. of lines in F	Possible original actors
Adult		
Orlando	304	Henry Condell?
Touchstone	273	Will Kemp?
Jaques	214	Richard Burbage?
Oliver	150	William Sly?
Duke Senior	109	Augustine Phillips?
Corin	79	Richard Cowley?
Silvius	76	Christopher Beeston??
		John Sincler??
Duke Frederick	70	John Heminges?
Adam	64	William Shakespeare?
Le Beau	50	Richard Burbage?
1 Lord	46 [+2?]	John Sincler?
Charles	40	Thomas Pope?
Jaques de Boys	17	John Heminges?
		John Duke?
Amiens	16	Thomas Vincent?
		John Duke?
Hymen	16	Richard Cowley?
		Shakespeare?
		Thomas Pope?
William	11	Shakespeare?
		Thomas Pope?
2 Lord	11	John Duke?
Sir Oliver Mar-text	5	William Sly?
		John Sincler?
		Thomas Pope?
Dennis	3	John Sincler?
Boy		
Rosalind	686	Alexander Cooke?
Celia	263	Robert Gough?
Phoebe	84	Nicholas Tooley?
		Ned?
Audrey	20	Ned?
		Nicholas Tooley?
1 Page	6	Thomas Belte?
2 Page	3	Will? (Ostler? Ecclestone? other?)

1   Line numbers are based on King, Table 57; the hypothetical cast list is deduced from research by Kathman ('*Sins*', 13–44).

Rosalind (Alexander Cooke?) and Celia (Robert Gough?)

The part of Rosalind, at 686 lines (cf. Cleopatra, 693; Portia, *Merchant*, 557; Helena, *All's Well*, 451; Isabella, *Measure*, 426; Viola, *Twelfth Night*, 284), is more than twice as long as Orlando's. Among Shakespearean parts for men, only Hamlet, the Duke in *Measure*, Iago, Othello, Lear (F), Macbeth, Antony and Coriolanus are longer. Celia's part is almost the same length as Touchstone's. Cooke and Gough may have been used to playing pairs of women (Portia and Jessica in *Merchant*, Beatrice and Hero in *Much Ado*; see Kathman, '*Sins*', 34), and could have played Rosalind and Celia.[1] Cooke, if born on 15 December 1583 in Sandwich (see Kathman, 'Apprentices', 28), was fifteen in 1599.

Orlando (Henry Condell?) and Oliver (William Sly?)

Condell and Sly played 'the young male leads of Ferrex and Porrex in *2 Seven Deadly Sins*' (Kathman, '*Sins*', 33), and may have taken Bassanio and Lorenzo in *Merchant*, Poins and Hotspur in *Henry IV, Part 2* and Claudio and Don John in *Much Ado*. In 1599 Condell, baptized in Norwich on 5 September 1576, would have been twenty-two, a suitable age for the 'young Orlando'. Sly's age is not known.[2]

Jaques and Le Beau (Richard Burbage?)

Burbage, who would have been thirty in 1599, is perhaps more likely to have played Jaques than Orlando.

Duke Senior (Augustine Phillips?)

A possible part for Phillips, who took the king's part in *Deadly Sins 2*.

---

1 Scott McMillin argues, as T.W. Baldwin did in 1927: 'There does appear to be a schedule to the 1604–5 female roles, and I think its purpose was to combine training with performance in the main parts' (McMillin, 243).

2 A William Sly was baptized in 1573, who may not have been the actor. 'W. Sly' is one of the players in the Induction written by John Webster for the revival in 1604 of Marston's *The Malcontent*.

Corin and Hymen (Richard Cowley?)

Cowley played Verges opposite Kemp's Dogberry in *Much Ado*, which may have been performed only a few months or even weeks before *As You Like It*. If he took Silence in *2 Henry IV* (Baldwin, *Company*, 395ff.), he may have acted opposite Kemp's Justice Shallow, and possibly partnered him again in *As You Like It* 3.2.

Silvius (Christopher Beeston? John Sincler?)

Beeston would have been eighteen or nineteen early in 1599, and may still have been acting with the Chamberlain's Men five months after *Every Man In*. But the part could have been taken by Sincler, who had played Gremio, a rejected suitor in *Shrew*, Robert Faulconbridge in *King John* and a beadle in *1 Henry VI* (see Dusinberre, '*TS*', 171–4), and could conceivably have played Sir Andrew Aguecheek in *Twelfth Night*. Silvius is a possibility, but if Sincler took the part it must have been high comedy. Whoever played Silvius would probably have doubled as a forester (see List of Roles, 15n.).

Duke Frederick (John Heminges?)

The role of Duke Frederick may have been played by the same actor who took Prince John in *2 Henry IV* (see 1.3.85n.). Heminges is a possible choice for the Duke, as he is on stage in 1.2 and 1.3 to rehearse Cooke (his apprentice) as Rosalind in her scenes with Celia (see Stern, *Rehearsal*, esp. 62–72); see Jaques de Boys below.

Adam and Hymen (Shakespeare?)

Theatrical tradition claims Adam as Shakespeare's part (see 2.7.167.1n.).

Charles and Hymen (Thomas Pope?)

Thomas Pope may have played Falstaff (Kastan, '*1H4*', 79). If he played Charles, the wrestler's part may have been a comic one.

Jaques de Boys (John Heminges? John Duke?)

Possibly doubled with Duke Frederick and taken by Heminges.

Amiens ((Thomas?) Vincent? John Duke?)

'Vincent' played a musician in *Deadly Sins 2*, so the singing role of Amiens may have fallen to him. Kathman ('*Sins*', 27) offers three possible identifications:

1   Thomas Vincent, named in the player Simon Jewell's will, so possibly another player
2   George Vincent, musician with travelling players in Germany and Poland in 1615–18
3   Thomas Vincent, mentioned in 1638 by John Taylor the water poet as 'one *Thomas Vincent* that was a Book-keeper or prompter at the Globe playhouse'.[1]

Thomas Morley, Gentleman of the Chapel Royal, and composer of 'It was a lover and his lass' (5.3), may have taken the part of Amiens in a court performance. However, Duke Senior addresses Amiens as 'cousin' (2.7.174), which might conceivably be a theatrical joke on the name of the actor John Duke.

William (Shakespeare? Pope?)

If the part were not in fact played by the dramatist, it may have been doubled with Charles the wrestler.

Sir Oliver Mar-text (William Sly? John Sincler? Thomas Pope?)

Sir Oliver Mar-text may have been doubled with Orlando's brother Oliver, both marrers of texts; both parts may have been played by Sly. However, Sir Oliver could have been a Sincler part (where a skinny physique would be in order), or the part could have been a comic one for Pope (a miserable hedge-priest, not a pope).

Dennis, Frederick's attendant (John Sincler?)

In *Deadly Sins 2* Sincler's parts are small and functional, but see *Silvius*.

---

1   Nungezer, 328, cited in Kathman, '*Sins*', 27.

Phoebe and Audrey (Ned? Nicholas Tooley?)

If Audrey was played by Edmund Shakespeare, in 5.1 he might, as a Warwickshire 'lass', have spurned his elder brother in the role of William, Audrey's rejected suitor.

Two Pages attendant on Duke Senior

1 *Thomas Belte:* Kathman suggests that Thomas Belte 'may have been the son of Thomas Belte, a Norwich city wait who was expelled from the city along with his wife and children on 16 November, 1594' (Kathman, '*Sins*', 42, 28). The waits were musicians who accompanied public functions and entertainments. A son might also have been musical and possibly the family was known to Morley, also a Norwich man (*New Grove*, 126–33, esp. 126–7).

2 *Will (Ostler? Ecclestone?):* Kathman notes that Will Ostler had been with the Children of the Chapel Royal in 1601, and was with the King's Men by 1610, as was Ecclestone ('*Sins*', 30).

Touchstone (Will Kemp)

If *As You Like It* was produced in February 1599, Touchstone would have been played by Kemp, as Robert Armin had not yet joined the company. Armin may later have taken over the role (see pp. 4, 45–6). The reasons for assigning this role to Kemp are related to the Marprelate controversy of the late sixteenth century.[1] Kemp's involvment is attested in the short *Theses Martinianae* (1589) assigned to 'Martin Junior', which viciously attacks the stage (implying, as many detractors did, its Catholicism): 'Feare none of these beastes, these pursuivants, these Mar-Martins, these stage-players, these prelates, these popes, these diuels, and al that they can do.' The reason for the warning is soon made clear: 'There bee that affirme, the rimers and stage-players, to haue cleane putte you out of countenaunce, that you

---

1   See Dusinberre, 'Topical', 239–51; and also 'Touchstone'.

dare not againe shew your face.' The players are condemned as 'poore seelie hunger-starued wretches . . . poor varlets . . . so base minded, as at the pleasure of the veryest rogue in England, for one poore pennie, they will be glad on open stage to play the ignominious fooles, for an hour or two together'. But the abuse does not hide the message, which is that the stage has put its victims out of countenance. The piece ends with a recommendation to cease pamphleteering, for the tract-writers are on a losing wicket:

> Otherwise thou shalt but commend thy follie and ignorance vnto the world to be notorious. Mar-martin, Leonard Wright, Fregneuile, Dick Bancroft, Tom Blan.o[f] Bedford, Kemp, Vnderhil, serue thee for no other vse, but to worke thy ruine, and to bewray their owne shame, & miserable ignorance.[1]

Here is Kemp, a Mar-martin, feared by Martinists, in a tract which attacks the theatre. The Martinists were afraid of the theatre, and in particular of Kemp.[2]

Kemp was renowned for the singing and dancing of jigs, an activity which became one of the commonest forms of satirical assault on the Martinists (Baskervill, 52). Kemp was a phenomenal dancer, and his *Nine Days' Wonder* describes his dance to Norwich in Lent 1600 when the theatres were closed. He is thought by many scholars, but not all (see Nielson; Dutton, *Licensing*, 34), to have left the Chamberlain's Men before he went on this dance. He was also a well-known composer of jigs. The song 'O sweet Oliver' with which Touchstone sings Sir Oliver Mar-text off the stage in 3.3 was a jig in fashion in London in 1584, about a year after the first pamphlets in the Marprelate controversy. It was entered in the

---

1   *Theses Martinianae*, sigs Di^v, Dij, Dij^v, Diij^v.
2   Kristen Poole also links Falstaff with the Marprelate controversy, and supports David Wiles's suggestion that Falstaff in *1 Henry IV* may have been played by Kemp: 'The original performances of *1 Henry IV* may also have invoked the Marprelate controversy through the casting of Will Kemp as Falstaff – the same actor likely to have portrayed Martin in the anti-Martinist theatres' (Poole, 34n.).

Stationers' Register in 1584, as 'A Ballat of. *O swete Olyuer Leaue me not behind the[e]*', and a reply entered within two weeks, which a couple of years later acquired a religious gloss: 'The answeare of "O sweete Olyuer" altered to ye scriptures' (Knowles, 198). The religious slant is interesting in view of the Marprelate controversy, possibly suggesting an early hostile connection between the jig and the tract-writers.

The Ardennes background of the Forest of Arden, together with its Warwickshire affinities, is a feature of *As You Like It*; the Flemish region was prominent in the theatrical biography of Will Kemp. In 1585 he left for the Low Countries with the Earl of Leicester, Sir Philip Sidney and the Earl of Essex, apparently as a guest performer with Leicester's players, a semi-detached position which may throw light on his relation with the Chamberlain's Men in 1599–1600. Kemp's fame as a comedian, dancer, 'tumbler' and 'instrumentalist'[1] (he played on the lute and virginals[2]) seems to have originated from his time in the Ardennes. The 'O sweet Oliver' jig may have associations with the four surviving texts of the 'Rowland' jigs from the period 1599–1603, which were also connected with the Low Countries and with Kemp.[3] Ross Duffin suggests an allusion to a Rowland jig at the end of 2.7 (see 2.7.199n.). Who fitter than Kemp to play the jester in *As You Like It* in company with old Sir Rowland's youngest son and the Mar-text priest?

In the Forest of Arden, where illicit Marprelate tracts were printed (see p. 58), Shakespeare may allow his clown a reprise of his best gag against a theatre-hating sect.[4]

---

1   Danish court records, cited in Baskervill, 129; see also Bald.

2   See 'Kempes Jigge' (lute music), in Cambridge MS Dd.2.11, fol. 99ᵛ, a volume which includes the originals of some Shakespeare songs, among them 'Hearts Ease' (fol. 44), which Peter (originally acted by Kemp) begs the musicians to play in *Romeo and Juliet* (4.5.100–1).

3   See Baskervill, 183, 224, 226n.; Wiles, 168. Like the Rowland jigs, 'O sweet Oliver' remained current in the Low Countries in the early seventeenth century, where its tune is included in a Leyden anthology by Thysius (Knowles, 198).

4   One of the earliest writers in the Marprelate controversy had been John Field (*A Godly Exhortation by Occasion of the Late Judgement of God*, 1583), father of a six-month-old infant who would become one of the Chamberlain's Men's most famous actors, Nathan Field (L. Carlson, 13; see also Brinkley, 6–7).

APPENDIX 3

BEN JONSON, *AS YOU LIKE IT* AND THE 'WAR OF THE THEATRES'

As You Like It, whether first played at court in February 1599, or at the Globe in the autumn/winter of 1599–1600, can be seen with hindsight to be held in some kind of equipoise between Ben Jonson's two 'humour' plays: *Every Man In His Humour*, first performed in September 1598, and *Every Man Out of His Humour*, probably first performed in November or December of 1599.[1] The word 'humorous', used of Duke Frederick at 1.2.255, though more in its modern sense of moody and volatile than in its Jonsonian context of the physiological 'humours', nevertheless rings with an awareness of Jonson's popular foray into a new kind of comedy based on the humours of men. The characteristic melancholy humour of Jaques in the Forest of Arden may have reminded some of Shakespeare's contemporaries of the volatile Ben Jonson. Shakespeare is named on the Folio cast list for *Every Man In*, and there are various correspondences between Jonson's comedy and *As You Like It*,[2] which may reflect Shakespeare's experience of acting in *Every Man In*. Although scholars have suggested a deliberate pattern of statement and retort between the two plays, assuming *As You Like It* to follow *Every Man Out* (which this edition does not), the interchanges between them do not depend on a theory of sequence, nor can that be reliably established.

---

1   Jonson, *EMI*, 1; Jonson, *EMO*, 39; see pp. 359, 350.
2   See 2.7.71n.; 3.3.91n.; 3.5.83n.; Epilogue, 11n., 18–19n. Shakespeare may have played Lorenzo Senior, and therefore have begun the whole play (Herford & Simpson, 3.403); though Robert Miola (Jonson, *EMI*) does not hazard a guess at the part taken by the dramatist.

Some of the notable characteristics of Jonson's *Every Man Out* might have grown from an admiration of *As You Like It*. Other echoes and parallels occur in *Cynthia's Revels* and *Poetaster*, and perhaps pre-eminently in *Epicoene*, where the boy actor plays a starring role. If *Every Man Out* were the later play, Jonson may have been responding to aspects of *As You Like It*. Jonson in *Every Man Out* explores the territory of what constitutes a 'gentleman', an area Shakespeare anatomized with ironic astuteness in *The Two Gentlemen of Verona*. This was, in an upwardly mobile society, a recurrent late-Elizabethan preoccupation (see Neill); but in *As You Like It* Shakespeare repeatedly scrutinizes the word 'gentle' and the concept of gentle behaviour (see pp. 31–3). In *Every Man Out* the figure of Sogliardo is satirized for social climbing, sometimes read as a slur on Shakespeare's acquisition of a coat of arms (see 1.2.64n.). The revised quarto ending of *Every Man Out* seems to draw on the epilogue of *As You Like It* (see Epilogue, 18–19n., and Dusinberre, 'Pancakes', 404–5). Helen Ostovich notes that the 'conversion' of Macilente into the figure of Asper – i.e. the abandonment of his stage character of satirist – is the same technique as Rosalind's remaining on stage as boy actor to speak her epilogue (Jonson, *EMO*, 5.4.40.2n.). More centrally, *As You Like It* partners *Every Man Out* in the awareness of stage space noted by Ostovich ('Seeing and judging'). The fruitful interaction evident between the three plays would support in some degree the rewriting of the tradition of Jonson's envy of Shakespeare (Donaldson, 'Myths'). It seems evident that each dramatist found the other's work a powerful stimulus to creativity, and that this need not have spelled hostility.

Nevertheless, there appears to have been hostility between Jonson and his fellow playwrights particularly during the years 1599–1602, which Jonson claimed began with his altercations with the young playwright John Marston: 'He had many quarrels with Marston: beat him, and took his pistol from him; wrote his *Poetaster* on him. The beginning of th[e]m [i.e. the

quarrels] were that Marston represented him in the stage'
('Drummond', ll. 235–7, p. 601). There has been some resistance
from scholars to the idea of a 'War of the Theatres' on the
grounds that it was largely an invention of a later age, but Tom
Cain delineates convincingly different elements in the quarrel
(Jonson, *Poetaster*, 30–6), and my account follows his in key
respects.

Jonson's identification of the beginning of a feud alludes to
Marston's play *Histriomastix* – probably written for the first
season in the autumn of 1599 of the reconstituted Children of
Paul's – in which the character 'Chrisogonus' has some of
Jonson's traits (Jonson, *Poetaster*, 31–2). Jonson in *Every Man
Out* retorts on Marston with the figure of 'Clove'. Marston's
Jack Drum's Entertainment (1600), his *What You Will* (1600–1?)
and Jonson's *Cynthia's Revels* (1601) participate further in the
skirmish. *Poetaster* (1602) attacks Jonson's fellow playwrights,
but he is finally brought to book in the routing of his alter ego,
the poet Horace, in Dekker's *Satiromastix* (1602). Cain suggests
(Jonson, *Poetaster*, 33, 36–8) that *Twelfth Night*, with Feste's
mockery of Malvolio (a figure in some ways comparable to
Macilente in *Every Man Out*), forms part of a sequence, in
which, however, he does not include *As You Like It*.

The figure of Jaques has been seen by some scholars as a
possible participant in the 'War of the Theatres'. Arthur Gray
argued in 1928 that when 'Kempe' in *The Return from Parnassus,
Part 2* alleges that Shakespeare has given Jonson a 'purge' (*2
Parnassus*, 4.3.1766–73), he is referring to Jaques in *As You Like
It*. This identification was touched on by C.H. Herford and
Percy Simpson in 1925 (1.28), and developed by Grace Tiffany
in 1994 (Tiffany, 214). However, James Bednarz (2001) claims
that the real purge is directed against Ajax in *Troilus and
Cressida*.[1]

---

1 Bednarz, 32–52; see Bevington, *TC*, 6–11.

One reason for believing that 'Kempe's' allegation relates to Jaques is that *if* Will Kemp played Touchstone he would know that he had offered a reproof which Jaques witnessed, and which fitted Jonson's behaviour, about fighting a duel instead of merely talking about fighting one. On 20 September 1598 Jonson was in a 'duel' with a fellow player, Gabriel Spenser, whom he killed, an event ruefully recorded by Philip Henslowe[1] and alluded to in Dekker's *Satiromastix* (4.3.202–4). Jonson escaped hanging by claiming 'benefit of clergy' – exemption from legal trial and sentence through the reading and translating of the opening of Psalm 51, known colloquially as the 'neck-verse'. If *As You Like It* was involved in the 'purging' of Jonson, Touchstone's excursions on how to avoid duelling with an 'if' (see 5.4.95–101) could be quite specifically levelled at the watching Jaques – a figure with characteristics which some scholars associate with Jonson.

None of these connections is incontrovertible, perhaps because Shakespeare's Jaques is more vital imaginatively than any of the external constituents in his creation. But at the end of the play a particular word may conjure up Jonson: 'I am for other than for dancing measures' (5.4.191), declares the solitary man who has resisted the coupling which takes others to Noah's ark.

A 'measure' is, according to the *OED*, 'a graduated rod, line, tape . . . used by builders, tailors' (*sb.* 4b). Early in 1599 Jonson renewed his association with the Bricklayers' Guild, though whether he actually undertook bricklaying again is questionable.[2] Another meaning of the word is the metre or rhythm of poetry (*OED sb.* 16). Jonson's scorn of 'dancing' measures (the

---

1   Letter from Henslowe to his son-in-law, the actor Edward Alleyn, 26 September 1598, in *Henslowe's Diary*, 285–6 (*Article 24*). A verbatim Latin report by the Middlesex Clerk of the Peace's Memorandum ('the parchment recently discovered in a fragmentary session roll at the Clerkenwell Sesssions House') is reprinted, with translation, in the *Athenaeum*, 6 March 1886 (see 'Ben Jonson'). The document states that Jonson fought with a rapier.

2   See Kathman, 'Apprentices', for the players' use of their Guild associations to further their theatrical activities.

'Measure' was indeed the name of a dance sequence) may also indicate his contempt for inferior verse, such as Sir John Harington's translation of Ariosto's *Orlando Furioso* (see p. 88); his own destiny was as a 'serious' classical writer. The *OED* also lists 'measure' (*sb.* 2e) as a term for the distance between two fencers, quoting *The Two Gentlemen of Verona*: 'Come not within the measure of my wrath' (5.4.125). But the ordinary meaning of 'measure' as a (unit of) measurement (*sb.* 5a) might have reminded the players of Jonson's boast that when he killed Gabriel Spenser his adversary's sword 'was ten inches longer than his'.[1] The *OED* records another usage of the word, as a verb (*v.* 2j), for which *As You Like It* (there dated 1600) provides the first and only example until 1852: 'And so we measured swords and parted' (5.4.86), words which mark Touchstone's finale to his evaded duel. This is not exactly a 'purge'; but it would be possible to read it as an admonition, *if* one so wished.

Another factor in the relation between Shakespeare and Jonson which is highlighted in discussions of the so-called 'War' turns on differences in the type of comedy they write. Both Bednarz and Tiffany see *As You Like It* as a response to Jonson's *Every Man Out* (which they assume to be the earlier play). Bednarz argues that the Shakespearean duo of 'nature' and 'folly' test the Jonsonian partnership of 'art and judgement' (*Poets' War*, 106). Tiffany claims that 'By lampooning mythic romance in *Every Man Out*, Jonson argues the artistic superiority of his new humors drama; conversely, by mocking satire in *AYL*, Shakespeare champions mythic comedy' (216–17). Jonson's attack on Shakespearean romantic comedy is a masculinist stance against the effeminization of comedy, in which an emotional response takes precedence over a rational one. Jonson repeatedly in his plays urges audiences to resist a 'group' response in favour of 'individual' detachment as a condition of critical arbitration:

---

1 'Drummond', ll. 202–3, p. 600, recorded in 1618/19 but no doubt contemporaneous with the event.

When we turn from Asper's stern directives in *Every Man Out*'s induction, which demand the playgoers' mutual disregard, to Rosalind's friendly address to the audience in the epilogue to *AYL*, we encounter their radical antithesis. For through the boy playing Rosalind – himself a kind of hybrid sexual 'monster' (to recall the Scrivener's word from *Bartholomew Fair*) – Shakespeare urges the commingled audience response that Jonson abhors: 'I charge you, O women . . .'

(Tiffany, 218)

Tiffany argues that the basis on which Shakespeare asks for approval of the play is through the shared '*ir*rational erotic sensibility that connects audience members', a phenomenon alien to Jonson and abhorred by him. This difference between the types of audience involvement is significant for understanding the effect of *As You Like It* on audiences. It is perhaps in this identification of crucial difference between Jonson and Shakespeare that the real interest of the 'War of the Theatres' lies.

However, a conviction that *As You Like It* indirectly admonishes Jonson in the person of Jaques seems to misread the tone of the play towards the dissident satirist. There is real regret in the Duke's valediction to the melancholy gentleman who has followed his fortunes to the Forest of Arden, and there is uncertainty that it will be a true farewell, as Jaques agrees to wait on the Duke's further pleasure at his cave.

APPENDIX 4

THE DOUAI MANUSCRIPT

The Douai manuscript (Bm de Douai, Ms 787 Anglais), dating from 1694 and 1695 and held in the Bibliothèque municipale in Douai,[1] is a transcription/adaptation of six of Shakespeare's plays: *Twelfth Night*, *As You Like It*, *The Comedy of Errors*, *Romeo and Juliet*, *Julius Caesar* and *Macbeth*, which are followed by Nathaniel Lee's *Mithridates* (1678), Dryden's *The Indian Emperor* (1667) and Part 2 of William Davenant's *The Siege of Rhodes* (enlarged version, 1663). *As You Like It*, the second play in the volume, though not the second to be transcribed,[2] is dated '169$^{4/5}$ 9° Martij' (fol. 65^{v}) – 9 March 1695, new-style dating.

The entry for the manuscript in the *Catalogue général des manuscrits des bibliothèques publiques* is as follows:

N° 787. 1° « Shakespeare's Twelfth night or What you will; As « you like it; The famous comedy of errors; Romeo and « Juliet; Julius Caesar; Macbeth. » – 2° (Fol. 210) « Nat. Lee's « Mithridates, king of Pontus. » – 3° (Fol. 252) « John Dry- « den's the Indian emperor. » – 4° (Fol. 287) « William Da- « venant's the Siege of Rhode. » – 1694 et 1695.

---

1 Situated south of Lille in the region of the Ardennes. The old name was Douay, changed to Douai in the eighteenth century.

2 Evans, 159; Hedbäck, 3; *Mithridates* is dated 1695. Pierre-Jacques Lamblin writes (private communication): 'On peut remarquer . . . qu'il n'y a pas de cadre de réglure fait au crayon comme dans *TN* et dans *CE*, mais que le copiste a tracé une marge en creusant un léger sillon avec une pointe arrondie (comme le faisaient beaucoup de copistes au Moyen-Âge). Ce petit détail tendrait à lui seul à prouver que les pièces n'ont pas été reliées dans l'ordre chronologique de leur copie.' ('One can notice . . . that there is no ruled frame drawn in pencil as with *TN* and *CE*, but the transcriber has traced a slight groove using a rounded-point tool (as did many transcribers in the Middle Ages). This little detail alone could prove that the plays were not bound in the chronological order of their printing.')

Provient sans doute de l'un des couvents anglais de Douai. G. 740, D. 740.

– Écriture cursive de trente à quarante ligne [*sic*]. – 1° Ces pièces de Shakespeare ont été imprimées dans les Oeuvres de Shakespeare. – 2°, 3°, 4° Idem dans les Oeuvres de Lee, de Dryden et de Davenant. – Bien conservé. Cartonné en parchemin. – 317 feuillets; papier; 220 millimètres sur 170.[1]

(Doubtless originating in one of the English convents [religious foundations] of Douai. G. 740, D 740. Cursive writing on thirty to forty lines. 1. These plays of Shakespeare have been printed in the Works of Shakespeare. 2, 3 and 4 idem in the Works of Lee, Dryden and Davenant. Well preserved. Vellum binding. 317 leaves; paper; 220 millimetres by 170.)

The volume was printed in Béthune in 1697 (Hedbäck, 2). The original binding carries the title 'English Transcripts / Comedys / and / Tragedys / Shakespear / Lee / Dryden / Davenant'. Ann-Mari Hedbäck offers the following bibliographical account:

The scribe has worked, as is usual with manuscripts, with sheets folded once. They are half sheets, and the leaves are the size of a contemporary play quarto in print. As a rule the scribe has used full quires, i.e., gatherings of four half sheets. At the end of a few plays

---

1   *Catalogue général des manuscrits des bibliothèques publiques*, vol. 6: *Manuscrits de la Bibliothèque de Douai*, ed. C. Dehaisnes (1978), 477–8; see Evans, 'Douai'. The manuscript was first noticed by B.M. Wagner in the *TLS* (4 October 1934, 675), but Wagner only knew of it through the entry in the nineteenth-century catalogue of Douai manuscripts (see n. 3, p. 381). On Wagner's authority Alfred Harbage mentioned it in *Annals of English Drama* (1940), and the *Macbeth* transcript was used by Evans himself, from microfilm only, in *Prompt-Books*, I.i.26–7. The manuscript has also been studied by Ann-Mari Hedbäck.

the scribe used gatherings of fewer sheets when he did not need a full quire to finish one transcript . . . *As You Like It* [covers] four full quires and one gathering of three half sheets . . . The scribe ruled the pages of the quires of *Twelfth Night* and similarly those of the third transcription [*CE*]. There are no rules, however, in the quires of the second play [*AYL*] or in those of numbers 4–9 above [*RJ*, *JC*, *Mac*, *Mithridates*, *The Indian Emperor*, *The Siege of Rhodes*].

(Hedbäck, 3)

There are two blank pages between *Twelfth Night* and *As You Like It*. The play ends on fol. 65ᵛ. A list of 'Drammatis Personae' is provided (fol. 32ᵛ; see notes on the List of Roles and Fig. 22).

All the manuscripts have been copied by the same scribe. A second hand, noted by G. Blakemore Evans and identified by Pierre-Jacques Lamblin as that of P.J. Guilmot (librarian in Douai from 1806 to 1834),[1] 'has written on fol. 2ʳ (right margin): "twelfth Night / or, What [of] you Will. / (La Soirée des Rois, / ou ce que vous voudrez.) / Comedie de Shakespear"' (Evans, 'Douai', 159), and has added some stage directions to *TN*, *RJ*, *JC*, and also probably to *CE*, but not to *As You Like It*. Evans suggests that the copy-text behind the manuscripts is the Second Folio (1632), which would account for archaic spelling (159), but also points out that 'there are a number of readings in the transcripts which either return to F1 or anticipate F3 or F4' (160, n. 6). This suggestion is reinforced by Hedbäck, who is less convinced of the F2 origin of the Shakespeare texts, and finds 'a large number of substantive variants which cannot be explained as attempts at modernizing the text or purging it of passages considered improper from a religious or moral aspect. Nor can

---

1 Guilmot 'also annotated the folios 1 and 21 of *Crispe* or *Crispus* in the manuscript Ms 772 Jésuites, Douai' (Lamblin); Evans observes that [of] has been 'scored through in the MS' ('Douai', 159n.).

they be misreadings' (5–6). She draws attention to the precision of the editing in the non-Shakespearean plays, finding 'in one variant in Davenant's *2 The Siege of Rhodes* a "more convincing emendation of a faulty word in the early editions than any of those suggested by later editions"',[1] a phenomenon apparent in one or two cases in *As You Like It*. In the case of *The Comedy of Errors* Evans argues that the Douai manuscript seems to be based on independent manuscript copy (163). The Douai scribe may conceivably have had access to a Restoration text of *As You Like It* (see p. 139).

The finesse with which the very clean text is presented suggests that this scribe was no mere copyist. Although two people may have been involved – a scribe and an 'editor-reviser' – Evans posits for the Shakespearean plays in the volume only one ('Douai', 164; see also Massai, 258). If so, this agent of transmission ought to be considered the first editor of *As You Like It*, anticipating Nicholas Rowe's first edition (1709) by fourteen years. Jonathan Bate has claimed such a role for Edward Ravenscroft's Restoration adaptation of *Titus Andronicus* (1687):

> Even if we wish to retain our faith in the possibility of providing an edition of some kind of 'original' text, whether a version of the author's foul papers or of the promptbook of the play's first performance, then at the very least, if an emendation that seems to recover some feature of that text was first made by a Restoration adaptor, why should the textual apparatuses of scholarly editions continue to ascribe that innovation to Rowe or some other eighteenth-century editor?

> (Bate & Massai, 133)

Bate's principle for adopting on occasion a Ravenscroft emendation on the grounds that it may represent a recovery of an earlier

---

1   Hedbäck, 16, cited in Massai, 258.

reading has been followed in this edition in relation to the Douai manuscript (copied only eight years after Ravenscroft's adaptation).

Particularly interesting anticipations of later editorial readings occur in the Douai manuscript (D) as follows:

1   2.4.1

     F–F4   O *Iupiter*, how merry are my spirits?

     D   Oh Jupiter, how weary are my spirits?

(TLN 784; fol. 41^v)

(Theobald, 1733)

2   1.2.261

     F   But yet indeede the taller is his daughter

     D   and yet indeed the lesser is his daughter

     (TLN 440; fol. 37 $^{\underline{bis}}$ = fol. 37 repeated and noted in MS)

This reading occurs first in the Cambridge Globe edition of 1864. Rowe emended 'taller' to 'shorter' in his third edition of 1714, creating an infelicitous internal rhyme with 'daughter'. By 1695 an Elizabethan use of 'taller' to mean 'boisterous' and 'masculine' may have been lost (see 1.2.261n., and Cam^2, 1.2.224n.), which could account for the change made by the Douai editor-reviser; but he may have had access to a manuscript which used the word 'lesser'.

3   Cases of error (common in F) in the use of pronouns, handled by the Douai editor-reviser in the following ways:

     1.1.104

     F, F2   hee [Celia] would haue followed her exile,

     F3   she would have followed their exile.

     D   she would have followed her exile.

(TLN 110; fol. 34^r)

This example might suggest that F2 is not being used as the copy-text, but nor is F3, because only one alteration ('she' instead of 'hee') has been made.

3.2.142

F–F4　*Helens cheeke, but not his heart,*

D　　　Helens cheek, but not her heart,

(TLN 1343; fol. 47^v)

D's emendation was made in Rowe's first edition (1709), which may reflect a change current in (presumed) Restoration performances of the play.

4　Some further substantive readings from the Douai MS adopted in this edition are:

4.3.56–7

F–F4　*He that brings this loue to thee,*
　　　　Little knowes this Loue in me:

D　　　» He that brings *these lines* to thee,
　　　　» Little knows this love in me.

(TLN 2205–6; fol. 58^r, my emphasis)

William Sidney Walker suggested (in his *Critical Examination of the Text of Shakespeare*, 1860) that F's repetition of '*this loue*' was probably a mistake (1.295); see 4.3.56nn.

4.1.17

F　　　the sundrie contemplation of my trauells,

D　　　the sundry computation of my travels,

(TLN 1934; fol. 54^v)

D's substitution of 'computation' for 'contemplation' (see 4.1.17n.) could not have arisen from religious scruples or propriety, as contemplation is a central part of Catholic worship; the speech is uncensored in the Valladolid Folio (see 3.4.12–16n.). 'Computation', a more difficult reading, may therefore be the older one.

3.2.143–4

F　　　Cleopatra's *Maiestie*;
　　　　Attalanta's *better part*

D   Atalanta's majesty
           Cleopatra's better part

(TLN 1344–5; fol. 47ᵛ)

The editor-reviser seems to have tried here to make some sense of the line 'Attalanta's *better part*', but in assigning it to Cleopatra has not been any more successful than other, later editors.

3.3.99–100

F–F4   'Tis no matter; Ne're a fantastical knaue of them all shal flout me out of my calling.

D   'Tis no matter; Nere a fantasticall knave of em all Shall flout me out of my calling.

(TLN 1706–7; fol. 51ᵛ)

The verse alignment is unique, and is reproduced in the present edition (see 3.3.99–100 and n.).

These examples demonstrate the richness of the Douai text of *As You Like It*.

Performance

There were in Douai four colleges which housed British recusants and educated the children sent abroad by their Catholic families. The English College, known as the Collège des Grands Anglais, was originally set up for training English Catholic priests for return to England to reconvert the country to Catholicism, and its missionary zeal was an important part of its character. Equally important was the Benedictine monastery which housed St Gregory's School for (English) boys, a foundation jointly set up in 1607 by English monks from Valladolid. In the same vicinity was the Collège des Écossais and the Collège des Irlandais. Some teachers in these establishments – and certainly in the Jesuit Collège d'Anchin, the English College and the Benedictine monastery – were peripatetic.[1] Extant records might suggest that children from the same families were educated in both the Benedictine monastery and the English College.[2] The Douai manuscript may have been jointly owned and used by both the English College and the Benedictine monastery.[3]

Many aspects of the manuscript suggest that it was used for performance, and this is supported by *The Douay College Diaries*, written in Latin and accessible in a selective English translation (1911), which span a period of about 150 years from the mid-sixteenth century to the first decade of the eighteenth. The earliest record of an individual performance is dated 26 August 1625:

> Publice in area exhibita fuit a scholaribus *Vita S*[ti] *Eustachii* in theatro, composito M[ro] Grayneo (hic Clarke) rhetoricae professore, quae summopere placuit.
> (*Douay Diaries*, 1.238)

> (In the public area was exhibited by the scholars the *Life of St Eustace* in the theatre, composed by Monsignor Grayne (here Clarke), professor of rhetoric, which gave much pleasure.)

A public performance was apparently given in a 'theatre', suggesting that dramatic performance at the English College was not simply a classroom exercise, but live performance in front of an audience, as in an entry for 1628:

> 17° Augusti, exhibita fuit in area nostra tragaedia de Mauritio Imperatore non sine magna laude, necnon omnium audientum applausu, quam composuit D[ns]

1 The English College reverted, on moving to St Jacques (see p. 382), to the custom of internal lectures on philosophy and theology, where previously students had attended those at the Collège d'Anchin (Milburn, 'Douai to Durham', 19).
2 Another group of English émigrés, the Franciscans known as the English Recollets, also set up their community in Douai, at the new church of St Jacques.
3 The *Catalogue descriptif et raisonné des manuscrits de la bibliothèque de Douai*, ed. H.R. Duthilloeul (librarian of the Bibliothèque municipale, Douai) (Douai, 1846), N° 740, p. 258, differs from the later catalogue in assigning the manuscript to the Benedictine monastery.

Bernardus Wrench (hic Edwardus Damfordus) Poesios Professor; in fine tragaediae adjecta fuit Comaedia, qua peracta, in humanioribus Classibus praemia merentibus dabantur.

(1.270)

(17th August, there was shown in our place the tragedy of the Emperor Mauritius, not without great praise, nor less than the applause of all the listeners, which was composed by Dom. Bernard Wrench (here known as Edward Damford) [assumed names were common because of spies] Professor of Poetry; at the end of which tragedy was added a Comedy, which was presented by the pupils who had achieved the highest merit in Classics and the Humanities.)

'Area nostra' appears to have been a 'theatrical' space for public performance, as was the Salle des Actes in the Jesuit Collège d'Anchin, specially built in 1613 for recitations, debates and dramatic performances (still standing in modern Douai). The English College, soon after moving premises in 1603 from more or less opposite the Collège d'Anchin to a building close to the church of St Jacques, built a new refectory which was used for dramatic performance (Milburn, 'Douai to Durham', 19). On 21 July 1628 the *Douay Diaries* record: 'In Refectorio nostro Tragico-Comedia privatim exhibita fuit' (1.270) ('In our Refectory a tragi-comedy was privately performed'), in contrast to the 'public' performance of the 1625 entry. As in hall staging in Shakespeare's theatre, performances could be given to an audience sitting in the Refectory, which probably, as in the Salle des Actes, had a raised platform at one end. An entry for 23 August 1754 notes that *The Tragedy of Crispus* was acted 'à une heure de l'après-midi pour les dames seulement et le lendemain à la même heure, pour les messieurs seulement' ('at one o'clock in the afternoon for ladies only and the next day at the same time, for gentlemen only'). This performance, open to the public, was followed by a comedy.[1]

Evidence of performance behind the Douai manuscript of *As You Like It* can be deduced from its list of 'Drammatis Personae' (missing in the Folios), from the addition of stage directions, and from the cutting and careful joining of text with suitable interpolations.

The Douai list of 'Drammatis Personae' for *As You Like It* (see Fig. 22) is the earliest in existence, resembling, in its detailed descriptions of characters and their function, the cast lists in F usually ascribed to the scrivener Ralph Crane rather than the less detailed list compiled by Rowe (1709). The Douai editor-reviser distinguishes between Duke Frederick's 'attendants' and Duke Senior's 'Companions', identifies Jaques as a 'melancholly Gentleman', not a lord, and describes Phoebe as 'a shepherdess beloved by Silvius' – comparable to Crane's '*Silvia: beloved of Valentine*' for *The Two Gentlemen of Verona*. Douai's 'Audrey a country Girle' matches Crane's '*Elbow, a simple Constable*' in *Measure for Measure*. Douai names Duke Senior 'Ferdinand Old duke of Burgundy Banish by his Brother', together with 'Frederick his Brother yᵉ Usurper of Burgundy' (comparable to Crane's description of Prospero and Antonio in *The Tempest*). 'Burgundy' for both dukes locates the play in the Ardennes, local to Douai, an emphasis increased by the cutting of 1.1.110–11 (fol. 34ʳ), with its reference to 'old Robin Hood of England'. The name Ferdinand is not used in the text of *As You Like It*, thus paralleling the case of 'Vincentio' for the Duke in Crane's list of actors for *Measure for Measure*. Jaques de Boys is named 'James' in the Douai list, as also at 1.1.5 (fol. 34ʳ), despite the reversion to '2ⁿᵈ Brother' (F '*Second Brother*') at 5.4.148.1. The curious anglicizing of the name avoids confusion with the melancholy

---

1   Douai Ms 772 Jésuites, Douai: *Crispe, Tragédie* (À Douay: Chez Jacques-François Willerval Imprimeur du Roi, 1754).

Jaques, but may also reflect the fact that English boys were playing the parts.

The likenesses between the *As You Like It* list of 'Drammatis Personae' – typical of all the Shakespearean plays in the volume – and Crane's practice could be explained simply by imitation. But there is an interesting correspondence also with Folger MS V.a.73 of *The Merry Wives of Windsor*, dating from *c.* 1660, which has the Douai editor-reviser's spelling of 'Drammatis Personae' as well as detailed descriptions of characters (Mowat, 'Rowe', 316–17). In the case of *Julius Caesar* Evans demonstrated that both the Folger MS V.a.85 and the Douai manuscript were derived from a common manuscript source based on the second Folio.[1] There may conceivably be comparable connections between Folger MS V.a.73 of *Merry Wives* and the Shakespearean plays in the Douai volume.

The Douai manuscript cuts completely 2.5, 5.1 and 5.3 (see p. 139). At 2.7.35–87 all of Jaques's satire disappears, but at 87 three new lines and a stage direction are inserted:

> D. [Duke Senior] Shall we sit down and tast the sweet
> provision bountifull fortune has bestowed on us.
> J. [Jaques] with all my heart my stomack's ready for
> you.
>
> They prepare to eate
Enter Orlando
(fol. 44^r)

The new lines read like Restoration insertions, but they may equally have been inserted by the Douai editor-reviser. At 3.3.5–25 Touchstone's lines on Ovid and poetry are cut, and new lines inserted. Instead of Audrey's question at 3.3.25: 'Would you not have me honest?', Touchstone (always given the SP 'Cl.' in the Douai text) has two new lines after 'some hope thou didst feign'

---

1 Evans, 'Douai', 160–1, and '*JC*'.

(3.3.23–4): 'If thou were [a poet] thou wert not honest; beauty and honesty can never lye coupled' (fol. 51ʳ), replacing lines 26–8. Touchstone's 'horns' speech (44–58) is cut and his interchange with Jaques about marriage (72–85) reduced:

> J. Wᵗ motley dost thou mean to be married [72]. Get
>   thee then to church and have a good priest and be
>   not botched up by such a bungler as this is. [77–81]
> Cl. If we be not well married, I shall have the better
>   excuse to leave my wife hereafter [84–5].
>
> (fol. 51ʳ)

Sir Oliver enters after 'Here comes Sir Oliver' (59), which follows directly on Touchstone's 'Amen' (44), but he has only one line to speak: 'Is there none to give her?' (63) (fol. 51ʳ). Touchstone's 'O sweet Oliver' (91–7) is cut. There are large cuts in Adam's difficult part in 2.3; many risqué jokes and allusions, especially in the speeches of Rosalind and Celia, disappear.[1] In 2.7 and 4.2 texts of the songs are replaced by the SD 'Musicke and Song' (fols 45ᵛ and 57ʳ respectively), suggesting that there may have been separate copy-text for them (see p. 128).

The cuts, by simplifying the language and creating a faster-moving narrative, make the play more manageable for boys to act. The big adult roles of 'Clowne' and 'melancholly Gentleman', which may have been associated in Shakespeare's theatre with particular actors (see Appendix 2), have been scaled down. Satire and the Marprelate controversy disappear, anticipating the text of *As You Like It* which would run in the

---

1 Charles Butler, an old student of the English College before the mid-eighteenth century, wrote in *Reminiscences* (1824) of the propriety demanded in Douai in the early eighteenth century: 'The boys were secluded from the world; every thing that could inflame their imagination or passions was kept at a distance . . . No classic author was put into their hands, from which every passage, describing scenes of love or gallantry, or tending, even in the remotest degree, to inspire them, had not been obliterated . . . Few works of English writers were permitted to be read; none, which had not been similarly expurgated. The consequence was, that a foreign college was the abode of innocence, learning and piety' (C. Butler, 5–6). What a welcome relief even an expurgated Rosalind must have been to the class of (?)1695.

theatre for virtually the next century and a half. But the Douai manuscript may also reflect a tradition of cutting adopted in the Restoration theatre, which possibly derived from the earlier practices of Shakespeare's own theatre (see p. 139).

The Douai editor-reviser has inserted a number of stage directions, also suggestive of performance. At 2.4.40 (fol. 42ʳ) an 'Exeunt' is marked for both Silvius and Corin; Corin re-enters after line 64 (fol. 42ᵛ), an adjustment probably caused by the lack of depth in a proscenium arch stage (at one end of the Refectory) for accommodating separate groups of players (see also 3.2.159 (fol. 37ᵛ) for a plural 'Exeunt' for Touchstone and Corin). At 2.7.167.1 the Douai manuscript contains the earliest example of 'Enter Orlando bearing [F '*with*'] Adam' (fol. 45ʳ). Rosalind's asseverations at 5.2.105–16 carry some SDs, although not as many as in modern texts of the play:

> I will help you if I can (to Sil:) I would love you if I
> could (to Ph:) and I'll marry you if ere I marry woman,
> and I will be married tomorrow. I will content you
> if what pleases you contents you and you shall be
> married tomorrow. As you love Rosalind, meet (to
> Orla:) as you love Phebe meet; (to S) and as I love no
> woman, I'll meet. So fare you well: I have left you
> comands [*sic*].
>
> (fol. 81ᵛ)

The presence of these SDs suggests performance. Rosalind's promise to Orlando, 'I will satisfy you, if ever I satisfied man' (110–11), is cut (perhaps for the reasons of propriety which influenced later editors).

Douai was a town with a thriving theatrical tradition. A manuscript catalogue from the nineteenth century in the Bibliothèque municipale lists plays performed every year between 1562 and 1754, and another volume lists plays right into the nineteenth century.[1] The list begins with Etienne Jodelle, and continues with an impressive roll-call of French classical drama: Robert Garnier, Alexandre Hardy, Georges de Scudéry, Corneille, Molière, Racine and many others. About ten or twelve plays seem to have been performed every year, quite where is not clear, but there was perhaps an earlier theatre on the present site of the remarkable eighteenth-century building, which was bought by the town, presumably having been privately owned by a nobleman. In the 1690s there may have been an eager audience for performances of Shakespeare by pupils at the English College and St Gregory's School.

The Douai manuscript is a fascinating document which has been underused by scholars. It may open a window on Restoration stage practices, themselves perhaps drawing on older theatrical traditions. Behind it is the hand of a highly intelligent reader and early editor of the texts, whose decisions anticipate those of many later editors. Who was this person? How did the manuscript get to Douai? What status ought to be accorded to its insights? This edition cannot answer the many questions raised by the manuscript. Instead, it presents the document as fully as possible from the conviction that here is a source which would repay further research.

---

1 *Catalogue général des manuscrits des bibliothèques publiques des départements*, vol. 41, Mss Nos 1251, 1256.

APPENDIX 5

POLITICAL AFTER-LIVES: VERACINI'S OPERA *ROSALINDA* (1744) AND CHARLES JOHNSON'S *LOVE IN A FOREST* (1723)

Rosalinda, the final opera composed by Francesco Maria Veracini (1690–1768), was premiered in London on 31 January 1744. Ten further performances took place during February and March. The musical score was later lost except for seven arias, published as a collection of *Favourite Songs* in 1744 (*SMC*, 1.113). Shakespeare's characters were reduced to six: Rosalind (Celia), Clelia (Rosalind), Constante (Orlando), Martano (Duke Frederick) and Selvaggio (Duke Senior), with the addition of Clelia's suitor Ernesto; Oliver is briefly mentioned (Hill, 45, 229). In effect the part of Ganymede, Rosalind's disguise role, is played in the opera by Clelia, who disguises herself as a shepherd.

Veracini may possibly have been inspired to adapt *As You Like It* for operatic performance because he had seen Charles Fleetwood's 1741 production of the play at the Theatre Royal, Drury Lane, London. The composer was criticized by the musicologist Charles Burney for basing the final aria of the opera *Rosalinda* on a Scots tune, 'The Lass of Patie's Mill', which had been used by John Gay in *The Beggar's Opera*, performed at Drury Lane in 1742. On 30 September 1742 Veracini had played a violin concerto in the interval of Gay's opera, and he was regularly employed by the Theatre Royal to provide entr'acte music (Hill, 46). Might he have played his violin during the interval at a performance of *As You Like It*, which continued at Drury Lane until 20 May 1741 (Odell, 1.228)? It seems plausible that he saw the production.

The Scots popular song which Veracini incorporated into the last aria of *Rosalinda* may have seemed indecorous in 1744 for a number of reasons. The Jacobite rebellion under Prince Charles Edward broke out in 1745, but can hardly have been unexpected; Veracini had himself been in London in the lead-up to the 1715 rebellion, which Katherine Scheil sees as background to Charles Johnson's adaptation in 1723 of *As You Like It* under the title of *Love in a Forest*. Veracini's librettist for *Rosalinda*, Paolo Rolli (an Italian Catholic like himself), has made the usurper Martano (Duke Frederick) not only a central figure in the opera but also an Italian Catholic, who leads an army and takes Rosalinda hostage. Martano is overwhelmed by Selvaggio (Duke Senior) and his life spared because of Clelia's devotion to Rosalinda (Hill, 230–1). The theme of rightful monarchy and exiled legitimate ruler is, in Veracini's opera, of equal prominence with the love story, and may have made the choice of a Scottish popular song to conclude the drama seem not only tasteless but also politically tactless because of its reminder of the Stuart Catholic sympathies of the Scots.

Charles Johnson's *Love in a Forest*, a free rendering of *As You Like It* with insertions from other Shakespearean comedies, was performed at Drury Lane on 9 January 1723 (and on the five following nights), and was probably a contributing factor to the full-scale revival of Shakespeare's play at the same theatre in 1741. Katherine Scheil has argued that Johnson's version grew from his immersion in the political coffee-house culture of eighteenth-century London, and was influenced by his conviction that theatre should support the government (Scheil 45–6). Johnson had already used *The Taming of the Shrew* in his play *The Cobler of Preston* (1716), which drew on the Jacobite rebellion of the previous year (Scheil, 47). In December 1722 and January 1723 lawless acts by the Blacks (groups of poachers and gentry seen as allied to Jacobite political interests) were reported almost daily, and the Black Act of 1723 by the Hanoverian government 'made it a felony to enter a forest under disguise or with a blackened face and to hunt, wound, or steal deer'. It was plain that the Black Act was an attempt to quell potentially political activity by Catholic Jacobites (Scheil, 51). Scheil demonstrates that some of Johnson's changes to the text of *As You Like It*, particularly in making Duke Senior complicit in Jaques's lament for the wounded deer in 2.1, had the effect of 'increasing support for government intervention in the forests' (54). By contrast, Veracini and Rolli expand the role of the usurper, Martano (Duke Frederick), and his adversary, Selvaggio (Duke Senior); they incorporate Jaques's melancholy into the role of Constante (Orlando), who becomes a figure as much devoted to honour, and the restoration of the rightful ruler, as to love. The opera *Rosalinda*, in its proximity to a second Stuart uprising one year later in 1745, offers – through its Italian Catholic composer and his librettist – a version of Shakespeare's play to answer the Hanoverian perspective of Johnson's adaptation.

The linking of poaching and rebellion which exercised the Hanoverian government gave an establishment slant to Johnson's version of *As You Like It* which, with hindsight, throws light on Shakespeare's own treatment of the exiles' hunting in the Forest. Shakespeare's play taps a political vein present in Elizabethan contemporary controversy about poaching (see 1.3.109n.).[1] Chris Fitter compares the treatment of hunting in *As You Like It*, especially Jaques's lament over the wounded stag, with Andrew Marvell's 'Nymph Complaining for the Death of her Fawn' (written after the beheading of Charles I in 1649) – a poem which he considers a companion piece to Marvell's 'Horatian Ode' in its 'wreathing ironies around regicide as its primary symbolic ground' (Fitter, 194). In an illuminating survey of Renaissance attitudes to hunting in

---

1   Fitter, 196–7; Fitter draws on Manning. See also E.P. Thompson, 64; Stallybrass, 'Liberty', 59–62; R. Wilson, 12.

relation to *As You Like It* Fitter suggests that 'deer hunting culture was . . . saturated in political symbolism' (198). Poaching raids were a form of social and political protest both between opposed members of the gentry and between commoners and aristocrats. Fitter interprets *As You Like It* 4.2, the triumphal bringing home of the slaughtered deer, as an 'exultant ritual of early demotic political transgression' in its 'open celebration of illegally taken deer slain by the outlaws' (207). But he also argues that Jaques's lament for the wounded stag in 2.1 participates in 'anti-authoritarian statements' (200), using the traditional lament of the wounded deer as a means of evading censorship. Fitter links the passage specifically to the suppression of satire in June 1599 (199–200).

If Shakespeare's Forest pastoral masks its own political and social commentary beneath a sylvan disguise, its subtle and discreet involvement nevertheless continues to be a part of later perceptions of *As You Like It*. The beheading of Charles I in 1649, the Jacobite rebellions of 1715 and 1745, and the exile of the Pretender, Prince Charles Edward, all have a place in its subsequent history. The uprising of 1715 forms part of the background to Johnson's adaptation of *As You Like It* in 1723. Veracini's opera, both in its time of playing (1744, one year before the 1745 rebellion), in its use of the contentious popular Scottish song from *The Beggar's Opera*, and in its reworking of Shakespeare's plot to foreground the struggle between the usurper and the legitimate monarch, belongs to the same narrative in the play's rich after-life.

ABBREVIATIONS AND REFERENCES

Throughout this edition, quotations from the First Folio are reproduced as closely as possible to the original, except that the long 's' is reduced. Quotations and references to Shakespeare plays other than *As You Like It* are from *The Arden Shakespeare Third Series*, where they exist as of this date; other quotations are from *The Arden Shakespeare: Complete Works*, ed. Richard Proudfoot, Ann Thompson and David Scott Kastan, rev. edn (2001). In all references, place of publication is London unless otherwise stated.

ABBREVIATIONS

ABBREVIATIONS USED IN NOTES

c	corrected state
conj.	conjectured by
edn	edition
Fc	corrected state of F
Fr.	French
Fu	uncorrected state of F
It.	Italian
Lat.	Latin
ms/MS	manuscript ('ms' in textual notes only)
n., nn.	note, notes
n.d.	no date
n.s.	new series
om.	omitted in
opp.	opposite
Q	Quarto
SD	stage direction
sig., sigs	signature, signatures
SP	speech prefix
subst.	substantially
this edn	a reading adopted for the first time in this edition
TLN	through line numbering in *The Norton Facsimile: The First Folio of Shakespeare*, prepared by Charlton Hinman (New York, 1968)

t.n.	textual note
( )	enclosing a reading in the textual notes indicates original spelling; enclosing an editor's or scholar's name indicates a conjectural reading
*	precedes commentary notes on readings which substantively emend F

WORKS BY AND PARTLY BY SHAKESPEARE

AC	*Antony and Cleopatra*
AW	*All's Well That Ends Well*
AYL	*As You Like It*
CE	*Comedy of Errors*
Cor	*Coriolanus*
Cym	*Cymbeline*
E3	*King Edward III*
Ham	*Hamlet*
1H4	*King Henry IV, Part 1*
2H4	*King Henry IV, Part 2*
H5	*King Henry V*
1H6	*King Henry VI, Part 1*
2H6	*King Henry VI, Part 2*
3H6	*King Henry VI, Part 3*
H8	*King Henry VIII*
JC	*Julius Caesar*
KJ	*King John*
KL	*King Lear*
LC	*A Lover's Complaint*
LLL	*Love's Lavour's Lost*
Luc	*The Rape of Lucrece*
MA	*Much Ado about Nothing*
Mac	*Macbeth*
MM	*Measure for Measure*
MND	*A Midsummer Night's Dream*
MV	*The Merchant of Venice*
MW	*The Merry Wives of Windsor*
Oth	*Othello*
Per	*Pericles*
PP	*The Passionate Pilgrim*
PT	*The Phoenix and Turtle*
R2	*King Richard II*
R3	*King Richard III*
RJ	*Romeo and Juliet*
Son	*Sonnets*

STM	*Sir Thomas More*
TC	*Troilus and Cressida*
Tem	*The Tempest*
TGV	*The Two Gentlemen of Verona*
Tim	*Timon of Athens*
Tit	*Titus Andronicus*
TN	*Twelfth Night*
TNK	*The Two Noble Kinsmen*
TS	*The Taming of the Shrew*
VA	*Venus and Adonis*
WT	*The Winter's Tale*

REFERENCES

EDITIONS OF SHAKESPEARE COLLATED

This section includes entries for scholars whose names appear in the textual notes as contributors to a listed edition.

Alexander	*William Shakespeare: The Complete Works*, ed. Peter Alexander (1951)
Andrews	*As You Like It*, ed. John F. Andrews and Michael Kahn, Everyman (1997)
Ard¹	*As You Like It*, ed. J.W. Holme, Arden Shakespeare (1914)
Ard²	*As You Like It*, ed. Agnes Latham, Arden Shakespeare (1975)
Bevington	*As You Like It*, ed. David Bevington (New York, 1988)
Boswell-Malone	*Plays and Poems*, ed. James Boswell, 21 vols (1821)
Brennecke	See under 'Other works cited: Other works'
Caldecott	Thomas Caldecott, *Hamlet and As You Like It* (1819; edition cited 1832)
Cam	*Works*, ed. William George Clark, John Glover and William Aldis Wright, 9 vols (Cambridge, 1863–6)
Cam¹	*As You Like It*, ed. Arthur Quiller-Couch and John Dover Wilson (Cambridge, 1926)
Cam²	*As You Like It*, ed. Michael Hattaway (Cambridge, 2000)
Capell	*Comedies, Histories, and Tragedies*, ed. Edward Capell, 10 vols (1767–8)
Collier	*Works*, ed. John Payne Collier, 8 vols (1842–4); includes manuscript annotations once thought to be by an 'Old Corrector' but probably by Collier, in Collier's copy (the Perkins–Collier–Devonshire copy of F2 in the Huntington Library), and entered by Collier in his own copy of the first of his editions, now in the Folger Shakespeare Library
Collier²	*Plays*, ed. John Payne Collier (1853)

Cowden Clarke	*Plays*, ed. Charles and Mary Cowden Clarke, Cassell's Illustrated Shakespeare, 3 vols (1874–8)
Craig	*Comedies*, ed. W.J. Craig, introductions by Algernon Charles Swinburne and Edward Dowden (Oxford, 1911)
Douai ms/MS	See under 'Other works cited: Manuscripts'
Douce	Francis Douce, contributor to Var 1793
Dowden	*As You Like It*, ed. Edward Dowden, International Shakespeare (1887)
Duffin	See Duffin, *Songbook*, under 'Other works cited: Other works'
Dyce	*Works*, ed. Alexander Dyce, 6 vols (1857)
Dyce²	*Works*, ed. Alexander Dyce, 6 vols (1863–7)
Dyce³	*Works*, ed. Alexander Dyce, 9 vols (1875–6)
F	*Comedies, Histories and Tragedies*, The First Folio (1623)
F2	*Comedies, Histories and Tragedies*, The Second Folio (1632)
F3	*Comedies, Histories and Tragedies*, The Third Folio (1664)
F4	*Comedies, Histories and Tragedies*, The Fourth Folio (1685)
Folger	*As You Like It*, ed. Barbara Mowat and Paul Werstine, New Folger Library Shakespeare (New York, 1997)
Furness	See Var 1890
Gargàno	W. Shakespeare, *A Piacer Vostro* (*As You Like It*), Testo riveduto, con versione a fronte, introduzione e commento a cura di G.S. Gargàno, nuova tiratura (Florence, 1947)
Gilman	*As You Like It*, ed. Albert Gilman, Signet (1963)
Globe	*The Works of Shakespeare*, ed. William George Clark and William Aldis Wright (Cambridge, 1864)
Halliwell	*Works*, ed. James O. Halliwell, 16 vols (1853–65)
Hanmer	*Works*, ed. Thomas Hanmer, 6 vols (1743–4)
Hanmer²	*Works*, ed. Thomas Hanmer, 6 vols (Oxford, 1771)
Heath	[Benjamin Heath], *A Revisal of Shakespeare's Text* (1765)
Hudson	*Works*, ed. Henry N. Hudson, 11 vols (Boston and Cambridge, Mass., 1851–6)
Hudson²	*Works*, ed. Henry N. Hudson, Harvard edn, 20 vols (Boston, 1880–1)
Johnson	*Plays*, ed. Samuel Johnson, 8 vols (1765)
Johnson²	*Plays*, ed. Samuel Johnson, 8 vols [2nd issue] (1765)
Jourdain	See under 'Other works cited: Other works'
Keightley	*Plays*, ed. Thomas Keightley, 6 vols (1864)
Kittredge	*As You Like It*, ed. George Kittredge (Boston, 1939)
Knight²	*Comedies, Histories, Tragedies, & Poems*, ed. Charles Knight, 12 vols, 2nd edn (1842–4)
Knowles	*As You Like It*, ed. Richard Knowles, New Variorum edn (New York, 1977)
Langford	*As You Like It*, ed. W.F. Langford, *Canadian Swan Shakespeare* (Toronto, 1964)

Lettsom	William Nanson Lettsom, contributor to Cam (1863) and editor of Walker
L.H.	Contributor to Theobald
Malone	*Plays and Poems*, ed. Edmond Malone, 10 vols (1790)
Marshall	*As You Like It*, ed. Cynthia Marshall (Cambridge, 2004)
Mason	John M[onck] Mason, *Comments on the Last Edition of Shakespeare's Plays* (1785)
Moberley	*As You Like It*, ed. Charles E. Moberley, Rugby edn (1872, first edn 1868)
Neil	*As You Like It*, ed. Samuel Neil, Collins School and College Shakespeare (1876)
Oliver	*As You Like It*, ed. H.J. Oliver, New Penguin Shakespeare (Harmondsworth, England, 1968)
Oxf	*Complete Works*, ed. Stanley Wells and Gary Taylor (Oxford, 1986)
Oxf[1]	*As You Like It*, ed. Alan Brissenden (Oxford, 1993)
Pinkerton	See under 'Other works cited: Other works'
Pope	*Works*, ed. Alexander Pope, 6 vols (1723–5)
Rann	*Dramatic Works*, ed. Joseph Rann, 6 vols (Oxford, 1786–[94])
Reed	*Plays*, ed. Isaac Reed, 21 vols (1803)
Ridley	*As You Like It*, ed. M.R. Ridley, New Temple (1934)
Ritson	Joseph Ritson, contributor to Var 1793
Riv	*The Riverside Shakespeare*, ed. G. Blakemore Evans (Boston, 1974)
Riv[2]	*The Riverside Shakespeare*, ed. G. Blakemore Evans, 2nd edn (Boston, 1997)
Robson	William Robson, contributor to Dyce[2]
Rowe	*Works*, ed. Nicholas Rowe, 7 vols (1709)
Rowe[2]	*Works*, ed. Nicholas Rowe, 7 vols [2nd edn] (1709)
Rowe[3]	*Works*, ed. Nicholas Rowe, 7 vols (1714)
Scott	Sir Walter Scott, conjecture in introduction to *Quentin Durward* (1823), recorded in Dyce[2]
Singer	*Dramatic Works*, ed. Samuel W. Singer, 10 vols (1826)
Singer[2]	*Dramatic Works*, ed. Samuel W. Singer, 10 vols (1856)
Sisson	*Works*, ed. Charles Jasper Sisson (1954)
Spedding	James Spedding, contributor to Cam
Staunton	*Plays*, ed. Howard Staunton, 3 vols (1858–60)
Steevens	*The Plays of William Shakespeare*, ed. George Steevens (1811)
Theobald	*Works*, ed. Lewis Theobald, 7 vols (1733)
Theobald[2]	*Works*, ed. Lewis Theobald, 8 vols (1740)
Theobald[3]	*Works*, ed. Lewis Theobald, 8 vols (1752)
Theobald[4]	*Works*, ed. Lewis Theobald, 8 vols (1757)

Theobald 1741	*As You Like It*: a comedy, as it is acted at the Theatre-Royal in Aungier-Street, Dublin (text based on Theobald and used in performance) (Dublin, 1741)
Thirlby	Styan Thirlby, manuscript annotations in a copy of Warburton
Tollet	George Tollet, contributor to Var 1778
Tucker & Holden	*As You Like It*, ed. Patrick Tucker and Michael Holden, Shakespeare's Globe Acting Edition (1991)
Upton	See under 'Other works cited: Other works'
Var 1773	*Plays*, ed. Samuel Johnson & George Steevens, 10 vols (1773)
Var 1778	*Plays*, ed. Samuel Johnson & George Steevens, 10 vols (1778)
Var 1785	*Plays*, ed. Samuel Johnson, George Steevens, and Isaac Reed, 10 vols (1785)
Var 1793	Plays, ed. George Steevens and Isaac Reed, 15 vols (1793)
Var 1890	*As You Like It*, ed. Horace Howard Furness, New Variorum Edition (Philadelphia, 1890)
Verity	*As You Like It*, ed. A. Wilson Verity, in *Works*, ed. Henry Irving and Frank Marshall, Henry Irving Shakespeare, 8 vols (1888–90)
Walker	William Sidney Walker, *A Critical Examination of the Text of Shakespeare*, ed. W. Nanson Lettsom, 3 vols (1860)
Warburton	*Works*, ed. William Warburton, 8 vols (1747)
Warwick	*As You Like It*, ed. J.C. Smith, Warwick Shakespeare (London and Glasgow, 1894)
White	*Works*, ed. Richard Grant White, 12 vols (1857–66)
Wright	*As You Like It*, ed. William Aldis Wright (Oxford, 1876)

OTHER WORKS CITED

Manuscripts

Adv. MS	NLS Advocates MS 5.2.14. Manuscript of Thomas Morley, 'It was a lover and his lass' (National Library of Scotland)
Adv.b.8.1	John Harington, a scribal MS of epigrams bound in with *OF* (1600), fols 2–30; Cambridge University Library
BL Add MS	British Library Additional Manuscript
Cambridge MS Dd.2.11	A compilation of songs and pieces [1600], some of which appear in the *Fitzwilliam Virginal Book*
Cambridge MS Dd.5.75	Commonplace book of Henry Stanford [*c.* 1600]
Douai ms/MS	Bm de Douai, Ms 787 Anglais. Manuscript transcript of *As You Like It*, dated 169$^{4/5}$, bound in with five other Shakespeare plays and mid-seventeenth-century dramas (Bibliothèque municipale de Douai)

Essex, 'Original Letters'	The Hulton Papers. BL Add MS 74286. ORIGINAL LETTERS from Robert Dudley, Earl of Leicester and Robert Devereux, Earl of Essex to QUEEN ELIZABETH. See Other works, Beal
Essex, 'Two Letters'	BL Add MS 48126. Two Letters. Robert Devereux, 2nd Earl of Essex, and Thomas Egerton, Lord Keeper [1598]
Macklin	Charles Macklin, partbook for Touchstone, Drury Lane, October 15, 1741 (Folger S.a.25); see Fleetwood, 1741
PRO	Public Record Office, Kew
PRO LC 5/12	A Catalogue of part of his Maties Servants Playes as they were formerly acted at the Blackfryers & now allowed of to his Maties Servants at ye New Theatre (1669) [margin: Playes Acted at the Theatre Royall]
PRO E351/543	Document in the Declared Accounts of the Treasurer of the Chamber (1599)
PRO E351/3223	Document in the Declared Accounts of the Office of Works (1588)
PRO E351/3230	Document in the Declared Accounts of the Office of Works (1595–6)
PRO E351/3234	Document in the Declared Accounts of the Office of Works (1598–9)

Other works

Abbott	E.A. Abbott, *A Shakespearian Grammar* (1873)
Adams, *Tables*	Francis Adams, *Writing Tables* (1594)
Almond	[Anon; Lyly?], *An Almond for a Parrot, Or Cuthbert Curry-knave's Alms* (1589), in Nashe
Altick	Richard D. Altick, *Paintings from Books: Art and Literature in Britain, 1760–1900* (Columbus, Ohio, 1985)
Arber	*A Transcript of the Registers of the Company of Stationers of London*, ed. Edward Arber, 5 vols (1875–94)
Ariosto	See Harington, *OF*
Aristotle, *Ethics*	Aristotle, *The Nicomachean Ethics*, in *The Rhetoric, Poetic, and Nicomachean Ethics of Aristotle*, trans. Thomas Taylor, 2 vols (1818)
Armin, *Fool*	Robert Armin, *Fool upon Fool or Six Sorts of Sots* (1600), in *The Collected Works of Robert Armin*, introduced by J.P. Feather, 2 vols (New York, 1972)
Arthur	Julia Arthur, *As You Like It* (promptbook) (New York and London, 1899)
Ascham	Roger Ascham, *The Schoolmaster* (1570), ed. Edward Arber (1923)
Astington	John H. Astington, *English Court Theatre 1558–1642* (Cambridge, 1999)
Auerbach	Nina Auerbach, *Ellen Terry, Player in Her Time* (1987)

Augustine, *City*	St Augustine, *The City of God*, trans. Henry Bettenson (Harmondsworth, England, 1984)
Axton	Marie Axton, *The Queen's Two Bodies* (1977)
Bacon, *Advancement*	Francis Bacon, *The Advancement of Learning* (1605), ed. G.W. Kitchin (1973)
Bacon, *Essays*	*The Essays or Counsels, Civil and Moral, of Francis, Lord Verulam, Viscount St. Alban* (1625)
Bald	R.C. Bald, 'Will, my Lord of Leicester's jesting player', *N&Q*, 204 (1959), 112
Baldwin, *Company*	T.W. Baldwin, *The Organization and Personnel of the Shakespearean Company* (Princeton, NJ, 1927)
Baldwin, *Evidence*	T.W. Baldwin, *Shakespeare's Love's Labor's Won: New Evidence from the Account Books of an Elizabethan Bookseller* (Carbondale, Ill., 1957); reviewed by G.K. Hunter, *RES*, n.s. 10 (1959), 412–13
Barlement	Noel van Barlement, *Colloquia et Dictionariolum Septem Linguarum* (Antwerp, 1586, reprinted 1598)
Barnaby	Andrew Barnaby, 'The political conscious of Shakespeare's *As You Like It*', *SEL 1500–1900*, 36 (1996), 373–95
Barnfield, *Shepherd*	Richard Barnfield, *The Affectionate Shepherd* (1594), ed. James Orchard Halliwell (1845)
Barroll	Leeds Barroll, *Politics, Plague and Shakespeare's Theater: The Stuart Years* (Ithaca, NY, 1991)
Barton, 'Parks and Ardens'	Anne Barton, 'Parks and Ardens', in *Essays, Mainly Shakespearean* (Cambridge, 1994), 352–79
Barton, 'King'	Anne Barton, 'The king disguised: Shakespeare's *Henry V* and the comical history' (1975), in *Essays, Mainly Shakespearean* (Cambridge, 1994), 207–33
Barton, 'Staging'	Anne Barton, 'Staging the Forest' and 'Let the Forest Judge', Clark lectures (2003), in *Shakespeare and the Forest* (Cambridge, forthcoming)
Baskervill	Charles Read Baskervill, *The Elizabethan Jig* (New York, 1965)
Bate	Jonathan Bate, *Shakespeare and Ovid* (Oxford 1993)
Bate & Massai	Jonathan Bate and Sonia Massai, 'Adaptation as edition', in D.C. Greetham (ed.), *The Margins of Text* (Ann Arbor, Mich., 1997), 129–51
Bath	Michael Bath, 'Weeping stags and melancholy lovers: the iconography of *As You Like It*, II. i', *Emblematica*, 1 (1986), 13–52
BCP	*The Book of Common Prayer* (1549: two differently paginated editions)
Beal	Peter Beal, *Elizabeth and Essex: The Hulton Papers* (Sotheby's Catalogue, 1992); see Essex, 'Original Letters' (Other works cited: Manuscripts)

Bednarz	James P. Bednarz, *Shakespeare and the Poets' War* (2001)
Bellard-Thomson	Carol Bellard-Thomson, 'Rabelais and obscenity, a woman's view', in Helen Wilcox, Keith McWatters, Ann Thompson and Linda R. Williams (eds), *The Body and the Text: Hélène Cixous, Reading and Teaching* (New York, 1990), 164–74
Belsey	Catherine Belsey, 'Disrupting sexual difference: meaning and gender in the comedies', in *Alternative Shakespeares*, ed. J. Drakakis (1985), 166–90
'Ben Jonson'	[Anon.], 'Ben Jonson convicted of felony', *Athenaeum*, no. 3045, 6 March 1886, 337–8
Benson	Lady [Constance] Benson, *Mainly Players* (1926)
Berry, *Hunt*	Edward Berry, *Shakespeare and the Hunt* (Cambridge, 2001)
Berry, 'Rosalynde'	Edward Berry, 'Rosalynde and Rosalind', *SQ*, 31 (1980), 42–52
Berry, P.	Philippa Berry, *Of Chastity and Power: Elizabethan Literature and the Unmarried Queen* (1989)
Bevington, *AC*	*Antony and Cleopatra*, ed. David Bevington (Cambridge, 1990)
Bevington, 'Review'	David Bevington, review of Donaldson, *Magic*, *BJJ*, 5 (1998), 317–20
Bevington, *TC*	*Troilus and Cressida*, ed. David Bevington, Arden Shakespeare, 3rd series (1998)
Bevington, *Tudor Drama*	David Bevington, *Tudor Drama and Politics* (Cambridge, Mass., 1968)
Bevington & Rasmussen	*Tamburlaine, Parts I and II, Doctor Faustus, A- and B-Texts, The Jew of Malta, Edward II*, ed. David Bevington and Eric Rasmussen (Oxford, 1995)
Bible	See Great Bible, Bishops' Bible, Geneva Bible
Billington, '*AYL*'	Michael Billington, '*As You Like It*', *Guardian*, 20 August 2003
Billington, 'Beggars'	Michael Billington, 'Beggars and choosers', *Guardian*, 23 April 1992
Birch	*Memoirs of the Reign of Elizabeth*, ed. Thomas Birch, 2 vols (1754)
Bishops' Bible	*The Holy Bible* (1568)
BJJ	*Ben Jonson Journal*
Black Books	*The Records of the Honorable Society of Lincoln's Inn, The Black Books*, 2 vols, vol 1: 1422–1586 (1897)
Blayney, *Folio*	Peter W.M. Blayney, *The First Folio of Shakespeare* (Washington, DC, 1991)
Blayney, 'Playbooks'	Peter Blayney, 'The publication of playbooks', in Cox & Kastan, 383–422

Boaden	James Boaden, *Memoirs of Mrs Siddons*, 2 vols (1827)
Boose	Linda E. Boose, 'The 1599 Bishops' ban, Elizabethan pornography, and the sexualization of the Jacobean stage', in Richard Burt and John Michael Archer (eds), *Enclosure Acts, Sexuality, Property, and Culture in Early Modern England* (Ithaca, NY, 1994), 185–200
Bowers, 'Rebellion'	Fredson Bowers, 'Essex's rebellion and Dekker's *Old Fortunatus*', *RES*, n.s. 3 (1952), 365–6
Bowers, 'Authority'	Fredson Bowers, 'Authority, copy, and transmission in Shakespeare's texts', in Georgiana Ziegler (ed.), *Shakespeare Study Today* (New York, 1986), 7–36
Bradley	David Bradley, *From Text to Performance* (Cambridge, 1992)
Brathwait, *Art Asleep?*	Richard Brathwait, *Art Asleep Husband? A Boulster Lecture by Philogenes Panedorium* (1640)
Bredvold	L.I. Bredvold, 'The naturalism of Donne in relation to some Renaissance traditions', *JEGP*, 22 (1923), 471–502
Brennecke	Ernest E. Brennecke, Jr., '"What shall he have that killed the deer?" A note on Shakespeare's lyric and its music', *Musical Times*, 93 (1952), 347–51
Breton, *Pasquill's Pass*	Nicholas Breton, *Pasquill's Pass, and Passeth Not* (1600), in *The Works of Nicholas Breton*, ed. A.B. Grosart, 2 vols (Blackburn, England, 1879)
Breton, '*Praise*'	Nicholas Breton, '*The Praise of Virtuous Ladies*' (1599), fifth discourse in *Will of Wit*
Breton, *Will of Wit*	Nicholas Breton, *The Will of Wit, Wit's Will, or Will's Wit, choose you whether* (1599), ed. James O. Halliwell (1860; first edition 1597)
Brinkley	Roberta Florence Brinkley, *Nathan Field* (New Haven, Conn., 1928)
Bristol	Michael D. Bristol, *Carnival and Theater: Plebeian Culture and the Structure of Authority in Renaissance England* (New York, 1985)
Brown, D.	D. Brown, 'Thomas Morley and the Catholics: some speculations', *Monthly Musical Record*, 89 (March–April 1959), 53–61
Brown, H.	Huntington Brown, *Rabelais in English Literature* (Cambridge, Mass., 1933)
Bruce	J. Bruce, 'Description of a pocket dial made in 1593 for Robert Devereux, earl of Essex', *Archaeologia*, 90 (1866), 343–56
Bruster	Douglas Bruster, 'In a woman's key: women's speech and women's language in Renaissance drama', *Exemplaria*, 4 (1992), 235–66
Bullough	Geoffrey Bullough, *Narrative and Dramatic Sources of Shakespeare*, 8 vols (1957–75)

Bulman, 'Gay theater'	James C. Bulman, 'Bringing Cheek By Jowl's *As You Like It* out of the closet: the politics of gay theater', *Shakespeare Bulletin*, 22 (2004), 31–46
Bulman, *Performance*	*Shakespeare, Theory, and Performance*, ed. James C. Bulman (1996)
Burton	Robert Burton, *The Anatomy of Melancholy* (1620), ed. Holbrook Jackson (1932)
Butler, C.	Charles Butler, *Reminiscences* (1824)
Butler, J.	Judith Butler, *Gender Trouble: Feminism and the Subversion of Identity* (1995)
Butler, M.	Martin Butler, 'Jonson's *News from the New World*, the "Running Masque," and the season of 1619–20', *MRDE*, 6 (1993), 153–78
Byrne	Sr. St Geraldine Byrne, *Shakespeare's Use of the Pronoun of Address: Its Significance in Characterization and Motivation* (Washington, DC, 1936)
Callaghan, 'Buzz Goodbody'	Dympna Callaghan, 'Buzz Goodbody: directing for change', in Jean Marsden (ed.), *The Appropriation of Shakespeare: Post-Renaissance Reconstructions of the Works and the Myth* (New York, 1991), 163–81
Callaghan, *Feminist*	*A Feminist Companion to Shakespeare*, ed. Dympna Callaghan (Oxford, 2000)
Callaghan, *Women*	Dympna Callaghan, *Shakespeare Without Women: Representing Gender and Race on the Renaissance Stage* (2000)
Calvin	John Calvin, *Institutes of the Christian Religion*, ed. John T. McNeill, trans. Ford Lewis Battles (1961)
Calvo, 'Celia'	Clara Calvo, 'In defence of Celia: discourse analysis and women's discourse in *As You Like It*', *Essays and Studies*, 47 (1994), 91–115
Calvo, 'Pronouns'	Clara Calvo, 'Pronouns of address and social negotiation in *As You Like It*', *Language and Literature*, 1 (1992), 5–27
Capell, *Notes*	Edward Capell, *Notes and Various Readings to Shakespeare*, 3 vols (1779–83; vol. 1 also issued separately 1774)
Capp, 'Arson'	Bernard Capp, 'Arson, threats of arson, and incivility in Early Modern England', in Peter Burke, Brian Harrison and Paul Slack (eds), *Civil Histories: Essays in Honour of Keith Thomas* (Oxford, 2000), 197–213
Capp, *Gossips*	Bernard Capp, *Where Gossips Meet: Women, Family, and Neighbourhood in Early Modern England* (Oxford, 2003)
Carlisle	Carol J. Carlisle, 'Helen Faucit's Rosalind', *SSt*, 12 (1979), 65–94
Carlson, L.	Leland H. Carlson, 'Martin Marprelate: his identity and his satire', in Leland H. Carlson and Ronald Paulson, *English Satire* (Los Angeles, 1972), 3–53

Carlson, S.	Susan Carlson, 'Women in *As You Like It*: community, change, and choice', *Essays in Literature*, 14 (1987), 157–69
Cave, *Cornucopian*	Terence Cave, *The Cornucopian Text: Problems of Writing in the French Renaissance* (Oxford, 1979)
Cave, *Pré-Histoires*	Terence Cave, *Pré-Histoires: Textes troublés au seuil de la modernité* (Geneva, 1999)
Cawdrey, *Table*	Robert Cawdrey, *A Table Alphabetical of Hard Usual English Words* (1604), introduction by Robert A. Peters (Gainesville, Fla., 1966)
Cercignani	Fausto Cercignani, *Shakespeare's Works and Elizabethan Pronunciation* (Oxford, 1981)
Chamberlain, *Letters*	*Letters of John Chamberlain*, ed. Sarah Williams, Camden Society (1861)
Chambers, *ES*	Sir Edmund Chambers, *The Elizabethan Stage*, 4 vols (Oxford, 1923)
Chambers, *MS*	E.K. Chambers, *The Medieval Stage*, 2 vols (Oxford, 1903)
Chambers, *WS*	E.K. Chambers, *William Shakespeare: A Study of Facts and Problems*, 2 vols (Oxford, 1930)
Chan	Mary Chan, *Music in the Theatre of Ben Jonson* (Oxford, 1980)
Chapman	Translation of Homer: see Homer/Chapman
Chapman, *Masque*	George Chapman, *The Memorable Masque of the Two Honourable Houses or Inns of Court; the Middle Temple and Lincoln's Inn* (1613)
Chaucer	*The Works of Geoffrey Chaucer*, ed. Thomas Speght (1598)
Chaucer, 'Knight'	Geoffrey Chaucer, 'The Knight's Tale', *The Canterbury Tales*, in Chaucer
Chaucer, 'Merchant'	Geoffrey Chaucer, 'The Merchant's Tale', *The Canterbury Tales*, in Chaucer
Chaucer, 'Nun's Priest'	Geoffrey Chaucer, 'The Nun's Priest's Tale', *The Canterbury Tales*, in Chaucer
Chaucer, 'Wife of Bath'	Geoffrey Chaucer, 'The Wife of Bath's Tale', *The Canterbury Tales*, in Chaucer
Chaudhuri	Sukanta Chaudhuri, *Renaissance Pastoral and Its English Developments* (Oxford, 1989)
Clare	Janet Clare, *Drama of the English Republic, 1649–60* (Manchester, 1988)
Clark	Alice Clark, *The Working Life of Women in the Seventeenth Century*, ed. Amy Louise Erickson (1992)
Clegg	Cyndia Susan Clegg, 'Liberty, license, and authority: press censorship and Shakespeare', in Kastan, *Companion*, 464–85
Coleman	D. Coleman, 'Montaigne's "Sur des vers de Virgile"', in Peter Sharratt (ed.), *French Renaissance Studies 1540–70* (Edinburgh, 1976), 137–40

Colie	Rosalie Colie, *Paradoxia Epidemmica*: *The Renaissance Tradition of Paradox* (Princeton, NJ, 1966)
Colvin	H.M. Colvin, *The History of the King's Works*, 6 vols (1963–82)
Cooper, H.	Helen Cooper, 'Did Shakespeare play the Clown?', *TLS*, 20 April (2001), 26–7
Cooper, *Thesaurus*	Thomas Cooper, *Thesaurus* (1578)
Cornwallis	Sir William Cornwallis, *Essays* (1600; edition cited 1606)
Cox & Kastan	*A New History of Early English Drama 1590–1642*, ed. John D. Cox and David Scott Kastan (Cambridge, 1997)
Craik	*King Henry V*, ed. T.W. Craik, Arden Shakespeare, 3rd series (1995)
Cressy	David Cressy, *Bonfires and Bells: National Memory and the Protestant Calendar in Elizabethan and Stuart England* (1989)
Crunelle-Vanrigh	Anny Crunelle-Vanrigh, '"What a case am I in then", Hymen and Limen in *As You Like It*', *Q-W-E-R-T-Y*, 7 (1997), 5–14
Cuffe, *Ages*	Henry Cuffe, *The Differences of the Ages of Man's Life* (1600; edition cited 1607)
Daley	A. Stuart Daley, 'Where are the woods in *AYL*?' *SQ*, 34 (1983), 172–80
Daly	Augustin Daly, *As You Like It*, promptbook for the production at Daly's Theatre, 17 December 1889, privately printed (New York, 1890)
Daniel, *Praise*	Samuel Daniel, *The Praise of Private Life*, a translation of Petrarch's *De Vita Solitaria* (1603, previously thought to be Harington's translation), in Harington, *Letters*
Daniel, *Queen's Arcadia*	Samuel Daniel, *The Queen's Arcadia: A Pastoral Trago-Comedy* (1606)
Dart, 'Catholics'	R. Thurston Dart, 'Morley and the Catholics: some further speculations', *Monthly Musical Record*, 89 (May–June 1959), 89–92
Dart, *Consort*	R. Thurston Dart, 'Morley's *Consort Lessons* of 1599', *Proceedings of the Royal Music Association*, 74 (1947–48), 1–9
Davies, *Nosce Teipsum*	Sir John Davies, *Nosce Teipsum* (1599; edition cited 1622)
Day, *Bees*	John Day, *The Parliament of Bees*, in Day, *Works*, vol. 1
Day, *Travels*	John Day, *The Travels of Three English Brothers* (1602), in Day, *Works*, vol. 2
Day, *Works*	*The Works of John Day*, ed. A.H. Bullen, 2 vols (1881)
Dean	Paul Dean, '"Comfortable doctrine": *Twelfth Night* and the Trinity', *RES*, n.s. 52 (2001), 500–16

de Grazia	Margreta de Grazia, *Shakespeare Verbatim: The Reproduction of Authenticity and the 1790 Apparatus* (Oxford, 1991)
Dekker, *Lantern*	Thomas Dekker, *Villainies Discovered by Lantern and Candlelight and the help of a New Crier called O per se O with Canting Songs never before printed* (1608; edition cited 1616)
Dekker, *Old Fortunatus*	Thomas Dekker, *Old Fortunatus* (1600), in Dekker, *Works*, vol. 4
Dekker, *Satiromastix*	Thomas Dekker, *Satiromastix* (1602), in Dekker, *Works*, vol. 1
Dekker, *Shoemaker's*	Thomas Dekker, *The Shoemaker's Holiday* (1599), ed. D.J. Palmer (1975)
Dekker, *Works*	*The Dramatic Works of Thomas Dekker*, ed. Fredson Bowers, 4 vols (Cambridge, 1953–61)
de Mourgues	Odette de Mourgues, *Metaphysical, Baroque and Précieux Poetry* (Oxford, 1953)
Dent	R.W. Dent, *Shakespeare's Proverbial Language: An Index* (1981)
Dering, *Catechism*	Edward Dering, *A Brief and Necessary Catechism or Instruction* (1590)
DiGangi	Mario DiGangi, *The Homoerotics of Early Modern Drama* (Cambridge, 1997)
Dillon	Janette Dillon, 'Shakespeare and the traditions of English stage comedy', in Dutton & Howard, 4–22
Dominik	Mark Dominik, '*As You Like It* and *Love's Labor's Won*', pamphlet (Beaverton, Oreg., 1998), 1–18
Donaldson, *Jonson*	*Ben Jonson*, ed. Ian Donaldson (Oxford, 1985)
Donaldson, *Magic*	Ian Donaldson, *Jonson's Magic Houses* (Oxford, 1997); see also Bevington, 'Review'
Donaldson, 'Myths'	Ian Donaldson, 'Looking sideways, Jonson, Shakespeare, and the myths of envy', *BJJ*, 8 (2001), 1–22
Donaldson, *World*	Ian Donaldson, *The World Upside Down: Comedy from Jonson to Fielding* (Oxford, 1970)
Donne, *Courtier's Library*	John Donne, *The Courtier's Library or Catalogus Librorum Aulicorum*, ed. Evelyn Mary Simpson (1930)
Dorsch	*The Comedy of Errors*, ed. T.S. Dorsch (Cambridge, 1988)
Douay Diaries	*The Douay College Diaries, Third, Fourth and Fifth, 1598–1654*, ed. E.H. Burton and T.L. Williams (1911)
Douce, *Illustrations*	Francis Douce, *Illustrations of Shakespeare and of Ancient Manners*, 2 vols (1807)
Dramatic Records 6	*Dramatic Records in the Declared Accounts of the Treasurer of the Chamber 1558–1642*, ed. David Cook and F.P. Wilson, MSR (Oxford, 1962)
Dramatic Records 10	*Dramatic Records in the Declared Accounts of the Office of Works 1560–1640*, ed. F.P. Wilson, R.F. Hill and G.R. Proudfoot, MSR (Oxford, 1977)

Drayton, *Elizium*	Michael Drayton, *The Muses' Elizium, Lately discovered by a new way over Parnassus* (1630)
Drayton, *Poly-Olbion*	Michael Drayton, *Poly-Olbion* (1612)
DSK	David Scott Kastan
Duffin, 'Catching'	Ross W. Duffin, 'Catching the burthen: a new round of Shakespearean musical hunting', *Studies in Music* (2001), 19–20
Duffin, *Songbook*	Ross W. Duffin, *Shakespeare's Songbook*, with a foreword by Stephen Orgel (New York, 2004)
Duncan-Jones, 'Bess Carey'	Katherine Duncan-Jones, 'Bess Carey's Petrarch: newly discovered Elizabethan sonnets', *RES*, n.s. 50 (1999), 304–19
Duncan-Jones, *Ungentle*	Katherine Duncan-Jones, *Ungentle Shakespeare: Scenes from his Life* (2001)
Dusinberre, 'As Who?'	Juliet Dusinberre, 'As *Who* Liked It?' *SS 46* (1994), 9–21
Dusinberre, '*AYL*'	Juliet Dusinberre, '*As You Like It*', in Dutton & Howard, 411–28
Dusinberre, 'Boys'	Juliet Dusinberre, 'Boys becoming women in Shakespeare's plays', *SS* (Tokyo), 36 (1999), 1–28
Dusinberre, 'Cleopatras'	Juliet Dusinberre, '"Squeaking Cleopatras": gender and performance in *Antony and Cleopatra*', in Bulman, *Performance* (1996), 46–67
Dusinberre, '*KJ*'	Juliet Dusinberre, '*King John* and embarrassing women', *SS 42* (1990), 37–52
Dusinberre, 'Much Ado'	Juliet Dusinberre, 'Much Ado About Lying', in Michele Marrapodi and A.J. Hoenselaars (eds), *The Italian World of English Renaissance Drama, Cultural Exchange and Intertextuality* (Newark, Del., 1998), 239–57
Dusinberre, 'Pancakes'	Juliet Dusinberre, 'Pancakes and a date for *As You Like It*', *SQ*, 54 (2003), 371–405
Dusinberre, 'Rival poets'	Juliet Dusinberre, 'Rival poets in the Forest of Arden', *Shakespeare Jahrbuch*, 139 (2003), 71–83
Dusinberre, '*TC*'	Juliet Dusinberre, '*Troilus and Cressida* and the definition of beauty', *SS 36* (1983), 85–95
Dusinberre, 'Topical'	Juliet Dusinberre, 'Topical forest: Kemp and Mar-text in Arden', in Ann Thompson and Gordon McMullan (eds), *In Arden: Editing Shakespeare. Essays in Honour of Richard Proudfoot* (2003), 239–51
Dusinberre, 'Touchstone'	Juliet Dusinberre, 'Touchstone and Kemp in *As You Like It*', *Shakespeare Newsletter*, 52 (2002/2003), 93–126
Dusinberre, '*TS*'	Juliet Dusinberre, '*The Taming of the Shrew*: women, acting, and power', in Dana E. Aspinall (ed.), *The Taming of the Shrew: Critical Essays* (New York and London, 2002), 168–85
Dusinberre, *Women*	Juliet Dusinberre, *Shakespeare and the Nature of Women*, 3rd edn (2003)

Dusinberre, 'Women and boys' Juliet Dusinberre, 'Women and boys playing Shakespeare', in Jean-Paul Débax and Yves Peyré (eds), *As You Like It: Essais Critiques* (Toulouse, 1998), 1–26; reprinted in Callaghan, *Feminist*, 251–62

Dusinberre, *Woolf's Renaissance* Juliet Dusinberre, *Virginia Woolf's Renaissance: Woman Reader or Common Reader?* (Basingstoke, England, 1997)

Dutton, *Licensing* Richard Dutton, *Licensing, Censorship and Authorship in Early Modern England: Buggeswords* (Basingstoke, England, 2000)

Dutton, *Mastering* Richard Dutton, *Mastering the Revels: The Regulation and Censorship of English Renaissance Drama* (1991)

Dutton, 'Sign' Richard Dutton, '*Hamlet*, an apology for actors, and the Sign of the Globe', *SS 41* (1989), 35–43

Dutton & Howard *A Companion to Shakespeare's Works* (4 vols), vol 3, *The Comedies*, ed. Richard Dutton and Jean Howard (Oxford, 2003)

Edmond, 'Burbages' Mary Edmond, 'Yeomen, citizens, gentlemen, and players: the Burbages and their connections', in S. Schoenbaum, S.P. Zitner, R.B. Parker and Sheldon P. Zitner (eds), *Elizabethan Theatre: Essays in Honor of S. Schoenbaum* (Newark, Del., 1996), 36–9

Edmond, *Hilliard* Mary Edmond, *Hilliard and Oliver* (1983)

Edwards Philip Edwards, *Last Voyages: Cavendish, Hudson, Ralegh* (Oxford, 1988)

Elam Keir Elam, 'As they did in the Golden World: Romantic rapture and semantic rupture in *As You Like It*', in Jonathan Hart (ed.), *Reading the Renaissance: Culture, Poetics, and Drama* (New York, 1996), 163–76

ELH *English Literary History*

Elizabeth I, *Works* Elizabeth I, *Collected Works*, ed. Leah S. Marcus, Janel Mueller and Mary Beth Rose (Chicago, 2000)

Ellacombe Henry H. Ellacombe, *Plant-Lore of Shakespeare* [1886]

ELR *English Literary Renaissance*

Elyot, *Governor* Sir Thomas Elyot, *The Book Named the Governor* (1531)

Empson, *Reviews* *Empson in Granta: The Book, Film and Theatre Reviews of William Empson*, introduction by Eric Griffiths (Tunbridge Wells, England, 1993)

Empson, *Versions* William Empson, *Some Versions of Pastoral* (Harmondsworth, England, 1966; first edition 1935)

England's Parnassus *England's Parnassus Compiled by Robert Allot, 1600*, ed. Charles Crawford (Oxford, 1913)

Erasmus, *Colloquies* *All the Familiar Colloquies of Desiderius Erasmus of Rotterdam*, trans. N. Bailey (1725)

Erasmus, *Folly* Desiderius Erasmus, *The Praise of Folly*, trans. Thomas Chaloner (1569), ed. Janet E. Ashbee (1901)

Erickson	Peter Erickson, 'Sexual politics and social structure in *As You Like It*', *Masssachusetts Review*, 23 (1982), 65–83
Erne	Lukas Erne, *Shakespeare as Literary Dramatist* (Cambridge, 2003)
Essex, *Apology*	*An Apology of the Earl of Essex, against those which jealously, and maliciously, tax him to be the hinderer of the peace and quiet of his country* (1603, 'Penned by himself in Anno 1598')
Essex, *Travel*	*Two Excellent Letters Concerning Travel: One written by the late Earl of Essex, the other by Sir Philip Sidney* (1633)
Evans, 'Douai'	G. Blakemore Evans, 'The Douai manuscript: six Shakespearean transcripts (1694–95)', *PQ* , 41 (1962), 158–72
Evans, '*JC*'	G. Blakemore Evans, 'Shakespeare's *Julius Caesar*: a seventeenth-century manuscript', *JEGP*, 41 (1942), 401–17
Faucit, *Characters*	Helena Faucit (Lady Martin), *On Some of Shakespeare's Female Characters* (Edinburgh, 1887)
Fellowes, 'Lover'	Edmund H. Fellowes, '"It Was a Lover and His Lass": some fresh points of criticism', *MLR*, 41 (1946), 202–6
Fellowes, *Madrigal*	E.H. Fellowes, *The English Madrigal Composers* (Oxford, 1921)
Feuillerat	*Documents Relating to the Office of the Revels in the Time of Queen Elizabeth*, ed. Albert Feuillerat (Louvain, 1908)
Ficino, *Commentary*	*Marsilio Ficino's Commentary on Plato's Symposium on Love*, trans. Sears Jayne, 2nd edn (Dallas, Tex., 1985)
Ficino, *Mind*	Marsilio Ficino, *Five Questions Concerning the Mind*, trans. Josephine L. Burroughs, in Ernst Cassirer, Paul Oscar Kristeller and John Herman Randall, Jr (eds), *The Renaissance Philosophy of Man* (Chicago, 1948)
Fisher	Will Fisher, 'The Renaissance beard: masculinity in early modern England and Europe', *RQ*, 54 (2001), 155–87
Fitter	Chris Fitter, 'The slain deer and political imperium: *As You Like It* and Andrew Marvell's "Nymph Complaining for the Death of her Fawn"', *JEGP*, 98 (1999), 193–218
Fitzwilliam Virginal Book	*The Fitzwilliam Virginal Book*, ed. J.A. Fuller Maitland and W. Barclay Squire, 2 vols (New York, 1979)
Fleay	Frederick Gard Fleay, *A Chronicle History of the Life and Work of William Shakespeare* (1886)
Florio, *World*	John Florio, *A World of Words* (1598)
Foakes	*King Lear*, ed. R.A. Foakes, Arden Shakespeare, 3rd series (1997)
Forker	*King Richard II*, ed. Charles A. Forker, Arden Shakespeare, 3rd series (2002)
Fraser, *AW*	*All's Well That Ends Well*, ed. Russell Fraser (Cambridge, 1985)

Fraser, '*Genesis*' Russell Fraser, 'Shakespeare's *Book of Genesis*', *Comparative Drama*, 25 (1991), 121–8

Frye Roland Mushat Frye, *Shakespeare and Christian Doctrine* (Princeton, NJ, 1963)

Fumerton Patricia Fumerton, '"Secret" arts: Elizabethan miniatures and sonnets', *Representations*, 15 (1986), 57–97

Furnivall F.J. Furnivall, 'Sir John Harington's Shakespeare Quartos', *N&Q*, 7th series, 9 (17 May 1890), 382–3

Gamelyn *Gamelyn*, in *Middle English Verse Romances*, ed. Donald B. Sands (New York, 1966)

Garber, 'Education' Marjorie Garber, 'The education of Orlando', in A.R. Braunmuller and James C. Bulman (eds), *Comedy from Shakespeare to Sheridan* (Newark, Del., 1986), 102–12

Garber, *Vested Interests* Marjorie Garber, *Vested Interests: Cross-Dressing and Cultural Anxiety* (1992)

Gardner, '*AYL*' Helen Gardner, '*As You Like It*', in Kenneth Muir (ed.), *Shakespeare: The Comedies* (Englewood Cliffs, NJ, 1965), 58–71

Gautier Théophile Gautier, *Mademoiselle de Maupin*, ed. Adolphe Boschot (Paris, 1955; first edn 1835)

Gaw, 'John Sinclo' Alison Gaw, 'John Sinclo as one of Shakespeare's actors', *Anglia*, 49 (1926), 289–303

Gay Penny Gay, *As She Likes It: Shakespeare's Unruly Women* (1994)

Gazzard Hugh Gazzard, 'Samuel Daniel's *Philotas*', *RES*, n.s. 51 (2000), 423–50

Geneva Bible *The Holy Bible* (Geneva, 1560)

George Eliot Letters *The George Eliot Letters*, ed. Gordon S. Haight, 9 vols (London and New Haven, Conn., 1954)

Gerard, *Herbal* John Gerard, *Herbal* (1597)

Gibbons Brian Gibbons, 'Amorous fictions in *As You Like It*', in *Shakespeare and Multiplicity* (Cambridge, 1993), 153–81

Girart de Roussillon *Girart de Roussillon* commenté par Marcel Thomas et Michael Zink, adaptation en français moderne de Roger-Henri Guerrard (Lyons, 1990)

GKH G.K. Hunter, private communication

Goldberg Jonathan Goldberg, *James I and the Politics of Literature: Jonson, Shakespeare, Donne, and Their Contemporaries* (Baltimore, Md., 1983)

Goodman Lizbeth Goodman, 'Women's alternative Shakespeares and women's alternatives to Shakespeare in contemporary British theatre', in Novy, *Cross-Cultural*, 206-26

Gosson, *Abuse* Stephen Gosson, *The School of Abuse* (1579)

Gray Arthur Gray, *How Shakespeare 'Purged' Jonson: A Problem Solved* (Cambridge, 1928)

Great Bible *The Holy Bible* (1539)

Greene, *Groatsworth*   Robert Greene, *Greene's Groatsworth of Wit, Bought with a Million of Repentance* (1592), ed. D. Allen Carroll, Medieval and Renaissance Texts and Studies, 114 (Binghamton, NY, 1994)

Greene, *Mamillia*   Robert Greene, *Mamillia* (1588), in *The Life and Complete Works in Prose and Verse of Robert Greene*, ed. Alexander B. Grosart, 15 vols (1881–6)

Greene, *Menaphon*   *Menaphon* (1589) by Robert Greene and *A Margarite of America* (1596) by Thomas Lodge, ed. G.B. Harrison (Oxford, 1927)

Greene, *Orlando*   Robert Greene, *The History of Orlando Furioso* (1599)

Greene, *Quip*   Robert Greene, *A Quip for an Upstart Courtier: Or A quaint dispute between Velvet breeches and Clothbreeches* (1592) (Gainesville, Fla., 1954)

Greer   David Greer, 'The lute songs of Thomas Morley', *Lute Society Journal*, 8 (1966), 25–37

Greg   W.W. Greg, *Dramatic Documents from the Elizabethan Playhouses: Documents* (Oxford, 1931)

Gregerson   Linda Gregerson, 'Rough wooing: French marriages, English history, and the comic interim', unpublished paper, ISA conference, Stratford-upon-Avon, 2002

Grimble   Ian Grimble, *The Harington Family* (1957)

Grose   Francis Grose, *The Antiquarian Repertory*, 4 vols (London, 1808)

Guarini, *Il pastor fido* Giovanni Battista Guarini, *Il pastor fido or The Faithful Shepherd*, trans. Sir Edward Dymock (1602)

Guarini/Tasso   Guarini's *Il pastor fido* and Torquato Tasso's *Aminta*, ed. Giacopo Castelvetro (1591)

Gurr, 'Historicism'   Andrew Gurr, 'A new theatre historicism', in Holland & Orgel, 71–88

Gurr, *Playgoing*   Andrew Gurr, *Playgoing in Shakespeare's London* (Cambridge, 1987)

Haber   Judith Haber, *Pastoral and the Poetics of Self-contradiction* (Cambridge, 1994)

Habicht, 'Shakespeare'   Werner Habicht, 'Shakespeare in West Germany', *SQ*, 29 (1978), 296–9

Habicht, 'Tree'   Werner Habicht, 'Tree properties and tree scenes in Elizabethan theater', *Renaissance Drama*, n.s. 4 (1971), 69–92

Hackel   Heidi Brayman Hackel, 'The "great Variety" of readers and early modern reading practices', in Kastan, *Companion*, 139–57

Hakluyt, *Navigations* Richard Hakluyt, *The Principal Navigations, Voyages, and Discoveries of the English Nation, with the victory achieved at Cadiz, 1596*, 3 vols (1598, 1599, 1600). 'The account of the Earl of Essex's voyage to Cadiz, which was ordered

411

suppressed in 1599, is lacking in some copies' (*STC* 1.552–3)

Hall, *Virgidemiarum* Joseph Hall, *Virgidemiarum, Six Books, First Three Books of Toothless Satires* (1597); *The Three Last Books of Biting Satires* (1599)

Hamer Mary Hamer, 'Shakespeare's Rosalind and her public image', *Theatre Research International*, 11 (1986), 105–18

Hammer Paul Hammer, *The Polarisation of Elizabethan Politics, The Political Career of Robert Devereux, 2nd Earl of Essex, 1585–1597* (Cambridge, 1999)

Hankey, 'Helen Faucit' Julie Hankey, 'Helen Faucit and Shakespeare: womanly theater', in Novy, *Cross-Cultural*, 50–69

Hannay Margaret Patterson Hannay (ed.), *Silent But for the Word: Tudor Women as Patrons, Translators, and Writers of Religious Works* (Kent, Ohio, 1985)

Harbage Alfred Harbage, *Annals of English Drama* (New York, 1940)

Harington, *Ajax* John Harington, *A New Discourse of a Stale Subject, called The Metamorphosis of Ajax* (1596), ed. Elizabeth Story Donno (1962)

Harington, *Apology* [*for Ajax*] John Harington, *An Apology*, in Harington, *Ajax*, 205–65

Harington, 'Apology of Poetry' John Harington, 'Apology of Poetry', prefaced to his translation of Ariosto; see Harington, *OF*

Harington, 'Epigrams 1600' See Adv.b.8.1 under 'Manuscripts'

Harington, *Epigrams 1618* John Harington, *Epigrams*, in four books (1618)

Harington, *Letters* *The Letters and Epigrams of Sir John Harington*, together with *The Prayse of Private Life*, ed. Norman Egbert McClure (Philadelphia, 1930)

Harington, *Nugae Antiquae* *Nugae Antiquae Being a Miscellaneous Collection of Original Papers in Prose and Verse by Sir John Harington*, selected by Rev. Henry Harington, 3 vols (1779)

Harington, *OF* John Harington, *Orlando Furioso* in English (1591; edition cited 1600). See also Adv.b.8.1 under 'Manuscripts'

Harington, *Salernum* *The School of Salernum, Regimen Sanitatis Salernitanum, The English Version by Sir John Harington (1608)* (Oxford, 1922)

Harington, *Succession* Sir John Harington, *A Tract on the Succession to the Crown (AD 1602)*, ed. Clements R. Markham (Roxburghe Club, 1880)

Harington Snr., *Friendship* John Harington, *The Book of Friendship of Marcus Tulli Cicero* (1550)

Harley Marta Powell Harley, 'Rosalind, the hare, and the hyena', *SQ*, 38 (1985), 335–7

Hart   W.H. Hart, 'The Parliamentary Surveys of Richmond, Wimbledon, and Nonsuch, in the County of Surrey, A.D. 1649', in *Surrey Archaeological Collections*, 5 (1871), 75–156

Hassel   R. Chris Hassel, Jr., *Renaissance Drama and the English Church Year* (Lincoln, Nebr., 1979)

Hattaway   Michael Hattaway, *Elizabethan Popular Theatre: Plays in Performance* (1982)

Hawkes, D.   David Hawkes, 'Idolatry and commodity fetishism in the antitheatrical controversy', *SEL*, 39 (1999), 255–73

Hawkes, T.   Terence Hawkes, 'Entry on Q', in Christy Desmet and Robert Sawyer (eds), *Shakespeare and Appropriation* (1999), 33–46

Hazlitt   William Hazlitt, *Characters of Shakespeare's Plays* (1915; first edition 1817)

Heaney   Seamus Heaney, unpublished Clark lectures no. 1, University of Cambridge, 1992

Hedbäck   Ann-Mari Hedbäck, 'The Douai manuscript reexamined', *PBSA*, 73 (1979), 1–18

Heffner   R. Heffner, 'Essex the ideal courtier', *ELH*, 1 (1934), 7–36

Hemming, 'Like a man'   Sarah Hemming, 'Taking it like a man', *Independent*, 20 November 1991

Hemming, 'Three Rosalinds'   Sarah Hemming, 'Three Rosalinds take to the stage this summer in new productions of Shakespeare's *As You Like It*', *Independent*, 15 April 1992

Henderson & Siemon   Diana E. Henderson and James Siemon, 'Reading vernacular literaure', in Kastan, *Companion*, 206–22

Henke   Robert Henke, *Pastoral Transformations: Italian Tragicomedy and Shakespeare's Late Plays* (Newark, Del., 1997)

Henslowe's Diary   *Henslowe's Diary* [1590–1604] *with supplementary material, introduction and notes*, ed. R.A. Foakes and R.T. Rickart (Cambridge, 1961)

Herford & Simpson   *Ben Jonson*, ed. C.H. Herford and Percy Simpson, 11 vols (Oxford, 1925)

Heywood, *Epigrams* (*300, 400, 500, 600*)   *The Works of John Heywood, Newly imprinted. A Dialogue, wherein are pleasantly contrived the number of all the effectual Proverbs in our English tongue. Together with three hundred Epigrams upon three hundred Proverbs. Also a fourth, fifth and sixth hundred of . . . Epigrams* (1598)

Heywood, *Weather*   John Heywood, *The Play of the Weather* (1533), in *The Plays of John Heywood*, ed. Richard Axton and Peter Happé (Woodbridge, England, 1991)

Hill   John Walter Hill, *The Life and Works of Francesco Maria Veracini* (Ann Arbor, Mich., 1979)

Hillebrand	Harold Newcomb Hillebrand, *The Child Actors* (New York, 1964)
Hilliard, *Limning*	*A Treatise Concerning the Art of Limning by Nicholas Hilliard* [1602?], ed. R.K.R. Thornton and T.G.S. Cain (Ashington, England, 1981)
Hilton	John Hilton, *Catch That Catch Can: A Choice Collection of Catches, Rounds, and Canons* (1652)
Hinman	Charlton Hinman, *The Printing and Proof-Reading of the First Folio of Shakespeare*, 2 vols (Oxford, 1963)
Hirsh	James Hirsh, 'Act divisions in the Shakespeare First Folio', *PBSA*, 96 (2002), 219–56
HLQ	*Huntington Library Quarterly*
Hobbes, *Philosophy*	Thomas Hobbes, *Elements of Philosophy. The first section concerning the body* (1656)
Hodgdon	Barbara Hodgdon, 'Sexual disguise and the theatre of gender', in Alexander Leggatt (ed.), *The Cambridge Companion to Shakespearean Comedy* (Cambridge, 2002), 179–97
Holdsworth	R.V. Holdsworth, 'Touchstone's butterwomen', *N&Q*, n.s. 31 [229] (1984), 196–7
Holland	Peter Holland, 'Theatre without drama: reading *REED*', in Holland & Orgel, 43–67
Holland & Orgel	*From Script to Stage in Early Modern England*, ed. Peter Holland and Stephen Orgel (Basingstoke, England, and New York, 2004), 151–72
Homer/Chapman	*The Whole Works of Homer; Prince of Poets in his Iliads and Odysses*, trans. George Chapman [1616?]
Homilies	*Certain Sermons or Homilies appointed to be read in Churches* (1547; edition cited 1623)
Honigmann, *'Lost Years'*	E.A.J. Honigmann, *Shakespeare: The 'Lost Years'* (Manchester, 1998)
Honigmann, *Texts*	E.A.J. Honigmann, *The Texts of 'Othello' and Shakespearian Revision* (1996)
Hope	Jonathan Hope, *Shakespeare's Grammar* (2003)
Hopkins	Lisa Hopkins, '*The Comedy of Errors* and the Date of Easter', *BJJ*, 7 (2000), 55–64
Howard, 'Crossdressing'	J.E. Howard, 'Crossdressing, the theatre, and gender struggle in early modern England', *SQ*, 39 (1988), 418–40
Howard, 'Scripts'	Jean Howard, 'Scripts and/versus playhouses: ideological production and the Renaissance public stage', *RD*, 20 (1989), 31–40
Howard-Hill, *Crane*	T.H. Howard-Hill, *Ralph Crane and Some Shakespeare First Folio Comedies* (Charlottesville, Va., 1972)
Howard-Hill, 'Editor'	T.H. Howard-Hill, 'Shakespeare's earliest editor, Ralph Crane', *SS 44* (1992), 113–29

Hughey	Ruth Willard Hughey, *John Harington of Stepney: Tudor Gentleman; His Life and Works* (Columbus, Ohio, 1971)
Hunting	[George Gascoigne], *The Noble Art of Venery or Hunting* (1575; edition cited 1611); attributed to George Turberville
Hutton	Ronald Hutton, *The Rise and Fall of Merry England: The Ritual Year 1400–1700* (Oxford, 1994)
Imitation	[Thomas à Kempis], *The Imitation of Christ*, trans. Thomas Rogers (1598)
ISA	International Shakespeare Association
Jackson	Russell Jackson, 'Perfect types of womanhood': Rosalind, Beatrice and Viola in Victorian criticism and performance', *SS 32* (1979), 15–26
Jacquot	Jean Jacquot, 'Harriot, Hill, Warner and the new philosophy', in Shirley, *Renaissance Scientist*, 107–28
James	M. James, 'At a crossroads of the political culture: the Essex revolt, 1601', in *Society, Politics and Culture: Studies in Early Modern England* (Cambridge, 1986), 416–65
Jamieson	Michael S. Jamieson, *Shakespeare, As You Like It* (1965)
Jankowski	Theodora A. Jankowski, *Pure Resistance: Queer Virginity in Early Modern English Drama* (Philadelphia, 2000)
Javitch	Daniel Javitch, *Proclaiming a Classic: The Canonization of Orlando Furioso* (Princeton, NJ, 1991)
JEGP	*Journal of English and Germanic Philology*
Jenkins	*Hamlet*, ed. Harold Jenkins, Arden Shakespeare, 2nd series (1982)
Johnson, *Forest*	Charles Johnson, *Love in a Forest* (1969; first edition 1723)
Jones	William M. Jones, 'William Shakespeare as William in *As You Like It*', *SQ*, 11 (1960), 228–31
Jonson, *Cynthia's Revels*	Ben Jonson, *The Fountain of Self-Love, or Cynthia's Revels* (1601), ed. W. Bang and L. Krebs (Louvain, 1908)
Jonson, 'Drummond'	Ben Jonson, 'Conversations with William Drummond of Hawthornden' [1618–19], in Donaldson, *Jonson*, 595–611
Jonson, *EMI*	Ben Jonson, *Every Man In His Humour* (1598), ed. Robert S. Miola (Manchester, 2000)
Jonson, *EMO*	Ben Jonson, *Every Man Out of His Humour* (1599), ed. Helen Ostovich (Manchester, 2001)
Jonson, *Epicoene*	Ben Jonson, *Epicoene or The Silent Woman* (1609), ed. R.V. Holdsworth (Manchester, 1979)
Jonson, 'Epitaph'	Ben Jonson, '*Epitaph on S* [*alamon*] *P* [*avy*]', in Donaldson, *Jonson*, 270
Jonson, 'Execration'	Ben Jonson, '*An Execration upon Vulcan*' (1632) (*The Underwood*), in Donaldson, *Jonson*, 365–70
Jonson, *Gypsies*	Ben Jonson, *A Masque of the Metamorphosed Gypsies* (1621), in Orgel, *Masques*, 316–73

Jonson, *Hymenaei*   Ben Jonson, *Hymenaei* (1606), in Orgel, *Masques*, 75–106

Jonson, '*Penshurst*'   Ben Jonson, '*To Penshurst*' [1611–12?] (*The Forest*), in Donaldson, *Jonson*, 282–5

Jonson, *Poetaster*   Ben Jonson, *Poetaster* (1602), ed. Tom Cain (Manchester, 1995)

Jourdain   W.C. Jourdain, 'Some proposed emendations in the text of Shakespeare and explanations of his words', *Transactions of the Philological Society* (1860–1), 133–44

Jowett   John Jowett, 'New created creatures: Ralph Crane and the stage directions in *The Tempest*', *SS 36* (1983), 107–20

Kastan, *1H4*   *King Henry IV, Part 1*, ed. David Scott Kastan, Arden Shakespeare, 3rd series (2002)

Kastan, *Book*   David Scott Kastan, *Shakespeare and the Book* (Cambridge, 2001)

Kastan, *Companion*   *A Companion to Shakespeare*, ed. David Scott Kastan (Oxford, 1999)

Kastan & Vickers   David Scott Kastan and Nancy J. Vickers, 'Shakespeare, Scève and "A Woeful Ballad"', *N&Q*, n.s. 27 [225] (1980), 165–6

Kathman, 'Apprentices'   David Kathman, 'Grocers, Goldsmiths, and Drapers: Freemen and Apprentices in the Elizabethan Theatre', *SQ*, 55 (2004), 1–49

Kathman, 'Boy actors'   David Kathman, 'How old were Shakespeare's boy actors?', *SS 58* (2005), 220–46

Kathman, '*Sins*'   David Kathman, 'Reconsidering *The Seven Deadly Sins*', *Early Theatre*, 7 (2004), 13–44

Kawachi   Yoshiko Kawachi, 'Transvestism in English and Japanese theatres: a comparative study', in *Shakespeare's Universe: Renaissance Ideas and Conventions*, ed. John M. Muraciolo (Aldershot, England, 1995), 108–20

Kay   Dennis Kay, unpublished lecture notes

Keats, *Letters*   *The Letters of John Keats*, selected by Hugh l'Anson Fausset (n.d.)

Keats, *Poems*   *The Poems and Verses of John Keats*, ed. John Middleton Murry (1949)

Kemp, *Nine Days'*   William Kemp, *Nine Days' Wonder* (1600) (Edinburgh, 1966)

Kerrigan   John Kerrigan, *Motives of Woe: Shakespeare and the 'Female Complaint'* (Oxford, 1991)

King   T.J. King, *Casting Shakespeare's Plays: London Actors and Their Roles, 1590–1642* (Cambridge, 1992)

Kinney   Clare Kinney, 'Feigning female faining: Spenser, Lodge, Shakespeare, and Rosalind', *MP*, 95 (1998), 291–315

Kirsch   Arthur C. Kirsch, *Jacobean Dramatic Perspectives* (Charlottesville, Va., 1972)

Knutson, 'Repertory'	Roslyn Lander Knutson, 'The Repertory', in Cox and Kastan, 461–80
Knutson, *Shakespeare's*	Roslyn Lander Knutson, *The Repertory of Shakespeare's Company 1594-1613* (Fayetteville, Ark., 1991)
Kökeritz	Helge Kökeritz, *Shakespeare's Pronunciation* (1953)
Koller	Kathrine Koller, 'Spenser and Ralegh', *ELH*, 1 (1934), 37–60
Kott	Jan Kott, *The Gender of Rosalind* (Evanston, Ill., 1992)
Lamb	Charles Lamb, 'On the tragedies of Shakespeare, considered with reference to their fitness for stage representation' (1811), in Edmund D. Jones (ed.), *English Critical Essays: Nineteenth Century* (1916), 81–101
Lamblin	Pierre-Jacques Lamblin, private communication
Laroque	François Laroque, *Shakespeare's Festive World*, trans. Janet Lloyd (Cambridge, 1991)
Leishman	*The Three Parnassus Plays (1598–1601)*, ed. J.B. Leishman (1949)
Leslie	Michael Leslie, '"Something nasty in the wilderness", entertaining Queen Elizabeth on her progresses', *MRDE*, 10 (1998), 47–71
Levi	Primo Levi, 'François Rabelais', in *Other People's Trades*, trans. Raymond Rosenthal (1989), 121–5
Levine	Laura Levine, *Men in Women's Clothing: Anti-theatricality and Effeminization, 1579–1642* (Cambridge, 1994)
Lewalski	Barbara Lewalski, *Writing Women in Jacobean England* (Cambridge, Mass., 1993)
Lily, *Grammar*	William Lily, *Brevissima Institutio, seu ratio Grammatices cognoscendae*, being the second part of *A Short Introduction of Grammar Generally to be Used* (Geneva, 1557)
Lockspeiser	Edward Lockspeiser, *Debussy: His Life and Mind*, 2 vols (1965), vol. 2, Appendix A, 247–52: 'Projects for "As You Like It"'
Lodge	Thomas Lodge, *Rosalynde: Euphues Golden Legacy* (1590) (Menston, England, 1970, from the 1592 edition)
Lodge, 'A reply'	*The School of Abuse* by Stephen Gosson and a reply by Thomas Lodge [*c.* 1580], prefaced by Arthur Freeman (New York, 1973)
Lodge, *Fig*	Thomas Lodge, *A Fig for Momus* (1595)
Lodge, *Margarite*	Thomas Lodge, *A Margarite of America* (1596); see Greene, *Menaphon*
Lodge, *Phillis*	Thomas Lodge, *Phillis, honoured with pastoral sonnets, elegies and amorous delights* (1593)
Lodge & Greene, *Looking-glass*	Thomas Lodge and Robert Greene, *A Looking-glass for London and England* (1594), in *The Dramatic and Poetical Works of Robert Greene & George Peele*, ed. Alexander Dyce (1861)

Loewenstein	Joseph Loewenstein, *Ben Jonson and Possessive Authorship* (Cambridge, 2002)
Loseley	*The Loseley Manuscripts*, ed. Alfred John Kempe (1835)
Love	Harold Love, *Scribal Publication in Seventeenth-Century England* (Oxford, 1993)
Lyly, *Endymion*	John Lyly, *Endymion* (1588), ed. David Bevington (Manchester, 1991)
Lyly, *Galatea*	John Lyly, *Galatea* (1592), ed. G.K. Hunter (Manchester, 1993)
Lyly, *Midas*	John Lyly, *Midas* (1592), ed. David Bevington (Manchester, 1993)
Lyly, *Sappho and Phao*	John Lyly, *Sappho and Phao* (1584), ed. David Bevington (Manchester, 1991)
McCabe	Richard A. McCabe, 'Elizabethan satire and the bishops' ban of 1599', *Yearbook of English Studies*, 11 (1981), 188–94
McCoy	Richard McCoy, *The Rites of Knighthood* (Berkeley and Los Angeles, 1989)
McDonald	Marcia A. McDonald, 'The Elizabethan Poor Laws and the stage', *MRDE*, 7 (1995), 121–44
McKenzie	D.F. McKenzie, 'Stretching a point: or, the case of the spaced-out comps', *Studies in Bibliography*, 37 (1984), 106–21
McMillin	Scott McMillin, 'The sharer and his boy: rehearsing Shakespeare's women', in Holland & Orgel, 231–45
Mann	David Mann, *The Elizabethan Player* (1991)
Manning	Roger B. Manning, *Hunters and Poachers: A Social and Cultural History of Unlawful Hunting 1485–1640* (Oxford, 1993)
Manningham	*The Diary of John Manningham of the Middle Temple 1602–23*, ed. Robert Parker Sorlien (Hanover, NH, 1976)
Manwood, *Laws*	John Manwood, *A Treatise of the Laws of the Forest* (1598)
Maplet, *Forest*	John Maplet, *A Green Forest* (1567)
Marcus, 'Heroines'	Leah Marcus, 'Shakespeare's comic heroines, Elizabeth I, and the political uses of androgyny', in Mary Beth Rose (ed.), *Women in the Middle Ages and the Renaissance: Literary and Historical Perspectives* (Syracuse, NY, 1986), 135–53
Marcus, *Puzzling*	Leah S. Marcus, *Puzzling Shakespeare: Local Reading and Its Discontents* (Berkeley, Cal., 1988)
Markham, *Horseman*	Gervase Markham, *Cavalrice, or The English Horseman* (1607), an amplification of *The Art of Horsemanship* (1593, reprinted 1598)
Marlowe	*The Complete Works of Christopher Marlowe*, ed. Roma Gill (Oxford, 1987), vol. 1: *Translations*

Marlowe, *Dido*   Christopher Marlowe, *Dido Queen of Carthage* (1594), in
                          Marlowe
Marlowe, *Elegies*   Christopher Marlowe, *All Ovid's Elegies* ([1598–9], 1600),
                          in Marlowe
Marlowe, *Faustus*   Christopher Marlowe, *Doctor Faustus* [A-Text 1604, B-
                          Text 1616], in Bevington & Rasmussen
Marlowe, *Hero and*   Christopher Marlowe, *Hero and Leander* (1598), in
  Leander   Marlowe
Marlowe, *Lucan*   Christopher Marlowe, *Lucan's First Book* (1600), in
                          Marlowe
Marlowe,   Christopher Marlowe, *Tamburlaine Part I* (1590), in
  Tamburlaine 1   Bevington & Rasmussen
Marston, *Antonio*   John Marston, *Antonio and Mellida, The First Part* (1602),
  and Mellida   ed. G.K. Hunter (1965)
Marston,   [John Marston], *Histriomastix, Or, The Player Whipped*
  Histriomastix   (1599; edition cited 1610)
Marston, *Insatiate*   John Marston and others, *The Insatiate Countess*, ed.
  Countess   Giorgio Melchiori (Manchester, 1984)
Marston, *Malcontent* John Marston, *The Malcontent* (1604), ed. Bernard Harris
                          (1967)
Marston, *Scourge*   John Marston, *The Scourge of Villainy* (1598) (Edinburgh,
                          1966, from the 1599 edition)
Marston, *What*   John Marston, *What You Will* (1607), in *The Works of John*
  You Will   *Marston*, ed. A.H. Bullen, 3 vols (1887), vol. 2
Massai   Sonia Massai, '"Taking just care of the impression": edi-
                          torial intervention in Shakespeare's Fourth Folio, 1685',
                          SS 55 (2002), 257–70
Masten, 'Ganymede'   Jeffrey Masten, 'Textual deviance: Ganymede's hand in
                          As You Like It', in Marjorie Garber, Paul B. Franklin and
                          Rebecca L. Walkowitz (eds), *Field Work: Sites in Literary*
                          and Cultural Studies (New York, 1996), 153–63
Masten, 'Pressing   Jeffrey Masten, 'Pressing subjects: or, the secret lives of
  subjects'   Shakespeare's compositors', in Jeffrey Masten, Peter
                          Stallybrass and Nancy Vickers (eds), *Language Machines:*
                          Technologies of Literary and Cultural Production (1997),
                          75–107
May, *Stanford*   Steven W. May, *Henry Stanford's Anthology: An Edition of*
                          Cambridge University Library Manuscript Dd.5.75 (New
                          York, 1988)
May & Ringler   Steven W. May and William A. Ringler, Jr., *Elizabethan*
                          Poetry, A Bibliography and First Line Index of English Verse,
                          1559–1603 (2004)
Melchiori   *The Merry Wives of Windsor*, ed. Giorgio Melchiori,
                          Arden Shakespeare, 3rd series (2000)
Mendelson &   Sara Mendelson and Patricia Crawford, *Women in Early*
  Crawford   *Modern England 1550–1720* (Oxford, 1998)

Merchant	Moelwyn Merchant, *Shakespeare and the Artist* (1959)
Milburn, 'Douai to Durham'	The Revd David Milburn, 'Douai to Durham: the second centenary of Crook Hall', *Northern Catholic History*, 35 (1994), 18–37
Milton, *Areopagitica*	John Milton, *Areopagitica*, in *Complete Prose Works of John Milton*, ed. Don M. Wolfe, 10 vols (New Haven, Conn., 1953–82), vol. 2
Milton, 'L'Allegro'	John Milton, 'L'Allegro', in *Complete Shorter Poems of John Milton*, ed. B.A. Wright (New York, 1961)
Modjeska	Helena Modjeska, *As You Like It* (promptbook, New York, 1882)
Montaigne	Michel de Montaigne, *The Essays 1603*, trans. John Florio (Menston, England, 1969)
Montemayor, *Diana*	Jorge de Montemayor, *Diana*, trans. Bartholomew Young (1598)
Montrose, 'Brother'	Louis Adrian Montrose, '"The place of a brother" in *As You Like It*: social process and comic form', *SQ*, 32 (1981), 28–54
Montrose, 'Elisa'	Louis Montrose, '"Elisa, Queen of shepheardes", and the pastoral of power', *ELR*, 10 (1980), 153–82
Moody, *Illegitimate*	Jane Moody, *Illegitimate Theatre* (Cambridge, 2000)
Moody, 'Romantic'	Jane Moody, 'Romantic Shakespeare', in Stanley Wells and Sarah Stanton (eds), *The Cambridge Companion to Shakespeare on Stage* (Cambridge, 2002), 37–57
Moore	John Moore, *As You Like It: Record of Productions* (New York, 1855–76)
More, *Utopia*	Thomas More, *Utopia*, in *The Complete Works of St Thomas More*, ed. Edward Surtz, S.J. and J.H. Hexter, 15 vols (New Haven, Conn., 1965), vol. 4
Morley, *Airs*	Thomas Morley, *First Book of Airs* (1600)
Morley, *Consort Lessons*	Thomas Morley, *First Book of Consort Lessons collected by Thomas Morley, 1599 and 1611*, ed. S. Beck (New York, 1959)
Morley, *Practical Music*	Thomas Morley, *A Plain and Easy Introduction to Practical Music* (1597; edition cited 1771)
Mowat, 'Rowe'	Barbara A. Mowat, 'Nicholas Rowe and the twentieth-century text', in Tetsuo Kishi, Roger Pringle and Stanley Wells (eds), *Shakespeare and Cultural Traditions* (Newark, Del., 1994), 314–22
Mowat, 'Theater'	Barbara A. Mowat, 'The theater and literary culture', in Cox & Kastan, 213–48
MP	*Modern Philology*
MRDE	*Medieval and Renaissance Drama in England*
MSR	Malone Society Reprints
Mucedorus	*Mucedorus* (1598), in Tucker Brooke

Munday & Chettle, *Death*	Antony Munday and Henry Chettle, *The Death of Robert Earl of Huntingdon*, MSR (Oxford, 1964)
Munday & Chettle, *Downfall*	Antony Munday and Henry Chettle, *The Downfall of Robert Earl of Huntingdon*, MSR (Oxford, 1964)
Murphy	P.J. Murphy, 'Shakespeare and *Company*: Beckett's *As You Like It*', in *Reconstructing Beckett: Language for Being in Samuel Beckett's Fiction* (Toronto, 1990), 144–53
N&Q	*Notes and Queries*
Nashe	*The Works of Thomas Nashe*, ed. R.B. McKerrow and F.P. Wilson, 5 vols (Oxford, 1958)
Nashe, *Pierce Penniless*	Thomas Nashe, *Pierce Penniless his Supplication to the Devil* (1592), in Nashe
Nashe, *Strange News*	Thomas Nashe, *Strange News of the Intercepting Certain Letters* (1592), in Nashe
Naylor	E.W. Naylor, *An Elizabethan Virginal Book* (1905)
Neill	Michael Neill, '"This gentle gentleman": social change and the language of status in *Arden of Feversham*', *MRDE*, 10 (1998), 73–97
Nelson	William Nelson, 'From "Listen, Lordings" to "Dear Reader"', *University of Toronto Quarterly*, 46 (1976–7), 111–24
New Grove	*The New Grove Dictionary of Music and Musicians*, ed. Stanley Sadie, 20 vols (1980), vol. 17
Nielson	James Nielson, 'William Kemp at the Globe', *SQ*, 44 (1993), 466–8
Nightingale	Benedict Nightingale, 'Subdued light on love's follies', *Life and Times*, 24 April 1992
Northall, *Word-Book*	G.F. Northall, *A Warwickshire Word-Book* (1896)
Novy, *Cross-Cultural*	*Cross-Cultural Performances: Differences in Women's Re-Visions of Shakespeare*, ed. Marianne Novy (Urbana and Chicago, 1993)
Novy, *Engaging*	Marianne Novy, *Engaging with Shakespeare: Responses of George Eliot and Other Novelists* (Iowa, 1998)
Nungezer	Edwin Nungezer, *A Dictionary of Actors* (New Haven, Conn., 1929)
OCT	*The Oxford Companion to the Theatre*, ed. Phyllis Hartmell (Oxford, 1983)
Odell	George C.D. Odell, *Shakespeare from Betterton to Irving*, 2 vols (New York, 1920)
OED	*Oxford English Dictionary*, ed. J.A. Simpson and E.S.C. Weiner, 2nd edn, 20 vols (Oxford, 1989)
Onions	C.T. Onions, *A Shakespeare Glossary* (Oxford, 1958)
Orgel, *Impersonations*	Stephen Orgel, *Impersonations: The Performance of Gender in Shakespeare's England* (Cambridge, 1996)

Orgel, *Masques*   *Ben Jonson: The Complete Masques*, ed. Stephen Orgel (New Haven, Conn., 1969)

Ormerod   David Ormerod, 'Orlando, Jaques, and Maurice Scève', *N&Q*, n.s. 36 [234] (1989), 325–7

Ornstein   Robert Ornstein, 'Donne, Montaigne and Natural Law', in John R. Roberts (ed.), *Essential Articles for the Study of John Donne's Poetry* (Hassocks, 1975), 129–41

Ostovich, 'Seeing and judging'   Helen Ostovich, '"To behold the scene full": seeing and judging in *Every Man Out of His Humour*', in Martin Butler (ed.), *Re-Presenting Ben Jonson: Text, History, Performance* (Basingstoke, England, 1999), 76–92

Ovid, *Ars Amatoria*   Publii Ovidius Nasonis, *De Arte Amande*, or *The Art of Love*, trans. Thomas Heywood (1625)

Ovid, *Heroides*   *The Heroical Epistles of Publius Ovidius Naso, in English verse*, trans. G. Turberville (1569, reprinted 1584, 1600)

Ovid, *Met.*   *The xv Books of P Ovidius Naso, entitled Metamorphosis*, trans. Arthur Golding (1567)

Owens   Anne Owens, '*As You Like It* or, The Anatomy of Melancholy', *Q-W-E-R-T-Y*, 7 (1997), 15–26

Paglia   Camille Paglia, *Sexual Personae* (New Haven, Conn., 1990)

Palmer   Daryl W. Palmer, 'William Kemp's *Nine Daies Wonder* and the transmission of performance culture', *Journal of Dramatic Theory and Criticism* (Spring 1991), 33–47

Panofsky   Erwin Panofsky, *Studies in Iconography* (1938)

Parker, L.   L.A. Parker, 'The Agrarian Revolution at Cotesbach 1501–1612', *Leicestershire Archaeological Society*, 24 (1948), 41–76

Parker, *Margins*   Patricia Parker, *Shakespeare from the Margins* (Chicago, 1996)

Parker, 'Tongue'   Patricia Parker, 'On the tongue: cross gendering, effeminacy, and the art of words', *Style*, 23 (1989), 445–65

2 Parnassus   *The Return from Parnassus, Part 2* (1601–2), in Leishman

Partridge   Eric Partridge, *Shakespeare's Bawdy: A Literary and Psychological Essay and a Comprehensive Glossary* (New York, 1948)

Paster   Gail Kern Paster, 'The humor of it: bodies, fluids, and social discipline in Shakespearean comedy', in Dutton & Howard, 47–66

Patterson   Annabel Patterson, *Pastoral and Ideology* (Oxford, 1988)

PBSA   *Papers of the Bibliographical Society of America*

Pennington   Michael Pennington, *Hamlet: A User's Guide* (1996)

Pepys   *The Diary of Samuel Pepys*, ed. R.C. Latham and W. Matthews, 11 vols (1995)

Percy, *Fairy Pastoral*   William Percy, *The Fairy Pastoral* or *The Forest of Elves*, ed. John Arthur Lloyd (Roxburghe Club, 1824; MS *c.* 1600)

Peters	Julie Stone Peters, *Theatre of the Book, 1480–1880: Print, Text and Performance in Europe* (Oxford, 2000)
Phelps	Samuel Phelps, promptbook for Sadler's Wells (29 November 1847)
Pinkerton	Robert Heron [John Pinkerton], *Letters of Literature* (1785)
Piper	D. Piper, 'The 1590 Lumley inventory: Hilliard, Segar and the early life of Essex (2 parts)', *Burlington Magazine*, 99 (1957), Part 1: 224–31, Part 2: 299–303
Pitcher	John Pitcher, 'Samuel Daniel and the authorities', *MRDE*, 10 (1998), 113–48
Playfair	Nigel Playfair, *The Story of the Lyric, Hammersmith* (1925)
Pliny	C. Plinius Secundus, *The History of the World*, commonly called *The Natural History*, trans. Philemon Holland (1634)
PMLA	*Publications of the Modern Language Association of America*
Poggioli	Renato Poggioli, *The Oaten Flute: Essays on Pastoral Poetry and the Pastoral Ideal* (Cambridge, Mass., 1975)
Pont, *Reckoning*	Robert Pont, *A New Treatise of the Right Reckoning of Years, and Ages of the World* (Edinburgh, 1599)
Poole	Kristen Poole, *Radical Religion from Shakespeare to Milton* (2000)
Poulton	Diana Poulton, *John Dowland* (1972)
PP	*Past and Present*
PQ	*Philological Quarterly*
Proclamations	*Book of Proclamations* (1600)
Proudfoot	Richard Proudfoot, 'The 1998 Globe season', *SS 52* (1999), 215–28
Prynne, *Histrio-Mastix*	William Prynne, *Histrio-Mastix, The Players' Scourge, or Actors' Tragedy* (1633)
Puttenham, *English Poetry*	George Puttenham, *The Art of English Poetry* (1589)
Raab	Felix Raab, *The English Face of Machiavelli* (1964)
Rabelais, *Gargantua*	François Rabelais, *Gargantua*, in *Les Oeuvres de François Rabelais*, vol. 1 (Lyons, 1573)
Rabelais, *Tiers Livre*	François Rabelais, *The Third Book*, in Rabelais/Urquhart
Rabelais/Urquhart	François Rabelais, *Gargantua and Pantagruel*, trans. Thomas Urquhart and Peter Le Motteux (1653) (1994)
Rackin, 'Androgyny'	Phyllis Rackin, 'Androgyny, mimesis, and the marriage of the boy heroine on the English Renaissance stage', *PMLA*, 102 (1987), 29–41
Rackin, 'Crossdressing'	Phyllis Rackin, 'Shakespeare's crossdressing comedies', in Dutton & Howard, 115–36
Ralegh, *History*	Walter Ralegh, *A History of the World* (1614)
Ralegh, *Letters*	*The Letters of Sir Walter Ralegh*, ed. Agnes Latham and Joyce Youings (Exeter, 1999)

Ralegh, *Writings*	Sir Walter Ralegh, *Selected Writings*, ed. Gerald Hammond (Harmondsworth, England, 1984)
Rasmussen	Eric Rasmussen, 'Editions and textual studies', *SS 56* (2003), 349–56
Record	Robert Record, *Arithmetic*, Part 2: *The Whetstone of Wit* (1557)
Records	*Records of the Court of the Stationers Company 1576 to 1602 ~ from Register B*, ed. W.W. Greg and E. Boswell, vol. 1 (1930)
Redgrave	Michael Redgrave, *In My Mind's Eye: An Autobiography* (1983)
RES	*Review of English Studies*
Rich	Adrienne Rich, 'Compulsory heterosexuality and lesbian existence', in *Blood, Bread and Poetry: Selected Prose 1979–85* (1987), 23–75
Riggs	David Riggs, *Ben Jonson: A Life* (Cambridge, Mass., 1989)
Ringler	William Ringler, 'The number of actors in Shakespeare's early plays', in Gerald Eades Bentley (ed.), *The Seventeenth-Century Stage* (Chicago, 1968), 110–34
Ringler & May	William A. Ringler and Steven W. May, 'An epilogue possibly by Shakespeare', *MP*, 70 (1972), 138–9
Roberts, 'Ralph Crane'	Jeanne Addison Roberts, 'Ralph Crane and the text of *The Tempest*', *SSt*, 13 (1980), 213–33
Roberts, *Wild*	Jeanne Addison Roberts, *The Shakespearean Wild: Geography, Genus, and Gender* (Lincoln, Nebr., 1991)
Robin Hood	*A Little Geste of Robin Hood* [1506?]
Robson, *Play-Goer*	William Robson, *The Old Play-Goer* (1846)
Ronk	M. Ronk, 'Locating the visual in *As You Like It*', *SQ*, 52 (2001), 255–76
Rosen	Edward Rosen, 'Harriot's science, the intellectual background', in Shirley, *Renaissance Scientist*, 1–15
RP	Richard Proudfoot, private communication
RQ	*Renaissance Quarterly*
RSC	Royal Shakespeare Company
Ruff & Wilson	Lillian M. Ruff and D. Arnold Wilson, 'The madrigal, the lute song and Elizabethan politics', *Past and Present*, 44 (1969), 1–51
Ruthrof	H. Ruthrof, 'The dialectic of aggression and reconciliation in *The Tale of Gamelyn*, Thomas Lodge's *Rosalynde* and Shakespeare's *As You Like It*', *University of Cape Town Studies in English*, 4 (1973), 1–14
Rutter	Carol Rutter, *Clamorous Voices: Shakespeare's Women Today*, ed. Faith Evans (1988)
Ryan	Kiernan Ryan, *Shakespeare*, 3rd edn (2002)
Saslow	James M. Saslow, *Ganymede in the Renaissance* (New Haven, Conn., 1986)

Saviolo, *Of Honor*	Vincentio Saviolo, *Of Honor and Honorable Quarrels* (1595); see Saviolo, *Practice*
Saviolo, *Practice*	*Vincentio Saviolo his Practice, In two Books: The first entreating of the use of the Rapier and Dagger. The second, of Honor and honorable Quarrels* (1595)
Scheil	Katherine West Scheil, 'Early Georgian politics: the Black Act and Charles Johnson's *Love in a Forest* (1723)', *SS 51* (1998), 45–66
Schleiner	Winifried Schleiner, '"Tis like the howling of Irish wolves against the moon": a note on *As You Like It*, V.ii.109', *English Language Notes*, 12 (1974), 5–8
Schoenbaum	S. Schoenbaum, *William Shakespeare, A Compact Documentary Life* (Oxford, 1977)
Scolnikov	Hanna Scolnikov, 'Here is the place appointed for the wrestling', in *The Show Within: Dramatic and Other Insets: English Renaissance Drama (1550–1642)*, ed. François Laroque, vol. 1 (Montpellier, 1992), 141–52
Scott-Warren, 'Bear-gardens'	Jason Scott-Warren, 'When theatres were bear-gardens; or, what's at stake in the comedy of humors', *SQ*, 54 (2003), 63–86
Scott-Warren, *Harington*	Jason Scott-Warren, *Sir John Harington and the Book as Gift* (Oxford, 2001)
Sedinger	T. Sedinger, '"If sight and shape be true": the epistemology of crossdressing on the London stage', *SQ*, 48 (1997), 63–79
SEL	*Studies in English Literature 1500–1900*
Sen	Sailendra Kumar Sen, '"And therefore look you call me Ganymede"', in Sukanta Chaudhuri (ed.), *Renaissance Essays* (Calcutta, 1995), 107–15
Shaaber	*The Second Part of Henry the Fourth: A New Variorum Edition of Shakespeare*, ed. Matthias A. Shaaber (Philadelphia, 1940)
Shaheen	Naseeb Shaheen, *Biblical References in Shakespeare's Comedies* (Newark, Del., 1993)
Shapiro, J.	James Shapiro, *1599: A Year in the Life of William Shakespeare* (2005)
Shapiro, M.	Michael Shapiro, *Gender in Play on the Shakespearean Stage* (Ann Arbor, Mich., 1994)
Shattuck	Charles H. Shattuck, *Mr Macready Produces AS YOU LIKE IT: A Prompt-book Study* (Beta Phi Mu, 1962)
Sherman	William Sherman, '"Gold is the strength, the sinnewes of the world": Thomas Dekker's *Old Fortunatus* and England's Golden Age', *MRDE*, 6 (1993), 85–102
Shibata	Toshihiko Shibata, 'Shakespeare in Tokyo', *SQ*, 31 (1980), 403–4

Shirley, *Harriot*	John W. Shirley, *Thomas Harriot: A Biography* (Oxford, 1983)
Shirley, *Renaissance Scientist*	*Thomas Harriot, Renaissance Scientist*, ed. John W. Shirley (Oxford, 1974)
Sidney, *Apology*	Sir Philip Sidney, *An Apology for Poetry* (1595), ed. Geoffrey Shepherd (1965)
Sidney, *Lady of May*	Sir Philip Sidney, *The Lady of May* [1578 or 1579], in *Miscellaneous Prose*, ed. K. Duncan-Jones and J. Van Dorsten (Oxford, 1973)
Sidney, *Old Arcadia*	Sir Philip Sidney, *The Countess of Pembroke's Arcadia (The Old Arcadia)* [1580], ed. Katherine Duncan-Jones (Oxford, 1985)
Sidney Papers	*Letters and Memorials of State in the Reigns of Queen Mary, Queen Elizabeth, King James, King Charles the First, part of the Reign of King Charles the Second, and Oliver's Usurpation, by Sir Henry Sidney*, ed. Arthur Collins, 2 vols (1746)
Sir Clyomon	*Sir Clyomon and Sir Clamydes* (1599), ed. J.S. Farmer, MSR (Oxford, 1913)
Sisson, *Lodge*	*Thomas Lodge and Other Elizabethans*, ed. Charles J. Sisson (Cambridge, Mass., 1933)
SM	Steven May, private communication
Smallwood	Robert Smallwood, *As You Like It* (2003)
SMC	*A Shakespeare Music Catalogue*, ed. Bryan N.S. Gooch and David Thatcher, 5 vols (Oxford, 1991)
Smith, B., 'E/loco'	Bruce R. Smith, 'E/loco/com/motion', in Holland & Orgel, 131–50
Smith, H., 'Contentation'	Henry Smith, 'The benefit of contentation', in *Three Sermons* (1599)
Smith, S., 'Apprentices'	Steven R. Smith, 'The London apprentices as seventeenth-century adolescents', *PP*, 61 (1973), 149–61
Smyth	John Smyth, *The Berkeley Manuscripts: The Lives of the Berkeleys, from 1066 to 1618*, ed. Sir John Maclean, 3 vols (Gloucester, 1883–5)
Sokol & Sokol	B.J. Sokol and Mary Sokol, *Shakespeare's Legal Language: A Dictionary* (2000)
Solomon	Maynard Solomon, *Late Beethoven: Music, Thought, Imagination* (Berkeley, Cal., 2003)
Sontag	Susan Sontag, *In America* (New York, 2000)
Soule	Lesley Anne Soule, 'Subverting Rosalind: cocky Ros in the Forest of Arden', *New Theatre Quarterly*, 7 (1991), 126–36
Spenser	*The Poetical Works of Edmund Spenser*, ed. J.C. Smith and E. de Selincourt (Oxford, 1912)
Spenser, *FQ*	Edmund Spenser, *The Faerie Queene* (1593, bks 1–3; 1596, bks 1–3, 4–6), in Spenser

Spenser, *Hymnes*   Edmund Spenser, *Fowre Hymnes* (1596), in Spenser
Spenser, *SC*   Edmund Spenser, *The Shepheardes Calender* (1579), in
                        Spenser
Spenser, *View*   Edmund Spenser, *A View of the Present State of Ireland*
                        (1598), in Spenser
Sprague   Arthur Colby Sprague, *Shakespeare and the Actors: The
                        Stage Business in His Plays (1660–1905)* (Cambridge,
                        Mass., 1945)
SQ   *Shakespeare Quarterly*
SS   *Shakespeare Survey*
SSt   *Shakespeare Studies*
Stallybrass, 'Liberty' Peter Stallybrass, '"Drunk with the cup of liberty": Robin
                        Hood, the carnivalesque, and the rhetoric of violence in
                        early modern England', in Nancy Armstrong and Leonard
                        Tennenhouse (eds), *The Violence of Representation:
                        Literature and the History of Violence* (1989), 45–76
Stallybrass,   Peter Stallybrass, 'Transvestism and the "body beneath";
  'Transvestism'   speculating on the boy actor?', in Susan Zimmerman
                        (ed.), *Erotic Politics: Desire on the Renaissance Stage* (1992),
                        64–83
Starkey   David Starkey, *Elizabeth: Apprenticeship* (2000)
Stationers' Register   See Arber
STC   *A Short-Title Catalogue of Books Printed in England,
                        Scotland, and Ireland 1475–1640*, compiled by A.W.
                        Pollard and C.R. Redgrave, 2 vols, 2nd edn (1976)
Stebbins   Emma Stebbins, *Charlotte Cushman: Her Letters and
                        Memories of Her Life* (1878)
Stern, *Making*   Tiffany Stern, *Making Shakespeare* (2004)
Stern, *Rehearsal*   Tiffany Stern, *Rehearsal from Shakespeare to Sheridan*
                        (Oxford, 2000)
Stern, 'Re-patching'   Tiffany Stern, 'Re-patching the play', in Holland & Orgel,
                        151–77
Stern, 'Small-beer'   Tiffany Stern, '"A small-beer health to his second day":
                        playwrights, prologues, and first performances in early
                        modern theatre', *Studies in Philology*, 101 (2004), 172–99
Stern, '*Totus*'   Tiffany Stern, 'Was *Totus Mundus Agit Histrionem* ever the
                        motto of the Globe Theatre?', *Theatre Notebook*, 51
                        (1997), 122–7
Stevenson & Sosanya   Juliet Stevenson and Nina Sosanya, 'Interpretations',
                        BBC Radio 4, 30 January 2003
Stirm   Jan Stirm, '"For solace a twinne-like sister": teaching
                        themes of sisterhood in *As You Like It* and beyond', *SQ*,
                        47 (1996), 374–86
Stoppard,   Tom Stoppard, *Rosencrantz and Guildenstern Are Dead*
  Rosencrantz   (1967)

Strachey	Charles Strachey, 'Shakspere and the Romany: a note on the obscurities in *As You Like It* – Act.ii.sc.5', *Journal of Gypsy Lore Society*, 3 (1891), 96–9
Strong, *Cult*	Roy Strong, *The Cult of Elizabeth: Elizabethan Portraiture and Pageantry* (1977)
Strong, *Elizabethan*	Roy Strong, *The Tudor and Stuart Monarchy, Pageantry, Painting, Iconography*, 2 vols, vol. 2: *Elizabethan* (Woodbridge, England, 1995)
Strong, 'Hilliard'	Roy Strong, 'Queen Elizabeth, the earl of Essex and Nicholas Hilliard', in Strong, *Elizabethan*, 181–6
Strong, 'Miniature'	Roy Strong, 'Nicholas Hilliard's miniature of the "Wizard Earl"', in Strong, *Elizabethan*, 187–98
Strong, 'Persian Lady'	Roy Strong, '"My weeping stagg I crowne": the Persian Lady reconsidered', in *Elizabethan*, 303–24
Strong, '*Young Man*'	Roy Strong, 'Hilliard's *Young Man amongst Roses*', in *The Cult of Elizabeth* (1977), 56–83
Strout	Nathaniel Strout, '*As You Like It*, *Rosalynde*, and mutuality', *SEL 1500–1900*, 41 (2001), 277–95
Sugden	Edward H. Sugden, *A Topographical Dictionary to the Works of Shakespeare and his Fellow Dramatists* (Manchester, 1925)
Szatek	Karoline Szatek, 'Engendering spaces: a study of sexuality in pastoral borderlands', *Classical and Modern Literature*, 18 (1998), 345–59
Tanitch	Robert Tanitch, *Gielgud* (1988)
Tarlton's Jests	*Tarlton's Jests* [1611] and *News out of Purgatory* [1590?], ed. James Orchard Halliwell (1844)
Tasso, *Aminta*	See Guarini/Tasso
Tasso & Tasso, *Marriage*	Hercule and Torquato Tasso, *Of Marriage and Wiving*, trans. R. T[ofte?] (1599)
Taylor, 'Butterwomen'	Gary Taylor, 'Touchstone's butterwomen', *RES*, n.s. 32 (1981), 187–93
Taylor, 'Expurgation'	Gary Taylor, ''Swounds revisited: theatrical, editorial, and literary expurgation', in Taylor & Jowett, 51–106
Taylor, 'Structure'	Gary Taylor, 'The structure of performance: act-intervals in the London theatres, 1576–1642', in Taylor & Jowett, 3–50
Taylor & Jowett	Gary Taylor and John Jowett, *Shakespeare Reshaped 1606–1623* (Oxford, 1993)
Tenney	Edward Andrews Tenney, *Thomas Lodge* (New York, 1935)
Terry	Ellen Terry, *Four Lectures on Shakespeare*, ed. Christopher St John (1932)
Theses Martinianae	[Martin Junior], *Theses Martinianae* [Wolston, England, 1589]

Thirsk	Joan Thirsk, *The Agrarian History of England and Wales*, vol 4: *1500–1640* (Cambridge, 1967)
Thomas Lord Cromwell	*Thomas Lord Cromwell* (1602), in Tucker Brooke
Thompson, A.	Ann Thompson, *Shakespeare's Chaucer* (Liverpool, 1978)
Thompson, E.P.	E.P. Thompson, *Whigs and Hunters: The Origin of the Black Act* (Harmondsworth, England, 1977)
Thompson & Roberts	*Women Reading Shakespeare 1600–1900: An Anthology of Criticism*, ed. Ann Thompson and Sasha Roberts (Manchester, 1997)
Thornber	Robin Thornber, '*As You Like It*', *Guardian*, 19 April 1977
Thorne	Alison Thorne, *Vision and Rhetoric in Shakespeare: Looking through Language* (2000)
Tiffany	Grace Tiffany, '"That reason wonder may diminish": *As You Like It*, androgyny, and the theater wars', *HLQ*, 57 (1994), 213–39
Tintner	Adeline R. Tintner, '*As You Like It* as George Sand Liked It', *Revue-de-Littérature-Comparée*, 60 (1986), 337–44
TL	Tom Lockwood, private communication
TLS	*Times Literary Supplement*
Traub	Valerie Traub, *Desire and Anxiety: Circulations of Sexuality in Shakespearean Drama* (1992)
Tucker Brooke	*The Shakespeare Apocrypha*, ed. C.F. Tucker Brooke (Oxford, 1918)
Turberville	George Turberville; see *Hunting*
TxC	*William Shakespeare, A Textual Companion*, ed. Stanley Wells and Gary Taylor with John Jowett and William Montgomery (Oxford, 1987)
Upton	John Upton, *Critical Observations on Shakespeare* (1746)
Vaughan & Vaughan	*The Tempest*, ed. Virginia Mason Vaughan and Alden T. Vaughan, Arden Shakespeare, 3rd series (1999)
Veracini, *Rosalinda*	*The Favourite Songs in the Opera Call'd Rosalinda by Sigʳ Veracini* [1744]
Vickers, '*Counterfeiting*'	Brian Vickers, '*Counterfeiting*' *Shakespeare: Evidence, Authorship, and John Ford's* Funeral Elegy (Cambridge, 2002)
Vickers, 'Rhetoric'	Brian Vickers, 'Shakespeare's use of rhetoric', in Kenneth Muir and S. Schoenbaum (eds), *A New Companion to Shakespeare Studies* (Cambridge, 1971), 83–98
Virgil, *Eclogues*	Vergil, *Eclogues*, ed. Robert Coleman (Cambridge, 1977)
Walker, A.	Alice Walker, 'The life of Thomas Lodge', *RES*, 9 (1933), 410–32
Walker, G.	Greg Walker, *The Politics of Performance in Early Renaissance Drama* (Cambridge, 1998)
Watkins	Ronald Watkins, *On Producing Shakespeare* (1950)

Watson	Robert N. Watson, 'As You Liken It: simile in the wilderness', *SS 56* (2003), 79–92
Watt	Tessa Watt, *Cheap Print and Popular Piety 1550–1640* (Cambridge, 1991)
Welsford	Enid Welsford, *The Fool: His Social and Literary History* (1935)
Werstine	Paul Werstine, 'Narratives about printed Shakespeare texts: "foul papers" and "bad" quartos', *SQ*, 41 (1990), 65–86
West	Anthony James West, *The Shakespeare First Folio: The History of the Book*, 2 vols (Oxford, 2001)
Whetstone, *Mirror*	George Whetstone, *A Mirror for Magistrates of Cities* (1584)
Whitworth	Charles Whitworth, 'Wooing and wedding in Arden, Rosalynde and *As You Like It*', *Etudes Anglaises*, 50 (1997), 387–99
Wilders	*Antony and Cleopatra*, ed. John Wilders, Arden Shakespeare, 3rd series (1995)
Wiles	David Wiles, *Shakespeare's Clown* (Cambridge, 1987)
Williams	Gordon Williams, *A Glossary of Shakespeare's Sexual Language* (1997)
Williamson	George Williamson, 'The libertine Donne', *PQ*, 13 (1934), 276–91
Wilson, E.C.	E.C. Wilson, *England's Eliza* (1939)
Wilson, J.	Jean Wilson, *Entertainments for Elizabeth* (Woodbridge, England, 1980)
Wilson, R.	Richard Wilson, '"Like the old Robin Hood": *As You Like It* and the Enclosure Riots', *SQ*, 43 (1992), 1–19
Wilson, *Rhetoric*	Thomas Wilson, *The Art of Rhetoric* (1560)
Wise	John Wise, *Shakspere, His Birthplace and His Neighbourhood* (1861)
Withals, *Dictionary*	John Withals, *A Short Dictionary in Latin and English, profitable for young beginners* (1586; reprinted 1599)
Woolf, *Orlando*	Virginia Woolf, *Orlando* (1928)
Wordsworth, *The Prelude*	William Wordsworth, *The Prelude (1805)*, in *William Wordsworth: The Major Works*, ed. Stephen Gill (Oxford, 1984)
Woudhuysen	*Love's Labour's Lost*, ed. H.R. Woudhuysen, Arden Shakespeare, 3rd series (1998)
Wright, *Dialect*	*The English Dialect Dictionary*, ed. Joseph Wright (1898)
Wyatt	Sir Thomas Wyatt, *The Complete Poems*, ed. R.A. Rebhoolz (Harmondsworth, England, 1978)
Yamada	*The First Folio of Shakespeare: A Transcript of Contemporary Marginalia in a Copy of the Kodama Memorial Library of Meisei University*, ed. Akihiro Yamada (Tokyo, 1998), 57–66 (*AYL*)

Yates   Frances A. Yates, *Astraea: The Imperial Theme* (1975)

Zemon Davis,   Natalie Zemon Davis, 'The reasons of misrule: youth
  'Misrule'   groups and charivaris in sixteenth-century France', *PP*, 50
                    (1971), 40–75

Zemon Davis,   Natalie Zemon Davis, 'Women on top: symbolic sexual
  'Women'   inversion and political disorder in early modern Europe',
                    in Barbara A. Babcock (ed.), *The Reversible World* (Ithaca,
                    NY, and London, 1978), 147–89

STAGE AND FILM PRODUCTIONS CITED

Productions are listed chronologically. The name of the actress playing Rosalind follows that of the theatre manager (eighteenth and nineteenth centuries), or director (twentieth and twenty-first centuries). The names of other actors are given in brackets where significant. All RSC productions are at the Royal Shakespeare Theatre, Stratford-upon-Avon unless otherwise specified. Theatres are in London unless otherwise identified.

Eighteenth-century productions

Johnson, 1723   Charles Johnson, *Love in a Forest* (adaptation), Theatre
                    Royal, Drury Lane

Fleetwood, 1741   Theatre Royal, Drury Lane (Charles Fleetwood); Peg
                    Woffington (Charles Macklin as Touchstone; see Macklin
                    under 'Other works cited: Manuscripts')

Swan, 1741   Aungier-Street Theatre, Dublin (Mr Swan); Mrs
                    Reynolds (James Quin as Jaques)

Sheridan, T.,   United Smock-Alley and Aungier-Street Theatres
  1751–2   (Thomas Sheridan); Peg Woffington (Thomas King as
                    Touchstone; see Fig. 13)

Sheridan, R., 1785 Theatre Royal, Drury Lane (Richard Sheridan); Sarah
                    Siddons

Sheridan, R., 1787 Theatre Royal, Drury Lane (Richard Sheridan); Dorothy
                    Jordan

Nineteenth-century productions

Macready, 1839   Covent Garden Theatre (William Charles Macready);
                    Helena Faucit

Macready, 1842   Theatre Royal, Drury Lane (William Charles Macready);
                    Louisa Nisbett (Macready as Jaques; see Fig. 16)

Maddox, 1845   Princess's Theatre (J.M. Maddox); Charlotte Cushman

Phelps, 1847   Sadler's Wells Theatre (Samuel Phelps); Mrs Charles
                    Young

Buckstone, 1871   Niblo's Theatre, New York (John Buckstone); Rose Evans
                    (James Mace as Charles the Wrestler)

Modjeska, 1882	Booth's Theatre, New York (Helena Modjeska, also as Rosalind; see Fig. 20)
Daly, 1889	Daly's Theatre, New York (Augustin Daly); Ada Rehan
Daly, 1897	Outdoor performance in grounds of Shakespeare Memorial Theatre, Stratford-upon-Avon (Augustin Daly); Ada Rehan
Arthur, 1898	Wallack's Theatre, New York (Julia Arthur, also as Rosalind)

Twentieth-century productions

Playfair, 1919	Shakespeare Memorial Theatre, Stratford-upon-Avon (Nigel Playfair); Athene Seyler
Bell & McNeill, 1922	St Leonards, Rye and Battle, East Sussex (Oliver Bell and Hugh McNeill); (John Gielgud as Orlando)
Williams, 1932	Old Vic (Harcourt Williams); Peggy Ashcroft (see Fig. 6)
Carroll, 1933	Open Air Theatre, Regent's Park (Sydney W. Carroll); Phyllis Nielson-Terry (George Grossmith as Touchstone)
Church, 1936	Old Vic (Esmé Church); Edith Evans (Michael Redgrave as Orlando); see Fig. 3
Czinner, 1936	Film (Inter-Allied) (Paul Czinner); Elizabeth Bergner (Laurence Olivier as Orlando)
Prentice, 1946	Shakespeare Memorial Theatre, Stratford-upon-Avon (Herbert M. Prentice); Ruth Lodge
Visconti, 1948	*Rosalinda, o Come vi piace*, Teatro Eliseo, Rome (Luchino Visconti, designed by Salvador Dali); Rina Morelli
Byam Shaw, 1952	Shakespeare Memorial Theatre, Stratford-upon-Avon (Glen Byam Shaw); Margaret Leighton
Byam Shaw, 1957	Shakespeare Memorial Theatre, Stratford-upon-Avon (Glen Byam Shaw); Peggy Ashcroft
Elliott, 1961	RSC (Michael Elliott); Vanessa Redgrave. Aldwych Theatre transfer, 1962 (Patrick Wymark replacing Colin Blakeney as Touchstone)
Jones, 1967	RSC (David Jones); Dorothy Tutin (Roy Kinnear as Touchstone)
Williams, 1967	National Theatre/Old Vic (Clifford Williams); Ronald Pickup
Jones, 1968	RSC (David Jones); Janet Suzman
Goodbody, 1973	RSC (Buzz Goodbody); Eileen Atkins
Roman, 1977	Theatre Clwyd, Mold, North Wales (George Roman); Penelope Beaumont
Masumi, 1979	Haiyuza Company, Sunshine Gekijo, Tokyo (Toshikiyo Masumi); Daishi Horikoshi
Hands, 1980	RSC (Terry Hands); Susan Fleetwood
Noble, 1985	RSC (Adrian Noble); Juliet Stevenson (Fiona Shaw as Celia); see Fig. 7

Hytner, 1986	Royal Exchange Theatre, Manchester (Nicholas Hytner); Janet McTear
Albery, 1989	Old Vic (Tim Albery); Fiona Shaw
Donnellan, 1991	Cheek by Jowl, Lyric Theatre, Hammersmith (Declan Donnellan); Adrian Lester (see Fig. 4)
Carson, 1992	Greenwich Theatre (James Robert Carson); Jemma Redgrave
Thacker, 1992	RSC (David Thacker); Samantha Bond
Pimlott, 1996	RSC (Steven Pimlott); Niamh Cusack
Bailey, 1998	Shakespeare's Globe (Lucy Bailey); Anastasia Hille

Twenty-first-century productions

Doran, 2000	RSC (Gregory Doran); Alexandra Gilbreath
Grandage, 2000	Crucible Theatre, Sheffield (Michael Grandage); Victoria Hamilton
Hall, 2003	Peter Hall Company, Theatre Royal, Bath (Peter Hall); Rebecca Hall
Thompson, 2003	RSC, Swan Theatre, Stratford-upon-Avon (Gregory Thompson); Nina Sosanya (see Fig. 5)

INDEX

References in italics refer to figures.

435